THE ILLUSTRATED ENCYCLOPEDIA
OF
DINOSAURS

THE ILLUSTRATED ENCYCLOPEDIA
OF
DINOSAURS

An original and compelling insight into life in the dinosaur kingdom

DR DAVID NORMAN

Colour restorations by
JOHN SIBBICK

GREENWICH EDITIONS

A SALAMANDER BOOK

This edition published by
Greenwich Editions
10 Blenheim Court
Brewery Road
London N7 9NT
A member of the Chrysalis Group

ISBN 0-86288-230-3

CREDITS

Editor:
Philip de Ste. Croix

Contributing authors (captions):
Dr Michael Benton; Dr Gillian King

Designers:
Nick Buzzard
Carol Warren

Colour dinosaur artwork:
John Sibbick © Salamander Books Ltd

Skeletal drawings:
Denise Blagden and David Nicholls
© Salamander Books Ltd

Diagram artwork:
Bob Chapman; Alan Hollingbery; Greg Jones;
Bernard Robinson; Tim Widdall
© Salamander Books Ltd

Filmset:
Modern Text Typesetting Ltd, England

**Colour and monochrome
reproduction:**
Culver Graphics Ltd, England

Printed in Italy:
G. Canale & C SpA, Turin

THE AUTHOR

Dr David Norman is a lecturer in Zoology at Brasenose College, Oxford, and also a Research Fellow of the University Museum, Oxford, where he specialises in researching the evolution of and the relationships between dinosaurs. He graduated from Leeds University in 1973, and conducted postgraduate research at King's College, London, and the British Museum (Natural History). He held a Royal Society Fellowship in Brussels for one year. He has been actively involved in many of the important palaeontological finds of recent years, and participated in an expedition to the 'outback' of Australia in 1978 which resulted in the discovery of a small armoured dinosaur which Dr Norman is currently preparing in the laboratory. He is research consultant at a new excavation at Nehden in West Germany, and is generally regarded as the world's foremost authority on *Iguanodon*. In addition to his technical and academic writing, on the more popular level he has written a *Spotter's Guide to Dinosaurs* and contributed to *Collins Guide to Dinosaurs*. At the moment he is working on a book dealing with the relationships between dinosaurs and other archosaur reptiles to be published by Oxford University Press in 1986.

THE ARTIST

John Sibbick undertook his art training in the early 1970s at Guildford Art School, Surrey, where he studied both graphic design and, latterly, illustration. He subsequently spent 4 years in various art studios in London 'learning the ropes' before going fully freelance. He has always been interested in dinosaurs, and over the last 10 years has worked on a number of dinosaur books before this one, which he considers his *pièce de résistance* with regard to the subject. Apart from his publishing commissions, he also works regularly for galleries and museums.

ACKNOWLEDGEMENTS

I would like to take this opportunity of thanking the many people who have contributed to this book over the months of its production. In particular, I am grateful to Dr Michael Benton and Dr Gillian King, who wrote many of the captions describing the individual pieces of artwork of dinosaurs; to Dr Angela Milner of the British Museum (Natural History) for her advice on the photography of Museum specimens; and, above all, to the author, Dr David Norman, who not only wrote the text, but also proved an invaluable source of advice and encouragement throughout the project.

Much of the impact of a book of this nature derives from the quality of its artwork, and the designer, Nick Buzzard, and I wish to thank all the artists (credited above) who produced it – notably, of course, John Sibbick, who painted all the colour restorations, and Denise Blagden and David Nicholls, who between them prepared all the skeleton drawings. In producing these, we have frequently consulted restorations of complete skeletons (or individual elements thereof) created by noted palaeontologists for scientific publication. A detailed acknowledgement of these reference sources is included on page 208. In addition the many museum archives, picture agencies, and private individuals who have kindly supplied photographs for publication are credited on the same page.

In conclusion, I would like to express my gratitude to Harry Coussins, who read the proofs; and to Stuart Craik, who compiled the index.

Philip de Ste. Croix

CONTENTS

AUTHOR'S FOREWORD

This book is intended to serve as an accurate and comprehensive review of dinosaurs for use by people of all ages. This is obviously a rather grand claim with which to begin, and one that will not necessarily be agreed with by all who read it. Nevertheless, it has been my genuine intention to try to encapsulate between the covers of this book much of the work that has led to our current understanding of the life and times of dinosaurs. I hope that I have done this in such a way that it neither over-simplifies things nor patronises the reader, but simply and clearly explains the present 'state of the art'.

A casual glance at the shelves of most bookshops will reveal a considerable number of dinosaur books; these, no matter how serious their content, are invariably confined to the 'children's section'. Many dinosaur books are indeed intended for the children's age-range and consist of large-format picture books with, in most cases, lurid illustrations of dinosaurs locked in 'mortal combat' which are frequently accompanied by fairly meaningless text. Over the last decade, however, things have changed; there have appeared a range of better illustrated and more professionally written books about dinosaurs. There are, however, relatively few serious works on dinosaurs currently available.

Some serious books of recent years do come to mind, all of which are more often than not lodged in the wrong areas of bookshops. These include Professor Edwin Colbert's *Men and Dinosaurs* (1968), a very fine historical review of the discovery of dinosaurs, and his subsequent *Dinosaurs: An Illustrated History* (1983); Adrian Desmond's *The Hot-Blooded Dinosaurs* (1975), a biased but lively review of the controversy that has been raging over the physiology of dinosaurs; Dr Beverly and Jenny Halstead's *Dinosaurs* (1981), a compendium of dinosaurs; David Lambert's *Collins Guide to Dinosaurs* (1983), which describes itself as 'the first comprehensive field guide to the subject'; Donald Glut's *The New Dinosaur Dictionary* (1982), an alphabetical listing of dinosaur genera; and Dr Alan Charig's *A New Look at the Dinosaurs* (1979). The latter is by far the most authoritative book on dinosaurs published in recent years, and has done much to put into perspective the work of the palaeontologists who study these creatures and laying to rest many popular misconceptions concerning dinosaurs.

At first sight it would seem that there is little scope for yet another book on dinosaurs. So why this one? Well, this book provides one of the most detailed and comprehensive layman's guide to the dinosaurs yet published. The core of the book (pages 38 – 169) provides extensive documentation on the various groups of dinosaurs currently recognised. Each group is described in considerable detail, and includes information ranging from the time and geography of the original discoveries through to detailed anatomical discussion, consideration of muscular reconstructions and the way of life of these ancient animals. In addition there are comments about their geological and geographic distribution, evolutionary history and any outstanding controversies. All this information is augmented by many extremely accurate and beautiful colour restorations of representative dinosaurs as they may have appeared in life. There are also detailed anatomical drawings of complete reconstructed skeletons and other key anatomical portions, 'life-style' reconstructions, and numerous photographs of fossil specimens. Never before has such detailed work been provided in a book of this type.

Another unique feature of this book is found in chapter 2, 'To Study a Dinosaur'. In order to appreciate how it is possible for palaeontologists to reconstruct dinosaurs in such remarkable detail, the reader is taken virtually step-by-step through the work of a palaeontologist. Starting with the initial discovery of fossil bones, this chapter shows how they are excavated, the problems of laboratory preparation and conservation, the detailed analysis and the painstaking build-up of information that goes into producing a full reconstructed dinosaur skeleton and flesh restoration, and finally how biological interpretations can be used to give us a picture of the way in which the dinosaur (in this case *Iguanodon*) may have looked and behaved when it was alive.

In addition to this wealth of information purely on dinosaurs, there are other chapters devoted to the history of dinosaur discoveries, geological phenomena and dinosaur origins, as well as dinosaur contemporaries during the 140 million years of their reign. Finally one chapter is devoted to the various controversies that surround the study of dinosaurs. This book is therefore clearly all about dinosaurs and their world. Most people, even professional palaeontologists, should learn something new about dinosaurs from this book, and will, I hope, find it interesting. With regard to the readership, I feel that the high quality of the dinosaur restorations alone will be enough to satisfy the young budding 'dinosaurologist' while all the supplementary information in the text and drawings can be dipped into at leisure by just about anybody else.

A word of warning. For reasons of space it has been impossible to provide colour illustrations of dinosaurs that were contemporary with one another in all cases. Thus while it is just about permissible to feature *Diplodocus* and *Apatosaurus* in the same landscape (they are both found in the same geological deposits), the inclusion of, for example, *Compsognathus* (late Jurassic), *Ornitholestes* (late Jurassic) and *Coelophysis* (late Triassic) in the same landscape is, from the point of view of the timescale, clearly not strictly accurate. I hope the reader will forgive these occasional compromises which allowed us to illustrate a greater range of dinosaur examples. I should also point out that throughout the central 'dinosaur section' of the book, the localities where the fossil remains of dinosaurs were discovered have been plotted on palaeogeographic maps of the world which show the positions of the continents as they were when the relevant dinosaur genera under consideration were abundant. However, in such cases as *Compsognathus*, *Ornitholestes* and *Coelophysis* which lived in greatly different time zones, we have again had to compromise and opt for the map which seems most generally appropriate.

In order to help readers find their way about the book, a few words of explanation about its structure may be useful. The first chapter is concerned with the history of dinosaur discoveries and introduces the reader to the world of dinosaurs in general. The second chapter explains how a palaeontologist studies a dinosaur, while the third is concerned with examining the line of evolution that led to the appearance of dinosaurs on the Earth.

The dinosaurs themselves will be found between pages 38 and 169. They are split into two main groupings (or Orders): Saurischia (pages 38 to 97) and Ornithischia (pages 98 to 169). As will be explained, these Orders are based on the structure of the animals' hips. Within these Orders, the dinosaurs are arranged into family groups according to the family tree that can be found on page 23. It will be seen that the colours of the branches on this family tree match the colours of the bands across the top of the pages in the dinosaur section, and also the colour of the individual family trees that appear alongside the colour drawings of the dinosaurs. It is hoped that this will help the reader to understand the internal structure of the book, and so to be able to use it as a reference with ease.

The final section is devoted to many of the animals that lived at the same time as the dinosaurs, and to a consideration of the major scientific controversies that surround this subject. Two appendices at the end of the book show where dinosaurs have been discovered around the world, and where the museums are that have dinosaur exhibits on display. While writing this book, I have tried to avoid using excessively technical language, but any unfamiliar terms may be looked up in the Glossary (pages 202-203).

David Norman   Oxford   August 1985

INTRODUCTION TO DINOSAURS

The name 'dinosaur' was first coined by Richard Owen (later Sir Richard), a famous British anatomist in 1841. The occasion was an annual meeting of the British Association for the Advancement of Science held at Plymouth (England). Owen had been asked to review all the fossil reptiles that had been described to that date from the British Isles. As a result of his anatomical training and expertise he was able to recognise from their meagre remains that three fossil reptiles, *Megalosaurus, Iguanodon* and *Hylaeosaurus,* were totally unlike any other fossil or living types. They were all very large (approximately elephant-sized), land-living creatures which had pillar-like legs that were tucked in beneath the body; this leg position was totally different from the splayed position of the legs typical of reptiles. Comparisons that Owen was able to make at the time suggested to him that these peculiar reptiles, which he named dinosaurs after the Greek words *deinos* and *sauros* or 'terrible reptiles', seemed to anticipate the form of the large pachydermal mammals (e.g. elephants, rhinoceroses and hippopotamuses) of today. Dinosaurs thus came to be regarded as the acme of the reptilian type of animal. The alleged similarity between the anatomical design of dinosaurs and large mammals seemed amply to confirm this view.

As it eventually transpired, Owen's model of the dinosaur proved rather inaccurate, although he was absolutely correct about the posture of these reptiles. Nevertheless, whatever the faults of his argument, Owen introduced dinosaurs to the world at large. Since that time (the 1840s) dinosaurs have held a deep and continuing fascination for generation after generation.

For the great majority of us it is a fascination that is intense but temporary: restricted to those formative years of childhood. Often it is the result of a first trip to a Museum, or a school project, or the purchase of a first picture book on dinosaurs. Whatever the stimulus, dinosaurs certainly make a big impression on children who very quickly learn their jaw-cracking names, their appearance, and even their feeding habits, as many parents and teachers will testify. The nature of their appeal obviously varies from individual to individual: it may be simply their immense size, or the grotesque appearance of their skeletons, or the inevitable associations that are drawn with a violent or blood-thirsty life-style. Whatever the cause, for a brief period the imagination of children all over the world (this is certainly not a phenomenon associated with just the western world) is kindled by these dramatic and awe-inspiring creatures. Today many museums have fine dinosaur skeletons on display to the public, so that their visual impact is immediate. However, even in the middle of the last century, before complete dinosaur skeletons had been discovered, interest in these former inhabitants of our world was intense.

For most of us though, the childhood fascination with dinosaurs is transient — it fades with the passing of the years. School curricula naturally demand skills other than the ability to recite the names and attributes of dinosaurs. Interest in dinosaurs, however, rarely dies completely — they are associated with crucial years in a child's development. I think that this is amply confirmed by the quite frequent appearance of 'dinosaur-inspired' stories in the media. New theories or discoveries concerning dinosaurs are still considered newsworthy even by the most sombre or serious-minded of newspapers or television programmes; dinosaurs even figure in advertising campaigns, though

Above: Richard Owen, (1804-1892) who first coined the term *Dinosauria* A leading comparative anatomist, he became the first superintendent of the British Museum (Natural History).

Below: Children are nearly always fascinated by dinosaurs. Here a crowd has gathered to watch the excavation of a large fossil reptile in the 'outback' of Queensland, Australia.

they almost always symbolise the epitome of something that is out-dated, badly-designed or inefficient (a view that will be firmly refuted in this book).

So, what is it that makes dinosaurs so innately interesting? Surely, so the argument goes, we should find something more relevant to our world instead of harking back to the ancient past. Why bother with creatures that lived over 64 million years ago when we have so many urgent and pressing problems in present-day society. Is it escapism — a way of taking our minds off the horrendous problems that face us from day to day? Many palaeontologists who have devoted their lives to the study of dinosaurs or other fossil creatures may sympathise with this point of view but would be tempted to offer the following rather more dispassionate scientific explanation.

We live in an incredibly complex biological world and have become (particularly through environmental issues) generally aware of our potential to affect the delicate balance of nature upon which we depend. The world that we now inhabit has taken at least 4,500 million years to reach its present state. During this time it has been altered by geological processes and

Hip Structure (right)
Top right is the pelvis of an early ornithischian dinosaur (*Heterodontosaurus*). Note the position of the pubis (in red). Below left is a typical saurischian pelvis (*Compsognathus*).

Below: This haunting reconstruction of *Diplodocus* is displayed in the Smithsonian Institution, Washington D.C. The eerie quality of the lighting in the photograph emphasises the aura of mystery and fascination that surrounds dinosaurs in general.

the organisms that have lived on this planet before us. Dinosaurs form a part, and quite a significant one since they lasted for over 140 million years, of the history of this planet. Perhaps by studying the rise, flourishing and eventual decline and extinction of this group we may learn more not only about long term evolutionary processes, but also about the complex interactions between these organisms and the Earth that they inhabited. We should perhaps be able to learn, from the example of the dinosaurs, how better to manage this world and so perhaps avoid the eventual fate of the dinosaurs. It also gives us an element of perspective about ourselves and the Earth. We are very probably temporary custodians of this planet, an integral part of the history of the Earth which has not only a past but a future. We should therefore concern ourselves with what we are doing to the planet at the present time and to what extent it will affect future generations and inhabitants, rather than selfishly pursuing short-term aims.

There is indeed a great deal of fundamental truth in these arguments. They do, however, run the risk of becoming very profound intellectually and at the same time potentially highly political.

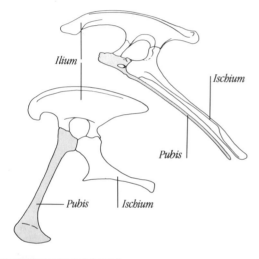

Ilium

Ischium

Pubis

Pubis

Ischium

Below: Even in today's 'high technology' culture, dinosaurs frequently catch the headlines in the world's press—particularly when the find is especially large or dramatic. This is again an indication of the powerful impression that they make on the human mind.

I do not particularly wish to avoid these issues but I do feel that another argument, concerned with human emotions and psychology, is probably of greater immediacy to the issue of why bother about dinosaurs.

Dinosaurs are very big—even awe-inspiring—and are all extinct; they are also the virtual personification of 'dragons' or other 'mythical beasts' that are associated with folk-lore traditions dating back long before dinosaurs were first described. This common factor of a human obsession with 'dragons', 'mythical beasts' or dinosaurs may be a key feature relating to the very essence of the human condition: the imaginative and creative aspects of the human intellect.

Dinosaurs, like other mythical beasts, require us to exercise both *imagination* and *creativity* in order to bring these extinct creatures back to life and give them a feeling of reality. One of the key features of Man is his ability to use his imagination and creativity in order to think ahead, predict or anticipate—from planning how to trap a rabbit for food, to designing a piece of industrial machinery or a new silicon 'chip'. All these and many other day-to-day activities are central to our ability to co-ordinate and regulate our lives.

Like many other skills, imagination and creativity are partly innate and partly learned, and all require *stimulation* to grow and develop. Perhaps it is in this area that dinosaurs have a limited but important rôle to play in stimulating the innate imaginative and creative potential in ourselves, particularly during those vital childhood years. It seems to me that dinosaurs (just like fairy tales, mythologies, space adventures, science fiction, etc) fall into this category of stimuli for the human imagination. None is *necessarily* relevant to the material needs of our present society but all may be of some importance in the maintenance of our essential humanness.

What Were Dinosaurs?

Before considering the dinosaurs as a whole, a few words of introduction should be offered on behalf of the dinosaurs themselves. There are very widespread misconceptions about the nature of dinosaurs, ranging on one hand from them being regarded as just any gigantic prehistoric animal to the notion that they are just one type of fossil animal. The truth is somewhere between these two extreme views.

Dinosaurs lived during the so-called Mesozoic Era of Earth history. The Mesozoic (literally 'middle life') comprises the Triassic, Jurassic

and Cretaceous Periods which lasted from about 225 until 64 million years ago. Thus animals that lived either before or after the Mesozoic are *not* dinosaurs. For example, giant woolly mammoths which went extinct within the last million years or so are not dinosaurs, nor are the large sail-backed reptiles of the Permian Period such as *Dimetrodon*.

Dinosaurs are also *reptiles* so that any fossil animals from the Mesozoic Era that are not reptiles (that is to say fish, amphibians, birds or mammals) cannot be dinosaurs either. To be even more precise dinosaurs were a rather special group of reptiles. All of them were land-living creatures. Of course a few ventured into shallow swamps to wallow, much as elephants do today, but none were particularly powerful swimmers or habitually lived in the sea. Thus the gigantic sea monsters of the Mesozoic, the plesiosaurs, ichthyosaurs and mosasaurs were not dinosaurs.

Similarly no dinosaurs were airborne fliers, so that the extraordinary flying reptiles of the Mesozoic, the pterosaurs, were not dinosaurs.

Dinosaurs are in fact members of a group of reptiles known as archosaurs ('ruling reptiles') which include well-known creatures like crocodiles, the extinct pterosaurs and those well-known archosaur descendants, the birds, as well as other less well-known extinct creatures such as the thecodontians.

The dinosaurs are distinct from other archosaurs for one main reason which is (as Owen rightly pointed out in 1841) that they are able to walk and run extremely efficiently; their legs are tucked in beneath the body rather than being held out from the sides. This change has left tell-tale marks in the form of changes in the structure of the hip, knee and ankle joint in their fossilised remains that serve to distinguish fairly clearly dinosaur remains from those of other archosaurs (see pages 36-37).

Hip Structure

Since the last half of the nineteenth century the dinosaurs have been split into two distinct groups, the *saurischian* ('reptile hipped') and *ornithischian* ('bird-hipped') dinosaurs. As their names suggest the hip structure of these two types is different.

Saurischian dinosaurs have hip bones arranged as shown in the diagram. The three bones on each side of the hip radiate outward from the hip socket. The upper bone (ilium) contacts the backbone forming a very firm attachment while the two lower bones (pubis and ischium) point forward and backward respectively and provide areas for the attachments of large leg-moving muscles. Examples of saurischian dinosaurs are the large plant-eating sauropods such as *Diplodocus* and *Brachiosaurus* and the meat-eating theropods such as *Allosaurus* and *Tyrannosaurus*.

Ornithischian dinosaurs have a rather differently shaped pelvis in which the pubis lies back against the ischium: an arrangement similar to that seen in birds (see diagram). In early ornithischians the hip bones are exactly as shown, but later on many seem to develop a new forwardly-directed pubis almost as if they were trying to replace the one they had lost. Ornithischians were *all* herbivores so far as we can tell and also tended to have a distinctive turtle-like beak at the tips of the jaws. Examples range from ornithopods such as *Hypsilophodon* to rather bizarre creatures such as the ceratopians (*Triceratops*), stegosaurs (*Stegosaurus*), ankylosaurs (*Euoplocephalus*) and 'bone-heads' such as *Pachycephalosaurus*.

Right: Baron Georges Cuvier (1769-1832) was the father of modern palaeontology and comparative anatomy. His description of the jaws of *Mosasaurus* paved the way for the scientific acceptance of extinction, and the first descriptions of dinosaurs by Buckland and Mantell.

Below: Deep in a chalk mine near Maastricht in Holland the jaws of the mighty *Mosasaurus* were unearthed in 1770. They provoked much interest and controversy. Cuvier eventually proving that they belonged to an extinct marine reptile.

Left: Dean William Buckland (1784-1856). Originally a scholar at Corpus Christi College, Oxford, he was appointed a Reader in Geology in 1818, and eventually became Dean of Westminster. It was he who described the remains of *Megalosaurus* in 1824.

Right: A portion of the lower jaw of *Megalosaurus bucklandi* which was part of the remains of this large carnivorous dinosaur, first described by Buckland. The remains are on view to this day at the University Museum, Oxford.

Below: *Scrotum humanum* was the caption provided for this piece of bone by R. Brooks in 1763. It was first illustrated by Robert Plot in 1676 who thought it belonged to a giant human. Though now lost, it may have been the lower end of the thigh bone of *Megalosaurus*.

The Discovery of Dinosaurs

The first descriptions of true dinosaurs date back to the 1820s and the work of the Revd. William Buckland and Gideon Mantell. However, several significant events led up to these discoveries which are instructive because they reveal why it was that such giant fossil reptiles remained 'undiscovered' until such a late date. Dinosaur skeletons must have been weathering out of the rocks for longer than Man has existed on Earth. The reason for the delay in finding them was essentially a religious one. Religious beliefs in the early nineteenth century and earlier included a concept known as the *plenum*. This supposed that God must have populated the Earth with every conceivable type of organism. Bearing this in mind, it seemed inconceivable that he would have allowed any of his creatures to become extinct. The discovery of fossilised animals in rocks therefore presented a potential problem because fossils may prove the reality of extinction. For the most part early fossil discoveries were regarded as dead members of presently existing species. However, in 1770 a remarkable discovery, the jaws of a huge fossil animal, was made in a chalk quarry in Maastricht (Holland). After much difference of opinion the jaws were eventually recognised by the eminent French anatomist Baron Georges Cuvier as those of a gigantic marine lizard (*Mosasaurus*—'Meuse reptile'). This was a clear example of a long extinct creature and supported Cuvier's long-held belief that there had been repeated extinctions of animals in earlier times.

The dramatic size and appearance of these mosasaur jaws seems to have stimulated much interest in gigantic extinct fossil reptiles in subsequent years and was probably a major contributory factor to the discovery and acceptance of the giant fossil reptiles discovered by Mantell and Buckland.

Right: Gideon Mantell (1790-1852), a country doctor in Sussex, described the first remains of *Iguanodon* (some teeth discovered by his wife) in 1822 before naming them in 1825.

Mantell and Buckland

In the early 1820s Gideon Algernon Mantell was a family doctor in practice at Lewes in Sussex (England). He was also an extremely enthusiastic amateur geologist who had spent much of his early life exploring and collecting fossils from rocks in the South Downs area of Sussex. Indeed he even had a small geological museum of the specimens he had collected aranged in his house. In about 1822, or perhaps a little earlier, several large and rather unusual teeth came into his collection. He actually described these teeth quite accurately in a large book that he published in 1822 called *The Fossils of the South Downs* and noted that it was his wife, Mary Ann Mantell, who had discovered them in some gravel. A rather appealing but unsubstantiated story has frequently been told of Mary Mantell discovering the teeth in piles of gravel on the roadside while accompanying her husband on one of his many doctor's calls to patients in the countryside. Whatever the actual events, the important point was that they eventually fell into Mantell's hands. He was able to trace the gravel, in which the teeth were embedded, to quarries in the Cuckfield area of Tilgate Forest and soon discovered more fragmentary remains.

At first Mantell was at a loss to identify these teeth. When shown to eminent anatomists of the time, such as William Buckland at Oxford and Georges Cuvier in Paris, they were sceptical about the supposed age of the rocks and regarded the teeth as being of no particular interest; perhaps they belonged to a large fish, or mammal such as a rhinoceros of fairly recent origin. Despite these authoritative comments Mantell suspected that Buckland and Cuvier were wrong. He *knew* that the teeth were from 'secondary' (Mesozoic) rocks and therefore really ought to be reptilian. Further work of his own, comparing his fossil teeth, revealed at last that they were similar to those of a South American lizard, the iguana. Thus it was that in 1825 Mantell finally published his description of these teeth as those of a gigantic, 40ft (12m) long herbivorous fossil lizard named *Iguanodon* ('iguana-tooth'), an extinct relative of the living iguana. The article included a handsome admission by Cuvier of his faulty earlier determination.

A year earlier (1824) William Buckland described the partial remains of a large carnivorous reptile (including the partial jaw bone illustrated above right) which was discovered near Stonesfield in north Oxfordshire and named *Megalosaurus* ('big reptile').

Both of these gigantic lizards seemed to fall into the *Mosasaurus* category of fossil reptile, except that both were land-dwellers rather than marine. Thus, although they were notable discoveries, their true significance was not fully appreciated. The same also applies to the partial skeleton of another reptile, this time armoured, named *Hylaeosaurus*. It was described by Mantell in 1833. Throughout the 1830s more fragments of these reptiles were discovered although no complete skeletons were found at this time.

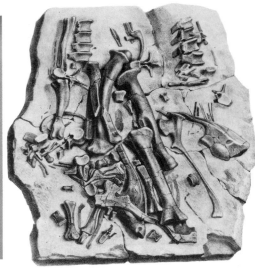

Above: This lithograph, from Owen's review of British fossil reptiles, is of the partial skeleton of *Iguanodon* found in a quarry at Maidstone in Kent. It was bought by friends for Gideon Mantell for the then princely sum of £25. These bones formed the basis of Mantell's early restoration of *Iguanodon* as a sort of giant lizard.

Left: Between 1852 and 1854 Richard Owen and the sculptor Waterhouse Hawkins produced several life-sized restorations of dinosaurs and other prehistoric animals for the grounds of the Crystal Palace exhibition centre at Sydenham. Just before they completed their task, Owen and Hawkins organised a special dinner party for 20 inside the incomplete body of an *Iguanodon*. As can be seen from the engraving of the occasion, the guests were rather cramped!

Richard Owen's Dinosauria

In 1841 Richard Owen, another comparative anatomist who had been inspired by the work of Cuvier, entered the scene. His review of British fossil reptiles revealed that *Iguanodon, Megalosaurus* and *Hylaeosaurus* were so unlike living lizards, with which they had been compared, that they deserved to be recognised as a separate 'tribe or suborder' as he called them—namely the *Dinosauria* ('terrible reptiles'). Owen's conception of the dinosaurs as huge elephantine reptiles proved extraordinarily powerful, generating interest in the group among the scientific community and the general public that has endured right up to the present day.

As our understanding of dinosaurs has gradually improved over the years, it has become clear that dinosaurs had been inadvertently discovered many years earlier than Mantell and Buckland's works. Robert Plot, a clergyman at Oxford University and Keeper of the Ashmolean Museum, described and illustrated part of a thigh-bone in 1676 which he thought must have belonged to a giant human. The drawing looks remarkably like a thigh-bone of

Buckland's *Megalosaurus*. Unfortunately there is now no trace of this bone. During the eighteenth century there are several reports of giant fossil bones having been discovered in rocks that have since yielded dinosaur remains.

In 1807-1809 fossil bones were recovered from Cuckfield in Sussex by William Smith during his geological survey of the British Isles. These have since been relocated in collections at the Institute of Geological Sciences in London by Dr Alan Charig and I was able to confirm that they belong to *Iguanodon*. This seems to be one of the earliest properly documented records of a dinosaur discovery.

Owen's view of dinosaurs as elephantine reptiles gained particular prominence in the early 1850s shortly after the Great Exhibition at Hyde Park of 1850-51. The enormous Crystal Palace in which the exhibition was held was moved to Sydenham Park in south-east London and Owen was asked to provide life-sized models of his prehistoric animals which could be placed in the park grounds. These models atracted enormous publicity at the time and are still standing today, and, inaccurate though we know them to be, they still create a strong impression on the viewer.

American Discoveries

Not long after Owen's elephantine models of his dinosaurs had been finished at Sydenham, discoveries of dinosaurs began to be made in North America. Scattered teeth found in 1855 in Montana seemed to resemble those of *Iguanodon* and *Megalosaurus* from Britain. Joseph Leidy named these teeth *Trachodon* and *Deinodon* respectively. A little later in 1858 Leidy examined a partial skeleton from Haddonfield, New Jersey. Very fortunately this creature, named *Hadrosaurus* (again with teeth reminiscent of those of *Iguanodon*), had both its fore and hindlimbs preserved intact. Leidy realised that unlike Owen's 'elephantine' dinosaurs, his *Hadrosaurus* must have had a more kangaroo-like posture and at a stroke took *Hadrosaurus* far closer to an accurate picture of this type of dinosaur than over 30 years of work by Mantell, Buckland and Owen had managed. Life-sized models of *Hadrosaurus* and a carnivore named *Laelaps* were constructed in kangaroo-pose in the newly created Central Park of New York in 1868 by Waterhouse Hawkins (the man who had assisted Owen with his Sydenham dinosaurs).

SKELETON OF THE GREAT FOSSIL LIZARD OF NEW JERSEY.
(Hadrosaurus Foulkii Leidy.)

SCIENCES IN PHILADELPHIA.
S. W. Cor. of Nineteenth and Race Streets.

Thus from early in their history dinosaurs had made a large public impact through the models in London and in New York, and the added 'spice' of a certain element of disagreement over the actual form of these animals. By the late 1870s further publicity was given to the dinosaurs as a result of virtually coincidental dinosaur discoveries in Europe and North America.

Above left: Across the Atlantic, Hawkins was commissioned to build models of the dinosaurs described by Joseph Leidy. This is the *Hadrosaurus* skeleton in the Philadelphia Academy of Sciences in 1868.

Above: The son of a Quaker family, Edward Drinker Cope (1840-1897) was a precocious child with a brilliant intellect. His scientific reputation was great even before he became interested in dinosaurs in the 1870s.

Above: Less brilliant than Cope, Othniel Charles Marsh (1831-1899) was fortunate to have George Peabody as his uncle. With his support Marsh became a professor at Yale College with ample time to study dinosaurs.

Below: In the early 1880s the dinosaur skeletons collected at Bernissart began to be reassembled in St George's Chapel, Brussels. Here we see the completion of the first skeleton, and the men involved.

Bernissart

In April, 1878 miners excavating a coal seam 1,056ft (322m) below ground at the small Sainte Barbe pit in the village of Bernissart (south-west Belgium) entered a clay-filled fissure. From this site were recovered the remains of almost 40 complete or partial *Iguanodon* skeletons. Excavation of these dinosaurs was handed over to research workers of the then Royal Museum of Natural History in Brussels (since re-named the Royal Institute of Natural Sciences). The recovery of these dinosaurs was the responsibility of Louis Depauw and the scientific description of these skeletons fell to Louis Dollo. Dollo was for the first time able to provide an accurate reconstruction of one of Owen's dinosaurs: *Iguanodon*. This finally confirmed that Leidy's views rather than Owen's were the more correct. Today over 30 of the Bernissart dinosaurs are exhibited to the public in enormous glass enclosures at the Royal Institute of Natural Sciences in Brussels (see also the following chapter 'To Study a Dinosaur').

Cope and Marsh

In 1877, just before the Bernissart discoveries were made, even richer deposits were discovered in Colorado. These dinosaur fossils were discovered quite independently by two school masters: one, Arthur Lakes, found bones on a ridge at Morrison, Colorado and sent them to Othniel Charles Marsh, a Professor at Yale College (later to become Yale University), while the other, O. W. Lucas, found his fossils in similarly aged rocks near Canyon City, Colorado and sent his fossils to Edward Drinker Cope in New Jersey.

The coincidence of these discoveries was remarkable for in the late 1870s Marsh and Cope were already great rivals. The starting point of their rivalry was, according to Adrian Desmond, an occasion in 1870 when Cope showed Marsh the skeleton of *Elasmosaurus*, a plesiosaur from Kansas that Cope had described

Right: The dinosaurs of China have rightly gained much attention in recent years. Seen here is the dinosaur hall at Beipei Museum with the fine skeletons of the stegosaur *Tuojiangosaurus* in the foreground, and the large sauropod *Omeisaurus* behind.

Below: In the 1920s several nests of eggs and young *Protoceratops* were found by the Central Asiatic expedition organised by the American Museum of Natural History. In recent years further Polish-Mongolian expeditions to this area have revealed more nests, like the one seen here.

a few years earlier. Upon examination Marsh noted that the head of the animal had been placed on the wrong end of the skeleton — a fairly dramatic error on Cope's part! Cope being a brilliant, but rather quick-tempered individual never forgave Marsh for pointing out this error and so their rivalry began.

The feud between Cope and Marsh was fuelled by these new dinosaur discoveries and the desire to be the first to describe any new dinosaur remains. From these beginnings in Colorado, teams of explorers hired by Marsh and Cope extended their excavations into Wyoming at Como Bluff (alongside the original Union Pacific Railroad) to Montana, the Connecticut Valley and New Mexico. Between 1877 and the late 1890s Cope and Marsh, driven by their intense rivalry, described about 130 new species of dinosaur, a veritable avalanche of types. Many of these fossils found their way into North American Museums, notably the Peabody Museum at Yale University, the Smithsonian Institution in Washington and the American Museum of Natural History (New York). Today they provide a testament to their mighty labours. The deaths of Cope in 1897 and Marsh in 1899 saw a change to much more careful and co-ordinated exploration of these North American localities.

In 1897/8 new expeditions to Como Bluff, Wyoming were undertaken by the American Museum of Natural History; these proved only moderately succesful but in 1898 a new locality, Bone Cabin Quarry, was discovered. The unusual name comes from the fact that a shepherd had built himself a small cabin out of the dinosaur bones that were strewn across the area. Between 1878 and 1905 the AMNH removed hundreds of bones of dinosaurs from this site.

In 1909 Earl Douglass of the Carnegie Museum (Pittsburgh) found one of the richest deposits of dinosaur skeletons that the world has ever known. The locality is in Utah, near Vernal in the Uinta mountains. This site was excavated from 1909-1923 by the Carnegie Museum and revealed magnificent skeletons of *Diplodocus, Apatosaurus, Camarasaurus, Stegosaurus, Allosaurus* and many other dinosaurs. In 1915 it became, by Presidential decree, 'Dinosaur National Monument' and today a working museum stands on the site. The steeply tilted fossil-bearing rocks form a mural with the fossils visibly in place.

Dinosaurs in Canada

The first Canadian dinosaur remains were discovered during geographical surveys of the Canadian border in the early 1870s. In 1884 Joseph Tyrrell made the first important discovery of a skull of the carnivorous dinosaur *Albertosaurus* in the valley of the Red Deer River, Alberta. By the late 1880s it was realised that the only way to collect dinosaurs in this area was by using a boat to travel down river. This procedure was used with moderate success through the late 1890s into the first decade of the twentieth century when the real Canadian dinosaur rush began.

In 1910 Barnum Brown of the American Museum of Natural History (New York) launched a broad-beamed barge on the Red Deer River, equipped with a large tent and fully equipped for an expedition. Using this as a base camp, Brown navigated the river stopping at points to explore the terrain and collect fossils systematically. The results were remarkably good and form an impressive record of late Cretaceous dinosaurs from North America. Two years after Brown started his collecting trip by boat, Canadians joined in. The Sternberg family, Charles H. (senior) and his three sons, Charles, Levi and George, built a similar barge and began prospecting in the same area of the Red Deer River. Both groups were very successful during the period 1912-1917 finding many fine dinosaur specimens which are now on display in museums both in North America and elsewhere around the world.

The African Dinosaur Rush

1907 saw the discovery of large dinosaur remains at Tendaguru in German East Africa (now known as Tanzania). These were excavated largely by native Africans under the supervision of scientists (Edwin Hennig and Werner Janensch) from the Berlin Museum of Natural History, during the period 1908-1912. Working under much more difficult conditions than those experienced in North America, the expedition recovered some remarkable dinosaurs including the gigantic, giraffe like *Brachiosaurus,* as well as *Dicraeosaurus* and the armoured dinosaur *Kentrosaurus.*

A British Museum expedition also went to Tanzania in the 1920s and recovered more dinosaur remains, but these were rather more fragmentary than the German discoveries.

Dinosaurs in Central Asia

In the early 1920s, following on from the phenomenal success that dinosaur collectors had had in North America through the preceding 40 years since the time of Cope and Marsh, an ambitious plan was hatched to send an expedition from the American Museum of Natural History into Mongolia.

The main aim of the expedition was to find more evidence concerning the origin of Man. The expedition (led by Roy Chapman Andrews, Henry Fairfield Osborn and Walter Granger) entered Mongolia for the first time in 1922. In the Gobi Desert they found some mammal remains, but by far the most significant discoveries made were of dinosaurs. Between 1922 and 1925 four expeditions managed to reach the Gobi and collected a fine array of dinosaurs: *Protoceratops, Pinacosaurus, Saurornithoides, Oviraptor, Velociraptor,* all of which were new to science. Most renowned of all these discoveries though were the nests of *Protoceratops* eggs — the first of any dinosaur to be discovered.

Political events in China in the 1920s and world events in the 1930s and 1940s prevented further exploration of Mongolia. However, in 1946 and 1948/9 Russian expeditions went back to Mongolia, led by I. Efremov and A. K. Rozhdestvensky. These revealed not only more *Protoceratops* and armoured dinosaurs, but also extended exploration into the Nemegt Basin where they found hadrosaurids like the North American *Saurolophus,* and *Tarbosaurus,* a form very close to the great North American *Tyrannosaurus.*

Further work in Mongolia followed in the 1960s and 1970s with the setting up of joint Russian-Mongolian and Polish-Mongolian collaborative expeditions to the Nemegt Basin and elsewhere; these have resulted in yet more new and interesting fossils being discovered, including not only abundant and varied dinosaurs, but also well-preserved and important early mammal remains.

Dinosaurs in China

Records of 'dragon bones' from Sichuan in China, where dinosaur remains are known to be abundant today, have been traced back almost to the time of the birth of Christ A.D. 265-317. However, the study of dinosaur fossils in China dates back to 1902 with the collection by a Russian colonel (Manakin) of large fossils that had been discovered by fishermen in northern China. This site was excavated by Russians in 1915-17 and produced the hadrosaurid *Mandschurosaurus,* a well-preserved skeleton of which is now in Leningrad.

After this time several expeditions ventured into China, notably Sino-French, Sino-Swedish and the AMNH on their way to Mongolia. However, from 1933 onward the Chinese have been the primary explorers of their country. Led by the German-trained Professor Yang Zhong-jian (C. C. Young to western palaeontologists!), explorations were carried out in Sichuan,

Yunnan, Xinjiang and Gansu and led to the discovery of the prosauropod *Lufengosaurus*.

After the People's Republic was formed in 1949, all research was concentrated on the Institute of Vertebrate Palaeontology at Beijing (Peking) which co-ordinated much of the palaeontological work done in China. 1950 saw the discovery of the remarkable hadrosaurid *Tsintaosaurus* in Laiyang, and 1952 and 1957 skeletons of the diplodocid *Mamenchisaurus* in Sichuan. In the 1960s the huge hadrosaurid *Shantungosaurus* was excavated in Shandong. In the 1970s Xigong Province yielded many new and interesting forms, *Omeisaurus, Szechuanosaurus* and the stegosaur *Tuojiangosaurus,* and then the rich fossil deposits of Sichuan were discovered; these latter deposits have yielded literally hundreds of dinosaurs, many of which are to this day still being excavated. In many ways China is now the area of the present 'dinosaur rush', its finds being as important as those in North America around the turn of the century.

South America and Australia

Dinosaur remains have been known in both South America and Australia for many years but there has been a significant rise in the number of finds in South America, particularly through the work of José Bonaparte (Argentina) and his collaborators, and in Australia through the work of Ralph Molnar, Tony Thulborn and colleagues in Brisbane, Sydney and Melbourne. All this points to the likelihood of new and dramatic discoveries in the near future. For example, one locality in southern Queensland has revealed literally hundreds of dinosaur tracks. Dinosaurs were obviously there in great abundance; it is surely just a matter of time before good fossil-bearing rocks are found.

The Geological Timescale

Dinosaurs are found only in the so-called Mesozoic Era. To explain what the Mesozoic Era was in terms of Earth history we have illustrated here the Geological Timescale.

It has been estimated that the Earth is about 4,600 million years old. The oldest rocks so far discovered are about 3,600 million years old; however, there must have been a considerable period of time before this when the hot molten Earth cooled sufficiently for a crust of rocks to form. By dating meteorites which were probably formed at the same time as the rest of our Solar System, a generally agreed upon age of the Earth of 4,600 million years has been arrived at.

Precise dating of rocks is obviously of great importance to palaeontologists because it tells them the age of the fossilised organisms. Herein lies a major problem. There are only two ways of dating rocks, *comparative* dating and *absolute* dating.

Comparative dating, as the name implies, involves comparisons. In this case the characteristic fossils of one rock sample are compared with those of another area. If they are found to be broadly similar then it would seem a fair supposition that they were of similar age. By drawing comparisons between many rock and fossil types the *degree* of similarity can be assessed. For example fossil sequences from different areas may have overlapping ranges of fossils so that a comparative sequence of ages can be arrived at. Fine though these comparative series are, they give no idea of precisely how old the fossils are. For this absolute dating techniques are employed.

Absolute dating of rocks can be done by analysing radioactive isotopes. many elements have radioactive isotopes; these isotopes are known to *decay* at an established rate so that half of the isotope breaks down into a more stable element in a fixed time (the 'half-life'). Therefore if we know in what proportions the radioactive isotope and its stable version were first formed and can analyse their proportions at the present time, we can calculate how long the rocks have been formed. One of the best isotopes for dating rocks from the age of dinosaurs is Potassium 40; this decays to produce Argon 40. The half-life for this decay is about 1,300 million years. However the ratio of Potassium 40-Argon 40 can only be measured in volcanic lava. In order to arrive at agreed dates for the Mesozoic we have to rely on a combination of Potassium-Argon absolute dating of the occasional lava rock sample in dinosaur-bearing rocks, and comparative dating of fossil sequences in the rocks between these absolute dates. As a result of these two methods we have arrived at this generally agreed geological timescale illustrated here.

As can be seen from the timescale dinosaurs were not the oldest known fossils. The oldest forms of life so far discovered are tiny bacteria-like creatures whose remains have been preserved in rocks 3,100 million years old. More complicated forms of life appear about 2,500 million years later. Some of these fossils, form the so-called Ediacara shales of Australia, include sea-living worm-like animals, jellyfish and primitive corals. This vast expanse of time before the first complex organisms start to appear is known as the Precambrian ('before the Cambrian'). Beyond the Precambrian, the last 600 million years of life on Earth is termed the Phanerozoic ('visible life') which is in turn divided into three Eras: these are known as the Palaeozoic ('ancient life'), Mesozoic ('middle life'), and Cenozoic—or Kainozoic—('recent life').

The **Palaeozoic Era** (600-225 million years ago) marks the appearance of most of the major groups of animals and plants that we recognise today, such as shellfish, insects, spiders, fish, amphibians, reptiles, and most plant types except for the flowering plants.

The **Mesozoic Era** (225-64 million years ago) marks the arrival of several modern groups, notably the mammals and birds as well as flowering plants and many modern groups of insect. More importantly from our point of view, the Mesozoic marks the arrival of dinosaurs and their rise to dominance throughout this Era.

The Mesozoic Era is divided into three Periods: the Triassic Period (225-200 million years ago), the Jurassic Period (200-135 million years ago) and the Cretaceous Period (135-64 million years ago). At the start of the Triassic there were no dinosaurs. Mammal-like reptiles were particularly abundant; these, however, died out toward the end of the Triassic to be replaced by the dinosaurs. Many kinds of dinosaur appeared throughout the remaining 140 million years of the Jurassic and Cretaceous Periods but they all mysteriously became extinct at the end of the Cretaceous Period 64 million years ago.

The **Cenozoic (Kainozoic) Era** (64 million years ago up to the present) saw the change to animals and plants more typical of today. Mammals, birds, insects and flowering plants are everywhere and, quite importantly, so far as we are concerned the first humans appear. Early Man however did not appear on Earth until a *mere* 2-3 million years ago—long after the dinosaurs went extinct.

Plate Tectonics

Ever since the first crude maps of the world were drawn, it must have seemed obvious that the continents could fit snugly together like the pieces of a gigantic jigsaw puzzle. For example the coastlines of North and South America seem remarkably similar to those of Europe and Africa on the other side of the Atlantic Ocean. No-one, however, took these observations to be particularly important because continents seem such firm and immovable things. Despite this, in 1915 Alfred Wegener proposed that the continents had in fact moved during the millions of years of Earth history: Europe and Africa had *drifted* apart from North and South America. He went on to show that if the continents were fitted back together, the rock types and mountain ranges often fitted together very neatly.

The notion of Continental Drift had one major problem in that it lacked a mechanism. What forces could have been responsible for

	YEARS AGO (MILLIONS)	
Maastrichtian	64	
	70	
Campanian		
Santonian	80	
Coniacian		
Turonian	90	
Cenomanian		
	100	
Albian		
	110	
Aptian		
Barremian	120	
Hauterivian		
Valanginian	130	
Ryazanian		
Purbeckian	140	
Portlandian		
Kimmeridgian	150	
Oxfordian		
Callovian	160	
Bathonian		
Bajocian	170	
Toarcian		
Pliensbachian	180	
Sinemurian		
	190	
Hettangian		
	200	
Rhaetian		
	210	
Norian		
	220	
Carnian		
	225	

CRETACEOUS / JURASSIC / TRIASSIC

The Geological Timescale (right and left)

The spiral (right) is an attempt to compress the immense age of the Earth into a meaningful form. Each twist of the spiral covers 570 million years! Starting at the bottom, the formation of the Earth from a cloud of dust occurred about 4,500 million years ago. The Earth then cooled allowing a crust to form, and large amounts of gas and water vapour were expelled to form a primitive atmosphere of dense cloud and poisonous gas. By about 3,000 million years ago the crust and atmosphere were sufficiently stable for the first living organisms to appear—simple, single-celled bacteria. The next 2,400 million years were dominated by relatively simple forms of life, mainly bacteria that fed on simple chemicals, and others ('blue-greens') that were able to use sunlight to make oxygen. The blue-green algae formed huge reef-like structures, stromalites, in these ancient oceans. The first complex organisms appeared about 600 million years ago after which evolution proceeded more rapidly as can be seen from the annotated events marked on the diagram. The age of the dinosaurs (225-64 mya) is visible on the topmost layer, and this period is shown in expanded form in the time chart (left). The individual geological stages marked are scientifically-agreed time zones. This chart figures on the opening spread of each dinosaur family group later in the book, where the distribution in time of the dinosaur genera is duly indicated.

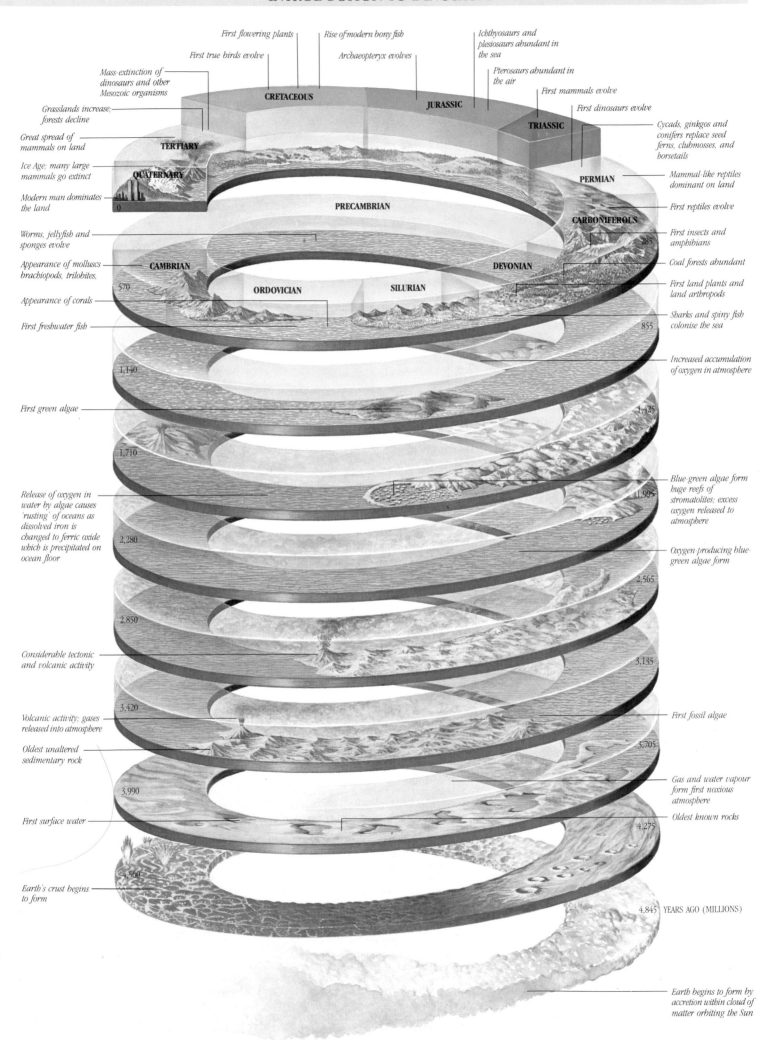

First flowering plants

Rise of modern bony fish

Ichthyosaurs and plesiosaurs abundant in the sea

First true birds evolve

Archaeopteryx evolves

Pterosaurs abundant in the air

Mass-extinction of dinosaurs and other Mesozoic organisms

First mammals evolve

CRETACEOUS

JURASSIC

First dinosaurs evolve

Grasslands increase; forests decline

TRIASSIC

Great spread of mammals on land

TERTIARY

Cycads, ginkgos and conifers replace seed ferns, clubmosses, and horsetails

Ice Age; many large mammals go extinct

QUATERNARY

PERMIAN

Mammal-like reptiles dominant on land

Modern man dominates the land

0

PRECAMBRIAN

First reptiles evolve

CARBONIFEROUS

Worms, jellyfish and sponges evolve

285

First insects and amphibians

Appearance of molluscs brachiopods, trilobites,

CAMBRIAN

DEVONIAN

Coal forests abundant

570

ORDOVICIAN

SILURIAN

First land plants and land arthropods

Appearance of corals

First freshwater fish

855

Sharks and spiny fish colonise the sea

1,140

Increased accumulation of oxygen in atmosphere

First green algae

1,425

1,710

Blue-green algae form huge reefs of stromatolites; excess oxygen released to atmosphere

1,995

Release of oxygen in water by algae causes 'rusting' of oceans as dissolved iron is changed to ferric oxide which is precipitated on ocean floor

Oxygen-producing blue-green algae form

2,280

2,565

2,850

Considerable tectonic and volcanic activity

3,135

3,420

Volcanic activity; gases released into atmosphere

First fossil algae

Oldest unaltered sedimentary rock

3,705

3,990

Gas and water vapour form first noxious atmosphere

First surface water

Oldest known rocks

4,275

4,560

Earth's crust begins to form

4,845 YEARS AGO (MILLIONS)

Earth begins to form by accretion within cloud of matter orbiting the Sun

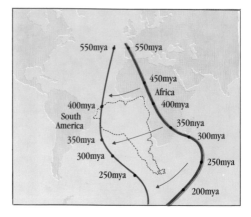

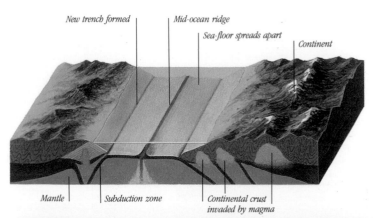

New trench formed   Mid-ocean ridge
                           Sea-floor spreads apart
                                        Continent

Mantle   Subduction zone   Continental crust
                               invaded by magma

Palaeomagnetism (left)
When plotted, the polar bearings of South America and Africa follow curved paths. Between 550 and 270 million years ago these curves were identical: the continents were joined then.

Sea-Floor Spreading (right)
Molten rock in the mantle rises to form a mid-ocean ridge, pushing the sea-floor apart before descending at a 'trench' along a land margin.

Right: Viewed from space, the Sinai peninsula, Red Sea, Egypt and Saudi Arabia show dramatically how areas of the Earth are splitting apart driven by convection in the the mantle. The Red Sea is the site of a new ocean which in several million years time may be as great as the Atlantic Ocean.

Below: This topographic relief map, produced from radar altimeter data from the Seasat satellite, lets us see the effects of sea-floor spreading. Note the deep ocean trenches off the coast of south-east Asia and the prominent mid-oceanic ridge in the Atlantic.

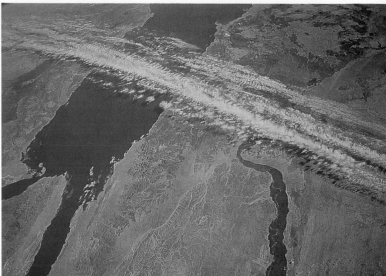

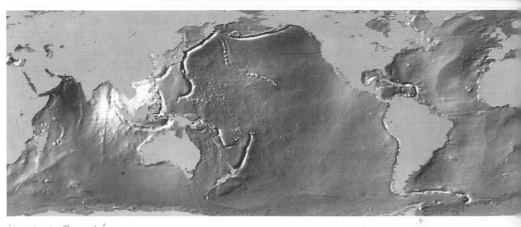

the movement of entire continents? At the time of Wegener no such forces were known, and so his theory was ignored or dismissed as preposterous. Since the early 1960s, however, much evidence has accumulated to support Wegener's ideas of Continental Drift. Notable among these are evidence of palaeomagnetism and sea-floor spreading.

Palaeomagnetism relies on the fact that some rocks contain magnetic iron particles. While these rocks are still molten, the particles point toward the magnetic pole just like compass needles. Once the rock has solidified, this magnetic bearing is preserved permanently. By studying such rocks the direction of the magnetic pole can be plotted. Obviously we would expect these 'fossil compasses' to point toward the present magnetic pole: but they do not! If we look at a series of differently aged rocks the 'compasses' point in a variety of directions which seem to plot the movement of the pole. In fact what it shows is the movement of the continent relative to the pole.

Sea-floor spreading observations have come from detailed studies of the sea-floor. These have shown that the oceans are divided up by a system of enormous underwater mountain ranges or 'ridges' and deep oceanic 'trenches'. These 'ridges' represent areas where new crust is being formed from molten rock rising from the centre of the Earth, while the 'trenches' are areas where the Earth's crust is slipping back downward into the molten mantle.

The great sheets of the Earth's crust (known as tectonic plates) are rather like gigantic, incredibly slow-moving (a few centimetres a year) conveyor belts; these carry the continents about on them. Incredible though it seems, the continents upon which we live are quite light compared with the Earth's crust and so are able to float along on their respective tectonic plates. The whole system appears to be powered by heat at the Earth's core; this causes the molten rock of the mantle to circulate, the movement of which in turn drags the Earth's crust along by friction.

The result of these remarkable revelations is that Wegener has now been proved to be quite correct, the continents have moved around quite considerably in geological time. This phenomenon can be demonstrated by looking at the positions of the continents during the Mesozoic Era.

In the Triassic Period the various continental blocks had, by pure chance, all bumped together to form the so-called supercontinent of Pangaea. Evidence for the existence of Pangaea comes from palaeomagnetic analysis and is strongly supported by the animals living on land in the Triassic. The strange, pig-like dicynodont *Lystrosaurus* is found in Australia, South Africa, India, China and Antarctica in the Triassic Period. Many other reptiles are very

widely distributed across the continents; all of which points to their being able to disperse across dry land, rather than breast great oceans! Early dinosaurs seem also to be widely distributed at the end of the Triassic.

The Jurassic Period does not seem to have allowed the continents to remain in contact for very long. Pangaea began to split into several large fragments. The southern continents, South America, Africa, India, Antarctica and Australia began to pull away from Europe and North America with the formation of a narrow sea-way. Despite this there must have been significant contact between these areas because various Jurassic dinosaurs, diplodocids (page 80), brachiosaurids (page 86) and iguanodontids (page 110), are found to be practically the same in Africa and North America in late Jurassic times. In addition to this sea-barrier, another sea (Turgai Sea) separated Europe from Asia in middle Jurassic times; However, this was not before a significant fauna of dinosaurs had begun to develop in Asia.

By early Cretaceous times the Atlantic Ocean had begun to develop and the northern and southern continents were completely separated and India began to separate from Africa. At this time we start to find that some dinosaur groups seem to show a restricted distribution, particularly those that evolved in the early Cretaceous. For example the dromaeosaurids (page 56) are restricted to the northern continents, which is presumably where they evolved. Thus we begin to see how geological events can affect the evolutionary history of particular groups of animals.

By late Cretaceous times the continents were beginning to move into more familiar positions. Africa and South America had begun to drift apart and India was rafting across the Indian Ocean. The northern continents, while not greatly separated physically, were nevertheless very subdivided by oceans in such a way that western North America and eastern Asia were in contact across the Bering Straits, while Europe and eastern North America were still in

Palaeogeographic Maps (left)

The study of continental drift has made possible the production of a series of maps showing continental positions as they were in the Mesozoic Era. In the Triassic Period (**1**) all the continents were joined together to form the supercontinent of Pangaea. This began to split in the Jurassic Period (**2**); a narrow Atlantic Ocean formed and sea separated Europe and Asia. By the time of the early Cretaceous (**3**), the continents were further removed, and shallow seas started to divide the southern continents. By late Cretaceous times (**4**), South America and Africa had begun to separate, India was rafting away across the Indian Ocean and Europe and North America were moving apart. Seaways also divided Europe and Asia, *and* western from eastern North America. This resulted in some curiously isolated fauna.

Sedimentation (below)

Weathering of upland areas is responsible for the formation of sedimentary rocks. Wind, water, rain and ice action erode exposed rock; the silt is carried to lakes, lagoons or deltas where it may be deposited in layers. Land-living animals are most likely to be buried and fossilised in such areas.

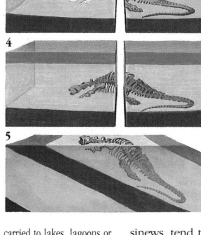

Fossilisation (left)

An essential requirement for the formation of a fossil is that after the organism dies (**1**) and the soft tissue rot away leaving (in this example) the bony skeleton, it should be rapidly buried by sediment (**2**). This normally occurs in rivers, lakes, or the sea into which the carcasses of land-living animals may be washed. Two processes may then occur (**3**). The organic material in the bones decays and may be replaced by minerals from water percolating through the sedimentary rocks: permineralisation (**left**). The bony structure may even be replaced entirely by minerals: petrification. Alternatively the bones may dissolve leaving a hollow mould (**right**) which may be filled later by minerals which form a solid replica of the bone: a natural cast (**4 right**). Land movements and erosion may then lead to exposure of the fossil (**5**).

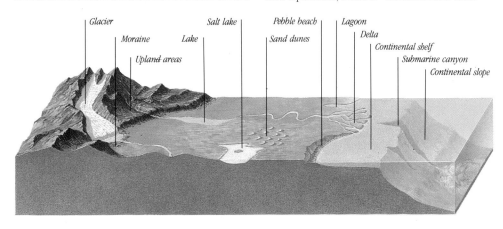

Glacier   Salt lake   Pebble beach   Lagoon
Moraine   Lake   Sand dunes   Delta
Upland areas   Continental shelf
Submarine canyon
Continental slope

sinews, tend to rot very quickly. However, on rare occasions even these may be fossilised. For example soft-bodied jellyfish and worms have been preserved as imprints on rocks that are 530 million years old (the Burgess Shales of British Columbia). These remarkable fossils were apparently formed as a result of mud-slides from underwater cliffs which buried animals living on the sea-floor—such preservation is extremely rare.

Hard parts such as bones and teeth can be preserved in a number of ways. Teeth are particularly resistant and are frequently preserved in their original state. Most other hard parts are changed to a greater or lesser extent. Bones have a considerable amount of organic material in them; when buried the organic material (mostly collagen) decays or is dissolved away. Relatively recent fossil bones are often found in this state and are very light and crumbly. In older fossils the spaces around the bone crystals are filled with new minerals from water seeping through the rocks. These can be minerals such as silica, calcite or iron pyrites. This process of mineral replacement is known as permineralisation and makes the bones much harder and heavier.

On occasions, the original mineral structure of the bone can be replaced by the minerals in the percolating ground waters. The bone is then said to have been petrified or turned to stone. Permineralised *and* petrified bones retain their original structure as can be seen if examined microscopically. This presumably reflects the fact that the percolating minerals replace the bone minerals virtually molecule for molecule.

Sometimes the original bone material may be completely dissolved by the percolating minerals, leaving a hollow mould. Although a mould is not part of the original animal, it is nevertheless still a fossil because it tells us a great deal about the original animal. Sometimes moulds such as this are filled at a later date by another mineral. The mineral will then take on the form of the original object and it will again become a petrified fossil. Fossils formed in this way are known as natural casts.

contact with each other. We find that dinosaur distributions reflect these connections with, for example, ankylosaurids (page 164), ceratopians (page 128) and advanced hadrosaurids (page 122) evolving in Asia and western North America, while nodosaurids (page 160), iguanodontids (page 110) and primitive hadrosaurids (page 116) persist in Europe and eastern North America.

The history of the continents and their geographic positions can thus be seen to play an important part in the evolutionary history of the dinosaurs. Without our knowledge of plate tectonics and continental drift some of their distribution would be very difficult to explain.

Fossilisation

The word fossil used to mean literally *anything* that was dug out of the ground. Nowadays its meaning has become more restricted to the preserved traces or remains of ancient organisms.

The essential requirement for fossilisation is that the organism (be it plant or animal) or evidence of its activities (such as footprints, droppings, gnawings, pollen grains etc.) should be covered in sediment of some kind before scavenging animals or the natural processes of erosion or decay completely destroy them. Rapid burial of this kind is most likely to occur in the sea where a continuous rain of debris (silt and fine sands) falls on to the sea floor. As a result there is a very strong bias in the Fossil Record toward sea creatures. Land-dwelling creatures such as the dinosaurs also get preserved as fossils when their carcasses are washed into lakes or into the sea and buried; this is a rather chancy affair, yet despite this fossilised dinosaur remains are in some cases (as will be seen later) surprisingly abundant. Some have even been preserved in sand-dunes.

It is usual for only the hard parts, shells, teeth and bones, to be preserved as fossils since these are the things that are most resistant to decay. Soft tissues, such as skin, muscles and

Trace Fossils

In addition to these conventional types of fossil there is also a group of fossils known as trace fossils. Trace fossils are those that reveal the former presence and activities of organisms, but not the organisms themselves. Trace fossils range from fossilised dung (*coprolites*) to gnawings, burrows and tubes. Some of the most abundant trace fossils are footprints and trackways, especially those of dinosaurs. In fact an entire sub-branch of palaeontology known as ichnology ('the study of footprints') has arisen solely devoted to the interpretation of fossilised footprints and tracks. Despite the fact that the makers of the trackways can never be identified with certainty, nevertheless a great deal can be learned from footprints. For example: whether it was a dinosaur that made them, whether they were four-footed (quadrupedal) or two-footed (bipedal), how heavy they were, how fast they were moving, whether they were showing herding behaviour, etc.

Discoveries and Excavations

Palaeontology, like other sciences, is based upon factual information; in this case, the raw material for these facts are the fossils themselves. The science of palaeontology today, however, is not limited by the rate of discovery of new fossil specimens. As will be made obvious in Chapter 2 a considerable amount of scientific work can be done on material that was discovered a long time ago. Techniques of fossil preparation have improved immeasurably over the last half century. Thus specimens studied by palaeontologists in the 1920s or earlier can be further prepared to reveal new and important facts about the structure of dinosaurs. Scientific approaches have also changed over the years. Different sorts of investigatory approaches are used and new interpretations can result from examining old materials.

However interesting it might be to re-study old material, there is always a need for new or better preserved specimens to add to our gradually accumulated picture of the history of life on our planet. New fossil material comes from a wide range of sources from accidental discoveries to the activities of highly organised fossil collecting expeditions.

Where To Look

Dinosaur fossils are obviously not just found anywhere. In order to understand where to look, we need to remember how and where fossils are most likely to form in the first place. If we know this then we should be able to predict where to look.

Dinosaurs were land-living creatures for the most part and the majority of these would be scavenged and their remains completely destroyed when they died. Events such as burial in volcanic ash (as at Pompeii) or sand dunes would preserve their remains, but are exceedingly rare. Occasionally animals may have died in or near water where their remains might be washed down-stream to be buried in lake sediments — some may even get washed out to sea before burial. In these sediments their remains are likely to become fossilised in the ways described.

So we should look in *sedimentary* rocks: clays, mudstones, limestones and sandstones; and preferably those that were deposited in rivers and lakes if we are looking for land-living animals. It is also important to look in rocks of the right age; it is obviously no use looking for

dinosaurs in rocks of Permian age. Finally it is necessary to find *exposures* of sedimentary rock. It is again of no use if the sedimentary rocks that contain dinosaurs are buried thousands of feet beneath the ground. We are helped here in a number of ways. Erosion by wind and rain wears away rock exposing lower layers; this process is assisted by earth movements. Tectonic activity results in the Earth's crust being folded and buckled in places, bringing deep layers of rock to the surface. Rivers cut into rocks exposing layer upon layer of earlier rocks; a similar thing is found on the sea-shore, where wave action batters and erodes the cliffs at a very rapid rate continually exposing new rocks. Man is also a fairly effective agent in rock exposure. Quarrying, cutting roads, railway lines and foundations for buildings all expose new rocks.

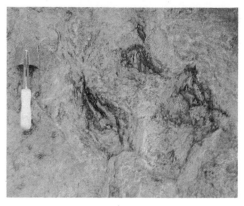

Above: We see clearly here the impression of a three-toed foot preserved in a rock. As can be appreciated from the size of the trowel, it is quite large and was probably made by *Iguanodon,* remains of which have been found in these rocks.

Right: Moving *Iguanodon* footprints can be quite a strenuous activity! This one literally fell out of the cliffs on the Isle of Wight, but such finds have to be collected quickly before they are pounded up by the action of the waves.

So, in order to find fossilised dinosaurs we need to be well-prepared in advance. It is necessary to know where to find sedimentary rocks of the right type (lake or river sediments), the right age (Mesozoic), and where they are exposed and preferably being eroded. All this information can be provided by the detailed work of geologists who have been involved for the last two centuries in studying and mapping the distribution of rock types all over the World.

Expeditions and Discoveries

All the back-up information indicated above can be used by palaeontologists and geologists in order to plan expeditions to find dinosaurs. Nowadays many expeditions tend to be large, expensive, often multinational projects involving teams of scientists. As such they require a great

deal of co-operation, not only among the scientists but also between the relevant Governments of the countries involved. Providing that these potential difficulties are successfully overcome then the 'nitty gritty' of prospecting and collecting can proceed.

In the 'field' likely exposures of rock are visited by teams of people who spend their time scouring the rocky outcrops for slivers of fossil bone or other tell-tale signs. This can be very disheartening — days can go by with nothing being found; this is partly because it takes some time to get your 'eye in' — that is to become able to recognise those tell-tale signs of fossil fragments.

One fairly standard way of looking for fossils is to walk along the bottom of exposures, cliffs or valleys, looking for bits of bone. If some are found then it is a matter of scrambling up the

exposures to see where they have come from; with luck this may lead to the discovery of a skeleton or part of a skeleton weathering out of the cliff-face.

Expeditions are not the only way to discover fossils. The most frequent, and often the most rewarding discoveries are made either by accident, or as a result of the activities of a dedicated and highly skilled band of amateur collectors.

Accidental discoveries are made by all sorts of people: quarrymen and miners, people building roads or digging foundations, farmers, holiday makers, or geologists during normal geological survey work. Most of these finds are reported back to museums for identification. Some of these may eventually lead to rather dramatic discoveries (such as Bill Walker's 'super claw' — see page 61).

Some other fossil discoveries result from the activities of fossil-collecting enthusiasts who spend their free time walking across well-known exposures on the look-out for new fossils. These 'amateurs' ('amateur' is hardly an appropriate term for these able, highly skilled enthusiasts) are extremely valuable to museums all over the world because they act as their 'eyes' and 'ears': keeping them in touch with the new finds and alerting them to new exposures. After all, museums cannot afford to keep their own staff on duty in this way. In many ways this dedicated band is continuing the work of early enthusiasts such as the pioneering figure of Gideon Mantell (see page 10).

Excavation Techniques

Having located a fossil skeleton the next problem is how to remove it without damage so that it can be prepared under laboratory conditions. The techniques adopted vary depending upon the size of the fossil. Small fossils are relatively easy to excavate. The important point to remember is not to get carried away in the excitement of your discovery. Ideally it should be labelled and then photographed in position in the rock, or at least careful notes and drawings made of its position; these may be of enormous value to palaeontologists at a later date (and also to you if some pieces become detached later).

Having recorded the position of the bone (or bones), the fossil is then prepared for removal. Usually some treatment is needed before it can be lifted. Often the remains are cracked or crumbly and need to be hardened using quick-setting resins or glues that can be painted or sprayed on. The fossils can then be either wrapped in paper and stored in sample bags, or if the bones are fragile protected in plaster or polyurethane foam jackets, so that they can be moved in relative safety.

Large fossils, such as dinosaur skeletons, are much more laborious to excavate. Quite often only a part of the skeleton is exposed on a cliff-face. To expose the skeleton completely, the 'overburden' — the rock lying above it — has first to be removed using picks, shovels and sometimes power hammers or even explosives! The overburden is removed to about 2-3in (5-8cm) above the level of the fossil and then fine hand-held tools are used to expose the upper surface of the skeleton. When fully exposed, the skeleton is then photographed and sketched and carefully labelled so that all of its parts can be clearly identified. The skeleton, since it cannot be lifted whole, is then carefully divided into blocks of manageable size each of which is plastered, re-labelled for identification back in the laboratory, and then removed.

Laboratory Preparation

The arrival in the museum laboratory of new specimens collected on expeditions marks the next phase of work. This involves careful removal of protective packaging and then painstaking preparation of the fossils from the rock so that detailed study can begin. Various techniques are used to remove the rock ranging from fine hand-held needles, to electrically powered vibropens, small pneumatic chisels or ultrasonic probes, or in some cases chemical techniques such as acid treatment to dissolve the encrusting sediments.

In some cases this treatment can produce magnificent specimens that resemble the freshly prepared skeletons of living animals rather than those of 100-million-year-old fossils.

Left: Successful expeditions require a lot of planning. Seen here are the closing phases of the excavation of the *Coelophysis* bone-bed in New Mexico. Large slabs of rock bearing the bones of this dinosaur have been exposed, lifted, coated in plaster-of-Paris, and are now being hauled away for the trip to the laboratory.

Above: Excavation of large specimens is complicated and laborious. Cyril Walker (BMNH) is here digging away the rock beneath a large ichthyosaur skeleton. Once this stage is completed, sections of the upper surface can be plastered, then the pillars broken and the fossil inverted so the underside can be plastered in turn.

Below: This old barracks on the upper University of Utah campus — the now defunct 'bone barn' — was the first home of the extensive collection of bones from the Cleveland-Lloyd Quarry. Often it is problems such as the storage of large numbers of fossils that can cause the biggest headaches after especially rich discoveries.

Classification

There are enormously large numbers of organisms living in the world today and countless millions have lived in the past. Faced with such a bewildering diversity of life we might be tempted to throw up our hands in horror and say it is just impossible to understand either the nature of life or the reasons why there should be such diversity in Nature. This is not the case, however. Many thousands of biologists devote their lives to this very set of problems; surely they cannot all be wrong!

One of the great advances in our attempt to understand Nature has come from the activities of people interested in classification; this is the art of listing or cataloguing organisms. There are a variety of ways in which this can be done. For example they could be catalogued in the order in which they were discovered, or perhaps by size. Such lists, however, would not tell us anything about the qualities of the individual organisms. In practice, these sorts of systems have not been adopted by biologists for this very reason. Instead a system was developed through the work of people such as Carolus von Linné or Linnaeus (in the middle of the eighteenth century) which relied upon measuring the degree of resemblance between different organisms. A careful and detailed survey of living organisms revealed that certain of them shared features in common which could be used to cluster them together into related sets or groups.

To take a familiar example, a large group of animals possess a bony backbone (known as a vertebral column). This particular feature is found only in fish, amphibians, reptiles, mammals and birds and allows them to be grouped together and called 'vertebrates'. In similar fashion if we look within the vertebrates we find that amphibians, reptiles, mammals and birds have four limbs (while the fish have fins) and can be grouped together as 'tetrapods' (four-footed vertebrates). Furthermore if we look within the tetrapods, we find that reptiles, mammals and birds all bear young that develop inside an egg-membrane known as the amnion, while the amphibians do not. The former types are therefore grouped together as 'Amniotes'. All organisms can be grouped together into larger or smaller sets on the basis of the shared possession of certain characters. Looking at as many organisms as possible it is possible to build up, using this classificatory procedure, an hierarchical tree-like picture of the relationships of all organisms. The demonstration of this rather 'organised' pattern of relationships in nature by Linnaeus in the 1750s gave rise to the belief that God had created this pattern of life. Therefore, by studying this 'tree of life' and clarifying any ambiguities, philosophers believed that they might get closer to an understanding of the mind of God.

These views were challenged on many occasions by various scientists in subsequent years, but with little effect until 1858-59 when Charles Darwin published his theory of evolution through natural selection. This flew in the face of orthodox religious beliefs in that it implied that organisms had not been placed on Earth in one divine act of Creation, but had gradually changed or evolved over an immense period of time through a mechanism called 'Natural Selection' (survival of the fittest).

Natural selection is a mechanism which relies on a number of factors. First, all organisms in a species tend to vary—no two human beings are identical (apart from rare

Above: Charles Darwin's theory of evolution (1858-9) envisaged natural selection as a mechanism for evolutionary change. This proposition allowed the tree of life to be interpreted as a genealogical tree instead.

identical twins of course). Given this variation within a species, then it is likely that under certain (perhaps harsh) environmental conditions some individuals will by chance possess features that allow them to survive better than others. Given long enough under these conditions, and provided that the favourable traits are inherited by their offspring, the organisms in the population of this species may exhibit a change in character (evolve): this is because surviving organisms will tend to be those with the favourable traits. Thus an environmental change can be seen to be one way of introducing a change in the characteristics of a species. Given that this seems to be a not unreasonable set of circumstances, effects such as this could result in change (or evolution) within a species in a few generations (think, for instance, of the resistance that some bacteria have evolved to antibiotics, or rats to the poison warfarin). If we then extrapolate from these small changes that have taken place in a short space of time to the millions of years that have elapsed since the origin of life (about 3,100 million years), then the possibility of dramatic changes in the form of organisms seems very reasonable.

Thus, with the advent of Darwin, the tree of life became, instead of just an interesting philosophical problem, a potential genealogy — literally the family tree of life. The prospect then arises of our being able to understand the pattern revealed in nature through the hierarchical classificatory scheme as a result of the evolution of one group from another in the course of time.

Up to this point, there had been no need to consider fossil organisms at all because the pattern of the classificatory tree was viewed as a static thing created by God in his infinite wisdom. However, if the tree of life could have been arrived at as a result of evolutionary events in the distant past, fossil organisms may provide clues to the process of evolution; they may even catch evolution 'in the act'.

Thus classification, often regarded as a dry and exceedingly boring branch of biology, can be seen to be an activity that is of considerable value to all those who are interested in the nature of the relationships between organisms. The following pages are devoted to the classification of the reptiles in general and the dinosaurs in particular.

The Reptile Family Tree

As was mentioned earlier, the reptiles are classified along with the mammals and birds as Amniotes because their young develop within the so-called amniotic membrane. Excellent though this characteristic is if we consider living tetrapods, it is practically useless when it comes to distinguishing fossil amniotes from amphibians. Soft anatomical features like egg-membranes are simply not fossilised. As a result a series of additional characters has to be agreed upon in order to distinguish fossil amphibians and reptiles. For example, some fossil amphibians have been preserved with gilled larvae or sensory grooves on the skull; both of these features are only found in amphibian tetrapods. Failing these, then a range of skeletal characters are used but these are open to much disagreement among palaeontologists.

At the present time there is general agreement that one of the earliest known reptiles was *Hylonomus* from the very earliest part of the late Carboniferous Period. This was a small (12in, 30cm long) lizard-like creature which probably fed on insects which it crunched up between the spiky teeth in its jaw. It also acts as an excellent starting point for the family tree of reptiles.

There are about 16 Orders of reptile currently recognised of which only four have survived to the present day (the crocodiles, lizards and snakes, *Sphenodon,* and turtles and tortoises). The sixteen Orders are divided into four major groupings or subclasses: the anapsids, synapsids, euryapsids and diapsids (see illustration). These subclasses are recognised by the pattern of openings that is developed at the back of the head, immediately behind the eye cavity.

Anapsids are generally regarded as the most primitive of reptiles, and have no opening in the skull roof at all. This is the condition seen in *Hylonomus* and also with a little modification in the skulls of turtles and tortoises, the only living representatives of this group. The earliest turtles date back to the late Triassic since when they have changed little. It would appear that the heavily armoured shell provided an exceptionally safe haven from all predators but rather hampered their chances of evolving into anything more exotic.

The **synapsids** or mammal-like reptiles are all extinct. They have skulls with a single opening relatively low down on the side of the skull. The earliest members of this group appear in the late Carboniferous as lizard-like creatures very similar to the anapsid *Hylonomus.* Synapsids reached their heyday in the late Permian and early Triassic times when they were by far the most abundant of terrestrial vertebrates. Towards the end of the Triassic they declined in number and variety becoming extinct at the close of that Period.

Euryapsids are characterised by having a single opening on the side of the skull, but higher in position than in the synapsid condition. The least satisfactory subclass, many palaeontologists believe that they are an unnatural group of reptiles that just happen to share this euryapsid condition by chance, rather than because of more fundamental genealogical reasons. Euryapsids are all marine reptiles and include the plesiosaurs, ichthyosaurs, placodonts and nothosaurs of the Mesozoic Era.

The **diapsids** have a pair of openings behind the skull and are one of the most diverse reptile groups. Again the earliest diapsid reptiles are known from the late Carboniferous Period. Diapsids include not only the highly successful

The Reptile Family Tree (right)

Reptiles can be subdivided into four major groups on the basis of the pattern of openings in the back of the skull. These are anapsids, synapsids, diapsids and euryapsids (see drawings below and main headings on chart). Anapsids seem to be the most primitive types of reptile since they have no special skull openings and appear earliest in the fossil record. *Hylonomus* is one of the earliest definite reptiles; it comes from late Carboniferous deposits of Nova Scotia. The only surviving anapsids are the turtles and tortoises. Synapsids have an impressive fossil record. The earliest forms, pelycosaurs, appeared in the late Carboniferous and are followed by the therapsids and cynodonts of the Permian and Triassic. Synapsid reptiles went extinct in the late Triassic or early Jurassic, but gave rise to the earliest mammals which survived the reign of the dinosaurs and then evolved rapidly. Diapsids can be divided into two groups: lepidosaurs (lizards and snakes) and archosaurs (crocodiles, dinosaurs and their kin). The archosaurs date back to the late Permian proterosuchians which were followed by the late Triassic phytosaurs and true crocodiles. The Triassic was the time of origin of all major archosaur groups from the thecodontians to the aerial pterosaurs and the dinosaurs (for whose family tree see page 23). Note that the birds are here related to theropod dinosaurs. Euryapsids are an uncertain group including the placodonts, ichthyosaurs, and plesiosaurs, all of which were swimming forms.

ANAPSID

SYNAPSID

DIAPSID

EURYAPSID

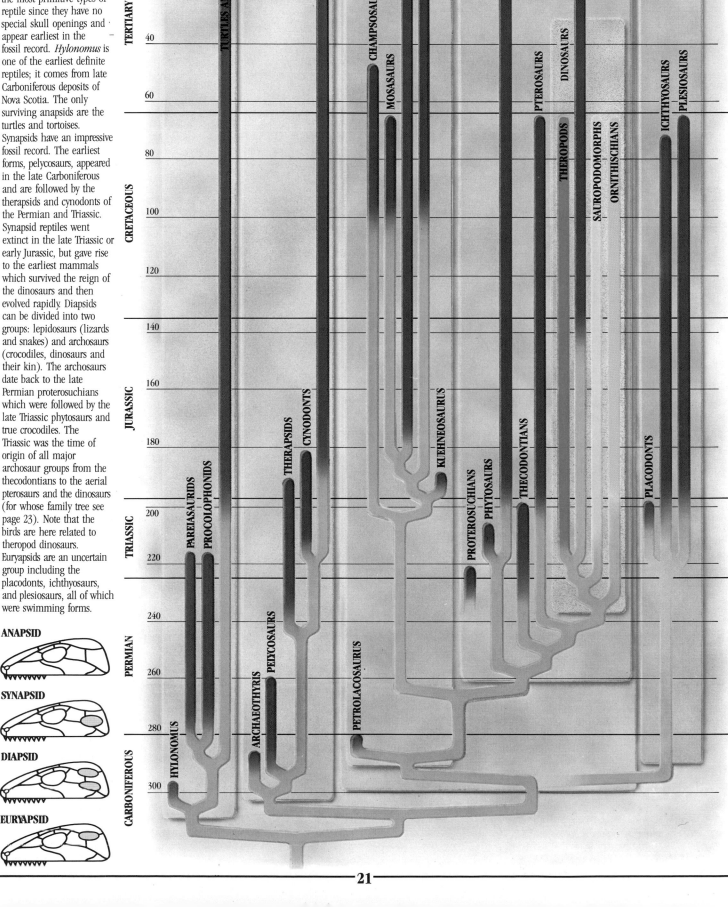

living forms, the lizards and snakes, but also the archaic lizard-like *Sphenodon* from New Zealand and the other great group the archosaurs ('ruling reptiles') represented today by the crocodiles and in the past by among others, the dinosaurs.

The archosaurs, dinosaurs on land and pterosaurs in the air, were particularly abundant and diverse during the Mesozoic Era, but suffered a major setback in the late Cretaceous when most non-crocodilian archosaurs went extinct. Since the end of the Cretaceous, the lizards and snakes have diversified and are now by far the most successful group of reptiles.

Skull Openings

The characteristic development of openings in the rear part of the skulls of reptiles was for a long time explained as providing areas for the muscles of the jaws to bulge when they contracted. Although this is indeed the case in living reptiles, it seems unlikely that this was the reason for their development in early anapsid reptiles. Tom Frazzetta provided an interesting alternative explanation that has been accepted by most. The openings are regarded as developing in order to lighten the skull to make it more flexible and manoeuvrable, and to provide areas for much more effective muscle attachment around the edges of the holes. So rather paradoxically the appearance of holes in the skull roof probably strengthened rather than weakened the bite of these reptiles!

The Dinosaur Family Tree

Dinosaurs, as mentioned above, are members of the archosaur group of reptiles; this includes the primitive thecodontians of the Permian and Triassic as well as the pterosaurs, crocodiles and dinosaurs which appear to have evolved from thecodontians. The archosaurs are recognised as such because they share several distinctive features that are not found in other diapsids. For example, the skull has, in addition to the 'diapsid' skull openings, another large triangular opening in front of the eye cavity and an opening in the side of the lower jaw as well. Archosaurs also tend to have rows of bony armour running down the middle of the back and, more often than not, have large, powerful back legs for running.

Turning to the dinosaurs, we can see from the family tree that dinosaurs are in fact divided into two distinct groups: the *Saurischia* ('reptile hipped') and the *Ornithischia* ('bird-hipped'). For many years after Richard Owen had christened the dinosaurs in 1841, they were regarded as a single group of reptiles. However, by 1887 enough material had been discovered to make it clear to Harry Govier Seeley that dinosaurs had either one type of hip arrangement or another, and so he coined these new names (see diagrams on page 9). The hip bones of saurischian dinosaurs do not differ very much from those of normal reptiles. Ornithischians by contrast have an unusual arrangement of hip bones whereby the pubis, which points forward and downward in reptiles, has swung backward to lie against the ischium. Curiously although this is the pattern seen in some early ornithischians, in later ornithischians (such as hadrosaurids or ceratopians) the pubis seems to develop a new forwardly-directed process; it is almost as if it were replacing the one that it had originally lost.

In addition to this very obvious difference in the structure of the pelvis, the two dinosaur groups differ in other ways. Notably the ornithischians are all herbivorous dinosaurs,

while saurischians are represented by both carnivorous and herbivorous types. Also the ornithischians are 'peculiar' in that unlike any other animal they have a predentary bone, a crescent-shaped piece of bone at the front of the lower jaw. The predentary has a sharp, toothless edge and was undoubtedly covered in horn (like a turtle's beak). Ornithischians are also unusual in that they have bony ligaments that form a trellis-like arrangement across the spines of the back.

The family tree indicates that in addition to this basic division into saurischians and ornithischians, dinosaurs can be further subdivided. The saurischians form a 'natural' division into mainly meat-eating theropods and plant-eating sauropodomorphs.

The theropods are nearly all bipedal animals which can be separated out into rather distinctive types. Just as today we recognise felids (cat-like meat-eating mammals), and canids (dog-like meat-eaters) and several other categories such as bears and weasels, so it is with the theropods. On the one hand there are the gigantic tyrannosaurids and at the other extreme there are the slender 'coelurosaurs', or yet again there are the peculiar toothless ostrich dinosaurs (ornithomimosaurs). These various subdivisions are represented here.

Similarly the herbivorous sauropodomorphs can be divided into clearly distinctive groups such as medium-sized prosauropods and gigantic sauropods and then further into more

Above: *Tyrannosaurus'* skull clearly shows the development of window-like openings in its sides characteristic of reptiles. These both lightened the head, and also improved the attachment areas for the jaw muscles, thereby increasing the power of the bite.

Below: This photograph shows the underside of the skull of one of the *Iguanodon* skeletons that were discovered at Bernissart in Belgium. The predentary bone characteristic of all ornithischian dinosaurs can be seen at the tip of the lower jaw.

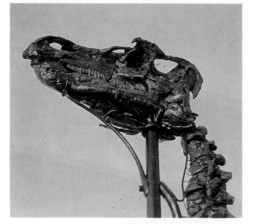

closely-related groups or families such as the diplodocids and brachiosaurids.

The ornithischians (despite their name) do not appear to be at all closely related to birds — in fact birds may be very closely related to saurischian theropods. The ornithischians are divided into several clearly distinct groups. There are the ornithopods ('bird feet') — a rather misleading name since their feet are not particularly bird-like! Most of these are bipedal though on occasions they were capable of walking on 'all-fours'. One rather distinctive group which may be close relatives of the ornithopods (there is some dispute about this) is the pachycephalosaurs ('thick headed reptiles').

There are also the stegosaurs ('plated reptiles'), the ankylosaurs ('fused [welded] reptiles') and the ceratopians ('horned faces'). Unlike the ornithopods these were predominantly quadrupedal (except for a few ceratopians).

The relationships between these dinosaur groups are indicated at right, and provide a framework for the cladograms that appear with the colour drawings of dinosaurs later in the book. (Cladograms are the family-tree-type drawings representing the possible evolutionary relationships of the dinosaurs).

Notes on Nomenclature

A variety of different names is used here for the various groupings of dinosaurs. These are arrived at as follows. The scheme starts with the species which are recognisable animal 'types', to put it rather simply. An example of this is the domestic cat, the scientific name for which is *Felis catus*. This consists of its 'particular' or species name, *catus*, and its 'group' or generic name, *Felis*. The generic, or genus, name indicates that domestic cats are members of a group of species of cat-like animals, such as the wild cat (*Felis sylvestris*) and the African bush cat (*Felis lybica*). Furthermore this genus *Felis* shows strong similarities to other cat-like carnivores such as the lion (*Panthera leo*) and the cheetah (*Acinonyx jubatus*); these can all be grouped together in the family *Felidae*.

We group related species of dinosaurs together in just the same way. For example *Iguanodon bernissartensis* is a particular *species* of ornithopod dinosaur. Other species of the genus *Iguanodon* are known: *I. mantelli, I. fittoni, I. dawsoni.* The genus *Iguanodon* is very similar to others such as *Camptosaurus, Ouranosaurus* and *Probactrosaurus*, so these are grouped together in the family *Iguanodontidae* (see the iguanodontids page 110). Beyond this level of grouping, the iguanodontid family shares features in common with several other families such as the hadrosaurids, hypsilophodontids and fabrosaurids and they are in turn grouped together in the Order Ornithopoda.

Thus we have a fairly clear hierarchy:

Order : Family : Genus : Species

In this book we will concentrate on these particular groupings: the Theropoda, and Sauropodomorpha of the Order Saurischia, and the Ornithopoda, Ceratopia, 'Pachycephalosaurs', Stegosauria and Ankylosauria in the Order Ornithischia. Within each of these major groupings the dinosaurs have, where possible, been clustered together into families (e.g. tyrannosaurids, hypsilophodontids etc.). Unfortunately this has not been possible in all groups as precise classification is currently almost impossible, and in this case the informal terms placed in quotation marks such as 'coelurosaurs' and 'carnosaurs' have been used. The reasons for this are explained in the relevant sections.

The Dinosaur Family Tree (right)

The major division of the dinosaurs is into the *Saurischia* and *Ornithischia*; it is based primarily on the differences in hip structure (see page 9). The *Saurischia* are further subdivided into *Theropoda* and *Sauropodomorpha*. The theropods included a wide variety of carnivorous dinosaurs all of which were bipedal. They range from small fast runners such as 'coelurosaurs', to the larger 'carnosaurs' and tyrannosaurids of the late Cretaceous. The sauropodomorphs were the large plant-eating dinosaurs of the Mesozoic. They include the partially bipedal prosauropods of the late Triassic and early Jurassic, and the massive quadrupedal sauropods of the later Jurassic and Cretaceous.

The *Ornithischia* were all herbivores. They can be further divided into a series of distinctive types: *Ornithopoda, Ceratopia, 'Pachycephalosaurs', Stegosauria* and *Ankylosauria*. Ornithopods first appeared in the early Jurassic with small, lightly-built creatures such as the fabrosaurids. They culminate in the late Cretaceous hadrosaurids. Ceratopians were a late Cretaceous group characterised by peculiar parrot-like beaks, horns and frills. Pachycephalosaurs were a strange group with oddly thickened skulls, while the stegosaurs and ankylosaurs were distinctively armoured types.

As can be seen, the various family groups have been given distinctive coloured bands (keyed below). They correspond to the colour bands across the top of the pages in the dinosaur section. The length of the coloured 'fingers' in this diagram corresponds to the geological time range in which we have found members of the family group.

THEROPODA

SAUROPODOMORPHA

ORNITHOPODA

CERATOPIA

'PACHYCEPHALOSAURS'

STEGOSAURIA

ANKYLOSAURIA

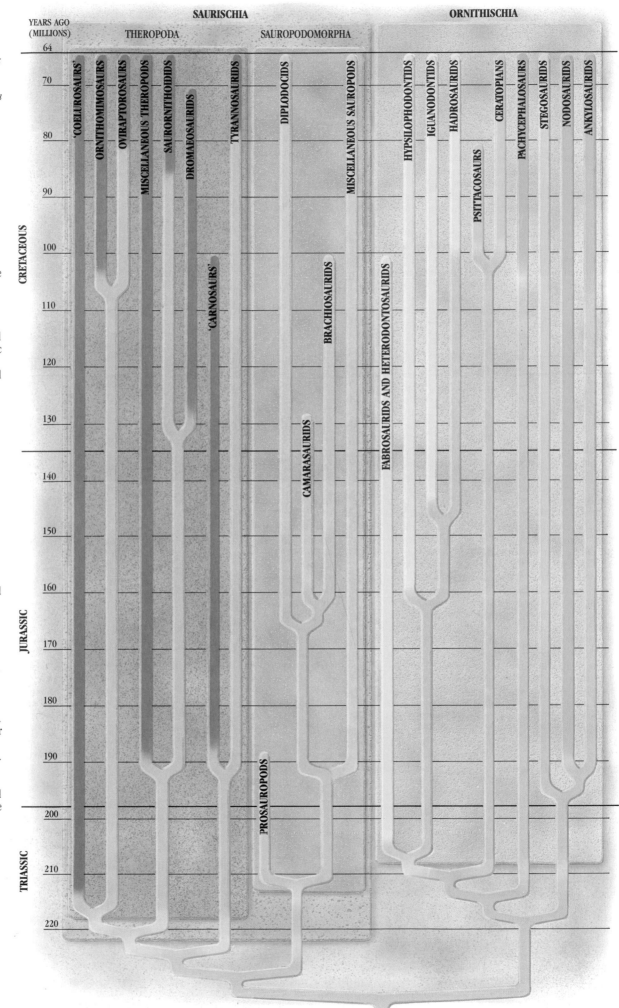

In this chapter we shall examine how a palaeontologist sets about studying a dinosaur, in this case *Iguanodon,* and show how research proceeds in a step-by-step way that involves several levels of intellectual activity in a fixed hierarchy. On the first level, the scientist analyses the fossils, taking into account the significance of where they were found, how they were excavated, and how they were prepared in the laboratory. By studying his laboratory specimens he can undertake the basic descriptive anatomy of the bones. From this stage, he can proceed to level two and make further anatomical deductions, such as how the skeleton might be put together and what this can tell us about the animal's musculature, its age, its nervous and blood systems, and likely methods of feeding and locomotion. Finally, the evidence from levels one and two is used to support higher level interpretations which may be concerned with how the dinosaur is related to other species, how this fits into the wider evolutionary framework, and what speculations we can make about the dinosaur as a living creature. So, let us proceed to study *Iguanodon,* starting at the first level outlined above.

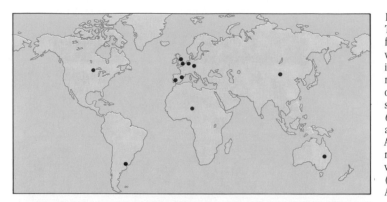

Iguanodon Finds (left)
The distribution of *Iguanodon* fossils has been reported to be very wide. However, on closer inspection many of the reports are found to be based on inadequate or misidentified specimens — for example, *Ouranosaurus* from Niger and *Muttaburrasaurus* from Australia. Definite *Iguanodon* remains are known in western Europe with possible (unsubstantiated) finds in Asia and North America.

Where is Iguanodon found?

Iguanodon remains are typically found in rocks which are of the Lower Cretaceous Period (about 100 million years ago — mya). However, although rocks of this age are known from every continent in the world, those containing remains that are definitely *Iguanodon* are only known across Europe and Asia (see map). There have been many other reports of *Iguanodon* in other countries, for example Spitzbergen in Norway, various parts of Africa, North America, South America and Australia, but these have been based on rather uncertain evidence such as footprint trackways (in Spitzbergen and South America) which are not diagnostic, or imperfect fragments of fossil bone, or teeth (in Africa). The evidence for *Iguanodon* in Australia was based on a partial skeleton of a dinosaur rather like *Iguanodon,* which on further inspection proved to be so different that it was given the name *Muttaburrasaurus* (see pages 110-111). The North American material is intriguing, but so far inconclusive. The material consists of a small piece of upper jaw with two teeth in it, and the end of a thigh bone (femur). Both of these specimens do indeed look rather like those of *Iguanodon.* Unfortunately there are several other known iguanodontids that also have such teeth and leg bones (*Camptosaurus* and *Ouranosaurus*) so at the moment we cannot be completely sure whether the North American specimens are of *Iguanodon.* This might seem to be an excessively cautious attitude to take to the evidence. However, as we shall see shortly, evidence such as the distribution of certain dinosaurs can be used to build up a much larger theoretical picture of the evolution and ecology of dinosaurs, and if the data base is not certain, this must be emphasized, otherwise it is possible that a completely inaccurate interpretation may be produced. The confusion resulting from this may take many years to resolve.

Looking in rather more detail at one of the areas where *Iguanodon* has been discovered, we can see that a considerable number of sites have yielded remains of this animal; these may range from isolated fragments of bone in some places, to partial or even complete skeletons in others. This locality data can reveal some interesting information. For example, if all the

The Wealden Area (right)
Illustrated here is a map of the Wealden area of south east England which includes parts of Sussex, Surrey and Kent. Plotted on the map are the sites where *Iguanodon* remains have been discovered as well as the geological formation from which they came. *Iguanodon* remains occur mainly in the Weald Clay (yellow) and Wadhurst Clay area (red). Orange signifies Tunbridge Wells Sand.

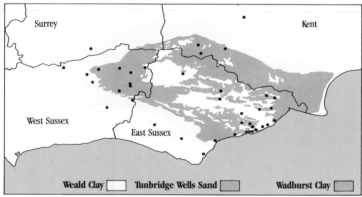

localities are plotted onto a geological map of the area, it can be seen that certain Wealden rocks, such as the Wadhurst Clay, the Tunbridge Wells Sand and the Weald Clay are the ones which tend to produce most of the fossils. We can, therefore, use this information to decide where to prospect for new fossil sites , and also take note of the range of time during which the fossils were laid down. For example, the Wadhurst Clay contains fossils of animals that lived much earlier than those of the Weald Clay, so we can ask whether there are any differences between the *Iguanodon* from these two periods which may reflect evolutionary changes.

In addition to the remains of *Iguanodon,* numerous other fossils have been discovered at these sites: other types of dinosaur, other reptiles, fish, even tiny shrew-like mammals and a vast array of plant remains. All of the latter information can be used to place *Iguanodon* into an ecological context. In attempting to reconstruct the environment in which *Iguanodon* might have lived, the geological nature of the deposits must be carefully reviewed to reassure ourselves that what we are

seeing is in fact a true community of animals and plants, and not the chance accumulation of these remains which have been washed together from their natural habitats which may have been widely separated.

What Fossils are They?

Iguanodon fossils come in a wide range of types which depend mainly upon the history and nature of the geological deposits in which they have been discovered. Wealden fossils were deposited in an area that we are confident was a fertile lowland plain across which many rivers and streams ran from upland areas to the north-east and south-west. At various times the land rose and fell, so that the Weald became periodically more marshy or lake-like. The dinosaurs living in the surrounding countryside naturally died and their remains may, or may not, have been washed into the river system and buried. As a result many fossils tend to be fragmentary, water-rolled specimens that are often quite hard to identify; these have undoubtedly come from rotted carcasses that

Right: This is an original drawing made by the mine workers (possibly even by Louis Depauw) at Bernissart. It is a carefully-drawn plan of a skeleton as it appeared when excavated.

Far right: Another drawing, this time by the artist Lavalette, made at the Museum in Brussels once the specimen (near right) had been reassembled and cleaned in the laboratories.

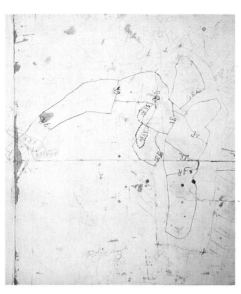

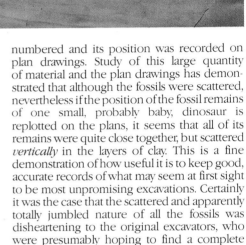

Above: This picture taken from Hanover Point beneath the cliffs on the southern coast of the Isle of Wight shows clearly the layers of Wealden rock that are being weathered away by wave action. Out of these rocks, which date from the Cretaceous Period, have fallen the remains of dinosaurs such as *Iguanodon*, *Polacanthus* and *Hypsilophodon*, as well as large sauropod and theropod dinosaurs.

Nehden Excavations (below and right)

Below we see early stages in the excavation of the new dinosaur quarry at Nehden in W. Germany. Beneath the protective awning, the clay deposit from which fossils have been recovered is being excavated systematically. The white posts act as markers so that a reference point can be given to each fossil as it is discovered and excavated prior to return to the Museum. Four plan drawings (right) taken at different levels within the quarry have here been super-imposed, using the original marker posts as reference points for each plan. The round dots on each level show the position of the remains of a baby *Iguanodon* which was evidently relatively undisturbed but scattered *vertically* rather than *horizontally*, as might have been expected.

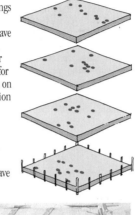

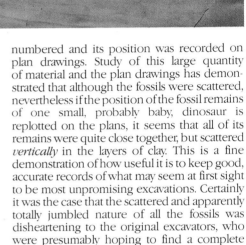

have been washed into a river and eventually fallen into pieces and the bones scattered and rolled among the pebbles and gravel of the river-bed. It is very rare that anything more complete than this is found; if it is, then it is almost invariably in the soft clays deposited under marshy conditions or in a lake. In this case, a carcass must have been rapidly washed downstream before sinking in a lake, and then being buried quickly in thick soft mud.

Much of the Wealden area has produced rather scrappy fragments, which caused early workers such as Mantell and Owen (see Chapter 1) so many problems. However, as early as 1871, an almost complete skeleton of an *Iguanodon* was discovered in the soft Wadhurst Clay near Hastings. Owen described various bits of it—but never realised that it was all part of the same animal! Unfortunately Owen, who never visited the site of the discovery relied on the amateur fossil collector, Samuel Beckles, to collect the skeleton, which consequently became rather mixed up. The specimen, now in the British Museum (Natural History) has lain unrecognised for over a century, yet it

could have anticipated much of Dollo's work on *Iguanodon* (see below).

Two other types of fossil discovery deserve mention: one of these at Nehden in West Germany is very recent (1980), the other at Bernissart is relatively old (1878).

The Find at Nehden

An abandoned open-cast quartz and gypsum quarry, near the village of Nehden, was found to contain, in a pocket of clay at its far end, some fragments of fossil bone. Eventually some teeth were found by Karl-Heinz Hilpert of the University Museum at Münster and identified as *Iguanodon*. Between 1980 and 1982 excavations were carried out at the new dinosaur site. They quickly revealed extremely rich fossil deposits. Much of the fossil bone, however, was disassociated. As a result it was decided to proceed with the excavations by removing horizontal layers of clay. The area to be excavated was mapped out using a grid of wooden posts at 20in (50cm) intervals and as each layer was excavated, each bone was

numbered and its position was recorded on plan drawings. Study of this large quantity of material and the plan drawings has demonstrated that although the fossils were scattered, nevertheless if the position of the fossil remains of one small, probably baby, dinosaur is replotted on the plans, it seems that all of its remains were quite close together, but scattered *vertically* in the layers of clay. This is a fine demonstration of how useful it is to keep good, accurate records of what may seem at first sight to be most unpromising excavations. Certainly it was the case that the scattered and apparently totally jumbled nature of all the fossils was disheartening to the original excavators, who were presumably hoping to find a complete skeleton.

Earlier Discoveries at Bernissart

An exceptional discovery was that made in 1878 at Bernissart, a small mining village in the Mons coal-field of south-west Belgium. The miners discovered a clay-filled fissure across a coal seam which was literally packed full of dinosaurs. However, rather than being fragmentary (as in the Wealden), or scattered (as at Nehden), the Bernissart fossils were of *complete* dinosaurs—as well as a whole range of fish, other reptiles and plant remains. These were discovered at a depth of 1,056ft (322m) in the mine. The remains of thirty-nine *Iguanodon*, many of them complete skeletons, were discovered at this site, before excavations were stopped in 1881. During the 1914-18 war, Bernissart was occupied by German forces, and the palaeontologist Otto Jaekel was sent from Berlin to supervise the reopening of the mine and the excavation of a new gallery. Just as the first fossiliferous layer was about to be uncovered, the Allies relieved Bernissart and work stopped. After the war, attempts were made to continue excavation, but regrettably the necessary money was not forthcoming and the mine had to be abandoned in 1921, after which it rapidly flooded. Many other skeletons, therefore, may still be buried underground.

As was the case at Nehden, very detailed records of the excavations undertaken between 1878 and 1881 were made. As each skeleton was discovered, it was given a letter of identification and its position in the mine was carefully drawn, so that it could then be divided up into manageable blocks which could be lifted. These were carried to the pit head and then transferred by rail to the Royal Museum of Natural History in Brussels where each entire animal was reassembled, rather in the manner of a giant jigsaw puzzle.

The detailed records that were made of both the position of each dinosaur in the mine, and of the geology of the mine itself, were kept in the archive and they have made it possible to reconstruct the arrangement of the dinosaurs in the mine and their relative geological positions. This entirely new analysis of all the data that was so carefully collected so many years ago has revealed some interesting details about the mode of deposition of these dinosaurs which as we shall see later has implications for most published comments on Bernissart and its *Iguanodon* collection.

Preserving Fossil Specimens

Preservation and conservation are subjects which do not normally receive much attention when dinosaur discoveries are discussed because fossilised bones are frequently both hard as stone and very stable. However, this is not always the case, as we shall see below. In the case of *Iguanodon,* these topics loom very large because the fossils recovered from both Bernissart and Nehden suffer, or have suffered in the past, from 'pyrite disease'. This is a condition in which the fossilised bone of the specimens appears spontaneously to crack and crumble away into fine pale-yellow powder. In earlier days this disastrous condition was thought literally to be caused by a disease that had 'infected' the fossil bones; thus various medical-type treatments were used in an attempt to 'kill' the infection. Such was the case at Bernissart. After the fossils had been excavated and were being transferred to Brussels between 1878 and 1881, they were constantly in danger of such decay. The procedure that was adopted to prevent and, it was hoped, cure the condition was to kill the 'disease' in the laboratories of the Museum in Brussels by using a rather dangerous mixture of alcohol saturated with arsenic and shellac — in order simultaneously to penetrate (alcohol), kill (arsenic), and harden (shellac) the fossils.

The record which was kept on the general state of preservation of the skeletons informs us that this attempt was not particularly successful. Between 1884 and 1890 the fossils continued to decay in their glass enclosure at the Museum and eventually all had to be returned to the laboratories for re-treatment.

We now know that the cause of 'pyrite disease' is *iron pyrites* (or 'fool's gold'), the chemical iron sulphide (FeS_2). At Bernissart (and at Nehden) the water in the clays where the dinosaurs were found contained this chemical which penetrated the bones. While the skeletons remain buried in the clay, they are relatively stable; there is no serious pyritic decay, although there can be the occasional growth of crystals of iron pyrites. However, once the fossils are removed from the clay during excavation, they begin to dry out. As a result the water content in the fossil bone falls from the usual level of saturation. At about 60% relative humidity some of the iron pyrites in the fossil (particularly the micro-crystalline variety) becomes unstable and is spontaneously converted to iron sulphate (the pale-green powder); free acids are also produced. Thus the 'disease' that affects these fossils is really a simple chemical process which is dependent only upon the amount of moisture in the air. What was happening in Brussels after the 'treatment' was that the alcohol-arsenic-shellac mixture helped to strengthen the fossils, but at the same time it

trapped moisture within the bones, so that instead of the bones drying out quite quickly with a small amount of pyritic decay taking place, the whole process was extended over a period of probably twenty to thirty years so that considerable damage was done. It is a great pity that the method that was used to preserve the marvellous collections of fossils from Bernissart actually resulted in their suffering more from the effects of 'pyrite disease' rather than less. However, at the time when this was done, nobody knew any better way of treating them. We can all be wise with hindsight. Having eventually 'dried out', the Bernissart material on display at the Royal Institute of Natural Sciences in Brussels (formerly the Royal Museum of Natural History) is now perfectly stable. In addition, large glass enclosures were built around the display in the 1930s which serve to stabilise the humidity around the specimens.

Nehden, the newest find of *Iguanodon,* presented the same problems as those faced at Bernissart: pyritic decay. The treatment of these fossils has been significantly different and reflects modern techniques of conservation. As soon as a fossil was exposed, it was coated with a weak epoxy-resin to prevent too much evaporative water loss. The specimen was then removed by cutting it out in a jacket of clay, and wrapping the whole in hessian cloths. In the laboratory the fossils were unwrapped and then placed in a large, purpose-built vacuum impregnator with polyethylene glycol granules. The vacuum pump dehydrates the specimens, and the temperature is gradually raised to 60°C to drive off any remaining moisture and to melt the polyethylene glycol which penetrates, seals and greatly strengthens the fossils, as well as the clay matrix. The latter has then to be removed rather laboriously using air- and/or electrically powered vibrating hammers. The resulting fossils, when full prepared, are extremely tough and very stable with a slightly 'waxy' feel.

Studying the Bones

The last, and in many ways the most important but also the most tedious, part of the process of collecting information about a fossil animal such as *Iguanodon* takes place in the laboratory.

The bones have to be sorted and glued together where necessary, and carefully cleaned; the latter may take a considerable amount of time if they are embedded in very hard rock and need to be prepared by mechanical or chemical means. However, when this is finally completed, the specimen is ready to be described. This is one of the most important stages in the study of any fossil species because it is the detail and accuracy of the description that will allow other scientists who are interested in similar animals to compare them closely and perhaps draw conclusions about their relatedness or about their general biology.

The scientific description takes the form of detailed drawings and photographs of individual bones in various views (dorsal, medial, ventral, lateral, proximal and distal) and in the case of some complicated specimens or teeth with much fine detail that are very difficult to draw, photographs in stereo pairs may be used so that the researcher, with the appropriate viewer, can see a three-dimensional picture of the specimen in question. The various illustrations are accompanied by a great deal of technical language which is used to describe particular important features of the bones, and also to make comparisons with other dinosaurs in order to demonstrate their similarities or differences.

In addition to the bone-by-bone description of the skeleton, various drawings are usually made of the reconstruction of certain parts of the body. This helps considerably to clarify the description. For example, it is all very well to describe each bone of the skull in minute detail, but it is practically impossible to fit these all together in your mind to visualise a complete skull.

All this rather dry and dusty work gives a very detailed knowledge of bony structures which does, on occasions, have rather unexpected benefits. A rather large, non-descript bony fragment, which had been discovered in a quarry in the Wealden, was unidentifiable until I re-discovered it. My detailed descriptive work meant that I immediately recognised it as a part of the rear of the head of a large *Iguanodon,* including the braincase. The fossil bone of the head was extremely poorly preserved but it was

Above: The detailed records that were kept by Louis Dollo of the condition of the Bernissart fossils that were put on display in the museum courtyard tell a sad story of continual pyritic decay.

Below: At Münster University, the fossils from Nehden were treated in a vacuum impregnator. This vertebra of *Iguanodon* has just been treated and shows the 'waxy' protective coating of polyethylene glycol covering it.

Right: Once the fossil has been collected and brought back to the Museum, the long task of preparation begins. More often than not the fossil is embedded in a slab of rock, with just a small portion exposed. The job then is carefully to remove the rock at the same time avoiding damage to the fossil. One of the standard preparatory tools is an electrically-powered vibrating needle which is being used here delicately to chip away the rock.

embedded in very hard rock so I decided to have the specimen sectioned in the hope that it might reveal parts of the endocranial cavity (the cavity for the brain). The specimen did indeed show evidence of the brain cavity; but more than this, further preparation revealed the presence of a brain cast, the cranial nerves, the blood system surrounding the brain and the structure of the inner ear (where the hearing and balancing senses are located). This exciting find would not have been made if it had not been for the underlying, painstaking work that had gone into studying the bones.

Having thus established a data-base, a 'body' of solid evidence concerning the detailed structure of *Iguanodon*, this evidence can then be 'used' in order to gain a more comprehensive idea of the way in which the animal lived—its biology—as far as possible. This is done largely by using comparisons with living animals and a measure of elementary mechanics and common sense. Let us see to what extent we can use these principles to understand more about the biology of *Iguanodon*.

The Shape of the Skeleton

In that there are complete skeletons of *Iguanodon* known from Bernissart, it is possible to build up quite an accurate picture of its general shape. It is frequently the case that palaeontologists have rather more fragmentary remains to deal with, so that their attempts must be inevitably more tentative.

It is surprising to see how much our idea of the general body-shape of *Iguanodon* has changed over the years. As we saw earlier, the first conception of *Iguanodon* as a gigantic lizard was very inaccurate and reflected the very fragmentary nature of the material at hand. Similarly Owen's conception (following the idea of Cuvier) that *Iguanodon* was a reptilian rhinoceros was wrong, but understandable at the time. The first restoration of the skeleton of *Iguanodon* based on complete skeletons was that of Louis De Pauw and Louis Dollo, which has become the standard restoration up to the present day. As we shall see below, I think that there are good reasons why the De Pauw-Dollo restoration is not correct; however, first of all let us consider why it was that De Pauw and Dollo chose this particular form for the body.

Between 1878 and 1882 (1882 was when the first restoration of *Iguanodon* was produced) Dollo and De Pauw had many complete skeletons and detailed drawings to study so that the anatomy was very clear. The prevailing scientific influence at that time was from the work of Thomas Henry Huxley (an influential

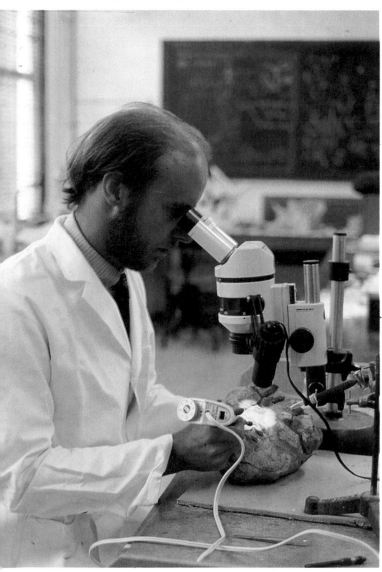

Endocranial Cast (right and below right)
This photograph shows the endocranial cast of *Iguanodon* after careful preparation. The specimen is seen here looking down on it from above and slightly behind the right ear of the dinosaur. The brain cast is the portion on the left side of the photograph. Various narrow pipes or tubes can be seen running to and from the brain cast and represent the passages for nerves and blood vessels. An outline drawing of the photograph shows more clearly some of the parts of the brain cast. The labels identify many of the parts. For example, os. lab. = osseus labyrinth, the cavity of the inner ear; jug = jugular vein; ol. lob. = olfactory lobes; vcd, v. par, Ts, vcm and sub. v refer to other blood vessels and the Roman numerals to nerves.

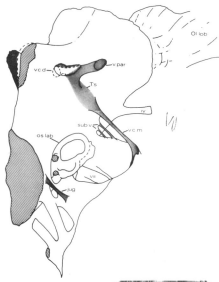

Iguanodon Skull (below)
This detailed drawing (a longitudinal section) shows the arrangement of bones inside the skull of *Iguanodon* and has been made possible by careful and painstaking work on lots of isolated bony fragments; these have been put together rather like a difficult jigsaw puzzle. At the top right is the area of the braincase, with the outline of the brain shown quite clearly.

Detailed Drawings (right)
These drawings are of the shin and ankle bones of *Iguanodon*. As can be seen these have been drawn in various views: a = dorsal, b = medial, c = ventral, d = lateral, e = proximal, f = distal. In this way a fairly detailed picture of the anatomy of the dinosaur can be built up and used for comparisons with other dinosaurs.

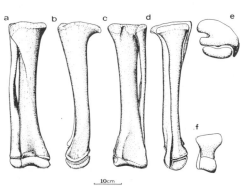

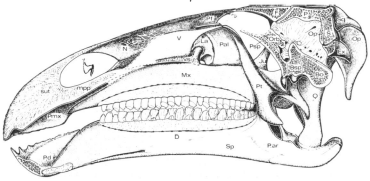

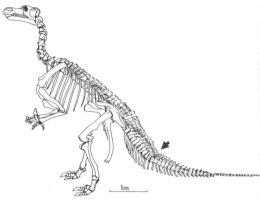

Left: This photograph taken in 1879/80 shows the first attempt to reconstruct the skeleton of *Iguanodon* from material at Bernissart. Note the small emu and wallaby skeletons for guidance. This workshop was in the Chapel of St George in Brussels, near the Natural History Museum.

The Bernissart Iguanodon (above) This finished version of *Iguanodon* was completed in about 1882 after the first attempts of 1878. This reconstruction was first published by Dollo in 1882. Note that the tail was broken in the area arrowed.

evolutionary biologist and palaeontologist). A decade earlier (in 1870), Huxley had been able to demonstrate that dinosaurs showed certain affinities with birds in the construction of the hip bones and hind leg, rather than with large pachydermal mammals as Owen believed. So Dollo and De Pauw not surprisingly chose an emu skeleton as one model upon which to base the reconstruction, because *Iguanodon* showed clearly the bird-like pelvis and the rather bird-like hind leg as Huxley had predicted. However, the resemblance was far from complete; unlike a bird, *Iguanodon* had a massive bony tail, and large forelimbs and hands. The only other living animals that fit these general proportions are members of the kangaroo family. Thus we see in photographs of the time the skeletons of an emu and a wallaby dwarfed alongside the massive bones and skeleton of the first *Iguanodon*. Not surprisingly then, the final version of the restored skeleton resembled, if anything, a giant wallaby, with a hint of emu in its bird-like neck. And indeed, this is how *Iguanodon* has been restored ever since, both as a skeleton and also as flesh restorations.

There are however, in my opinion, several anatomical features which suggest that all is not well with this particular restoration. Let us consider them point by point.

The tail As can be seen from the beautiful drawings made at the time, and also in several of the skeletons in Brussels today which are laid out as they were found in the mine, the tail was normally held out in a straight line behind the hips; it was held straight by a series of long bony rods (the remnants of long tendons of the muscles of the back). However, if we look at the De Pauw—Dollo restoration we can see the kangaroo-like sweep of the tail. Looking carefully at the original skeleton it is possible to see that the tail of *Iguanodon* has been artificially curved. This point is very important because straightening the tail produces great changes in the form of the body. If the tail is straightened, the front part of the body has to be lowered so that the backbone is more horizontal and the animal is balanced at the hips; this in turn explains why the long bony tendons of the back are continued into the tail: they acted as powerful cable-like hawsers to prevent the backbone from sagging while the long, heavy tail counterbalanced the front end of the body. This cantilevered design is a very simple and yet mechanically efficient system of support which would undoubtedly have been

necessary for an animal measuring between 30 and 33ft (9-10m) in length and weighing somewhere between 1·5 and 2 tonnes.

The repercussions caused by altering the posture to one in which the vertebral column was held more horizontally are interesting. The first consideration relates to the forelimbs. If the front end of the vertebral column is lowered, the forelimb is brought quite close to the ground, certainly close enough to touch the ground with ease. The question then is whether *Iguanodon* was able to use its front legs for walking, or whether it tucked them out of the way, rather like a kangaroo does when it is hopping at speed. To try to solve this question we can use various lines of investigation. Here we will concentrate on a few areas.

The hand The structure of the hand may well indicate the range of ways in which it can be used. As can be seen from the diagram, the hand of *Iguanodon* is the normal five-fingered structure with which we are already familiar in our own hands. However, if we look a little closer, then we can appreciate several rather unusual characteristics. Firstly the thumb is modified into a large, conical spike which sits upon the side of the wrist. In fact it can only move across the wrist in a sweeping movement,

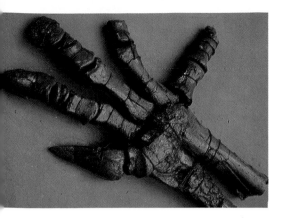

Above: This isolated hand found in the mine at Bernissart is very well-preserved and clearly shows some of the unusual features of the hand: note particularly the large spike on the thumb, the broad hooves on its middle fingers, and its slender fifth finger.

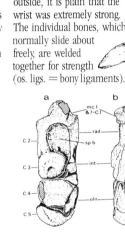

Left: In Brussels Natural History Museum two large glass enclosures are used to display the *Iguanodon* skeletons from Bernissart. In one there are 11 skeletons mounted in standing position, while the other (seen here) has the remains of 20 skeletons laid out roughly in the positions that they were found.

The Wrist Bones (below)
Seen here in two views (a) end on, and (b) from the outside, it is plain that the wrist was extremely strong. The individual bones, which normally slide about freely, are welded together for strength (os. ligs. = bony ligaments).

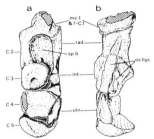

Chest Bones (right)
Looked at from beneath, the bones of the shoulders and chest are clearly visible. The two hatchet-shaped bones lie in the area of the breast, while the two saucer-shaped bones are parts of the shoulders. Between these lies an irregular bone which may have strengthened the chest for walking on all-fours.

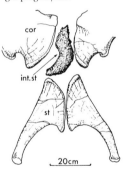

Flexing the Hand (above)
By adjusting the bones of the hand, it can be arranged in a 'fully-flexed' position as shown here. The fingers cannot be closed properly to make a 'fist', although the 5th finger can be flexed across the hand quite well, as shown here.

The Walking Hand (left)
By contrast, the middle three fingers can be hyperextended and form a very effective weight-supporting arrange-ment. The broad and rather twisted hooves on these fingers seem well adapted for walking on, rather than for grasping objects.

and it seems to have nothing to do with the other fingers which it cannot touch. The second, third and fourth fingers are also rather oddly arranged. The three long bones that form the palm of the hand are held together very rigidly and the toes on the ends tend to splay outward, away from one another towards their tips. In addition, and perhaps most significantly, if the joints between the finger bones are analysed for movement it can be seen that these fingers cannot be closed to make a tight 'fist' for holding objects (plant food etc.) but they can be bent backwards (hyperextended) on themselves. Finally, the tips of the second and third fingers are not narrow and curved as they are in typical prehensile hands, but are broad, flattened and twisted, in this way they resemble the toe bones of the walking legs of animals such as the rhinoceros or hippopotamus.

Unlike the others, the fifth finger is quite long and, judging by the way the individual bones are jointed together, very flexible. Certainly this would have been much more finger-like in our sense than any of the other fingers; perhaps it was used to hook up or manipulate pieces of foliage into the mouth.

As can be seen in the diagram, the hand can be reconstructed both in a grasping position

(rather unconvincing because the fingers do not meet, but rather diverge) or in a splayed position, as if resting on the ground. The latter position, with fingers splayed is so similar to the splayed, weight-bearing arrangement in the foot that this seems to be the most reasonable position.

The wrist In a mobile, grasping hand, the wrist bones are usually well-developed and allow considerable movement to take place between the hand and the forearm. Obviously the hand should be as flexible as possible. In a hand used for walking upon, the bones of the wrist perform the function of shock absorbers and tend to be quite flattened, and reduce the range of movement between hand and forearm to that of a simple hinge so that the likelihood of dislocating the wrist while running, or even walking, is minimised.

In *Iguanodon* the wrist bones are quite extraordinarily modified. The individual wrist bones can just about be distinguished, but they are all cemented together by the growth of a lot of spongy bone and the alteration of normally tough, cord-like ligaments which wrap around the wrist, into sheets of bony fibres. The hand and forearm bones are wedged into the wrist to create quite a firm

structure with a very limited range of movement.

The forearm and upper arm These are quite stout bones and are also proportionally rather long (ie 70% of the length of the back leg). The stoutness and length of the front legs are not typical of an animal which uses its hands to pick up objects; again, those bones tend to be rather light and slender so that the arms are more mobile.

The shoulders Again, the shoulder bones are very large, reflecting the size of the arm and hand. However, although we would expect the shoulder bones to be quite large in such animals whether they were walking on two or four legs, there is one peculiarity in the shoulder girdle of *Iguanodon*. In several of this specimens from Bernissart in Belgium, there is a peculiar irregular bone in the centre of the chest (see diagram). This completely novel bone, not usually found in dinosaurs of this type, requires some explanation. If we add together the information from above, then there is one possible explanation at least for why it is there.

Putting all the information together, we have an animal with a hand that is incredibly specialised. The thumb is stiletto-like and was most probably used rather like a gangster's stiletto-knife for fighting at close-quarters with large predatory dinosaurs such as *Megalosaurus* (pages 62-67). The middle three fingers formed a solid centre to the hand, and were hoofed and able to bend backward to form a weight-supporting arrangement. Finally, the fifth finger was a highly mobile, prehensile structure which may indeed have been used to grasp objects. Add to this the stiff wrist, the long, powerful arm bones and shoulders and it seems almost inevitable that *Iguanodon* used to walk on all-fours at least for part of the time. Obviously it must also have been able to use its front legs as ordinary hands, by swinging the front part of the body upwards, perhaps to browse on foliage, or to defend itself against predators. However, I suspect that fully-grown animals may have spent much of their time on 'all-fours' because this would account for the peculiar bone found in the centre of the chest. The knobbly texture of this bone, and its rough and quite variable shape suggests that it may be a pathological development. I think that this bone may well have formed because the fully-grown animals were walking on their front legs for considerable periods of time. The weight carried by the front legs, during walking especially, would be transmitted alternately through the left and right halves of the shoulder bones at each stride; this would inevitably cause twisting across the chest between the shoulders, where the tissues were probably of cartilage and, compared with bone, quite weak. The new bone may therefore have formed in the cartilage of the chest to help prevent the chest from being literally pulled apart while walking. You may well ask, why don't other four-footed dinosaurs have this problem and also develop peculiar chest bones? The answer seems to be that at least some did; it has recently been reported that some ankylosaurs have similar irregular chest bones.

As was mentioned earlier, it seems that the nearer to full adult size that *Iguanodon bernissartensis* grew, the more likely it was to walk or rest on all-fours. This implies that smaller and presumably younger individuals spent more of their time walking bipedally. The reason for believing this can be found by looking at leg and arm proportions in small and large *Iguanodon* skeletons. Curiously if the lengths of the forelimb and hindlimb are compared in small and large specimens, the small individuals seem to have proportionally shorter arms than the larger specimens! Therefore as the animals grew to full size, their front legs got longer as if they were anticipating being used to walk upon. This rather strange observation may perhaps be explained by the way of life of the animal. As relatively peaceable plant eaters, *Iguanodon* undoubtedly fell prey to the large, predatory dinosaurs of the time such as *Megalosaurus* or *Altispinax* (pages 62-67) or even 'super-claw' (pages 56-61). Small *Iguanodon* would probably not have had the physical strength to defend themselves against large predators, and probably relied upon their agility and speed to escape. The larger, heavier and less agile adults would have used an alternate strategy; they were large and powerful and could have stood their ground against predators, using the stiletto-like thumb-spike as a devasting weapon at close-quarters.

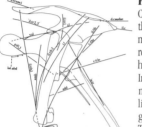

Hip Muscles (left)
Careful study of the surface of the pelvis and leg bones makes it possible to attempt a reconstruction of the main hip muscles of *Iguanodon*. In this diagram, the main muscles are indicated as lines and their names are given in abbreviated form. The arrangement is quite like that of birds and crocodiles.

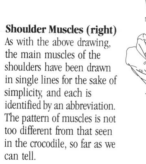

Shoulder Muscles (right)
As with the above drawing, the main muscles of the shoulders have been drawn in single lines for the sake of simplicity, and each is identified by an abbreviation. The pattern of muscles is not too different from that seen in the crocodile, so far as we can tell.

Reconstructing Muscles

In addition to analysing the skeletons to make bone-by-bone reconstructions, it is also possible to study certain areas of the body (the hips, shoulders and head in particular) for evidence of muscle attachment. This is possible because areas where muscles and ligaments are attached to bone frequently develop characteristic surface markings or muscle scars. Some muscles even cause the development of ridges or crests of bone especially for their attachment. In areas of the body where large and powerful muscles are attached, such as around the hips, shoulders and head, the pattern of muscle scars can be quite distinctive, even in fossil bone. So, how do we interpret the muscle scars? Well, just as in the case with the reconstruction of the skeleton from its bones, we use a judicious mixture of comparison with modern living relatives, and a certain amount of commonsense.

The hips As can be seen in the diagram the muscles of the hip of *Iguanodon* can be reconstructed to show remarkable complexity. The basis for this is firstly the pattern of muscle scars on hip and femur. These are then compared with the known arrangement of muscle attachments of hip and leg muscles in living crocodiles and birds. The reasons for using these two groups for comparison are as follows: crocodiles, as archosaurs, are the only living reptilian relatives of the dinosaurs (see pages 20-21) and would therefore perhaps be expected to show some fundamental resemblances in muscle arrangement with a dinosaur such as *Iguanodon*; birds seem also to be not only extremely close relatives of the dinosaurs (pages 191-194) but also show a very similar arrangement of their hip bones (*Iguanodon* being after all an ornithischian or 'bird-hipped' dinosaur).

Of course the pattern of muscle scars on the hips of *Iguanodon* does not *exactly* conform to the pattern seen in either the crocodile or the bird, so the final reconstruction represents a compromise which, in the opinion of the expert, seems to be the most reasonable interpretation of the evidence available. Obviously the skeletal reconstruction and proposed method of locomotion will influence the final choice. I should say that bearing all

these factors in mind, the final interpretation should not be too far from the truth.

The shoulders Exactly the same technique is used to interpret the muscles of the shoulder region as well. However this time we cannot use the crocodile *and* the bird for comparison. The bird would be a very unwise choice for comparison because it has forelimbs that are modified into wings. This means that although the pattern of bones in the arm and shoulder are roughly comparable with those of *Iguanodon*, the muscles are highly modified for flapping—a movement that is not very important to a terrestrial animal.

Again, as in the hip region, it is possible to come up with a fairly clear pattern of muscles, which should be consistent with the proposed way of life of the animal.

The head The muscles of the head are principally those necessary for feeding. In most cases these muscles are quite complicated in their arrangement. The reason for this is that the majority of animals bite their food quite precisely (just think how carefully and delicately or powerfully you can move your teeth and jaws); to do this many different muscles are needed (the more the better, it would seem!). The illustrations show details of the structure of *Iguanodon*'s head.

Feeding Habits

Just as the muscles of the hips can be useful to support or confirm ideas about the method of locomotion of an animal, so too can the jaw muscles help to work out how such an animal chewed its food. In the case of carnivores the teeth and jaws are mainly concerned with killing (large stabbing teeth) and biting off chunks of meat which can be swallowed quickly so that the flesh can be digested in the stomach. Herbivores face a much greater problem: plant food is far less nutritious than meat, which can be quickly broken down in the stomach, and therefore they have to spend a lot of time 'processing' it. That is to say pounding up the plant fibres so that they will release their nutrients, just as cows now 'chew the cud'.

By any standards *Iguanodon* was a large herbivore and would probably therefore have been quite efficient about the way in which it

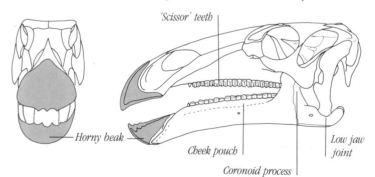

'Scissor' teeth

— Horny beak —

Cheek pouch

Low jaw joint

Coronoid process

Clothing in Muscles and Skin (left)
It is possible to clothe the skeleton of *Iguanodon* in the muscles of the shoulders, hips and head from the analysis so far given. Add to this the general muscles of the neck, belly and tail (middle picture) and we can wrap it in skin and provide a restoration of the animal as a living creature. (From Mark Hallett's drawings.)

Beak and Jaws (above)
The diagrams above show the likely form of the horny beak that covered the front of the upper and lower jaws of *Iguanodon* in life. This sharp, continually-growing beak would have been very effective for nipping off tough twigs and shoots of horsetails, cycads and conifers that may well have been the staple diet of this herbivorous creature.

Right: A heavily worn tooth is seen near right. The upper, wider part is worn flat and the right hand side is broken off. Note the long, slender root. The middle tooth is a newly emerged crown; the surface is shiny with its hard enamel coating and the coarse serrations can be seen on its front and back edges. Far right is a partly worn tooth, and below are teeth embedded in the jaw.

dealt with its food. Looking at the skull we can see that the front of its jaws lacked teeth but had instead a turtle-like horny beak which would have been ideal for cropping vegetation, and has the added advantage of never wearing out! The teeth are very numerous (100 or so) and are found in parallel rows; the teeth in each row lock together to form a continuous cutting edge. The teeth are also inset, that is to say that there is a depression along the outside of both the upper and lower jaws which formed a cheek pouch. At the back of the lower jaw there is a large prong of bone, the coronoid process, to which many of the large jaw muscles were attached; behind this again the jaw drops down sharply to the jaw joint which means that all teeth would meet simultaneously as the jaws close.

The jaw muscles would close the jaws very powerfully, so that the teeth in each jaw meet and slide past one another. In doing this a most remarkable thing happens. Because the upper

teeth slide at an angle past the *outside* of the lower teeth, the upper jaw on either side is pushed apart; it is able to do this because instead of its head being solid, as is usually the case, it has joints running down either side of it. The movement seems to have been controlled by special ligaments or muscles.

This extraordinary system whereby the upper jaw can move sideways is very interesting, and was probably very important to *Iguanodon* because it allowed this dinosaur to chew its food very efficiently. Large herbivorous mammals (cows or horses or people for example) chew their food by moving the *lower* jaw not only up and down but also from side-to-side in a rotatory movement. The side-to-side part of the movement is very important because it means that the lower teeth can grind against the upper teeth and so break up the plant fibres. Reptiles generally cannot chew food like this, and *Iguanodon* is no

exception; they do not have the special muscles that allow mammals to move the lower jaw from side to side. However, although *Iguanodon* can only move its lower jaw simply up and down, because its upper jaw splays outwards, the upper teeth are able to make the all-important grinding movement against the lower ones. This is rather a fine example of a completely unexpected alternative solution developed by the dinosaurs to the problem of how to chew plants efficiently. As can be appreciated, the presence of the peculiar joints in the skull of *Iguanodon* may have remained completely inexplicable if we had not had the mammalian example of chewing for comparison.

Nervous and Blood Systems

The endocranial cast referred to earlier clearly shows the general shape of the brain cavity of *Iguanodon*, (as well as lots of other interesting details), which give an insight into aspects of the life of the animal that are very rare in any fossil species.

Careful analysis of the cast reveals the degree of development of the nervous system — the system that governed sensitivity (sight, hearing, taste etc), co-ordination and behaviour. This reveals that rather than being stupid, slow-witted creatures as is the popular image of dinosaurs, they had quite large brains by reptilian standards and were highly sensitive, well co-ordinated, and probably capable of quite elaborate behaviour. With regard to behaviour, many living reptiles, crocodiles especially, show remarkable complexity, particularly that associated with breeding and care of the young hatchlings.

In addition, the endocranial cast has brought to light unexpected details of the blood supply to the brain and surrounding tissues. All of this is really quite amazing detail when you consider that fossils of *Iguanodon* are over 100 million years old.

Variability and Sex

One particular problem that bedevils palae-ontological research is sexual dimorphism. That is to say if we find some differences between the fossilised skeletons of two otherwise very similar animals, can we prove that the differences are just (i) the normal range of variation for the species (just think of the range of shapes and sizes that human beings come in!), or (ii) that they show the differences to be expected between male and female of the same species, or (iii) that they are in fact truly different species?

These are virtually insoluble problems, because the ultimate solution could only be found if we had the living animals to study. In the end, decisions of this type are to some degree arbitrary, reflecting the opinion of the expert in question.

In the case of *Iguanodon* we again have a rather interesting situation. In Bernissart many skeletons were discovered at the same site, and therefore may represent a local 'population' or fauna of this species. It should therefore be possible to investigate the skeletons for tell-tale signs of normal individual variability or sexual differences. What has been discovered is that there are two different 'types' of *Iguanodon*: one named *Iguanodon bernissartensis* is very large, (30-33ft, 9-10m long) and stoutly built, as might be expected of an animal weighing about 2 tonnes; the other is named *Iguanodon mantelli* and is quite a lot smaller,

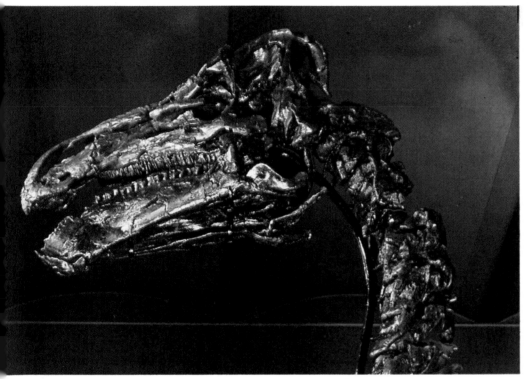

Above: This specimen in Brussels is very well preserved and little disturbed. The shiny reflective surface of the bones is caused by coatings of preservative. Note here the shape of the skull with its large beak, long, tooth-lined jaws, inset teeth for a cheek pouch, low jaw joint and coronoid process, all of which helped it to chew tough plants.

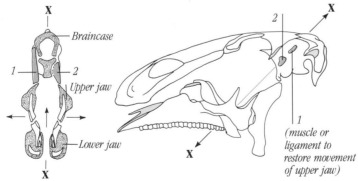

Skull and Jaw Movements (above)

These drawings attempt to show how these animals were able to chew tough plants very efficiently. Above, the lower jaw has been removed, and the remainder of the skull has been separated into two portions. One bears the teeth: the upper jaw and other attached bones; the other being the remainder of the skull roof and braincase. These two portions are jointed together along the blue areas so that the upper jaw on each side can swing in and out. Above left we see a cross-section along the line x-x in the previous diagram. It demonstrates how closing the jaws pushes the upper jaws apart, allowing the upper teeth to slide past the lower, so creating a grinding motion.

(muscle or ligament to restore movement of upper jaw)

(16·5-20ft, 5-6m long) and more gracefully built (weighing about 0·7 tonne).

These two species can be distinguished by several anatomical differences: the shape of the skull, the bones of the hand, the pelvis and foot. So, what is the significance of these differences? Well, since they are consistent (even when you compare similar sized individuals), at first sight the differences can be used to propose that the skeletons are of separate species (therefore *I. bernissartensis* and *I. mantelli* are sufficiently distinct to be given names that recognise the differences). It does not seem reasonable to regard these two 'types' as representing variations within a single species (the differences are regarded as too great and too consistent for that). However, that leaves the last option, which is to decide whether they represent male and female versions of the same species. Here 'expert' opinions are divided, several workers have proposed that the two 'species' are male and female. Some regard the small type *(I. mantelli)* as the male, others regard it as the female (i.e. if we use modern reptiles for comparison, some male lizards and crocodiles are larger than the females, whereas female turtles are usually larger than the males).

The present interpretation that I shall give is rather ambiguous, because the answer is not clear. The anatomical differences between these specimens are sufficiently clear-cut to allow them to be defined as species. Therefore, I think that the names *I. bernissartensis* and *I. mantelli* should remain. However, in saying this I am proposing that two species of very similar-sized dinosaurs, which are obviously closely related, lived at the same time and probably in the same area. Is this reasonable from a biological and ecological point of view? The answer is a *probable* no! It would need to be demonstrated that the two 'types' of *Iguanodon* are separated ecologically, so that they were not competitors for the same niche.

Thus there are two outstanding problems: firstly, can the differences between the two 'types' of *Iguanodon* be proved to be sexual, and secondly, can the two 'types' be separated ecologically? Neither question can be answered satisfactorily. For the time being, therefore, the two types are recognised as species, but they may be sexual forms of just one species.

Higher Level Interpretations

There are a number of ways in which the evidence that has been accumulated throughout this chapter can be brought together to help us draw more wide-ranging conclusions and generate new theories. I will elaborate a few of these.

Anatomy and relationships The detailed anatomical studies can be used for comparison with other dinosaurs of a similar type in order to get an idea of its evolutionary relationships with the other forms. The strictly anatomical data can be used to generate a pattern of relationships (see cladogram of iguanodontids on page 111). This can then be superimposed upon the geological timescale so that we can tie the relationships into an evolutionary pattern. By this means we can then begin to ask questions about how and why the pattern of relationships may have arisen through evolution, or indeed perhaps whether the relationships that have been proposed are indeed correct!

One way of using this sort of approach is to compare the pattern of relationships that have been deduced with the *geographical* distribution of the species involved. That is to say, is there any broad correlation between geographical separation of species (through continental drift for example) and the evolutionary pattern that has been deduced?

In the case of *Iguanodon* and related ornithopod dinosaurs, there does seem to be some measure of agreement between the evolutionary relationships that have been proposed and continental movements. The evolutionary pattern suggests that the hadrosaurids (pages 116-127) may have evolved from the iguanodontids (pages 110-115) in the Jurassic, with the latter being confined to Europe and the western continents, while the hadrosaurids evolving in the east spread back into the west sporadically in the Cretaceous.

Ecology Information on the local flora and fauna associated with *Iguanodon* can be used to build up a fairly comprehensive picture of the general life-style of the animal: the way it fitted into the ecology of the time and whether it is comparable with any modern animals in the sort of rôle which it fulfilled.

One rather misleading aspect of the way of life of *Iguanodon* relates to the discoveries at Bernissart. The concentration of skeletons at Bernissart has been used as evidence that these animals lived in herds, and in the case of Bernissart that they plunged into a ravine after being stampeded by a predator, or some other dramatic event. Unfortunately, appealing though the story is, it is certainly not what happened at Bernissart. Re-study of the material has shown that there was no ravine to fall into, the skeletons simply collected in a marshy or lake-like depression; furthermore there was no large herd, but rather there were separate phases of deposition, with carcasses being washed in and buried from time to time.

Right: This photograph gives a vivid impression of the incredible display of *Iguanodon* from Bernissart as they can be seen today behind vast glass panels at the Royal Institute of Natural Sciences in Parc Léopold. Most of these are *Iguanodon bernissartensis;* however the skeleton of *I. mantelli* is in the centre near the far side of the enclosure.

Below: Taken in 1883, this photograph, from Dollo's original account of the species, shows the one well-preserved skeleton of *Iguanodon mantelli* from Bernissart. This individual is 20ft (6m) long and appreciably more slender than the 33ft (10m) long *Iguanodon bernissartensis.*

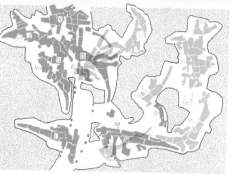

Bernissart Excavation (left)
This map shows the position of the *Iguanodon* skeletons as found in the mine. They seem to have been deposited in two distinct orientations (red is the lower, older level) probably at different times. This may mean that the direction of the flow of current carrying the bodies altered between depositions.

Patterns and processes Another way of looking at evolutionary processes is to attempt to carry out population censuses (counting fossil specimens). This is admittedly rather a hazardous approach to use because the number of fossils that may be found at any one place at any one time must be subject to enormous variables. Nevertheless, sometimes undeniable patterns do emerge, which demand some attempted explanation. One such pattern reflects what appears to be the history of the ornithopod dinosaurs.

During much of the Jurassic Period the ornithopods were neither particularly numerous nor particularly diverse; they seem if anything to be relatively small to medium-sized herbivores when compared with the numerous giant sauropods. The Cretaceous Period, however, shows a major change in fortunes. The sauropods appear to decrease in number and variety, while the ornithopods increase quite dramatically. Not only are there several different types, but locally they can be very abundant. *Iguanodon* is, by any standards, very abundant in Europe. By the end of the Cretaceous Period the ornithopod hadrosaurids were clearly one of the most diverse and abundant groups, particularly in North America and Asia. What caused this remarkable change in the fate of the sauropods and ornithopods? One answer may be seen in the way that ornithopods chewed

their food. The advanced ornithopods, such as the hypsilophodontids, iguanodontids and hadrosaurids, all show the development of the peculiar chewing mechanism described earlier for *Iguanodon*. It could well be that the replacement of the sauropods by ornithopods hinged on an ability to chew food. Sauropods had teeth that were used rather like 'rakes' to gather up leaves and twigs. These were swallowed without being chewed and then pounded up in a muscular gizzard which was lined with pebbles. It is quite possible that a vegetation change, perhaps linked to the rise of the flowering plants (angiosperms) which occurred at the beginning of the Cretaceous Period, promoted the decline of the stomach-grinding sauropods and the rise of the mouth-grinding ornithopods.

These are admittedly tenuous proposals, but I hope that it can be appreciated how such interesting broad-scale or *macroevolutionary* observations can arise from such mundane work as the counting of fossils!

Drawing Conclusions

As a result of all the foregoing work, we can build up a fairly—perhaps surprisingly—comprehensive picture of our fossil animal, in this case *Iguanodon*. Starting with our pile of bones, we have pieced them together to build a skeleton, deduced how it would have supported itself and moved around; clothed it in muscles and analysed the way in which it would have fed; we have also gained an insight into its intellectual abilities, and even pondered the problems of sex! Having built up a picture of *Iguanodon*, we have then taken all this information and 'processed' it in an attempt to bring this animal to life: discussing its ecology, relationships and evolution in time and space. One area of this research has led us to use the geological timescale to speculate upon a rather curious pattern of faunal replacement which seems to have occurred at about the time that *Iguanodon* lived (the replacement of the sauropods by ornithopods as abundant herbivores). The explanation for the replacement may have it origins in the rise of flowering plants and the rather peculiar way in which *Iguanodon* and other ornithopod dinosaurs chewed their food.

Therefore, we do seem to know a surprising amount about the general biology and way of life of this extinct animal. However, at this point it would be best to remind ourselves that there is also a considerable amount of information

that we do not and cannot ever know about such animals. This can perhaps be best appreciated by comparing our information on *Iguanodon* with that available for a living lizard, the *Iguana* (see table at foot of column).

Thus we can learn virtually all there is to know about the *Iguana* because it is alive and amenable to study both in the 'field' (in its natural surroundings) and the laboratory. As soon as a species goes extinct, a considerable amount of information is lost. A very recently extinct *Iguana*, for example, would be not much better than *Iguanodon* (extinct 100 million years ago) from the point of view of information that can be retrieved. This should be borne in mind when looking at the rest of the book. The pictures represent our best attempt to bring them back to life, and rely on a combination of fact, interpretation, and scientifically inspired guesswork. For example, how do we know what colours they were? The answer is simply that we have no idea of their colour. However, by looking at animals around today we realise that colours are important and quite variable; they are used for camouflage (either by causing an animal to blend in with the background or by being disruptive to confuse a potential predator or prey), as warning colours, for sexual attractiveness, territorial behaviour, or more general social behaviour. The colours used here are, therefore, educated guesses based on a comparison with living forms.

COMPARATIVE KNOWLEDGE		
IGUANA		IGUANODON
	Anatomy and Physiology	
complete	bone structure	complete
complete	musculature	partial
complete	soft anatomy	very little
complete	locomotion	partial
complete	feeding and digestion	little
complete	sensory systems	very little
complete	reproduction	very little
complete	water balance	none
complete	blood systems	very little
complete	metabolism	none
	Ecology	
complete	field studies	none
complete	laboratory	none
	Behaviour	
complete	field studies	none
complete	laboratory	none
	Evolution and	
fairly complete	**relationships**	partial

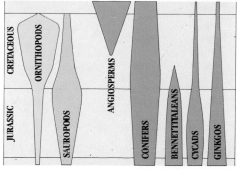

Large-scale Evolution (left)
This chart shows how the fortunes of various groups varied during the Mesozoic Era. Sauropods were notably abundant in Jurassic times, but declined in the Cretaceous. The reverse seems true of the ornithopods. Is this linked to changes in plant types (near left) and food-processing techniques?

Right: *Conolophus,* the land-iguana of the Galapagos Islands, allows us a great opportunity to study all aspects of its biology. Many of these we can only guess at in the case of dinosaurs like *Iguanodon.*

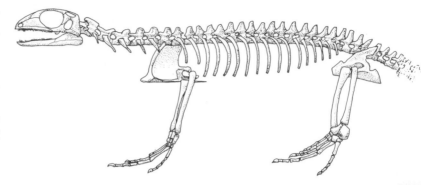

As described earlier, dinosaurs are related to a very large group of so-called 'two-arched' or diapsid reptiles. The diapsids are a very diverse group of reptiles ranging from dinosaurs to living forms such as lizards, snakes and crocodiles, as well as the extinct flying reptiles, the pterosaurs, and less well-known groups such as the thecodontians and rhynchosaurs.

In order to trace the history and origins of dinosaurs we must briefly dwell on some of these groups, because in them we find some clues to dinosaur ancestry.

The Earliest Diapsids

The first diapsid known is an animal named *Petrolacosaurus* which comes from the Carboniferous of Kansas in North America. It is a remarkably lizard-like creature with, if anything, rather disconcertingly long legs. These evidently agile animals very probably fed upon the insect life in the dry upland areas surrounding the coal-swamp forests which were very widespread at this time in the Earth's history. These were evidently very successful little animals because animals of just this type (modern lizards!) are still widespread and abundant, particularly in the tropics. However, the success of this early diapsid was of crucial importance because its survival acted as a springboard for the evolution of a considerable variety of diapsids in the Carboniferous and Permian Periods. It would appear from the study of the diapsids found in rocks of these times that there was an early separation into two quite distinctive groups of diapsid. One of these, the lepidosaurs, remained virtually unchanged as generally small, very lizard-like creatures; the other group, the archosaurs, were generally larger predatory creatures with heavier bodies, particularly powerful hindlimbs and tails, and a pronounced tendency to develop armour plating over the back. It is the latter group (the archosaurs) that particularly interest us, because it is from them that the dinosaurs finally evolved towards the end of the Triassic Period. However, before looking at the archosaurs let us briefly look at the lepidosaurs. After all, dramatic though the dinosaurs were, they went extinct, whereas the lepidosaurs (as lizards and snakes) have continued to evolve right through to the present day.

The Lepidosaurs Most of the history of lepidosaurs revolves around their small-size and insectivorous habit (with one particularly noteworthy exception). They can generally be said to live a very economical life-style. The heat of the Sun is used to maintain body temperature within tolerable limits and strong, widely-spread legs and sinuous body movements are combined to move extremely quickly over short distances — to catch prey and avoid predators. They also feed on small highly nutritious packets of food (i.e. insects). The main evolutionary innovation of the lepidosaurs is in fact an adaptation linked to feeding. Comparing the skull of *Petrolacosaurus* with that of a modern lizard, we can see that the lower temporal arch has been lost: a feature peculiar to lepidosaurs. Its loss means that the skull bones can develop remarkable flexibility. As a result food can be manipulated with great precision while in the mouth. The skull mobility is thought to be one of the reasons for the continued success of lepidosaurs. The snakes have taken skull flexibility to almost ridiculous extremes in that their heads are so flexible that they can swallow prey much larger than their own heads (see also page 181).

Petrolacosaurus Skeleton (above)
This small reptile comes from the late Carboniferous rocks of Kansas. In its general proportions it resembles most other lizard-like reptiles, although its legs are rather long. Very probably *Petrolacosaurus* was a fast-moving predator of insects.

Petrolacosaurus Skull (right)
These views show the two openings behind the eye socket that characterise diapsid reptiles. The teeth are small and spiky, well suited to a diet of insects. The drawings are based on the work of Dr Robert Reisz.

Euparkeria Skull and Skeleton (right and below)
Euparkeria is a good example of an early archosaur reptile. Based on the work of Dr Rosalie Ewer, this reconstruction shows a highly active creature which grew to about 3·3ft (1m) in length. As shown here, the tail is used to counter-balance the body for short sprints on its hind legs. The skull shows the typical archosaur pattern of openings in front of the eye and in the lower jaw.

Petrolacosaurus Skull

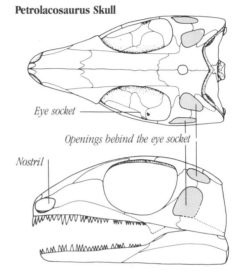

Eye socket

Openings behind the eye socket

Nostril

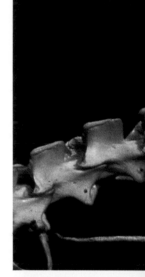

Euparkeria Skull

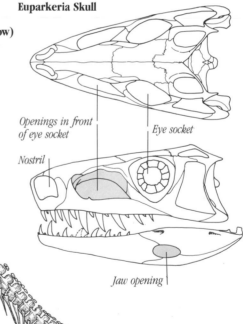

Openings in front of eye socket

Eye socket

Nostril

Jaw opening

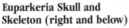

Right: This cast of the skull of *Riojasuchus*, a South American thecodontian, is in the collection of the British Museum (Natural History). As in the case of *Euparkeria* (below left), the typical archosaur skull openings in the upper and lower jaws are well shown. The powerful jaws and serrated teeth of both these creatures testifies to their predatory habits.

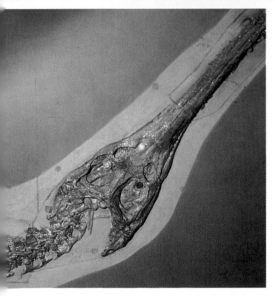

Above: The varanid lizards of today (the monitor lizards) appear to be distant living relatives of the gigantic mosasaurs of the late Cretaceous seas. This specimen shows very clearly the detailed structure of the skull. The loss of the lower temporal arch behind the eye allows such reptiles great jaw flexibility.

Leg Postures (below)
This sequence, adapted from Dr Alan Charig's work, shows the sprawling posture of most living reptiles (far left). In the centre is the semi-erect posture adopted by thecodontians and living crocodiles. On the right is the fully-erect posture typical of dinosaurs, birds and mammals.

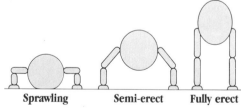

Sprawling **Semi-erect** **Fully erect**

Above: The skull of a phytosaur, an early but short-lived group of archosaurs. These large aquatic reptiles looked very similar to crocodiles. They lived in late Triassic times only. They were predominantly fish-eating types with long, narrow snouts lined with sharply pointed teeth. One notable feature of these animals is that whereas crocodiles have nostrils at the tip of the snout, in phytosaurs they were situated on a mound just above their eyes.

The mosasaurs of the Cretaceous Period are one exception to the general rule that states that lepidosaurs are small. These were huge sea-going lizards which appear to have been giant relatives of the monitor lizards of Africa and South-East Asia. Most present-day lizards are adept swimmers, but the mosasaurs took this to an extreme because their legs had developed into broad paddles.

The Thecodontians The earliest archosaurs so far known are really quite large animals from the end of the Permian Period, such as *Proterosuchus* and *Erythrosuchus*. However, rather than use these as examples of a typical early archosaur, I shall use the relatively small Triassic thecodontian *Euparkeria*. This particular genus is well-known and well illustrates the principal attributes of all early archosaurs.

The skull of *Euparkeria* shows several of the distinctive characters of the archosaur: the head is relatively large and has deeply-rooted teeth with sharp serrated edges; there is also an additional opening, in the form of a broad depression on the side of the head immediately in front of the eye socket; there is another aperture in the side of the lower jaw as well. None of these features is found in typical lepidosaurs. Along the backbone, there is also a double row of bony plates—the beginnings of armour-plating, another archosaur feature. Finally and very importantly as we shall see shortly, there are some rather subtle rearrangements found in the hips and hind leg. These changes reflect an ability to alter the angle that the back leg makes between the body and the ground during a normal stride. The upper leg bone (femur) is distinctively curved and the hip-joint is socketed in such a way that the leg can be held either straight out from the side of the body as in a lizard or alternatively the leg can be held partly beneath the body. The latter position enables the belly of the animal to be raised from the ground so that it does not drag and walking is therefore more easy and efficient. The ability to use a so-called 'variable gait'—to hold the leg in positions other than just the typical sprawling posture—seems to have been of considerable importance to the evolution of the thecodontians as a whole and to that of their eventual successors, the dinosaurs, in particular.

Holding the legs at least partly beneath the body has one immediate advantage: it means that larger body-sizes can be attained because the weight of the body can be carried by the legs rather than through the belly resting on the ground. Thus, by altering the range of leg positions, the archosaurs immediately opened up a range of body sizes that could not possibly be achieved by lepidosaurs. However, large size does have its side-effects. In the case of the thecodontians it resulted in the modification of the ankle joint. With the legs held out from the sides of the body, as in typical lizards, the ankle is subjected to considerable twisting during the normal range of movement between foot and leg. While animals are relatively small, and the forces involved in moving are small, there is no particular requirement for great strength and stability in the ankle bones. However, large size and variable gait, as in thecodontians, demands much greater strength and stability of the ankle joint—to prevent unwanted dislocation for example. The solution found variously in thecodontians is to develop a rather unusual ankle joint with, instead of rows of small bones that slide past one another, a strong ball-and-socket joint between the ankle bones (see diagram on page 36). Ankles of this general type are found in all thecodontians and can be taken as a reflection of the greater power exerted by the hindleg on the foot.

Thus what we appear to see in early archosaurs is a suite of characteristics that distinguishes them from their 'cousins' the lepidosaurs—how did these new characters arise? The usual explanation offered is that the early thecodontians (*Proterosuchus* is a good example) became at least partially aquatic (generally crocodile-like) in their way of life. In water a powerful tail and large hind legs are advantageous for swimming powerfully to capture other animals and they can also grow larger because their weight is buoyed up by water. It is proposed therefore that these thecodontians became large aquatic predators with big tails and long back legs. Later on, these 'types' reverted to living on land, but although

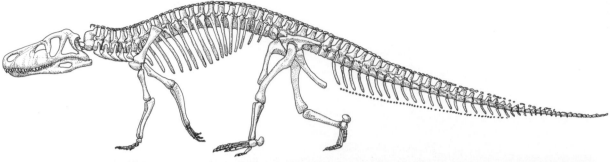

large, they had powerful back legs to support the body and a large counterbalancing tail which suited them well to a terrestrial rather than an aquatic way of life.

This theory fits in well with the known fossil record, but it does not strike me as a totally convincing explanation. I can much more readily imagine that the earliest archosaurs appeared in upland areas as small or medium-sized carnivores which had developed a variable gait as a means of moving more efficiently to catch prey, and simultaneously giving them the opportunity to grow into much larger predators. The early archosaur 'type' would then be a *Euparkeria*-like animal. The problem with *Euparkeria* being an actual animal of this type is that unfortunately it lived too late in time. I consider that similar active, predatory archosaurs must have existed in the upland areas in late Permian/early Triassic times, but as yet we just have not found them. If this is the case, *Proterosuchus* and other large aquatic thecodontians may then be seen as early representatives of an evolutionary radiation of archosaurs into the watery habitat; this was eventually to be colonised by the extremely successful archosaur group, the crocodiles. I therefore see the development of the archosaur ankle joint in particular as a consequence of developing a variable gait for more efficient locomotion and support on *land* rather than it developing in *water* as others have proposed. Clearly, the explanation that we can provide for archosaur origins is not clear-cut but relies on opinion and personal preference. However, what is not in doubt is the fact that archosaurs did possess the suite of anatomical features listed above and that their arrival coincided with a very noticeable change in the types of animal to be found in the world at this time.

The Rise of the Dinosaurs

Throughout the Triassic a considerable variety of thecodontians are found almost world-wide, ranging from small *Euparkeria*-like animals to very large crocodile-sized forms such as *Saurosuchus* from Argentina or *Ticinosuchus* from Germany. All in all they seem to have been very successful carnivorous forms.

However, in order to understand the processes that were taking place in the Triassic and led to the appearance of the dinosaurs at the very end of the Triassic, we must briefly chart the events of the Triassic as a whole. In the early part of the Triassic, the thecodontians were not very abundant, but lived alongside a very diverse fauna of herbivorous (dicynodont) and carnivorous (cynodont) mammal-like reptiles. By the middle of the Triassic the dicynodonts had been replaced by diademodontoids (herbivorous cynodonts) and also by the rhynchosaurs, a short-lived but meanwhile very numerous group of diapsid reptiles. The thecodontians meanwhile persisted as generally large-bodied carnivores. At the end of the Triassic there was a rather abrupt change in fortunes: the majority of the mammal-like reptiles went extinct, as did the rhynchosaurs, while the dinosaurs and other late thecodontian groups rose to a dominant position. The age of the dinosaurs begins.

The explanations for the observed change in fortunes of the mammal-like reptiles and archosaurs at the close of the Triassic has provoked considerable debate. For the moment, we will merely accept the fact that it happened, although those that are interested may turn straight to page 186 for more information. However, before going on in the next chapter to

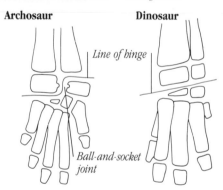

discuss in some detail the anatomy and biology of the dinosaurs that are presently known, a few more words about dinosaur anatomy are in order.

Dinosaur Anatomy

To recap briefly on the distinction that was introduced in the 'dinosaur family tree' section of Chapter 1, the dinosaurs that evolved from the thecodontians at the end of the Triassic can readily be divided into two types: saurischian ('reptile-hipped') dinosaurs and ornithischian ('bird-hipped') dinosaurs.

Saurischian dinosaurs include both carnivorous and herbivorous representatives and are characterised by having a pelvis in which the three bones (ilium, ischium and pubis) radiate outwards from one another in different directions from the hip joint or socket like most other reptiles. However, unlike most other reptiles there is an opening in the hip socket and above the opening an outwardly-directed lip against which the femur was firmly pressed. Also, the pubis and ischium are very long and directed downward between the legs. The legs in turn are tucked in pillar-like beneath the

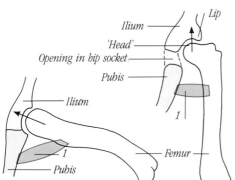

Hip Joints (left)

In semi-erect archosaurs (far left) the femur is angled inward against the hip socket and muscle 1 swings the leg forward quite easily. In dinosaurs the femur is upright and has a 'head' that fits against a lip on the socket. Muscle 1, which works well for the semi-erect archosaur, is too short to work effectively for the dinosaur.

Dinosaur Hips (below)

These diagrams, based on the ideas of Dr Alan Charig, attempt to explain the range of dinosaur hip structures (pubis: blue; muscles: red). In *Ticinosuchus* (far left), a thecodontian included for comparison, the normal hip muscles operate effectively because the femur is angled inward. In the quadrupedal sauropod *Diplodocus* muscle 1 still operates because the

femur does not swing far forward. Muscle 1 works more effectively for a bipedal theropod like *Ceratosaurus* because the pubis is tilted up and away from the femur. In *Scelidosaurus*, an early quadrupedal ornithischian, the pubis has moved backwards and muscle 1 is attached to the ilium. In the bipedal *Hypsilophodon* a new pubic bone has grown for the attachment of muscle 1.

Above left and above: Seen here are an ornithischian dinosaur (*Stegosaurus*, above left), and a saurischian one (*Tarbosaurus*, above). The pelvis of *Stegosaurus* has a backwardly-pointing pubis, while that of *Tarbosaurus* points forward and down from the hip socket. However, *Stegosaurus*, like many late ornithischians, has also developed a new forwardly-pointing pubic bone.

Ticinosuchus   **Diplodocus**   **Ceratosaurus**   **Scelidosaurus**   **Hypsilophodon**

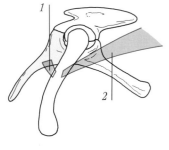 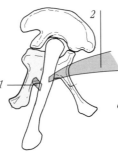 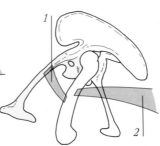 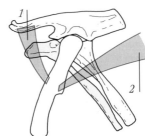 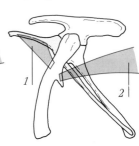

body and show several changes from the thecodontian plan. The femur has a distinct 'head' which sticks out at right-angles to the shaft. The 'head' fits into the deep hip socket, and rests against the lip. The knee joint is a simple hinge, as is the ankle joint. The ankle does not have to withstand the great twisting forces that were found in the variable-gaited thecodontians, so it can become a very strong, simple hinge, rather than having a complicated ball-and-socket joint as in the thecodontian.

The saurischian dinosaurs are in turn divided into two distinct groups, the theropods (bipedal carnivores of various sizes) and the sauropodomorphs (generally quadrupedal plant eaters of very large size).

Ornithischian dinosaurs resemble saurischian dinosaurs in the structure of the legs: they have a similarly off-set head to the femur as well as hinge-like knee and ankle joints. However, the pelvis, although it has a perforated socket, and a lip, is notably different. The pubis lies parallel to the ischium as it does in living birds (hence the name ornithischian). In some later ornithischians the pubis develops another anterior spine which resembles but should not

be confused with the saurischian one. In addition to the difference in hip structure, ornithischians also possess a lattice of bony rods on either side of the spines of the back and a peculiar horn-covered bone (predentary) at the tip of the lower jaw. These three differences serve readily to distinguish ornithischian from saurischian dinosaurs. Ornithischians were *all* herbivorous and are represented by the more bizarre looking type of dinosaur, such as the plated stegosaurs, the tank-like ankylosaurs, the horned ceratopians and the crested hadrosaurs.

Why is it that dinosaurs have such distinctive hips? One novel explanation provided by Dr Alan Charig (London) (in fact the only one that has ever been put forward) is that it is to do with the way the leg muscles worked in thecodontians and dinosaurs. It is briefly as follows: in thecodontians the main leg moving muscles were attached to the pubis and to the tail (muscles 1 and 2 in diagram). Muscle 1 pulled the leg forwards, while muscle 2 pulled it back (the main walking muscle). However, if we imagine this arrangement operating in a dinosaur, then there are a couple of unexpected problems. The main one is that with the legs

fully 'tucked-in', as in the typical dinosaur, the femur is brought very close to the pubis — in fact too close for muscle 1 to be able to work properly. Therefore the earliest dinosaurs seem to have been faced with a problem: how to avoid having the femur too close to the pubis. The dinosaurs seem to have 'solved' the problem in at least three different ways. The huge sauropodomorph saurischians simply stayed as they were and exploited the option of moving slowly with their legs acting as pillars and having a small range of leg movement. The theropod saurischians became bipedal and by doing so swung the body and pubis upwards and away from the femur so that the leg muscles continued to work effectively. The ornithischians seem to have 'decided' early on, to abandon the pubis altogether; it was therefore swung backwards out of the way against the ischium and the leg-moving muscle was moved to the long spike on the front end of the ilium. The redevelopment of a pubic spine in later ornithischians may well be associated with the development of bipedality which moves the anterior spike on the ilium to a rather unfavourable position for leg muscle 1.

The saurischian dinosaurs are a fairly mixed group of animals which all share the general features associated with a re-organisation of the hindlimb and pelvis for a fully erect position (see pages 36-37). It is possible to break down the saurischians into at least two quite distinct groups: the **Theropoda** ('beast feet') and **Sauropodomorpha** ('reptile-type feet'). The theropods tend to be bipedal carnivores of various shapes and sizes, while the sauropodomorphs tend to be either omnivores (ie. eating a mixed diet) or herbivores. We shall use this division to look at the saurischian types over the next few pages: theropods (pages 38-73) and sauropodomorphs (pages 74-97).

The theropods are a group of carnivorous dinosaurs of bewildering variety. They are all grouped together because of their shared predatory habits and associated skeletal form. Unfortunately their relationships are not at all clear and can only be hinted at here in the

Compsognathus (below)
One of the smallest dinosaurs of all, some *Compsognathus* reached a total length of only 28in (70cm) or so. Most of this length was made up by the long slender tail, so that an adult *Compsognathus* was no heavier than a hen. The tail was used as a balancing rod during fast running. The neck was quite long like that of *Coelophysis*, and *Compsognathus* had only two clawed fingers on its hand, an unusual feature.

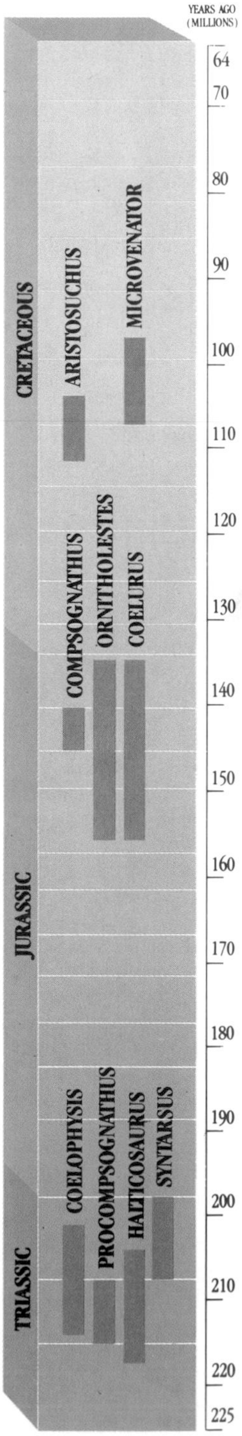

Coelophysis (below)
This is one of the earliest and most primitive dinosaurs. *Coelophysis* was very slim and it could have run on its hind legs, or walked on all-fours. The hands were equipped with three strong fingers that were probably used for attacking smaller prey animals such as the small lizard-like reptiles that lived at the same time. Some of the skeletons of *Coelophysis* that were found in a mass burial at Ghost Ranch, New Mexico, in 1947 contained the bones of juveniles of the same species. It was thought that these were babies ready to be born, but they are rather too big for that so *Coelophysis* may have been a cannibal.

Time Chart (left)
This chart shows that there were lots of 'coelurosaur'-type theropods living throughout much of the reign of the dinosaurs, although they seem to show a fairly sharp decline towards the end of the Cretaceous Period.

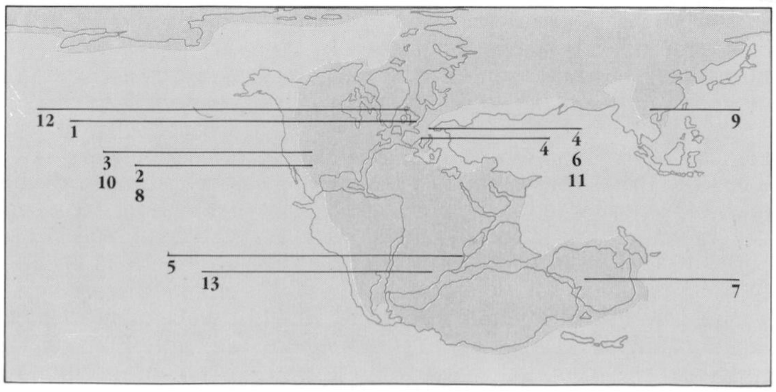

Map (left)
1 *Aristosuchus*
2 *Coelophysis*
3 *Coelurus*
4 *Compsognathus*
5 *Elaphrosaurus*
6 *Halticosaurus*
7 *Kakuru*
8 *Longosaurus*
9 *Lukousaurus*
10 *Ornitholestes*
11 *Procompsognathus*
12 *Saltopus*
13 *Syntarsus*

vaguest way. The reason for this uncertainty is the relative rarity of good theropod fossils. There are many isolated theropod fossil bones and teeth, but (as we shall see) these tend to *add* to the confusion, rather than helping to clarify our understanding of the groups and their relationships. We shall be looking at good examples of 'coelurosaurs' (pages 38-43), ornithomimosaurs (pages 44-49), miscellaneous small theropods (pages 50-55), dromaeosaurids (pages 56-61), 'carnosaurs' (pages 62-67) and tyrannosaurids (pages 68-73). The terms 'coelurosaur' and 'carnosaur' are deliberately used in quotation marks as the precise relationships of the dinosaurs included in these groups are virtually impossible to untangle.

'Coelurosaurs'

As explained above, the first group of saurischian dinosaurs with which we shall be dealing are the theropods ('beast feet'). All theropods were carnivores (although there are one or two examples such as the ornithomimosaurs—pages 44-49—which lacked teeth and may have had a rather specialised diet); they also all tend to be two-legged (bipedal) runners. As you will see over the next few sections, this sort of body plan is surprisingly constant in all theropods. Comparing these creatures with living animals, it is difficult to find obvious counterparts. The most familiar living carnivores are the quadrupedal (four-footed) mammals such as the various dogs, bears and cats. The only two-legged carnivores are found among the birds (kestrels, kites, eagles, etc), but these winged and feathered animals can hardly be compared to the ground-dwelling theropods of the dinosaur era. This is an observation which poses an obvious but difficult question. Why was it that dinosaurs produced so many obviously successful ground-dwelling *bipedal* predators, whereas today the ground-dwelling predators are all *quadrupeds?*

Before we try to answer this question, let us look at some representatives of the geat variety of theropod dinosaurs. Firstly there are the 'coelurosaurs' ('hollow-tailed reptiles').

The 'coelurosaurs' that we shall be looking at here are a rather odd mixture of generally small, lightly-built theropods. They are clearly not all close relatives when looked at in detail, but are described together in this section simply as a matter of convenience. All of these theropods are slender, fast-running predators with small heads (the jaws of which are lined with small, sharp teeth), long flexible necks and long arms with sharply-taloned grasping hands. Unfortunately, although animals of this general type must have been quite abundant throughout the 140 million year reign of the dinosaurs, the very fact that they were both small and lightly-built greatly reduces the probability of their being preserved at all well as fossils. Small animal carcasses tend to rot very quickly and their skeletal remains are liable to be scavenged and

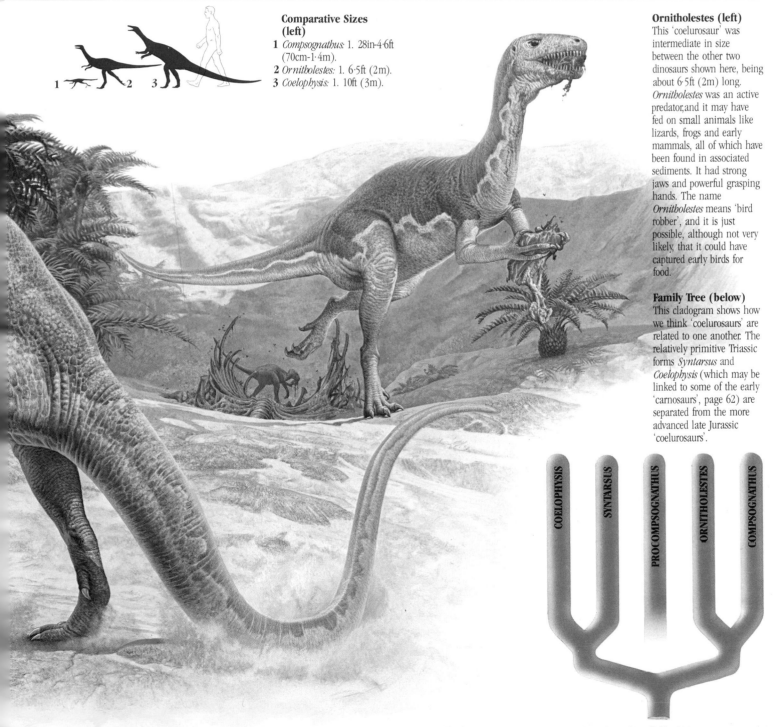

Comparative Sizes (left)
1 *Compsognathus*: 1. 28in-4·6ft (70cm-1·4m).
2 *Ornitholestes*: 1. 6·5ft (2m).
3 *Coelophysis*: 1. 10ft (3m).

Ornitholestes (left)
This 'coelurosaur' was intermediate in size between the other two dinosaurs shown here, being about 6·5ft (2m) long. *Ornitholestes* was an active predator, and it may have fed on small animals like lizards, frogs and early mammals, all of which have been found in associated sediments. It had strong jaws and powerful grasping hands. The name *Ornitholestes* means 'bird robber', and it is just possible, although not very likely, that it could have captured early birds for food.

Family Tree (below)
This cladogram shows how we think 'coelurosaurs' are related to one another. The relatively primitive Triassic forms *Syntarsus* and *Coelophysis* (which may be linked to some of the early 'carnosaurs', page 62) are separated from the more advanced late Jurassic 'coelurosaurs'.

COELOPHYSIS

SYNTARSUS

PROCOMPSOGNATHUS

ORNITHOLESTES

COMPSOGNATHUS

scattered, or completely destroyed. As a result, the fossil record of coelurosaur-type dinosaurs is extremely patchy. Their remains are found throughout the reign of the dinosaurs, but the vast majority of their fossils are isolated bones and teeth. This makes for great problems when it comes to looking at or trying to investigate their biology and relationships. It also creates problems which we will see recur throughout this section; these relate to the naming of dinosaurs. Quite often in the past, dinosaur names have been given to extremely scrappy pieces of fossil. In later years it has become obvious that the material is either so poor that it cannot be used for strictly scientific comparison with other more complete skeletons (*Mono-clonius*— page 134 — may be a good example of this); or it turns out that several names have been proposed for various pieces of just one dinosaur (*Brontosaurus* which is now known as *Apatosaurus*— pages 80-81 — is a good example of this). In the case of the 'coeluro-

saurs' we shall concentrate on three, rather different, but nevertheless well-preserved specimens: *Coelophysis*, *Compsognathus* and *Ornitholestes*, in order to illustrate the main characteristics of this group of dinosaurs.

Coelophysis Described

The remains of *Coelophysis* ('hollow form') were first discovered by an amateur fossil collector named David Baldwin. Baldwin was originally a collector of fossils employed by Othniel C. Marsh, but later in his career he began to work for Edward D. Cope. Compared with many of the North American fossil collectors of the late 19th century, Baldwin was unusual because he worked alone rather than in larger working parties. Baldwin collected fossils from New Mexico where there are good exposures of Permian and Triassic rocks. In Triassic rocks near Abiquiu in north-western New Mexico, Baldwin discovered some scraps

of early dinosaurs in 1881. These bones were shipped back to Cope in Philadelphia who immediately recognised them as the bones of a small, very lightly-built carnivorous dinosaur. In fact he claimed that he was able to recognise *three* species of this dinosaur among these scrappy remains: *Coelophysis bauri*, *Coelophysis willistoni* (named after George Baur and Samuel Wendel Williston, both of whom were assistants of O.C. Marsh) and *Coelophysis longicollis*. These rather incomplete remains comprised various vertebrae, leg bones, and pieces of pelvis and rib, and they remained all that was known of one of the earliest discovered dinosaurs for the next sixty years. Then, in 1947, an expedition organised by the American Museum of Natural History re-visited the area of New Mexico explored by David Baldwin. From the field notes Baldwin made at the time, the expedition was able to discover the original *Coelophysis* locality, now on a property known as Ghost Ranch. The team

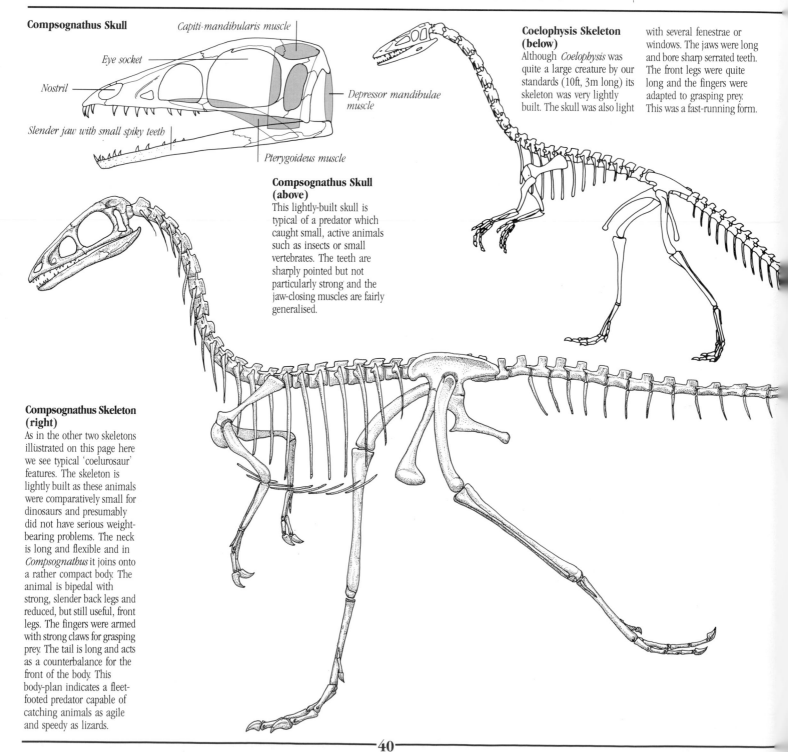

Compsognathus Skull

Capiti-mandibularis muscle

Eye socket

Nostril

Slender jaw with small spiky teeth

Depressor mandibulae muscle

Pterygoideus muscle

Compsognathus Skull (above)
This lightly-built skull is typical of a predator which caught small, active animals such as insects or small vertebrates. The teeth are sharply pointed but not particularly strong and the jaw-closing muscles are fairly generalised.

Coelophysis Skeleton (below)
Although *Coelophysis* was quite a large creature by our standards (10ft, 3m long) its skeleton was very lightly built. The skull was also light with several fenestrae or windows. The jaws were long and bore sharp serrated teeth. The front legs were quite long and the fingers were adapted to grasping prey. This was a fast-running form.

Compsognathus Skeleton (right)
As in the other two skeletons illustrated on this page here we see typical 'coelurosaur' features. The skeleton is lightly built as these animals were comparatively small for dinosaurs and presumably did not have serious weight-bearing problems. The neck is long and flexible and in *Compsognathus* it joins onto a rather compact body. The animal is bipedal with strong, slender back legs and reduced, but still useful, front legs. The fingers were armed with strong claws for grasping prey. The tail is long and acts as a counterbalance for the front of the body. This body-plan indicates a fleet-footed predator capable of catching animals as agile and speedy as lizards.

explored the area and found large numbers of bone fragments, but no good skeletons. Eventually it was decided to excavate a large section of the hillside, down to the layer where the bones seemed to be weathering out. As this layer was exposed, it revealed one of the most amazing dinosaur graveyards. Literally dozens of skeletons were discovered all lying across one another. It seems as though some local catastrophe had struck a herd of these animals; perhaps they were caught in a flash-flood and their carcasses were swept downriver on to a sand bar near the mouth of a river. Whatever the reason, the phenomenon has left for us some of the best evidence of any Triassic dinosaur. In this remarkable accumulation of skeletons can been seen animals of all ages from very young to fully-grown. These show that Cope was wrong to name three different species of *Coelophysis;* all that he had done was recognise the differences caused by growth between individuals.

As can be seen in the illustrations, *Coelophysis* was a slender creature; its skeleton was very lightly-built, with a long tail counterbalancing the front part of its body. The head was long and pointed, the eyes were large and the long jaws were armed with sharp, serrated teeth. As with all 'coelurosaurs', the neck was very slender and flexible. The arms were moderately long and had sharp clawed hands for grasping prey. The back legs were quite long and slender, and designed for running fast in pursuit of prey.

Life-Style and Habits

The general life-style of *Coelophysis* is fairly obvious. With its lightly-built skeleton, long back legs, grasping hands and sharp tooth-lined mouth, it was undoubtedly a nimble predator of the late Triassic. Its potential victims were probably quite varied. Growing to a maximum length of 10ft (3m), *Coelophysis* may well have preyed upon the small, fleet-footed ornithopods of the time: *Lesothosaurus, Heterodontosaurus* and *Scutellosaurus* (see pages 98-99), all of which were no more than 3-5ft (1-1.5m) long. In fact they probably had a fairly varied diet, as many carnivores do today, taking large and small insects, amphibians and lizards.

The Ghost Ranch discoveries also give a rather gruesome insight into the feeding habits of *Coelophysis.* Some of the skeletons reveal the presence of small *Coelophysis* skeletons inside the ribcage of adult animals. At first it was supposed that the young skeletons were those of unborn infants. Unfortunately this is unlikely. All dinosaurs seem to have laid eggs, rather than bearing live young. The supposed embryos are, however, too large and well-formed to have been from embryos within eggs; they must therefore represent the last *meal* of the adult *Coelophysis!* This example of cannibalism probably reflects the fact that *Coelophysis* adults would tend to eat *any* small creatures that they could catch—even their own kind!

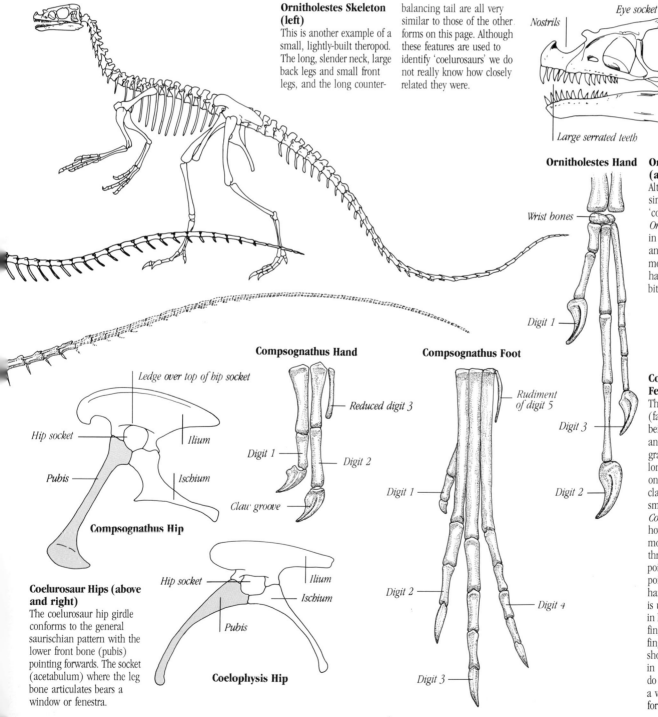

Ornitholestes Skeleton (left)
This is another example of a small, lightly-built theropod. The long, slender neck, large back legs and small front legs, and the long counter-balancing tail are all very similar to those of the other forms on this page. Although these features are used to identify 'coelurosaurs' we do not really know how closely related they were.

Ornitholestes Skull (above)
Although its skeleton is very similar to that of other 'coelurosaurs', the skull of *Ornitholestes* is rather different in being more heavily built and having shorter jaws and more robust teeth. It may have had a more powerful bite than other forms.

Nostrils

Eye socket

Large serrated teeth   *Heavy jaw*

Ornitholestes Hand

Wrist bones

Digit 1

Compsognathus Hand

Reduced digit 3

Digit 1

Digit 2

Claw groove

Compsognathus Foot

Rudiment of digit 5

Digit 1

Digit 2

Digit 4

Digit 3

Digit 3

Digit 2

Coelurosaur Hands and Feet (left)
The hand of *Compsognathus* (far left) is rather peculiar in being so short, since an animal which presumably grasped its prey would need a longer hand to do so. Also only two of the fingers are clawed and the third is very small indeed. The foot of *Compsognathus* (middle left), however, is quite typical of most 'coelurosaurs' with three long, slender, forward-pointing toes and a fourth pointing backwards. The hand of *Ornitholestes* (left) is unusual for 'coelurosaurs' in having two especially long fingers and a short first finger. It is possible that this short finger could be turned in towards the others, as we do with our thumb, providing a very effective mechanism for gripping prey.

Ledge over top of hip socket

Hip socket

Ilium

Pubis

Ischium

Compsognathus Hip

Hip socket

Ilium

Ischium

Pubis

Coelophysis Hip

Coelurosaur Hips (above and right)
The coelurosaur hip girdle conforms to the general saurischian pattern with the lower front bone (pubis) pointing forwards. The socket (acetabulum) where the leg bone articulates bears a window or fenestra.

The Discovery of Compsognathus

Another of the few well-preserved 'coelurosaurs', *Compsognathus* ('pretty jaw') remains have been discovered in rocks of late Jurassic age from southern Germany and France. It was a small creature, the remains so far discovered indicate an animal of between 28in and 4·6ft (70cm-1·4m) in length.

The first remains of *Compsognathus* to be discovered consisted of a beautifully preserved, virtually complete skeleton from the lithographic limestone of the Riedenburg-Kelheim area of southern Germany (Bavaria). The precise area where this was discovered is now unknown because Dr Oberndorfer who collected this specimen in the late 1850s was rather vague about where he had found it; this may have been because he did not want other amateur collectors to discover his locality. Many amateur fossil collectors in Germany scoured the lithographic limestone quarries because they produced some of the finest preserved fossils of pterosaurs (see pages 170-173) and *Archæopteryx* (pages 191-193) which could be sold to State museums for a great deal of money. Since this time only two other specimens of *Compsognathus* have been reported. One consists of a few toe bones from the same area. The other is an almost complete skeleton discovered in rocks of a similar age near Nice in southern France in 1972.

The first *Compsognathus* skeleton is by far the best known specimen and has recently been redescribed by Professor John Ostrom (Yale). It represents an animal of about 28in (70cm) body length, preserved lying on its right-hand side. The skeleton is virtually undisturbed. (The hand bones are a little scattered, probably drifted in currents as the carcass rotted, and there is some evidence that the belly was breached, perhaps by the build up of gases within the decomposing cadaver.)

The death position of the animal is characteristic of many skeletons with the head and neck strongly arched over the back. The likely cause of this contorted posture is the contraction in *rigor mortis* of the neck muscles and ligaments which would have been very powerful in these long-necked animals.

As can be seen from the skeletal reconstruction, the proportions of *Compsognathus* are very similar to those of *Coelophysis*. A long tail counterbalances its front, and the hindlimbs are strong and slender, indicating that it was a fleet-footed biped. The back of the animal is relatively shorter than that of *Coelophysis*, giving it a more 'compact' appearance, but the neck and head are very similar in general shape.

The forelimbs deserve particular mention. Firstly, they are unusually short for an animal that presumably used them to grasp prey; and secondly, they exhibit only two clawed fingers on each hand, whereas *Coelophysis* has three, and a remnant of a fourth.

Life-Style and Habits

The life-style of *Compsognathus* is reasonably self-evident. It was a fleet-footed, bipedal predator of small animals: presumably insects and small vertebrates of various types. Very fortunately, we can be more certain of the probable feeding habits and abilities of *Compsognathus* than of most other dinosaurs, because, like *Coelophysis*, the remains of its last meal are preserved within the ribcage of this animal as well.

John Ostrom was able to study the stomach contents of *Compsognathus* and showed that it consisted of the skeleton of a small lizard named *Bavarisaurus*. (O.C. Marsh, who first noted that stomach contents were present in the ribcage, suggested that they represented embryos.) Judged by the proportions of its limbs and its long tail, Ostrom deduced that *Bavarisaurus* must have been an extremely fast-running, agile ground-dwelling lizard. Since *Compsognathus* undoubtedly caught the *Bavarisaurus* we have a testimony to its abilities. In order to catch this type of creature it would need keen sight, rapid acceleration, high speed, manoeuvrability and quick reactions.

In 1972 a new species of *Compsognathus* (*C. corallestris*) was described, based on a fairly complete skeleton of a larger animal in almost the same preserved position. The new specimen was given the new specific name because it was larger than the German skeleton and also because it seemed to have flipper-like front legs. A flesh reconstruction of *Compsognathus corallestris* was produced in Dr Beverly Halstead's book *The Evolution and Ecology of the Dinosaurs* in 1975. It was envisaged that this species of *Compsognathus* lived in and around coral lagoons and that the 'flippers' on its forelimbs enabled it to swim more efficiently in the lagoons, either in pursuit of prey or to avoid predators.

Unfortunately the evidence upon which the 'flipper' reconstruction is based is extremely dubious. The forelimbs of this skeleton are quite poorly preserved, and the area around the forelimbs which is supposed to show the flipper impression does not look very different from other areas of the slab of rock upon which this animal is preserved. Careful comparison of the two good skeletons by Professor Ostrom proved fairly conclusively that the French specimen was simply a larger version of the same species of *Compsognathus* from Germany and that there was no good evidence for a flipper on the forelimb.

The 'Bird Robber'

This third type of 'coelurosaur' — *Ornitholestes* ('bird robber') — was discovered in late Jurassic rocks at Bone Cabin Quarry near Como in Wyoming (North America) in 1900. This specimen, which consists of a partial skeleton including the skull, jaws and many other parts, was first described by Henry Fairfield Osborn in 1903 and in more detail in 1916. To this day it is still only known from this specimen and an incomplete hand from another individual.

Again a quick glance at *Ornitholestes*, *Coelophysis* and *Compsognathus* reveals the very strong similarity between all three of these dinosaurs. The body of *Ornitholestes* is similarly balanced at the hips and the neck is slender and flexible. The skull and forelimbs are, however, sufficiently different to merit some brief comments. The skull is rather more robustly constructed than the previous two examples, being both deeper and shorter-snouted. The teeth are also numerous and quite large. This arrangement of skull and teeth suggests greater mechanical strength and that *Ornitholestes* had a rather more powerful bite than either of the other two. Perhaps *Ornitholestes* was capable of tackling larger and more active prey than either *Compsognathus* or *Coelophysis*. The hand, which was represented by several finger bones in the original skeleton and two other complete fingers from another individual, is rather unusually proportioned. The second and third fingers are long, slender and almost equal in length while the first finger is very short. The arm is also relatively long in proportion to that

of *Coelophysis* and *Compsognathus*. Both of these features suggest an enhanced prehensile ability of the forelimb for reaching and grasping prey more powerfully and effectively. The difference in length between the first and the second and third fingers is linked to the ability to turn the first finger inwards against the other two like a thumb. The hand could therefore grip its prey very powerfully indeed. The structure of the hand is rather similar to that of dromaeosaurids (pages 56-61).

Other 'Coelurosaurs'

The three examples that we have looked at so far are fairly representative of a bewildering variety of lightly-built theropods that are found throughout the reign of the dinosaurs. We shall look at some of the more bizarre types of small theropod over the next few sections. There are, however, a considerable number of small theropods which are, for the most part, rather

Above: A reconstruction of the skeleton of *Ornitholestes* that has been prepared by the Tyrrell Museum of Palaeontology in Alberta. The skull is quite deep and obviously fairly robust, implying that *Ornitholestes* was a predator that was equipped with quite a powerful bite.

Below: This beautifully preserved specimen of *Compsognathus* is from the lithographic limestone of the Riedenburg-Kelheim area of Bavaria. We know something of the feeding habits of this nimble predator as the remains of *Bavarisaurus*, a lizard, were found in its stomach.

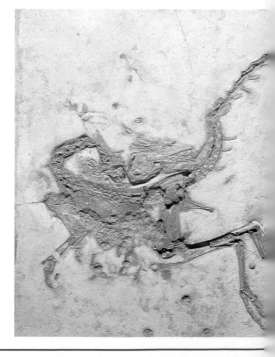

poorly known and whose biology and relationships to the above dinosaurs are naturally difficult to assess.

(i) Possible relatives of *Coelophysis* include *Procompsognathus* ('before pretty jaw') a very fragmentary fossil from the Triassic of West Germany, and *Halticosaurus* ('nimble reptile') a much larger but again rather poorly preserved skeleton from the same site, and *Longosaurus* ('Long's reptile') based on some of Cope's original *Coelophysis longicollis*. In addition to these species there are *Syntarsus* ('fused ankle'), a partial skeleton from the late Triassic of Zimbabwe; *Saltopus* ('leaping foot') which is an imperfectly known small form from the late Triassic of Scotland; and *Lukousaurus* ('Lu-Kou reptile') a peculiar horned form from the late Triassic of southern China.

Several other genera such as *Avipes* ('bird foot'), *Dolichosuchus* ('long crocodile') and *Velocipes* ('speedy foot') are dubious forms based on rather poor material. *Spinosuchus* ('spiny crocodile') from Texas is a thecodontian, not a dinosaur at all.

(ii) Relatives of *Compsognathus* are not presently known, although many authors have related *Compsognathus* to the *Ornitholestes*-type 'coelurosaurs' listed below.

(iii) Possible relatives of *Ornitholestes*, generally known as coelurids, include *Coelurus* ('hollow tail') from the late Jurassic of Wyoming in North America: *Aristosuchus* ('top crocodile'), a fragmentary type from the early Cretaceous of southern England; *Elaphrosaurus* ('light reptile'), a moderately well-preserved but headless skeleton from the late Jurassic of Tendaguru (Tanzania); *Microvenator* ('small hunter') from the early Cretaceous of Montana, as well as possibly *Stokesosaurus* ('Stokes' reptile') from the late Jurassic of Utah; *Iliosuchus* ('crocodile pelvis') from the late Jurassic of England; and *Kakuru* ('rainbow lizard'), a genus based on a tibia from South Australia. Relations may also exist with dromaeosaurid theropods.

Dubious Genera

Numerous extremely dubious coelurids are known including: *Coeluroides* ('Coelurus form'), *Compsosuchus* ('pretty crocodile'), *Inosaurus* ('In reptile'), *Jubbulpuria* ('from Jabalpur'), *Laevisuchus* ('lucky crocodile'), *Ornithomimoides* ('Ornithomimus form'), *Sinocoelurus* ('Chinese hollow tail') and *Teinurosaurus* ('extended reptile'). The latter are all based on undiagnostic remains which may or may not be of small theropod dinosaurs.

An example of the problems that have been created as a result of the very poor state of some of these fossils is given by *Aristosuchus* from southern England. Fragmentary remains of this little creature have been given at least five different names over the years: *Calamosaurus, Calamospondylus, Thecocoelurus, Thecospondylus* and *Coelurus*. All of these are invalid, but cause enormous confusion to people studying these creatures.

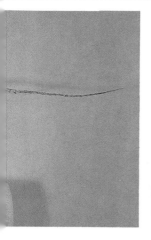

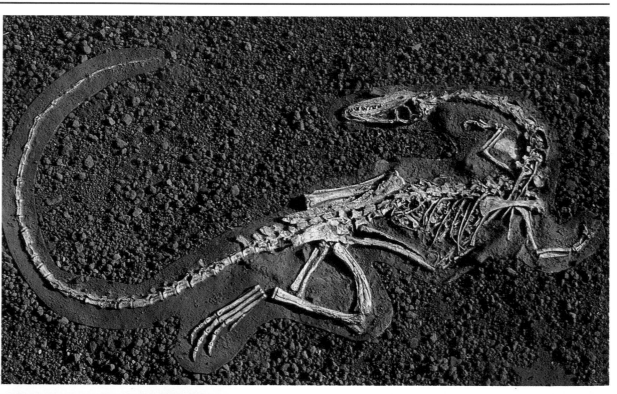

Below: It is not easy to find counterparts of the small theropods in the natural world today, but their behaviour may have paralleled that of the Secretary Bird seen here, which is also a long-legged, and fleet-footed predator the feeds upon ground dwelling reptiles.

Above: *Coelophysis* is a typical 'coelurosaur' with its long jaws, sharp teeth, and long, slender limbs. The curved-back position of the head was probably caused by the contraction of the neck muscles as *rigor mortis* set in.

The Lagoon Dweller (below)
An intriguing suggestion has been advanced that one species of *Compsognathus* (*C. corallestris*) may have been equipped with flipper-like forelimbs which would have allowed it to adopt an amphibious way of life, venturing into lagoons to find food or avoid its natural enemies, as below. Recent study of the skeleton, however, casts doubt on the evidence of flippers and seems to rule out this interpretation.

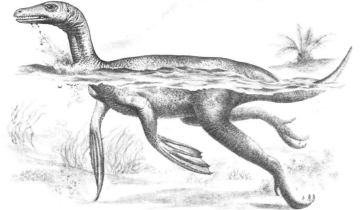

ORNITHOMIMOSAURS & OVIRAPTOROSAURS

Struthiomimus (right)
This was a medium-sized ostrich dinosaur, being 10-13ft (3-4m) long. The proportions of the body of *Struthiomimus*, and many of the more detailed features of its anatomy are remarkably convergent with present-day ostriches. The limbs are very similar, and palaeontologists speculate that the ostrich dinosaurs could have run just as fast as a modern ostrich. The most obvious differences are that *Struthiomimus* had no feathers (as far as we know) and that it used its long tail for balancing while running. Ostriches use their reduced wings for this purpose.

Having introduced the theropods as fleet-footed predatory dinosaurs, it must seem a little odd to find that the very next example after the 'coelurosaurs' should be that of theropods that have lost their teeth! Nevertheless, both the ornithomimosaurs ('bird mimic reptiles') and the relatively less well-known oviraptorosaurs ('egg-stealing reptiles') have this rather dubious distinction.

Ornithomimosaurs

Also known as 'ostrich dinosaurs' for fairly obvious reasons (see below), ornithomimosaur remains are reasonably abundant in late Cretaceous rocks of Western North America and East Asia (Mongolia). Ornithomimosaurs seem to be very similar in size and appearance, reaching body lengths of about 10-13ft (3-4m), and bearing a strong resemblance to modern ground-dwelling birds such as the ostrich or emu.

Time Chart (left)
The ornithomimosaurs are notable for their general appearance in the late Cretaceous, the earliest form seeming to date from the middle Cretaceous, provided it has been correctly identified. Some authors have proposed that they are related to *Elaphrosaurus* of the Late Jurassic. The oviraptorosaurs are exclusively late Cretaceous in age. Their origins are unknown.

Family Tree (below)
The relationships of the ostrich dinosaurs are not at all clear. The North American forms are all very similar and show strong affinities to *Gallimimus*. Ornithomimosaurs may have their origins in the middle Cretaceous from forms like *Archaeornithomimus*. The oviraptorosaurs occupy a related but separate branch of the cladogram.

The first ornithomimosaur remains consisted of the imperfect foot of a dinosaur which was discovered in 1889 by George Cannon in late Cretaceous rocks near Denver, Colorado. Marsh described this material in 1890 as *Orni thomimus velox* ('speedy bird mimic') and, in addition, named two other species *O. tenuis* (a partial foot and hindlimb) and *O. grandis* from other fragmentary remains. Both of the latter had been discovered by J. B. Hatcher in Montana, in the later 1880s. More fragmentary material was described by Marsh in 1892 *(O. sedens* and *O. minutus)* and he recognised from the remains of the pelvis of *Ornithomimus sedens* that these animals were not ornithopods (pages 98 to 127) as originally suspected, but theropods of a hitherto unknown sort. The precise relationships of these remains to other theropods were very uncertain; they represented relatively large animals and were therefore thought to belong to the carnosaurs rather than the smaller coelurosaurs.

A clear picture of the really unusual nature of these animals did not emerge, however, for several years. In 1902 Lawrence Lambe described another specimen from the late Cretaceous of Red Deer River, Alberta as *Ornithomimus altus;* this was again rather fragmentary, comprising hindlimbs, feet and pelvic bones. It was not until 1917 that the first reasonably complete skeleton of an ornithomimosaur was described by Henry Fairfield Osborn. This skeleton consisted of a more-or-less completely preserved animal, lacking only parts of the head, some of the vertebrae and a few limb bones. It allowed the first accurate skeletal reconstruction to be drawn.

On the basis of this fine specimen, Osborn proposed that it was virtually indistinguishable from Lambe's *Ornithomimus altus* but suggested that a new generic name *Struthio mimus* ('ostrich mimic') *altus* be used. Osborn claimed that *Struthiomimus* was from a geologically earlier period than *Ornithomimus*,

and also differed in that *Struthiomimus* still had a small splint-like remnant of a fourth toe on its hindfoot which *Ornithomimus* lacked.

Osborn's description and discussion of the anatomy and biology of *Struthiomimus* was wide-ranging and perceptive. He recognised the very strong similarity between the proportions of *Struthiomimus* and the large running birds of today (small head, long neck, and legs)—although there is the obvious lack in living birds of a long, bony tail and long, clawed arms. The really unexpected characteristic of this form, however, was the absence of teeth in its jaws. The resemblance in shape and texture of the jaw bones to those of birds suggests that the jaws were sheathed in a horny beak.

The thin and light structure of ornithomimosaurs' skull bones makes it highly probable that the skulls of these creatures were *flexible*. Certainly many living birds are able to tilt the upper beak upward or downward while moving the lower jaw. This, allows them to

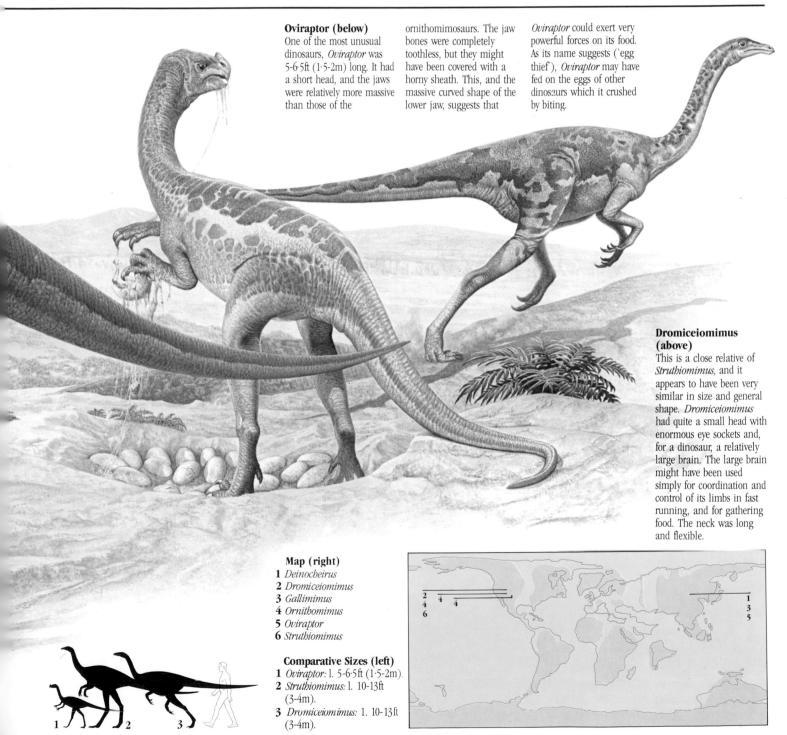

Oviraptor (below)
One of the most unusual dinosaurs, *Oviraptor* was 5-6·5ft (1·5-2m) long. It had a short head, and the jaws were relatively more massive than those of the ornithomimosaurs. The jaw bones were completely toothless, but they might have been covered with a horny sheath. This, and the massive curved shape of the lower jaw, suggests that *Oviraptor* could exert very powerful forces on its food. As its name suggests ('egg thief'), *Oviraptor* may have fed on the eggs of other dinosaurs which it crushed by biting.

Dromiceiomimus (above)
This is a close relative of *Struthiomimus,* and it appears to have been very similar in size and general shape. *Dromiceiomimus* had quite a small head with enormous eye sockets and, for a dinosaur, a relatively large brain. The large brain might have been used simply for coordination and control of its limbs in fast running, and for gathering food. The neck was long and flexible.

Map (right)
1 *Deinocheirus*
2 *Dromiceiomimus*
3 *Gallimimus*
4 *Ornithomimus*
5 *Oviraptor*
6 *Struthiomimus*

Comparative Sizes (left)
1 *Oviraptor:* l. 5-6·5ft (1·5-2m).
2 *Struthiomimus:* l. 10-13ft (3-4m).
3 *Dromiceiomimus:* l. 10-13ft (3-4m).

manoeuvre food in the mouth with great precision. A good example is a parrot; parrots and budgies are able to hold nuts between their jaws and by carefully moving upper and lower beaks and tongue in unison, remove the unpalatable husks with great delicacy. Ornithomimosaurs seem to have had the same abilities, because their skulls were so light. Whether this allowed them to consume a wider range of food in their diet, or represented a special adaptation to a specific type of food is uncertain.

The neck was long and slender and the bones were very flexibly jointed to permit great mobility, whereas the back seems to have been held rather stiffly. The spines of the backbone are scarred by powerful ligaments which held them in place. The ribs are also well formed and were apparently connected to an extensive series of belly ribs (gastralia). The combination of ribs enclosing the entire chest and belly region, plus the stiffening ligaments of the back, undoubtedly conferred great rigidity

upon this part of the body. The spine is jointed very firmly to the pelvis, and the tail, which was evidently long, is unusually modified towards its back end. The narrow prongs of bone (zygapophyses) which jut out from the top of the individual vertebrae and help to control the movements of the tail bones are unusually long. As a result of this, the end of the tail must have been held quite stiffly, although the part of the tail nearer the hips was quite normally flexible.

The front legs are remarkably slender and elongate, ending in three very long, clawed fingers. Compared with *Ornitholestes* (see page 41) the proportions of the fingers are different and the claws are much less sharply curved. Osborn was particularly struck by the similarity in proportion and arrangement between the forelimbs of *Struthiomimus* and those of the three-toed sloth *(Bradypus tridactylus)*.

The hindlimbs are remarkably long and slender, and obviously well designed for fast running. The feet, which are also long and

slender, end in three toes with narrow, flattened claws, rather similar to those on the feet of large running birds.

Habits of Struthiomimus

Osborn reviewed the various proposals that had been made up to then (1917) concerning the habits of ornithomimosaurs. These seemed to him to present certain problems. On the one hand *Struthiomimus* resembled ostrich-like running birds in the structure of its head, neck and legs; while on the other, its forelimbs were most similar to those of the sloths (which hang from branches).

That *Struthiomimus* was a running creature seems incontrovertible; its tail counterbalanced the front part of its body, the stiffening of its back end apparently most readily explained if it were used as a dynamic stabiliser for rapid changes of direction, as well as straight running. This particular adaptation seems to be quite

---

Belly Ribs of Struthiomimus (below)
Belly ribs, or gastralia, are found in various reptile groups although they are absent from mammals. They are not formed in the same way as vertebral ribs and should not strictly be called by the same name. No-one really knows what their function is but there have been several suggestions. They may help to support the abdomen, especially important in an herbivore with a large gut.

Gastralia

Struthiomimus Skeleton (right)
This skeleton is an odd mixture of rigidity and flexibility. The neck was long, slender and presumably highly mobile but the vertebrae of the back were held stiffly in place by strong ligaments. The end of the tail was also very stiff since the prongs of bone which joined the vertebrae together were very long and so restricted movement. The front legs were relatively long, and very slender.

Struthiomimus Hand and Foot (right)
The foot (far right) provides evidence that *Struthiomimus* was a running creature. The toes are rather long and slender, but the upper foot bones (metatarsals) are very elongate. The foot bears an obvious resemblance to that of large running birds such as ostriches. The claws are narrow and flattened and may have provided traction with the ground to stop the foot slipping as it was thrust backwards during running. The hand is rather lightly built but looks as though it would form a useful gripping mechanism, perhaps for bending down the branches of trees, and so bringing them within range of *Struthiomimus'* slender toothless beak.

Struthiomimus Skull (left)
The long slender, toothless jaw and large eyes give this skull a very bird-like appearance. It is also probable that the jaws were covered with horn. The lightness and thinness of the skull bones suggest that they may have been flexible, allowing movement in the skull, as in modern birds.

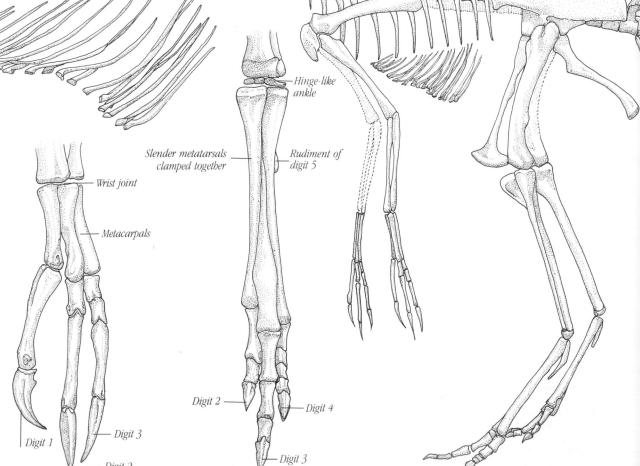

Ring of bones supporting the eye

Nostril

Toothless beak   *Eye socket*

Nostril

Jaw muscles attached here

Hinge-like ankle

Slender metatarsals clamped together   *Rudiment of digit 5*

Wrist joint

Metacarpals

Digit 2   *Digit 4*

Digit 1

Digit 3

Digit 2

Digit 3

widespread among fleet-footed dinosaurs. Dromaeosaurids (pages 56-61) show an extreme development of stiffening rods of the sort seen in *Struthiomimus* while hypsilophodontids (pages 104-109) used a sheath of ossified tendons to achieve the same sort of structure.

As far as their likely diet is concerned, William Beebe proposed that ornithomimosaurs were insectivores, perhaps the equivalent of the anteaters of today. Osborn rejected this theory because the forelimbs of *Struthiomimus* were clearly not powerful enough to undertake the sort of digging activities needed to grub up anthills. Certainly there is no evidence of the powerful shoulder muscles characteristic of modern anteaters, nor was there any evidence of a long, sticky tongue. Furthermore the hindlimbs were adapted for fast running rather than digging.

Another theory arose when Barnum Brown noted that the remains of ornithomimosaurs

are usually found in coastal shore deposits, and proposed that these creatures may have waded along shores feeding on small crabs and shrimps. They may then have used their forelimbs for scraping sand, moving rocks and probing crevices to catch these animals. Osborn also rejected this theory, although his reasons for doing so are not nearly as convincing as he obviously thought they were. Firstly, he suggested that the beak and hands were not adapted for catching shrimps and the like. This is obviously a matter of opinion, rather than being based on a logical argument. Secondly, he stated that the forelimbs were not adapted either for digging or holding struggling prey. Again in what sense this is supposed to provide a conclusive rebuttal of Brown's proposal is not obvious.

Thirdly, neither the structure of the beak nor that of the feet resembles that of living wading birds. This argument may have a little more weight because Osborn is at least making a

statement of comparison. However, whether the structure and habits of small wading birds can be realistically compared with those of a 10-13ft (3-4m) long shore-dwelling dinosaur must be open to doubt.

Having reviewed and rejected previous theories, Osborn proposed his own—the ostrich theory—which was that *Struthiomimus* was a browsing herbivore. He suggested that the forelimbs were used as grapples for bending down branches, so that young shoots and buds could be bitten off. This type of life-style seems to explain the combination of long grasping hands and arms, and the long flexible neck which would have allowed the head to be moved with accuracy between branches and twigs, there to peck at food. The shape of the beak seems well suited to this type of feeding. And finally the feet are similar to those of the big ostrich-like birds.

A fourth interpretation of the habits of *Struthiomimus*, proposed by Dr William King

---

Dromiceiomimus Skull (right)

This is another lightly built ornithomimosaur skull. It is very similar to that of *Struthiomimus*. In fact, it is the body skeleton of *Dromiceiomimus* which really distinguishes it from other ornithomimosaurs: the short back, slender front leg, and slightly differently arranged pelvic bones. The eye socket is very large (see also photograph on page 49).

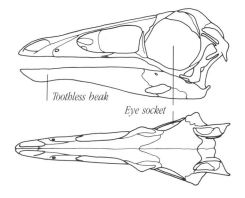
Toothless beak
Eye socket

Oviraptor Skulls (right)

Several skulls belonging to this genus have been described and they exhibit quite a lot of variety. The top two skulls have been assigned to the species *philoceratops*, yet one has a small bump in the nasal region, while the other has a large crest. The third and fourth drawings show another species from Mongolia which has yet to be described. Its large eye sockets and smooth bone contours suggest that it is a juvenile animal.

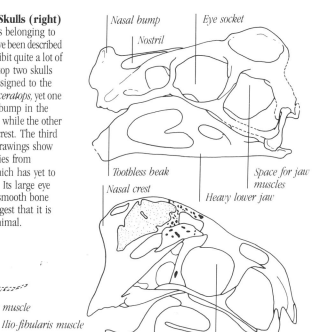
Nasal bump | *Eye socket*
Nostril
Toothless beak | *Space for jaw muscles*
Nasal crest | *Heavy lower jaw*
Eye socket

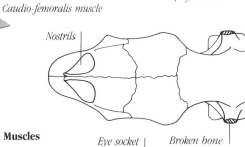
Nostrils

Ilio-tibialis muscle
Ilio-fibularis muscle
Caudio-femoralis muscle

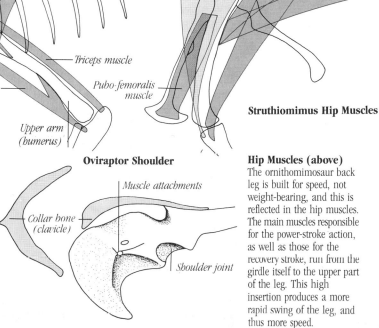

Scapulo-humeralis muscle
Coraco-brachialis muscle
Triceps muscle
Biceps muscle
Pubo-femoralis muscle
Upper arm (humerus)

Struthiomimus Shoulder

Struthiomimus Hip Muscles

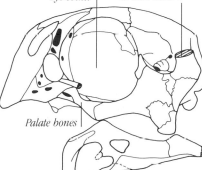
Eye socket | *Broken bone*
Palate bones

Struthiomimus (above) and Oviraptor (right) Shoulders

The muscles reconstructed on the *Struthiomimus* shoulder are fairly generalised and would have permitted quite a wide range of movement. The shoulder girdle of *Oviraptor* shows that a collar bone is present in this theropod at least. It is shown in top view (near right) and in side view.

Oviraptor Shoulder

Muscle attachments
Collar bone (clavicle)
Shoulder joint

Hip Muscles (above)

The ornithomimosaur back leg is built for speed, not weight-bearing, and this is reflected in the hip muscles. The main muscles responsible for the power-stroke action, as well as those for the recovery stroke, run from the girdle itself to the upper part of the leg. This high insertion produces a more rapid swing of the leg, and thus more speed.

Gregory, is essentially similar to Osborn's, only differing in one or two respects. Gregory concurs with Osborn in envisaging these animals as very fast-running ground dwellers which used their arms and hands as grapples to obtain food. However, Gregory proposed a much more catholic diet for *Struthiomimus*, suggesting it was an omnivore, taking fruits and seeds as well as small vertebrates (mammals, reptiles, amphibians) and larger invertebrates (millipedes, flying insects etc). Gregory also came up with the novel suggestion that they may have had skin flaps (patagia) between the arms and body; these, he proposed, served to prevent the animal from toppling forward when running fast with arms outstretched. This last suggestion has never really been taken seriously, and it could only be proved if a well-preserved skin impression were to be found.

To sum up, although Brown's sea-shore theory has not been effectively disproved, the general consensus today supports the opinions of Osborn and Gregory. Ornithomimosaurs were probably ground-dwelling, omnivorous dinosaurs which were capable of running very fast—perhaps as fast as living ostriches (31 mph, 50 kph). Their fleetness of foot and probable great manoeuvrability permitted them not only to escape larger predators, but also to catch fast-moving prey, such as lizards, small mammals or flying insects.

Recent Discoveries

Since the early years of this century, several significant discoveries of ornithomimosaurs have been made both in North America and Asia. In the early 1920s a fragmentary skeleton, *Struthiomimus brevitertius,* came to light. Then in 1926 a new specimen was discovered near Steveville on the Red Deer River, Alberta. This new find consisted of the front part of the skeleton (including a fine head) of an ornithomimosaur, which was described and named *Struthiomimus samueli* by William Parks in 1928. This was the first ornithomimosaur with a well-preserved skull. In the early 1970s Osmolska, Roniewicz and Barsbold described a completely new ornithomimosaur: *Gallimimus* ('chicken mimic') from Mongolia.

In 1972 Dale Russell (Ottawa) provided a much needed review of the North American ornithomimosaurs and reassessed the various species that had been proposed since the 1890s. This was valuable because many authors had tended to regard *Ornithomimus* and *Struthiomimus* as the same animal, and used *Struthiomimus* as the generic name for almost all the material.

Russell's research revealed that there were *three* genera of ornithomimosaurs in the late Cretaceous of North America:

(i) *Ornithomimus* (based on Marsh's original type material, *O. sedens,* and another fine skeleton lacking only the tail—originally named *Struthiomimus currelli*—from the Red Deer River). *Ornithomimus* is distinguished from the two other genera, *Struthiomimus* and *Dromiceiomimus,* by the length of its back, the proportions of its forelimbs (longer than *Struthiomimus*) and hindlimbs (shorter than both *Struthiomimus* and *Dromiceiomimus*) and the shape of its hands.

(ii) *Struthiomimus* (based primarily on the skeleton described by Osborn in 1917 and other related, but relatively poorly preserved, material) is distinguished from the other two genera by the length of its body, the proportions of its limbs (longer legs and shorter arms than *Ornithomimus*), and hand and pelvis shape.

(iii) *Dromiceiomimus* ('emu mimic'). This new genus, proposed by Dale Russell, is based on material from Alberta originally described as *Struthiomimus brevitertius* and *Struthiomimus samueli* by William Parks. *Dromiceiomimus* has a relatively short back, a comparatively slender and long forearm and hand, and somewhat differently arranged pelvic bones.

Russell also reviewed the possible habits of ornithomimosaurs and proposed that they may well have been solely carnivorous, perhaps feeding upon eggs and other small animal material obtained by scooping from the ground or digging. Since ornithomimids were defenceless, they would have relied upon their sprinting abilities (and possibly camouflage) to avoid predators which may well have been the more heavily built but less agile tyrannosaurids (pages 68-73).

Ornithomimosaurs may well have originated from the lightly-built theropods ('coelurosaurs') such as *Elaphrosaurus,* a relatively large, lightly-built theropod from the later Jurassic of Tanzania. Unfortunately the head of *Elaphrosaurus* is not known, so it is uncertain whether it possessed teeth in its jaws or had the horny bill typical of ornithomimosaurs. However, numerous small theropod teeth are known from the same locality. Another species, originally named *Ornithomimus asiaticus,* from the early Cretaceous of Mongolia, which has since been re-named *Archaeornithomimus* ('ancient bird mimic'), may also be an early ornithomimosaur, but at the moment this form is only known from a few fragmentary bones of the hand, foot and backbone.

Gallimimus, the Asian ornithomimosaur, comes from the late Cretaceous of Mongolia. It has been described from at least three quite well-preserved skeletons and differs from the North American forms in the shape of its skull and the proportions of its limbs.

Garudimimus (Garuda [a mythical bird] mimic') is another ornithomimosaur from the late Cretaceous of Mongolia. It is known from a well-preserved skull and other fragments described by Rinchen Barsbold in 1981. This dinosaur was placed in a group all of its own: the garudimimidae. This was because it had an unusually shaped beak, notched at its tip, and a peculiar bony ridge just above its eyes. It seems at this stage more probable that *Garudimimus* simply represents a distinctive ornithomimosaur rather than a totally new group of toothless dinosaurs.

Deinocheirus ('terrible hand') is a remarkable fossil from the late Cretaceous of Southern Mongolia. *Deinocheirus* consists of just two huge arms that were discovered by the Polish-Mongolian expedition (see photograph). In their general arrangement and proportions, these puzzlingly large arms most closely resemble those of the ornithomimosaurs. The arms are long, and for their size, relatively

Above: As its name suggests, *Struthiomimus* (and other ornithomimosaurs) probably resembled today's ostrich to some degree, both being fast-running and well balanced creatures.

Left: A cast of a skull of the Mongolian ornithomimosaur *Gallimimus* in the British Museum (Natural History) collection. Note the long, toothless jaws and the relatively large size of the eye socket.

Browsing Herbivores (right)
A number of suggestions have been advanced with regard to the likely feeding habits of ornithomimosaurs. While it is impossible to be certain, their basic body shape would seem to be well adapted to a plant-eating life-style. The long arms and hands might be used to grasp branches while the beak could nip off buds and leaves. Of course these attributes would also suit a speedy omnivore with a wider and more catholic diet.

slender, and end in three-fingered hands. The fingers themselves are huge, but are of practically equal length, a characteristic of ornithomimosaurs. However, the first finger shows no obvious thumb-like ability to fold inwards to form an effective grip, as in ornithomimosaurs. Exactly what the rest of the animal looked like is a complete mystery.

Oviraptorosaurs

These equally extraordinary creatures — egg-thieves as their name suggests — are at the moment rather poorly-known, toothless theropod dinosaurs. However, this situation should improve greatly in the next few years as new Mongolian material is described.

The first remains of fossils of this type of dinosaur were those named *Oviraptor* ('egg thief') and were discovered during the American Museum of Natural History— Mongolian expedition in the early 1920s. The

remains consisted of one partial skull and skeleton discovered in 1923 by Mr George Olsen, at the *Protoceratops* (see pages 128-133) locality of Shabarakh Usu, Southern Mongolia. The skull (illustrated on page 47), although rather badly fractured, was preserved in a nodule of sandstone, so that a clear idea of its shape and the arrangement of its bone was obtained. It is notable for the large number of openings in its sides and the curious horn-like prong on the tip of its snout. As in the ornithomimosaurs (with which group these dinosaurs have been linked by many), this skull possesses no teeth and presumably compensated for this by having horn-covered jaws. However, unlike the skulls of ornithomimosaurs, this skull is rather short-snouted, with a very deep and strong lower jaw.

Associated with the skull, that was described by Osborn in 1924, was a partial skeleton consisting of fragmentary neck vertebrae, various ribs, the shoulder bones, left arm and

hand, and most of the right hand. The hand was well enough preserved to reveal that there were three elongate fingers ending in large, sharp claws. However, the proportions of the fingers are different from those of ornithomimosaurs, in that they have more sharply-curved claws and the first finger is considerably shorter than the other two. In fact the hand is rather similar in shape to that of *Ornitholestes* (page 41) and the dromaeosaurids (pages 56-61). The arms and shoulders do not disclose much concerning the biology of this creature, but there is one unexpected bone preserved in the shoulder— a modified collar-bone or clavicle. A few years ago no dinosaur was supposed to possess a bony collar bone. It was believed that they had been lost early in the history of the reptile group from which dinosaurs were thought to have evolved.

Since the original description of this new dinosaur by Osborn, five better preserved skulls and skeletons of *Oviraptor* have been discovered by a joint Soviet-Mongolian expedition in 1972. These are to be described by Dr Rinchen Barsbold (Ulan Bator, Mongolia) in the near future. However, some preliminary comments and illustrations of these dinosaurs were published in 1983 which confirmed the presence of the unusual collar-bone in the shoulder. The curious feature is that instead of comprising a pair of bones, one on each side of the shoulder girdle, the two bones are welded together to form a single curved bone. This arrangement is strikingly like that seen in living birds whose collar bones are fused together to form the 'wish-bone' (furcula). This discovery has added much fuel to the debate over the origin and relationships of birds and dinosaurs (see pages 191-193).

According to Dr Barsbold, the remainder of the skeleton of *Oviraptor* is very similar to that of most theropods, and this reassurance has formed the basis for the flesh restoration of *Oviraptor* on pages 44-45. Some inaccuracies will undoubtedly be revealed when full skeletal descriptions have been published.

Both the Polish-Mongolian expedition of 1970-71 and the Soviet-Mongolian expedition of 1972 recovered *Oviraptor* material. This has revealed quite a wide range of skull shape and degree of horn development. Many of these differences may be due to the degree of maturity of the specimen.

Oviraptor may also provide a clue to an unusual bird-like jaw from the late Cretaceous of Alberta, Canada. Originally this was described as the lower jaw of *Caenagnathus* ('recent jawless'), and was thought to be that of an unusual bird. The jaw was unlike anything previously described as bird-like. However, as Halszka Osmolska rightly pointed out in 1976, the jaw of *Caenagnathus* closely resembles that of *Oviraptor* and very probably represents a North American species of this unusual group of animals.

The circumstances of preservation of the original specimen of *Oviraptor* described by Osborn in 1924 provided the reason for its name: *Oviraptor philoceratops* ('egg thief, fond of ceratopian eggs'). Its skull and skeleton were found lying on top of a clutch of *Protoceratops* eggs! Perhaps the unfortunate creature had died at the very moment of robbing a nest, or its skull was crushed after being caught by an enraged parent. We shall never know. It is certainly possible that *Oviraptor* preyed upon ceratopian eggs, which it cracked open with its horny beak. Perhaps, like the ornithomimosaurs, they were general predators or scavengers of anything dead or alive.

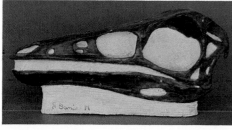

Left: *Dromiceiomimus* ('emu mimic') *brevitertius* is known from the late Cretaceous of Alberta in Canada. Again the size of the eye socket is really remarkable, and may imply that these creatures possessed a particularly acute sense of vision.

Above: The gigantic forearms of *Deinocheirus mirificus* being mounted at the Institute of Palaeobiology in Warsaw. We can only speculate what the rest of this remarkable creature may have looked like: very possibly a giant ornithomimosaur.

Over the last decade in particular a large variety of enigmatic theropods have been discovered and described. For the most part these have been rather poor or incomplete specimens of dinosaurs which do not seem to fit readily into any of the groups currently recognised. Described below are *some* of these new and enigmatic animals. It is quite likely that when more and better preserved fossils of these creatures are recovered, many will fall into some of the better established groups; others, however, may prove to be totally new dinosaur types.

Segisaurus

Discovered in 1933 in early Jurassic rocks of Arizona, *Segisaurus* ('reptile from Segi Canyon') was described by Dr Charles Camp in 1936. The fossil remains of this animal consist of a fragmentary, headless skeleton which includes a few back vertebrae, some ribs, the shoulder girdle, incomplete arms, legs and parts of the pelvis. The animal as reconstructed is small (about 3·3ft, 1m long) and ran on slender hind legs. The fore legs were apparently short, with sharp-clawed fingers. The feet and hands are reminiscent of those of 'coelurosaur'—type theropods. However, *Segisaurus* does have a collar bone (clavicle) preserved on one shoulder which, as we saw earlier (pages 48-49), is quite rare in dinosaurs. Until better material of *Segisaurus* is recovered it is probably best to regard it as a rather curious small theropod.

Chirostenotes

Chirostenotes ('slender hand') consists of two imperfectly preserved, sharply-clawed hands which were discovered in late Cretaceous rocks of the Red Deer River, Alberta. The fingers are of unequal length and quite closely resemble those of the late Jurassic 'coelurosaur' *Ornitholestes* (see page 41) and the dromaeosaurids (pages 56 to 61). Indeed *Dromaeosaurus* is known from the same area, so this material may well belong to this genus. In addition to these two hands, several other teeth and a lower jaw were referred to *Chirostenotes*. These were found a few miles from the hands, so their reference to this genus is necessarily cautious, but they do, with the benefit of hindsight, resemble dromaeosaurid jaws.

Macrophalangia

Macrophalangia ('large toes') is another theropod from the Red Deer River of Alberta. First described by Charles Sternberg in 1932, *Macrophalangia* is known from a partial foot which looks very much like that of an ornithomimosaur (see pages 44-49). It has long and slender toes ending in flattened but quite pointed claws. However, unlike the three-toed ornithomimosaur foot, the foot of *Macrophalangia* has four toes: three long, slender ones and a smaller first toe typical of the great majority of theropods. The question, therefore, is: does *Macrophalangia* represent a primitive type of ornithomimosaur? If it does, then its appearance in late Cretaceous rocks is unexpected. Alternatively, these remains may indicate a completely new group of slender-toed theropods in the late Cretaceous.

Elmisaurus

Elmisaurus ('foot reptile'), another poorly preserved theropod, this time from the late Cretaceous of the Gobi Desert, was described in 1981 by Dr Halszka Osmolska. Known as it is from portions of hands, feet and odd leg bones, this new dinosaur may provide vital clues to the relations of both *Chirostenotes* and *Macrophalangia*. The hand of *Elmisaurus* seems, from its proportions, to resemble closely that of *Chirostenotes* (as well as that of *Ornitholestes* and dromaeosaurids). The foot, however, is most similar to that described as *Macrophalangia*; the toes are quite long and slender and are arranged very similarly to those of *Macrophalangia* and ornithomimosaurs, except that as in *Macrophalangia* there appear to be *four* toes. The interpretation that can be made from this combination of features is that the remains of *Chirostenotes*, *Macrophalangia* and *Elmisaurus* represent the remains of a new type of theropod in the late Cretaceous. Osmolska proposed that these all be referred to as elmisaurids, a new family of theropod dinosaurs. These dinosaurs seem to combine the grasping hands of the rapacious dromaeosaurids with the fleetness of foot of ornithomimosaurs. Unfortunately at the moment very little is known about the rest of the skeleton or the skull, so that accurate life-like restorations of these creatures are impossible.

Avimimus

In 1981 Dr Kurzanov (Moscow) described the partial skeleton of a remarkably bird-like theropod dinosaur, *Avimimus* ('bird mimic'), discovered during the joint Soviet-Mongolian expedition. This dinosaur was of very slender build, with slim legs and long bird-like feet, as well as a long slender, bird-like neck. The tail was typically long and dinosaurian (unlike the short 'Parson's Nose' of a bird) so as to counterbalance the front part of the body. Dr Kurzanov noted that there were a considerable number of bird-like characters found in *Avimimus* and proposed that this was a small,

'A Segnosaur' (right)
It must be emphasized that what you see here is an hypothetical animal. At present we know the structure of the skull of *Erlikosaurus* along with some of its neck vertebrae and feet. Added to this we have part of a jaw, legs, a pelvis and hands and feet of *Segnosaurus*. These have been used to provide an outline of what a segnosaur may have looked like. The unusual combination of a toothless beak, bird-like hips, theropod hands and rather broad feet is most perplexing. One suggestion is that they were fish eaters and had webbed hind feet as shown here.

Segisaurus (right)
Another unusual theropod is the early Jurassic form known as *Segisaurus* found in Arizona. Unfortunately the skeleton was found to be headless though the remainder was reasonably well preserved. As seen here *Segisaurus* was quite small and was lightly constructed as a presumably agile runner. Most probably *Segisaurus* fed upon small vertebrates (lizards and amphibians) or larger insects. The teeth are not preserved so we cannot be absolutely sure of its diet.

Time Chart (left)
Segisaurus from the lower Jurassic is one of the earliest of these theropod forms; this is then followed by a range of peculiar theropods clustered into the late part of the Cretaceous Period which was possibly a time of 'experimentation' in theropod design—perhaps reflecting unusual climatic conditions at the time.

YEARS AGO (MILLIONS)

CRETACEOUS			
	AVIMIMUS	ERLIKOSAURUS	NOASAURUS

64
70
80
90
100
110
120
130
140
150
160
170
180
190
200
210
220
225

JURASSIC — SEGISAURUS

TRIASSIC

feathered, bird-like dinosaur of the late Cretaceous. Among the skeletal remains there is an incomplete forelimb which is of particular interest. Kurzanov analysed the bones of the forelimb in some detail and demonstrated that the humerus (upper arm bone) was extremely bird-like with all the ridges and bumps for attachment of the main flight muscles, and a wing-folding mechanism. In addition, and perhaps more intriguing still, Kurzanov demonstrated that one of the forearm bones (ulna) had a distinctive bony ridge running along its rear edge. No other theropod is known to possess such a bony ridge. Birds however do have a rather similar series of small bony 'pimples' running along this forearm bone. These 'pimples' are developed at the point of attachment of the flight feathers (secondaries). *Avimimus* does not have a series of pimple-like attachment points, but rather a long bony ridge; nevertheless such a structure is very suggestive of the presence of feathers on the forelimbs. As

Dr Kurzanov rightly points out, there is no direct evidence of feathers as there is in the case of the famous fossils of *Archaeopteryx*, but the bird-like structure of the skeleton and the possible feather attachment ridge on the bone of the forearm are very suggestive. Kurzanov proposes that *Avimimus* was a member of a very late group of bird-like theropod dinosaurs named avimimids; these were small, fleet-footed creatures living perhaps upon insects. The feather covering is supposed to be associated primarily with body insulation rather than flight. Kurzanov believes that these were small highly-active creatures which would have generated their own body heat internally, rather than relying upon the Sun to keep them warm as reptiles usually do. Since they were small, avimimids would have needed some form of insulation to control the rate at which they lost heat, and feathers may have been what they used. As others have suggested in the past, a small, highly-active, ground-running creature

such as this may have been a first stage in the origin of powered flight. Kurzanov visualises *Avimimus* occasionally fluttering into the air when pursuing flying insects, or alternatively using short airborne jumps as a way of avoiding larger fleet-footed predators.

Avimimus is obviously an interesting and highly controversial animal at this moment. As with most fossils, its remains are frustratingly incomplete. It would be nice to know what the complete structure of the head, the shoulder bones, the remainder of the arm and hand and the hips were like; all of which would help to clarify the true nature of this animal. If *Avimimus* was truly a *feathered* theropod dinosaur, then it would provide an extraordinary and unexpected insight into the process of evolution because it suggests that a structure as complicated as a bird's feather may have evolved twice: once producing true birds in the Jurassic, and a second time producing the avimimids of the late Cretaceous. Unless,

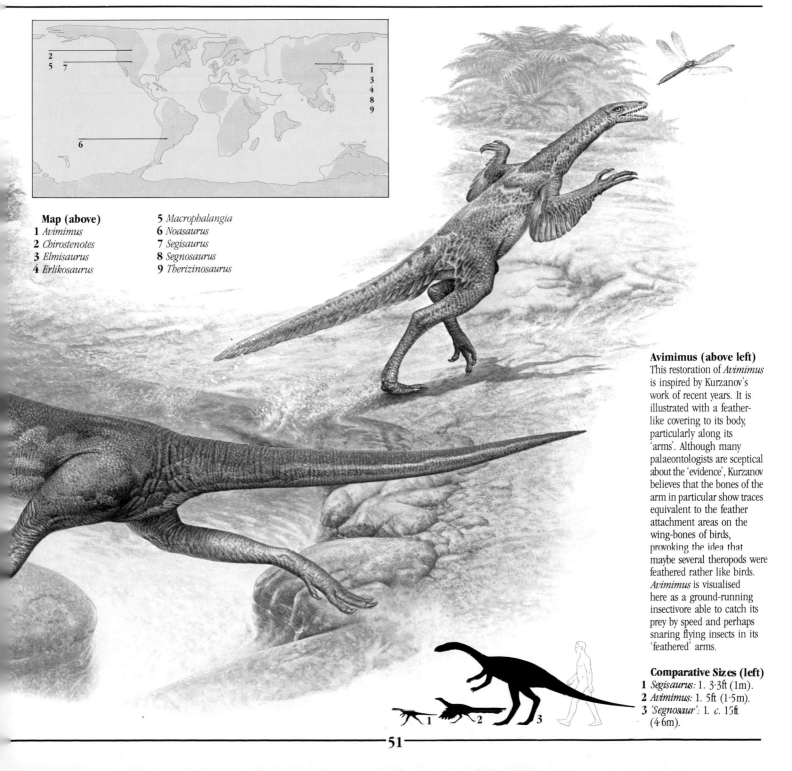

Map (above)

1 *Avimimus*
2 *Chirostenotes*
3 *Elmisaurus*
4 *Erlikosaurus*
5 *Macrophalangia*
6 *Noasaurus*
7 *Segisaurus*
8 *Segnosaurus*
9 *Therizinosaurus*

Avimimus (above left)
This restoration of *Avimimus* is inspired by Kurzanov's work of recent years. It is illustrated with a feather-like covering to its body, particularly along its 'arms'. Although many palaeontologists are sceptical about the 'evidence', Kurzanov believes that the bones of the arm in particular show traces equivalent to the feather attachment areas on the wing-bones of birds, provoking the idea that maybe several theropods were feathered rather like birds. *Avimimus* is visualised here as a ground-running insectivore able to catch its prey by speed and perhaps snaring flying insects in its 'feathered' arms.

Comparative Sizes (left)
1 *Segisaurus*: 1. 3·3ft (1m).
2 *Avimimus*: 1. 5ft (1·5m).
3 'Segnosaur': 1. c. 15ft (4·6m).

of course, all small theropods were feathered! In the past most evolutionary biologists have argued that a structure as complex as a feather was very unlikely to have evolved more than once. At the moment I am rather sceptical of Dr Kurzanov's proposals.

Segnosaurids

The first segnosaurid remains were described in 1979 by Dr Altangerel Perle and also by Dr Rinchen Barsbold (Ulan Bator, Mongolia) from material discovered during the Soviet-Mongolian expeditions. As with the previous examples, the fossil remains are incomplete and merely provide an interesting glimpse of other dinosaur types. So far three Mongolian segnosaurids have been named: *Segnosaurus* ('slow reptile'), *Erlikosaurus* ('King of the Dead [Erlik] reptile') and an un-named form, all of which come from the late Cretaceous Bayn Shireh horizon of south-eastern Mongolia.

Segnosaurus, the first of these dinosaurs to be described, was based on a partial skeleton including a lower jaw, parts of the legs and backbone, and a complete pelvis. Several other fragments including a forelimb have also been discovered in the same area which provide a little more evidence of the structure of this animal. Several features of *Segnosaurus* deserve mention. First and most obviously, the pelvis is very unusual for a theropod. As can be seen right, the pubis lies parallel to the ischium below the hip socket; this arrangement is very similar to that seen in ornithischian dinosaurs and birds. Secondly, the jaws are unusual for theropods in that the front part of the jaw was toothless and the teeth at the back of the jaw were quite small and pointed, rather than being like large serrated daggers. The front end of the jaws was probably covered by a horny beak, again rather like that of ornithischian dinosaurs. The head, at least as judged from the size of the jaw, was quite small relative to the size of the body. The forelimb was short and ended in three slender, clawed fingers. The hindlimb was quite sturdy and ended in a rather short and broad four-toed foot. Again the foot is most unusual for a theropod, the toes of which are usually slender and bunched together in a distinctly bird-like arrangement.

Clearly *Segnosaurus* was a most unusual theropod. The remains indicate an animal of 20-23ft (6-7m) in length with a small head, horny beak, small cheek teeth, short forelimbs, bird-like pelvis and stout, broad-footed hindlimbs. *Segnosaurus* must have been a rather slow-moving theropod with a very specific diet. One suggestion is that *Segnosaurus* was an aquatic fish eater; this may explain the small pointed teeth and broad (perhaps webbed) feet of this animal, though why it should possess a horny beak is a complete mystery.

Erlikosaurus from Baysheen Tsav in Mongolia is known from a skull, some neck vertebrae, a humerus and both feet. Smaller than *Segnosaurus, Erlikosaurus* was described by Barsbold and Perle in 1980. The skull shows the same toothless beak at the front of the jaws, and small, pointed teeth behind. The hind foot is rather similar to that of *Segnosaurus* in that there are four toes which are rather short, but end in sharp claws.

In general shape the jaws, neck vertebrae and feet of these two animals are very similar.

However *Erlikosaurus* is smaller than *Segnosaurus,* has a greater number of teeth, a larger beak and narrower claws on its feet. The shape of the pelvis in *Erlikosaurus* is entirely unknown at present, but is assumed to have resembled that of *Segnosaurus.*

'Un-named reptile' from Khara Kutul consists of a pelvis alone. This resembles that of *Segnosaurus* except that it is slightly smaller; there are also a few differences in detailed structure including the welding together of pubis and ischium. These differences have been deemed sufficient to recognise the existence of another segnosaurid from the late Cretaceous of Mongolia. However, it is at present not sufficiently well known to exclude the possibility that it is either the pelvis of *Erlikosaurus* or a variation of *Segnosaurus,* so very wisely a name has not yet been given.

Nanshiungosaurus ('Nanshiung reptile') which has been referred to the segnosaurids is fragmentary material that may be of a sauropod.

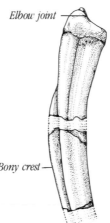

Elbow joint

Bony crest

Avimimus Arm Bone (above)

This incomplete arm bone (the ulna) is one of the most interesting (and controversial) pieces of evidence relating to the biology of *Avimimus.* The crest of bone indicated has been interpreted as an area for the attachment of wing feathers.

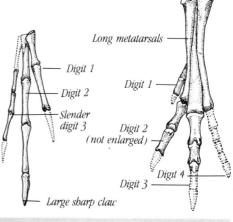

Elmisaurus Hand and Foot (right)

The hand of *Elmisaurus* is quite well preserved and in its proportions fairly closely resembles that of dromaeosaurids such as *Deinonychus.* It has a very powerful first finger and a long slender third finger. The foot by contrast is more similar to that of the ornithomimosaurs in that the toes are long and slender, and there is no enlargement of the second toe as a slashing claw.

Long metatarsals
Digit 1
Digit 2
Slender digit 3
Large sharp claw
Digit 1
Digit 2 (not enlarged)
Digit 3
Digit 4

Above: The North American Road Runner is a very fleet-footed creature. It has long back legs somewhat like those of *Avimimus,* which may have had a similar life-style.

Right: This photograph of *Avimimus* was provided by Dr Kurzanov of the Moscow Academy of Sciences and is one of the most recent reconstructions of this creature. As seen here it is surprisingly bird-like with long back legs, long neck and no tail. The forelimbs are short, but rather poorly preserved. The apparent absence of a tail is most intriguing.

In 1985 Greg Paul made the rather controversial suggestion that segnosaurids may be late surviving relatives of early prosauropods and ornithischians. This is a contentious claim which is bound to provoke much argument.

Noasaurids

Fragmentary remains of *Noasaurus* ('reptile from Noa' — Noa=N.W. Argentina) were described by José Bonaparte and Jaime Powell in 1980. They come from late Cretaceous rocks of the El Brete area of north-west Argentina and include parts of the skull, some vertebrae, and two foot bones — including a large claw. Careful comparison of these remains with those of known theropods seems to suggest that *Noasaurus* belongs to another new group of theropods: the noasaurids. However, this suggestion should be treated with great caution until better material is discovered. One rather interesting point noted by Bonaparte and Powell is that, if correctly identified, the foot claw seems to be of the large slashing type seen on the foot of dromaeosaurids (pages 56-61). However, the form of the claw is such that it could not have evolved from the type of claw seen in dromaeosaurids, but must have evolved quite independently.

Therizinosaurids

A large amount of dinosaur material was collected by a Soviet-Mongolian expedition to the southern Gobi Desert in 1948 which included some very large bony claws. These latter were described as *Therizinosaurus* ('scythe reptile') and were associated with some large flattened ribs. Later in 1957, 1959 and 1960 more large claws were discovered in Khazakhstan, Transbaykalia and Inner Mongolia. The latter consisted of not only a large claw, but also a partial forelimb, the incomplete hindlimbs and a tooth. These remains were of a large theropod dinosaur and finally proved that the claws of *Therizinosaurus*, originally thought to belong to turtle, were those of a dinosaur. The large flattened ribs finally proved to be ribs of a large sauropod dinosaur. As was the case with *Deinocheirus* (page 49), the remains of *Therizinosaurus* hint at some extraordinary late Cretaceous dinosaur from Asia. One of the claws from the hand measures approximately 28in (70cm) in length — this does not include the horny part of the claw which would have made it even longer! Precisely what these huge claws were used for is a mystery. They may have been formidable weapons for slashing through the skin of their prey or, as has been suggested by others, they may have been used to tear open termitaria (anthills). However, it does seem rather hard to believe that such a large animal lived on just termites or ants! Once again we have a desperate need to discover more of these amazing and perplexing fossil creatures.

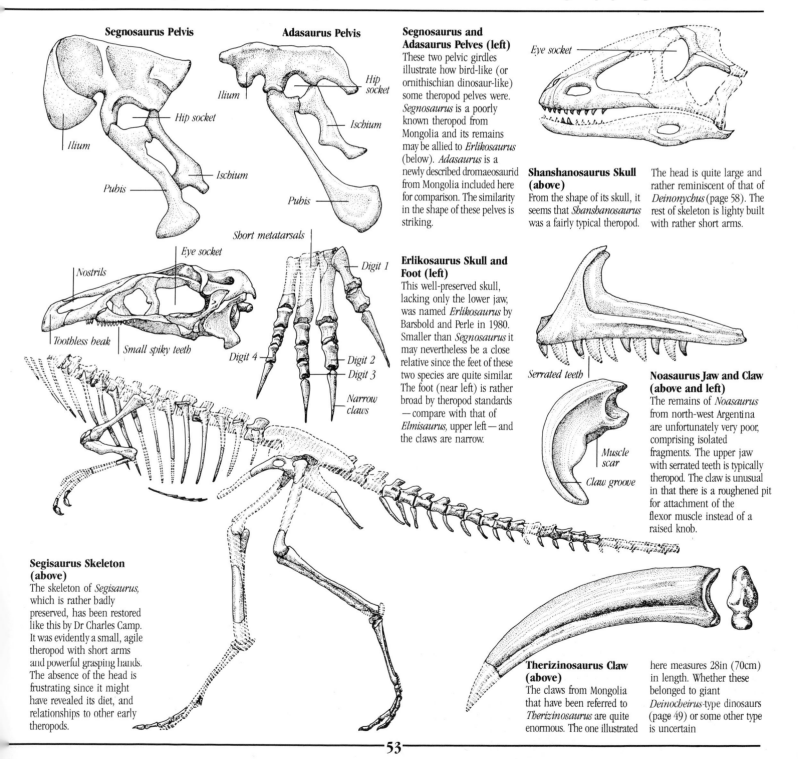

Segnosaurus and Adasaurus Pelves (left)
These two pelvic girdles illustrate how bird-like (or ornithischian dinosaur-like) some theropod pelves were. *Segnosaurus* is a poorly known theropod from Mongolia and its remains may be allied to *Erlikosaurus* (below). *Adasaurus* is a newly described dromaeosaurid from Mongolia included here for comparison. The similarity in the shape of these pelves is striking.

Erlikosaurus Skull and Foot (left)
This well-preserved skull, lacking only the lower jaw, was named *Erlikosaurus* by Barsbold and Perle in 1980. Smaller than *Segnosaurus* it may nevertheless be a close relative since the feet of these two species are quite similar. The foot (near left) is rather broad by theropod standards — compare with that of *Elmisaurus*, upper left — and the claws are narrow.

Shanshanosaurus Skull (above)
From the shape of its skull, it seems that *Shanshanosaurus* was a fairly typical theropod.

The head is quite large and rather reminiscent of that of *Deinonychus* (page 58). The rest of skeleton is lighty built with rather short arms.

Noasaurus Jaw and Claw (above and left)
The remains of *Noasaurus* from north-west Argentina are unfortunately very poor, comprising isolated fragments. The upper jaw with serrated teeth is typically theropod. The claw is unusual in that there is a roughened pit for attachment of the flexor muscle instead of a raised knob.

Segisaurus Skeleton (above)
The skeleton of *Segisaurus*, which is rather badly preserved, has been restored like this by Dr Charles Camp. It was evidently a small, agile theropod with short arms and powerful grasping hands. The absence of the head is frustrating since it might have revealed its diet, and relationships to other early theropods.

Therizinosaurus Claw (above)
The claws from Mongolia that have been referred to *Therizinosaurus* are quite enormous. The one illustrated here measures 28in (70cm) in length. Whether these belonged to giant *Deinocheirus*-type dinosaurs (page 49) or some other type is uncertain

In 1923 Henry Fairfield Osborn described the incomplete remains of a bird-like theropod dinosaur from late Cretaceous rocks at Bayn Dzak (=Shabarakh Usu) in the Gobi Desert. These included the major part of a skull found in one sandstone nodule and, a little way away from this, parts of the backbone, pelvis, legs and feet. All of these remains were collected in 1923 by a Chinese assistant on the Central Asiatic Expedition of the American Museum of Natural History.

This new dinosaur was named *Saurornithoides mongoliensis* ('bird-like reptile from Mongolia') and was at first supposed to be an early toothed bird, because its skull had a long, rather bird-like, narrow muzzle. In general shape and proportions the skull is rather similar to that of *Velociraptor* (page 56) which was incidentally described at the same time and came from the same area of Mongolia. However, the teeth (in particular) are rather different; those of *Saurornithoides* are smaller and more numerous with 38 teeth in the upper jaw, while *Velociraptor* had no more than 30 teeth. The teeth were also unusual in that only their back edges were serrated whereas both front and back edges of *Velociraptor's* were serrated. The incomplete hind foot showed that the toes were arranged in typical theropod fashion with a small, spur-like first toe and three longer walking toes. The original drawings of the specimen show that the second toe of the foot had a somewhat enlarged claw which could have been raised clear of the ground. However, this was not appreciated at the time when it was first described and its significance was realised only much later.

Osborn concluded that *Saurornithoides* must have been a small, carnivorous theropod which was neither as fleet-footed nor as voracious as *Velociraptor*.

Somewhat later (in 1932) some more bones were described by Charles Sternberg; these came from the late Cretaceous near Steveville on the Red Deer River, Alberta. The remains included a complete foot, several hand bones and a few vertebrae. The hand bones were rather similar to those of *Ornitholestes* (pages 46-47) and *Chirostenotes* (pages 50-51) with uneven finger lengths. The foot, however, was rather unusual because, although it showed the typical bird-like arrangement of toes, the second toe was somewhat shorter than the third and fourth toes and had an unexpectedly large, sharply-curved claw. The third and fourth toes were both quite long and almost equal in length with smaller but still sharply-curved claws. As was hinted at above in relation to the foot of *Saurornithoides*, the second toe was jointed in such a way that it could be held clear of the ground, instead of being used for walking upon. Again the significance of the unusual second toe and its claw was missed. At the time Sternberg concluded that this foot belonged to a new type of theropod which may have evolved from animals like *Ornitholestes*; he named this material *Stenonychosaurus* ('slender clawed' reptile) *inequalis*.

It was not until the discovery of *Deinonychus* (see page 56) in the mid 1960s and the research work of Professor John Ostrom (Yale) that the possibility of a relationship between *Saurornithoides* and *Stenonychosaurus* was appreciated. Ostrom recognised that *Deinonychus* had a very large claw on the second toe of its foot; he believed that this was used as an offensive weapon. Detailed comparison with other theropod feet showed that *Saurornithoides* and *Stenonychosaurus* had smaller, but similar, offensive claws. At first, both of

these dinosaurs were included with other dromaeosaurids. However, in 1974 Rinchen Barsbold (Ulan Bator, Mongolia) described more material of *Saurornithoides* which had been discovered at Bugeen Tsav in Mongolia. This material, ascribed the name *Saurornithoides junior* ('younger bird-like reptile'), was found in slightly earlier rocks and was 30 per cent larger than Osborn's species, while the number of teeth in the jaws was also greater. Apart from these differences, which may eventually prove to be simply due to growth, the two species seem remarkably similar.

The new *Saurornithoides* material included a well-preserved skull. The latter showed some rather curious swollen areas in the ear region and in the floor of the braincase. These features, plus the quite small size of the claw on the second toe of the foot, and the fact that their teeth were relatively smaller, more numerous and only serrated along their back edges, prompted Barsbold to propose that *Saurornithoides* and *Stenonychosaurus* should not be included in the dromaeosaurid family as proposed by Ostrom. Instead he placed them in a family of their own, and they became known as saurornithoidids. In 1978 Hans-Dieter Sues added another fragmentary form, *Saurornitholestes* ('reptile-like bird robber'), to the saurornithoidid group, although this small, lightly-built creature (found in Alberta, Canada) may in fact be a dromaeosaurid. Other supposed saurornithoidids include *Bradycneme* ('heavy shin') and *Heptasteornis* ('seven star bird') both from Rumania and originally thought to belong to birds; both of these are extremely dubious since they are based on very poor material. *Pectinodon* ('comb tooth') is another possible saurornithoidid.

The 'Dinosauroid'

In 1982 Dale Russell and R. Séguin (Ottawa) published an interesting article on *Stenonycho-*

	YEARS AGO (MILLIONS)
CRETACEOUS	64
	70
	80
	90
	100
	110
	120
	130
	140
	150
	160
JURASSIC	170
	180
	190
	200
TRIASSIC	210
	220
	225

SAURORNITHOIDES — STENONYCHOSAURUS — SAURORNITHOLESTES

Time Chart (left)
Another of the exclusively late Cretaceous groups, the saurornithoidids are only known so far from western North America and East Asia. At this time the two areas were connected via the Bering Straits and many of their dinosaurs are similar. These forms will probably only be found in these parts of the world.

Stenonychosaurus (right)
This has been credited as the most intelligent dinosaur. Compared with most other dinosaurs, it had a relatively large brain, but most of this excess brain volume was probably not concerned with reasoning and other activities that we would call 'intelligence'. *Stenonychosaurus* had large eyes, slender flexible fingers, and a light body. The brain was probably concerned mainly with its highly developed senses, fine control of its limbs, and fast reflexes, which were used in hunting small and elusive prey.

The 'Dinosauroid' (right)

Is this what *Stenonychosaurus* might have looked like if it had continued evolving to the present day? Russell and Séguin assumed for it an enlarged brain, and the short neck and upright posture were arrived at as a way of balancing the head more efficiently. In turn, the vertical posture removed the need for a tail. The legs were modified by lowering the ankle to the ground and the foot was lengthened. Although fictional, given the right conditions, such changes would be quite feasible.

saurus. A new partial skeleton of this dinosaur was discovered in Alberta in 1967, and this provided the basis for the first skeletal and flesh restoration of *Stenonychosaurus*. The detailed work that went into building this first model was described and illustrated in Russell and Séguin's paper. However, in addition to this work, they also indulged in an imaginative thought experiment. They posed the question: what might these dinosaurs have looked like if they had continued to evolve and not gone extinct at the end of the Cretaceous Period?

Stenonychosaurus proved to be an interesting choice of dinosaur for this type of 'experiment' because it was one of the largest-brained and therefore presumably one of the most intelligent of all dinosaurs. The result of this experiment was the so-called 'dinosauroid' restoration seen here.

One interpretation of the probable habits of *Stenonychosaurus* (and saurornithoidids in general) is that they were lightly-built active hunters of small prey—perhaps small lizards and mammals. The long grasping hands, and the very large eyes which pointed partly forward and therefore gave reasonable stereoscopic vision, may indicate that these were nimble predators which were active at dusk or even at night, when many of the small nocturnal mammals of the time would have been active.

The 'dinosauroid' was constructed by extrapolating from these attributes. It was visualised as a highly intelligent and 'manipulative' dinosaur. What it would have lacked in fleetness of foot (since it is more 'flat-footed' than *Stenonychosaurus*) it would have made up for through its greater intellect. This would have allowed it to avoid potential predators by 'outwitting' them rather than by showing them a 'clean pair of heels'. As a predator it may have been able to catch prey both by endurance running and perhaps by making simple weapons—much as primitive man must have done. Such an idea is an obviously fanciful, though provocative thought.

Saurornithoides (below)

Like *Stenonychosaurus*, *Saurornithoides* had a large brain and a slender body. Its large saucer-like eyes might have been used for hunting small mammals at dusk, when other predatory dinosaurs would have been unable to see properly.

Saurornithoides had small sharp teeth, but these were serrated only on the posterior edges. On its foot, there was a slightly enlarged claw which was normally folded back, but which could be used to slash at potential prey. In this it resembles *Deinonychus*.

Map (right)
1 *Saurornithoides*
2 *Saurornitholestes*
3 *Stenonychosaurus*

Comparative Sizes (left)
1 *Stenonychosaurus*: l. 6·5ft (2m).
2 *Saurornithoides*: l. 6·5ft (2m).

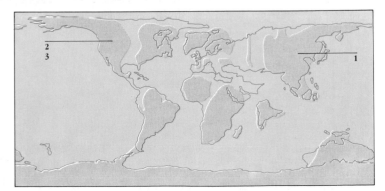

DROMAEOSAURIDS

Our knowledge of the dromaeosaurids has until quite recently been rather patchy in nature. The first dromaeosaurid remains to be described were those of *Dromaeosaurus* ('running reptile') *albertensis,* which were discovered near the Red Deer River by Barnum Brown in 1914. Unfortunately, as is often the case with many fossil species, the specimen that Brown collected was far from complete; it consisted of the partial head, lower jaws and an assortment of foot bones of a small carnivorous dinosaur. During the next fifty years nothing more was discovered of this dinosaur. Many scientists referred to this specimen but were unsure of its real nature and relationship with the other types of carnivorous dinosaurs then known, because so many parts of its skeleton were still undiscovered. Consequently *Dromaeosaurus* was grouped by some people with the huge 'carnosaurs' (the tyrannosaurids or megalosaurs) while others suggested that it was related to the small, slender 'coelurosaurs'

Deinonychus (below)
To date this is the best known of all dromaeosaurids, several partial skeletons having been described in great detail by Professor Ostrom. The distinctive characteristics of dromaeosaurids are shown very clearly here. The head is large with backwardly curved teeth; the arms are long and powerful, and the feet have the extraordinary sickle-like second toe. As can be seen here, the 'terrible claw' is shown raised off the ground. It was, in life, in such a position to protect the sharp point of the claw.

Velociraptor (below)
Fossil remains of this dinosaur have been discovered in the Djadochta Formation of Shabarak Usa, in Mongolia. Although illustrated with

Dromaeosaurus and *Deinonychus* here, remains of *Velociraptor* have not been found so far in geological deposits at the same sites as the other two, so in life they probably never met!

Velociraptor can be distinguished from other dromaeosaurids by its very low and narrow head. The difference in head shape and size may well reflect differences in the diets.

Time Chart (left)
The dromaeosaurids are very restricted in their time of appearance in the fossil record. One of the earliest known, after *Phaedrolosaurus,* is the new 'Surrey dinosaur' which is still being prepared at the British Museum. It dates from rocks of latest Lower Cretaceous age. *Deinonychus* is known from rocks that are a little younger, and is followed onto the scene by *Velociraptor, Dromaeosaurus* and *Hulsanpes* in the Upper Cretaceous.

YEARS AGO (MILLIONS)

CRETACEOUS — 64, 70, 80, 90, 100, 110, 120, 130, 140

JURASSIC — 150, 160, 170, 180, 190, 200

TRIASSIC — 210, 220, 225

VELOCIRAPTOR
DROMAEOSAURUS
HULSANPES
DEINONYCHUS
'SURREY DINOSAUR'
PHAEDROLOSAURUS

Comparative Sizes (left)
1 *Dromaeosaurus:* l. 6ft (1·8m).
2 *Velociraptor:* l. 6ft (1·8m).
3 *Deinonychus:* l. 10-11ft (3-3·3m)

(e.g. *Compsognathus* or *Coelurus*). If anything, its small size tended to favour the latter interpretation.

This rather unsatisfactory state of affairs was considerably improved by the discovery in 1964, by Grant Meyer and Professor John Ostrom of Yale University, of a new fossil locality in southern Montana. During the next two years excavations at this site unearthed several hundred bones of an entirely new carnivorous dinosaur: *Deinonychus* ('terrible claw') *antirrhopus*. The study of this dinosaur, which is now known from several almost complete (or complimentary) skeletons, has revealed many new and exciting facts: not only about this extraordinary kind of dinosaur, but also about its kinship with *Dromaeosaurus*. The peculiarities of *Deinonychus* help to show why it had been so difficult for earlier researchers to pin-point its affinities with *Dromaeosaurus*. Both *Dromaeosaurus* and *Deinonychus* share characteristics with both 'carnosaurs' and

'coelurosaurs', as well as exhibiting features that are unique; hence the confusion. One of their most characteristic features is the huge, sickle-like claw on the second toe of the foot. Once the unusual nature of the feet of these dinosaurs was appreciated, it became possible to draw comparisons with another dinosaur known since 1924, *Velociraptor* ('speedy predator') *mongoliensis*, which also had a sickle-like claw on its hind foot. A remarkable discovery made more recently in Mongolia is that of an almost complete *Velociraptor* skeleton preserved, apparently in combat position, clutching the skull of a *Protoceratops* skeleton with its forelimbs; this may be one of the few pieces of real evidence we have of the feeding habits of predatory dinosaurs.

Dromaeosaurids are now known from well preserved remains of the Upper Cretaceous of North America (*Dromaeosaurus* and *Deinonychus* in particular) and Mongolia (*Velociraptor*). In addition, other rather frag-

mentary remains have been described; these are *Hulsanpes* ('foot from Khulsan') *perlei*, which consists only of the incomplete hind foot of a very small dromaeosaurid from the Upper Cretaceous of Mongolia, and *Phaedrolosaurus* ('gleaming reptile') *ilikensis* from the Lower Cretaceous of China. *Phaedrolosaurus* consists of some scattered teeth and leg bones which do not all derive from the same animal; none of these shows *clear* evidence that it comes from a dromaeosaurid and should therefore be ignored until better material is discovered. '*Adasaurus*' is another recently discovered dinosaur from southern Mongolia that is thought to be a dromaeosaurid. It has not yet been fully described.

One of the most exciting recent discoveries was made in southern England. In 1982 a quarryman, Bill Walker, discovered a very large, sickle-shaped claw in a quarry in Surrey. The claw (three-times larger than that of *Deinonychus!*) was taken to the British Museum

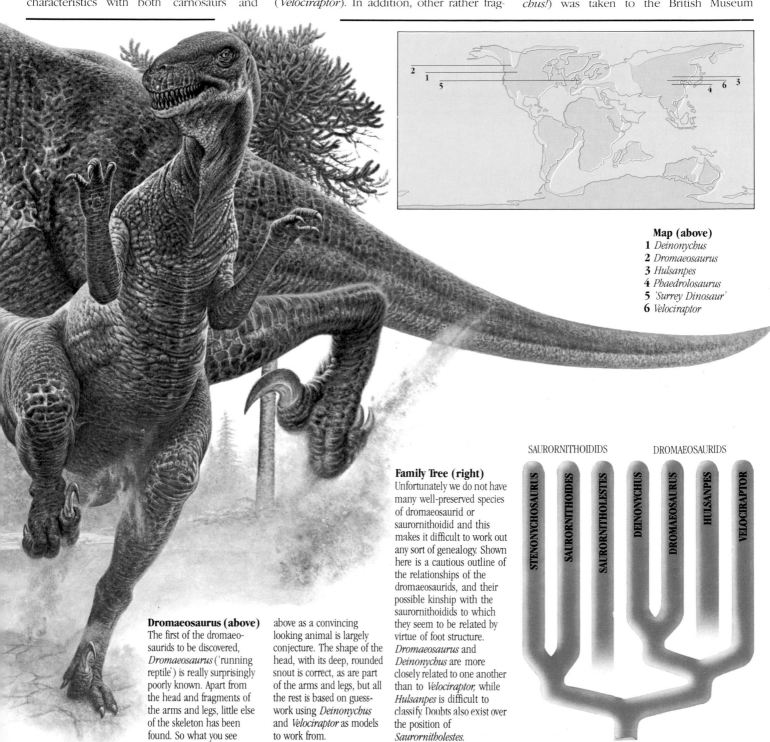

Map (above)
1 *Deinonychus*
2 *Dromaeosaurus*
3 *Hulsanpes*
4 *Phaedrolosaurus*
5 '*Surrey Dinosaur*'
6 *Velociraptor*

SAURORNITHOIDIDS   DROMAEOSAURIDS

STENONYCHOSAURUS · SAURORNITHOIDES · SAURORNITHOLESTES · DEINONYCHUS · DROMAEOSAURUS · HULSANPES · VELOCIRAPTOR

Family Tree (right)
Unfortunately we do not have many well-preserved species of dromaeosaurid or saurornithoidid and this makes it difficult to work out any sort of genealogy. Shown here is a cautious outline of the relationships of the dromaeosaurids, and their possible kinship with the saurornithoidids to which they seem to be related by virtue of foot structure. *Dromaeosaurus* and *Deinonychus* are more closely related to one another than to *Velociraptor*, while *Hulsanpes* is difficult to classify. Doubts also exist over the position of *Saurornitholestes*.

Dromaeosaurus (above)
The first of the dromaeosaurids to be discovered, *Dromaeosaurus* ('running reptile') is really surprisingly poorly known. Apart from the head and fragments of the arms and legs, little else of the skeleton has been found. So what you see

above as a convincing looking animal is largely conjecture. The shape of the head, with its deep, rounded snout is correct, as are part of the arms and legs, but all the rest is based on guesswork using *Deinonychus* and *Velociraptor* as models to work from.

(Natural History) in London where it immediately attracted a great deal of interest. A team of scientists from the museum visited the site and in 1983 an excavation was arranged, which recovered the major part of a very large dromaeosaurid. At present the specimen is being carefully prepared in the palaeontology laboratory of the British Museum so that it can be scientifically described. Meanwhile the palaeontological world will have to wait patiently for the results of this work.

Turning to the distribution of dromaeosaurids, at present these dinosaurs are only known in the northern continents: North America, Europe and Asia; this suggests two possible explanations. Firstly these dinosaurs may have also lived on the southern continents, but have simply not been found there to date. Alternatively, and more likely to my mind, is the possibility that these dinosaurs are *restricted* to the northern continents. The earliest record we have of dromaeosaurids is from the approximate

middle of the Cretaceous Period; at this time Tethys, a large ocean, separated Europe and Asia from Africa, Australia and India. Seaways also separated North from South America and had probably done so for several millions of years. Therefore, if dromaeosaurids had evolved in the northern hemisphere in Lower or Middle Cretaceous times, then they would have been able to spread across these continents relatively easily because they were still linked, but would have been less likely, or perhaps unable, to cross the seas and reach the southern continents. Thus their distribution may well be explicable in terms of their time of origin and the relative positions of continents then.

The relationship of dromaeosaurids to other carnivorous dinosaurs is still a vexed question. Their nearest relatives would seem to be the saurornithoidids (see pages 54-55); these are dinosaurs which also exhibit a smaller version of the peculiar sickle-shaped toe claw. However the saurornithoidids do not possess the

peculiar stiffened tail or the same hips as dromaeosaurids, and are separated from them for these reasons. The general consensus regarding the relationships between dromaeosaurids and other carnivorous dinosaurs are indicated in the cladogram diagram. On balance the dromaeosaurids share slightly more characteristics with 'coelurosaurs' than with the 'carnosaurs' and could be thought of, perhaps, as rather special, highly predatory dinosaurs that evolved from simpler coelurosaurian ancestors.

Deinonychus Described

The best example of the dromaeosaurid type of dinosaur is without doubt *Deinonychus*, because it is known from well preserved material and has been very thoroughly described by Professor John Ostrom. Detailed study of its anatomy has revealed a number of quite remarkable features.

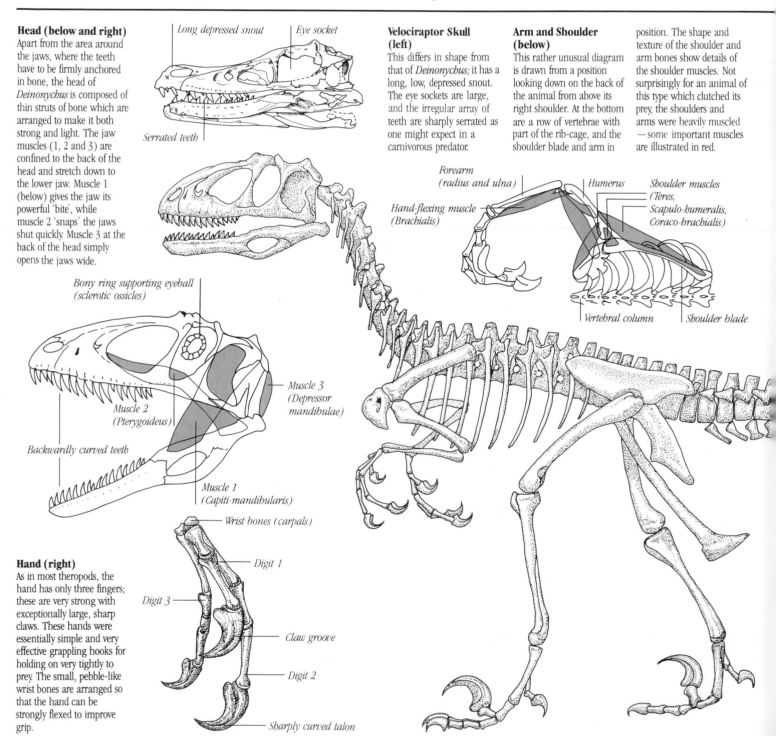

Head (below and right)
Apart from the area around the jaws, where the teeth have to be firmly anchored in bone, the head of *Deinonychus* is composed of thin struts of bone which are arranged to make it both strong and light. The jaw muscles (1, 2 and 3) are confined to the back of the head and stretch down to the lower jaw. Muscle 1 (below) gives the jaw its powerful 'bite', while muscle 2 'snaps' the jaws shut quickly. Muscle 3 at the back of the head simply opens the jaws wide.

Long depressed snout

Eye socket

Serrated teeth

Velociraptor Skull (left)
This differs in shape from that of *Deinonychus*; it has a long, low, depressed snout. The eye sockets are large, and the irregular array of teeth are sharply serrated as one might expect in a carnivorous predator.

Arm and Shoulder (below)
This rather unusual diagram is drawn from a position looking down on the back of the animal from above its right shoulder. At the bottom are a row of vertebrae with part of the rib-cage, and the shoulder blade and arm in position. The shape and texture of the shoulder and arm bones show details of the shoulder muscles. Not surprisingly for an animal of this type which clutched its prey, the shoulders and arms were heavily muscled — some important muscles are illustrated in red.

Forearm (radius and ulna)

Hand-flexing muscle (Brachialis)

Humerus

Shoulder muscles (Teres, Scapulo-humeralis, Coraco-brachialis)

Vertebral column

Shoulder blade

Bony ring supporting eyeball (sclerotic ossicles)

Muscle 3 (Depressor mandibulae)

Muscle 2 (Pterygoideus)

Backwardly curved teeth

Muscle 1 (Capiti-mandibularis)

Wrist bones (carpals)

Hand (right)
As in most theropods, the hand has only three fingers; these are very strong with exceptionally large, sharp claws. These hands were essentially simple and very effective grappling hooks for holding on very tightly to prey. The small, pebble-like wrist bones are arranged so that the hand can be strongly flexed to improve grip.

Digit 1

Digit 3

Claw groove

Digit 2

Sharply curved talon

Looking first at the skull, *Deinonychus* has a large head but it is a quite lightly built with large openings in its sides for the eyes and muscles of the jaws. The teeth are large, with serrated edges for cutting through flesh, and are curved backwards. Putting these facts together we can deduce that this animal was probably a sharp-eyed predator which used its large jaws and teeth to overcome and eat its prey very efficiently. The thin bony framework of the skull made it very light and manoeuvrable for its size, and also provided ample room for large jaw muscles to give the animal a fearsome bite. The muscles of the jaws were arranged so that one set (the capiti-mandibularis) was able to drive the jaws together really powerfully when they were nearly closed, while another set (the pterygoideus) worked best when the jaws were wide open and gave a sharp snapping bite. Both of these muscles were very large and powerful in *Deinonychus*. The backward curvature of the teeth also suggests that

Deinonychus was able to tear large chunks of flesh from its prey by tugging backwards while it was biting. Unfortunately the top of the skull of *Deinonychus* is not well preserved. However in *Dromaeosaurus* a narrow hinge runs across the head just behind the eyes; this probably served as a shock-absorber which may even have prevented it from jarring its brain when it snapped its jaws together.

Deinonychus' neck is quite slender, sharply curved and flexible so that the head had a very wide range of movement. The back by contrast (and especially the tail, as we shall see later) was held quite stiffly by powerful ligaments; these were necessary because when the animal walked and ran, its back was held horizontally and needed constant support to prevent the animal from collapsing.

The arms are unusually long and the three-fingered hands are very large with powerful, sharply curved talons. The strong arms and hands were obviously used to catch

and hold prey very firmly. The upper arm bone (humerus) is broad and has roughened areas for the attachment of powerful chest and arm muscles; this reinforces the supposition that the arms were used to hold actively struggling prey. Indeed the development of such powerful muscles and long arms may be explained by the extraordinary way in which these animals caught and killed their prey.

The hind leg of *Deinonychus* is clearly its most striking possession. Looking first at the leg as a whole, the upper leg bone (femur) is quite short, shorter than the shank (tibia and fibula), which is a feature usually associated with animals that are capable of running very fast. The foot bones are, however, short and stout—not as long as might be expected in a fast runner—but are modified, for a very good reason. Instead of having three forwardly pointing toes of roughly equal length as is usually the case, it has two toes (the third and fourth) which it used for walking, while toe

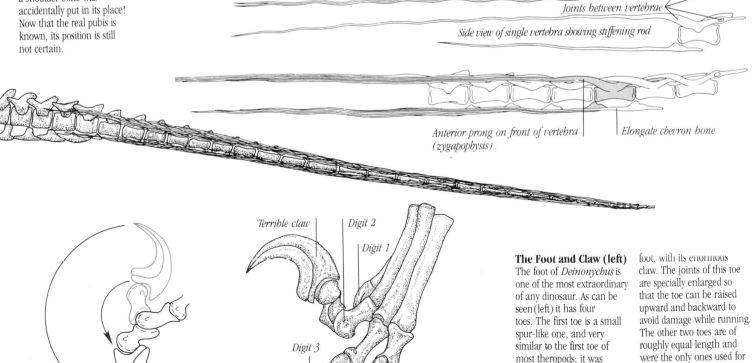

Deinonychus Skeleton (below)

The colour restoration of *Deinonychus* on the previous page is based on this detailed skeletal restoration. The large head is balanced on a slender, almost bird-like neck which was evidently very flexible. The chest was quite short and horizontal. The arms are shown held folded in their resting position against the flanks, rather like the wings of a bird at rest. The hip bones have been a matter of some controversy, especially the shape and size of the pubis. Early on, the pubis was not known at all, in fact a shoulder bone was accidentally put in its place! Now that the real pubis is known, its position is still not certain.

Femur

Leg-raising muscle (Ilio-femoralis)

Tibia

Fibula

Leg-straightening muscle (Femoro-tibialis)

Toe-flexing muscles (Gastrocnemius. Flexor digitorum longus)

Ischium

Pubis

Leg-kicking muscle (Ischio-trochantericus)

Leg (left)

Deinonychus' main weapon of attack would have been the leg with its huge claw, rather than the jaws and teeth of the typical predator. As can be seen (left) the muscles of the leg are quite complicated (these are just a few of them!) and most seem to have been arranged in a way that is typical for most dinosaurs. However, the femur has an unusual ridge near its top end. This may well have served as the point of attachment for a special leg-kicking muscle.

Tail (below)

As can be seen in the full skeleton (left) the part of the tail nearest the hips is quite normal in structure, with simple, block-like vertebrae. However, the remaining three-quarters of the tail is surrounded by a sheath of fine bony rods. As can be seen below, these rods are developed from each tail bone and served as muscle attachment sites and stiffeners. Muscles in the base of the tail attach to the bony rods so the tail may be held very still when running.

Top view of single vertebra

Joints between vertebrae

Side view of single vertebra showing stiffening rod

Anterior prong on front of vertebra (zygapophysis)

Elongate chevron bone

Terrible claw

Digit 2

Digit 1

Digit 3

Digit 4

The Foot and Claw (left)

The foot of *Deinonychus* is one of the most extraordinary of any dinosaur. As can be seen (left) it has four toes. The first toe is a small spur-like one, and very similar to the first toe of most theropods; it was probably held clear of the ground and may have been used for gripping food or prey. The second toe is the most striking feature of the

foot, with its enormous claw. The joints of this toe are specially enlarged so that the toe can be raised upward and backward to avoid damage while running. The other two toes are of roughly equal length and were the only ones used for running upon. The toes could be flexed through a very wide arc (far left) to penetrate the flesh of the prey.

number two is modified into a large sickle-shaped claw, and toe one is a small backward-pointing spur. The explanation for this large claw seems to be that it was used as a formidable weapon of attack. The drawing below shows how the hind leg may have been used. The femur has a special process (posterior trochanter) to which was attached a muscle which came from the ischium; this muscle was used specially for kicking backwards and downwards with the foot to slash open the soft belly of its prey. This special hip muscle may have been developed because had *Deinonychus* used its normal leg-pulling muscles, which are attached to the tail, it would have inevitably twitched its tail as it kicked, causing it to become unbalanced or perhaps to fall over!

Deinonychus' Tail

Another unusual feature of *Deinonychus* is to be found in the tail. As can be seen, the tail bones near the hips have the usual set of short knobs and spines, so that they can move one against another without becoming dislocated. Farther back down the tail, however, the vertebrae change their appearance quite dramatically. Beneath and between each vertebra are small wedge-shaped bones called chevrons; these develop a pair of long, thin forwardly-pointing rods of bone, which overlap several vertebrae in front. Similarly, above the vertebrae processes which are normally quite short and stout are developed into enormously elongate forwardly-pointing rods. The effect of these rod-like structures is to produce a sheath of

bony rods, where the rods of neighbouring vertebrae overlap, which almost completely surrounds the tail of the animal. Despite the fact that these bony rods seem almost to encase the tail bones, it nevertheless remains flexible because the joints between the individual vertebrae are still well developed and not welded together by bone. It seems most likely that the tail rods were formed from long, thin, tail muscles. Such muscles are found in the tails of living lizards and even long-tailed mammals such as kangaroos. In *Deinonychus* these long thin muscles, which are largely tendinous, appear to have been converted into bone. Such a conversion is not as remarkable as it sounds because a thin sheet of soft tissue, which covers the surface of bones and is continuous with muscles which are attached to bone, is the area where bone-forming cells are found and these can (and quite often do) readily migrate into the tendons of muscles. It would seem most probable that the ends of the bony rods in the tail of *Deinonychus* had muscles attached to them. Thus the tail was remarkably specialised: near the hips, the tail was quite flexible because there were no overlapping bony rods; the far end of the tail, however, could either be held extremely stiffly as the muscles attached to the bony rods pulled it taut or, conversely, relaxation of the tail-rod muscles would endow the tail with some slight flexibility. The reason for such complexity in the tail is very probably associated with its predatory life-style. First of all, the tail is long in order to counterbalance the weight of the front half of the body. Secondly, the stiffened tail may well have acted not only as

a dynamic stabiliser when running at speed, but also as a means of allowing a rapid change of direction when chasing fleet-footed and evasive prey. Swift alterations of direction could be made by swinging the tail to one side and using it to rotate the front end of the body, even when running at full speed. Damage to the tail by 'whip-lash' while performing this manoeuvre would have been prevented by keeping the tail very stiff, using the tail rods and muscles.

Patterns of Behaviour

So, what do all these observations tell us about the probable life-style of this animal. Well, they suggest a great deal about one aspect of its life as a predator. *Deinonychus* was apparently quite small, the total length of an adult may not have been much more than 10-11 feet (3-3.3m) judging by the remains found to date. Living at the same time as *Deinonychus* were herbivorous sauropods (titanosaurs), ankylosaurs (*Sauro-*

Above: A skeleton of *Dromaeosaurus* in the final stages of reconstruction at the Tyrrell Museum of Palaeontology, Alberta. The characteristic sickle-shaped claws on the hind feet are very evident.

The Hunting Pack (left)
To overcome large prey like *Tenontosaurus*, *Deinonychus* may have hunted in predatory packs. Some would slow the potential victim by grasping its tail and hind quarters while others would aim lethal kicks at its underside.

Hunting Hypsilophodon (below)
This sequence shows how an individual *Deinonychus* may have hunted a similarly fleet-footed prey, such as the ornithopod *Hypsilophodon*, in a one-to-one chase. Both animals are capable of high-speed running and jinking, but once *Deinonychus* has closed with its prey, it uses its arms and teeth to subdue the struggling creature. The *coup de grâce*, however, is administered by the fearsome claws on *Deinonychus'* hind feet.

pelta) and the hypsilophodontid *Tenontosaurus*, as well as other predators including a large 'carnosaur' and a small ornithomimosaur. All the herbivores were the potential prey of *Deinonychus* in one way or another: let us consider the various ways in which *Deinonychus* may have stalked and killed its prey.

(i) **Sauropods** Obviously fully grown, 65 feet (20m) long titanosaurs are unlikely to have been preyed upon by small *Deinonychus*. However, just as is the case today with the large cats hunting zebra and wildebeest in Africa, the usual target is not the strong adult, but the young, and old or sick individuals. Similarly *Deinonychus* may have stalked young titanosaurs in the same way as the big cats. There is much circumstantial evidence from footprint trackways of herding in sauropods, the young animals clustering at the centre of the herd protected by the adult individuals. One can imagine small predatory packs of *Deinonychus* waiting patiently for a young titanosaur to wander a little way from the main herd in search of more succulent vegetation where, unprotected by the adults, it might be pounced upon by a ferocious pack of *Deinonychus*.

(ii) **Ankylosaurs** A rather different proposition for *Deinonychus*, the nodosaurid *Sauropelta* (page 160) would have relied on its heavy dermal armour to resist attack. For the most part *Sauropelta* was probably impregnable. The only possible tactic would have been for *Deinonychus* to attempt to turn the animal on to its back to expose its relatively unprotected belly. Adult *Sauropelta* were sufficiently large and heavy to be beyond the scope of *Deinonychus*; however, as with the sauropods, young *Sauropelta* may well have fallen prey to *Deinonychus*.

(iii) **Ornithopods** The most numerous fossils found in the quarries that have yielded *Deinonychus* remains are those of *Tenontosaurus tilletti* (page 104); this was a medium-sized unarmoured herbivore, and would undoubtedly have been the main species upon which *Deinonychus* would have preyed. Both young and fully adult individuals of *Tenontosaurus* were likely targets, although the method of attack was probably different in each case.

Small *Tenontosaurus* were lightly built, agile creatures with relatively long slender legs and, curiously like *Deinonychus*, special tail-stiffening bony rods. These little animals were therefore quite nimble and fleet-footed; the stiffened tail would again have acted both as a dynamic stabiliser and as an inertial beam so that they could jink from side to side when running at high speed to evade predators. Lone *Deinonychus* are likely to have stalked young *Tenontosaurus* in order to get close enough to make a short sprint to catch them. If alerted, young *Tenontosaurus* probably stood a fair chance of escaping as it probably had a slightly greater top-speed. The reason for believing this is that *Deinonychus*' massive sickle-claw required a foot that was short and strong to absorb the stresses imposed by its very powerful kick (one specimen has been found with a toe bone [phalanx] of the big claw that had been broken and then healed during the life of the animal). *Deinonychus* could not therefore have such a slender ('fleet') foot as *Tenontosaurus*.

Larger, adult specimens of *Tenontosaurus* may well have attracted hunting packs of *Deinonychus*. Professor Ostrom noted when the first remains of *Deinonychus* were recovered that bones from three partial skeletons were found quite close to a skeleton of *Tenontosaurus*, and suggested that *Deinonychus* may have hunted in packs, rather like Cape hunting dogs. This seems to me a reasonable proposition. Certainly a fully grown *Tenontosaurus* was considerably larger than *Deinonychus* so it is unlikely that a single *Deinonychus* could bring down a *Tenontosaurus* alone. However, a concerted attack by several individuals would undoubtedly have resulted in success and large quantities of food as a reward.

Deinonychus' principal weapon was almost certainly its hind leg and claw. Small animals would have been grasped very securely by the large, powerful and very sharply taloned hand. Instead of being held close to the body so that it could be bitten, the prey would have been held out at arms' length. (The arms and hands of *Deinonychus* are extraordinarily long by the standard of most other theropods.) In this way the foot and its huge claw could be drawn forward so that it could be kicked against the belly of its prey. The arms and hand are therefore vitally important for not only grasping prey, but also holding it secure, keeping it at a distance to allow 'kicking room', and also to steady the prey against the impact of the kick. It seems likely, therefore, that the foot claw was used to kill the prey by disembowelling and that the teeth were used primarily for feeding. Most of the teeth are backwardly-directed, rather than being downwardly pointing, stabbing teeth as is the case in predators that use them to kill. Instead *Deinonychus*' teeth seem to have served for biting off large chunks of meat; this being effected by violent backward tugs of the head and body, while the jaws were clamped onto a piece of flesh.

All in all, *Deinonychus* (as well as the other dromaeosaurids) must be one of the most extraordinary predatory animals ever to have lived: its most remarkable feature of all being the enormous sickle-like claw on its hind foot which seems to have totally changed its method of attacking prey from that adopted by all other carnivorous dinosaurs.

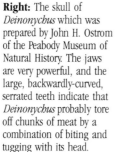

Right: The awesome claw of the 'Surrey dinosaur' which measures 12in (31cm) around its outside edge. About half the skeleton of this theropod has been recovered including much of the skull, limbs and girdle.

Right: The skull of *Deinonychus* which was prepared by John H. Ostrom of the Peabody Museum of Natural History. The jaws are very powerful, and the large, backwardly-curved, serrated teeth indicate that *Deinonychus* probably tore off chunks of meat by a combination of biting and tugging with its head.

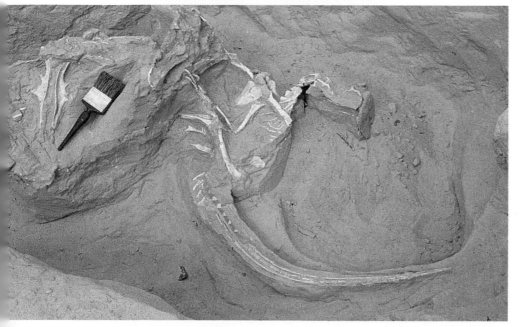

Below: This remarkable find was uncovered by the 1971 Polish-Mongolian expedition at Toogreeg in the Gobi Desert. It reveals the skeleton of *Velociraptor mongoliensis* interlocked with that of *Protoceratops andrewsi* (on the left, its skull being the triangular feature apparently gripped by *Velociraptor*'s hands and feet). Did they die in combat, perhaps as *Velociraptor* was trying to plunder eggs from the ceratopian's nest?

The 'carnosaurs' are, with the 'coelurosaurs', the other major group of theropod dinosaurs described in most popular dinosaur books. They differ quite markedly in their bodily proportions when compared with the various types of theropod that have been described over the previous pages. 'Carnosaurs' were typically large theropods, 20ft (6m) or more in length, and were heavily built, with stout, pillar-like hindlegs, rather feeble forelimbs and very large heads perched upon short, very powerful necks. Most of the 'carnosaurs' described over the next few pages share these characteristics. However, there is very little agreement among palaeontologists about the degree to which they are all related to one another. Part of this uncertainty stems from the fact that very few of these heavily-built theropods are known from anything like a complete skeleton. It is also quite likely that smaller theropods tend to share common design features (i.e. slender legs, long arms,

small heads etc) while larger theropods all tend to have pillar-like legs, large heads and short arms. We may, therefore, simply be grouping together animals which share the same design constraints, rather than those which are closely related in a genealogical sense.

In order to cope with these problems, I shall describe some of the best-known examples of these large theropods ('carnosaurs') in order to provide some basic information about their structure and biology. Below can be seen life-like restorations of three quite well-known theropods: *Allosaurus* ('strange reptile'), *Ceratosaurus* ('horned reptile') and *Dilophosaurus* ('two-crested reptile'). All three are known from the Jurassic Period. *Allosaurus* and *Ceratosaurus* seem to have been contemporaries, their remains having been found in the same late Jurassic quarries of North America. *Dilophosaurus*, however, is one of the very few well-preserved early Jurassic dinosaurs. It also was found in North America.

Allosaurus ('strange reptile') has rather confused origins, like many other dinosaurs. The remains of an *Allosaurus*-like theropod were first discovered in 1869 by Dr Ferdinand Hayden in Grand County, Colorado. This consisted of a single broken tail bone, which was described in some considerable detail by Joseph Leidy in 1870. Leidy was able to show that this single broken bone resembled those of other large carnivorous dinosaurs known from Europe, and at first he referred to it as *Poicilopleuron* ('varying cavity') after a European genus. A little later Leidy gave this bone the new name *Antrodemus*. Somewhat later (in 1877) Benjamin Mudge, one of O. C. Marsh's trusted field assistants, discovered the partial remains of another large carnivorous dinosaur in Fremont County, Colorado. To these imperfect remains Marsh gave the name *Allosaurus*. Unfortunately Marsh then decided to abandon Mudge's quarry in Fremont County and return to Wyoming where better fossils were being

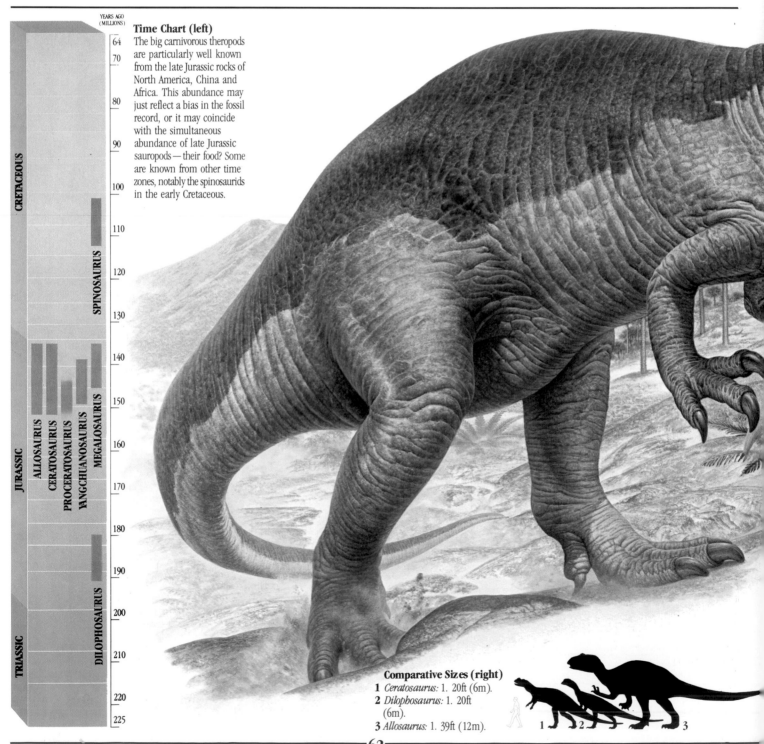

Time Chart (left)
The big carnivorous theropods are particularly well known from the late Jurassic rocks of North America, China and Africa. This abundance may just reflect a bias in the fossil record, or it may coincide with the simultaneous abundance of late Jurassic sauropods — their food? Some are known from other time zones, notably the spinosaurids in the early Cretaceous.

YEARS AGO (MILLIONS)

CRETACEOUS — 64, 70, 80, 90, 100, 110, 120, 130

JURASSIC — 140, 150, 160, 170, 180

TRIASSIC — 190, 200, 210, 220, 225

SPINOSAURUS
ALLOSAURUS
CERATOSAURUS
PROCERATOSAURUS
YANGCHUANOSAURUS
MEGALOSAURUS
DILOPHOSAURUS

Comparative Sizes (right)
1 *Ceratosaurus*: 1. 20ft (6m).
2 *Dilophosaurus*: 1. 20ft (6m).
3 *Allosaurus*: 1. 39ft (12m).

Allosaurus (below)
This large carnivore lived in North America at the same time as the first bird, *Archaeopteryx* (shown here) lived in Germany. An adult *Allosaurus* was up to 39ft (12m) long, and the skull could be 3ft (90cm) long.

The jaws were lined with recurved dagger-like teeth which had serrated edges back and front, just like the blade of a steak knife. *Allosaurus* had strong claws on its hand and feet with which to hold down and tear at its prey.

found, so that little more of this animal was discovered. In 1883 another of Marsh's assistants (M.P. Felch) returned to the 'Garden Park' Quarry and resumed where Mudge had left off—with spectacular results.

Between 1883 and 1884 Felch excavated an almost complete *Allosaurus* skeleton from this quarry as well as several partial skeletons and various isolated fragments. Many of these remains were described by Marsh in subsequent years. Much of this material was carefully prepared in the early part of this century at the Smithsonian Institution in Washington and was finally described by Charles Gilmore in 1920 under the name of *Antrodemus!* Gilmore decided that the single fragment of backbone described by Leidy was diagnostic of this dinosaur and therefore referred all the material, including that described by Marsh as *Allosaurus,* to *Antrodemus.* Clearly Gilmore's decision was mistaken; he should not have based his dinosaur on such

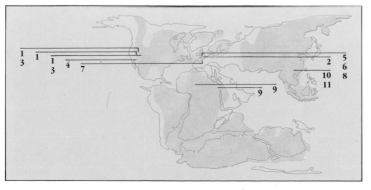

Ceratosaurus (above)
Similar to *Allosaurus* in some respects, *Ceratosaurus* was smaller, and had four-fingered hands. The most striking feature of *Ceratosaurus* is the fact that it had a sizeable bony bump on its snout which was shaped rather like a rhinoceros horn. The function of the bony bump is uncertain. It probably was not for protection against other predators, but may have been used by males in fighting each other for mates. *Ceratosaurus* has fewer teeth than *Allosaurus.*

Map (below)
1 *Allosaurus*
2 *Altispinax*
3 *Ceratosaurus*
4 *Dilophosaurus*
5 *Eustreptospondylus*
6 *Megalosaurus*
7 *Priveteausaurus*
8 *Proceratosaurus*
9 *Spinosaurus*
10 *Szechuanosaurus*
11 *Yangchuanosaurus*

Dilophosaurus (above)
This is the earliest large carnivorous dinosaur. *Dilophosaurus* had a crest on its head which was made from two thin ridges of bone situated side by side, and shaped rather like half dinner plates set up on end.

Dilophosaurus was also different from the other two later 'carnosaurs' shown here since its jaws were weak and slender. They probably could not have withstood the stresses of dealing with struggling prey, and it has been suggested that *Dilophosaurus* was a scavenger rather than an active predator.

Family Tree (right)
The 'carnosaurs' have been split into the primitive *Ceratosaurus* group (which may have included early 'coelurosaurs'), and the more advanced spinosaurids, and *Allosaurus* and related theropods.

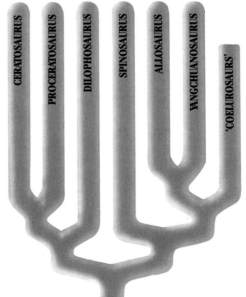

CERATOSAURUS PROCERATOSAURUS DILOPHOSAURUS SPINOSAURUS ALLOSAURUS YANGCHUANOSAURUS 'COELUROSAURS'

poor original material. Today the genus *Allosaurus* is the one that is recognised and is based on the virtually complete skeleton discovered by M. P. Felch in 1883. Since that time more *Allosaurus* material has been recovered from late Jurassic rocks of North America. One of the most spectacular of these discoveries was made in Utah in 1927 at the so-called Cleveland-Lloyd Dinosaur Quarry.

First exploration of this site by the University of Utah yielded over 800 dinosaur bones in just a few weeks, after which no further interest was shown. In 1939 further excavations by Princeton University resulted in the collection of a further 1,200 bones. Finally in 1960 the University of Utah, under the guidance of Dr Jim Madsen and William Stokes, organised a co-operative dinosaur project. By this means various institutions from around the world donated money or materials to aid an extensive series of excavations at the Cleveland-Lloyd Quarry (1960-1965) and received partial or complete

dinosaur skeletons in exchange. In 1967 the Cleveland-Lloyd Quarry was designated a 'Natural Landmark' and is now protected by federal law through the United States Department of the Interior. A permanent working exhibit of the excavation site, rather similar to that created at Dinosaur National Monument (also in Utah) is planned for the near future.

To date the quarry has revealed a diverse fauna of dinosaurs: ornithopods, stegosaurs, ankylosaurs, sauropods and theropods of several types including *Allosaurus* and *Ceratosaurus*. Curiously, *Allosaurus* is by far the most common dinosaur, being represented by at least 44 individuals which range in size from 39ft (12m) in length down to juveniles 10ft (3m) long. The one unfortunate feature of the Cleveland-Lloyd Dinosaur Quarry is that all the skeletal material is scattered. There is not one articulated skeleton.

The skull of *Allosaurus* was far longer than that of any of the theropods described so far.

Several skulls are known which range in length from 24-36in (60-90cm). The jaws are very large and lined with many long, curved, serrated teeth. Above the jaws, the skull, although large, is surprisingly lightly constructed. There are several large lateral spaces in front and behind the eye. These must have served a purpose and it seems most likely that they helped to lighten the skull so that it was easier for the animal to move its head around. There are really only two areas of skull that cannot be lightened much by removal of bone; these are the jaws, which have to anchor the teeth, and the area at the rear of the skull where the muscles that operate the jaws attach. Between these two areas of the skull there is a rather complicated series of bars or struts of bone which presumably served to transmit the forces exerted on the bones of the skull during biting and tugging at prey. It must seem a little curious that the very large skulls of predatory dinosaurs should have proportionately less bone in them than some of the smaller

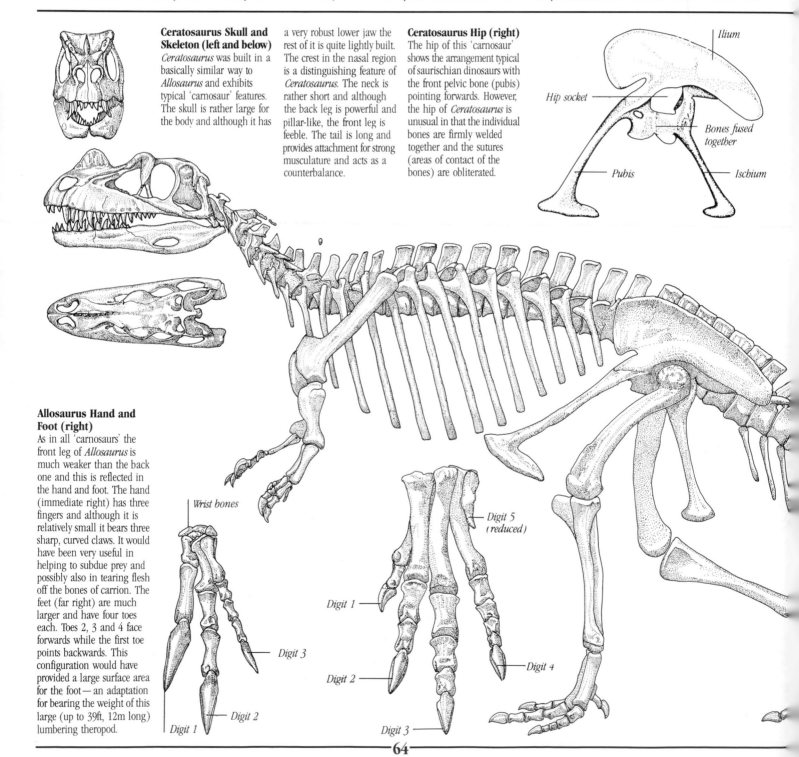

Ceratosaurus Skull and Skeleton (left and below)
Ceratosaurus was built in a basically similar way to *Allosaurus* and exhibits typical 'carnosaur' features. The skull is rather large for the body and although it has

a very robust lower jaw the rest of it is quite lightly built. The crest in the nasal region is a distinguishing feature of *Ceratosaurus*. The neck is rather short and although the back leg is powerful and pillar-like, the front leg is feeble. The tail is long and provides attachment for strong musculature and acts as a counterbalance.

Ceratosaurus Hip (right)
The hip of this 'carnosaur' shows the arrangement typical of saurischian dinosaurs with the front pelvic bone (pubis) pointing forwards. However, the hip of *Ceratosaurus* is unusual in that the individual bones are firmly welded together and the sutures (areas of contact of the bones) are obliterated.

Ilium

Hip socket

Bones fused together

Pubis

Ischium

Allosaurus Hand and Foot (right)
As in all 'carnosaurs' the front leg of *Allosaurus* is much weaker than the back one and this is reflected in the hand and foot. The hand (immediate right) has three fingers and although it is relatively small it bears three sharp, curved claws. It would have been very useful in helping to subdue prey and possibly also in tearing flesh off the bones of carrion. The feet (far right) are much larger and have four toes each. Toes 2, 3 and 4 face forwards while the first toe points backwards. This configuration would have provided a large surface area for the foot—an adaptation for bearing the weight of this large (up to 39ft, 12m long) lumbering theropod.

Wrist bones

Digit 3

Digit 2

Digit 1

Digit 1

Digit 2

Digit 3

Digit 5 (reduced)

Digit 4

theropods. However, it does highlight the point that a skull of solid bone would have rendered the head incredibly heavy and unwieldy in life. Large size does have the added cost to the animal of greater weight and, as will be seen in some of the very large sauropod dinosaurs (pages 80-97), some went to extraordinary lengths in order to reduce the weight of bone in their bodies.

Another curious feature of *Allosaurus*' skull is the large roughened ridge just above and in front of the eye. The centre of this bone is hollowed out, but no-one is really sure why. It may have housed a salt gland or alternatively provided some sort of distinctive feature that allowed individual *Allosaurus* to recognise one another (unusual or elaborate head-gear is known in many dinosaurs—see the hadrosaurids and ceratopids for examples).

Behind the head the body was typically 'carnosaur'. The massive pillar-like legs supported the squat body which was balanced over the hips by the massive tail. The neck, although short, was strongly curved so that the head was held almost above the shoulders rather than extended forward. The long ribs and blunt roughened spines on the neck indicate that powerful muscles were attached here, which undoubtedly assisted with feeding. The back too was short and powerfully constructed, and the spines of each vertebra are broad and very roughened where powerful back muscles and ligaments were attached. The forelimbs are quite small compared with the hindlimbs but they were evidently very powerful, and ended in three viciously curved claws.

Possible Life-Style

All in all, *Allosaurus* was an extremely well-equipped predatory dinosaur. The huge jaws were lined with large, stabbing and cutting teeth, both for killing and dismembering their prey. The powerful neck and back would have aided the jaws in tearing off large chunks of flesh, and the large claws on the hands and feet undoubtedly helped to subdue their victims. Precisely what their prey and predatory habits were is something of a mystery. Unlike the majority of 'coelurosaurs', these animals were not built for high-speed pursuit; they were much larger lumbering creatures. They probably fed upon the larger ornithischians such as *Camptosaurus* (page 110) and *Stegosaurus* (page 152) as well as the larger sauropods: *Diplodocus* and *Apatosaurus* (pages 80-81).

Camptosaurus was a moderate sized (16.5-23ft, 5-7m long) ornithopod which was presumably quite nimble although defenceless; it may well have been captured by ambush rather than hot pursuit tactics. *Stegosaurus* with its defensive tail spikes may have posed greater dangers to *Allosaurus* even though it was a much slower moving prey. The large sauropods could well have been attacked by *Allosaurus* operating in hunting groups. It seems possible

---

Dilophosaurus Skeleton (below)

Dilophosaurus was about 20ft or 6m long—about the same length as *Ceratosaurus*. Both were probably more agile than *Allosaurus* which was very much larger. Again in *Dilophosaurus* we see the typical 'carnosaur' features of the large head, weak front leg, powerful back leg and long tail. In this form the neck was longer and more flexible than usual, but it was still controlled by powerful muscles attached to the neck and ribs. These were probably necessary to support the large head.

Dilophosaurus Skull (below)

This is a typical 'carnosaur' skull, being large relative to the body and lightly built except for the strong lower jaw. The crests on the skull give this animal its name.

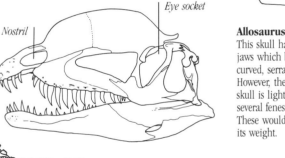
Nostril *Eye socket*

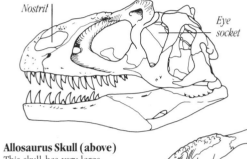
Nostril *Eye socket*

Yangchuanosaurus Skull (below)

This is the skull of a Chinese form from the Jurassic deposits of Sichuan. It is very similar to that of *Allosaurus* to which it might be related.

Allosaurus Skull (above)

This skull has very large jaws which bear many long curved, serrated teeth. However, the rest of the skull is lightly built with several fenestrae or windows. These would have reduced its weight.

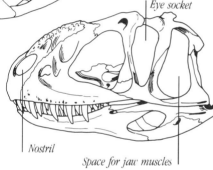
Eye socket
Nostril *Space for jaw muscles*

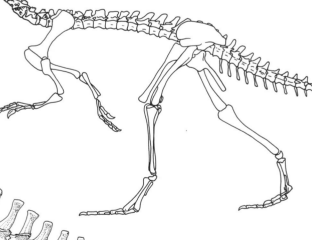

Neural spine
Transverse process
1

Muscle scar
2

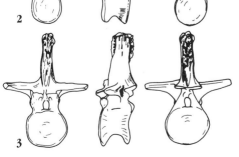
3

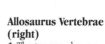

Allosaurus Vertebrae (right)

1 The top row shows a vertebra from the neck region. It is relatively small and has a low neural spine and short transverse processes. Its design lets the neck move freely.

2 The middle row shows a vertebra from the shoulder region. The neural spine is taller and shows muscle attachment scars. The rib is double-headed and contacts the transverse process and the body of the vertebra itself.

3 The bottom row shows a vertebra from just in front of the hip region where the largest vertebrae occur. The tall neural spine is very rough where muscles attached. The transverse process is almost horizontal unlike that of the shoulder.

that several *Allosaurus* could bring down even the largest sauropods in a determined attack; although the main victims may well have been the less powerful juveniles. The evidence of strong herding tendencies among sauropods is probably a reflection of the threat posed by large predatory theropods such as *Allosaurus*.

Like the large predatory cats of today, *Allosaurus* were probably opportunistic scavengers of carrion—not only devouring long-abandoned carcasses, but also driving small theropods away from their own kills.

Ceratosaurus Described

The first skeleton of *Ceratosaurus* ('horned reptile') was discovered in 1883/4 by M. P. Felch at the same quarry in which the fine skeleton of *Allosaurus* was excavated in Fremont County, Colorado. A large part of the skeleton of this theropod was recovered which provided O. C. Marsh with very good information with which to describe another new type of theropod, which was both smaller and clearly different from *Allosaurus*.

Ceratosaurus seems to have reached a maximum body length of 20ft (6m) and stood about 6·5ft (2m) high. In its general proportions *Ceratosaurus* resembles *Allosaurus*: it has a large head, a short neck, relatively short arms and pillar-like legs. However, there are several notable differences. In the skull the jaws are massive and the teeth are sharp and curved. Again the sides of the skull are cut away to produce large open spaces enclosed by a bony framework of struts. There is also a large, hollowed-out ridge just above the eye similar to that of *Allosaurus*. However, unlike *Allosaurus*, there is a very prominent bony horn on the snout; also there are fewer teeth in the jaws and the back of the skull is larger and deeper.

The remainder of the skeleton of *Ceratosaurus* also shows several subtle differences from that of *Allosaurus*. In particular the hand has four well-developed fingers, unlike *Allosaurus* which has only three. The bones of the pelvis are also rather unusual in that they are all firmly welded together by bone, rather than remaining separate as is normally the case. Rather unexpectedly, the *Ceratosaurus* skeleton was also found to possess the remains of a narrow row of bony plates which seem to have run down the middle of the back.

Compared with *Allosaurus, Ceratosaurus* would seem to have been a smaller, more lightly-built and agile predator. Skeletal remains of *Ceratosaurus* are quite rare in late Jurassic rocks, and most probably this implies that it was a more versatile and perhaps solitary predator, unlike the gregarious *Allosaurus*.

The Discovery of Dilophosaurus

Unlike the two previous theropods, *Dilophosaurus* ('two-ridged reptile') is from the early Jurassic. Its remains were first discovered in 1942 during an expedition to Northern Arizona organised by the University of California. The team were led to the site by a Navajo Indian, Mr Jesse Williams, where they discovered the remains of three individuals: one was an almost complete 20ft (6m) long skeleton, the other two consisted of rather badly eroded fragments.

After careful preparation in the laboratory, this dinosaur was finally described by Dr Sam Welles in 1954 as a new species of 'Megalosaurus'. *Megalosaurus* is a well known, but unfortunately very fragmentary, large theropod dinosaur from the late Jurassic of England (see later). First analysis of Welles' new dinosaur suggested strong similarities to the English theropod. In 1964 Welles returned to the area in which his 'Megalosaurus' was found and was fortunate to discover another skeleton of a similar theropod. Unlike the previous examples, this skull was quite well preserved and revealed a pair of thin bony crests that ran along its top. Clearly this was no ordinary theropod, and in 1970 Welles gave it the new name of *Dilophosaurus* in recognition of the unusual crests on its head.

In 1984 Sam Welles published a very detailed description of *Dilophosaurus*. As seems typical of 'carnosaurs', the skull of *Dilophosaurus* is large in proportion to its body, and is quite delicately constructed. Welles concluded that the long slender teeth at the front of the snout were probably used for plucking and tearing at the flesh of their victims rather than biting, while the more posterior teeth were used for cutting and slicing flesh. The function of the tall crests on the skull remains a mystery; most likely they were associated with some aspect of the behaviour of the animal—perhaps visual signalling for recognition purposes.

The neck, although long and flexible, was controlled by powerful muscles attached to the ribs and spines. The long tail counterbalanced the animal so that it could walk and run on its hind legs which were long and powerful. The forelimbs were short but strong, and the hand had four fingers, the first three of which bore sharp claws. The first finger was shorter and more powerful than the other two.

The Variety of 'Carnosaurs'

There are in addition to *Allosaurus, Ceratosaurus* and *Dilophosaurus* many other carnosaurs from the Jurassic and Cretaceous rocks of most countries. Unfortunately many of them are known from very scrappy material, such as odd serrated teeth or claws; this has led to the naming of large numbers of species on very dubious evidence indeed. One of the best examples of the problems created by imperfect or scrappy material causing a proliferation of names is the renowned dinosaur *Megalosaurus*.

Megalosaurus ('big reptile') is particularly famous because it was the first dinosaur to be named and scientifically described. The remains of *Megalosaurus* (*M. bucklandi* as it was later to be known) were discovered in a quarry at Stonesfield in Oxfordshire, England in the early years of the 19th Century; they represent parts of a large theropod dinosaur 23-26·2ft (7-8m) long that lived in late Jurassic times. The skeleton, first described by William Buckland in 1824, included parts of the jaws, several vertebrae, and parts of the pelvis and hindlimbs. In the years following the original description, any fragmentary remains of a carnivorous dinosaur found in Jurassic or Cretaceous rocks were referred to as *Megalosaurus*! Thus *Megalosaurus* remains were reported from Europe (France, Belgium, Germany, Portugal), Australia and North America (later to be renamed *Dilophosaurus*!). In fact much of this material is either obviously not referrable to *Megalosaurus* or too fragmentary to be diagnosed as anything more than 'the remains of a large theropod'.

For example, one well-preserved skeleton from Wolvercote, near Oxford, was for a long time referred to as another species of *Megalosaurus* (*M. cuvieri*). It consisted of a considerable part of the skeleton of a 16·5-20ft (5-6m) long theropod. After detailed study of this and other material, Dr Alick Walker (Newcastle) was able to show that this species was totally unlike *M. bucklandi* and deserved a completely new name: *Eustreptospondylus oxoniensis* ('Oxford's true reversed backbone'). To add further confusion to the situation, Alick Walker referred another specimen (an incomplete braincase from Dives [France] from similarly aged rocks) to *Eustreptospondylus* (*E. divesensis*). Re-study of this material led Dr Philippe Taquet and Sam Welles to propose that *E. divesensis* was so different from *E. oxoniensis* that it deserved to be renamed *Priveteausaurus divesensis* ('Priveteau's reptile from Dives')!

Another poorly known species of *Megalosaurus* (*M. dunkeri*) from the early Cretaceous near Hastings in Sussex is remarkable for the height of the spines on its backbones; these are quite unlike those on the back of *M. bucklandi*. In 1926 Friedrich Freiherr von Huene renamed this species *Altispinax* ('tall spines'). Yet another *Megalosaurus* (*M. parkeri*), based on a partial skeleton from the Jurassic of Dorset, was also notable for its high spines and was later renamed *Metriacanthosaurus* ('long spined reptile') by Dr Alick Walker.

These are just a few examples of the confusion that has arisen through the unfortunately widespread use of 'Megalosaurus' as a 'dustbin' for any large theropod remains; this arose primarily because most theropod fossils are isolated fragments and because the original *Megalosaurus* was a very imperfect specimen. Up to the present time at least 26 different names have been created for large, poorly-preserved *Megalosaurus*-like theropods. As we shall see later, such a profusion of names can cause great problems of classification.

Spinosaurids

Spinosaurids ('spine reptiles') are a group of relatively tall-spined theropods. They include such forms as *Altispinax* and *Metriacanthosaurus*. The family was founded on the remains of *Spinosaurus* which come from the late Cretaceous of Niger (Africa) and Egypt. The original material is again somewhat incomplete, including parts of the jaw, and some neck, back and tail vertebrae, but it indicates a large

theropod 33-39·4ft (10-12m) long with spines up to 6ft (1·8m) long! *Acrocanthosaurus* ('top spined reptile') is yet another large 42·6ft (13m) high-spined theropod from the early Cretaceous of Atoka County, Oklahoma. *Saurophagus* ('reptile eater') from the same general area may well be referrable to *Acrocanthosaurus*.

Although relatively little is known of spinosaurids as a whole, the extraordinary height of the spines does require some explanation. Their exaggerated size has two likely explanations: they were either used as behavioural signals for recognition purposes (mates or rivals), or they may have served as solar panels or radiators of heat to regulate the body temperature. Standing sideways on to the Sun, blood passing through the skin of the sail-like array of spines would have been warmed to raise the body temperature. Alternatively, by facing into the Sun, the sail could have acted as a radiator to dissipate heat.

Chinese Theropods

Since 1942, the only large theropod known from China was *Szechuanosaurus* ('reptile from Szechuan') described on the basis of four large serrated teeth dated at late Jurassic. Obviously this is insufficient material upon which to base a new species, but it at least records the existence of large theropods in China. The situation has improved greatly in recent years as a result of the parties organised through Beijing (Peking), which have collected new fossils in various parts of China. In 1978 a new theropod was described as *Yangchuanosaurus* ('Yang-ch'uan reptile'). *Yangchuanosaurus* was based on a nearly complete skeleton from the late Jurassic of Sichuan Province. The skull and skeleton are very similar to that of *Allosaurus* and seem to indicate that these two forms are very closely related. Since then another skull and partial skeleton have been discovered which have also been referred

to the genus *Yangchuanosaurus,* but in this particular instance as a new species.

Other Large Theropods

Excluding the tyrannosaurids (pages 68-73), which are all late Cretaceous species and quite distinct from the majority of large theropods, a variety of 'carnosaur' names are commonly used; valid and dubious names are listed below.

Most of the dubious genera, although undoubtedly based on the remains of theropods, are not sufficiently well preserved for useful scientific comparisons to be made. Their only justification is in instances where they provide a record of theropods on other continents. For example **Rapator* is a theropod from the early Cretaceous of Australia and as such may provide useful evidence about the geographic distribution of theropods at this time. All those which provide this type of information are marked with an asterisk (*).

Spinosaurus (left)
Spinosaurids are an especially interesting group of 'carnosaurs' that developed long dorsal spines that seem to have acted as supports for a large sail of skin. We see here *Spinosaurus*, an *Allosaurus*-sized theropod known from Africa whose spines grew to a length of 6ft (1·8m). It is possible that the spinal sail acted as a heat exchanger allowing the dinosaur to warm its blood rapidly when standing in the Sun, or to dissipate heat when the sail was angled out of direct sunlight. Similar spines are found on the iguanodontid *Ouranosaurus*, also from Niger. Perhaps some climatic factor caused this common development.

'CARNOSAUR' GENERA
Valid
Acrocanthosaurus
Allosaurus
Altispinax (?)
Ceratosaurus
Dilophosaurus
Dryptosaurus (?)
Erectopus
Eustreptospondylus
Marshosaurus
Megalosaurus
Metriacanthosaurus
Piatnitzkysaurus
Poekilopleuron
Priveteausaurus
Proceratosaurus
Spinosaurus
Torvosaurus
Yangchuanosaurus

'CARNOSAUR' GENERA
Dubious
Aggiosaurus
Antrodemus (=*Allosaurus*)
Apatodon (=*Allosaurus*)
Arctosaurus
Bahariasaurus
Carcharodontosaurus
Chienkosaurus
*Chingkankousaurus
Coelosaurus
Colonosaurus
Creosaurus (=*Allosaurus*)
Diplotomodon
Dryptosauroides
*Embasaurus
Empaterias (=*Epanterias*)
Epanterias (=*Allosaurus*)
Epantherias (=*Epanterias*)
Gwynneddosaurus
Kelmayisaurus
Labrosaurus (=*Allosaurus*)
Laelaps (=*Dryptosaurus*)
Macrodontophion
Majungasaurus
Orthogoniosaurus
Palaeosauriseus
Paronychodon
Pneumatoarthmus
Poicilopleuron (=*Allosaurus*)
Polyodontosaurus
*Rapator
Sarcosaurus
Saurophagus (=*Acrocanthosaurus*?)
Szechuanosaurus
Tichosteus
*Unquillosaurus
Walgettosuchus (=*Rapator*?)
Zapsalts

*=Significant geographically

Right: Part of the skull of *Proceratosaurus*, a fossil found at Mitchinhampton, Gloucestershire in 1910. The typically curved teeth, open framework of bones, and small bump on the snout would suggest that this was a fairly close relative of *Ceratosaurus*. The fossil is now in the British Museum (Natural History).

Right: *Yangchuanosaurus shangyouensis*, a 20ft (6m) long theropod from China now exhibited in Beipei Museum. The general shape of the skeleton suggests it is related to *Allosaurus*.

Left: *Allosaurus* attacking *Camptosaurus*, an iguanodontid. We can see clearly how massive the skull of *Allosaurus* is, but also how window-like openings are let into it to save weight. Note the three-fingered hand. This superb mount is in the Los Angeles County Museum.

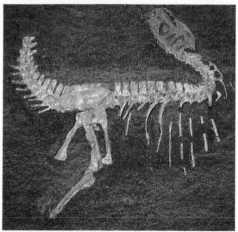

Tyrannosaurids, undoubtedly the best known of all dinosaurs, are a family of large (20-46ft, 6-14m long) theropod dinosaurs whose remains have been found in late Cretaceous rocks in North America and Central Asia. There are four well established species of tyrannosaurid: *Tyrannosaurus rex, Daspletosaurus torosus* and *Albertosaurus libratus,* which come from North America, and *Tarbosaurus bataar* from the Nemegt Basin of Mongolia.

The tyrannosaurids were not recognised as a distinct group of theropods until 1906, shortly after the first reasonably complete skeleton of *Tyrannosaurus* was discovered in Montana in 1902. Prior to this, numerous teeth and other generally indeterminate fragments of large theropods (probably tyrannosaurids) had been discovered in the middle and late part of the nineteenth century. The earliest of these was a selection of large theropod teeth collected from Montana in the 1850s. Joseph Leidy, the

pioneering palaeontologist who described many of the early dinosaur finds from North America, described these teeth as *Deinodon horridus* ('horrifying terrible tooth'). A little later (1866) E. D. Cope renamed these teeth *Dinodon,* and then in 1869 Leidy selected some of these teeth, because they differed in shape, and decided that they came from a new form, *Aublysodon.* The names *Laelaps* and *Teinurosaurus* were also applied to this material in subsequent years. This welter of names represents an inauspicious beginning for such a renowned group of dinosaurs, and provides yet another example of how dangerous it can be to name new species on the basis of inadequate material. One of the problems with the *Deinodon* teeth was that some were from near the front of the jaws, while others were from the back. Because tyrannosaurid teeth tend to vary in shape along the length of the jaw, those from the front look markedly different from those at the back. In isolation it would

seem reasonable to give differently shaped teeth different names (as Leidy did) in the belief that they came from different animals. If these scientists had resisted the temptation to name the teeth until better material, such as a skull and jaws has been discovered, much confusion would have been avoided.

Tyrannosaurus ('tyrant reptile') was first described by Henry Fairfield Osborn in 1905 from a partial skeleton discovered in late Cretaceous rocks in Dawson County, Northern Montana. The skeleton (discovered in 1902) consisted of the jaws and parts of the skull, back bones, shoulders, pelvis and the hindlimbs of a very large theropod. In addition to this material, another very large partial skeleton of a theropod was discovered in Wyoming; this was described as *Dynamosaurus* ('dynamic reptile'). Although equally as large as *Tyrannosaurus, Dynamosaurus* was at first regarded as a distinct species because there seemed to be some evidence of bony armour plating along its back like that

YEARS AGO (MILLIONS)

Time Chart (left)
The tyrannosaurids seem to have a very limited distribution at the end of the Cretaceous Period. Indeed *Tyrannosaurus* is one of the very last dinosaurs known. They would appear to have replaced the more conventional 'carnosaurs' as the main predators of this time. It is possible that they existed earlier, but as yet we have not seen any fossil evidence to substantiate this.

Daspletosaurus (right)
This tyrannosaurid was smaller than *Tyrannosaurus,* but with a total body length of 29·5ft (9m), it was still a fearsome carnivore. *Daspletosaurus* had a massive head with strong jaws which were lined with dagger-like teeth. It has been suggested that it fed on the quadrupedal armoured ceratopids and these would have been difficult animals to overwhelm. *Daspletosaurus* would probably have tried to sink its teeth into the unprotected flanks of its prey: once it had locked its jaws shut, the ceratopid probably could not have shaken itself loose.

Albertosaurus (right)
One of the more lightly built tyrannosaurids, being only 29·5ft (9m) long, *Albertosaurus* might have been able to hunt the

active hadrosaurids. These were unarmoured, and *Albertosaurus* could have killed its prey with a strong bone-crushing bite on the back of the neck.

In addition, *Albertosaurus* could probably have delivered a fierce and disabling kick with its sharply-clawed hind foot when at close quarters.

Map (left)
1 *Albertosaurus*
2 *Alectrosaurus*
3 *Alioramus*
4 *Daspletosaurus*
5 *Genyodectes*
6 *Indosuchus*
7 *Itemirus*
8 *Labocania*
9 *Prodeinodon*
10 *Tarbosaurus*
11 *Tyrannosaurus*
12 *Unquillosaurus*

Comparative Sizes (right)
1 *Tyrannosaurus:* l. 46ft (14m); h. 18·5ft (5·6m).
2 *Daspletosaurus:* l. 29·5ft (9m).
3 *Albertosaurus:* l. 29·5ft (9m).

Time chart scale: 64, 70, 80, 90, 100, 110, 120, 130, 140, 150, 160, 170, 180, 190, 200, 210, 220, 225

CRETACEOUS — JURASSIC — TRIASSIC

TYRANNOSAURUS / DASPLETOSAURUS / ALBERTOSAURUS / TARBOSAURUS

Tyrannosaurus (left)
This famous dinosaur, 46ft (14m) long, was the biggest carnivorous dinosaur. It might have hunted its prey actively, but there is strong evidence that it, and the other tyrannosaurids, lived by scavenging as well. *Tyrannosaurus* was so massive that it is hard to imagine it being capable of running down its prey over long distances. When a dinosaur died naturally or because of an accident, its carcass would have given off a powerful smell that might have attracted the giant meat-eaters for miles around.

noted in *Ceratosaurus* (pages 62-63). In 1906 Osborn referred the *Dynamosaurus* material to *Tyrannosaurus* (although whether the dermal armour is truly associated with this species is not certainly established), as well as an extremely dubious theropod vertebra, named *Manospondylus* by E. D. Cope in 1892.

The combination of all the *Tyrannosaurus* material then known allowed Osborn to reconstruct the skeleton of this animal with some confidence. Indeed modern reconstructions do not differ very significantly from Osborn's original attempt. In 1908 another far more complete skeleton including a perfect skull was discovered by researchers from the American Museum of Natural History in the same area of Northern Montana. This made *Tyrannosaurus* one of the best known of all theropod dinosaurs. The only areas of doubt which remain today about the skeleton of *Tyrannosaurus* concern the structure of the hand (the two-fingered hand is based on that of

Family Tree (above)
Tyrannosaurids are a closely knit group of late Cretaceous theropods. *Albertosaurus* separates as a lightly-built genus compared with the other heavily-built forms. *Daspletosaurus*, *Tyrannosaurus* and *Tarbosaurus* are very similar types; some have even suggested that *Tarbosaurus* and *Tyrannosaurus* are congeneric.

ALBERTOSAURUS DASPLETOSAURUS TYRANNOSAURUS TARBOSAURUS

'CARNOSAURS'

the related tyrannosaurid *Albertosaurus*—see below) and the length of the tail.

Some reconstructions of *Tyrannosaurus*, especially the later ones of Osborn, tend to show a very elongate tail dragging along the ground. However, as can be seen in the drawing of the skeleton, large sections of the end of the tail are unknown. As reconstructed here, the tail is given an 'average' length for a theropod and is shown held off the ground as a counterbalance. This pose was first proposed by Barney Newman (S. Africa) who was at one time involved in mounting the cast of a *Tyrannosaurus* skeleton in the original dinosaur gallery of the British Museum (Natural History).

Tyrannosaurus Anatomy

The skull of *Tyrannosaurus* is not of the type seen in *Allosaurus* (page 65), a similarly-sized theropod of the Jurassic Period. The *Allosaurus* skull is notable for the large window-like openings which give it a very open, airy appearance, apparently combining strength and lightness as far as possible. *Tyrannosaurus* by contrast has a skull which is far more massive. The window-like openings are still present, but they are not nearly as large, and the bony framework that surrounds them is thick and heavy. Nature would not normally add such a weight of bone to the skull of such a creature without good reason, because such additions would be very costly to the animal in terms of the amount of energy that it would have to expend simply to carry such a heavy head around. The enormous weight and apparent great strength of the skull must be a reflection of the feeding habits of *Tyrannosaurus*, which are discussed below.

The massive head is supported by a very short powerful neck, the vertebrae of which are very thick and bear stout spines for the attachment of powerful ligaments and muscles used to hold the head in position. The ribs are also very long for the attachment of more muscles used to twist the neck and swing it from side to side. The bones of the back are larger and stronger than those of the neck and acted in life like a massive girder. The block-like bodies of each vertebra withstood enormous compression forces because of the great weight of the body, while the roughened and ridged edges and tops of the spines projecting from the top of each vertebra were the sites for attachment of extremely powerful ligaments and muscles; these would have acted rather like hawsers holding the bones in place, while at the same time allowing them to move within the normal range of body movements.

An indication of just how enormous these forces on the backbone must have been is provided by the skeleton itself. In the skeleton discovered in 1908, two pairs of vertebrae in the back have become welded together. This is not a normal condition but a pathological one; the great compression forces had evidently col-

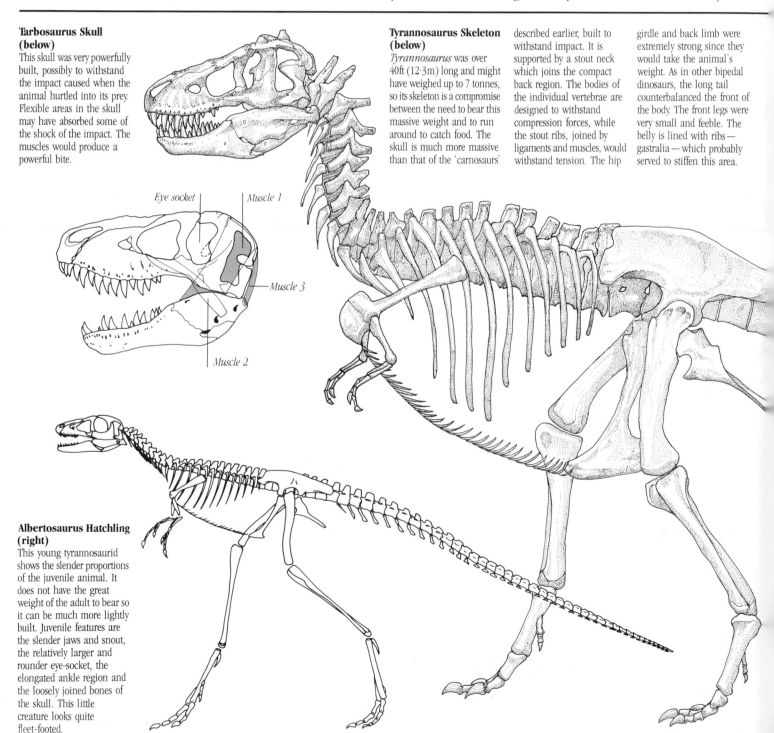

Tarbosaurus Skull (below)
This skull was very powerfully built, possibly to withstand the impact caused when the animal hurtled into its prey. Flexible areas in the skull may have absorbed some of the shock of the impact. The muscles would produce a powerful bite.

Eye socket   Muscle 1

Muscle 3

Muscle 2

Tyrannosaurus Skeleton (below)
Tyrannosaurus was over 40ft (12·3m) long and might have weighed up to 7 tonnes, so its skeleton is a compromise between the need to bear this massive weight and to run around to catch food. The skull is much more massive than that of the 'carnosaurs' described earlier, built to withstand impact. It is supported by a stout neck which joins the compact back region. The bodies of the individual vertebrae are designed to withstand compression forces, while the stout ribs, joined by ligaments and muscles, would withstand tension. The hip girdle and back limb were extremely strong since they would take the animal's weight. As in other bipedal dinosaurs, the long tail counterbalanced the front of the body. The front legs were very small and feeble. The belly is lined with ribs—gastralia—which probably served to stiffen this area.

Albertosaurus Hatchling (right)
This young tyrannosaurid shows the slender proportions of the juvenile animal. It does not have the great weight of the adult to bear so it can be much more lightly built. Juvenile features are the slender jaws and snout, the relatively larger and rounder eye-socket, the elongated ankle region and the loosely joined bones of the skull. This little creature looks quite fleet-footed.

lapsed the originally flexible joints between these vertebrae so that these backbones began to rub together, causing no doubt severe arthritic pain, until the bones finally welded themselves together.

Despite the enormous forces acting on the bones of the back, several vertebrae at the base of both the neck and the back possess cavities in their sides (known as pleurocoels) which undoubtedly served to reduce the weight of bone in the back wherever possible.

The pelvic bones are very large to allow for the attachment of big leg muscles and also to provide a strong socket for the hip joint itself. The huge blade-like upper pelvic bone (ilium) has a rather complex pattern of ridges and rough-edged patches (see below) which mark the areas of attachment to the stout ribs (sacral ribs) of the backbone. Six bones of the back are welded together to produce a massive and strong bar of bone; this had to be strong because the entire weight of the body — perhaps

6-7 tonnes — had to be carried across this joint to the hindlimbs. The legs are naturally very large and heavy-boned in order to support the large body. The feet are quite broad with three forward-pointing toes which end in sharply-curved talons, and a small backwardly-directed spur-like first toe.

The arms and hands of *Tyrannosaurus* are one of its most bizarre features. We noted earlier that the forelimbs of 'carnosaurs' tend to be relatively short, certainly when compared with those of 'coelurosaurs'. In *Tyrannosaurus* and tyrannosaurids generally this trend seems to be taken to a ridiculous extreme. The shoulder bone is moderately large, but the limb is minute and ends in a small two-clawed hand.

As with most theropods there is an array of ribs lying in the wall of the belly; in life these probably connected via ligaments (or possibly directly) to the ends of the chest ribs enclosing the chest and belly, and thereby making this part of the body fairly stiff and inflexible.

Other Tyrannosaurids

Albertosaurus ('reptile from Alberta') is another North American tyrannosaurid. Like *Tyrannosaurus* it has had a rather chequered history. Two partial skulls of large theropods were discovered on the Red Deer River of Alberta in the early 1890s; these were first referred to *Laelaps* by E. D. Cope (1892). Subsequently Lawrence Lambe transferred them to Marsh's genus, *Dryptosaurus* ('wounding reptile'). Both of these genera, as we have already seen, were based on inadequate material. However, in 1905 the remains of large theropods were reviewed by H. F. Osborn; in his article Osborn created yet another name for these remains: *Albertosaurus sarcophagus*. Knowledge of this type of dinosaur was greatly improved by C. H. Sternberg's discovery in 1913, near Berry Creek on the Red Deer River, Alberta, of a very well-preserved skeleton of a large theropod dinosaur. The remains included not

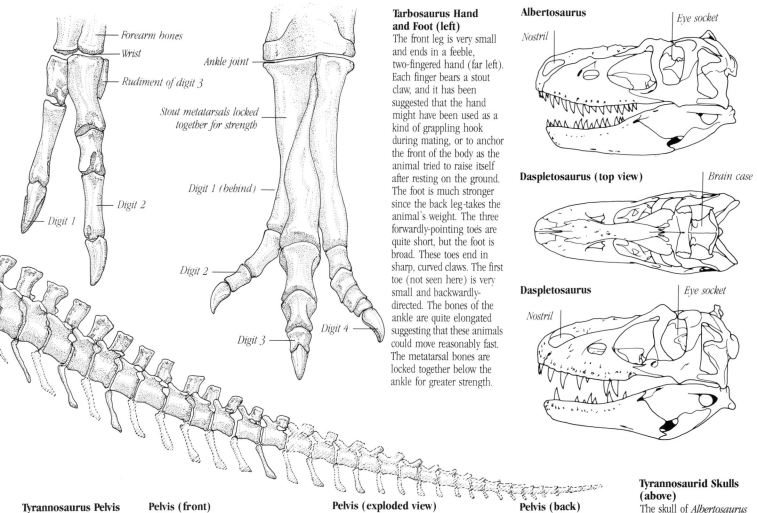

Tarbosaurus Hand and Foot (left)
The front leg is very small and ends in a feeble, two-fingered hand (far left). Each finger bears a stout claw, and it has been suggested that the hand might have been used as a kind of grappling hook during mating, or to anchor the front of the body as the animal tried to raise itself after resting on the ground. The foot is much stronger since the back leg takes the animal's weight. The three forwardly-pointing toes are quite short, but the foot is broad. These toes end in sharp, curved claws. The first toe (not seen here) is very small and backwardly-directed. The bones of the ankle are quite elongated suggesting that these animals could move reasonably fast. The metatarsal bones are locked together below the ankle for greater strength.

Forearm bones
Wrist
Rudiment of digit 3
Digit 1
Digit 2

Ankle joint
Stout metatarsals locked together for strength
Digit 1 (behind)
Digit 2
Digit 3
Digit 4

Albertosaurus
Nostril
Eye socket

Daspletosaurus (top view)
Brain case

Daspletosaurus
Nostril
Eye socket

Tyrannosaurus Pelvis (right)
In these views of the pelvis it is possible to see the upper pelvic bone (ilium) and the vertebrae which attach to it (sacral vertebrae). The lower pelvic bones are not shown. In the exploded view of the pelvis (middle, top and bottom) the wide, plate-like nature of the ilium is seen. This gives plenty of area for muscle attachment. The sockets for the sacral ribs (arrowed) are also visible in the middle drawing.

Pelvis (front)
Ilium
Ilium

Pelvis (top)

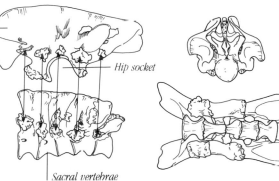

Pelvis (exploded view)
Hip socket
Sacral vertebrae

Pelvis (back)

Pelvis (bottom)

Tyrannosaurid Skulls (above)
The skull of *Albertosaurus* (top) is very similar to that of *Tyrannosaurus*. It is massively built with smaller skull windows surrounded by thicker struts of bone. The teeth are sharp and recurved (pointing backwards), typical of a carnivore. *Daspletosaurus* (middle and bottom) also has the typical tyrannosaurid build. It is distinguished by its teeth which, although fewer in number, are particularly large. All tyrannosaurid skulls show marked similarities.

only a fine, if slightly squashed skull, but a major part of the remainder of the skeleton including the forelimb. In 1914 this skeleton was given the name *Gorgosaurus (Albertosaurus) libratus* ('free dragon reptile'). At this time the skeleton had only been partly prepared. However, the forelimb was sufficiently distinctive to merit some early comment.

In the majority of theropods (although see *Compsognathus* for an exception) the hand has three clawed fingers. In *Gorgosaurus (Albertosaurus)* Lambe note only two clawed fingers (digits 1 and 2) both of which were quite small and a remnant of the third finger (a small splint of bone pressed up against the base of the second one). The very small forelimb and reduced hand is now one of the characteristics that distinguish the tyrannosaurids as a whole.

In 1917 Lambe completed a detailed study of *Gorgosaurus* and provided a first skeletal reconstruction. This revealed a theropod which was a little smaller than *Tyrannosaurus,* but otherwise its proportions were very similar. It was not directly related to *Tyrannosaurus* at the time because (for one reason) Osborn had reconstructed the skeleton of *Tyrannosaurus* in 1916 with three clawed fingers on the hand. He had no evidence for this at the time, but was presumably simply copying the arrangement that he had already described in *Ornitholestes* (pages 40-41) and *Struthiomimus* (pages 46-47). Like *Tyrannosaurus* the skeleton of *Gorgosaurus* was that of a large and quite heavily-built theropod with a massive skull, short forelimbs and heavy, pillar-like legs ending in bird-like feet. Similarly the belly ribs were particularly well-developed, as was the lower end of the pubis in the pelvis; the end of this bone is distinctly enlarged ('footed') and this feature may be linked to the habits of these creatures.

In 1970, Dale Russell reviewed the large theropods of Western Canada. He concluded that the material of *Albertosaurus* originally described by Osborn as *A. sarcophagus* was practically the same as the *Gorgosaurus libratus* material described by Lawrence Lambe and therefore referred *Gorgosaurus* to the genus *Albertosaurus* as *A. libratus.* Another almost complete skeleton described as *Gorgosaurus sternbergi* in 1923 was also referred to as a juvenile of *A. libratus.* The differences between *A. libratus* and *G. sternbergi* included small size (*G. sternbergi* was only 60 per cent of the size of *A. libratus*), more slender jaws and snout, and a rounder eye socket. In addition the bones of the skull were not firmly joined together and the lower part of the leg was more elongated. All of these features are ones that can be associated with juvenility in this specimen. On this basis, and from the fragmentary remains of *Albertosaurus* collected throughout Canada, Russell was able to project backwards in time to estimate the size of a hatchling *Albertosaurus.* This shows the rather slender and delicate proportions of young tyrannosaurids (see page 70). *Albertosaurus sarcophagus* comes from geologically younger rocks in Western Canada and is therefore probably not referrable to *A. libratus* but may represent a descendant species.

Daspletosaurus torosus ('frightful flesh-eating reptile') comes from the Red Deer River near Steveville, Alberta. Most of the skeleton was found by C. M. Sternberg in 1921. At first this was referred to as '*Gorgosaurus*' being of about the same size (29·5ft, 9m long) as the specimen described by Lambe. However, the skeleton is that of a much more heavily-built

animal than *Albertosaurus.* The forelimb, although small as in all tyrannosaurids, is larger than that of all other known species.

As Dale Russell pointed out, almost all *Daspletosaurus* remains are from large, presumably fully adult specimens, while the remains of more than half of the *Albertosaurus* skeletons found to date are of immature individuals. The coexistence of two species of large theropods may indicate that there were at least two discrete ecological niches for them. Dr Russell proposed that *Daspletosaurus* preyed upon the larger and heavier ceratopids (pages 134-145) while the lighter and perhaps more fleet-footed *Albertosaurus* preyed upon the smaller, more agile hadrosaurids (pages 116-127). It is certainly true that hadrosaurids and *Albertosaurus* are both very abundant at this particular time, while *Daspletosaurus* and the ceratopids are markedly less so, but whether these ratios are merely a matter of chance, or indicate the biological interactions suggested, is an open question.

Tarbosaurus bataar ('alarming reptile from Bataar`), a large tyrannosaurid from the Nemegt Basin of the Gobi Desert in Mongolia, was first described in 1955. The remains of at least seven individuals were collected by the Palaeontological Institute of the Academy of Sciences of the Soviet Union. In addition, at least six more skeletons were collected during the Polish-Mongolian expeditions. Although this dinosaur has not been described in detail, the information released to date suggests that *Tarbosaurus* was practically identical with *Tyrannosaurus,* although there are a few relatively minor differences in the structure of the skull bones that serve to distinguish the two forms. Apparently fully adult specimens never attained the size of the largest *Tyrannosaurus* specimens. Despite the relatively enormous distance that separates *Tyrannosaurus* and *Tarbosaurus* geographically, it is very tempting to place them in the same genus: this would certainly have been done had the *Tarbosaurus* remains actually come from Canada.

Probable Life-Style

Lawrence Lambe was one of the first palaeontologists to offer comments on the likely life-style of a tyrannosaurid (*Albertosaurus*). He proposed that *Albertosaurus* was a very slow-moving creature of sluggish habits. He noted that the well-developed belly ribs and the large 'foot' on the pubis could have been adaptations for lying prone on the ground. When driven by hunger, *Albertosaurus* would raise itself to its feet and slowly pace about in search of food, relying principally upon scavenging the carcasses of dead animals. Such a view is held by some (but not all) palaeontologists today.

Looking at the skeleton of *Tyrannosaurus,* the impression gained is one of a fairly dynamic animal. The tail is massive and counterbalances the trunk and head very effectively; the legs are indeed pillar-like in construction, as is necessary in an animal of relatively great weight. This, however, does not necessarily mean that tyrannosaurids were slow, lumbering creatures. A rhinoceros also possesses pillar-like legs to support its immense body weight, yet it can run extremely fast (22-25mph, 35-40kph). The ability of an animal to run fast depends not only upon the proportions of its limbs, but also on their overall length. Longer-legged animals (such as tyrannosaurids) take long strides and are therefore able to cover the ground very quickly, even though their legs do not move as fast as a more fleet-footed creature.

In view of these factors it would seem that tyrannosaurids may well have been predators which were able to move quite quickly, but only over short distances. It is hard to imagine a 6 tonne tyrannosaurid chasing a hadrosaurid at speed for several kilometres in the way that a Cape Hunting Dog may pursue wildebeest on the African plains. What seems more probable is that tyrannosaurids were lurking predators waiting in ambush for their prey and catching them after a short chase.

The heavily reinforced skull of tyrannosaurids may also confirm the suggestion that these animals were devastating predators. The powerful structure of the skull probably implies that the head had to withstand the violent impact of the jaws against the body of the prey; the shock of a tyrannosaurid hitting a hadrosaurid at 12-20mph (20-30kph) would have been borne by the skull. Perhaps related to this method of hunting is the presence of regions of flexibility at the back of the skull

Above: This display in the British Museum (Natural History) emphasises the massive construction of *Tyrannosaurus'* skull, and the fearsome array of teeth that it possessed.

Below: This fine skeleton of *Tarbosaurus bataar* is in the Palaeontological Institute of Moscow. Its close kinship with *Tyrannosaurus* can readily be appreciated.

where the lower jaw is supported. These areas may have allowed the skull bones to move passively under great stress (either under impact, or as a result of the prey struggling violently), so that the very large forces experienced would not break the skull bones.

Once subdued, the prey would have been very rapidly dismembered. The jaws, armed with large serrated teeth, would have sliced through the skin and flesh of the carcass. Violent twisting and tugging of the head aided by the powerful neck and legs would have torn the most powerful of sinews, so that great chunks of flesh and bone could have been swallowed whole.

One persistent puzzle of tyrannosaurid anatomy has been the ridiculously small arms of these formidable creatures. The hands seem to be of little potential use for dismembering prey, unlike those of other large theropods (see *Allosaurus* pages 62-63). Neither does it seem likely that they could reach the creature's

mouth. Two suggestions only seem feasible, both of which may have some merit. Osborn proposed that they may have been used as grapples during mating so that the male was able to hold on to the female; this could well have been important for relatively unstable two-legged creatures.

An alternative, or perhaps ancillary, function for the forelimb was proposed by Barney Newman. He suggested that if *Tyrannosaurus* were to adopt a prone position while resting — as Lambe suggested on quite reasonable evidence — then it may have been faced with a rather unexpected problem. When trying to raise itself from the ground, it would have needed to anchor the front part of the body against the ground, otherwise in attempting to straighten its legs it would have tended to pitch forward onto its nose. The front limbs therefore served to anchor the chest so that the legs could be straightened before the head and body were tilted backwards, allowing the upper

part of the animal to be brought upwards into the normal standing position.

Dubious Tyrannosaurids

A number of fragmentary fossil finds have been referred to the tyrannosaurid family, although the evidence for such a classification remains inconclusive. These dubious tyrannosaurids include *Genyodectes* ('received under jaw'): partial snout from the late Cretaceous of Patagonia; *Labocania* ('from La Bocana'): late Cretaceous of Baja California; *Indosuchus* ('Indian crocodile'): late Cretaceous of India; *Unquillosaurus* ('Unquillo reptile'): late Cretaceous of Argentina; *Prodeinodon* ('before terrible tooth'): late Cretaceous of Mongolia; *Alioramus* ('other branch'): late Cretaceous of Mongolia; *Alectrosaurus* ('single reptile') late Cretaceous of Mongolia; and *Itemirus* ('from Itemir'): late Cretaceous of central Kyzylkum, Central Asia.

Right: A skeleton of *Tarbosaurus bataar* being excavated from the late Cretaceous sandstone of Nemegt, Gobi Desert, during the 1970 Polish-Mongolian expedition.

Below: This view of *Albertosaurus* enables us to see particularly well the tiny forelimbs that are characteristic of tyrannosaurids, and the 'footed' lower end of the pubis in the pelvis.

Hunting Methods (above)
Tyrannosaurid skulls are heavily reinforced, and this suggests that they may have attacked their prey, such as this hadrosaurid, by running into it jaws agape, the shock of such a collision being absorbed by the skull bones.

Functional Arms (below)
The minute size of tyrannosaurid forelimbs is a puzzling phenomenon. One explanation envisages them being used as props to help the animal rise from a prone position. They would secure the front of the body while the rear legs were straightened; the upper body would then be tilted back to bring the tyrannosaurid upright.

Prosauropods are an interesting, but also rather puzzling group of saurischian dinosaurs. They existed in the late Triassic and early Jurassic and were distributed practically worldwide, their remains having been discovered on every continent except for Antarctica; they also tend to be found extremely abundantly in rocks of this age. In fact they seem to represent the first major evolutionary radiation among the dinosaurs—indeed among the archosaurs (dinosaurs, crocodiles, pterosaurs, thecodontians, etc)—to exploit plant food. Until the late Triassic the world had been dominated by various herbivorous types of mammal-like reptile. During the Permian and Triassic Period the archosaurs were, with very few exceptions, exclusively carnivores of various shapes and sizes.

The prosauropods were, therefore, a very important group of early dinosaurs which, in a sense, paved the way for the evolution of the gigantic and closely related sauropod dinosaurs.

The fossil record of prosauropods suffers many of the problems previously encountered in the theropods. Numerous species have been established upon totally inadequate fossil material. In order to learn something of the nature and biology of prosauropods we shall, therefore, consider a few of the better-known species. Prosauropods have been divided into three families: the anchisaurids, melanorosaurids and yunnanosaurids all of which are discussed below.

Anchisaurids

The vast majority of all prosauropods known to date fall into this family which derives its name from *Anchisaurus* ('close reptile'), a small (8·2ft, 2·5m long), lightly-built prosauropod from early Jurassic rocks of the Connecticut Valley of eastern North America. The earliest discovery of *Anchisaurus* was made in 1818. These fragmentary remains, at first thought to be human,

were not confidently identified as reptilian until 1855! And it was not until 1912, when Richard Swan Lull was reviewing the fossils discovered in the Connecticut Valley, that the material was referred to as those of the prosauropod dinosaur *Anchisaurus*. Between the time of the first discovery and its final identification, other material was discovered in adjoining areas of the Connecticut Valley. Edward Hitchcock (who collected large numbers of fossil footprints in this area) reported bones from Springfield, Massachusetts; this skeleton was named *Megadactylus polyzelus* by his son E. Hitchcock Jr, and subsequently renamed *Amphisaurus* by Marsh in 1882 (because another animal had already been named *Megadactylus*), and then again in 1885 renamed *Anchisaurus polyzelus* by Marsh because the name *Amphisaurus* was also preoccupied!

The most productive site in the Connecticut Valley proved to be a quarry near Manchester,

YEARS AGO (MILLIONS)

Map (left)
1 *Ammosaurus*
2 *Anchisaurus*
3 *Coloradia*
4 *Lufengosaurus*
5 *Massospondylus*
6 *Melanorosaurus*
7 *Mussaurus*
8 *Plateosaurus*
9 *Riojasaurus*
10 *Yunnanosaurus*

Time Chart (left)
The prosauropods were exclusively late Triassic/ early Jurassic creatures. They represent the first radiation of early high-browsing dinosaurs, and their abundance in the fossil record may be a reflection of the fact they could feed on high trees without significant competition. Their disappearance seems to imply that they were eventually displaced from this niche by the longer-necked sauropods.

Comparative Sizes (left)
1 *Anchisaurus*: 1. 8·2ft (2·5m).
2 *Plateosaurus*: 1. 20-26·25ft (6-8m).

Connecticut, this produced three well-preserved prosauropod skeletons and a few other fragments. These skeletons were described in some detail by O. C. Marsh in the early 1890s as *Anchisaurus major, A. colurus* and *A. solus. A. major* was subsequently renamed *Ammosaurus major* and *A. colurus* became *Yaleosaurus colurus* just to add to the general confusion! Other prosauropod material comes from the Navajo Sandstone of northern Arizona and consists of the partial remains of *Ammosaurus* ('sand reptile').

Anchisaurus remains have also been described from the earliest Jurassic rocks of Orange Free State, South Africa. Originally described as *Hortalotarsus, Thecodontosaurus* and *Gyposaurus*, Drs Peter Galton and Mike Culver redescribed this partial skeleton of *Gyposaurus* and noted that it was virtually indistinguishable from the North American *Anchisaurus* and so renamed it *Anchisaurus capensis*.

Plateosaurus (left)
This was the first large dinosaur, reaching a length of up to 26·25ft (8m). *Plateosaurus* fed on plants at ground level and on leaves of tall trees. *Plateosaurus* could stand on its hind legs or on all-fours, and its long neck would have allowed it to seek food over a wide area. The hands are characterised by their strong fingers, and particularly the thumb which was furnished with a broad scythe-like claw. This thumb was probably used to rake up plants on the ground, or to tear leaves down from the trees, or possibly as a defensive weapon.

ANCHISAURUS
LUFENGOSAURUS
PLATEOSAURUS
COLORADIA
YUNNANOSAURUS
RIOJASAURUS
MELANOROSAURUS

Family Tree (above)
Anchisaurus and its allies are generally slender, mostly bipedal forms. *Yunnanosaurus* may represent a group of prosauropods that developed sauropod-like teeth. *Melanorosaurus* represents a group of large sauropod-like prosauropods.

Anchisaurus (above)
One of the smaller prosauropods, the early Jurassic form *Anchisaurus* was a successful early herbivore. It had blunt pencil-shaped teeth spaced out along its jaw, and there have been long arguments about whether it ate meat, plants or both. The balance of evidence seems to favour a vegetarian diet. *Anchisaurus* was lightly built and probably agile, so that it could escape the attentions of the contemporary theropod predators.

The skeleton of *Anchisaurus*, based on material from the Connecticut Valley, consists of the major part of the skeleton lacking only the tail and much of the neck. As can be seen in the drawings the skull of *Anchisaurus* was quite small in proportion to the body, with a relatively long and slender snout. The teeth were quite slender and pencil-shaped and may well have had rough serrations down the front and back edges. These serrations are not like the fine, sharp serrations of typical theropod teeth, but rather large, coarse ridges which were evidently suited to shredding plant fibres.

The neck and back of *Anchisaurus* are reconstructed partly by reference to other prosauropods, such as the well-preserved *Plateosaurus*. The neck was probably long, slender and flexible, as was the back, giving these animals a rather long-bodied look—particularly when compared with theropods. The tail was undoubtedly long, and helped to counterbalance the front part of the body over the hips.

The limbs are of slightly unusual construction. The hindlimbs are relatively sturdy and were evidently well-designed to carry the bulk of the weight of the animal when walking. The foot also was quite broad with four well-developed toes and the rudimentary remains of the fifth. The forelimbs and shoulders, however, were also remarkably well-developed. The shoulders are stout and the arms relatively long and were evidently capable of touching or resting on the ground with ease; this suggests that *Anchisaurus* may have walked on all fours on occasions. The hand is rather curious in that the outer fingers (4th and 5th) are quite small and slender and may not have borne claws, while the inner fingers are well developed, particularly the first finger which has a much enlarged sharply-curved claw.

Plateosaurus Described

Another of the anchisaurid-type of prosauropods, *Plateosaurus* ('flat reptile') was con-siderably larger (20·26·25ft, 6-8 m body length) and comes from the late Triassic rocks of western Europe (Federal Republic of Germany, the German Democratic Republic, France and Switzerland). Today *Plateosaurus* remains are known to occur in mass concentrations of relatively complete remains, notably at Trössingen in the FRG, Halberstadt in the GDR and La Chassagne in France.

The first remains of *Plateosaurus* were described by Hermann von Meyer in 1837 from fragments of a skeleton. However, during 1911-12, 1921-23 and in 1932 extensive excavations at Trössingen were carried out by the Palaeontological Institute of the University of Tübingen. These revealed a massive accumulation of complete and partial skeletons of *Plateosaurus*. These were described in considerable detail by Friedrich Freiherr von Huene, a palaeontologist from Tübingen.

As can be seen from the skeletal reconstruction which is taken from von Huene's work

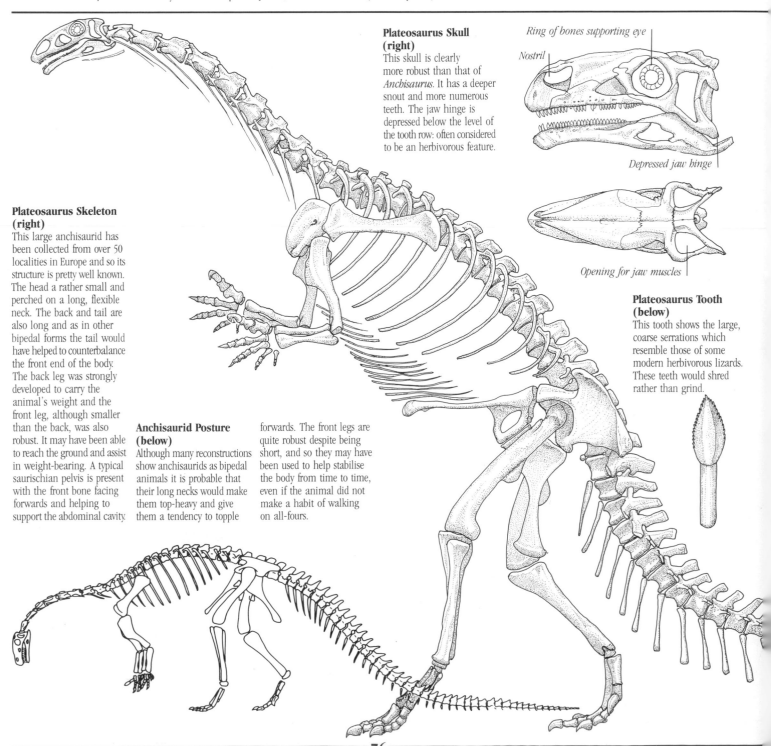

Plateosaurus Skull (right)
This skull is clearly more robust than that of *Anchisaurus*. It has a deeper snout and more numerous teeth. The jaw hinge is depressed below the level of the tooth row: often considered to be an herbivorous feature.

Ring of bones supporting eye

Nostril

Depressed jaw hinge

Opening for jaw muscles

Plateosaurus Skeleton (right)
This large anchisaurid has been collected from over 50 localities in Europe and so its structure is pretty well known. The head a rather small and perched on a long, flexible neck. The back and tail are also long and as in other bipedal forms the tail would have helped to counterbalance the front end of the body. The back leg was strongly developed to carry the animal's weight and the front leg, although smaller than the back, was also robust. It may have been able to reach the ground and assist in weight-bearing. A typical saurischian pelvis is present with the front bone facing forwards and helping to support the abdominal cavity.

Plateosaurus Tooth (below)
This tooth shows the large, coarse serrations which resemble those of some modern herbivorous lizards. These teeth would shred rather than grind.

Anchisaurid Posture (below)
Although many reconstructions show anchisaurids as bipedal animals it is probable that their long necks would make them top-heavy and give them a tendency to topple forwards. The front legs are quite robust despite being short, and so they may have been used to help stabilise the body from time to time, even if the animal did not make a habit of walking on all-fours.

of 1926, *Plateosaurus* was larger and consequently more robustly constructed than *Anchisaurus*, although the general body proportions are remarkably similar. The skull is somewhat more heavily built, with a deeper snout region; the teeth are also more numerous. Also deserving of comment is the position of the jaw joint in *Plateosaurus*; this is sited *below* the level of the teeth, while in *Anchisaurus* the jaw joint is on practically the *same* level as the teeth. The teeth of *Plateosaurus* have coarse serrations running down the edges of the crown, as do the teeth of almost all other prosauropods.

The remainder of the skeleton is very similar to that of *Anchisaurus*. The natural pose of these anchisaurid prosauropods has been the subject of some disagreement in the past. In the 1890s O. C. Marsh produced the restoration of *Anchisaurus* seen below. The body in this pose does seem rather unbalanced; the tail looks to be too small effectively to counterbalance the front part of the body in this position. However, the arm and hand do not seem to be designed for walking upon. In particular the fingers are relatively slender and have narrow claws which would have enabled them to be used for grasping objects. A very similar posture was used by von Huene in his 1926 reconstruction of *Plateosaurus*. Peter Galton proposed a somewhat different posture for all prosauropods (shown in the drawing at bottom left) after reviewing the anatomy of the hand and the general body proportions of prosauropods. As was mentioned above, the relatively long neck and trunk of these animals does not give them a perfect balance at the hips; there is a strong tendency for the body to pitch forward on to all-fours. The arms and shoulders are quite long and robustly constructed, so that their use as weight-bearing legs would not have been prohibited; and on careful investigation the hands were found to be quite sophisticated in the range of movements that they could make.

Not only could the fingers be flexed to grasp objects, but the fingers could also be *hyperextended* (bent backwards) so that the fingers of digits II, III and IV could rest on the ground like the toes of a foot. The enlarged claw on the first finger was probably held clear of the ground in order to protect it from damage.

Anchisaurid Biology

The way of life and probable diet of prosauropods has generated a lot of discussion in the past. Opinions as to the primary food of prosauropods has ranged from purely meat (regarding them as 'scavenger-predators'), to an omnivorous or mixed diet of plant and animal tissues, to one that is purely of plants.

The main problem here has been one of simple interpretation based on the characteristics of the teeth combined with the general body shape and head size. For example, prosauropod teeth are serrated; serrations are

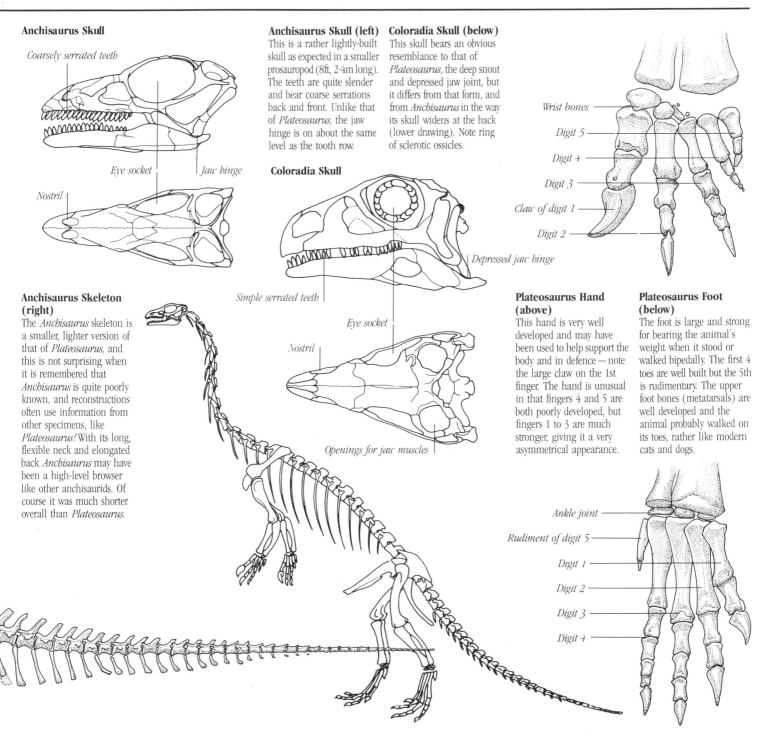

Anchisaurus Skull

Coarsely serrated teeth

Eye socket   *Jaw hinge*

Nostril

Anchisaurus Skull (left)
This is a rather lightly-built skull as expected in a smaller prosauropod (8ft, 2·4m long). The teeth are quite slender and bear coarse serrations back and front. Unlike that of *Plateosaurus*, the jaw hinge is on about the same level as the tooth row.

Coloradia Skull (below)
This skull bears an obvious resemblance to that of *Plateosaurus*, the deep snout and depressed jaw joint, but it differs from that form, and from *Anchisaurus* in the way its skull widens at the back (lower drawing). Note ring of sclerotic ossicles.

Coloradia Skull

Depressed jaw hinge

Simple serrated teeth

Eye socket

Nostril

Openings for jaw muscles

Anchisaurus Skeleton (right)
The *Anchisaurus* skeleton is a smaller, lighter version of that of *Plateosaurus*, and this is not surprising when it is remembered that *Anchisaurus* is quite poorly known, and reconstructions often use information from other specimens, like *Plateosaurus!* With its long, flexible neck and elongated back *Anchisaurus* may have been a high-level browser like other anchisaurids. Of course it was much shorter overall than *Plateosaurus*.

Wrist bones

Digit 5

Digit 4

Digit 3

Claw of digit 1

Digit 2

Plateosaurus Hand (above)
This hand is very well developed and may have been used to help support the body and in defence—note the large claw on the 1st finger. The hand is unusual in that fingers 4 and 5 are both poorly developed, but fingers 1 to 3 are much stronger, giving it a very asymmetrical appearance.

Plateosaurus Foot (below)
The foot is large and strong for bearing the animal's weight when it stood or walked bipedally. The first 4 toes are well built but the 5th is rudimentary. The upper foot bones (metatarsals) are well developed and the animal probably walked on its toes, rather like modern cats and dogs.

Ankle joint

Rudiment of digit 5

Digit 1

Digit 2

Digit 3

Digit 4

also found on theropod teeth; theropods were carnivores. Therefore, the argument runs, prosauropods are likely to have been carnivorous as well. Add to this the small size of the head and the quite large, cumbersome body, then the most reasonable interpretation would suggest that it could not have been a devastatingly aggressive predator like the large 'carnosaur'-type theropods, but may perhaps have scavenged its meat from abandoned carcasses, or caught smaller slower-moving animals.

Other research workers have proposed a mixed diet for prosauropods implying that from an evolutionary point of view they were a sort of intermediate type of dinosaur: neither wholly carnivorous like the theropods, nor wholly herbivorous like the sauropods. In this way the theropod-type teeth and the sauropod body proportions of these creatures makes some sort of sense.

The third explanation, and the one preferred here, is that they were completely herbivorous. Dr Peter Galton (Bridgeport) has recently reviewed the arguments concerned with the diets of prosauropods in response to a paper presented in 1981 by Dr Mike Cooper (Zimbabwe) in which the scavenger-predator hypothesis was proposed very strongly. Galton observed that the serrations on the teeth of prosauropods were not the same as those on the teeth of theropod dinosaurs; as noted earlier they are relatively large and coarse compared with those of theropods and, in fact, resemble those on the teeth of the herbivorous land iguanas living in South America today. Rather than showing adaptations for slicing meat therefore, these teeth seem well-suited for shredding up plant material. The curious low position of the jaw joint is also of some significance in this argument because this feature is also seen in the herbivorous ornithischian dinosaurs (and in a modified form in herbivores living today) and seems to be an adaptation which improves the effectiveness of the teeth along the jaw during jaw closure in the process of eating.

Another important piece of evidence relating to the diet of prosauropods is the observation by Dr John Attridge (University of London) that the prosauropod *Massospondylus* ('massive vertebra') had a gastric mill ('stomach stones' – gastroliths). These sizeable pebbles, which were probably lodged in the muscular walls of a 'gizzard' or an equivalent region of the stomach of these dinosaurs, could have provided an area where plant material would have been ground to a pulp; it could then be more easily digested. Gastric mills would have been important for herbivores such as these because, unlike modern herbivorous mammals and many ornithischian dinosaurs, prosauropod dinosaurs did not have the complicated teeth or jaws designed for chewing food. This is a distinct disadvantage for herbivores because most of the nutritious parts of the plants are locked inside the enzyme-resistant cellulose plant cell walls. In order to extract the nutritious parts from plant tissues, the plant cell walls have to be crushed and broken either by chewing (the usual method), or by the use of gastric mill-stones. Crushing and pulping of plant food allows the animal to absorb the plant cell tissues more easily, and also provides an opportunity for special cellulose-digesting bacteria which live in the gut of herbivores to break down the plant cellulose; this can also be directly or indirectly absorbed by the animal. (Incidentally the presence of a large, stone-laden stomach may also have upset its posture.)

As Dr Galton pointed out, with their long necks and legs the prosauropods were probably adept 'high browsing' dinosaurs and as such may well have been the first group of reptiles to evolve the ability to feed on relatively high vegetation. Until the appearance of the prosauropods, all herbivores had been squat, short-necked creatures that would have been incapable of reaching high foliage. So, not only were they the first herbivorous dinosaurs, they were also the first high browsers as well.

The preponderance of prosauropod fossils at some Triassic and Jurassic localities has prompted the suggestion that many, perhaps all, species lived in herds. In fact the local abundance of *Plateosaurus* at Trössingen prompted von Huene to speculate vividly upon the circumstances which led to the mass accumulation. He proposed that vast herds of such creatures may have wandered through the ancient highlands of southern Germany, and that rather like the wildbeest of Africa, they underwent seasonal migrations during the dry season in search of water. Trössingen represented to von Huene a place where a large herd had perished on just such a journey. In 1982 Dr David Weishampel (Miami) re-investigated the Trössingen *Plateosaurus* quarry and was able to demonstrate that rather than being the remains of a single vast herd, many of the *Plateosaurus* skeletons were buried over a considerable period of time. These probably represented the chance fossilisation of normal deaths of individuals of a very abundant dinosaur living in this area. However, hidden within this record there were also two 'spikes', that is narrow geological bands which seem to have unexpectedly high numbers of skeletons. Weishampel interpreted these 'spikes' as representing catastrophic deaths of large numbers of individuals. What the cause of these might have been is uncertain; one possibility is that they were animals caught in flash-floods rather than members of herds that died during seasonal droughts.

The 'Mouse Reptile'

Mussaurus patagonicus ('mouse reptile from Patagonia') is a remarkable prosauropod-like dinosaur. Several incomplete skeletons and two small eggs of this type of dinosaur were found in late Triassic rocks from the Province of Santa Cruz in Patagonia, southern Argentina in the late 1970s. These remains were described by Dr José Bonaparte and Martin Vince and are most remarkable for their size. The best preserved skeleton of *Mussaurus* is so small that it sits comfortably in the palm of a man's hand! The total body length was approximately 8in (20cm) allowing for a reasonable length of tail. Bonaparte and Vince concluded that they must have discovered a nest with the hatchlings of a prosauropod dinosaur. Certainly, looking at the skeleton, the bones seem typical of a juvenile animal, and in the skull the eye socket is extremely large which is a very common juvenile feature (see *Psittacosaurus* page 129).

The discovery of *Mussaurus* is very interesting because it adds to the knowledge of juvenile dinosaurs, which are quite rare in the fossil record. Unfortunately it is not possible to be sure of the precise relationship of *Mussaurus* to other prosauropods because most of these are represented by adults, and at present we have no idea what adult *Mussaurus* may have looked like. It has been tentatively suggested that *Mussaurus* may be hatchlings of *Coloradia*, another newly-described prosauropod known from a skull and jaws found in this formation.

Other Groups

Another major group of prosauropods may be the melanorosaurids ('black reptiles'). Unlike the anchisaurids, these prosauropods are larger and much more heavily built. The melanorosaurids are based upon animals such as *Melanorosaurus* which is an assortment of large limb bones from South Africa. These seem to indicate the existence of a large, heavily-built prosauropod which walked on all-fours rather like the later sauropods (see pages 80 to 97). Another fairly well known form is *Riojasaurus* ('reptile of Rioja') from the late Triassic of Rioja, Argentina. *Riojasaurus* was a very large prosauropod up to 36ft (11m) long. At present it is known from postcranial remains which indicate a large and heavily-built prosauropod. The forelimbs are notably larger and more robust than those of anchisaurids which seems to suggest that it walked on all-fours all of the time. Unfortunately there is no cranial material known for any melanorosaurid, so whether they had typical anchisaurid-type skulls and teeth is unknown. The long slender neck of *Riojasaurus* does tend to suggest a relatively small skull.

Yunnanosaurids ('reptiles from Yunnan') are a special group of prosauropods devoted to a single species at present (*Yunnanosaurus huangi*) which was found in Yunnan Province, China, and described by Dr C. C. Young in 1942. Apparently smaller and less heavily-built than the melanorosaurids, the yunnanosaurids are

Above: A left lateral view of the skull of *Massospondylus carinatus* which was excavated at Blikana Mountain in the District of Herschel, Cape Province, South Africa. *Massospondylus* was one of the most widespread of the dinosaurs in this region in late Triassic/early Jurassic times (see Time Chart).

notable for one particular feature: the structure of their teeth. In his review of prosauropod diets Peter Galton separated out *Yunnanosaurus* because it did not have the coarsely-serrated teeth typical of most prosauropods; its teeth were in fact reminiscent of those of true sauropods. They are cylindrical but somewhat flattened from side to side, presenting a somewhat chisel-like appearance. The tip of the tooth tends to be worn off at an angle forming quite a sharp cutting edge

Yunnanosaurus seems therefore to have developed a full set of truly sauropod-type teeth; they are in fact strikingly similar to those of the giant sauropod *Brachiosaurus* (see page 88) both in their shape and the way they are worn down. If only teeth had been found, they would almost certainly have been classified as belonging to an early sauropod dinosaur. However, the skeleton of *Yunnanosaurus* is quite typical of that of an anchisaurid prosauropod. This suggests that at least some of the prosauropods developed feeding techniques similar to those of the spectacularly successful sauropods of the late Jurassic.

It has been suggested that another *Plateosaurus*-like prosauropod from Yunnan Province, *Lufengosaurus* ('reptile from Lu-feng'), is in fact synonymous with *Yunnanosaurus*, but this is not the case.

General Conclusions

The prosauropods were a very abundant and varied group of late Triassic and early Jurassic herbivorous dinosaurs. They seem to have evolved along several lines

(i) The anchisaurids seem for the most part to have been relatively agile bipedal and quadrupedal types capable of browsing on high foliage, using to advantage their long necks and hind legs. Their teeth were coarsely serrated and capable of shredding plant fibres reasonably effectively. A 'gastric mill' served further to pulp the otherwise indigestible plant tissues. Many of these herbivores may have been gregarious, living in herds in order to provide communal protection from some of the large predatory thecodontians of the late Triassic, such as *Saurosuchus* for instance, or large theropod dinosaurs (see *Dilophosaurus*, page 63) of the early Jurassic. The large claw on the hand may well have been used as a close-quarters defensive weapon.

(ii) The melanorosaurids may have represented an early attempt by prosauropods to use large size to become relatively invulnerable to predatory attack. Unfortunately these types are still rather poorly understood; for example it is not known whether they may even have developed sauropod-like teeth as did the third group, as mentioned below.

(iii) The yunnanosaurids retained the body form of the typical anchisaurid but developed a rather specialised dentition closely resembling that of the later sauropods.

Below: The Chinese prosauropod *Lufengosaurus huenei* broadly resembles *Plateosaurus,* and they were probably quite closely related. Its discovery in southern China bears witness to the wide geographical distribution of prosauropods in the late Triassic/early Jurassic.

Right: An extremely well preserved skull (now in the Humboldt Museum) of *Plateosaurus engelhardti* that was excavated from the Upper Triassic rocks of Halberstadt, Germany. The coarsely-serrated teeth seem well adapted to shredding plant material.

Left: Tübingen University's skeleton of *Plateosaurus* is restored in a bipedal pose, although recent research suggests that prosauropods may also have walked on all-fours. The long neck is an adaptation that would have allowed *Plateosaurus* to browse comfortably on high vegetation.

Right: The South African Museum's cast of the skeleton of *Massospondylus carinatus.* This dinosaur stood some 13ft (4m) tall, and the picture emphasises the generally small size of its head and jaws in relation to the overall body proportions. It is possible that its food was pulped by a gastric mill of stomach stones.

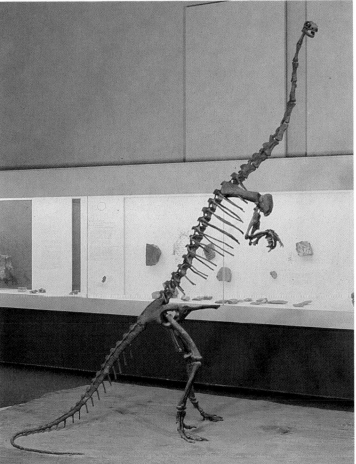

PROSAUROPOD GENERA

Valid

Ammosaurus
Anchisaurus
Aristosaurus
Azendohsaurus (?)
Coloradia
Efraasia
Euskelosaurus
Lufengosaurus
Massospondylus
Melanorosaurus
Mussaurus
(?= Coloradia)
Plateosaurus
Riojasaurus
Sellosaurus
Sinosaurus (?)
Thecodontosaurus
Yunnanosaurus

Dubious

Aetonyx
Agrosaurus
Amphisaurus
Avalonia
Avalonianus
Basutodon
Clepsysaurus
Dimodosaurus
Dinosaurus
Dromicosaurus
Eucnemesaurus
Gresslyosaurus
Gryponyx
Gyposaurus
Hortalotarsus
Leptospondylus
Megadactylus
Nyasasaurus
Orosauravus
Orosaurus
Pachysauriscus
Pachysaurus
Pachyspondylus
Palaeosauriscus
Palaeosaurus
Picrodon
Thotobolosaurus
Yaleosaurus
Zanclodon

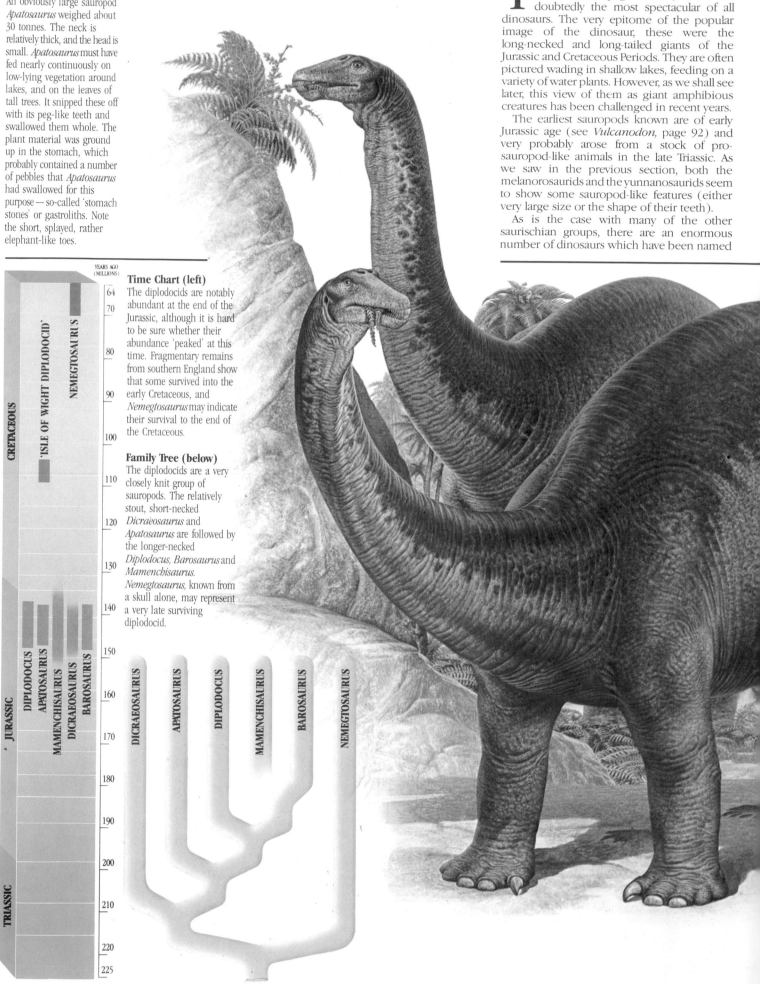

Apatosaurus (below right)

An obviously large sauropod *Apatosaurus* weighed about 30 tonnes. The neck is relatively thick, and the head is small. *Apatosaurus* must have fed nearly continuously on low-lying vegetation around lakes, and on the leaves of tall trees. It snipped these off with its peg-like teeth and swallowed them whole. The plant material was ground up in the stomach, which probably contained a number of pebbles that *Apatosaurus* had swallowed for this purpose — so-called 'stomach stones' or gastroliths. Note the short, splayed, rather elephant-like toes.

The sauropods which are described in this section (pages 80-97) were undoubtedly the most spectacular of all dinosaurs. The very epitome of the popular image of the dinosaur, these were the long-necked and long-tailed giants of the Jurassic and Cretaceous Periods. They are often pictured wading in shallow lakes, feeding on a variety of water plants. However, as we shall see later, this view of them as giant amphibious creatures has been challenged in recent years.

The earliest sauropods known are of early Jurassic age (see *Vulcanodon*, page 92) and very probably arose from a stock of pro-sauropod-like animals in the late Triassic. As we saw in the previous section, both the melanorosaurids and the yunnanosaurids seem to show some sauropod-like features (either very large size or the shape of their teeth).

As is the case with many of the other saurischian groups, there are an enormous number of dinosaurs which have been named

Time Chart (left)

The diplodocids are notably abundant at the end of the Jurassic, although it is hard to be sure whether their abundance 'peaked' at this time. Fragmentary remains from southern England show that some survived into the early Cretaceous, and *Nemegtosaurus* may indicate their survival to the end of the Cretaceous.

Family Tree (below)

The diplodocids are a very closely knit group of sauropods. The relatively stout, short-necked *Dicraëosaurus* and *Apatosaurus* are followed by the longer-necked *Diplodocus, Barosaurus* and *Mamenchisaurus. Nemegtosaurus,* known from a skull alone, may represent a very late surviving diplodocid.

YEARS AGO (MILLIONS)

TRIASSIC · JURASSIC · CRETACEOUS

64 70 80 90 100 110 120 130 140 150 160 170 180 190 200 210 220 225

'ISLE OF WIGHT DIPLODOCID'

NEMEGTOSAURUS

DIPLODOCUS
APATOSAURUS
MAMENCHISAURUS
DICRAEOSAURUS
BAROSAURUS

DICRAEOSAURUS · APATOSAURUS · DIPLODOCUS · MAMENCHISAURUS · BAROSAURUS · NEMEGTOSAURUS

on the basis of imperfect material and are consequently very hard to discuss in any meaningful way. I shall therefore restrict the coverage given to these sauropods to a survey of some of the better known and most distinctive types. A table of valid and dubious sauropod genera, which includes diplodocids, is given on page 97.

The First Discoveries

Scientific study of *Apatosaurus* ('deceptive reptile') began in an extremely confused and confusing way in 1877. Much of this confusion has its origins in the rivalry between two palaeontologists: Othniel Marsh and Edward Drinker Cope. In the July of that year, O. C. Marsh described a large, incomplete section of hip bones found by Arthur Lakes near Morrison, Colorado; to this he gave the name *Titanosaurus montanus* only to discover that *Titanosaurus* ('giant reptile') had already been used

for a sauropod from India. Later that year he coined the name *Atlantosaurus* ('Atlas reptile') for this material. In the same publication, Marsh also used the name *Apatosaurus ajax* for more hip and back bones found in another quarry in the Morrison area by Lakes. Incidentally this latter specimen was originally sent to Marsh's great rival, E. D. Cope, but Cope was obliged to send it to Marsh when he learned that Marsh had already bought the fossils from Lakes. Over the next few years more material of *Apatosaurus ajax,* and another larger skeleton named *Atlantosaurus immanis,* was recovered from the second quarry. This collection included fragments of a skull, which were later to prove to be of considerable importance. In 1879 two more of Marsh's collectors, W. H. Reed and E. G. Ashley, discovered two more sauropod skeletons at Como Bluff, Wyoming; these were from rocks of the same age as the previous find. One of these, an almost complete skeleton lacking only the skull, was described as

'*Brontosaurus*' (=*Apatosaurus*) *excelsus* by Marsh in 1879, the other was named *B. amplus* (*Brontosaurus*: 'thunder reptile'). In 1883 Marsh produced the first ever reconstruction of any sauropod, based on his '*Brontosaurus*' *excelsus*, but unfortunately used several limb bones as well as the feet of *Camarasaurus* (page 87). As a result the animal was given rather graceful, slender forelimbs, as opposed to the much more stout, robust limbs that it actually had. *Camarasaurus*, or '*Morosaurus*' as it was then known, was also used as the model for the neck which was given 12 neck vertebrae, instead of the 15 that we now know there to be. Marsh was also unaware that '*Brontosaurus*' had a long whip-like end to its tail comprising more than 80 vertebrae, almost twice the number found in the tail of *Camarasaurus*.

Because of the confusion generated by Marsh in distinguishing between his '*Brontosaurus*' and the *Camarasaurus* skeleton, he also reconstructed '*Brontosaurus*' with a

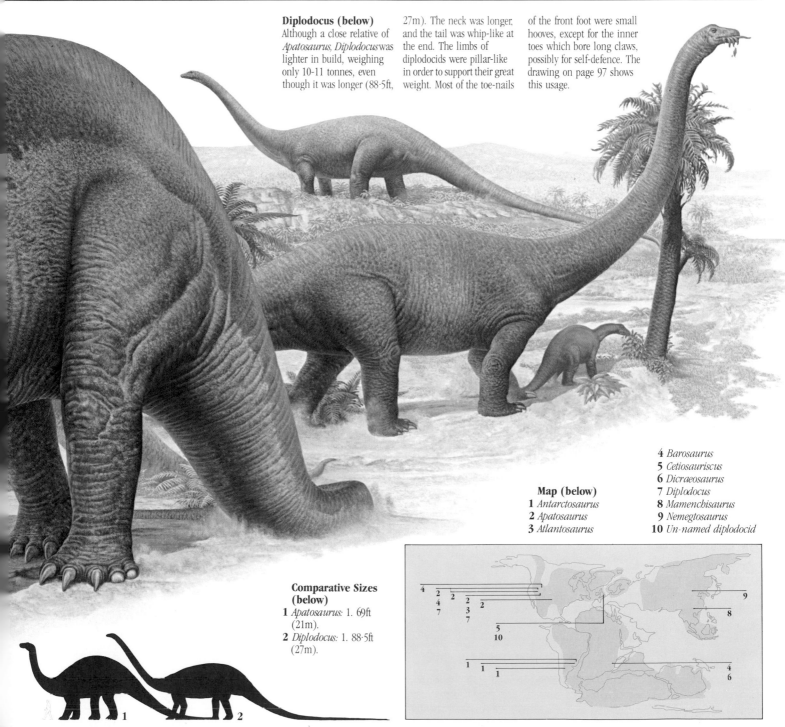

Diplodocus (below)
Although a close relative of *Apatosaurus, Diplodocus* was lighter in build, weighing only 10-11 tonnes, even though it was longer (88·5ft,

27m). The neck was longer, and the tail was whip-like at the end. The limbs of diplodocids were pillar-like in order to support their great weight. Most of the toe-nails

of the front foot were small hooves, except for the inner toes which bore long claws, possibly for self-defence. The drawing on page 97 shows this usage.

Map (below)
1 *Antarctosaurus*
2 *Apatosaurus*
3 *Atlantosaurus*
4 *Barosaurus*
5 *Cetiosauriscus*
6 *Dicraeosaurus*
7 *Diplodocus*
8 *Mamenchisaurus*
9 *Nemegtosaurus*
10 *Un-named diplodocid*

Comparative Sizes (below)
1 *Apatosaurus*: 1. 69ft (21m).
2 *Diplodocus*: 1. 88·5ft (27m).

Camarasaurus-type head based upon a partial skull recovered from another quarry at Como Bluff, and incidentally from geologically older rocks which had only yielded several sauropod skeletons, but none that could be identified as Apatosaurus ('Brontosaurus').

Extensive collections of sauropod remains were recovered from south eastern Wyoming around the turn of the century, particularly at Como Bluff and Bone Cabin Quarry. These, however, were largely of disarticulated remains rather than well-preserved skeletons, and tended to add to the confusion rather than clarifying relationships between names and skeletal types. For example the hindlimbs of Camarasaurus ('Morosaurus') and Apatosaurus ('Brontosaurus') were regularly confused, as were the forelimbs of Diplodocus and 'Morosaurus'.

One rather interesting consequence of this confusion can be seen in many museums around the world! Casts of a magnificent skeleton of Diplodocus carnegiei were sent to various museums around the world at the beginning of this century. In order to complete the skeleton in preparation for casting, a complete foot of Camarasaurus ('Morosaurus') identified as 'Diplodocus' by Henry Fairfield Osborn, was sent from the American Museum of Natural History to the Carnegie Museum. As a result many of the museums of the world have Diplodocus skeletons with front feet which are modelled on the hind feet of Camarasaurus!

Better-preserved material of Apatosaurus and careful work on the original material revealed that there were a number of inconsistencies in the early work on sauropods that had been undertaken by Marsh and others. As a result it was agreed that (i) Apatosaurus was the valid name for material described either as 'Atlantosaurus' or 'Brontosaurus'; (ii) Camarasaurus was the valid name for material also referred to as 'Morosaurus'; and (iii) that there were more similarities between the skeletons of Apatosaurus and Diplodocus than there were between Apatosaurus and Camarasaurus.

The latter point is of some significance because despite this observation, until very recently (1975) the skeletons of Apatosaurus have always been restored with a Camarasaurus-like head, following Marsh's original drawings. This is slightly surprising, for in 1915 and 1924 W. J. Holland, a noted expert on the sauropods of North America, claimed that Apatosaurus very probably had a Diplodocus-type skull. He based his argument upon the overall similarities in their skeletons and the observation that a partial Diplodocus-like skull was discovered very close to two Apatosaurus skeletons recovered from Dinosaur National Monument (Utah). This claim seems to have been completely ignored by the scientific community until 1975 when the issue was re-examined by Dr Jack McIntosh (Wesleyan University), one of the leading experts on

Diplodocus Skeleton (below)

The skeleton of this form was considerably lighter than that of Apatosaurus although in other respects very similar. The very small head, long neck and long tail are hallmarks of the diplodocids. The rather slender neck is composed of 15 vertebrae, the back 10, and the tail about 70. Because of these proportions some workers suggest that Diplodocus had the body plan of a walking cantilever bridge! Both front and back legs (the pillars of the bridge) and their girdles were extremely strong to bear the animal's weight. Despite the large belly area, there is no evidence of gastralia.

Diplodocid Skulls (right)

These three skulls were found in very different places yet they all show basic diplodocid features. The eyes are far back in the head and the nostrils right on top of the skull. The snout is long and broad with a cluster of rather feeble-looking teeth at the front. Nemegtosaurus (near right, top) is from the late Cretaceous rocks of Mongolia. Dicraeosaurus (near right, bottom) was found in late Jurassic rocks of Tanzania. Antarctosaurus is from the Jurassic of Argentina, not Antarctica as its name suggests! It would seem that the jaw muscles of all these diplodocids were relatively feeble.

Nemegtosaurus Skull

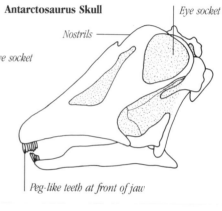

Nostrils

Eye socket

Dicraeosaurus Skull

Nostrils

Eye socket

Antarctosaurus Skull

Eye socket

Nostrils

Peg-like teeth at front of jaw

Diplodocus Skull (left)

Here the features of the diplodocids are seen clearly. In side view (top drawing) note the large eye-socket and fine pencil-like teeth at the front of the snout. In top view (lower drawing) you can see the unusual position of the nostrils.

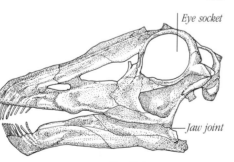

Eye socket

Jaw joint

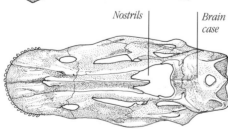

Nostrils

Brain case

Diplodocus Hand (below)

The hand is broad and rather short as expected in such a massive animal. It is possible that only the first finger bore a large curved claw, and that the other fingers were finished off with a blunt pad, probably of horn.

Diplodocus Hand

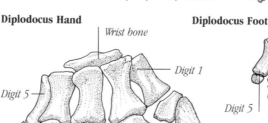

Wrist bone

Digit 1

Digit 5

Diplodocus Foot (below)

Like the hand, the foot is short and broad with five rather stubby toes. Although the foot is often drawn with three clawed toes, at least one well-preserved specimen of Diplodocus carnegiei shows that only toes 1 and 2 bore claws.

Diplodocus Foot

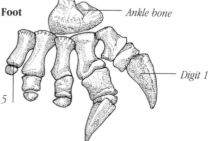

Ankle bone

Digit 1

Digit 5

Claw

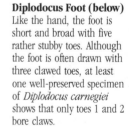

sauropod dinosaurs, and Dr David Berman (Carnegie Museum). They were able to demonstrate convincingly, that *Apatosaurus* probably possessed a skull that was virtually indistinguishable from that of *Diplodocus*. They were also responsible for bringing to light the reason for much of the confusion surrounding the early work on sauropods toward the end of the last century. In fact if Marsh had studied the skull fragments found in Colorado in the late 1870s, he could have avoided all this confusion.

Dinosaur National Monument

In 1936 Charles Whitney Gilmore—one of the most productive and respected of research workers on dinosaurs in the early half of this century—described an almost complete skeleton of *Apatosaurus* (*A. louisae*, named in honour of the wife of Andrew Carnegie, the benefactor of the Carnegie Museum that is situated in Pittsburgh, Pennsylvania).

This particular skeleton was of considerable importance because of its key role in the establishment of Dinosaur National Monument. In 1909 Earl Douglass of the Carnegie Museum discovered the remains of the skeleton which was to become *A. louisae* which was weathering out on a sandstone ledge near Jensen on the Green River. Upon excavation, this specimen proved to be almost complete and while it was being dug out other specimens were discovered, one after another. Excavations led by the Carnegie Museum continued without a break until 1922, and the quarry was still far from exhausted of its fossils. In the early years permits for excavation were granted on an annual basis by the Department of the Interior. Finally the Carnegie Museum attempted to 'file a claim' for the site to prevent it from being exploited by unscrupulous collectors. This was refused on the grounds that fossil bones were not deemed to be minerals. However, this action provoked no less a person than President

Woodrow Wilson on 4th October 1915 to set aside 80 acres in and around the quarry as an area to be preserved as an 'American Antiquity' and to be known as Dinosaur National Monument.

After the major excavations of the Carnegie Museum (1909-1922), further excavations were undertaken by the Smithsonian Institution (Washington D.C.) and the University of Utah to extract more skeletons before the exposure was enclosed in a huge permanent building. This remarkable site and Museum (opened in 1958) offers an almost unparalleled opportunity for visitors to visit a dinosaur excavation site 'in action'.

Apatosaurus Described

The head of *Apatosaurus* is now thought to be like that of *Diplodocus* which is described below, in concordance with the views of Holland, McIntosh and Berman. The neck is

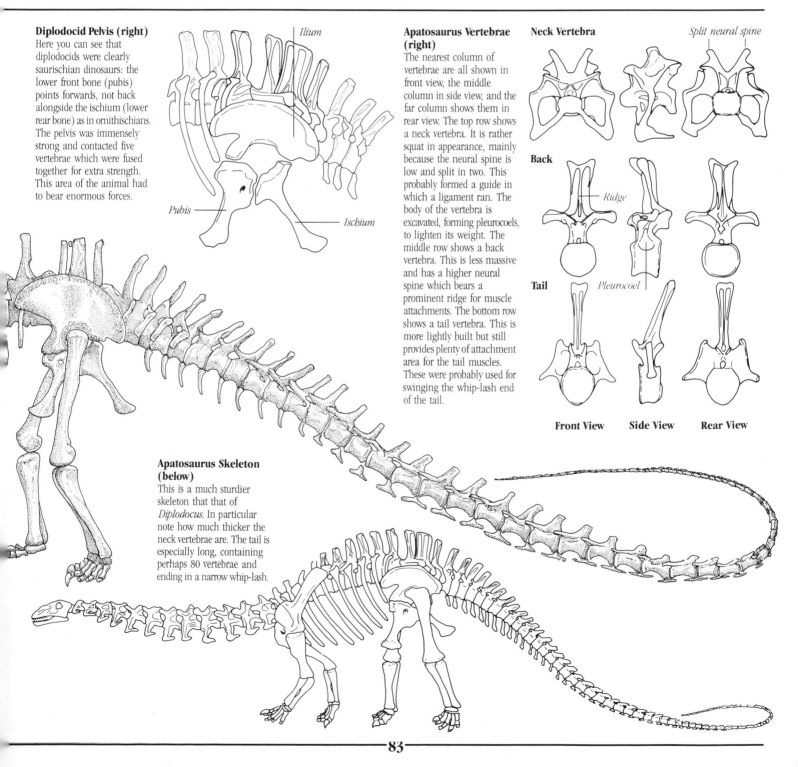

Diplodocid Pelvis (right)
Here you can see that diplodocids were clearly saurischian dinosaurs: the lower front bone (pubis) points forwards, not back alongside the ischium (lower rear bone) as in ornithischians. The pelvis was immensely strong and contacted five vertebrae which were fused together for extra strength. This area of the animal had to bear enormous forces.

Ilium
Pubis
Ischium

Apatosaurus Vertebrae (right)
The nearest column of vertebrae are all shown in front view, the middle column in side view, and the far column shows them in rear view. The top row shows a neck vertebra. It is rather squat in appearance, mainly because the neural spine is low and split in two. This probably formed a guide in which a ligament ran. The body of the vertebra is excavated, forming pleurocoels, to lighten its weight. The middle row shows a back vertebra. This is less massive and has a higher neural spine which bears a prominent ridge for muscle attachments. The bottom row shows a tail vertebra. This is more lightly built but still provides plenty of attachment area for the tail muscles. These were probably used for swinging the whip-lash end of the tail.

Neck Vertebra
Split neural spine

Back
Ridge
Pleurocoel

Tail

Front View   **Side View**   **Rear View**

Apatosaurus Skeleton (below)
This is a much sturdier skeleton that that of *Diplodocus*. In particular note how much thicker the neck vertebrae are. The tail is especially long, containing perhaps 80 vertebrae and ending in a narrow whip-lash.

rather thick, certainly by comparison with that of *Diplodocus*; it consists of 15 vertebrae to which the ribs—which no doubt anchored the powerful muscles which moved the neck—are firmly fused. The sides of the neck vertebrae and those of the back are deeply excavated to form cavities (pleurocoels—see also the theropods). As was the case with the larger theropods, these cavities undoubtedly served to lighten the bones of the back of the animal in order to reduce the total body weight of these gigantic creatures. The spines of the neck, although they seem in profile to be relatively short when compared with those of the back, are nevertheless connected to extremely powerful muscles and ligaments used for raising the neck. As in *Diplodocus*, the spines near the base of the neck are divided down the middle and probably provided a pulley-like guide for a massive ligament that ran along this groove.

The back vertebrae are less elaborately sculpted than the neck vertebrae, but have extremely tall spines which are prominently ridged and scarred for the attachment of powerful muscles. At the hips, five of the backbones are fused together to form a massive support for the pelvic bones in order to transmit the enormous weight of the body into the pillar-like legs. The tail is surprisingly long for a quadrupedal animal (82 vertebrae are known in one specimen), almost half of which consists of a very slender whip-lash.

Both fore and hindlimbs are massively built and pillar-like in order to support effectively the weight of the animal. The feet have relatively short toes which are splayed rather like those of an elephant. The fore feet, as in the majority of sauropods, have a single clawed inner toe, the other four ending in blunt pads. The hind foot has three claws, the outer two toes again presumably ending in blunt pads.

Discovering Diplodocus

Diplodocus ('double beam'), another of the great and well-known sauropods from the late Jurassic of North America, was also initially described by O. C. Marsh. The first remains were found by Samuel Wendell Williston near the ranch of M. P. Felch not far from Canyon City, Colorado in 1877.

Williston managed to collect parts of a hind limb and numerous tail vertebrae. Marsh described these remains as *Diplodocus longus* in 1878. The name 'double beam' refers to the unusual form of the chevron bones which hang beneath the tail vertebrae; these are shaped like a pair of skids joined together at either end and were thought at the time to be unique to *Diplodocus*, though they have now been recognised in *Apatosaurus* and *Cetiosauriscus*. In subsequent years further fragmentary remains of sauropods, including *Diplodocus*, were recovered from Jurassic rocks in Colorado and Wyoming; however, it was not until 1899 that reasonable articulated skeletons were discovered, this time at Sheep Creek, Albany, County, Wyoming. Two partial skeletons were recovered which, together with the previously discovered remains, enabled John Bell Hatcher to provide a reasonably accurate reconstruction of the skeleton. This was modified in later years by further specimens described by W. J. Holland.

The skull of *Diplodocus* is surprisingly small for an animal of such large size. The snout is quite long and broad, and the teeth, which are narrow and pencil-like, are clustered closely together to form a fringe around the front of the mouth only. The eyes are situated quite far back on the side of the head and, rather curiously, the nostrils are located right on top of the head almost between the eyes, rather than in their usual position at the tip of the snout. The positioning of the eyes and nose gives a rather 'cramped' impression to the rear portion of the skull where the brain seems to have been relatively small, as were the jaw muscles. The joint between the head and neck suggests that the head was held at a distinct angle to the neck, rather than in-line with it.

As in *Apatosaurus*, there are 15 neck vertebrae; these, however, are somewhat longer, giving the neck a rather more slender appearance. The neck ribs are relatively short and fused to the vertebrae, while the vertebrae have extensive and complicated excavations in their sides to reduce their weight. The spines of the posterior neck vetebrae also have a V-shaped trough running down the centre which undoubtedly acted as a guide for a very powerful neck ligament.

Like *Apatosaurus* there are 10 back vertebrae with long, complexly-sculpted spines and deeply-excavated pleurocoels. In the tail slightly fewer, 73 or so, tail bones are known and again the posterior portion of the tail is developed into a thin whip-lash. At the base of the tail, the sides of the vertebrae have deep, vertical plates of bone; these may well provide areas for the insertion of massive muscles (*M. ilio-caudalis*) used for swinging the whip-lash end of the tail.

The ribs extending from the back of *Diplodocus* are very long and enclose a huge chest and belly cavity. Rather curiously there are no good records of these animals having bony gastralia (ribs lining the belly region) as are found extensively in prosauropods and theropods.

The shoulders and forelimbs are large and strong to carry the immense weight of these animals and provide areas for the attachment of powerful leg and shoulder muscles. The forelimb is pillar-like and ends in a rather short, broad foot. It would appear that only the inner toe of the foot bore a large curved claw, the remainder of the toes ending in blunt, possibly horny pads rather like the toes of elephants. This type of fore foot seems to have been common to almost all sauropods. However, owing to the confusion that prevailed concerning the identity of these sauropods at the end of the last century, *Diplodocus* and *Apatosaurus* are often illustrated with 3-clawed *Camarasaurus*-type feet!

The huge pelvis is firmly attached to the vertebral column by means of five fused vertebrae. As with the forelimb, the hindlimb is pillar-like, although it is slightly longer; as a result the back slopes down from the hips to the shoulders. The feet are again short, and five-toed. In one fine skeleton of *Diplodocus carnegiei*, the five-toed hind food is well preserved and appears to show that only *two* inner toes bore claws. However, as was the case with the fore foot, the reconstructions that have appeared in books and in dinosaur exhibitions persist in showing a foot bearing three claws which resembles that of both *Apatosaurus louisae* and *Camarasaurus lentus!*

Sauropod 'Heels'

Notwithstanding the confusion over the type of feet that these sauropods possessed, the proportions of the toes do bear a remarkable resemblance to those of living elephants. In elephants, the feet are supported by a thick wedge of fibrous tissue which lies beneath the rear of the foot—rather like the heel of a modern shoe. As a result, the toes of elephants do not lie flat on the ground when they walk, but rest on the fibrous pad at an angle to the ground. By developing this wedge-heel arrangement, elephants have solved one of the 'problems' which we face when walking. Our toes lie flat along the ground and the ankle joint with the lower leg is a right-angle one. As a result, every time we take a step we have to lift our heel off the ground so that the weight of our bodies is supported on the ball of the foot. When we walk we therefore tend to bob up and down with each stride. This is in fact quite tiring, although we do not consciously realise this. It is one reason why shoes with moderate heels, which save some of the energy we would have used to lift the body up and down, are so comfortable. Elephants (being considerably heavier than humans) face this problem as well: they are heavy and therefore need broad, flat feet to bear their weight. However, they would tire very quickly if they rested the entire length of their toes on the ground when they walked, and 'bobbed' in the way that we do. They therefore have developed 'built-in' heels to save energy. Sauropods must have done the same sort of thing. The broad stubby toes were undoubtedly supported behind by a thick wedge of tissue which acted as a 'heel'.

Drs David Berman and Jack McIntosh, who have done a great deal of work on the sauropod dinosaurs in recent years, have concluded that of the great variety of sauropods that have been described, at least a few share characteristics in common with those seen in *Diplodocus*

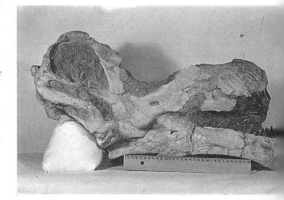

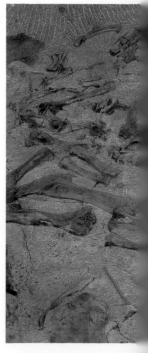

Above: The skull of *Nemegtosaurus mongoliensis* which was found at Altan Ula in the Gobi Desert during the 1965 Polish-Mongolian Expedition. It comes from late Cretaceous rocks, which is significant because most other diplodocids are known from the strata of late Jurassic formations. This may indicate that they survived throughout much of the age of the dinosaurs.

Right: The Dinosaur National Monument Quarry is one of the world's largest deposits of Jurassic fossils. The sediments containing the fossils are steeply inclined so that as they are exposed by the team of preparators they form a natural mural which can be studied by visitors. These scattered bones are principally of *Apatosaurus*.

and *Apatosaurus*. These include the shape of the head and teeth, peculiar skid-like chevron bones on the tail, a whip-lash tail and the relatively short front legs. These sauropods are referred to as diplodocids (members of the *Diplodocus* family) and include the following less well-known genera.

Barosaurus ('heavy reptile') was first described by O. C. Marsh in 1890. It comes from the late Jurassic of North America. It is a sauropod that is practically indistinguishable from *Diplodocus* except for the fact that it has very long neck vertebrae. It may even be a variant of *Diplodocus* rather than a different genus (see also table on page 97).

Cetiosauriscus ('whale-like reptile') is a genus named by Friedrich Freiherr von Huene in 1927 on the basis of a partial skeleton of a sauropod from the late Jurassic Oxford clay of Peterborough. Again it shows all the salient characters of other diplodocids (including the whip-lash tail and the skid-like chevrons).

Another presently un-named diplodocid from the Isle of Wight (England) was also described by Dr Alan Charig (British Museum — Natural History) in 1980. So far this is only known from a characteristically skid-like chevron bone from the tail. However, it shows that diplodocids were also around in the early Cretaceous of England at least.

Mamenchisaurus ('Mamenchi reptile') from the late Jurassic of Sichuan Province, China was another very long-necked diplodocid, although it is not known from complete skeletons. Most of the skeletal reconstructions known appear to be composite skeletons. *Mamenchisaurus* possesses several dipodocid characteristics and is also cautiously referred to this group of dinosaurs.

Dicraeosaurus ('forked reptile') from the late Jurassic of Tendaguru (Tanzania) was described by Werner Janensch in 1929 on the basis of an almost complete skeleton. Again, although it differs in some details from other diplodocids, it clearly possesses the characteristically shaped head as well as the skid-like chevrons and whip-lash tail.

Nemegtosaurus ('reptile from Nemegtu') is currently only known from a skull found in the late Cretaceous rocks of the Nemegt basin of Mongolia. As can be seen from the drawing the skull is very similar to that of other diplodocids. If it was a diplodocid, then it shows that members of this group persisted until the very end of the Cretaceous Period.

Antarctosaurus ('Antarctic reptile') from the Jurassic of Argentina may also represent another imperfectly-known diplodocid. The skull certainly shows all the typical diplodocid features.

Amphicoelias ('paired cavities') from the late Jurassic of the Morrison area of Colorado was first described by Cope in 1887 on the basis of isolated vertebrae. These are considered to be 'diplodocid' by McIntosh and Berman but beyond that are not identifiable.

Above: Denver Museum's fine skeleton of *Diplodocus longus*. This specimen was excavated at Dinosaur National Monument and shipped to Denver in the matrix in 1936. The work of articulating the skeleton was directed by Philip Reinheimer. The overall length of this *Diplodocus* is 75·5ft (23m) and it stands 12·6ft (3·8m) high at the hips. Note the pleurocoels in the vertebrae.

Below: The extraordinarily long neck of *Mamenchisaurus* is evident in this view of the skeleton in Beijing. The neck accounts for 33ft (10m) of the creature's total body length of 72ft (22m).

Another reasonably well known group of sauropod dinosaurs are the camarasaurids, based mainly upon *Camarasaurus* ('chambered reptile'). As we saw in the previous section, *Camarasaurus* which was first described by E. D. Cope in August 1877, was much confused with early discoveries of *Apatosaurus* and *Diplodocus*.

These dinosaurs all come from the same late Jurassic deposits of North America. E. D. Cope described *Camarasaurus supremus* on the basis of an imperfect series of vertebrae which were collected by O. W. Lucas from Canyon City, Colorado in 1877. In December of that year O. C. Marsh described more sauropod material (including an imperfect skull with major parts of a skeleton of an immature sauropod) as *Apatosaurus grandis,* and another partial skeleton of a more mature sauropod which he named *Apatosaurus ajax;* both of these specimens came from Como Bluff, Wyoming. In the following year more material from Como

Bluff was described as *Morosaurus robustus* and *M. impar* by Marsh, while from Colorado Cope described *Caulodon leptoganus* and *C. diversidens.* Another genus *Uintasaurus douglassi* was described on the basis of a partial skeleton recovered from Dinosaur National Monument, Utah, by W. J. Holland, in 1924. When this material was subsequently reviewed by Dr Theodore E. White in 1958, all these species (apart from *Apatosaurus ajax*) were referred to Cope's genus *Camarasaurus.* The relationships of other possible members of the camarasaurid family are again difficult to pin down with any degree of certainty. A table of valid and dubious camarasaurid genera is included at the end of the section concerned with sauropods (pages 96-97).

Camarasaurus Described

In 1925, shortly after Holland's description of '*Uintasaurus*' was published, Charles W. Gilmore

described the beautifully preserved, almost complete skeleton of a young *Camarasaurus* that had been discovered by the Carnegie Museum excavations at Dinosaur National Monument, Utah. The skeleton was preserved almost completely intact, with just a few bones missing or lying slightly out of natural position. It must be supposed that the carcass of this animal was buried very rapidly beneath the shifting sand-bars of a deltaic area at the mouth of a large river; if not, the rotting carcass would surely have been scavenged by carnivores or have simply fallen to pieces and its bones been scattered as its flesh slowly rotted. Around the carcass, between the ribs in particular, was found a thin layer of carbon which probably represented remains of the skin of *Camarasaurus.* Unfortunately no details of the scaly surface of the skin were preserved in this layer.

The skull of this animal is very different in appearance from that of the diplodocids seen earlier. It is much deeper and the snout region

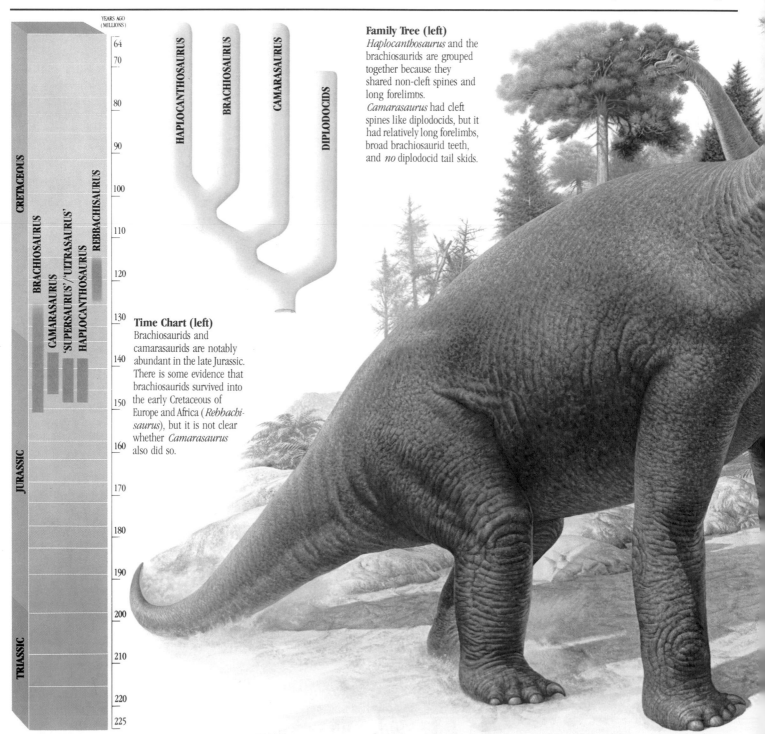

Family Tree (left)
Haplocanthosaurus and the brachiosaurids are grouped together because they shared non-cleft spines and long forelimbs.
Camarasaurus had cleft spines like diplodocids, but it had relatively long forelimbs, broad brachiosaurid teeth, and *no* diplodocid tail skids.

Time Chart (left)
Brachiosaurids and camarasaurids are notably abundant in the late Jurassic. There is some evidence that brachiosaurids survived into the early Cretaceous of Europe and Africa (*Rebbachisaurus*), but it is not clear whether *Camarasaurus* also did so.

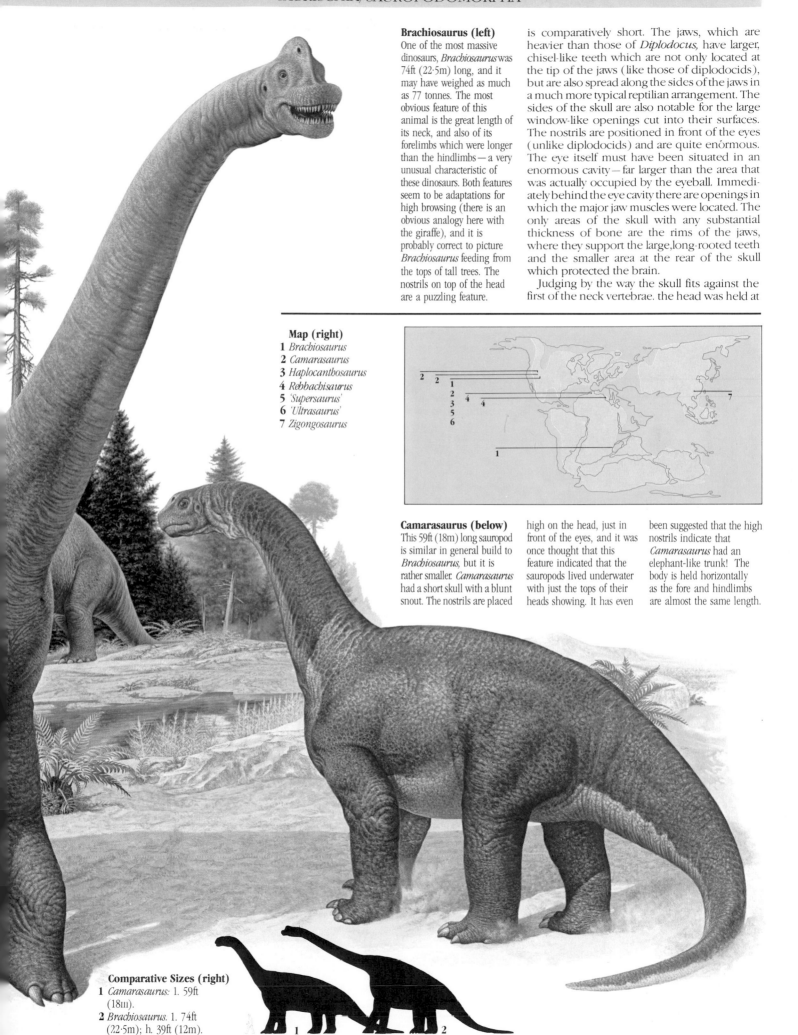

Brachiosaurus (left)
One of the most massive dinosaurs, *Brachiosaurus* was 74ft (22·5m) long, and it may have weighed as much as 77 tonnes. The most obvious feature of this animal is the great length of its neck, and also of its forelimbs which were longer than the hindlimbs—a very unusual characteristic of these dinosaurs. Both features seem to be adaptations for high browsing (there is an obvious analogy here with the giraffe), and it is probably correct to picture *Brachiosaurus* feeding from the tops of tall trees. The nostrils on top of the head are a puzzling feature.

is comparatively short. The jaws, which are heavier than those of *Diplodocus,* have larger, chisel-like teeth which are not only located at the tip of the jaws (like those of diplodocids), but are also spread along the sides of the jaws in a much more typical reptilian arrangement. The sides of the skull are also notable for the large window-like openings cut into their surfaces. The nostrils are positioned in front of the eyes (unlike diplodocids) and are quite enormous. The eye itself must have been situated in an enormous cavity—far larger than the area that was actually occupied by the eyeball. Immediately behind the eye cavity there are openings in which the major jaw muscles were located. The only areas of the skull with any substantial thickness of bone are the rims of the jaws, where they support the large, long-rooted teeth and the smaller area at the rear of the skull which protected the brain.

Judging by the way the skull fits against the first of the neck vertebrae. the head was held at

Map (right)
1 *Brachiosaurus*
2 *Camarasaurus*
3 *Haplocanthosaurus*
4 *Rebbachisaurus*
5 *'Supersaurus'*
6 *'Ultrasaurus'*
7 *Zigongosaurus*

Camarasaurus (below)
This 59ft (18m) long sauropod is similar in general build to *Brachiosaurus,* but it is rather smaller. *Camarasaurus* had a short skull with a blunt snout. The nostrils are placed

high on the head, just in front of the eyes, and it was once thought that this feature indicated that the sauropods lived underwater with just the tops of their heads showing. It has even

been suggested that the high nostrils indicate that *Camarasaurus* had an elephant-like trunk! The body is held horizontally as the fore and hindlimbs are almost the same length.

Comparative Sizes (right)
1 *Camarasaurus:* 1. 59ft (18m).
2 *Brachiosaurus.* 1. 74ft (22·5m); h. 39ft (12m).

an angle to the neck as in diplodocids. The neck is somewhat shorter than that of *Apatosaurus* and *Diplodocus,* consisting of 12 vertebrae which are relatively short and compact. Unlike the diplodocids, the neck ribs are quite long and slender, and overlap one another quite considerably. The spines near the base of the neck, and at the front of the trunk are, as in other sauropods, deeply cleft to accommodate large ligaments which supported the neck. The 12 trunk vertebrae have relatively short, thick and heavily-scarred spines, and as in other sauropods the sides of the vertebrae are deeply excavated to form weight-saving pleurocoels. Unlike the neck ribs, those of the trunk are exceptionally long and stout, enclosing an enormous space for the chest and belly.

Five large back vertebrae are welded together in the hip region to support the massive pelvic bones which carry much of the weight of the animal. The tail is quite short compared with that of the diplodocids; there seem to have

been 53 tail bones in the complete tail of the very well-preserved skeleton of *Camarasaurus* as distinct from the 82 of *Apatosaurus* and 73 of *Diplodocus.* The tail is also appreciably shorter because it lacks the thin whip-lash end so characteristic of the diplodocids.

The forelimb and hindlimb resemble those of other sauropods remarkably closely; the forelimb possessed one claw on its inner toe, while the hind foot bore claws on its three inner toes. One slightly unusual feature of *Camara-*

saurus' limbs is their relative porportions. Whereas in diplodocids the humerus (upper foreleg bone) is only ⅔ the length of the femur (thigh bone),in *Camarasaurus* the humerus is very nearly equal to the femur in length (⅘ actually!). In the first reconstruction of *Camarasaurus* by H. F. Osborn and C.C. Mook in 1921, this observation so strongly affected their judgement that they restored the skeleton with shoulders that were higher than the hips. They had in fact exaggerated the natural pose of the animal by altering the position of the shoulder girdle. In 1925 Gilmore was able to correct Osborn and Mook's first attempt on the basis of the more-or-less complete Carnegie Museum skeleton of *Camarasaurus.* But even so the back of the animal has to be constructed practically horizontally, rather than sloping down toward the shoulders as is the case in diplodocids. This *trend* towards greater length of the forelimbs in some sauropods is taken to the extreme in brachiosaurids.

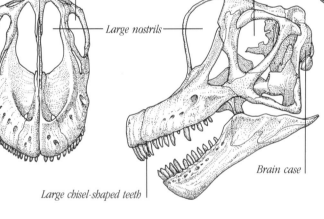

Brachiosaurus Skeleton (right)
This reconstruction of *Brachiosaurus* was made by Werner Janensch from the material collected at Tendaguru (1908-1912). A complete skeleton is mounted in the Museum of Natural History, Berlin. The similarity to a giraffe is quite striking with the long front legs lifting the shoulders above the hips and the neck raising the head to over 42ft (13m) in the original specimen. The spines on the neck are heavily scarred for the attachment of muscles to raise and hold the neck in position. The rib cage is quite narrow and deep, as in an elephant, and the feet are similarly narrow and compact. Unlike most sauropods, the tail is relatively short.

Brachiosaurus Rib

Attachment to vertebra · Pneumatic opening

Attachment to vertebra

Rib shaft

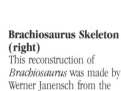

Nostril cavity · *Eye socket*

Muscle attachment areas

Chisel-like teeth

Camarasaurus Skull (above)
The skull of *Camarasaurus* is compact compared with that of diplodocids. The jaws are stout and support a closely packed array of chisel-like teeth. Above the level of the jaws the skull is high and spaciously designed. The large opening at the front of the skull is for extremely large nostrils. Immediately behind the nostril is the eye socket.

Brachiosaurus Skull (right)
In profile, this skull shows certain similarities to that of *Camarasaurus.* The jaws are stout and support large chisel-shaped teeth. The signs of heavy wear on these teeth suggest that these animals preferred abrasive plants. The unusual size of the nostrils may indicate either a powerful sense of smell, a resonating device or a cooling surface for the blood.

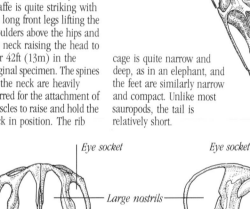

Eye socket · *Eye socket*

Large nostrils

Brain case

Large chisel-shaped teeth

Camarasaurus Skeleton (right)
The skeletal reconstruction seen here is based on the work of Charles Gilmore. The proportions of the skeleton are notably different from the diplodocids. The skull is relatively large and deep, and is supported on a short neck which was evidently quite flexible. The ribs of the neck are long and slender and no doubt provided for the attachment of large muscles. The short neck means that the range of plants available to *Camarasaurus* must have been limited to the lower branches of trees and plants closer to ground level. As reconstructed here the shoulder region is at the

same height as the hips and this is a reflection of the greater length of the forelimbs of *Camarasaurus.* In recent years it has been proposed that many sauropods were able to rear up on their hindlimbs in order to reach higher foliage. The large forelimbs and relatively short tail makes it seem unlikely that *Camarasaurus* could have done this.

Brachiosaurus

Brachiosaurus ('arm reptile') takes its name from the prodigious length of its arms (forelegs) when compared with its hindlimbs. *Brachiosaurus* was first described by Elmer S. Riggs on the basis of a very incomplete skeleton that was discovered in 1900 at the Grand River Valley, Western Colorado. The original material,which was collected by the Field Museum of Chicago, consisted of various parts of the vertebral column, the pelvis, ribs,shoulder girdle and, most importantly from the point of view of diagnosis, the humerus and femur. Judging by the way the remains were preserved on site, it appeared that the original carcass of the animal probably settled into the sediment of a lake or river system in this area, but was disturbed somewhat later, perhaps by flood water, so that various parts of it were washed away as the carcass disintegrated, and so lost to us for ever.

The distinctive features of the bones of this large sauropod dinosaur were several. The vertebrae were large with the big pleurocoel cavities typical of all sauropod skeletons. Indeed these cavities were in some cases so large that the wall of bone down the middle of the vertebrae was practically paper thin, and was even broken through in some places. A striking feature of these vertebrae compared with those of most other sauropods is the absence of forked spines to accommodate a large neck ligament. The vertebrae also show rather complicated joints at the foot of the neural spines which served greatly to strengthen the joint between individual back vertebrae, and also provided them with an unexpected degree of flexibility. The pelvis is supported by five vertebrae, as in other sauropods. Unusually two tail bones,apparently coming from close to the hips, did not show any sign of pleurocoels. The dimensions of the humerus (80in, 204cm) and the femur (79·5in, 203cm) are, however,

the most unusual among sauropods, in which the femur is always longer than the humerus, other than in this case. In fact so unusual was this feature that Riggs at first identified the humerus as a 'femur'. It was only after careful preparation and repair back in the laboratory that the true identity of these enormous bones emerged.

On the basis of this imperfect skeleton Riggs speculated upon the biology and habits of *Brachiosaurus* in an article in 1904. In this, he proposed that contrary to popular opinion of the time,the gigantic sauropods were probably not amphibious marsh dwellers, but were fully terrestrial animals comparable in most respects with animals such as the elephants of today. He based his argument upon the shape of the limbs and feet of these animals, rather narrow and deep chest, and the peculiar excavations and complexities of the vertebrae. The legs of large amphibious creatures such as hippos are relatively short and their feet are broad, the chest is barrel-shaped and their vertebrae

---

Brachiosaurus Rib (left) and Sectioned Vertebrae (right)

Brachiosaurus has many weight-saving features. The ribs in the chest region have a pneumatic opening near the top which leads to an air passage down the shaft of the rib. The cross section through a neck vertebra (top right) reveals the remarkable system of air spaces, while that of the back vertebra shows the extensive pleurocoels separated by a very thin sheet of bone (bony areas shown in red). The vertebra closely resembles an I-section girder.

Neck Vertebra (cross section)

Bone | Bone cavity

Back Vertebra (cross section)

Bone | Pleurocoel

Neck Vertebra

Spine

Back Vertebra

Cross section taken here

Muscle scars

Rib

Pleurocoel

Brachiosaurus Vertebrae (left)

The neck vertebrae are long, narrow, elongated structures with a low spine on which muscles attached. The front end of the neck vertebra has a rounded surface that forms a strong and flexible joint against the cup-shaped depression on the rear of the vertebra in front of it. The back vertebrae are taller and squatter to withstand supporting the weight of this animal. The tall spine is scarred for the attachment of muscles; the large 'wings' projecting from its foot support the ends of the ribs. The red lines show where the cross sections are taken.

Brachiosaurus Hand (from above)

5
4
3
2
1

Metacarpal 2

Metacarpal 3

Metacarpal 4

Metacarpal 1

First claw

Block-like bones

Brachiosaurus Hand (left)

This hand is remarkably specialised with very long metacarpals which are clustered closely together as can be seen in the top drawing. The toes (so far as they are known) have just one small bone on the end of each metacarpal except for the 1st toe which bears a small claw.

Camarasaurus Foot (below)

Camarasaurus' right foot has five short toes which are widely splayed to form a broad weight-bearing arrangement. The inner toe is larger and possesses a narrow curved claw which may have been used for self-defence. The foot of *Brachiosaurus* is only known from isolated bones.

Ankle bone

Large first claw

Digit 5

Digit 4

Digit 3

Digit 2

---

show none of the complexity seen in the giant sauropods. Riggs reasoned from these observations that sauropods were terrestrial rather than amphibious creatures. He even proposed that creatures such as *Diplodocus* and *Apatosaurus* were capable of rearing up on their hind legs, perhaps to browse on high foliage.

Bearing these characters in mind, Riggs suggested that *Brachiosaurus* was a peculiarly specialised sauropod with exceptionally long front legs, a strong yet flexible back and (he *guessed*) a relatively short tail. Riggs' conclusions have proved to be extremely far-sighted and accurate. Sadly, however, they were ignored by the majority of palaeontologists when they were first published, and it was not until the early 1970s that Riggs' comments were strongly supported by Robert T. Bakker (see later).

Tendaguru and Brachiosaurus

Tendaguru is 40 miles (64km) inland from the east coast of Africa in Tanzania, which in 1907 was known as German East Africa. A series of very fortunate circumstances resulted in a very dramatic dinosaur discovery being made there — the African equivalent of Como Bluff or Dinosaur National Monument in the USA.

As recounted by Professor Edwin Colbert, in 1907 Herr W. B. Sattler, an engineering geologist prospecting for minerals in this largely uncharted part of the world, discovered weathered fragments of enormous fossil bones at Tendaguru. He reported these finds to the company he worked for. Very fortunately Professor Eberhard Fraas from Stuttgart, a noted authority on fossil reptiles, was in the colony at this time and was requested to visit the new site. Fraas established that the locality was incredibly rich in fossil vertebrates. He was able to collect several very fine fossil specimens and returned with them to Germany. These remains fired the interest of Dr W. Branca, then director of the Berlin Museum of Natural History, who determined to raise an expedition to collect the fossils from Tendaguru. In due course Drs Werner Janensch and Edwin Hennig of the Berlin Museum were put in charge of it.

The expedition, which lasted from 1908-1912, needed remarkable energy and co-ordination on the part of all participants and proved to be extremely expensive, both in terms of wages for the workers and in the necessary food and supplies. During the four year period over 250 tonnes of fossil bone were removed from the 4·5 square mile site at Tendaguru and carried on the heads and backs of native porters to the coastal port of Lindi for shipment to Berlin. This was obviously a colossal enterprise, but it was highly successful and it was matched by the dedication of the scientists in Berlin who put an enormous amount of effort into the preparation and study of the fossils.

The immense energy and skill that went into the Tendaguru Expedition was certainly rewarded handsomely. Among dinosaurian remains collected from Tendaguru which included *Kentrosaurus, Elaphrosaurus, Dicraeosaurus,* there was the skeleton of *Brachiosaurus.* Erected in the Natural History Museum (now in East Berlin) this must be the most impressive skeleton of any dinosaur in the world; it stands nearly 39ft (12m) tall, and the body is some 74ft (22·5m) long.

As Rigg surmised, *Brachiosaurus* is indeed an unusual sauropod. Its pose is totally unlike that of other sauropods because its back slopes upward from the hips to the shoulders, the forelimbs being considerably longer than the hindlimbs. The tail is quite short by the

standard of diplodocid sauropods; and while the back vertebrae are massive and also deeply excavated by pleurocoels, the spines near the base of the neck and in the neck itself are not cleft to accommodate a large ligament. The neck vertebrae, of which there are 12 (as in *Camarasaurus*), are notably elongated; their sides are deeply excavated, the spines are relatively low and heavily scarred for muscle attachment, and the ribs are fused firmly to their sides.

The limbs and girdles which support this immense frame are stout and pillar-like. The forelimb ends in a rather narrow elephant-like five-toed foot which bears a single claw on its inner toe. The hindlimb is very similar to that of other sauropods, with the three inner toes of the foot bearing enlarged claws.

The head is similar in general shape and proportions to that of *Camarasaurus.* The jaws are quite sturdy and are lined with large, chisel-shaped teeth. Above the jaws the snout is quite flat and then rises in front of the eye region into enormously enlarged nostrils. Large recesses, which were apparently associated with the nostrils, extend forward on to the roof of the snout. There are also large cavities both in front and behind the eye, and the braincase is restricted to a relatively small area at the back of the skull.

Other Brachiosaurids

In addition to the impressive remains of *Brachiosaurus* from North America and Africa, several other *Brachiosaurus*-like sauropods are known which constitute the brachiosaurid family.

Haplocanthosaurus ('single spined reptile') is based on two partial skeletons described by J. B. Hatcher in 1903. The remains were excavated from the Canyon City site in Colorado that was first exploited by M. P. Felch and O. C. Marsh in the 1870s. Although far from complete, the remains of the vertebrae are similar to those of *Brachiosaurus* and may perhaps justify placing this genus with other brachiosaurids.

'Supersaurus', a fragmentary skeleton discovered in 1972 by Jim Jensen in western Colorado, seems to have been even larger than *Brachiosaurus.* Estimates based on comparisons between the neck vertebrae and shoulder bones of these two dinosaurs suggest that *'Supersaurus'* may have stood 54ft (16·5m) tall with a body length of anywhere between 82-98ft (25-30m)! The name *'Supersaurus'* is used in quotation marks because it has not yet been scientifically described and named.

'Ultrasaurus' was found in 1979 in the same general area of Colorado as *'Supersaurus'* again by Jim Jensen, and it proved to be an even larger brachiosaurid. Still undescribed, the remains of this creature are rumoured to indicate an animal in excess of 98ft (30m) in length. Extrapolating from *Brachiosaurus,* which is estimated to have weighed anything up to 70 tonnes, *'Ultrasaurus'* may have tipped the scales at a staggering 130 tonnes.

Rebbachisaurus ('Rebbachi reptile') from Morocco and Tunisia and *Zigongosaurus* ('Zigong reptile') from Sichuan have also been referred to as brachiosaurids by some workers. Other brachiosaurid attributions are more dubious. *Astrodon* ('star tooth') based on spoon-shaped camarasaurid or brachiosaurid-type teeth, has been reported from Europe and North America over the past century but cannot be clearly allied to any particular group in isolation. *Pleurocoelus* ('side cavity'), based on cavernous vertebrae or isolated teeth, is again a

The Underwater Dinosaur? (above)
For some years it was thought that *Brachiosaurus* might have favoured an aquatic way of life, the nostrils on the top of its head acting as a snorkel. Recent analysis, however, indicates that *Brachiosaurus'* lungs would not have survived the water pressure that they would have experienced if this had been the case.

Left: *Camarasaurus lentus* in the Carnegie Museum of Natural History, Pittsburgh, Pennsylvania. The skeleton is in the position in which it was found.

practically meaningless genus. *Pelorosaurus* ('monster reptile'), based on a moderately large humerus from the Weald of Southern England, must be a very dubious brachiosaurid in the absence of any associated skeleton. Similarly, a large excavated vertebra from southern England referred to as *Ornithopsis* ('bird like'), originally likened to the vertebrae of birds and of flying reptiles such as pterosaurs, and similar vertebrae from Madagascar referred to as *'Bothriospondylus'* ('excavated vertebra') must both be considered dubious genera based on poor material.

Probable Life-Style

Brachiosaurus' way of life has been the subject of much debate in recent years, as a result of which the long-forgotten views of Elmer Riggs have been unwittingly resurrected. For much of this century sauropods were thought to have been gigantic amphibious creatures that wallowed in swampy habitats. Several observations contributed to this view. Firstly, animals of this size and weight were not thought able to support themselves on land. Consequently they simply had to live in water where their bodies would have been buoyed up by displacement. Secondly, the position on the nostrils was widely interpreted as an adaptation for an aquatic way of life, allowing *Brachiosaurus* to breathe while almost completely submerged. Thirdly, their teeth were allegedly weak and only capable of cutting soft water plants.

Present-day opinions, however, all favour a land-living life-style for sauropods. This change of view was precipitated in 1971 by the publication of Robert T. Bakker's article which reassessed the evidence advanced in support of the amphibious way of life. Bakker showed that the pillar-like legs and relatively narrow feet, the deep, narrow rib cage, and the specially strengthened back were all features that were only consistent with land-living creatures. He argued that the long neck enabled these creatures to browse on high foliage rather like giraffes. Contrary to common belief, the teeth of *Camarasaurus* and *Brachiosaurus* do show evidence of having been quite heavily abraded, while many land animals have nostrils positioned near the top of the head (some aquatic ones do not for that matter!).

Further support for the terrestrial sauropod interpretation can be derived from the observation made by Professor Kenneth Kermack (London) in 1951 that if sauropods had lived in water they would have been unable to breathe! The water pressure at such depths, 33-39ft (10-12m) in the case of *Brachiosaurus*, would have collapsed its lungs, while the enormously high blood pressure would have caused heart failure. The deep-water snorkelling *Brachiosaurus*, so convincingly depicted by artists like Zdenek Burian and others, was thus utterly impossible.

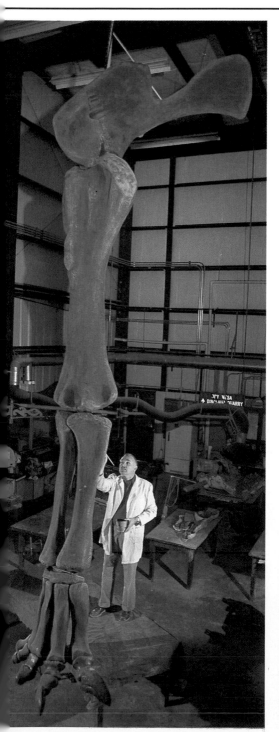

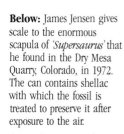

Left: James Jensen working on the front leg of the dinosaur popularly known as 'Ultrasaurus'. In life this extraordinary creature may have been more than 98ft (30m) long, almost a third larger even than *Brachiosaurus*!

Below: This skeleton of *Brachiosaurus* in the Humboldt Museum, Berlin, is about 39ft (12m) tall. Discovered at Tendaguru in Tanzania, it is the largest mounted dinosaur skeleton in the world. Note the length of the forelimbs.

Below: James Jensen gives scale to the enormous scapula of 'Supersaurus' that he found in the Dry Mesa Quarry, Colorado, in 1972. The can contains shellac with which the fossil is treated to preserve it after exposure to the air.

Above: The skull of a *Camarasaurus* being excavated by Tobe Wilkins, a preparator at the Dinosaur National Monument in Utah. This picture shows particularly well the long chisel-like teeth lining *Camarasaurus'* jaws.

In addition to the reasonably well represented and distinctive sauropods such as the diplodocids, camarasaurids and brachiosaurids described earlier, a large number of less well-known sauropods are known, whose fossil remains have been reported from practically every continent. Some of these will be discussed below, while many others are listed on page 97 as either 'valid' or 'dubious' genera, depending on how well-preserved the material is. In addition, several factors relating to the general biology or way of life of sauropods will be discussed.

Opisthocoelicaudia ('posterior cavity tail') is a recently described sauropod from Mongolia. The incomplete skeleton of *Opisthocoelicaudia* was discovered in 1965 during a Polish-Mongolian Expedition to the Gobi Desert. The carcass of the animal had evidently been buried before it had time to disintegrate; however neither the head nor the neck was recovered from the site. Magdalena Borsuk-Bialynicka,

Vulcanodon (below)

This restoration shows what we think the sauropods of the early Jurassic looked like; this is *Vulcanodon,* but *Barapasaurus* probably looked very similar. The animal is shown with a bulky body and pillar-like legs in accordance with the

information that we have on these dinosaurs. In neither case is a skull known and so the head illustrated is of necessity somewhat conjectural. Teeth found near *Vulcanodon's* remains are those of a carnivore, but they probably belonged to a predator not *Vulcanodon.*

who described the skeleton in 1977, suggested that the carcass may have been attacked by carrion feeders (perhaps tyrannosaurids since *Opisthocoelicaudia* comes from rocks of late Cretaceous age). Some of the fossilised bones (femur and pelvis) apparently show some evidence of gnawing, so this may explain the absence of both the head and neck!

The skeleton of *Opisthocoelicaudia* is rather like that of most non-brachiosaurid sauropods in its general shape and proportions. The back vertebrae have well-developed pleurocoels and the ones near the neck have deeply-cleft spines to accommodate a large neck ligament (ligamentum nuchae). In addition, the individual spines of more posterior vertebrae have swollen and roughened sides and tops which indicate the areas of attachment of other powerful ligaments and muscles. In their general shape and proportions the back vertebrae most resemble those of *Camarasaurus.* Six vertebrae are fused together to form a sacrum for

Family Tree (below)

This cladogram must be approached with caution, as it is very difficult to sort out the relations of this group of poorly known sauropods. *Barapasaurus* and

Vulcanodon are separated from the others as they are distinct geologically and to some extent anatomically. *Opisthocoelicaudia* occupies its own branch because of its unusual tail vertebrae.

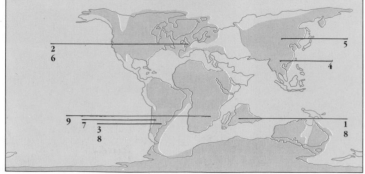

Time Chart (left)

Barapasaurus and *Vulcanodon* date from the earliest Jurassic and no doubt lived alongside some of the later prosauropods. Many and varied sauropods are known, albeit imperfectly, in the late Jurassic and again a considerable number are known in the Cretaceous Period. *Saltasaurus* and *Opisthocoelicaudia* are from the late Cretaceous.

Map (left)

1 *Barapasaurus*
2 *Cetiosauriscus*
3 *Laplatasaurus*
4 *Omeisaurus*
5 *Opisthocoelicaudia*
6 *Ornithopsis*
7 *Saltasaurus*
8 *Titanosaurus*
9 *Vulcanodon*

attachment of the pelvis. Beyond this area, the tail as preserved consists of 34 vertebrae. These bear chevrons which are similar to those of *Camarasaurus* rather than the skid-like chevrons characteristic of diplodocids. The curious feature of the tail vertebrae, which is responsible for the tongue-twisting name of this creature, is the fact that the front end of each has a large hemispherical dome which fits into a deep socket on the rear of the preceding vertebra. The joints between the vertebrae are, as a consequence, remarkably strong. By contrast, the joints between the tail bones of most sauropods are much more simple, having practically flat surfaces. Borsuk-Bialynicka also noted that the spines of the tail vertebrae were exceptionally swollen and roughened for the attachment of powerful muscles and ligaments equivalent to those noted in the back. The forelimbs and hindlimbs are characteristically stout and pillar-like to carry the great weight of these creatures. The number of clawed toes on

the feet of this dinosaur are unknown at present. In terms of limb proportions, a factor that Jack McIntosh and David Berman consider of importance in at least some sauropods, the humerus is reported to be about three-quarters of the length of the femur. This falls mid-way between typical diplodocid and typical camarasaurid limb proportions.

Biology and Probable Habits

The well-preserved nature of the limb and girdle bones of *Opisthocoelicaudia* allowed Borsuk-Bialynicka to attempt muscular restorations of both fore and hindlimbs. This showed that, unusually, there was little or no evidence for the massive and powerful muscles which run along the sides of the tail and insert upon the hindlimb (caudi-femoralis muscle). This is a muscle which almost always provides the main source of power for the stride in dinosaurs and most other reptiles. In *Opistho-*

Opisthocoelicaudia (above)
In its general body proportions *Opisthocoelicaudia* resembles *Camarasaurus* but it does have a number of peculiarities. The heavy pillar-like legs support a bulky body; the tail is held out straight and the shoulders are quite high. Unfortunately the head and neck are unknown; here we have speculatively given it a *Camarasaurus*-type, but it may have had a more slender-snouted *Nemegtosaurus*-type head. Until more material is found, this must remain a matter of conjecture.

Comparative Sizes (left)
1 *Opisthocoelicaudia*: 1. 39ft (12m)
2 *Saltasaurus*: 1. 39ft (12m).
3 *Vulcanodon*: 1. 21ft (6·5m)

Saltasaurus (above)
Saltasaurus, quite a recent discovery, is of great interest because it shows that some sauropods bore bony armour. Large round plates of bone are scattered across the hide and between them lie masses of small nodules. As shown the tail was flexible and could have supported the body when *Saltasaurus* reared on its back legs in its efforts to obtain food.

coelicaudia, however, the posterior portion of the ilium (pelvic bone) in notably enlarged and roughened as if for the attachment of unusually powerful muscles; perhaps these were the main propulsive muscles instead? Quite why *Opisthocoelicaudia* should have had such an unusual arrangement of limb muscles is not immediately obvious.

The structure of the back vertebrae, particularly those close to the neck, led Borsuk-Bialynicka to suggest that the neck was not only flexible but that the vertebrae were relatively short, as they are in the neck of *Camarasaurus*. The evidence also pointed towards the back being held in an essentially horizontal position, or with perhaps a very slight downward slope from the shoulders to the hips.

The tail, which is shorter even than that of *Camarasaurus*, appears to have created the greatest problems of interpretation. Firstly, the tail bones when articulated naturally tend to rise slightly passing backwards from the hips,

instead of falling toward the ground as in other sauropods. Secondly, the ball-and-socket joint between each tail vertebra is rare. Examples of some living reptiles with tail vertebrae of this type include a variety of fresh-water turtles; some of these are reported to use their tails as anchors to prevent themselves from being carried away in fast-flowing streams. Such a use in the case of *Opisthocoelicaudia* is plainly absurd. Other uses of this type of tail include its apparent function as a prop when on land. Borsuk-Bialynicka favoured this latter notion. The tail and rear legs were envisaged as a tripod arrangement which would allow these animals to rear up and reach higher branches for browsing. In fact she drew a parallel between *Opisthocoelicaudia* and the giant extinct ground-sloths (such as *Megatherium*) of South America. The latter seem to have been shuffling high browsers, which spent their time permanently balanced on their hind legs and tail, leaving their forelimbs free to grasp

vegetation. A *permanent* tripodal posture was not suggested for *Opisthocoelicaudia*, merely that this was perhaps a favoured position for feeding.

Sauropod Relations

Apart from the peculiarities in the tail, the greatest resemblance seems to lie with the *Camarasaurus*-like sauropods, and this possibility underlies the placing of it in the camarasaurid section of the table on page 97. If this is so, then it must be a very late representative of this predominantly late Jurassic group. However, the evidence so far is inconclusive, and so, while advancing this hypothesis, it seems sensible to adopt a cautious approach, and include the colour and skeletal restorations of *Opisthocoelicaudia* in this section of miscellaneous sauropods.

One outside possibility is that this skeleton belongs to the diplodocid sauropod *Nemegto-*

Sauropod Armour (below)

Recent work in Argentina has resulted in the discovery that some sauropods had bony armour plating. The first plates to be described are those of *Saltasaurus* and *Laplatasaurus*, and some are shown below. One type of plate with a low mid-line ridge has been referred to *Laplatasaurus*; the others are regarded as typical of *Saltasaurus*. These are variable in size and shape ranging from large, ridged plates (below middle) to the sheets of densely-packed, tiny nodular bones illustrated below right.

Omeisaurus Skull (right)

This skull is unusual when compared with those of other sauropods. It is wedge-shaped in side view and has typically sauropod struts of bone dividing large skull spaces. However, the nostrils are much nearer the front of the snout than in other sauropods. Though appearing to be toothless, there are sockets for at least 32 teeth in the upper jaw and 28-34 in the lower. The drawing is based on one included in Dong Zhiming's 1983 review of dinosaurs of south-central China.

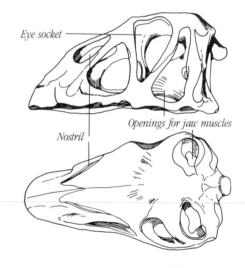

Eye socket

Nostril

Openings for jaw muscles

Laplatasaurus

Saltasaurus

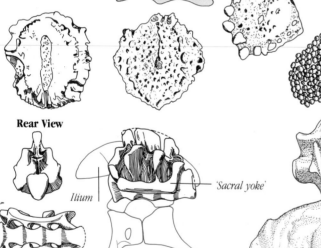

Rear View

Ilium

'Sacral yoke'

Underside View

Side View

Barapasaurus Sacrum and Pelvis (above)

There are four vertebrae in the sacrum, all firmly fused together. On either side, the ribs are short, stout and welded together to form a sacral yoke. This attached firmly to the inner surface of the ilium.

Ornithopsis Vertebra (below)

Seen here in three views (rear, side and front), this vertebra is very similar to that of *Brachiosaurus*, and may indicate a relationship. The large weight-saving pleurocoels are particularly noticeable.

Pleurocoel

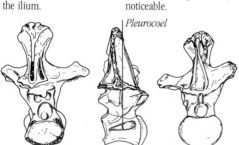

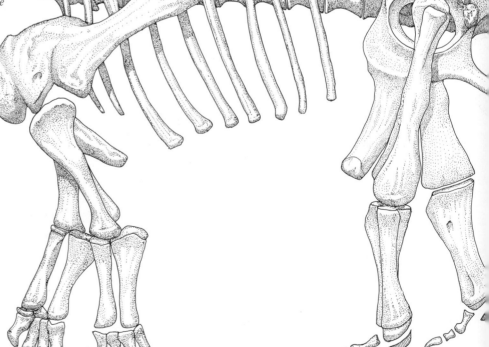

saurus. Both *Nemegtosaurus* and *Opisthocoelicaudia* are found in the same geological formation of the late Cretaceous. Since *Nemegtosaurus* is known only from a skull and *Opisthocoelicaudia* is known only from a headless skeleton, the temptation to place the head with the skeleton is great. However, I feel that the story of the head of *Apatosaurus* provides a salutary warning against taking anatomical short-cuts such as this. The fact that *Brachiosaurus, Camarasaurus, Diplodocus, Apatosaurus, Barosaurus* etc are all approximate contemporaries in the late Jurassic surely indicates that several distinct types of sauropod may well have lived together in the late Cretaceous.

Remains of an unusual sauropod *Saltasaurus* ('reptile from Salta Province') were first reported by José Bonaparte and Jaime Powell in 1980. They come from late Cretaceous rocks in north western Argentina and although incomplete provide unexpected evidence

concerning the appearance of some sauropods. The remains of *Saltasaurus* appear to derive from several individuals, rather than an isolated skeleton. The general proportions and construction of the main skeletal elements (backbone and limbs) are typically sauropod-like. Points worthy of mention include spines in the neck and back region which are not cleft, tail vertebrae which are rather stout and have a reversed ball-and-socket arrangement, and chevrons which are not skid-like. However, of greatest interest was the discovery of two types of bony armour associated with these remains: fairly large, oval plates which were perhaps rather widely scattered in the skin; and a dense layer of smaller round or angular bony studs which were apparently widely spread across the back and sides of the animal.

This first clear record of armour-plating in sauropods may well prove to be an important one because it could lead to the re-identification of several supposed ankylosaur specimens

elsewhere in the world. For example, *Titanosaurus* ('Titan reptile'), another sauropod from Argentina first described in 1893, was later redescribed in 1929 along with some fragments of bony armour found in the same area; these latter were referred to as an ankylosaur *Loricosaurus*. The supposed ankylosaur remains almost certainly belong to the sauropod *Titanosaurus*. There are also considerable similarities between *Titanosaurus* and *Saltasaurus*, although Bonaparte and Powell were not prepared to say that *Saltasaurus* and *Titanosaurus* belong to the same genus.

Described in 1972 by Mike Raath (Zimbabwe), *Vulcanodon* ('Volcano tooth') was found in early Jurassic rocks in Zimbabwe. It is of some importance because it may be one of the earliest sauropods to have been discovered to date. Unfortunately the skeleton, which was completely redescribed by Mike Cooper (Zimbabwe) in 1984, is far from complete. Cooper was able to demonstrate that *Vulcano-*

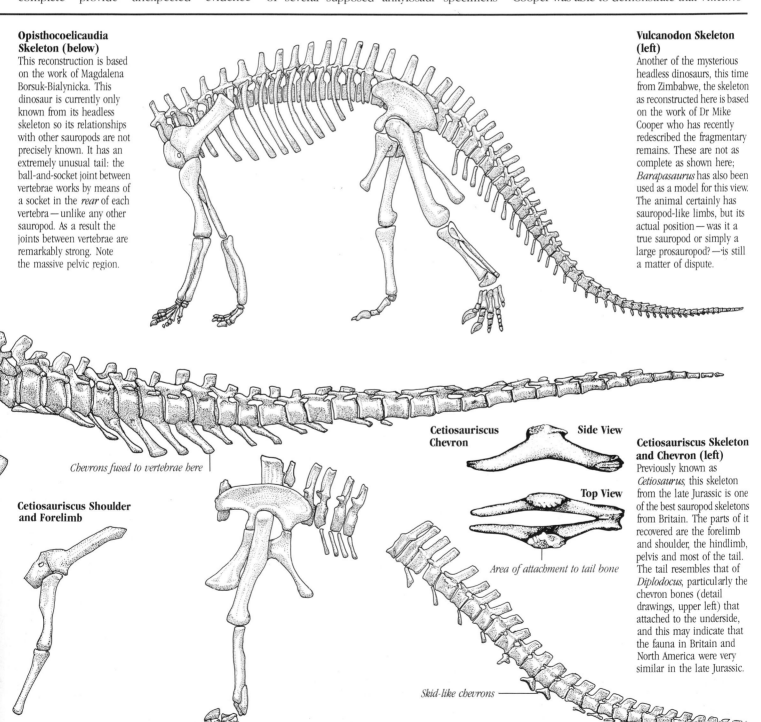

Opisthocoelicaudia Skeleton (below)
This reconstruction is based on the work of Magdalena Borsuk-Bialynicka. This dinosaur is currently only known from its headless skeleton so its relationships with other sauropods are not precisely known. It has an extremely unusual tail: the ball-and-socket joint between vertebrae works by means of a socket in the *rear* of each vertebra — unlike any other sauropod. As a result the joints between vertebrae are remarkably strong. Note the massive pelvic region.

Vulcanodon Skeleton (left)
Another of the mysterious headless dinosaurs, this time from Zimbabwe, the skeleton as reconstructed here is based on the work of Dr Mike Cooper who has recently redescribed the fragmentary remains. These are not as complete as shown here; *Barapasaurus* has also been used as a model for this view. The animal certainly has sauropod-like limbs, but its actual position — was it a true sauropod or simply a large prosauropod? — is still a matter of dispute.

Chevrons fused to vertebrae here

Cetiosauriscus Shoulder and Forelimb

Cetiosauriscus Chevron   Side View

Top View

Area of attachment to tail bone

Cetiosauriscus Skeleton and Chevron (left)
Previously known as *Cetiosaurus*, this skeleton from the late Jurassic is one of the best sauropod skeletons from Britain. The parts of it recovered are the forelimb and shoulder, the hindlimb, pelvis and most of the tail. The tail resembles that of *Diplodocus*, particularly the chevron bones (detail drawings, upper left) that attached to the underside, and this may indicate that the fauna in Britain and North America were very similar in the late Jurassic.

Skid-like chevrons

don was a very large, quadrupedal saurischian dinosaur. It shows several prosauropod features, particularly in the hips, but he claimed that in other ways (particularly in subtle changes in the structure of the vertebrae), *Vulcanodon* was very much what might be expected of an early sauropod. Obviously Cooper's arguments are based primarily on shades of opinion rather than clear and unambiguous fact. Yet again, better preserved material may help to clear up the status of *Vulcanodon*.

Barapasaurus ('big reptile') is another sauropod from the early Jurassic, but this time of India. The remains of *Barapasaurus* which were apparently very abundant (300 fossils were recovered in 1961) indicated the presence of a *Diplodocus*-sized sauropod. At present *Barapasaurus* is not completely described by Dr S. L. Jain and colleagues (Calcutta), but from preliminary reports it would appear that it had typical sauropod limbs and girdles; and although cavernous excavations in the sides of the neck and back vertebrae are not developed fully, there are depressions in these areas indicating the beginnings of pleurocoels.

Unfortunately no skull material is known so far. Serrated-edge theropod-like teeth have been reported near the remains of both *Barapasaurus* and *Vulcanodon,* but rather than supposing that these teeth came from these dinosaurs, current opinion considers that they belonged to predatory dinosaurs that were feasting upon these remains.

Possible Life-Style

In the 1830s when the first sauropod bones were collected in Oxfordshire and came into the possession of Dean William Buckland at Oxford University, they were identified as whale bones by Georges Cuvier. At the time Cuvier was the world's leading comparative anatomist and his views were widely respected. However, by the early 1840s Richard Owen had noticed that these remains, rather than being of whales (which are mammals), were more likely to have been those of whale-like reptiles—perhaps gigantic whale-sized crocodiles. He therefore coined the name *Cetiosaurus* ('whale-reptile') for these remains. A few years later (1848) more limb bones of *Cetiosaurus* were discovered; these looked remarkably like those of land-living dinosaurs that Owen had described, rather than whale-like reptiles. Finally in 1869 a fairly complete skeleton was discovered in the same area of Oxfordshire by Professor John Phillips (Buckland's successor); these showed clear dinosaur affinities. Despite the weight of this evidence, Owen was very reluctant to abandon the aquatic life-style that he proposed for his cetiosaurs. One of the main reasons for this was the absence of a well-preserved hip region in this creature (one of Owen's key dinosaur characteristics). It was T. H. Huxley who finally asserted that *Cetiosaurus* was a dinosaur in 1869.

Despite the long-held belief that sauropods were amphibious creatures, the majority of palaeontologists now support the idea that they were primarily terrestrial creatures similar to the elephants of today. Riggs and Bakker have provided powerful arguments in favour of this view based on the structure of the limbs and rib cage. In addition sauropods display several other structural characteristics of note.

(i) Pneumatic ducts and cavities. The large and extensive pleurocoels in the neck and back vertebrae have been mentioned previously, and such features undoubtedly served to lighten the skeleton as far as possible. This is clearly an adaptation associated with living on land where bodily support under the effects of gravity are critical in large animals. Large aquatic animals (e.g. whales) have vertebrae equally as large as sauropods but these show no developments of pleurocoels or comparable weight-saving devices because their body weight is buoyed up by displacement. The particularly large sauropods such as *Brachiosaurus* even go so far as to develop pneumatic openings into the ribs in order to save weight. It seems most likely that these so-called pneumatic spaces or openings were air-filled. Living birds (and extinct pterosaurs) which also need to save weight in their bodies in order to fly efficiently, have similar openings and excavations in their vertebrae and limb bones. These we know are filled with air by connections from their complicated lung/air-sac system; it seems likely that sauropods had a similar type of arrangement.

(ii) Energy-saving ligaments. Another fairly common feature among non-brachiosaurid sauropods is the development of cleft spines in the neck and back vertebrae. The cleft spines provide a deep trough in which probably lay a thick, rope-like ligament, roughly equivalent to the ligamentum nuchae of quadrupedal mammals, such as the horse. In horses this powerful ligament runs from the spines in the shoulder region along the back of the neck to insert on the rear edge of the skull. It effortlessly holds the head in its normal raised position. By this means the horse and many relatively heavy-headed quadrupeds save a great deal of muscular energy expenditure that would otherwise have to be used merely to hold the head in its normal position. In the case of sauropods it is not the head that is heavy, but rather the inordinately long neck. The massive neck ligament served therefore to hold the long, heavy neck of sauropods clear of the ground effortlessly. The neck ligament was also very probably connected via the tops of the back and hip spines to the tail vertebrae so that the neck and tail vertebrae tended to counterbalance one another. Such a system whereby the tail and neck were suspended against one another may have held the tail as well as the neck clear of the ground while on land, and may account for the rarity of tail-drag markings associated with sauropod footprint trackways.

Having gone to some lengths to 'prove' that sauropods were indeed terrestrial creatures, the reader must not suppose that I exclude sauropods from water altogether: just as elephants today wallow, so may have sauropods in the Mesozoic. Incontrovertible proof of this comes from some remarkable sauropod footprints unearthed by Roland T. Bird in the late 1930s in Texas. One remarkable series of footprints found in Bandera County shows a sauropod apparently walking on its front legs alone! No traces of its hindfeet are seen. Evidently the animal was floating in moderately deep water and moving along by kicking the bottom with its front feet. A little way along the track one large, clawed hindfoot was kicked down leaving its clear mark and the forefoot prints change direction: its back legs were obviously being used to steer the animal along!

Footprint trackways discovered by R. T. Bird and others have also provided an insight into other aspects of the biology of sauropods. Bird found other tracks in Bandera County which showed that more than 20 large sauropods had been moving together across an open area in the same direction; this evidence seems to indicate herding behaviour in these animals. Bob Bakker proposed that herding would have been a reasonable behaviour pattern for such creatures. While fully adult sauropods would undoubtedly have been almost immune to attack by even the largest of 'carnosaurs', juveniles may well have provided easy prey. Thus when moving to new feeding grounds, sauropods may well have clustered together in herds, with the vulnerable young individuals in the centre of the herd protected by the larger adult animals.

Defence, Diet and Reproduction

In the case of diplodocids, the long, whip-lash tail very likely served as a weapon of defence against predatory 'carnosaurs'. In addition, most non-brachiosaurid sauropods could probably rear up onto their hind legs so that the massive forelimbs could be used as weapons. The curious feature of all sauropods is that they retain one enlarged, curved claw on the inner toe of the forefoot. The only obvious explanation for the persistence of this claw in an otherwise highly specialised elephantine foot is that it served as an important defensive weapon. Quite how brachiosaurids dealt with predators is uncertain; they had relatively short tails and were probably unable to rear on to their hind limbs. It is possible that like elephants today, brachiosaurids were so large that they were virtually invulnerable to attack.

The immense size of sauropods and their disproportionately small heads and simple teeth has prompted considerable speculation concerning their likely diet. In the days when sauropods were considered to be amphibious swamp dwellers, a diet of soft aquatic water weeds was popular; this seemed to fit well with the weak, pencil-like teeth of forms such as *Diplodocus*. Some early alternative suggestions arose from the belief that plant material could not have been sufficiently nutritious for animals of such immense bulk; thus they became variously fish eaters (piscivores) [Tornier] or oyster eaters (molluscivores) [Holland]. Neither of these latter proposals found much favour in subsequent years and most interpretations now suggest a diet of terrestrial plants. The argument about the weak teeth and jaws of sauropods has been partly deflected by the proposal that the

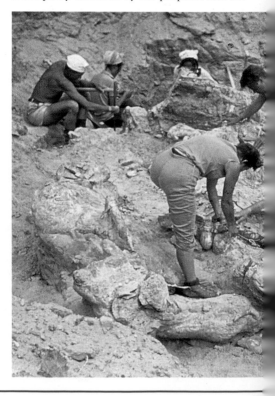

teeth served as rake-like devices in order to strip leaves or pine-needles from branches and twigs. Instead of chewing these items, they were simply swallowed and passed to a powerful muscular gizzard containing sharp, abrasive pebbles; these, rather than teeth, were used to pulp the tough plant tissues in readiness for digestion. The true stomachs of sauropods were probably like huge fermentation tanks in which vast quantities of plant matter were slowly broken down to release their nutrients—somewhat similar to the large complex stomach of cattle.

Two main types of teeth have been noted among sauropods, the narrow pencil-like teeth of diplodocids and the broader, spoon-like teeth of camarasaurids and brachiosaurids. These differences probably reflect different dietary preferences in these groups of sauropods; however at the moment the differences in tooth structure cannot be directly correlated with specific plant types.

With regard to reproductive behaviour, the enormous size of sauropods has frequently provoked the suggestion that these creatures, unlike the majority of reptiles, gave birth to live young. It seems inconceivable that a 30 or 40 tonne female sauropod could lay a clutch of eggs without crushing them. Nevertheless sauropod eggs are occasionally discovered. Aix-en-Provence (France) has produced numerous eggs attributed to the sauropod *Hypselosaurus* and in the Willow Creek Formation, Montana, from which hadrosaurid nests were recovered, Jack Horner also found some smaller sauropod-like eggs. The curious observation that Horner was able to make about both egg localities was that at least one sauropod seemed to be laying its eggs in batches of two in straight lines, presumably laying them while on the move! Perhaps this unusual technique avoided the almost inevitable prospect of crushing the eggs if full clutches were laid at a single nest site.

DIPLODOCID GENERA

Valid
Apatosaurus
Barosaurus
Cetiosauriscus
Dicraeosaurus
Diplodocus
Mamenchisaurus
Nemegtosaurus

Dubious
Amphicoelias
Atlantosaurus
Brontosaurus
(=*Apatosaurus*)
Elosaurus
(=*Apatosaurus*)

BRACHIOSAURID GENERA

Valid
Brachiosaurus
Pelorosaurus (?)
Rebbachisaurus
'*Supersaurus*'
'*Ultrasaurus*'
Zigongosaurus (?)

Dubious
Astrodon
Bothriospondylus
Dinodocus
'*Hughenden sauropod*'

CAMARASAURID GENERA

Valid
Camarasaurus
Euhelopus
Opisthocoelicaudia (?)
Tienshanosaurus

Dubious
Asiatosaurus
Caulodon
Chiayüsaurus
(=*Euhelopus*)
Morosaurus
Uintasaurus

'CETIOSAUR' GENERA
A poorly defined group of sauropods (mainly Jurassic): relatively short necks, no cleft spines, few pleurocoels.

Valid
Austrosaurus
Cetiosaurus
(in part)
Haplocanthosaurus (?)
Patagosaurus
Rhoetosaurus
Volkheimeria
Zizhongosaurus (?)

Dubious
Amygdalodon
Chinshakiangosaurus
Cardiodon
Dystrophaeus
Shuosaurus

'TITANOSAUR' GENERA
A poorly defined, mainly Cretaceous group of sauropods: proportions similar to 'cetiosaurs', tail vertebrae have cupped front surface, possibly armoured.

Valid
Antarctosaurus
Hypselosaurus
Laplatasaurus
Saltasaurus
Titanosaurus

Dubious
Aegyptosaurus
Aepisaurus
Alamosaurus
Algoasaurus
Argyrosaurus
Bothriospondylus
Campylodoniscus
Lametasaurus
Loricosaurus
(=*Saltasaurus?*)
Macrurosaurus
Microcoelus

PRIMITIVE SAUROPOD GENERA
(early Jurassic forms)

Valid
Barapasaurus
Shunosaurus
Vulcanodon (?)

OTHER SAUROPODS
This table lists names of other sauropods, mostly poorly preserved, whose names have figured in the scientific literature, but whose status is very dubious. Accurate classification is practically impossible

Chondrosteosaurus
Chubutisaurus
Clasmodosaurus
Datousaurus
Dinodocus
Gigantosaurus
Hoplosaurus
Hypsibema
Ishyrosaurus
Mongolosaurus
Morinosaurus
Nanshiungosaurus
Neosodon
Ohmdenosaurus
Omeisaurus
(=*Euhelopus?*)
Oplosaurus
Ornithopsis
Parrosaurus
(=*Hypsibema*)
Pleurocoelus
Sanpasaurus
Succinodon
(a mollusc!)
Tapinosaurus

Below: Excavation at Altan Ula in the Gobi Desert in 1965 of *Opisthocoelicaudia skarzynskii*. Frustratingly neither the head nor neck of this sauropod were recovered from the site.

Above: The discovery of footprint trackways seems to indicate that, like elephants today, sauropods were herding animals. The fully grown adults probably protected the young.

Fending off Predators (below)
While the sheer size of an adult sauropod probably rendered it virtually immune from attack by carnivorous predators, it is possible that in the event of such an attack the large claw on the inner toe of each front foot could be used as a defensive weapon, the sauropod rearing onto its hind legs using its tail as a counterbalance.

FABROSAURIDS & HETERODONTOSAURIDS

As described earlier ornithischian dinosaurs are all herbivores and can be recognised by several peculiar features: (i) a bird-like pelvis—from which the group gets its name; (ii) a peculiar horn-covered predentary bone at the tip of the lower jaw; (iii) a trellis-like arrangement of long bony tendons along the backbone. There is also in most ornithischians a peculiar bone (palpebral) in the eye cavity. There are several distinct types of ornithischian dinosaur: ornithopods, ceratopians, pachycephalosaurs, stegosaurs and ankylosaurs.

Ornithopod Dinosaurs

These are generally very abundant ornithischians found in rocks that date from the late Triassic until the very end of the Cretaceous. The early ones are typically small, agile creatures that run bipedally on their long back legs and have small front legs; later ones tend to be much larger although they are still mostly bipedal. The pachycephalosaurs ('bone-heads', pages 146-151) are often included with the ornithopods, but two Polish workers (Maryanska and Osmolska) consider them to be so unusual that they have separated them off from all other ornithopods.

The earliest ornithopod (possibly a heterodontosaurid) is claimed to be an animal named *Pisanosaurus* ('Pisano's reptile') from the late Triassic of Argentina. However, the very fragmentary remains of this animal do not make it clear even if it is an ornithischian, let alone an ornithopod, so we should perhaps note the existence of this fossil and hope that more material is discovered that will prove exactly what sort of animal this is.

Fabrosaurids have been known for a surprisingly long time. Well over a century ago, Sir Richard Owen described several small jaws and teeth which had been found in quarries in the Purbeck area of Dorset in southern England by an amateur collector of fossils, Samuel Beckles.

These jaws were small and slender and the teeth had long, narrow roots and leaf-shaped crowns, with spiky edges. Owen supposed that these belonged to a small herbivorous lizard since they were so small and gave them the name *Echinodon becklesii* which literally means 'Beckles' spiky-tooth'.

Unfortunately no more remains of *Echinodon* have been found since Owen's first description. Another fragmentary piece of jaw with a few teeth was found much later (1964) in southern Africa. The teeth look remarkably like those of *Echinodon*, however this fossil came from rocks which were dated at the boundary between Upper Triassic and the Lower Jurassic, while those of *Echinodon* are from Upper Jurassic/Lower Cretaceous boundary. The African fossil was named *Fabrosaurus australis* ('Fabre's southern reptile') and eventually gave its name to the Family.

It was not until the early 1970s that anyone had any clear idea of the true appearance of

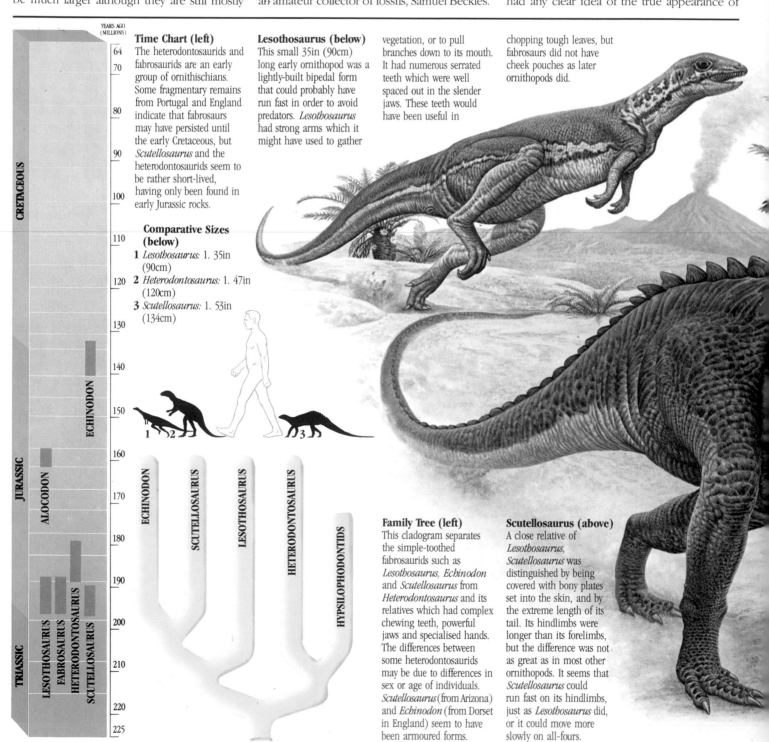

Time Chart (left)
The heterodontosaurids and fabrosaurids are an early group of ornithischians. Some fragmentary remains from Portugal and England indicate that fabrosaurs may have persisted until the early Cretaceous, but *Scutellosaurus* and the heterodontosaurids seem to be rather short-lived, having only been found in early Jurassic rocks.

Comparative Sizes (below)
1 *Lesothosaurus*: 1. 35in (90cm)
2 *Heterodontosaurus*: 1. 47in (120cm)
3 *Scutellosaurus*: 1. 53in (134cm)

Lesothosaurus (below)
This small 35in (90cm) long early ornithopod was a lightly-built bipedal form that could probably have run fast in order to avoid predators. *Lesothosaurus* had strong arms which it might have used to gather vegetation, or to pull branches down to its mouth. It had numerous serrated teeth which were well spaced out in the slender jaws. These teeth would have been useful in chopping tough leaves, but fabrosaurs did not have cheek pouches as later ornithopods did.

Family Tree (left)
This cladogram separates the simple-toothed fabrosaurids such as *Lesothosaurus*, *Echinodon* and *Scutellosaurus* from *Heterodontosaurus* and its relatives which had complex chewing teeth, powerful jaws and specialised hands. The differences between some heterodontosaurids may be due to differences in sex or age of individuals. *Scutellosaurus* (from Arizona) and *Echinodon* (from Dorset in England) seem to have been armoured forms.

Scutellosaurus (above)
A close relative of *Lesothosaurus*, *Scutellosaurus* was distinguished by being covered with bony plates set into the skin, and by the extreme length of its tail. Its hindlimbs were longer than its forelimbs, but the difference was not as great as in most other ornithopods. It seems that *Scutellosaurus* could run fast on its hindlimbs, just as *Lesothosaurus* did, or it could move more slowly on all-fours.

YEARS AGO (MILLIONS): 64, 70, 80, 90, 100, 110, 120, 130, 140, 150, 160, 170, 180, 190, 200, 210, 220, 225

CRETACEOUS — JURASSIC — TRIASSIC

ECHINODON — ALOCODON — LESOTHOSAURUS — FABROSAURUS — HETERODONTOSAURUS — SCUTELLOSAURUS

ECHINODON — SCUTELLOSAURUS — LESOTHOSAURUS — HETERODONTOSAURUS — HYPSILOPHODONTIDS

either *Echinodon* or *Fabrosaurus*. It had been recognised that Owen had been wrong about *Echinodon* being a lizard. Its teeth had long roots which were borne in deep sockets in the jaw bones; this feature made it an archosaur rather than an ancient lizard and, more specifically, the leaf-shaped and spiky-edged crown to the tooth was typical of those seen in ornithischian dinosaurs. New information about these mysterious fabrosaurids came from an expedition to southern Africa organised by Professor Kermack of University College, London. Among the many fossils collected during the expedition, were the remains of the partial skeleton of a small animal which came from the Upper Triassic 'Red Beds' of Lesotho. Preparation of this fossil revealed the true appearance of a fabrosaurid. Being of the same geological age as the original *Fabrosaurus* and having teeth which seemed virtually identical, this new animal was also named *Fabrosaurus australis* when it was finally described in detail

Heterodontosaurus (left)

As the name suggests ('mixed tooth reptile'), *Heterodontosaurus* is distinguished by its differentiated teeth. That is, unlike most other dinosaurs, we can recognise three quite distinctive kinds of teeth in each jaw: sharp cutting teeth at the front, fangs just behind these, and broad ridged teeth in the cheek region. *Heterodontosaurus* fed on tough vegetation which it nipped of with its 'incisors', punctured with its 'canines', and ground up with its cheek teeth.

Map (below)

1 *Abrictosaurus*	6 *Gongbusaurus*
2 *Alocodon*	7 *Lanasaurus*
3 *Echinodon*	8 *Lesothosaurus*
4 *Fabrosaurus*	9 *Nanosaurus*
5 *Geranosaurus*	10 *Scutellosaurus*
	11 *Trimucrodon*

by Dr Tony Thulborn. However, since then this animal has undergone a name change! It is now claimed that the original material of *Fabrosaurus*, since it is only a small piece of jaw with a few teeth, cannot be closely compared to the newer skeleton so it is impossible to know exactly how similar these animals really were. To be safe, the new skeleton was renamed *Lesothosaurus australis*. (Indeed, if you look back in some older dinosaur books, you may well find this dinosaur illustrated and described as *Fabrosaurus*).

Lesothosaurus is the best example of a fabrosaurid dinosaur known to date and in fact establishes a very common body shape for all later ornithopod dinosaurs. *Lesothosaurus* was a small (about 35in, 90cm from head to tail), lightly-built animal with extremely slender, long hind legs and rather short forelimbs; its tail was long, and counterbalanced the front part of its body so that it could stand and run on its hind legs, leaving its hands free to perform other duties. Unfortunately, the hand of *Lesothosaurus* is not well-preserved; most probably it had five rather stubby little fingers ending in small claws which would have been ideal all-purpose hands, a little like our own.

Looking at the skeleton in more detail (see below), the head is rather small and triangular in outline, with a very large eye cavity and large open spaces behind for the jaw muscles. There is also a fairly large opening in front of the eye which may have been for a salt gland. The snout is short and quite pointed, with a very slender lower jaw tipped by the horn-covered predentary bone, and the teeth are small, leaf-shaped and separate. This general shape and arrangement suggests that these animals were probably herbivorous, although they may have taken a little carrion or perhaps even insects on occasions. The horn-covered predentary bone at the front of the lower jaw would have formed a very effective device for chipping off pieces of foliage. In life, these animals may well have used their narrow snout and beak to feed on small succulent shoots of plants. They did not really chew up their food because their teeth and jaws were apparently not designed to do this; they simply broke the food into small pieces before swallowing it. (As we shall see later, some of the more advanced ornithopods chewed their food a great deal.) There are reptiles living today that have very similar teeth and jaws to those of *Lesothosaurus*, and they give us a clue to the way that it may have fed.

Conolophus, the land iguana of the Galapagos, has small, leaf-like teeth, slender jaws and a short snout. It feeds on plants, including cacti, and occasionally takes small animals. Like (we suppose) *Lesothosaurus*, the land iguana does not chew its food, but merely bites off small pieces which it then swallows. One result of not chewing up plant food is that most of the nutrients are locked inside the tough plant tissues and they therefore have to spend a very long time in the stomach and gut, being

Heterodontosaurus Skeleton (right)

The reconstructed skeleton of *Heterodontosaurus* shows it to be a lightly-built, agile animal, typical of the early ornithopods. In particular notice how the foot bones (metatarsals) and lower leg bones are elongated relative to the upper leg bone (femur). This kind of long, slender hind leg is a sure sign of a fleet-footed runner which presumably relied on speed to escape from its predators. The long, tapering tail acted as a counterbalance for the front half of the body and was probably held out almost horizontally above the ground when the animal ran. The front limbs are very robust compared with those of *Lesothosaurus* and in particular the fingers and wrist bones are well-developed. Also visible are the bony rods lying along the backbone, which are characteristic of bipedal ornithischians; they were present in order to stiffen the back, hips and tail.

Lesothosaurus Skeleton (right)

This animal is another typical early ornithopod but it does not show the specialisations of a robust front leg and fused lower hind leg bones seen in *Heterodontosaurus*. In that form the front leg may have been used for digging or in defending itself or possibly even in tearing down vegetation. In both forms the neck is long and flexible, perhaps useful for getting the head into vegetation to pick off shoots or buds, or for keeping an eye out for predators. The long tail is typically ornithopod.

Ornithischian Hip (left)

Ornithischians have a distinctive hip structure. The front bone of the pelvis, the pubis, which projects forwards in other reptiles, has been rotated backwards to lie alongside the rear bone of the pelvis, the ischium. A similar configuration also occurs in birds and gives ornithischians their popular name: 'bird-hipped dinosaurs'. Some later ornithischians developed a 'replacement' anterior spine in this area.

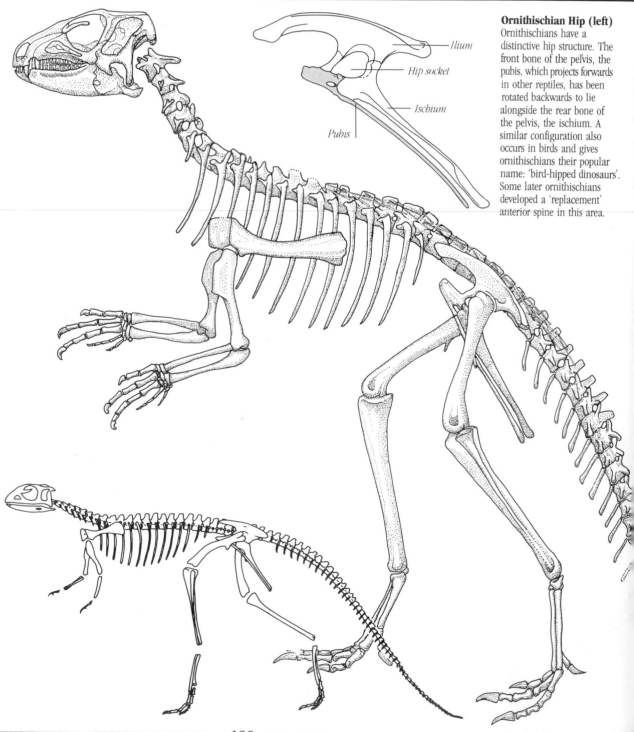

Ilium
Hip socket
Ischium
Pubis

fermented and digested. Both of these animals have quite a large belly. The iguana is very stout bodied and has a large belly slung between its front and back legs while *Lesothosaurus*'belly is situated between its legs underneath the hips so that it can maintain its balance and run unhindered on its hind legs. This point is important because while *Lesothosaurus* may well have fed like *Conolophus,* that is about as far as the comparison goes. *Conolophus* is a very sluggish reptile, in many respects it does not need to be anything else, after all its food does not need to be chased and it has no natural predators (apart from Man) to escape from. *Lesothosaurus* however, relied upon its speed and agility to survive in the world of the late Triassic.

Looking at the remainder of the skeleton, we see a pattern common to all later ornithopods. The neck is quite long, slender and was presumably very flexible. The back, hips and tail were stiffened and supported by narrow, bony

tendons and the tail was long in order to balance the body over the hips. The forelimbs are quite short compared to the hindlimbs and have a small grasping hand. The hind legs of this animal are very long with the skin and toes being particularly elongate. These proportions are typical of fast running animals, such as antelopes and gazelles living today. We therefore suspect that fabrosaurids were an improbable mixture: iguana-like in feeding habits, and yet the equivalent of small gazelle-like creatures of the late Triassic and early Jurassic periods. Indeed, unprotected as it was by either bony armour or defensive weapons such as large teeth or claws, *Lesothosaurus* would have relied heavily upon its great turn of speed and agility to avoid being caught by the large and fearsome thecodontians and the smaller and equally agile theropod dinosaurs that inhabited their world. One could easily imagine these animals living a life very similar to that of gazelles in the African bush, nervously picking off shoots and

leaves from low shrubs and constantly on the lookout for predators.

Another rather unusual fabrosaurid, *Scutellosaurus* ('bony-plate reptile'), was discovered and described only very recently by Professor Edwin Colbert. Discovered in Arizona, but from rocks of an age similar to those in which *Lesothosaurus* and *Fabrosaurus* were found, this animal is peculiar because it has very well-preserved bony plates (or scutes) rather like those found on the back of a crocodile. Perhaps what we are seeing here is an alternative strategy for survival to that of *Lesothosarus*. *Scutellosaurus* is armour-plated as well as being moderately fleet of foot, judging by its limb proportions, and could be thought of as balancing two alternative ways of surviving predation: one technique would be to be extensively armour-plated—this makes an animal both heavier and slower and therefore more easily caught, but its armour would make it unpalatable (the armadillo uses just this type of

Heterodontosaurus Hand (below)
This is particularly well-made for a bipedal dinosaur. The individual finger bones are long and slender, and bear well-developed claws. The smallest finger does not seem to be quite so off-set as in some ornithischians, so the hand appears more symmetrical. The wrist bones are small and numerous, suggesting flexibility. *Heterodontosaurus* was probably able to manipulate vegetation quite adeptly.

Heterodontosaurus Foot (below right)
The foot bones are long and slender, reflecting that the animal possessing them was both a runner, and small and light—the foot did not have to be specially strengthened to bear the animal's weight. Notice how the smallest toe is reversed relative to the others. This may have given the foot extra surface area for bearing the animal's weight. The metatarsal bones are particularly elongated.

Heterodontosaurus Skull (left)
In this form the teeth may have chewed up food, rather than simply cropping it. There are various theories about how the chewing action was produced: it might have been caused by back and forwards movement of the lower jaw, but perhaps more likely, the lower jaw might have rotated relative to the upper jaw as it closed. The large tusks are probably a male characteristic.

Lesothosaurus Skull (left)
The cheek teeth here are much more slender and leaf-like, used perhaps for shredding food, but not chewing it. This form may have had a salt-gland and if so this could indicate that the animal lived in an arid environment, needing to conserve its body water. Doing this leads to a build-up of body salts which must be disposed of by the salt-gland. Note how the small teeth are separated.

Tuskless Heterodontosaurus Skull (left)
The lack of tusks in this specimen may indicate that it is a female of a tusked *Heterodontosaurus* since in other respects it is almost identical (compare with skull shown at top left). If this is so then it shows that even if the tusks were used in feeding, they were also used as a sexual signal— distinguishing males from females. The muscles shown on the skull are responsible for closing the jaw and also for producing the forces which cause the chewing action of the jaw.

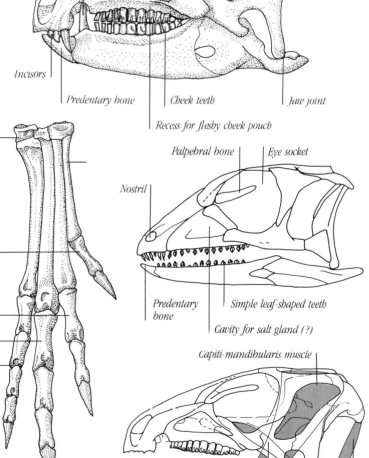

Heterodontosaurus Hand labels: Digit 5, Wrist bones, Digit 1, Digit 2, Digit 3, Digit 4

Heterodontosaurus Foot labels: Ankle bones, Digit 1, Digit 2, Digit 3, Digit 4

Heterodontosaurus Skull labels: Palpebral bone, Eye socket, Brain case, Canines, Nostril, Predentary bone, Cheek teeth, Jaw joint, Incisors, Recess for fleshy cheek pouch

Lesothosaurus Skull labels: Palpebral bone, Eye socket, Nostril, Predentary bone, Simple leaf-shaped teeth, Cavity for salt gland (?)

Tuskless Heterodontosaurus Skull labels: Capiti-mandibularis muscle, Depressor mandibulae muscle, Pterygoideus muscle

technique). Alternatively, the less armour an animal carries, the greater its agility and speed and the better its chances of avoiding capture altogether, but if it is captured it is completely unprotected. *Scutellosaurus* seems almost caught in the act of balancing these strategies.

In addition to the quite well-preserved skeletons of *Lesothosaurus* and *Scutellosaurus,* there are several other fabrosaurids known: *Echinodon,* represented by a few jaws and teeth from the late Jurassic of southern Britain; *Fabrosaurus,* a single broken jaw with some teeth from the late Triassic of southern Africa; *Nanosaurus* ('dwarf reptile'), an incomplete jaw and some skeletal fragments from the later Jurassic, Colorado, North America; *Alocodon* ('wing tooth') and *Trimucrodon* ('three-pointed tooth'), some tooth fragments from the Jurassic of Portugal; and *Gongbusaurus* ('reptile from Gongbu') from the Jurassic of China; *Azendohsaurus* ('reptile from Azendoh'), another jaw fragment from Morocco may even be prosauropod.

Heterodontosaurids

Heterodontosaurids are only known from the late Triassic and earliest Jurassic of southern Africa and North America. As was the case in the fabrosaurids, the earliest known heterodontosaurid fossil (described in 1911) was a jaw fragment with several teeth embedded in it. It came from southern Africa; this was named *Geranosaurus* ('crane reptile'). Somewhat later, another jaw was discovered, but this time was thought to belong to a mammal-like reptile and was named *Lycorhinus angustidens* ('wolf snout with sharp teeth'). It has a large pointed caniniform, or stabbing, tooth, at the front of the jaw and behind it a row of heavily worn cheek teeth. This specimen lay unrecognised as a dinosaur until 1962 when yet another new dinosaur from southern Africa was described and named *Heterodontosaurus* ('mixed-tooth reptile'). This too was discovered by an expedition from Britain organised this time by Dr Alan Charig of the British Museum (Natural History), and Dr John Attridge and Dr Barry Cox of the University of London. The animal, which has only recently be described, is apparently the same size and the same in general shape as the fabrosaurids above. However, there are, if we look a little closer, several striking differences.

The head is quite similar in shape to that of *Lesothosaurus,* but the teeth are notably different. At the front of the lower jaw there is a familiar horn-covered predentary, and immediately behind this there is a very large tusk-like tooth—like the one seen in *Lycorhinus*—and then a row of chisel-edged cheek teeth. The same arrangement is found in the upper jaw except that in front of the big tusk there are two small spiky teeth and then a gap at the front end of the snout which was probably covered by a horny pad to match the one on the predentary.

The remainder of the skeleton is similarly built to that of *Lesothosaurus* except that the hands are particularly large and strong with sharp claws, and the bones of the lower leg are welded together, a rather unusual feature which does not seem to occur in many other dinosaurs.

So what we seem to have are small, agile, bipedal ornithopod dinosaurs with several rather special features that distinguish them from their contemporaries, the fabrosaurids. They had special chisel-like cheek teeth behind the tusks; these were used to chew up food very finely, not at all like the simple feeding technique that was used by *Lesothosaurus;* and, associated with the chewing teeth, they probably possessed fleshy cheeks so that the food did not fall out of their mouths while they were chewing. The large tusks may also have had a defensive function. Large stabbing teeth are usually found in carnivores such as the big cats, where they are used for killing. In animals such as these heterodontosaurids which are herbivores, big tusks are usually used as defensive weapons and/or as feeding aids. Wild pigs and warthogs, for example, have teeth that are used both for digging and for defence. In some instances, such tusks can become long and very curly in males and are then used as social signals to establish a dominance hierarchy and to attract mates. The same sort of functions have been proposed for these teeth in heterodontosaurids.

In addition to *Heterodontosaurus,* there are several other heterodontosaurids: *Geranosaurus* and *Lycorhinus,* small pieces of jaw from the late Triassic of southern Africa; *Abrictosaurus* ('wide-awake reptile'), a moderately well-preserved skull which does not possess the large tusks seen in *Heterodontosaurus* (although in all other respects it is rather similar) again from the late Triassic of southern Africa; and *Lanasaurus* ('woolly reptile'), an upper jaw with some teeth, which appears to be distinct from other heterodontosaurids.

Such a variety of heterodontosaurids living at approximately the same time and in the same part of the world seems a little improbable; this seems particularly true when the different types are based largely upon tooth characters. Teeth are known to vary in shape tremendously within a single species of reptile, and even during the life of a single animal! One interesting possibility that has been suggested is that *Abrictosaurus* (the skull without the large tusks) may be a female, while *Heterodontosaurus* (with the tusks) is a male of the same species. Unfortunately, we cannot 'prove' in the strict sense whether one is a male and the other female, but it is certainly a possibility.

The general picture then of heterodontosaurids is that they are fleet-footed, agile bipeds, similar to the fabrosaurids that lived at the same time. However, unlike the fabrosaurids, they were able to chew a much greater variety of plant food much more efficiently using special cheek teeth and fleshy cheeks to hold the food

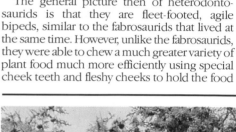

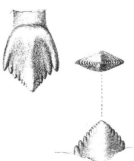

Left: The skull of a *Conolophus* (land iguana) killed by dogs on the Galapagos Islands. The similarity between its small, leaf-shaped teeth and those of fabrosaurids is immediately apparent. This suggests that their feeding habits were probably also similar.

Below: A detail of a 19th Century lithograph showing the teeth and fragments of jaw of the fabrosaurid *Echinodon becklesii* which were found in Dorset by Samuel Beckles. Compare the narrow roots and leaf-shaped crowns with those of the contemporary land iguana, *Conolophus* (left).

Above: A male African warthog displaying his huge tusks. It is tempting to draw a parallel between these animals and heterodontosaurids which also possessed large tusk-like teeth which were presumably used for defensive purposes and also for social display.

in the mouth; they also had large tusks for use both in defence against predators and perhaps for social display, especially if, as has been suggested, tusks were confined to males only; their hands were also surprisingly large and powerful and may have been used for digging as well as in defence.

Aestivation Controversy

One interesting controversy that has broken out recently concerns the biology and way of life of fabrosaurid and heterodontosaurid dinosaurs. In 1978, Dr Tony Thulborn devoted a long article to the possibility that in the late Triassic and early Jurassic of southern Africa, there was an annual dry season during which both fabrosaurids and heterodontosaurids lay dormant or *aestivated*. The evidence for this suggestion came from a number of areas.

First of all, the so-called 'Red Beds' — the rocks of the Stormberg Series of southern Africa — are characteristically red in colour. The red colour is interpreted as indicating generally warm climatic conditions which were marked by alternating wet and dry seasons. Thus, if the interpretation is correct, then there will be times of the year (the dry season) when the vegetation will be in short supply during which both groups of ornithopods might have aestivated.

Secondly, Thulborn has found remains of fabrosaurids in a fossil assemblage which includes jaw bones bearing sharp and practically unworn teeth, together with others which were apparently discarded and heavily worn. He explains this occurrence by proposing that these individuals continued to grow and replace their teeth while they were aestivating. Fortunately, for us at least, in this instance the individuals perished while aestivating thereby preserving this unique record of their life-style.

Thirdly, Thulborn noted that the heterodontosaurids seem to have most unusual grinding cheek teeth. He was unable to find any evidence of tooth replacement in the family and also noted that the cheek teeth were worn in such a way that the wear facets on each tooth form a single flat cutting surface in each jaw. Thulborn claimed that the flat cutting surface could only have been produced if the lower jaw of heterodontosaurids moved forward and backward when they chewed their food, rather than in a more typical up and down movement. This in itself is not unreasonable because several living animals (notably rodents and elephants) also chew their food by moving the lower jaw backward and forward. However, he went on to develop his argument as follows. If these animals used this kind of chewing mechanism, then they cannot conform to the normal reptilian pattern of continual tooth replacement because if teeth periodically fall out and are replaced, then the whole chewing action would be disrupted: the jaws would in effect keep jamming. Therefore heterodontosaurids would seem to be unable to replace their teeth so long as they continued to feed. In addition to this, the degree of wear on the teeth seen in several heterodontosaurids is very severe, which implies that these animals fed on very abrasive plant food.

To Thulborn's mind, the heterodontosaurids are presented theoretically with a dilemma; they cannot continually replace their cheek teeth because it would impair their ability to feed, and yet they feed on abrasive food material which necessitates tooth replacement at least periodically. Again, the solution to their dilemma is found in aestivation. The teeth are worn down during each wet season and then replaced, *en masse,* during a short dry season while these animals lay dormant. The new set of teeth would be worn down rapidly to produce a smooth cutting blade once these animals re-emerged in the next wet season.

All in all, these proposals seem convincing and rather neatly and elegantly link environmental, geological and anatomical factors together to gain an insight into the life-style of these animals. However, elegant though this explanation may be, there are dissenting voices. Jim Hopson from Chicago has re-studied much of the heterodontosaurid material. He has demonstrated that these animals show definite evidence of tooth replacement, although it does seem to slow down in older individuals; also he argues that heterodontosaurids do not show fore and aft grinding movement of the lower jaw, but chewed in typical reptile fashion by simply opening and closing the jaws. By demonstrating these two points, Hopson has removed Thulborn's main arguments for proposing that heterodontosaurids replace their teeth completely once a year during a period of aestivation. This, of course, still leaves the evidence of the fabrosaurid assemblage of two individuals caught in the act of aestivating, but even this has been doubted as a reliable record because the presence of a saurischian tooth with the others suggests that the 'assemblage' might in fact be a chance accumulation of fossils.

Therefore, a very familiar story has emerged of the fossil record affording us a small glimpse of the world and behaviour of dinosaurs. But as always, the glimpse is a fleeting one and potentially misleading. If you are not careful it can lead to a quite erroneous view of the world of dinosaurs, or at least to one that is not justified by the evidence. Here, for example, it is still quite conceivable that seasonal climates prevailed in the late Triassic and early Jurassic and that some of the dinosaurs aestivated in the dry season — one simply cannot prove it!

Self Defence (above)
The fabrosaurids and heterodontosaurids seem to show a full range of strategies for survival against predators. *Lesothosaurus* was very swift and agile and would flee; *Scutellosaurus* was moderately fleet of foot but also partly armoured; *Heterodontosaurus* was speedy, but agressive in defence when cornered.

Left: A lateral view of the skull of *Heterodontosaurus tucki* which was excavated from the northern slopes of Krommespruit Mountain in South Africa. Note tusk-like tooth and cheek teeth.

Below: This skeleton of *Heterodontosaurus* provides us with a fine view of the dinosaur's strong, clawed hands and the fused bones of its lower leg.

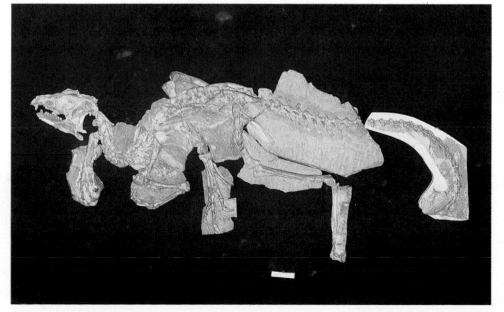

HYPSILOPHODONTIDS

The hypsilophodontids are a family of small-to-medium sized (6·6-16·5ft, 2·5m in length) ornithopod dinosaurs. In outward appearance at least, they are not unlike the fabrosaurids described earlier. However, unlike the fabrosaurids, which seem to have been most abundant at the earliest stages of the history of the ornithischians—in the latest Triassic and early Jurassic—the hypsilophodontids first make their appearance in Middle Jurassic times (see time chart below). The first remains are rather scrappy, consisting of tooth fragments and pieces of limb bones from Oxfordshire. Indeed they are so poor that they are simply referred to as 'hypsilophodontid', by which we mean that although the material belonged to a hypsilophodontid dinosaur, it is not well enough preserved to give it a proper scientific name.

Shortly after this, in the Upper Jurassic, several much better preserved hypsilophodontids are known. In particular, *Dryosaurus*

('oak reptile') from North America and *Dysalotosaurus* ('lost wood reptile') from Tanzania in East Africa. These two dinosaurs have recently been very carefully compared bone-by-bone and are now considered by some workers to be so similar that they have been given the same name: *Dryosaurus*, the North American form being called *Dryosaurus altus* and the East African form *Dryosaurus lettowvorbecki* after the German General, von Lettow-Vorbeck. In addition to these two species, there is another quite well preserved but unfortunately incomplete skeleton which has been named *Othnielia* (after Othniel Charles Marsh).

In the Cretaceous Period various types of hypsilophodontids have been found. Lower Cretaceous forms include *Hypsilophodon* ('high-ridged tooth') from the Isle of Wight, England, represented by several excellent skeletons, also *Valdosaurus* ('reptile from the Wealden'), a very fragmentary species from southern England; *Zephyrosaurus* ('west wind reptile'), a partial

Time Chart (left)

		YEARS AGO (MILLIONS)	

Hypsilophodontids are found fairly widely in the fossil record. The earliest of the remains date from the late Jurassic, and they persist as small to medium-sized forms right up to the late Cretaceous. The largest of these types, *Tenontosaurus* of the early Cretaceous of North America, bore a considerable resemblance to the contemporaneous large iguanodontids.

Dryosaurus (right)

A large hypsilophodontid, 10-13ft (3-4m) long, *Dryosaurus* had long powerful hind legs, and strong arms, each with five fingers. Its tail was stiff, and it could have been used for balance when the animal ran. *Dryosaurus* had sharp ridged cheek teeth, but there were no teeth at the front of the jaw. It probably nipped vegetation off with its bony 'beak' and then chopped the leaves and shoots with its cheek teeth. *Dryosaurus* was a wide-ranging dinosaur: its remains have been found in North America and East Africa, and it could probably migrate long distances.

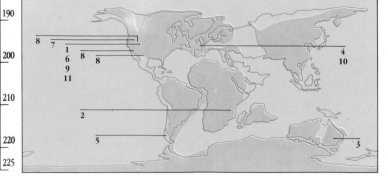

Map (left)

1 *Dryosaurus*
2 *Dysalotosaurus*
3 *Fulgurotherium*
4 *Hypsilophodon*
5 *Loncosaurus*
6 *Othnielia*
7 *Parksosaurus*
8 *Tenontosaurus*
9 *Thescelosaurus*
10 *Valdosaurus*
11 *Zephyrosaurus*

Tenontosaurus (below)
This was a much larger animal than its relative *Hypsilophodon;* it is estimated that it weighed up to 1 tonne. It has been classified as an iguanodontid, but it shows the same specialisations of the teeth as do other hypsilophodontids. *Tenontosaurus* was a strongly-built ornithopod and it had a massive powerful tail which might have been used at times to defend itself from packs of predatory *Deinonychus*.

skull from Montana; and the larger and heavier *Tenontosaurus* ('sinew reptile') represented by many skeletons from various areas in North America. Finally, in the Upper Cretaceous, there are two imperfectly known types: *Parksosaurus* ('Parks' reptile'), an incomplete skull and *Thescelosaurus* ('beautiful reptile') known from several part skeletons and skulls.

From their first appearance in the Middle Jurassic until their extinction at the end of the Cretaceous, the hypsilophodontids appear to have changed very little. In particular, *Othnielia* of the Upper Jurassic is remarkably similar to *Hypsilophodon* of the Lower Cretaceous, which is in turn very like *Thescelosaurus* of the late Cretaceous. It seems as though these animals evolved a particularly successful structure (and way of life) and simply retained that design to the end. The only obviously abberrant form would seem to be *Tenontosaurus* which is simply a hypsilophodontid grown rather large so that it resembles a small iguanodontid.

The geographic distribution of the hypsilophodontids seems to show a fairly easily understood pattern. Undoubtedly these animals were present in middle Jurassic times, perhaps even a little earlier—after all it is exeedingly unlikely that we would find the very first member of this or any other family in the fossil record. Anyway, at this time there were land links to all the continents, except perhaps eastern Asia, so that early representatives could have spread almost worldwide. The presence of *Dryosaurus* in both North America and East Africa demonstrates the likelihood of such widespread dispersal. In fact, we might predict that hypsilophodontids will eventually be found in Upper Jurassic rocks in South America, Australasia and India. In the Cretaceous, intercontinental seaways divided the land masses leading to the evolution in isolation, of distinctive hypsilophodontids on each continent: *Tenontosaurus, Parksosaurus* and *Thescelosaurus* in North America; *Hypsilophodon*

Hypsilophodon (left)
One of the best known and most successful of the small ornithopods, *Hypsilophodon* was a comparatively small dinosaur. It had short arms, each with five fingers, and long legs, each with four toes. *Hypsilophodon* was probably an agile and fleet-footed creature, and it may have used its long stiff tail as a stabiliser when running. It was once thought that *Hypsilophodon* lived in trees, but there is little evidence for this.

Family Tree (right)
Hypsilophodon is very like *Thescelosaurus* and *Zephyrosaurus*. *Tenontosaurus* seems to be larger relative of *Hypsilophodon*, while *Dryosaurus* and *Valdosaurus* are medium-sized forms that show certain similarities to the iguanodontids.

HYPSILOPHODON
THESCELOSAURUS
ZEPHYROSAURUS
TENONTOSAURUS
DRYOSAURUS
VALDOSAURUS
IGUANODONTIDS

HETERODONTOSAURUS

Comparative Sizes (left)
1 *Hypsilophodon:* 1. 6·6ft (2m).
2 *Dryosaurus:* 1. 10-13ft (3-4m).
3 *Tenontosaurus:* 15-21·3ft (4·5-6·5m).

and *Valdosaurus* in Europe. There are also new reports of two fragmentary Cretaceous hypsilophodontids from Australia (*Fulgurotherium,* 'Lightning Ridge beast') and South America (*Loncosaurus,* 'Lonco reptile') which, if confirmed, would support the prediction about the near worldwide dispersal.

So, having suggested that the hypsilophodontids had apparently hit upon a successful design as a reason for their not having changed very much in appearance, the obvious question is: what are the hypsilophodontids and how do they differ from their predecessors, the fabrosaurids?

For the most part, the skeletons of hypsilophodontids do not differ very much from that of fabrosaurids. They both are small, lightly-built, bipedal animals with long, slender, four-toed hindlimbs and quite short forelimbs with stubby, five-fingered hands. The real difference is only apparent when we look carefully at the head, and the jaws and teeth in particular. The skull of *Lesothosaurus* (a fabrosaurid) is small, light and roughly triangular in shape, as is that of *Hypsilophodon.* However, whereas the teeth of *Lesothosaurus* are separate and leaf-shaped and set in slender jaws, *Hypsilophodon* has broader, chisel-like teeth that lock together with their neighbours to form a continuous sharp cutting edge. The jaws are also quite massive and there is a cheek pouch alongside the teeth on each side of the head to store food while it is being chewed.

What we have, in effect, is a much more efficient chewing machine. The hypsilophodontids evolved more sophisticated teeth and jaws with cheek pouches to chew up plant food more efficiently and so extract more nutrients than the fabrosaurids could ever do. Thus, although these two groups look very similar, there is a world of difference between them in one vitally important respect: the design of their jaws. It seems quite likely that the hypsilophodontids rapidly replaced the majority of fabrosaurids in the small agile herbivore niche from mid-Jurassic times, with the few remaining fabrosaurids surviving as perhaps specialist feeders on young plants shoots.

Hypsilophodon Described

Although there are many hypsilophodontids, we shall look in detail only at *Hypsilophodon,* because it is the best preserved and described. The first remains of any hypsilophodontid to be discovered were found in a slab of sandstone from the south-west coast of the Isle of Wight, England, in 1849. The remains, which consisted of a partial skeleton, were first described by Gideon Mantell, and later by Sir Richard Owen, as those of a young *Iguanodon.* By 1868, several other skeletons had been recovered from the same locality by the Reverend William Fox, a noted amateur collector of fossils. The new material displayed several characteristics not previously seen in *Iguanodon* and prompted

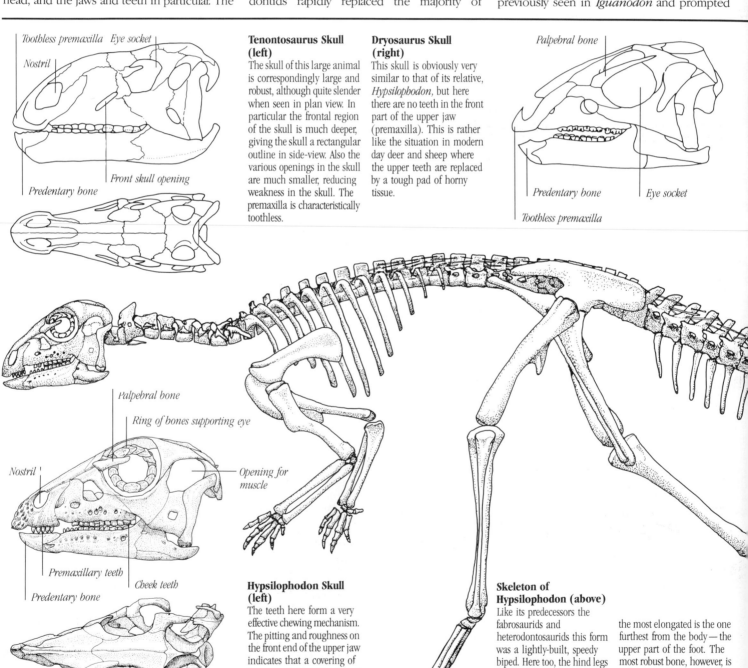

Toothless premaxilla Eye socket

Nostril

Predentary bone

Front skull opening

Tenontosaurus Skull (left)
The skull of this large animal is correspondingly large and robust, although quite slender when seen in plan view. In particular the frontal region of the skull is much deeper, giving the skull a rectangular outline in side-view. Also the various openings in the skull are much smaller, reducing weakness in the skull. The premaxilla is characteristically toothless.

Dryosaurus Skull (right)
This skull is obviously very similar to that of its relative, *Hypsilophodon,* but here there are no teeth in the front part of the upper jaw (premaxilla). This is rather like the situation in modern day deer and sheep where the upper teeth are replaced by a tough pad of horny tissue.

Palpebral bone

Predentary bone Eye socket

Toothless premaxilla

Palpebral bone

Ring of bones supporting eye

Nostril

Opening for muscle

Premaxillary teeth

Cheek teeth

Predentary bone

Hypsilophodon Skull (left)
The teeth here form a very effective chewing mechanism. The pitting and roughness on the front end of the upper jaw indicates that a covering of horn was present. The ring of small bones, or ossicles, in the eye is often found in reptiles and may be part of the focussing mechanism for sharp eyesight.

Skeleton of Hypsilophodon (above)
Like its predecessors the fabrosaurids and heterodontosaurids this form was a lightly-built, speedy biped. Here too, the hind legs show adaptations typical of cursorial (or running) animals. All segments of the leg (upper, lower, ankle, foot) are elongated, but the segment which is relatively the most elongated is the one furthest from the body — the upper part of the foot. The most robust bone, however, is that nearest the body, the upper leg. Because of these features the leg acts like a pendulum which has a long length but a small 'bob'. Such a pendulum has a short

Owen to propose that the animal represented a new species, *Iguanodon foxii*. However, it was Thomas Henry Huxley who first recognised that this dinosaur was totally unlike *Iguanodon*. Among the many differences, Huxley was struck by the shape of the teeth, which were smaller, narrower and more sharply pointed than those of *Iguanodon*. These prompted Huxley to re-name the dinosaur *Hypsilophodon foxii* ('Fox's high-ridged tooth').

In order to understand the anatomy of this animal more closely, let us look at one particular suggestion that was made about the way of life of this curious little dinosaur. In 1882 James Hulke completed the first description of *Hypsilophodon* and concluded that this dinosaur was adapted to climb on rocks and trees because it had long fingers and toes. From this observation, it was accepted as established fact that *Hypsilophodon* was an arboreal dinosaur (i.e. it lived in trees) and that this perhaps represented the primitive type of life-style of

ornithopod dinosaurs. Many life-like restorations made earlier in this century show *Hypsilophodon* perched, bird-like, on the branch of a tree (see overleaf).

In addition to Hulke's original comments, numerous other 'facts' were used to support the proposal that *Hypsilophodon* was a tree-dweller and comparable to the tree-kangaroo, *Dendrolagus*, of Australasia. The list of anatomical characteristics is quite impressive: (i) the first toe of the foot was supposed to be reversed so that it could grip on to branches; (ii) the claws on the hindfoot were strongly arched and sharp so that movement on the ground would have been difficult; (iii) the bones of the forearm were bowed like those of the tree-kangaroo; (iv) the great range of movement that was possible at the shoulder; (v) the hindlimb muscles were so arranged that the animal could not run fast, but were well suited to climbing and balancing; and (vi) the tail was rigid and so served as a balancing aid.

Peter Galton reviewed these statements critically in order to find out whether it was possible to confirm that *Hypsilophodon* was arboreal. Let us go through the points one by one to see how convincing they are.

(i) The authenticity of the idea of a grasping toe on the foot depends on whether the first toe of the foot pointed backwards, as it does in a bird's foot, to grip a branch. As can be seen in the drawing overleaf, the first toe does *seem* to be reversed but it is rather short compared to that of a bird and, more importantly, looking back at the original fossil, it can be seen that the claw on the end of the toe has been reversed by the artist! In life the first toe of *Hypsilophodon* pointed in the same direction as all the other toes, and therefore could not be used to grip on to branches.

(ii) The curved claws on the hind feet are not in fact strongly arched and would certainly not have prevented this animal from walking and running on the ground.

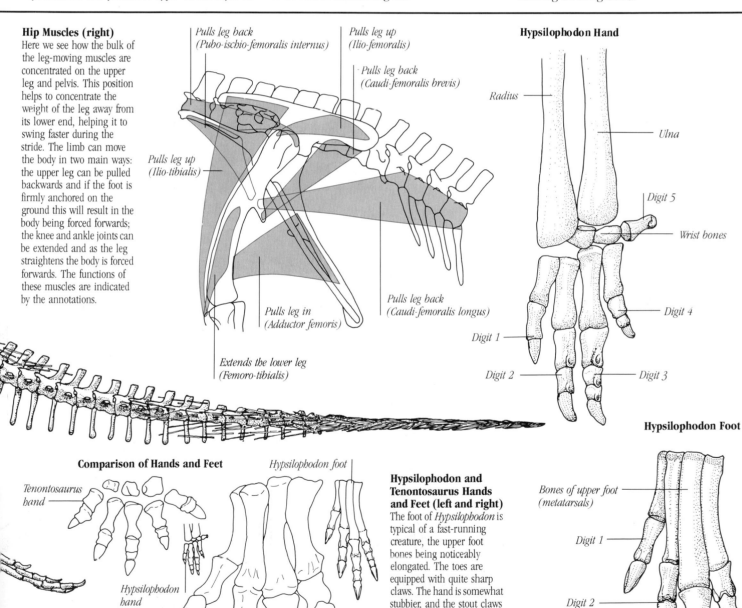

Hip Muscles (right)

Here we see how the bulk of the leg-moving muscles are concentrated on the upper leg and pelvis. This position helps to concentrate the weight of the leg away from its lower end, helping it to swing faster during the stride. The limb can move the body in two main ways: the upper leg can be pulled backwards and if the foot is firmly anchored on the ground this will result in the body being forced forwards; the knee and ankle joints can be extended and as the leg straightens the body is forced forwards. The functions of these muscles are indicated by the annotations.

Pulls leg back (Pubo-ischio-femoralis internus)

Pulls leg up (Ilio-femoralis)

Pulls leg back (Caudi-femoralis brevis)

Pulls leg up (Ilio-tibialis)

Pulls leg in (Adductor femoris)

Pulls leg back (Caudi-femoralis longus)

Extends the lower leg (Femoro-tibialis)

Hypsilophodon Hand

Radius

Ulna

Digit 5

Wrist bones

Digit 4

Digit 1

Digit 2

Digit 3

Comparison of Hands and Feet

Tenontosaurus hand

Hypsilophodon foot

Hypsilophodon hand

Tenontosaurus foot

period or swing-time, so during the stride the hind leg can swing backwards and forwards very rapidly — obviously useful for a fast runner. The characteristic bony rods are present along the backbone and in the tail.

Hypsilophodon and Tenontosaurus Hands and Feet (left and right)

The foot of *Hypsilophodon* is typical of a fast-running creature, the upper foot bones being noticeably elongated. The toes are equipped with quite sharp claws. The hand is somewhat stubbier, and the stout claws may have been used for tearing of scratching. The drawings (left) compare the hands and feet of *Tenontosaurus* and *Hypsilophodon*; while the relative dimensions vary considerably, they are basically very similar in design, suggesting close relationship.

Hypsilophodon Foot

Bones of upper foot (metatarsals)

Digit 1

Digit 2

Digit 3

Digit 4

(iii and iv) The forearm bones are not particularly strongly bowed compared with other dinosaurs, indeed they are less strongly bowed than those of *Iguanodon* and nobody believes that *Iguanodon* lived in trees! Similarly, point (iv) about the greater range of movement possible at the shoulder does not hold up to detailed comparison with other dinosaurs.

(v) The arrangement of muscles in the hindlimb of *Hypsilophodon* is unlikely to have hindered movement; in fact they are arranged in such a way that the legs could be moved very quickly.

(vi) The rigid tail of *Hypsilophodon* is due to the fact that its end is sheathed in bony tendons (rather similar to the arrangement seen in *Deinonychus*, page 59). Such a stiff tail would have been most useful as a stabiliser during fast running and in rapid changes of direction, rather than for tree-dwelling where it may even have got in the way. Quite often tree-dwelling animals have long, flexible, prehensile tails to aid climbing and grip.

Peter Galton concluded that there was no good evidence for *Hypsilophodon* being arboreal and in fact presented rather convincing evidence that it was a very fleet-footed ornithopod. Comparing the proportions of the limbs in known fast-running animals alive today (horses, gazelles and antelopes), it was found that *Hypsilophodon* had limb proportions typical of very fast-running animals, such as some of the smaller antelopes.

Family Members

Looking briefly at other hypsilophodontids, *Tenontosaurus* was a much larger animal (c. 15ft, 4·5m in length) that lived in North America at about the time that *Hypsilophodon* lived in Europe. As should be expected, its limbs are much more heavily built than those of *Hypsilophodon* to support its greater body weight. It has a sheath of tendons encasing the end of its tail, but unlike *Hypsilophodon* it appears to have walked on all four legs, although it probably ran on its back legs alone, with its great long tail stuck straight out to counterbalance the heavy chest and belly. Linked to the greater size of *Tenontosaurus,* the head is large and deeper to permit a more considerable intake of food and provide room for powerful jaw muscles.

Tenontosaurus remains have been found in the same quarries as *Deinonychus*. Unfortunately, *Tenontosaurus* relied on its large size to deter predators, coupled with its ability to run away at speed, since it had no defensive weapons. Neither of these ploys was likely to have been very successful against sophisticated and fast-moving predators such as *Deinonychus*.

Dryosaurus and *Dysalotosaurus* of the late Jurassic are very similar to *Hypsilophodon* in size and shape, although there are consistent differences in their anatomy. For example, there are no teeth at the front of the upper jaw in *Dryosaurus* and *Dysalotosaurus*, while there are five in *Hypsilophodon;* also the arrangement of the bones of the hips is rather different, and there are only three toes on the hindfoot while *Hypsilophodon* has four.

One intriguing observation that has been made relates to the similarity between *Dryosaurus* from western North America and *Dysalotosaurus* from Tanzania. As noted above,

it has been proposed that these forms are so similar that they should both be named *Dryosaurus*. This has prompted one author to speculate that Africa and North America were linked by a land route in the late Jurassic so that animals could move from one area to the other unhindered. Geographical maps that reconstruct that period, however, seem to indicate that seaways separated America from Africa at this time. Perhaps there is not great problem here though. In middle to late Jurassic times the northern and southern continents were linked, so that their faunas were undoubtedly very similar. By late Jurassic times, the faunas were only recently separated so there had been relatively little time for evolutionary divergence in the faunas to come about. This is reflected in the fact that although one or two similar genera are found in western North America and Tanzania: *Drysosaurus, Brachiosaurus* (see page 86), and (doubtfully) *Ceratosaurus* (page 62) and *Allosaurus* (page 62), they are still

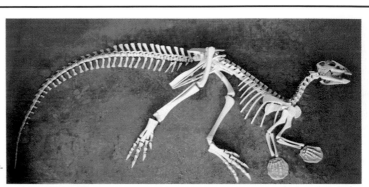

Right: This reconstruction of *Hypsilophodon foxii* is based on skeletal material held in the Sandown Museum, Isle of Wight. It is made of polyester resin reinforced with fibreglass, and was built under the supervision of Stephen Hutt. It is about 4·6ft (1·4m) in length and thus probably represents an immature individual, rather than a fully-grown specimen.

Right: The graceful lines and agile build of a typical hypsilophodontid are well displayed in this skeleton of *Dryosaurus altus* that is in the Carnegie Museum of Natural History in Pittsburgh. The relative dimensions of fore and hindlimbs are readily apparent, as is the absence of teeth from the front of its upper jaw. *Dryosaurus* is very similar to the East African form *Dysalotosaurus.*

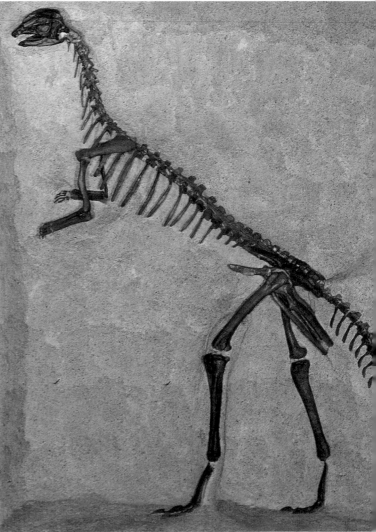

Above: This shattered skull of *Tenontosaurus* still semi-encased in its plaster jacket shows how much work often has to be put in to the task of reconstructing a dinosaur. *Tenontosaurus* has a fairly deep skull with plenty of room for the attachment of large jaw muscles. Though similar in size and shape to a small iguanodontid, it seems to be more closely related to the smaller *Hypsilophodon.*

different enough to be called separate species. Also other groups, for example, the stegosaurs, other sauropods and 'coelurosaurs' are represented by quite distinctive genera indicating that some of the dinosaurs are not common to both continents, thereby supporting the idea of a seaway separating these two areas. As always, a balanced view, weighing all the facts *pro* and *contra,* is necessary to any interpretation.

Life-Style

Returning to *Hypsilophodon,* about twenty-three partial or complete skeletons have been discovered on the Isle of Wight; all of these have come from a small area of the cliffs, the so-called '*Hypsilophodon* bed' from which virtually nothing else has been discovered. Many of the skeletons are beautifully preserved with all the bones in position, and several skeletons are practically touching. Why there should be such a rich concentration of these small dinosaurs in

one place is a mystery. One suggestion is that the animals preserved there represent part of a small herd that became trapped and perished in inter-tidal quick-sand. This is certainly a novel explanation, but it does have some merit. We would normally expect that the process leading to the fossilisation of any animal is quite a long and chancy one. The animal dies or is killed; its remains are left to rot and may be scavenged so that bits are lost before it is either finally destroyed, or buried in sediments, or washed into a river. Thus we should normally expect only very incomplete or fragmentary remains to be preserved. The *Hypsilophodon* bed, however, reveals complete and beautifully preserved skeletons; they must have been buried very rapidly at the time of death, allowing no time for scavenging or dipersal through rotting. Burial in quick-sand is certainly one way in which this could have happened.

So, what sort of a picture can we build up of hypsilophodontid dinosaurs and their possible

way of life? The typical hypsilophodontids were small, agile and extremely fleet-footed creatures of the Jurassic and Cretaceous Periods. In this, however, they did not differ greatly from either of their predecessors of the late Triassic and early Jurassic, the fabrosaurids and heterodontosaurids. However, although the fabrosaurids survived until the end of the Jurassic so far as we can tell, they were never very abundant once the hypsilophodontids appeared. The heterodontosaurids fared even worse; they do not seem to have survived beyond the earliest part of the Jurassic Period.

The explanation for this evolutionary change advanced in the section on fabrosaurids compared the way in which these animals chewed plant food. Fabrosaurids have rather simple, well-separated teeth and slender jaws well suited to chipping off pieces of foliage or soft shoots and swallowing them directly, while hypsilophodontids have teeth which overlap one another to form a long cutting blade, have much heavier jaws, more powerful jaw muscles *and* cheeks. With this rather complicated arrangement, these animals could mince up tough plants by repetitively chewing them up and the food would not be lost from the sides of the mouth each time they chewed because of the presence of retentive fleshy cheeks.

From an evolutionary point of view, the hypsilophodontids can be seen to be more advanced than the fabrosaurids in terms of the efficiency with which they chewed plant food, and perhaps it was this development that allowed them to replace the fabrosaurids as the dominant small-to-medium size plant eaters in the fossil record. This argument seems convincing enough, but it does have its flaws because it does not take account of the other important group of early ornithopods, the heterodontosaurids. As we have seen, these were small, agile, fleet-footed creatures of the late Triassic and earliest Jurassic. However, like hypsilophodontids, these animals also had a blade-like arrangement of teeth in the jaws, heavy jaws and jaw muscles, and cheeks. So the question remains: why did the heterodontosaurids die out so early in the Jurassic when they appear to have had such an efficient mechanism for chewing food? The simple answer is that we do not know! One possibility is that heterodontosaurids evolved their special jaws and teeth to deal with a very particular type of plant growing in the late Triassic and that this plant died out early in the Jurassic Period. Such an explanation is very unsatisfactory because it can never be proved or disproved. It is biologically plausible because it is known that certain animals do have a very specific food preference, i.e. pandas only eat bamboo, and koala bears only eat some varieties of eucalyptus leaf. In both cases, if the plants died, so would the animals because they are unable to change their diet. However, this observation does not mean that heterodontosaurids necessarily had such precise dietary requirements.

I hope that this problem emphasizes how careful one has to be when formulating a particular theory to explain an observation. When dealing with living animals it is usually possible to test a theory by direct experimentation. When considering the fossil record, it is very easy to propose all manner of theories to explain a particular observation, but these theories are impossible to test in any practical way. If any preference is made, then it is usually based on a judicious mixture of personal experience, biological plausibility and the application of plain commonsense.

Left: The nearest parallels to the hypsilophodontids in the natural world today would appear to be very speedy and agile runners such as this Thomson's Gazelle. Comparison of the dimensions of their bones shows that the proportions of the limb bones of hypsilophodontids are very similar to those of fleet-footed antelopes, and thus their behaviour may also be similar.

The Tree-Dweller (left and below)

The drawing (left) is based on Othenio Abel's 1912 illustration of the foot of *Hypsilophodon.* The reversed first toe was thought to be evidence that it was a tree-dweller and prompted restorations like Neave Parker's (below). In fact Abel had misinterpreted the data: *Hypsilophodon's* first toe pointed in the same direction as the others.

IGUANODONTIDS

Iguanodontids are ornithopod dinosaurs of medium-to-large size (16·5-33ft, 5-10m long) which range in time from the late Jurassic to the end of the Cretaceous Period. They appear to have co-existed quite happily with the hypsilophodontids in the late Jurassic and early Cretaceous, but the appearance of the most advanced ornithopods, the hadrosaurids, resulted in a marked decline in the abundance and diversity of the iguanodontids. In fact they all but go extinct everywhere in the world except in Western Europe where, for some reason (perhaps geographic isolation), the hadrosaurids never seem to have become firmly established.

A general comparison with the hypsilophodontids shows that these are all rather large, clumsy animals with massive hindlimbs and broad feet to support their heavy bodies and quite large shoulders and forelimbs; the fingers of the hand show modification such that the claws are broad and flattened and rather

hoof-like, as if they were used predominantly for walking rather than for grasping objects, as seemed to be the case in most hypsilophodontids. Many of these features are simply size-related characteristics, as can be appreciated if we look back and compare them with the only really large hypsilophodontid, *Tenontosaurus*. However, that is not to imply that iguanodontids are really just overgrown hypsilophodontids. There are a number of characteristic features of the iguanodontids, particularly in the structure of their skulls, teeth, forelimbs and hips, that set them apart as a distinct group and support the idea that they form a family of their own.

The illustrations below show clearly that iguanodontids retain the basic ornithopod characteristics: the body is counterbalanced by the tail and they walk on their hindlegs. It should be noted though that they are also perfectly capable of walking or resting on 'all-fours'—notice the large, blunt, hoof-like

Muttaburrasaurus (below)

This animal was about 23ft (7m) long and the skeleton shows affinities with *Camptosaurus* and *Iguanodon,* although it is not very well preserved. *Muttaburrasaurus* is very important because dinosaurs from Australia are still poorly known, and the new find extends our knowledge of the palaeogeographic distribution of iguanodontids which are otherwise

mainly known from the northern hemisphere. *Muttaburrasaurus* had a low broad head, with a heavy bony lump above the snout, and it has been suggested that its teeth could have been used for chopping plants or meat. This idea has yet to be confirmed.

Time Chart (left)

Like the hypsilophodontids, the iguanodontids seem to arise in the late Jurassic with such forms as *Camptosaurus* in North America and Europe. These medium-sized ornithopods were fairly abundant in the early Cretaceous of Europe, Asia, Africa and Australia, but in the late Cretaceous were limited to just Europe and possibly Africa.

Camptosaurus (right)

This ornithopod is known from a number of skeletons, and these include both juvenile and adult specimens ranging in length from 4-23ft (1·2-7m). *Camptosaurus* is the earliest iguanodontid that is known from skeletons. It is more primitive than the typical Cretaceous iguanodontids in being smaller, in having four toes on the foot (*Iguanodon* had three) and in lacking a fully developed spiked thumb. Like other iguanodontids, *Camptosaurus* had small hooves on both its fingers and toes, and this suggests that it often walked on all-fours.

Comparative Sizes (right)

1 *Camptosaurus:* l. 16·5-23ft (5-7m)
2 *Ouranosaurus:* l. 23ft (7m).
3 *Muttaburrasaurus:* l. 23ft (7m).
4 *Iguanodon:* l. 33ft (10m)

Time Chart columns

YEARS AGO (MILLIONS)

CRETACEOUS

KANGNASAURUS
MOCHLODON
MUTTABURRASAURUS
OURANOSAURUS
PROBACTROSAURUS
IGUANODON
CAMPTOSAURUS

JURASSIC

TRIASSIC

64
70
80
90
100
110
120
130
140
150
160
170
180
190
200
210
220
225

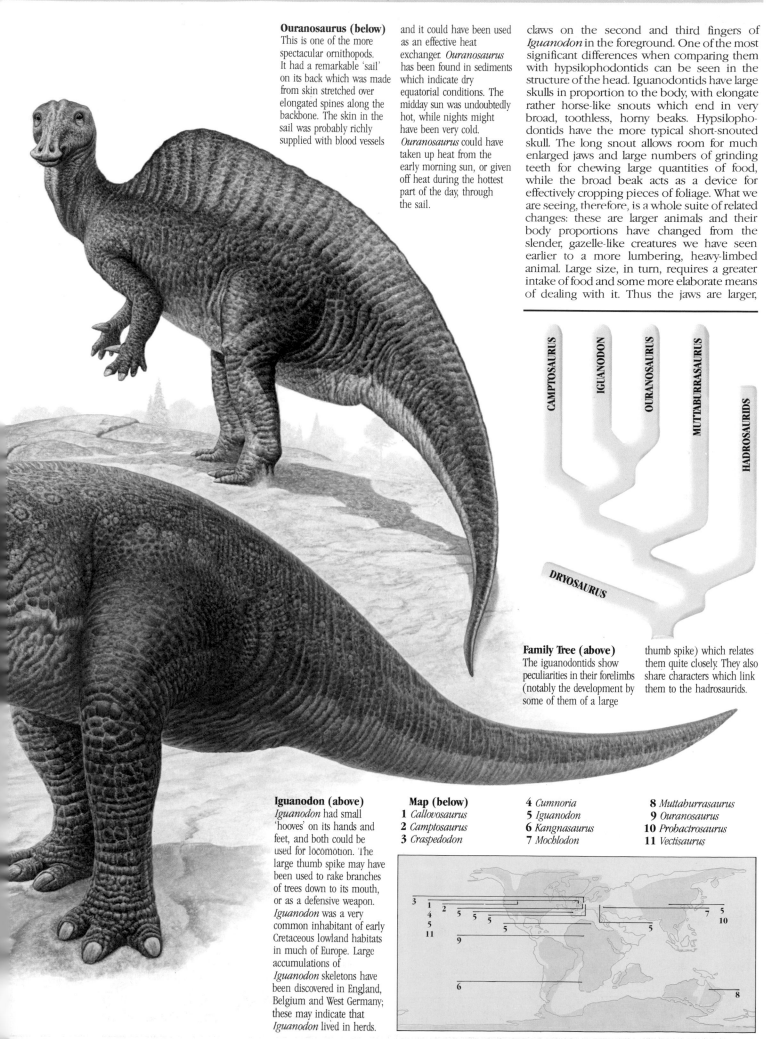

Ouranosaurus (below)
This is one of the more spectacular ornithopods. It had a remarkable 'sail' on its back which was made from skin stretched over elongated spines along the backbone. The skin in the sail was probably richly supplied with blood vessels and it could have been used as an effective heat exchanger. *Ouranosaurus* has been found in sediments which indicate dry equatorial conditions. The midday sun was undoubtedly hot, while nights might have been very cold. *Ouranosaurus* could have taken up heat from the early morning sun, or given off heat during the hottest part of the day, through the sail.

claws on the second and third fingers of *Iguanodon* in the foreground. One of the most significant differences when comparing them with hypsilophodontids can be seen in the structure of the head. Iguanodontids have large skulls in proportion to the body, with elongate rather horse-like snouts which end in very broad, toothless, horny beaks. Hypsilopho-dontids have the more typical short-snouted skull. The long snout allows room for much enlarged jaws and large numbers of grinding teeth for chewing large quantities of food, while the broad beak acts as a device for effectively cropping pieces of foliage. What we are seeing, therefore, is a whole suite of related changes: these are larger animals and their body proportions have changed from the slender, gazelle-like creatures we have seen earlier to a more lumbering, heavy-limbed animal. Large size, in turn, requires a greater intake of food and some more elaborate means of dealing with it. Thus the jaws are larger,

CAMPTOSAURUS

IGUANODON

OURANOSAURUS

MUTTABURRASAURUS

HADROSAURIDS

DRYOSAURUS

Family Tree (above)
The iguanodontids show peculiarities in their forelimbs (notably the development by some of them of a large thumb spike) which relates them quite closely. They also share characters which link them to the hadrosaurids.

Iguanodon (above)
Iguanodon had small 'hooves' on its hands and feet, and both could be used for locomotion. The large thumb spike may have been used to rake branches of trees down to its mouth, or as a defensive weapon. *Iguanodon* was a very common inhabitant of early Cretaceous lowland habitats in much of Europe. Large accumulations of *Iguanodon* skeletons have been discovered in England, Belgium and West Germany; these may indicate that *Iguanodon* lived in herds.

Map (below)
1 *Callovosaurus*
2 *Camptosaurus*
3 *Craspedodon*
4 *Cumnoria*
5 *Iguanodon*
6 *Kangnasaurus*
7 *Mochlodon*
8 *Muttaburrasaurus*
9 *Ouranosaurus*
10 *Probactrosaurus*
11 *Vectisaurus*

creating the long snout, and the horny beak is broader to collect more food with each bite. Having found a modern equivalent of the fabrosaurids and hypsilophodontids among the small gazelles and antelopes of today, perhaps the most appropriate comparison for the iguanodontids would be with the larger type of equid (i.e. horses), which are large-bodied and have strong legs and large, long-snouted skulls.

Turning back to look at the evolutionary history of the iguanodontids, we find that the earliest fossils come from the late Jurassic of North America and Western Europe. The earliest remains so far reported are of an animal named *Callovosaurus* ('Callovian reptile') from the late Jurassic of Northampton, England, which consists of a femur. The assignment of this specimen, which is crushed in the middle, must be uncertain for it could easily belong to a *Dryosaurus*-like animal as it is quite slender, unlike typical iguanodontids.

Apart from *Callovosaurus*, the earliest iguanodontids belong to the genus *Camptosaurus* ('flexible reptile') which is known from several skeletons discovered in 1879 in the late Jurassic of Wyoming, North America; these animals seem to range in size from about 16·5-23ft (5-7m) in length. As was the case with the two hypsilophodontid dinosaurs named *Dryosaurus* and *Dysalotosaurus*, there is another genus named *Cumnoria* which was also discovered in 1879 in late Jurassic rocks at Cumnor, near Oxford in England. This has recently been redescribed by Dr Peter Galton and Philip Powell and renamed *Camptosaurus* since it is virtually identical with the North American species. As in the case of *Dryosaurus* and *Dysalotosaurus*, the similarity between these dinosaurs from North America and Europe testifies to a land connection between these two areas well into the late Jurassic.

In early Cretaceous times a variety of iguanodontids appear in various parts of the world. *Iguanodon* ('iguana tooth') which has given its name to the family, is found abundantly right across western Europe, from Spain, Portugal and Britain in the West, to the Urals in the East. Other well-preserved genera are *Ouranosaurus* ('brave reptile') which was discovered quite recently (1965) in Niger, West Africa. Although very like *Iguanodon* in most respects, *Ouranosaurus* has a very distinctive head and extraordinarily high spines on its back. *Muttaburrasaurus* ('reptile from Muttaburra') is another newly discovered iguanodontid from Queensland, Australia. Although not as well preserved as some of the other iguanodontids, this form does appear to have an extraordinary bump on its nose, which is reminiscent of that seen in the hadrosaurid *Kritosaurus* (page 117). There are several other rather fragmentary remains that have been described including *Probactrosaurus* ('before the Bactrian reptile') from Mongolia (which may in fact be *Iguanodon* judged by what is so

Skull Comparison (below)
The skulls of these iguanodontids show considerable differences, despite all being large compared to the body, having long snouts, and ending in a broad, toothless beak. The *Iguanodon* skull has a generalised structure but that of *Camptosaurus* is lower at the back and has a comparatively narrower snout. The skull of *Muttaburrasaurus* is the most peculiar, with a remarkable bump above and behind its nostrils. We do not know what this was for but it may have been implicated in sexual recognition. The Mongolian form, *Iguanodon orientalis*, has a similar protruberance. These three forms represent a wide distribution for iguanodontids, coming from Europe, North America and Australia respectively.

Jaw Muscles (below)
The jaw muscles of *Ouranosaurus* are large and powerful as expected in a large ornithopod. Muscle 1 arises from a large opening in the skull and it has a firm insertion on to a projection of the lower jaw (coronoid process). This insertion increases the moment arm of the muscle, a measure of the force which it can produce.

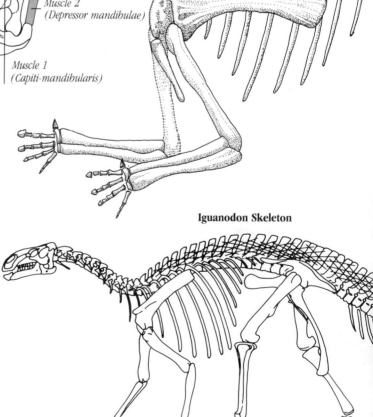

Ouranosaurus Skeleton

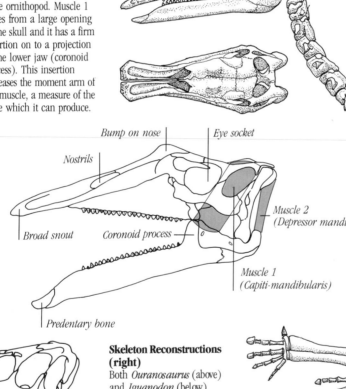

Bump on nose | Eye socket
Nostrils
Muscle 2 (Depressor mandibulae)
Broad snout | Coronoid process
Muscle 1 (Capiti-mandibularis)
Predentary bone

Skeleton Reconstructions (right)
Both *Ouranosaurus* (above) and *Iguanodon* (below) have fairly typical ornithopod skeletons. They are both bipedal, with the front legs reduced in size, but *Ouranosaurus* differs from the basic ornithopod plan in its large vertebral spines. They are both large animals, powerfully built compared with some ornithopods, and with particularly strong front legs. These may have been used in walking or resting on all-fours, rather like modern day kangaroos. This use of the front legs is quite different from that seen in the earlier ornithopods, and in fact iguanodontids are much more robust, less agile animals all round.

Iguanodon Skeleton

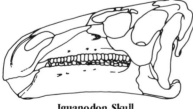

Iguanodon Skull

Camptosaurus Skull

Muttaburrasaurus Skull

far known); *Vectisaurus* ('Isle of Wight reptile') from the Isle of Wight, which is definitely just *Iguanodon; Anoplosaurus* ('unarmoured reptile') from England, a very fragmentary skeleton; and *Kangnasaurus* ('Kangna's reptile') from a tooth and femur from Southern Africa that may be an iguanodontid.

The late Cretaceous seems to show a marked decline in the abundance and diversity of iguanodontids worldwide. The only record that these forms survived at all is some teeth from the late Cretaceous of Western Europe that have been named *Craspedodon* ('edge tooth'), and several incomplete skeletons of a small iguanodontid named *Mochlodon* ('bar tooth') from Rumania.

The evolution of the iguanodontids seems to tie in quite well with their biogeography. They first appear in the fossil record in the late Jurassic, and probably evolved sometime around the middle Jurassic at which time they would have been able to disperse practically

worldwide, since the continents were then in contact. This is supported, partly at least, by the fact that *Camptosaurus* is found in western North America and Europe in the late Jurassic. In the early Cretaceous, seaways had begun to separate the various continents so that each was able to evolve its own distinct iguanodontid. Except, that is, for East Asia which may have received neither hypsilophodontid nor iguanodontid dinosaurs because of a sea barrier in the Jurassic. Thus the various continents show an interesting variety and abundance of iguanodontids: *Iguanodon* (Europe), *Ouranosaurus* (Africa), *Muttaburrasaurus* (Australia) and perhaps even *Kangnasaurus* (Southern Africa). However, the dispersal and evolution of iguanodontids seems to have been rapidly curtailed by the appearance of hadrosaurids in the late Cretaceous. After this time they seem to have become confined to just western Europe, where few hadrosaurids are found.

While the fortunes of the iguanodontids seem to have been adversely affected by the appearance of the hadrosaurids, they do not seem to have been so affected by the hypsilophodontids, which first appear at about the same time in the fossil record. This difference may indicate that the hypsilophodontids did not *compete*, in an ecological sense, with iguanodontids, whereas the hadrosaurids did. This means that the hypsilophodontids probably did not feed on the same sorts of plants, or generally live in the same sort of way, as did iguanodontids. This would seem reasonable because the two groups are not only very different in size, but their jaws and teeth are different. Probably they were able to co-exist quite happily. By contrast, the hadrosaurids exhibit the same body size range as the iguanodontids and their jaws and teeth are quite similar; the only real difference seems to be that the hadrosaurids have a more efficient arrangement for food grinding. The

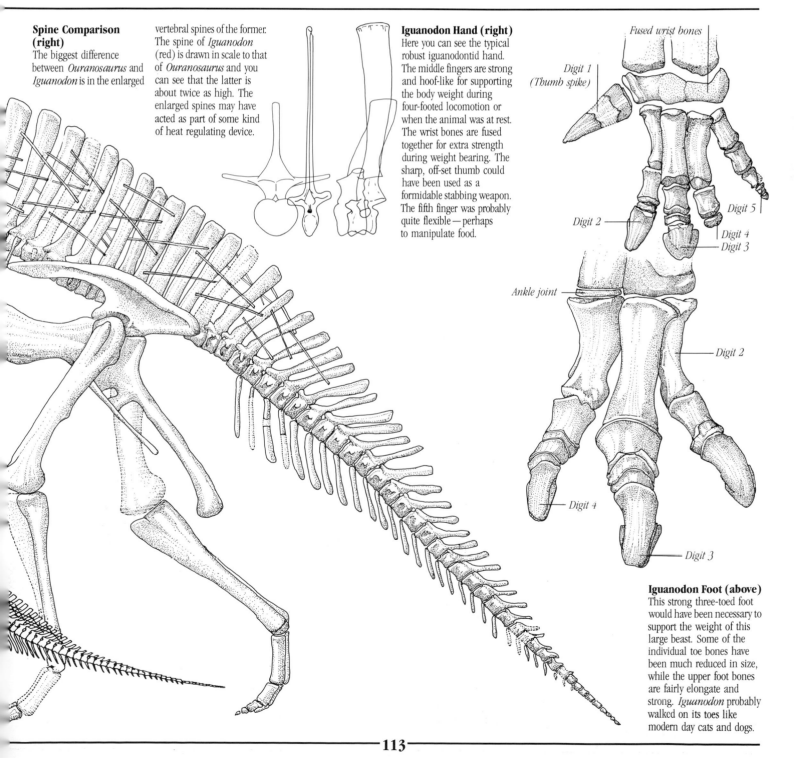

Spine Comparison (right)

The biggest difference between *Ouranosaurus* and *Iguanodon* is in the enlarged vertebral spines of the former. The spine of *Iguanodon* (red) is drawn in scale to that of *Ouranosaurus* and you can see that the latter is about twice as high. The enlarged spines may have acted as part of some kind of heat regulating device.

Iguanodon Hand (right)

Here you can see the typical robust iguanodontid hand. The middle fingers are strong and hoof-like for supporting the body weight during four-footed locomotion or when the animal was at rest. The wrist bones are fused together for extra strength during weight bearing. The sharp, off-set thumb could have been used as a formidable stabbing weapon. The fifth finger was probably quite flexible — perhaps to manipulate food.

Fused wrist bones

Digit 1 (Thumb spike)

Digit 2

Digit 5

Digit 4

Digit 3

Ankle joint

Digit 2

Digit 4

Digit 3

Iguanodon Foot (above)

This strong three-toed foot would have been necessary to support the weight of this large beast. Some of the individual toe bones have been much reduced in size, while the upper foot bones are fairly elongate and strong. *Iguanodon* probably walked on its toes like modern day cats and dogs.

suspicions then are that these two groups probably fed on similar sorts of food and had similar sorts of life-style. Rather than peacefully co-existing, it is highly probable that these two groups of animals were so similar that they actively competed for the same resources. In this case, the most advanced or behaviourally best adapted would be expected to survive, and the less efficient to perish.

Ouranosaurus

We have already looked at *Iguanodon* in some considerable detail in Chapter 2, so here we shall consider *Ouranosaurus*, the rather bizarre ornithopod from Niger. An almost complete skeleton of *Ouranosaurus* was discovered in 1966 near Elrhaz in Niger (West Africa). This was carefully excavated by a team of palaeontologists from the National Museum of Natural History, Paris, France, led by Dr Philippe Taquet. The skeleton was prepared and finally described in detail in 1976 by Dr Taquet.

The head of *Ouranosaurus* is very large and long, and this is especially striking when it is compared with a typical hypsilophodontid skull. In particular, the jaws are very long and have many more large teeth, while the end of the snout is very broad, flattened and toothless; in life this would have been covered by a large horny beak. The nostrils, which are formed just above the beak, are also extremely large. Immediately behind the nostrils there are a pair of low, broad bumps. The significance of these bumps is a mystery. It seems unlikely that they would have been used for defensive purposes, the most likely explanation would seem to be that they were of some behavioural significance, perhaps to aid recognition of members of the same species, or members of the opposite sex. Another rather curious feature, found in nearly all ornithischians, is the palpebral bone, which juts out across the cavity for the eye. Precisely why this should be where it is, and what it does there, is a total mystery. Behind the eye, there are large openings at the back of the skull through which passed the jaw muscles; these

must have been large and powerful because of the great size of the jaws that they had to move. Associated with this arrangement is the presence of a large bony projection that sticks upward towards the back end of the lower jaw. This projection, named the coronoid process, was the point at which most of the large jaw muscles attached. In fabrosaurids there is no coronoid process and even in heterodontosaurids it is quite small. However, in the large-jawed iguanodontids (and the hadrosaurids) the coronoid process is very large. The reason for this is that it not only provides a greater attachment area for the large jaw muscles, but also greatly improves the leverage of the muscles on the jaws so that they can close the jaws more powerfully, and therefore chew food more efficiently. Of course, this all relates to the problems of being a large animal and having to feed on large quantities of plant food.

The neck is of the usual ornithopod type, and is highly flexible. The back, hips and tail, however, have the most enormous spines which form a high, almost sail-like, ridge down the back of the animal. Yet again, this animal presents us with a mystery: what are they for? One suggestion is that the skin covering the 'sail' on its back was used rather like a solar panel. Blood in the skin could be warmed by the Sun's rays so that these animals might warm up their bodies quickly—perhaps after enduring a cold night. Equally, the sail could be used as a radiator to cool the animal down in the heat of the day, or after very strenuous activity. This sort of function has recently been proposed for the plates of *Stegosaurus* (page 152), where it is supported by a lot of additional evidence. In the case of *Ouranosaurus* it is not quite so clear-cut, although a heat-regulating function is quite possible. It is also interesting to note that the carnivorous dinosaur *Spinosaurus*, which appears to have lived at the same time and in the same area as *Ouranosaurus*, also had tall spines on its back. Presumably both dinosaurs grew spines for a similar reason, although the actual cause, whether physiological, behavioural or ecological, is not yet clear.

In most respects the forelimb of *Ouranosaurus* is very similar to that of *Iguanodon*. It is fairly long in comparison with the hindlimb and could have reached the ground quite easily. The claws on its second and third fingers are also very broad and hoof-like for use when walking or resting on 'all-fours'. In addition, the wrist bones are very large and welded together so that the weight of the body would not dislocate them when the hands were used for walking. As in *Iguanodon*, the hand is equipped with a very large thumb-spike that would have made a formidable defensive weapon against large predatory theropods. The fifth finger is quite long and flexible, and may well have been used for holding or plucking plant stems or twigs.

The hindlimb of *Ouranosaurus* is much more heavily built than that of *Hypsilophodon*. The individual bones are much more massive to support the great weight of the body, while the proportions of the bones are rather different. The femur (upper leg bone) is longer,

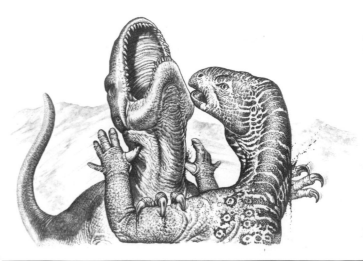

Left: On display in the Palaeontological Institute of the Academy of Sciences in Moscow, this is *Probactrosaurus mongoliensis*. Although the skull is not completely known, the dinosaur seems very similar to—and may even be—*Iguanodon*. The pose is interesting; it suggests quadrupedal motion.

Above: This skeleton cast of *Iguanodon* in Frankfurt's Senckenberg Museum is seen in a more conventional bipedal posture. It illustrates the generally massive build of these creatures, and the special nature of the hands with their thumb spikes for defence against predators, and 'hoofed' digits.

Self Defence (below)
A fully grown iguanodontid must have posed a formidable challenge to any potential predator. Here we see a 'carnosaur' being viciously stabbed by an *Iguanodon* using its thumb spike to good effect. At close quarters, *Iguanodon* was probably more than a match for most attackers.

while the tibia (lower leg) is shorter and the foot is much shorter, more compact and only has three toes. All these changes indicate that the legs were designed primarily to act as pillars, rather than to move the animal quickly as was the case with hypsilophodontids.

Camptosaurus and Muttaburrasaurus

Of the other iguanodontids, *Camptosaurus* from North America and Europe is well described and resembles quite closely both *Iguanodon* and *Ouranosaurus*. The main differences are to be found in the head, hands, hips and feet. The head of *Camptosaurus* is long, but quite low when compared with *Iguanodon,* and it lacks *Ouranosaurus'* bumps on the nose and its very broad muzzle.

The backbone is much more ordinary and 'Iguanodon-like' in its construction, with no tall spines. The forelimb differs slightly from that of *Iguanodon* in that the hand has a short spur-like first finger, rather than a distinct spike; also the claws on fingers two and three are more curved and less hoof-like. However, *Camptosaurus* does possess the large bony wrist to enable it to walk on all-fours.

As far as the hips are concerned, the pubis has a very long, narrow, posterior rod, which reaches the end of the ischium. In *Iguanodon* and *Ouranosaurus,* the posterior rod of the pubis only reaches about half-way down the ischium. Finally, its foot possesses four, well-developed toes, while there are only three in *Iguanodon* and *Ouranosaurus.*

Muttaburrasaurus is not known from such well-preserved material as the other iguanodontids mentioned above, but those features that have survived seem to share similarities with the iguanodontids, and in particular with *Camptosaurus.* However, unlike *Camptosaurus,* the head has a large bump between the nostrils at the front of the snout—different from the double bumps seen *behind* the nostrils in *Ouranosaurus.* Unfortunately, the hand is not completely known, so it is not certain that it possessed a large thumb-spike as did *Iguanodon* or *Ouranosaurus.* The illustration on page 110 shows it with a thumb spike, but this is speculative.

Life-Style

Iguanodontids, therefore, would seem to represent the first group of large-bodied ornithopods to evolve. They show characteristic differences when compared to the hypsilophodontids (and fabrosaurids), changes which are largely explicable in terms of the greater size of these animals and the simple physical and biological changes that this entails. The sort of life that these particular creatures led is not too difficult to deduce. Their larger size rendered them slower and less agile than the previous groups and much more liable to attack from the large, megalosaur-type predators of the time: *Allosaurus, Ceratosaurus Altispinax, Spinosaurus* etc. Rather than being evasive, these dinosaurs seem to have used defensive weapons to repel predators. All of them (except perhaps *Muttaburrasaurus* for which evidence is not yet available) had a spur-like claw on the first finger of the hand which would have been a surprisingly effective weapon. All of the large predatory dinosaurs named above possess characteristically massive heads, perched on quite short but powerful necks and relatively short forelimbs. This means that in order to make an attack, these predators would have to lunge at their prey from close-quarters, bringing them into range of the iguanodontid's forelimb spur. At close-quarters the spur, swung with all the weight of the massive body behind it, could cause hideous injuries to the eyes, face or neck of the predator.

Large accumulations of skeletons of *Iguanodon* in Belgium and Germany, and tracks of footprints from England, provide circumstantial evidence of the social behaviour of this type of dinosaur. Large numbers of fossil skeletons suggest that they were very numerous and by implication quite successful for their time. Footprint trackways, particularly in southern England, seem to show several dinosaurs moving about in the same direction at the same time—perhaps as a herd. Herding, if it did take place, is another important method of gaining protection from predators (see also sauropod herding, page 97). Looking at *Iguanodon,* the largest fully grown individuals were 33ft (10m) or more in length and probably sufficiently large to be practically invulnerable to attack. The prime subjects for attack would undoubtedly have been old or infirm individuals or the smaller, less powerful, young ones. Herding allows animals to protect themselves, and particularly the more vulnerable individuals, by structuring the herd so that the young (and perhaps pregnant females) stay near the centre, while the larger adults (perhaps exclusively the males if they are the larger) patrol the edges as 'look-outs' in order to give the alarm and defend the herd from predators.

The remains of *Iguanodon* are frequently found in lowland, marshy or estuarine areas in Britain and Europe and it seems quite possible that these animals lived in herds in such areas, feeding on the rich vegetation that would be expected to grow in such conditions. The plants growing in these areas were probably primarily horsetails (*Equisetum*), ferns, cyads, bennettitaleans and various conifers; many of these, although we do not know exactly which, would have formed the diet of these animals.

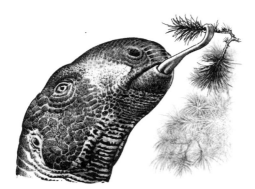

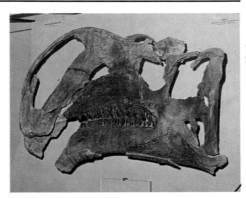

Reptilian Giraffe? (above) This drawing is based on Gerhard Heilmann's 1928 restoration that pictured *Iguanodon* with a prehensile tongue being used to gather foliage. Heilmann was influenced by Louis Dollo who had noticed an opening at the front of *Iguanodon's* lower jaw and surmised that its tongue could extend through it. In fact the hole was broken bone; there is no evidence to support Dollo's view.

Above: This fine skull of *Iguanodon orientalis* from Mongolia is very similar to European *Iguanodon* except for its enormous bulbous 'nose'. This is a totally unexpected feature and of great scientific interest.

Below: The impressive skeleton of *Ouranosaurus nigeriensis* in the Museo Civico di Storia Naturale, Venice. The remarkable dorsal 'sail' may have acted like a solar panel for temperature regulation.

Hadrosaurids were the last group of Hornithopods to evolve, appearing as they did in the middle of the Cretaceous Period. Despite their relatively short time of existence—they perished along with all other dinosaurs at the end of the Cretaceous Period (some 30 million years later)—hadrosaurids evolved spectacularly into a remarkable variety of types. As you will see by looking carefully at the variety of hadrosaurids illustrated in the following pages, the main differences between the many species are found in the shape of the heads of these creatures; the bodies of virtually all the hadrosaurids are remarkably similar. Indeed, hadrosaurid body shape is just the same as seen in the earlier iguanodontids apart from a few relatively minor changes. For example, hadrosaurids have no thumb at all and have slightly differently shaped hip-bones.

The first hadrosaur skeleton was described in 1858 by Joseph Leidy, an American palaeontologist. The remains were excavated by William Parker Foulke from a marl pit at Haddonfield, New Jersey. Apparently Foulke had heard that many large reptile bones, probably vertebrae, had been excavated from the pit about twenty years earlier, but these remains had been scattered and lost. So in 1858 Foulke re-located the pit, which had been filled in and was overgrown again, and re-excavated it in the hope of finding more of the same animal. At a depth of about 10 feet (3m) a pile of fossil bones was discovered including twenty-eight vertebrae, teeth and bones of the forelimb, hindlimb and pelvis; these remains were described by Leidy in 1858 and if complete would probably have resembled *Kritosaurus* ('chosen reptile') below. Leidy immediately recognized similarities between the shape of the teeth of this new animal (which he named *Hadrosaurus foulkii*, 'Foulke's big reptile') and the then known British dinosaur *Iguanodon*. However, as noted earlier, *Iguanodon* was at this time rather poorly known, having only

Bactrosaurus (below)
This is one of the earliest hadrosaurs. Although *Bactrosaurus* lacked a crest, it seems to be related to later 'lambeosaurine' hadrosaurs such as *Corythosaurus* and *Parasaurolophus* (see pages 122-123). Like all other hadrosaurs, *Bactrosaurus* had batteries of cheek teeth set well back in the mouth which could have ground up very tough plant material. *Bactrosaurus* was a fairly small hadrosaur, being only 20ft (6m) long.

Time Chart (left)
The uncrested hadrosaurine hadrosaurs are notably abundant in the very last part of the Cretaceous. Perhaps they were better able to cope with the harsher climate and vegetation than the crested lambeosaurine forms (see pages 122-127).

Anatosaurus (below)
This was a common hadrosaur, and it is one of the best known 'crestless' forms. It was a large animal, normally c. 33ft (10m) long, and weighing about 3 tonnes. The massive limbs and the broad 'duck bill' are very clear in this front view. *Anatosaurus* could have gathered up large amounts of vegetation in its broad mouth, and it had batteries of strong cheek teeth.

Comparative Sizes (left)
1 *Bactrosaurus*: l. 13-20ft (4-6m).
2 *Kritosaurus*: l. 30ft (9m).
3 *Anatosaurus*: l. 33-42ft (10-13m).
4 *Edmontosaurus*: l. 33-42ft (10-13m).

YEARS AGO (MILLIONS)

64
70
80
90
100
110
120
130
140
150
160
170
180
190
200
210
220
225

CRETACEOUS
JURASSIC
TRIASSIC

HADROSAURUS
ANATOSAURUS
EDMONTOSAURUS
KRITOSAURUS
BACTROSAURUS

been described from fragmentary remains, and was believed to look rather like a giant reptilian rhinoceros. Leidy quickly recognized that although *Hadrosaurus* had teeth like those of *Iguanodon,* it did not look at all like a reptilian rhinoceros because its front legs were much shorter than its back ones. Indeed he suggested that the animal might have stood upright when feeding, rather like a kangaroo resting on its back legs and tail, dropping down on to 'all-fours' to creep along the ground in a rather toad-like manner.

So it was that Leidy was able to provide a much more accurate picture of the shape and proportions of ornithopod dinosaurs such as *Iguanodon* and *Hadrosaurus* from the fortunate discovery of a single incomplete skeleton—a feat that neither Mantell nor Owen had managed despite having studied remains of *Iguanodon* for nearly forty years. The discovery of complete skeletons of *Iguanodon* in 1878 finally proved the correctness of Leidy's views.

Another of the earliest hadrosaurids known is *Bactrosaurus* ('reptile from Bactria') from Mongolia pictured below; it comes from rocks dated at the early part of the Upper Cretaceous Period. In its general appearance this animal resembles iguanodontids very strongly. It does, however, show, in the structure of its teeth in particular, the development of a grinding battery. Unfortunately the fossilized remains so far discovered do not include its hands, so it is uncertain whether this dinosaur possessed an iguanodontid thumb-spike or whether it was like all other hadrosaurids and had only four fingers on its hand.

At least two types of early hadrosaurid are known from Mongolia, the other is known as *Gilmoreosaurus* (named after Charles Witney Gilmore, the palaeontologist who first described this fossil in the 1930s). As with *Bactrosaurus, Gilmoreosaurus* is not at all well preserved so that its detailed anatomy is very unclear. After these early first appearances, hadrosaurids seem to

Kritosaurus (left)
A medium-sized crestless hadrosaur, *Kritosaurus* is very similar to *Hadrosaurus* in many respects.
Kritosaurus had a deep narrow face with a rounded hump in front of the eyes which was probably covered with thick skin in life.
It has been suggested that female *Kritosaurus* did not have this bump, so that it might have been a sexual recognition character.

Map (below)
1 *Anatosaurus*
2 *Bactrosaurus*
3 *Brachylophosaurus*
4 *Edmontosaurus*
5 *Hadrosaurus*
6 *Kritosaurus*
7 *Secernosaurus*
8 *Shantungosaurus*

Family Tree (right)
Bactrosaurus is the most primitive hadrosaur known to date. The other hadrosaurine hadrosaurs show no great development of specialised head-gear as is seen in later forms, such as the lambeosaurines (page 122).

BACTROSAURUS
ANATOSAURUS
EDMONTOSAURUS
BRACHYLOPHOSAURUS
KRITOSAURUS
HADROSAURUS
'SAUROLOPHINES/LAMBEOSAURINES'

Edmontosaurus (above)
A large animal, up to 42ft (13m) long, *Edmontosaurus* was closely related to *Anatosaurus. Edmontosaurus* had about a thousand strong teeth in the cheek region.
The low area on top of the skull near the front might have been covered with loose skin which could have been inflated to make a loud bellowing call.

IGUANODONTIDS

have evolved very rapidly producing a considerable variety of different species (including *Anatosaurus*, 'duck reptile', and *Edmontosaurus*, 'reptile from Edmonton' seen here), which are found quite widely distributed.

Hadrosaurid Life-Style

In addition to the perceptive comments that he made on the structure of hadrosaurids, Leidy also made several observations concerning the way of life of *Hadrosaurus* which deserve some consideration. He proposed that *Hadrosaurus* was probably an amphibious creature, living in and around water courses. Quite why he thought this is not clear from what he wrote; perhaps the notion that it crawled along like a giant toad, in combination with his observation that it had a rather deep, paddle-like tail convinced Leidy of this way of life. Whatever the reasons, his ideas were adopted wholeheartedly by later palaeontologists working on

these animals. In 1883, Edward Drinker Cope went so far as to state that hadrosaurids had very weak, broad, horny beaks and small loosely attached teeth in their jaws which could only have been used for scooping up and chewing soft aquatic plants. Indeed he proposed that they probably habitually waded in deep water upon their long legs rather like gigantic flamingoes. Further evidence for the supposed aquatic or semi-aquatic way of life of hadrosaurids came from the discovery of 'mummified' remains of another hadrosaurid (*Anatosaurus*) in 1908 by C.H. and C.M. Sternberg. Both of these skeletons showed evidence of a mitten-like covering of skin over the hand giving it the form of a paddle. The evidence then would seem to be very persuasive in favour of Leidy's original proposal that *Hadrosaurus* was amphibious. Indeed many books on dinosaurs feature hadrosaurs wallowing in lakes or on the banks of rivers, chewing water plants. However, there is an

argument that favours a way of life for hadrosaurids away from lakes and rivers. This is based on a careful analysis of the geological nature of the rocks in which hadrosaurids have been found, evidence from the plant fossils preserved with these dinosaurs and a detailed analysis of their anatomy.

(i) The geological evidence suggests that hadrosaurids in North America lived in areas that were coastal plains, close to sea-level with swamps and large meandering rivers. This fits well with the notion that they were amphibious creatures. However, it would also be a reflection of the environment in which the carcasses of these animals were deposited after they had died and been washed down into swampy or lake areas.

(ii) One of the main pieces of evidence concerning the environment in which hadrosaurs lived comes from the plants preserved with these dinosaurs. An analysis of these plant fossils has suggested that they grew in warm

Hadrosaurid Teeth (below)

Hadrosaurid jaws contain a formidable array of hundreds of teeth arranged in batteries on either side of both upper and lower jaws. These teeth acted like a rasping file and could deal with tough vegetation. The front end of the jaws was formed into a wide beak. The drawing below is a cross section through top and bottom jaws, showing how an up-and-down chewing action would cause the teeth to rub abrasively past one another and so crush the plant food. The drawing lower right is solely of the lower jaw. It clearly shows the tooth batteries.

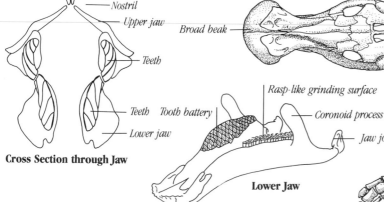

Nostril
Upper jaw
Teeth

Broad beak

Teeth *Tooth battery*
Lower jaw

Cross Section through Jaw

Rasp-like grinding surface
Coronoid process
Jaw joint

Lower Jaw

Predentary bone

Hadrosaurid Skulls (right)

The skulls drawn here and on page 125 show the tremendous variety in the hadrosaurid skull. The three forms here belong to the 'hadrosaurines'. These had large duck-like beaks but little development of the crest, as you can see if you compare the regions coloured red here, which delineate the area of the nasal passages, with those on page 125. The back of the skull in all forms does not change very much which is surprising when you consider what is happening at the front! Even the three crestless

forms here show some variation in their snouts: *Bactrosaurus* is very generalised, rather like an iguanodontid, *Kritosaurus* has an unusual bump on its nose and *Anatosaurus* has an extremely long, broad snout, which gave rise to the description 'duck-billed'.

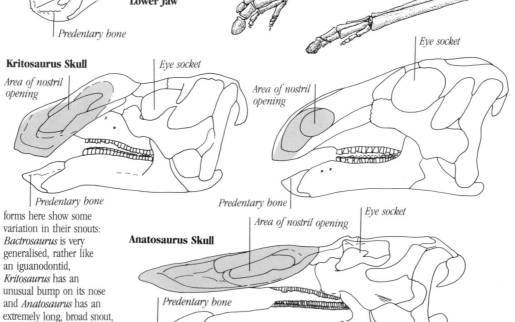

Kritosaurus Skull
Area of nostril opening
Eye socket
Predentary bone

Area of nostril opening
Eye socket
Predentary bone

Area of nostril opening
Eye socket
Anatosaurus Skull
Predentary bone

temperate or subtropical conditions in humid, lowland areas. The plants themselves, however, are represented by very *few* aquatic or marginal pond weeds but by abundant remains of lowland forest trees and shrubs: dominated by conifers, poplars, willows and oaks. Thus most plant food seems to have been on land.

(iii) The animals living (or rather preserved as fossils) with the hadrosaurids include hypsilophodontids, ankylosaurids, ceratopians, sauropods, tyrannosaurids, and other smaller theropods. Very few of these types of dinosaur have ever been thought of as being aquatic or amphibious — only the sauropods, but there is quite convincing evidence that these animals probably only ventured into water occasionally.

(iv) The anatomical evidence consists of two main lines of enquiry. Firstly, what their diet may have been? And secondly, are there any anatomical features that clearly demonstrate that these animals were either *exclusively* amphibious or terrestrial?

Hadrosaurid Diets

Cope's claim that hadrosaurids had soft, weak, beaks and fragile teeth seems to have been mistaken, and probably reflected the poor state of the material that he had to work on at the time. The teeth of hadrosaurids are anything but weak (see below); they are in fact arranged in dental batteries, each with hundreds of teeth in each jaw. The teeth are cemented together by bony tissue and form a long grinding surface (rather like a rasp, a carpenter's coarse file) which could have been used to pound up tough plants, even woody twigs. The teeth of hadrosaurids do not therefore predispose them to feed upon soft, succulent aquatic plants. Similarly the horny beaks can hardly be regarded as weak either. The obvious comparison that has been drawn here is between hadrosaurid beaks and ducks' bills (hence the common name for these dinosaurs: 'duck-billed dinosaurs'). The impli-

cation is that hadrosaurids grovelled about in muddy ponds and streams for small shrimps and water weeds as do ducks today. However, the outward similarity between a duck's bill and the beak of a hadrosaur is contradicted by the lack of teeth in the duck's jaws compared with the massive tooth batteries of hadrosaurids. Also a duck-like existence does seem a little improbable for a 2-3 tonne hadrosaurid! A far better comparison, particularly with regard to the beak, would be with the turtles and tortoises which have sharp, horny beaks. Such a tough, sharp and continuously growing beak would have been well suited to nipping off twigs and stripping leaves from branches.

However, the most convincing piece of evidence of all was that provided by Kräusel who, in 1922, analysed the fossilized stomach contents of one of the hadrosaur 'mummies' (now preserved in the Senckenberg Museum, West Germany). This showed that its stomach contained conifer needles and twigs, seeds and

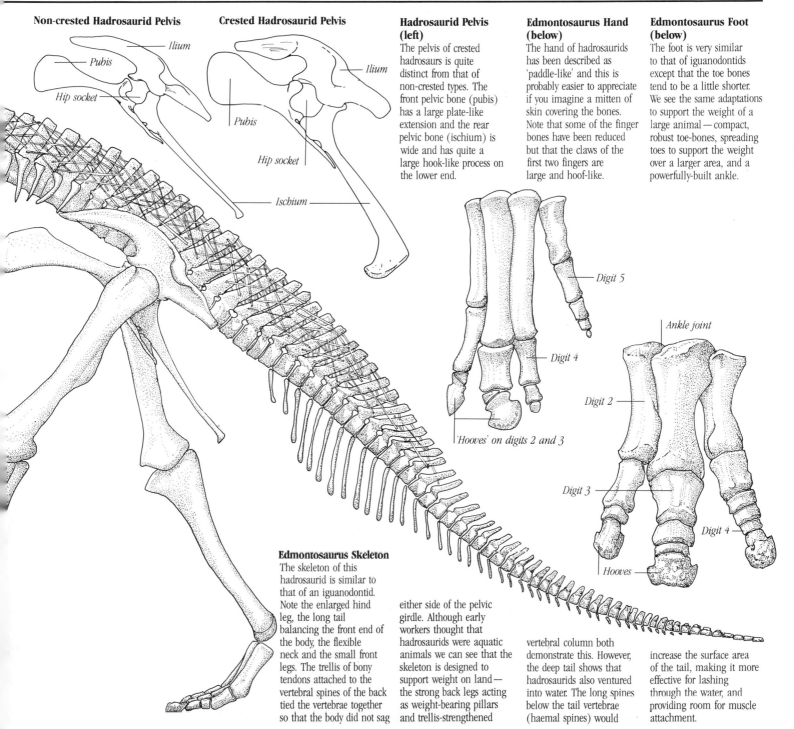

Non-crested Hadrosaurid Pelvis

Ilium
Pubis
Hip socket

Crested Hadrosaurid Pelvis

Ilium
Pubis
Hip socket
Ischium

Hadrosaurid Pelvis (left)
The pelvis of crested hadrosaurs is quite distinct from that of non-crested types. The front pelvic bone (pubis) has a large plate-like extension and the rear pelvic bone (ischium) is wide and has quite a large hook-like process on the lower end.

Edmontosaurus Hand (below)
The hand of hadrosaurids has been described as 'paddle-like' and this is probably easier to appreciate if you imagine a mitten of skin covering the bones. Note that some of the finger bones have been reduced but that the claws of the first two fingers are large and hoof-like.

Digit 5
Digit 4
'Hooves' on digits 2 and 3

Edmontosaurus Foot (below)
The foot is very similar to that of iguanodontids except that the toe bones tend to be a little shorter. We see the same adaptations to support the weight of a large animal — compact, robust toe-bones, spreading toes to support the weight over a larger area, and a powerfully-built ankle.

Ankle joint
Digit 2
Digit 3
Digit 4
Hooves

Edmontosaurus Skeleton
The skeleton of this hadrosaurid is similar to that of an iguanodontid. Note the enlarged hind leg, the long tail balancing the front end of the body, the flexible neck and the small front legs. The trellis of bony tendons attached to the vertebral spines of the back tied the vertebrae together so that the body did not sag either side of the pelvic girdle. Although early workers thought that hadrosaurids were aquatic animals we can see that the skeleton is designed to support weight on land — the strong back legs acting as weight-bearing pillars and trellis-strengthened vertebral column both demonstrate this. However, the deep tail shows that hadrosaurids also ventured into water. The long spines below the tail vertebrae (haemal spines) would increase the surface area of the tail, making it more effective for lashing through the water, and providing room for muscle attachment.

other land plants. All of this evidence points to hadrosaurids having a diet of land plants rather than one exclusively of soft aquatic plants.

Anatomical Features

The main anatomical evidence for the likely environment of hadrosaurids comes from the posture of the animal. The body is balanced at the hips, as in typical ornithopods, and the hindlimbs are long and arranged so that they act as pillars, so as to support the weight of the body most effectively. The foot is also arranged so that the three toes splay outward, forming a broad contact with the ground for good grip and balance. In addition, the ankle region is very powerfully built, presumably in order to prevent dislocation of this joint during walking and running. Another curious feature of hadrosaurids, and all other ornithopods as well, is the presence of a trellis-like arrangement of bony rods (ossified tendons or ligaments) found alongside the spines on the back, in front of, and behind the hip region of the animal (see below right). These rods most probably acted like hawsers supporting the backbone of the animal which would have naturally tended to sag on either side of the hips. Indeed we can turn to engineering for a comparable arrangement. The trellis-like arrangement of bony rods is precisely like that of the supporting struts of a balanced cantilever bridge. Thus we have another list of features that seem most readily explicable if these animals lived on land rather than in the water.

However, against this evidence, there is the undoubted paddle-like structure of the hand and the very deep tail. It has also been claimed that the extraordinary tubes and crests found on the heads of some hadrosaurids (pages 122-123) served as 'snorkels' for underwater breathing, as reserve 'air tanks', or as 'air-traps' to prevent water flooding the lungs. However, each of these suggestions is untenable. The 'snorkel' idea relied on the presence of holes in the tops of the crests—there were none; the 'air tank' idea is implausible because the crests could only have stored a minute amount of air; and the 'air-trap' idea simply would not work! The most likely function of the peculiar head-gear of hadrosaurids is discussed on pages 126-127.

Drawing Conclusions

So, having looked at the various features that may have a bearing on the way of life of hadrosaurids, is there a satisfactory interpretation? Well, the answer seems to be yes, there is! Hadrosaurids were probably land living browsers, feeding on the abundant vegetation of the fertile lowland areas of North America, and elsewhere. Their bodies were clearly designed to cope with the problems of support and movement on land, and their jaws and teeth were well able to cope with the abundant woody plant material available at the time. This is confirmed by the discovery of fossilized stomach contents in one example. The presence of the deep tail and paddle-like hand indicates that these animals were certainly capable of swimming; however, they may not have swum *habitually.* One suggestion which seems quite plausible is that hadrosaurids may have retreated into deep water to escape from predators such as the large tyrannosaurids. Hadrosaurids had no notable defensive weapons; they had no large teeth, claws or spikes to fight with and had lost the large thumb-spike so characteristic of the earlier iguanodontids; they were also probably far too

large and heavy-footed to be able to outrun predators, so that an ability to escape into deeper swamps may have been very useful.

Feeding and Evolution

Having seen that hadrosaurids were capable of feeding on very tough plant food such as conifer needles and twigs, let us look in a little detail at precisely how they were able to do this. As has been seen earlier in the iguanodontids, these animals have rather long snouts and heavy jaws with many teeth, which in hadrosaurids are cemented together to form batteries. Chewing of tough plant fibres wears the teeth down to produce a flat grinding surface. Precisely how these animals moved their jaws while chewing has been studied in some detail.

At first it was thought that hadrosaurids were able to slide their lower jaw backwards and forwards to produce a grinding action on the food trapped between the teeth. This was

supposed to be possible because the jaw hinge was quite loose to allow the jaw to slide, and because they had special muscles that were able to pull the jaw backwards and forwards. This model indicated that these animals chewed their food in the same way that rats and elephants do today. However, further detailed study of hadrosaurid teeth and jaws proved that their jaws could not have worked in this way. The arguments are quite detailed, but put very simply can be expressed in this way. The grinding ability of teeth depends on their roughness. The example of the carpenter's rasp is a very good one. Teeth can create this 'roughness' by being made of different materials (enamel which is very hard and covers your teeth, and dentine which is slightly softer). As teeth are worn down with use, they develop ridges of resistant enamel separated by grooves of softer dentine. In hadrosaurids the ridges of enamel are found arranged along the length of the jaw. If the jaws moved only backwards and

Above: A restoration of the skeleton of an infant *Maiasaura;* this specimen is about 3ft (1m) long, whereas an adult grew to about 29ft (9m) in length. The discovery of infants in a nesting colony suggests that *Maiasaura* actively cared for their young.

Below: Still encased in half its supporting field jacket of plaster of paris and burlap (sacking), this skull of *Edmontosaurus* is from the Belly River Formation of Alberta, Canada. It was excavated in the 1920s by Charles Sternberg junior, and is now in the British Museum (Natural History).

Signalling Devices (left) These drawings show how *Edmontosaurus* may have been equipped with an inflatable sac on its nose that it could use as a resonator to produce distinctive calls to attract or warn members of its group, rather in the manner that elephant seals do today.

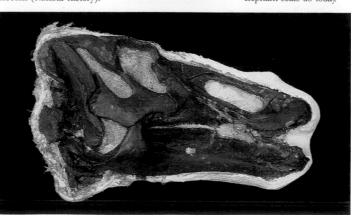

forwards the enamel ridges on the teeth in one jaw would wear against the softer dentine of the teeth in the other jaw, producing huge grooves; such grooves are *never* seen in hadrosaurid teeth. However, if the jaws move in the normal way up-and-down rather than backwards and forwards, the ridges of enamel in the jaws rub past one another, crushing and slicing the food trapped between them and also maintaining even wear across the grinding surface.

Very powerful jaw muscles and abrasive batteries of teeth seem to have been very important developments in later ornithopods, such as the iguanodontids and hadrosaurids, and in fact may be largely responsible for the dramatic evolution of these animals in the Cretaceous Period: both these groups becoming very abundant (hadrosaurid fossils are extremely common in late Cretaceous rocks in North America and Asia). It is possible that the increase in abundance of hadrosaurids (with their very efficient jaws) mirrors changes that

took place in the type of plants living in the world during the Cretaceous Period. This time marks the arrival of the first flowering plants and the disappearance of more primitive plants such as the bennettitales and seed ferns, so that soon the plant kingdom was dominated by mainly flowering plants, coniferous trees and ferns. This changeover seems, perhaps by accident or maybe by design, to coincide with changing fortunes of the plant-eating dinosaurs. The earlier part of the reign of the dinosaurs (the Jurassic Period) was marked by an abundance of earlier plants and big sauropod dinosaurs, whereas the Cretaceous sees the decline of the earlier plants and the sauropods which presumably fed upon them and the rise to dominance of the flowering plants and the later ornithopods. Although it is practically impossible to prove, it is tempting to propose that the apparent success of the ornithopods was a reflection of their greater ability to feed upon the newly-evolved flowering plants.

Care of the Young

In 1978 a remarkable discovery was made in western Montana. The fossilized remains of fifteen baby *Maiasaura* ('good mother reptile') hadrosaurids were found in and around a mound-shaped structure. The presence of many fragments of eggshell and the fact that the dinosaurs were obviously young, being only 3 feet (1m) long, suggested that what had been discovered was a dinosaur nest. Apart from the very famous *Protoceratops* nests from Mongolia, very few dinosaur nests or hatchlings are known and it was generally supposed that dinosaurs tended to lay their eggs in inaccessible upland areas and were unlikely to survive as fossils.

This discovery, reported by John Horner and Robert Makela, not only provided evidence about the existence of nest sites for hadrosaurids but also gave some indication of family structure in these dinosaurs. The young dinosaurs found around the nest were seen to have well-worn teeth and were considerably larger than newly hatched individuals. This indicated that the young dinosaurs had stayed together for some time which implies a degree of parental care. Either food was brought to the nest-site by the adults, or the young went out of the nest in search of food and subsequently returned. If the latter was the case, then it seems unlikely that the young would have returned to the nest without parental supervision. Such care of the young is perhaps not as surprising as it at first seems because crocodiles, distant relatives of the dinosaurs, show considerable care of their young—for example, moving the hatchlings to 'nursery' pools and guarding them against predators until they are large enough to defend themselves.

Further excavation and exploration of the Montana nest site in following years has revealed another nest with even smaller hatchlings (approximately 20in, 50cm long) and another six unoccupied nests with lots of egg-shell fragments. The nests that have been discovered so far seem to indicate that these animals would return and rebuild their nests year after year, and that the nests are approximately 23ft (7m) apart (a distance equal to the length of an adult hadrosaurid). John Horner has concluded that what has been discovered is not just a few odd nest sites, but in fact a nesting colony of hadrosaurids. He suggests that hadrosaurids probably used colonial nest sites because such an arrangement may have provided protection against predators (because of the continual presence of adult hadrosaurids) and also that the young most probably stayed in the nests waiting for the parents to bring food to them. This arrangement would enable the young to grow very quickly, and may explain why two nests had large numbers of young preserved within. The instinct to stay in the nest would have been very strong, so that the accidental loss of parents, perhaps killed by predators or by some other agent, would have resulted in the young, devoid of parental protection, starving to death in the nest.

In addition to this hadrosaurid nesting colony, Horner has found other nests at a different site, which seem to be those of a small hypsilophodontid dinosaur. These remains show very clearly that these animals returned to the same nest year after year and also reveal the way in which their eggs were laid, with the pointed end directed into the soil so that the hatchling could emerge from the rounder top end of the egg.

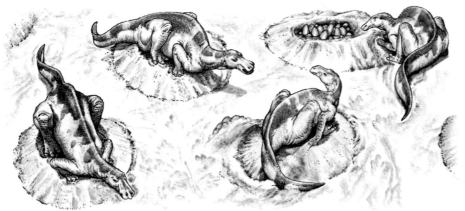

Left: Part of the upper jaw of a hadrosaur from the Oldman Formation of Alberta, Canada. Hadrosaurs were equipped with extensive batteries of teeth that enabled them to pound up thoroughly their food of tough plants and woody vegetation.

Parental Care (above)
The work of Horner and Makela on the fossilized eggs, hatchlings, and infant *Maiasaura* found in Montana has provided us with a major insight into a dinosaur community. Evidently some hadrosaurs looked after their young in a nesting colony. Here we see a female digging out a nest (front right) while the central dinosaur adopts an aggressive posture to defend her territory. At the back, newly-laid eggs are being covered with sand by the mother reptile. The fourth *Maiasaura* sleeps on the nest.

Below: The Royal Ontario Museum's fine panel mount of the skeleton of *Hadrosaurus*, a dinosaur that could grow to a length of c. 30ft (9m). Note the rounded bump above the nostrils, and the mass of reinforcing bony rods along the spines of the back.

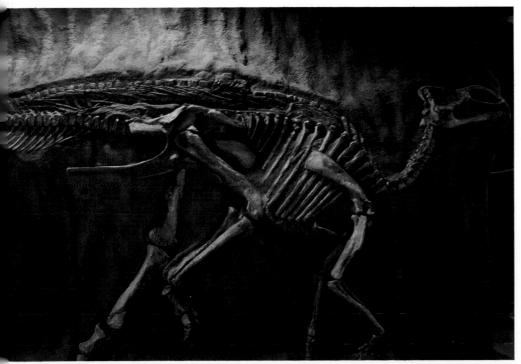

Hadrosaurid fossils are known in western and eastern North America, Central and South America, Europe and Asia (Mongolia, China and Japan). This type of distribution pattern is now quite familiar (see the dromaeosaurids, pages 56-7), with these animals being distributed across most of the northern continents, but almost completely absent from the southern continents. The most likely reason for the northerly distribution of hadrosaurids would seem to be the relative position of the various continents at the time when they first evolved. In the mid-Cretaceous the southern continents, Gondwanaland (South America, Africa, India, Australia and Antarctica), were separated from the North (Laurasia) by a large sea composed of Tethys to the east and the beginnings of the Atlantic Ocean to the west. This sea barrier would have prevented the hadrosaurids from spreading from their probable northerly area of origin southward. The spread of hadrosaurids across the northern

continents may have been partly impeded by a shallow seaway, the Turgai sea, which separated Europe and America on one side from Asia on the other, but this cannot have been a complete barrier to hadrosaurids, which could almost certainly swim (especially across a shallow sea), because they are found in both areas anyway. That the North-South barrier was not absolute is also proven by the recent discovery of hadrosaurids in South America (*Secernosaurus*, 'divided reptile' from Argentina). These hadrosaurs were probably able to migrate to South America across an island chain which then ran between the southernmost part of North America and the South American mainland. So far there are no reports of hadrosaurid dinosaurs elsewhere on Gondwana but fresh discoveries on, say, India or Australia might mean that we will have to re-think our ideas about the origin and evolution of hadrosaurids.

Towards the end of the Cretaceous Period the geographic situation was further complicated

by the expansion of the Atlantic Ocean, the development of yet another seaway, the Western Interior Sea, which split North America into western and eastern regions and the establishment of a link between North America and Asia across the Bering Straits.

Anatomical Observations

The hadrosaurids themselves are rather conservative ornithopods if we look at their skeletons. They continue the typical anatomical plan seen in the iguanodontids with relatively few changes. However, looking carefully at the two hadrosaurids that are illustrated as skeletons, it is possible to distinguish some subtle differences. *Edmontosaurus* is rather more lightly built than *Parasaurolophus* ('beside ridged reptile') and has lower spines along the backbone, while the bones of the pelvis have a strikingly different shape. The really obvious differences between the various species of

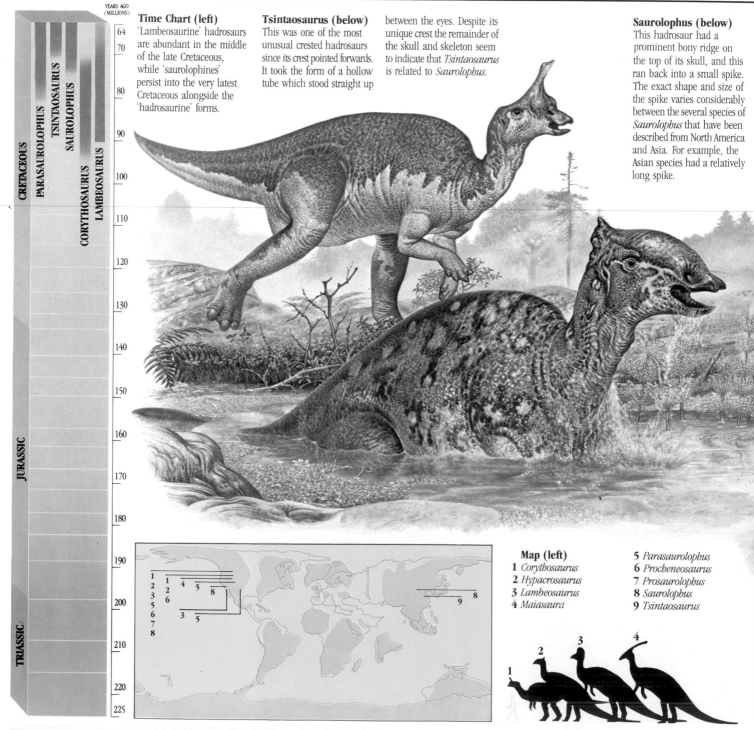

Time Chart (left)
'Lambeosaurine' hadrosaurs are abundant in the middle of the late Cretaceous, while 'saurolophines' persist into the very latest Cretaceous alongside the 'hadrosaurine' forms.

Tsintaosaurus (below)
This was one of the most unusual crested hadrosaurs since its crest pointed forwards. It took the form of a hollow tube which stood straight up between the eyes. Despite its unique crest the remainder of the skull and skeleton seem to indicate that *Tsintaosaurus* is related to *Saurolophus*.

Saurolophus (below)
This hadrosaur had a prominent bony ridge on the top of its skull, and this ran back into a small spike. The exact shape and size of the spike varies considerably between the several species of *Saurolophus* that have been described from North America and Asia. For example, the Asian species had a relatively long spike.

Map (left)
1 *Corythosaurus*
2 *Hypacrosaurus*
3 *Lambeosaurus*
4 *Maiasaura*
5 *Parasaurolophus*
6 *Procheneosaurus*
7 *Prosaurolophus*
8 *Saurolophus*
9 *Tsintaosaurus*

hadrosaur, however, are to be found in their heads. Some hadrosaurs, such as *Edmontosaurus, Anatosaurus, Bactrosaurus* and *Kritosaurus* — so-called 'hadrosaurines' — have very broad, duck-like beaks, quite large nostrils but very little development of elaborate ridges or crests of bone on the head. At most there developed a low bump on the nose as in *Kritosaurus*. Other types of hadrosaurid, however, possess all manner of strange head-gear. 'Saurolophines' such as *Saurolophus* ('ridged reptile'), *Maiasaura* ('good mother reptile'), and *Tsintaosaurus* ('reptile from Tsintao') show the development of a spine-like outgrowth from the top of the head. The spine of *Tsintaosaurus* is particularly odd because, unlike the others of this general type, the spine projects forward from the top of the head, just like the horn of the legendary unicorn. The other variety of hadrosaurids is the so-called 'lambeosaurines' which have much larger hollow or tubular crests or bone on their

Parasaurolophus (right)
This hadrosaur probably had the most striking crest of all. It was a long tube that extended back for a distance of up to 3·3ft (1m) behind the skull. Palaeontologists at first thought that *Parasaurolophus* used this as a snorkel, but this could not be so as there was no opening at the end of it.

Corythosaurus (left)
A well-known crested hadrosaur which was up to 33ft (10m) long, *Corythosaurus* had a crest which was shaped like a large dinner plate set up on end on top of the skull. Inside the crest there was a rather complex system of breathing tubes running from the nostrils at the tip of the snout to the back of the throat.

Family Tree (below)
The division here is into hadrosaurs with big tubular crests ('lambeosaurines') and those with a spike-like structure or excavated nasal region ('saurolophines').

SAUROLOPHUS
PROSAUROLOPHUS
MAIASAURA
TSINTAOSAURUS
PARASAUROLOPHUS
CORYTHOSAURUS
LAMBEOSAURUS

'HADROSAURINES'

Comparative Sizes (left)
1 *Tsintaosaurus*: 1. 23ft (7m)
2 *Saurolophus*: 1. 30-40ft (9-12m).
3 *Corythosaurus*: 1. 33ft (10m).
4 *Parasaurolophus*: 1. 33ft (10m).

heads—*Parasaurolophus* ('beside ridged reptile') and *Corythosaurus* ('Corinthian helmet reptile') are quite typical examples.

Before looking at other aspects of the biology of these animals, let us briefly examine the geographic distribution and relative evolutionary success of these different types of crested or crestless dinosaurs. The earliest known types of hadrosaurids seem to be the crestless 'hadrosaurines'; these are found on all continents and appear to rise in abundance until the very end of the Cretaceous. The 'saurolophines' seem never to have been particularly abundant at any time in their history in North America, apparently going extinct before the end of the Period, but they may have been more successful in Asia. Finally the 'lambeosaurines' (those hadrosaurids with large, hollow crests) seem to have been particularly abundant, outnumbering all other hadrosaurids in the middle part of the late Cretaceous of western North America but declining rapidly toward the end of the

Period. Curiously, to date there are no reliable fossils of any 'lambeosaurines' from Asia.

The curious waxing and waning of these groups of hadrosaurid may simply be caused by biases of the collectors of fossils. However, if they are a reflection of the natural numbers of these animals, then they suggest some interesting questions. Why were the crested 'lambeosaurine' hadrosaurids so successful earlier than the flat-headed types? Why were the 'saurolophines' never particularly abundant in North America and why do 'lambeosaurines' appear not to have inhabited Asia? To attempt to answer these questions, we need to propose new theories. These theories can then be 'tested' by further investigation of the fossils in order to try to either 'prove' or 'disprove' them. In this way we hope gradually to get closer to the real explanation. For example it should be possible to find out, by renewed collecting, if the differences in the abundance of some of these dinosaurs was due to the biases of past

collectors or whether apparent absences, such as the lack of definite 'lambeosaurines' in Asia, simply reflects the fact that people have not looked hard enough in the past.

Hadrosaurid Crests

By far the most intriguing aspect of hadrosaurid anatomy is their crests: why do some have them and others not, and what was their purpose? As we shall see a little later, numerous theories have been put forward to explain the function of hadrosaurid crests. However, one of the first real discoveries in this area resulted from the work of Dr Peter Dodson of the University of Pennsylvania. Dr Dodson conducted a very detailed series of measurements in order to make an analysis of the shape of the heads of a large range of 'lambeosaurine' hadrosaurids. As a result of this work he was able to propose that many species of 'lambeosaurine' were in fact simply female, male

Female Parasaurolophus Skull

Parasaurolophus Skeleton (below)
This skeleton is rather heavily built, especially the shoulder girdle and front leg, and looks as though

Parasaurolophus would have made a good deal of use of its front legs in walking or wading. This form shows the special pelvic structure of the crested hadrosaurids with the

enlarged front pelvic bone (pubis) and back pelvic bone (ischium). These expanded bones would have probably provided more area for hip muscle attachment. The tail

here shows the flattening typical of hadrosaurids. The drawing (left) is of the skull of a female *Parasaurolophus*; notice the crest is much less developed.

Skull Muscles (below)
This drawing shows a female *Parasaurolophus*. Compare the shape of her crest to the male's (right). An efficient muscle set-up is present here to make full use of the powerful tooth batteries. The capiti-mandibularis muscle runs from a prominent lower jaw process to a crest along the top of the skull. The adductor muscle is short and close to the jaw hinge and so probably acted as a 'tie' to stabilise the hinge.

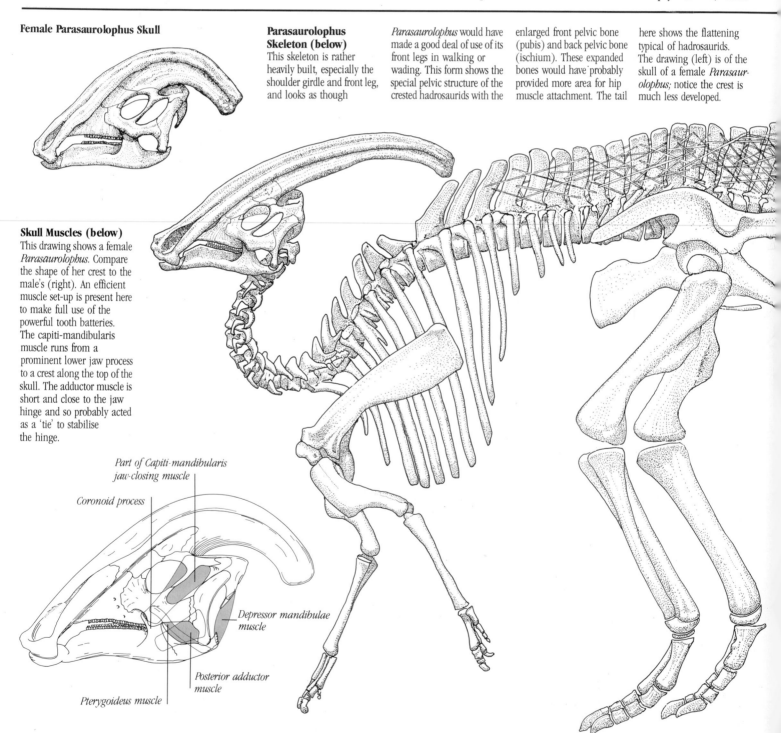

Part of Capiti-mandibularis jaw-closing muscle

Coronoid process

Depressor mandibulae muscle

Posterior adductor muscle

Pterygoideus muscle

or young individuals of a small number of species of hadrosaurid. For example, of the 'lambeosaurines' with helmet-shaped crests, *Corythosaurus casuarius* and *Corythosaurus intermedius* are now thought to be male and female respectively of the same species, while other species, known previously as *Procheneosaurus erectofrons*, and *Procheneosaurus cranibrevis* along with *Corythosaurus excavatus*, *Corythosaurus bicristatus* and *Corythosaurus brevicristatus* are all juveniles of the same species. This sort of very careful analysis is of vital importance to palaeontology because it greatly reduces the confusion that can be created by naming so many different fossil species. Almost at the stroke of a pen, Dodson has reduced the number of one type of 'lambeosaurine' in one area of North America from seven to one. In this same area of North America (The Old Man Formation of Alberta in Canada) Dodson has identified just two other 'lambeosaurines': *Lambeosaurus* ('Lambe's reptile') with a

somewhat more full and pronounced helmet-like crest, and the tubular-crested *Parasaurolophus*, where previously there had been thirteen different species. From a simple biological viewpoint, it is far easier to imagine three species of ecologically distinct hadrosaurids living in approximately the same area at the same time, rather than thirteen distinct species of similar types of dinosaur.

Thus the crests have had one very useful function, in that they have given us a clue about growth stages in the life of hadrosaurids and the differences between males and females of same species. However, this does not explain why some hadrosaurids had crests while others did not, nor what the crests were used for.

The Function of Crests

The extraordinary variety of crest shape displayed by hadrosaurids has provoked a considerable number of theories relating to

their probable function. Some of these are described and discussed below.

(i) Underwater feeding. The long, curved tubular crest of *Parasaurolophus* was thought to act as a snorkel so that the animal could breathe while feeding on submerged plants. It was supposed that the tip of the crest had a small hole, through which air could pass, as with a true snorkel. Unfortunately no such hole exists in any of the crests of *Parasaurolophus* so far discovered. Even if such a hole had existed, the snorkel explanation could not have been readily applied to other hadrosaurids, for example *Corythosaurus* whose crest was nothing like a snorkel.

An alternative to the snorkel theory was the proposal that the crests served as air-storage 'tanks', so that these animals could stay submerged for long periods while feeding. However, the amount of air that could have been stored in the crests was really very small, and is unlikely to have permitted crested

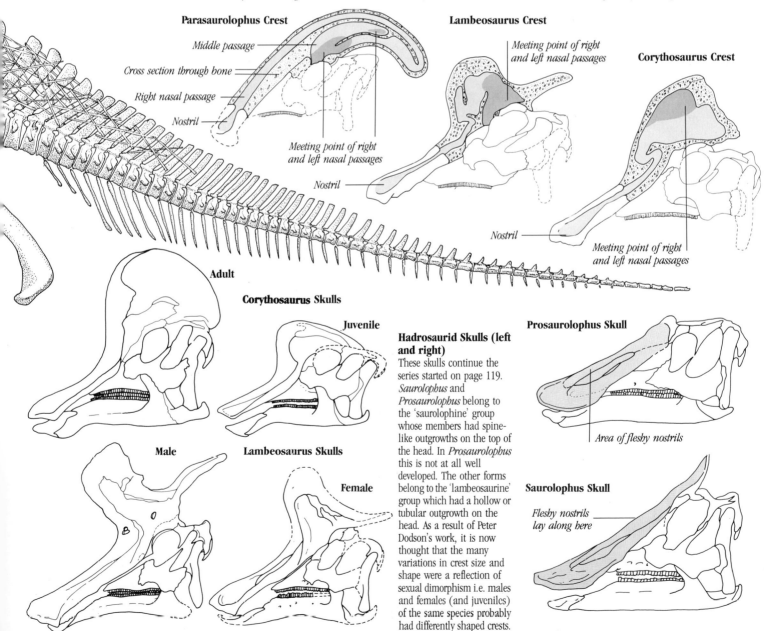

Sections through Crests (below right)
These drawings show the internal anatomy of the crests of three 'lambeosaurine' hadrosaurs: *Parasaurolophus cyrtocristatus, Lambeosaurus clavinitialis* and *Corythosaurus excavatus.* The areas marked in red are the nasal cavities. Many intriguing theories have been advanced concerning the function of these remarkable crests, ranging from snorkels for underwater feeding to foliage deflectors. The most probable explanation supposes that they were visual signals to allow members of individual species to recognise one another. In addition to this, it is likely that the tubular cavities inside the crests would serve as resonators, allowing these hadrosaurs to produce distinctive calls. 'Saurolophines' and 'hadrosaurines' could probably also make noises by inflating flaps of skin over their nostrils. Possibly these spaces also allowed for a greater area of sensitive skin and thus an improved sense of smell.

Parasaurolophus Crest
Middle passage
Cross section through bone
Right nasal passage
Nostril
Meeting point of right and left nasal passages

Lambeosaurus Crest
Meeting point of right and left nasal passages
Nostril
Meeting point of right and left nasal passages

Corythosaurus Crest
Nostril
Meeting point of right and left nasal passages

Corythosaurus Skulls
Adult
Juvenile

Lambeosaurus Skulls
Male
Female

Hadrosaurid Skulls (left and right)
These skulls continue the series started on page 119. *Saurolophus* and *Prosaurolophus* belong to the 'saurolophine' group whose members had spine-like outgrowths on the top of the head. In *Prosaurolophus* this is not at all well developed. The other forms belong to the 'lambeosaurine' group which had a hollow or tubular outgrowth on the head. As a result of Peter Dodson's work, it is now thought that the many variations in crest size and shape were a reflection of sexual dimorphism i.e. males and females (and juveniles) of the same species probably had differently shaped crests.

Prosaurolophus Skull
Area of fleshy nostrils

Saurolophus Skull
Fleshy nostrils lay along here

hadrosaurs to stay submerged for very much longer than their crestless counterparts. Nor does this theory readily explain why the crests should be so variable in shape.

The third proposal concerned with underwater feeding suggested that the loop in the air passages inside the crests acted as 'air-locks' to prevent water from flooding into the lungs when the head was underwater. In this case such an 'air-lock' just would not have worked in life, and in any case most aquatic animals have special muscular valves around their nostrils to stop water from rushing into their lungs. Therefore, most of these proposals seem improbable when considered in detail, which reinforces the earlier argument that hadrosaurids were not primarily aquatic plant feeders.

(ii) Salt glands. An alternative suggestion concerning the function of the cranial crests is that they were occupied by salt glands. Many living reptiles, especially those that feed on plants and those that live in the sea, have well developed salt glands in the cavity for the nose or the eye to regulate the salt balance in their bodies (the perpetual tears in the eyes of turtles on land are produced by these salt glands). It therefore seems reasonable to suppose that such large herbivorous reptiles also had well-developed salt glands. Whether the salt glands were housed in the large bony crests is at present not at all certain. Again the problem encountered in this explanation is, if they were to house salt glands alone, why are the crests so variable in shape, and how did the crestless hadrosaurs survive?

(iii) The sense of smell. Another proposal, somewhat similar to the last one, is that the tubular cavities inside the crests, which are continuous with the nostrils, may have provided space for a much enlarged sensory area which endowed these animals with a very acute sense of smell. This idea is quite appealing because it seems to fit in with the proposed life-styles of these animals. As defenceless, moderately mobile herbivores, it would have been extremely advantageous for them to have very acute senses of hearing, sight and smell to give them adequate warning of the approach of predators such as the large tyrannosaurids.

As with previous theories, there still remains the difficulty of explaining precisely why the crests of 'lambeosaurines' are so varied if they were simply providing more area for nasal lining, *and* why do some 'hadrosaurines' lack crests altogether and yet others ('saurolophines') have solid crests?

(iv) Foliage deflectors. One extremely novel suggestion concerning crest function in 'lambeosaurines' was made by Dr Andrew Milner of London University. Dr Milner's explanation relied upon an observation which he made on the skeleton of *Parasaurolophus*. He noticed that at the base of the neck, the spines show a peculiar flattened structure. A slight adjustment in the position of the neck in the preserved skeleton allows the extremely long tubular crest of this species to rest against this notch. The suggestion which was made was that if *Parasaurolophus* was indeed able to lock its crest onto this notch in its neck, then the smooth contours of the head and back would form an ideal deflector of low branches. Perhaps, therefore, some 'lambeosaurines' such as *Parasaurolophus* lived in quite heavily wooded areas and used the 'deflector' arrangement in order to crash through heavy foliage in order to escape from predators, without damaging their heads. As an extension of this idea, the elaborate crests of 'lambeosaurines' may have correlated with their living in quite dense forests, while the flat-headed forms lived in open areas where deflectors were not necessary. An interesting observation in this respect comes from the habits of the cassowary, a large flightless bird from the forested area of Northern Queensland, Australia. This curious bird has a large helmet-like crest on its head which very closely resembles the crest of *Corythosaurus*. When disturbed, this bird can run very quickly through dense undergrowth to escape. To do this, the cassowary lowers its head and deflects low branches with its helmet-clad head, neck and back.

Although this is a very interesting proposal there are a number of problems associated with it. At the moment it is impossible to tell whether 'lambeosaurines' were indeed confined to heavily forested areas. Also it is not possible in all cases to reconcile the crest shape of hadrosaurids with the proposed deflector function. An obvious example of the latter would be the long, slender, unicorn-like spike of *Tsintaosaurus* which would certainly not survive impacts against branches.

(v) Signalling devices. The last proposal we shall consider interprets the head structures of hadrosaurids as features that may reflect their behaviour. The crests are regarded as visual

Left: *Tsintaosaurus spinorhinus,* a 23ft (7m) tall 'saurolophine', in the Institute of Vertebrate Palaeontology, Beijing. This specimen is from late Cretaceous rocks of Laiyang County, Shandong Province, China. Its most distinctive feature is the unicorn-like, forwardly-pointing crest extending from the top of the skull.

Below: *Lambeosaurus lambei* being prepared for display at the Tyrrell Museum of Palaeontology in Alberta; the reason for the rather odd posture is that in the final exhibit it will be shown drinking water from a pool. Evidence from trackways, however, does suggest that large hadrosaurids were quadrupedal for much of the time.

Beating A Retreat (left)
Although the general consensus now is that hadrosaurids were not primarily aquatic animals, their characteristic deep tails and paddle-like hands is evidence that they were certainly capable of swimming. It is possible that when threatened by a tyrannosaurid predator they would retreat to the safety of deep water just as these *Parasaurolophus* are doing with some alacrity.

signal structures and as resonators for producing distinctive calls. Both of these functions would serve to help individual hadrosaurids recognize members of their own species, which would be especially useful in courtship and mating.

Visual Signals

In order to support this proposal, Dr Jim Hopson of Chicago University made a series of predictions which should be confirmed if the above proposal is to be considered plausible. Firstly, hearing and sight would be expected to be acute in hadrosaurids. As expected, the eye socket is very large in these animals. Also there is fossil evidence of a bony ring of thin bones in the eye (the sclerotic ring) which seems to demonstrate that hadrosaurids did indeed have very good eyesight. Several hadrosaur skeletons have also been found with a very thin, delicate ear bone in position at the back of the skull, confirming that they had quite acute hearing.

Secondly, and this has a bearing on proposals (ii) and (iii), the shape of the crest should not necessarily closely follow the shape of the cavities within. That is to say that the external shape of the crest was more important than its internal structure, because it acted as a visual signal. This prediction is borne out by *Corythosaurus*, in which the internal passages are clearly not the same shape as the crest. In fact several of the cranial crests give the heads very distinctive shapes, as can be appreciated by looking at the colour drawings.

Thirdly, if the crests acted as visual signals, then they would be expected to be specific to each species, that is they should be visually very distinct, and males and females should be indentifiable. This prediction seems to be strongly supported by Dodson's work (see above) which shows that in the Old Man Formation there are three very distinct species of 'lambeosaurine': *Corythosaurus, Lambeosaurus* and *Parasaurolophus*, and that males and females of at least the first two species have been tentatively identified. Unfortunately only one individual of *Parasaurolophus* is known in this area at the present time so that no conclusion can yet be drawn about its status.

Fourthly, if several species are found in the same area then they should exhibit great differences in head shape. This would have prevented any confusion when animals were trying to meet members of the same species, at mating time for example. This prediction seems to be amply confirmed. Again in the Old Man Formation there are known to be at least six hadrosaurid species—the three very distinctive 'lambeosaurines' seen above, one 'saurolophine' (*Prosaurolophus*) and two species of 'hadrosaurine'. The latter are again quite distinctive as *Kritosaurus* and the unusual plate-headed *Brachylophosaurus* ('short ridged reptile'). By contrast, in other Formations such as the Lance or Hell Creek, although many hadrosaurid specimens are known, they are all of one type: the flat-headed species *Anatosaurus*.

The fifth and final prediction postulated that the crests should become much more prominent as time passed. This, however, is certainly not supported in the case of 'lambeosaurines', although there may be some evidence for a trend of increasing spike length in the crests of 'saurolophines'.

Thus Hopson's predictions generally seem to be fulfilled and the variable form of the crests in these dinosaurs seems to fit with the idea that they provided visual cues connected with social behaviour in these animals.

This idea has been further elaborated in order to explain likely behavioural differences between crestless and crested dinosaurs. Hopson proposed that a hadrosaurid like *Kritosaurus* probably used the hump on its nose as a crude weapon for fighting during male butting contests. In other flat-headed species such as *Brachylophosaurus*, the flat, shield-like roof to the head allowed these animals to indulge in head-to-head pushing contests of strength. However, in all the other hadrosaurids the 'combat' was ritualized; instead of physical fighting, the animals relied upon sight and sound displays. The 'lambeosaurines' and 'saurolophines' used their distinctive cranial crests as visual signals to establish a dominance hierarchy. In the 'lambeosaurines' this was probably accompanied by noisy honking or bellows. David Weishampel of Florida State University has demonstrated that the tubular crest of *Parasaurolophus* served as a resonator for producing distinctive calls, and has suggested that the helmet-crest *Corythosaurus* and *Lambeosaurus* were also able to produce distinctive sounds.

'Hadrosaurines' such as *Anatosaurus* and *Edmontosaurus,* and 'saurolophines' such as *Saurolophus* and *Tsintaosaurus* probably possessed inflatable flaps of skin over their nostrils which may not only have served as resonators to produce loud snorts (perhaps rather like the roars produced by elephant seals which have very bulbous noses), but also have formed inflatable (perhaps highly coloured) display structures. Such visual signals play a prominent part in the lives of present day reptiles; many (for example *Anolis*) have highly colourful dewlaps that are used as flash signals for courtship and various other behaviours.

The most convincing explanation of the purpose of cranial crests seems to be that of Jim Hopson. It serves to explain all the crested or non-crested forms so far known. If he is right, the late Cretaceous must have been a colourful and noisy time in the Earth's history!

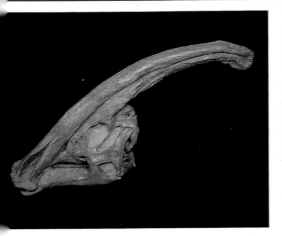

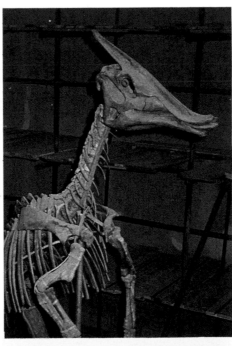

Above: A plaster cast of the skull of *Parasaurolophus walkeri,* a species from the Red Deer River area of Alberta. The great tubular crest of this creature could grow to a length of up to 6ft (1·8m).

Right: *Saurolophus angustirostris,* a large hadrosaurid from Mongolia. The fact that this is virtually identical to North American species shows the wide geographic dispersal of hadrosaurs.

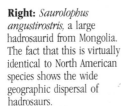

PSITTACOSAURS & PROTOCERATOPIDS

The ceratopian ('horned-face') dinosaurs were a group whose history was confined to the latter part of the reign of the dinosaurs: the late Cretaceous. During this last 35 million years or so, however, these dinosaurs became particularly abundant. Some areas of North America have yielded literally hundreds of remains (including complete skeletons) of these dinosaurs; this must be a reflection of their great abundance in the world at this time.

The distinctive characteristics seen in most of the ceratopians are the facial horns, the distinctive parrot-like, hooked beak and the large frill, a bony ruff projecting from the back and sides of the head. The great majority of ceratopians were also quadrupedal and bear quite a strong resemblance to the living rhinoceroses of Africa and South East Asia. *Centrosaurus* ('sharp point reptile') (pages 134-137) and *Chasmosaurus* ('cleft reptile') (pages 140-143) are typical representatives of the ceratopian type of dinosaur. Illustrated

below (and on the next four pages), however, are several rather less typical ceratopians.

Psittacosaurus ('parrot reptile') illustrated below does not really resemble the general description of ceratopian dinosaurs. The remains of *Psittacosaurus* were first discovered during an expedition to the Mongolian Peoples' Republic organized by the American Museum of Natural History between 1922 and 1925. During this expedition, two quite well preserved skeletons were discovered in the Oshih Formation (early Cretaceous) of Mongolia. These were first described as different animals and named *Psittacosaurus* and *Protiguanodon*. The fact that neither of the skeletons was complete, and both were not completely cleared of matrix, caused a certain amount of confusion; they are now both recognised as specimens of *Psittacosaurus*.

For many years *Psittacosaurus* was thought to be a member of the ornithopod group of dinosaurs (hence the name *Protiguanodon*

coined for one skeleton) as a fairly close relative of *Hypsilophodon*. I think it should be fairly obvious why this was believed. Just like *Hypsilophodon* and its relatives, *Psittacosaurus* was a small (6·6ft, 2m long) bipedal, fairly lightly built creature, with a long tail counter-balancing its body over the hips; its front legs were also equipped with blunt-clawed hands which seem to have been 'multi-purpose', serving both to walk upon and to grasp foliage for feeding. The head, supported on the long flexible neck, was apparently unadorned by the horns or frills so characteristic of ceratopians generally. The key to the affinities of *Psittaco-saurus*, however, does lie in the head—in the beak to be exact! As the name suggests, these animals had a sharp, narrow, parrot-like beak typical of all other ceratopians. More important than the shape of the beak was the fact that beneath the horn-covered part of the upper beak there is found a characteristic bone known as the rostral bone which is only found

Time Chart (left)

Some of the earliest known ceratopians (a late Cretaceous group) are the psittacosaurs from Mongolia. After this, the protoceratopids appeared and they persist right through to the end of the Cretaceous. They vary from typical quadrupedal types such as *Protoceratops* to small bipeds like *Microceratops* and *Leptoceratops* which is a North American form.

Map (left)
1 *Bagaceratops*
2 *Leptoceratops*
3 *Microceratops*
4 *Montanoceratops*
5 *Protoceratops*
6 *Psittacosaurus*

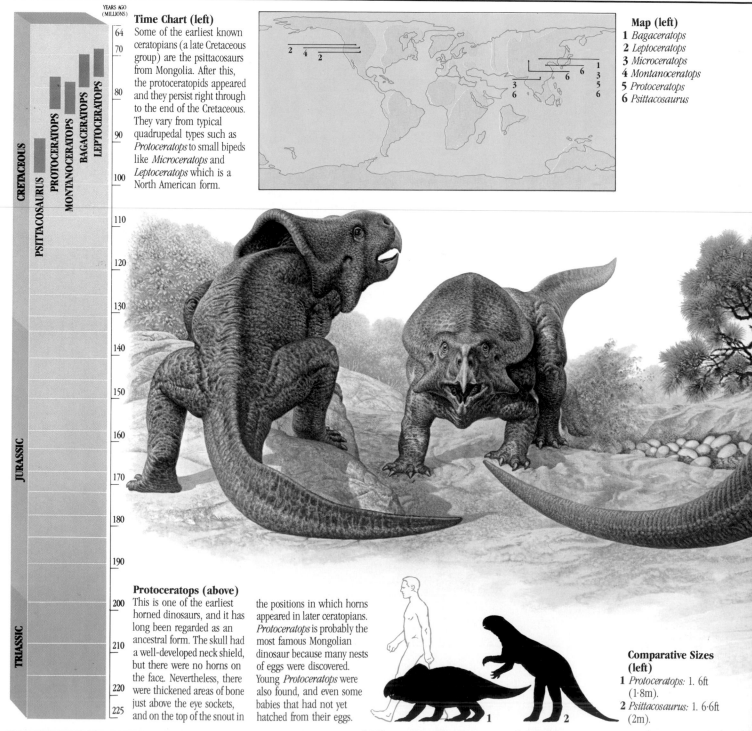

Protoceratops (above)

This is one of the earliest horned dinosaurs, and it has long been regarded as an ancestral form. The skull had a well-developed neck shield, but there were no horns on the face. Nevertheless, there were thickened areas of bone just above the eye sockets, and on the top of the snout in the positions in which horns appeared in later ceratopians. *Protoceratops* is probably the most famous Mongolian dinosaur because many nests of eggs were discovered. Young *Protoceratops* were also found, and even some babies that had not yet hatched from their eggs.

Comparative Sizes (left)
1 *Protoceratops*: 1. 6ft (1·8m).
2 *Psittacosaurus*: 1. 6·6ft (2m).

in ceratopian dinosaurs. The remarkable overall similarity between *Psittacosaurus* and hypsilophodontids, and the fact that *Psittacosaurus* pre-dates all other ceratopians, seems to suggest quite strongly that ceratopians *evolved* from hypsilophodontid types of dinosaur. Precisely why ceratopians should have appeared when they did and why the peculiar rostral bone appeared in the upper beak is not at all clear. My best guess (and it is only a guess) would be that the rather subtle changes in the proportions of the skull, which follow on from the development of the parrot-like beak at the front of the mouth, may perhaps reflect one of two things: either a new type of plant had evolved which required this type of beak to crop it, or perhaps the parrot-beak was a new 'invention' that allowed the ceratopians to feed on plants which had previously been inedible to most dinosaurs. The appearance of the ceratopian dinosaurs coincides very roughly with the time of appearance of the first angiosperms — or

Psittacosaurus (left)
An important early ceratopian, *Psittacosaurus* was quite a small dinosaur, about 6·6ft (2m) long, and it has been considered particularly significant because it seems to show characteristics that are intermediate between the ornithopods and the ceratopians. The long hindlimbs, short forelimbs with grasping hands, and the powerful skull all seem to be ornithopod characters. However, *Psittacosaurus* has a curved parrot-like beak which is a ceratopian characteristic, although it lacks the neck frill that is seen in *Protoceratops*.

Family Tree (right)
The relations of early ceratopians have been studied by Paul Sereno (New York) and are shown here. *Psittacosaurus* is clearly the most primitive known ceratopian. *Leptoceratops* of the late Cretaceous seems to be a persistently primitive type while *Bagaceratops*, *Protoceratops* and *Montanoceratops* show a clear trend towards the characteristics of the larger quadrupedal ceratopids.

PSITTACOSAURUS   LEPTOCERATOPS   BAGACERATOPS   PROTOCERATOPS   MONTANOCERATOPS   CERATOPIDS flowering plants—is this the key to the problem? At the moment we have no positive evidence of the true diet of ceratopians, so this suggestion can be neither supported nor denied.

In 1980 Walter Coombs Jnr reported that among the collections from the Asiatic expeditions of 1922-1925 in the American Museum of Natural History he had found some more *Psittacosaurus* material. This comprised the skull of one individual, and the skull with several parts of the skeleton of another individual. The remarkable thing about these specimens however was their size. The skulls of the two individuals were tiny: 1·6in (42mm) and 1·1in (28mm) long respectively. A simple size-for-size comparison between the original skeletons of *Psittacosaurus* and these tiny ones suggests that they could only have been about 16in (40cm) and 10in (25cm) in total length when complete. These are some of the smallest dinosaur remains so far discovered. Various

features of these two specimens, such as the very large size of their eyes and the incomplete way in which the bones of the back are arranged, tell us that these were hatchling dinosaurs. Even at this tiny size, these young dinosaurs were evidently quite independent because their teeth show signs of wear which indicates that they were already feeding on abrasive plant food. Dr Coombs suggested that the minute size of these hatchlings and the fact that they already had worn teeth indicated that there was unlikely to be parental care of the young. Attempts to feed such small young, it was claimed, would most likely result in their being stepped on. However, this type of argument does not seem very convincing, because we already know that adult crocodiles (which are considerably larger than their hatchlings) show considerable parental care—even ferrying them to favoured nursery pools between their jaws. As was suggested in the case of the hadrosaurid *Maiasaura*, *Psittaco-*

saurus parents may well have brought plant food to the nest for the young hatchlings.

Since *Psittacosaurus* was a herbivore it probably relied upon its fleetness of foot to escape from predatory dinosaurs, in the same way that hypsilophodontids were able to. This strategy however would not have been available to another rather primitive early ceratopian dinosaur *Protoceratops* ('first horned-face').

Protoceratops

While *Psittacosaurus* has so far only been discovered in Asia, *Protoceratops* and its close relatives (together known as protoceratopids) are known from the late Cretaceous of Asia and North America. Protoceratopids are typically small ceratopians (maximum length about 6·6ft, 2m) which have the characteristic parrot-like beak seen in *Psittacosaurus*, and also a well-developed bony frill which overhangs the neck. Although the areas over the eyes and the

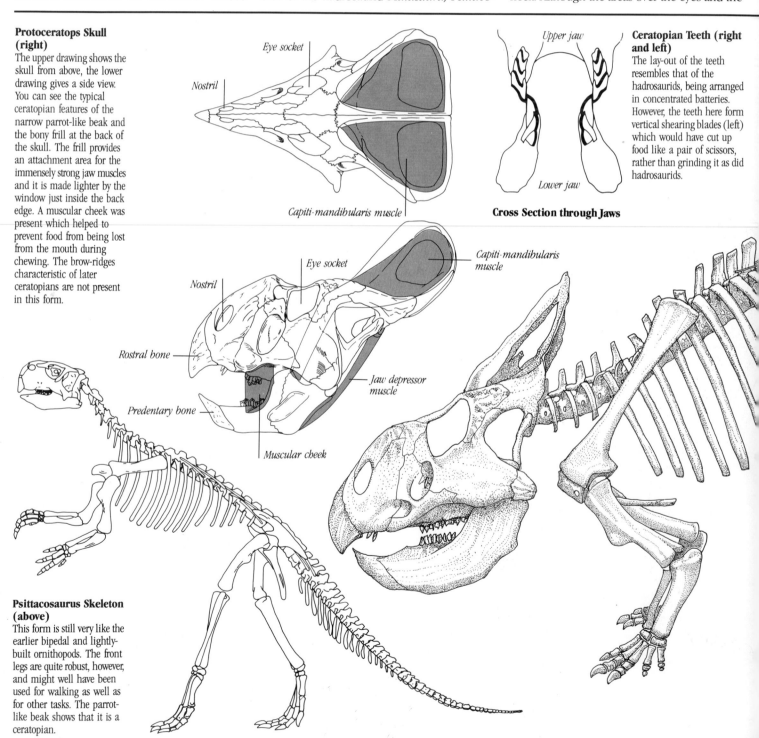

Protoceratops Skull (right)
The upper drawing shows the skull from above, the lower drawing gives a side view. You can see the typical ceratopian features of the narrow parrot-like beak and the bony frill at the back of the skull. The frill provides an attachment area for the immensely strong jaw muscles and it is made lighter by the window just inside the back edge. A muscular cheek was present which helped to prevent food from being lost from the mouth during chewing. The brow-ridges characteristic of later ceratopians are not present in this form.

Eye socket

Nostril

Capiti-mandibularis muscle

Ceratopian Teeth (right and left)
The lay-out of the teeth resembles that of the hadrosaurids, being arranged in concentrated batteries. However, the teeth here form vertical shearing blades (left) which would have cut up food like a pair of scissors, rather than grinding it as did hadrosaurids.

Upper jaw

Lower jaw

Cross Section through Jaws

Eye socket

Nostril

Capiti-mandibularis muscle

Rostral bone

Jaw depressor muscle

Predentary bone

Muscular cheek

Psittacosaurus Skeleton (above)
This form is still very like the earlier bipedal and lightly-built ornithopods. The front legs are quite robust, however, and might well have been used for walking as well as for other tasks. The parrot-like beak shows that it is a ceratopian.

snout tend to be rather raised and roughened there is no strong development of the brow or nose horns as there is in later ceratopians.

The first protoceratopid to be discovered was *Protoceratops,* another trophy of the expedition to Mongolia in the early 1920s. In fact, of all the new and dazzling fossil discoveries made in Mongolia during these expeditions, the discoveries of *Protoceratops* were the most renowned. This was because the remains found in the Djadochta Formation in the Gobi Desert included dozens of complete skulls and skeletons of individuals that ranged from newly emerged hatchlings right through the age-range to elderly specimens. In addition to this, the first nests of dinosaur eggs were discovered with these skeletons. Many of the nests were very well preserved, and showed clearly that the eggs had been laid in ring-shaped clutches in shallow depressions scooped out of the sand. The discovery of such a great abundance of skeletons of all ages and numerous nests

suggests very strongly that this is another nesting site, like the hadrosaurid one described by Horner and Makela. It seems that at least towards the end of the Cretaceous some dinosaurs were notably gregarious creatures, indulging in a variety of group activities such as using colonial nesting sites. These patterns of behaviour are more reminiscent of the birds of today than most reptiles, and give us a rather different perspective on dinosaur life-styles.

Indeed the discovery of this rich collection of fossil skeletons of *Protoceratops* has provided another of those, unfortunately rare, occasions when palaeontologists have been able to look a little closer at the biology of these animals. Peter Dodson from the University of Pennsylvania carried out a very detailed analysis of the skulls of twenty-four of the best preserved *Protoceratops.* His method of analysis was to take a series of measurements of various parts of the skull. For example, the height of the nose, the diameter of the eye, the length and

width of the frill, etc. Having done this, he was then able to analyse his results mathematically, in order to see whether there are certain parts of the skulls which could help him to distinguish between young individuals, males and females. In the sample that Dodson used, he was able to identify with certainty 7 adult females and 8 adult males using key measurements such as the height of the nose, the width of the frill and the total height of the skull. You can see the difference in skull shape between adult male and female skulls on page 133.

This study has also revealed something rather unexpected, which has repercussions upon long-held beliefs about the general function of the frill in ceratopians. For a long time it was thought that the purpose of the frill at the back of the skull was solely to provide a large area for attachment of powerful jaw muscles. As can be seen clearly in the drawing of the skull, the main jaw-closing muscles seem to have run forward and downward from an

---

Tooth Battery

Protoceratops Skeleton (below)

The *Protoceratops* skeleton has changed quite a lot from the basic ornithopod plan, producing an animal which probably moved much more slowly. *Protoceratops* moved around on all-fours and the front legs are nearly the same length as the hind legs, although, as in most land

vertebrates, the hind leg is still much the bigger. This probably has something to do with it being the source of power during locomotion, whereas the fore leg acts much more as a shock absorber as the body is forced forwards. Even though the front leg now supports the front of the body, there are still trellis-like bones spanning

the vertebrae, helping to prevent the body sagging. The long tail and rotated pubic bones, typical of all ornithischians, are seen here too. The feet and hands are well built and the fingers and toes rather splayed out, helping to support the weight of this fairly bulky animal on land. The head is quite low.

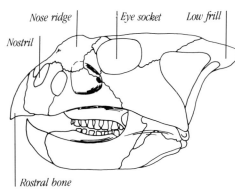

Bagaceratops Skull (above)

This form has the sharp beak and bony frill typical of ceratopians, although the frill is small and not lightened by a window. Brow ridges are not developed, but there is an unusual bony boss above the nose. Perhaps this supported a horn in life, possibly making the animal something like a rhinoceros in appearance and lifestyle.

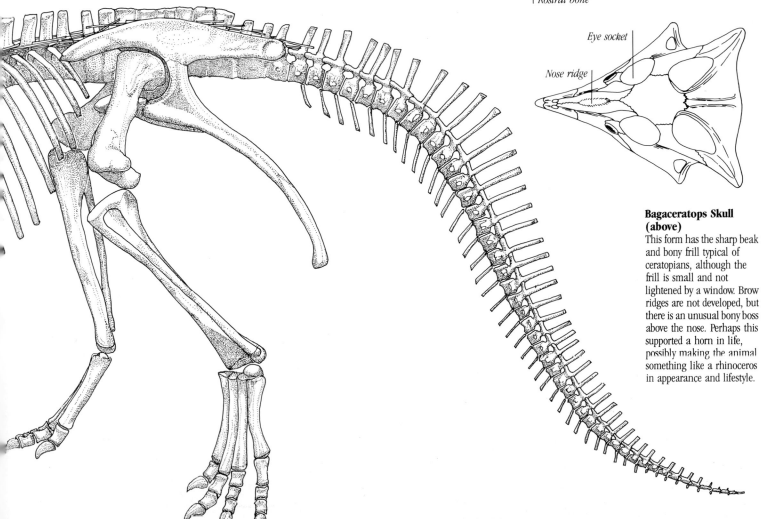

area of attachment around the margins of the frill. The edge of the frill is thickened to withstand the stresses and strains of muscular attachment. The area immediately in front of the back edge of the frill has a large, window-like opening on either side, which at first sight seems rather strange if large muscles are attached to the frill. However, the muscle would almost certainly have only been firmly attached to the edges of the frill and the edges of the 'windows', and in fact these 'extra' edges make the attachment stronger rather than weaker. There is another advantage to these openings in the frill which is slightly more obvious: they make the head and frill lighter and more easy to carry than it would be if it were a solid sheet of bone.

To return to these jaw muscles, they run forward and downward from the edge of the frill into long, slit-shaped holes on either side of the back of the skull. From here they run straight downward to attach to the raised bone on the lower jaw behind the teeth. The large bulk of such a muscle — far greater than that of any of the plant eaters we have seen so far, even those such as the hadrosaurids with their grinding batteries of teeth — is most impressive, and suggests that ceratopians had an immensely powerful bite. The strong jaw muscles also make sense when we look at the teeth of ceratopians which are rather similar to those of the hadrosaurids; at least insofar as there are many replacement teeth stacked together to form a *tooth battery.* However, one notable difference is the fact that instead of forming sloping wear surfaces as they do in hadrosaurids, ceratopians' teeth form vertical shearing blades — just like an enormous pair of scissors. They must have chewed their food rather differently than did the hadrosaurids. Hadrosaurids seem to have used their teeth and jaws like grindstones to pulverise plants. Ceratopians with their scissor-like tooth blades would presumably have chopped their food into short, uncrushed lengths of twig or leaf. Like most other ornithischians, ceratopians seem to have had muscular or fleshy cheeks which would have prevented the food from spilling out of the sides of the mouth when they were slicing it up. The implications of this method of chewing are interesting because plant foods are very difficult to digest. One of the best ways to prepare food for digestion is to chew it throroughly in the mouth so that it is

completely broken up. If ceratopians only sliced up their food into short lengths, then they may have had either to keep the food in the stomach for a very long time so that it could be fermented; or perhaps have used stomach stones to pound up the tough plant tissues. Either that or ceratopians were feeding on very juicy, succulent, nutritious plants which needed only to be chopped into neat lengths to release all their goodness. Once again we seem to be stumped for a convincing answer!

To return to the issue of the function of the bony frills in *Protoceratops:* while it is not, I think, seriously doubted that the frill served as a site for jaw-muscle attachment, nevertheless Dr Dodson was able to show, through his careful study of the shape of the frill in *Protoceratops,* that its shape was not in all circumstances controlled by the need for powerful jaw muscles. After all if this had been the only requirement then both males and females would surely have had exactly the same shaped

frills — which they do not! There is more discussion of ceratopian frill shape and function on pages 144-145.

Other Protoceratopids

Other protoceratopid dinosaurs known to date all show a general similarity in size and shape to *Protoceratops. Leptoceratops* ('slender horned face') is a rare type from the very late Cretaceous of Alberta and Wyoming. By comparison with *Protoceratops, Leptoceratops* is smaller and more lightly built, and may well have been at least partially bipedal; its hindlimb was long and well-suited to running, while its forelegs were quite short and had small, grasping-type hands. The head of this animal was also less elaborate than *Protoceratops.* There was no high nose-ridge, the face sloped down quite steeply toward the snout. The frill at the back of the skull was also very little developed, with none of the window-like openings seen in

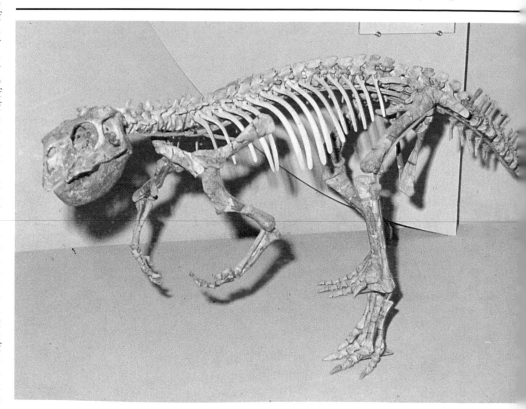

Above: This skeleton of *Psittacosaurus mongoliensis* illustrates the generally light build of this bipedal dinosaur, the clawed hands, and the distinctive parrot-like beak from which it derives its name. This specimen is in the Moscow Academy of Sciences' Palaeontological Institute.

Left: *Protoceratops* is known from the Late Cretaceous of both Asia and North America. This is a North American specimen on display in the Field Museum of Natural History, Chicago. The quadrupedal posture seems more typically 'ceratopian', as does the well-developed bony frill above the animal's neck. The pelvic structure is shown well here.

Protoceratops. In fact if it were not for its very late time of appearance in the fossil record, *Leptoceratops* would be very much the sort of creature that might have been expected to have evolved from *Psittacosaurus.*

Montanoceratops ('horned-face from Montana') was another North American protoceratopid. From Montana, as its name indicates, this creature was similar in size and shape to the Mongolian *Protoceratops.* The main difference lies in its possession of a quite prominent nose-horn. Otherwise, the very close resemblance between these two forms is striking, and suggests that they may have been quite close relatives.

More material of protoceratopids has recently been collected from Mongolia during joint Polish-Mongolian expeditions in the early 1970s. This includes the moderately well-preserved remains of *Microceratops* ('tiny-horned-face'). The parts of it that are known indicate that its skull had a better developed frill

than *Leptoceratops.* The remainder of the skeleton is very slender and light with the very long hind limbs and slender feet of a fast runner. Rather unusually, for an animal that ran on its hindlegs, its front legs were also quite long. Quite why this was so is not certain.

Finally there is *Bagaceratops* ('small horned-face') a recently (1975) described protoceratopid from the Khermeen Tsav formation of Mongolia. So far this new species is only known from several skulls. These range in size from 1·5-10in (4-25cm) in length. The skull on page 131 is 6in (15cm) long and shows the main characteristics of this new type. The frill is solid and only slightly developed, although it is somewhat larger in the biggest skulls. As is the case in *Montanoceratops,* there is quite a well developed horn on the nose, which gives *Bagaceratops* a rather similar appearance. It will be interesting to see, when new and more complete skeletons of *Bagaceratops* are eventually discovered, whether or not these apparent

similarities indicate any relationship between these two types of dinosaur.

Looked at together, the psittacosaurids and protoceratopids seem to represent an interesting intermediate step in the evolutionary line that led to the large and very powerful horned dinosaurs that appear in the late Cretaceous. Psittacosaurids retain many of the features of ornithopod dinosaurs such as the hysilophodontids as well as the very beginnings of the ceratopian features: notably the parrot-like beak. The protoceratopids in many ways seem to continue this 'trend'; some of them became essentially slower-moving, four-footed animals with well developed bony frills and the first rudiments of horns: very much smaller versions of the later ceratopids. Others, such as *Microceratops* and possibly *Leptoceratops,* seem to have persisted with the more active lifestyle of the psittacosaurids. These latter, however, seem never to have become as successful as the larger four-footed forms.

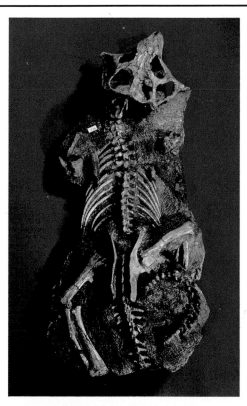

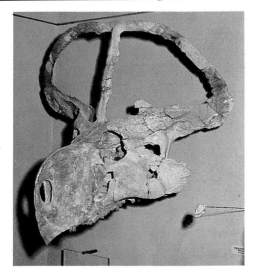

Left: A dorsal view of *Psittacosaurus sinensis,* a Chinese fossil from Shandong Province, now in the IVPP, Beijing. The length of the hind legs is particularly evident, an indication that this dinosaur may have resembled *Hypsilophodon* in its speed and agility.

Right: The size of the frill suggests that this skull is that of an adult male *Protoceratops andrewsi.* The tiny skull to its right is that of a small *Bagaceratops rozhdestvensky.* This Mongolian form has a small horn on its nose, rather like *Montanoceratops.*

Below: This cast of a nest of *Protoceratops* eggs is in the British Museum (Natural History). It seems that female *Protoceratops* would lay their clutches of eggs in concentric rings in hollowed-out depressions in the ground, much as we see here.

Sexual Dimorphism (below)
These drawings are based on the work of Dr Peter Dodson who has carefully analysed the skulls of several *Protoceratops* discovered at the same site. His research has shown that adult males

(lower drawing) have more erect frills and a more prominently humped snout than females. These differences may be related to social and sexual behaviour — the larger the frill, the more sexually attractive the male might appear to the female.

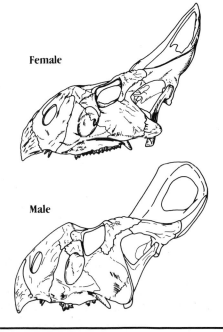

Female

Male

The larger and more typical ceratopian or horned dinosaurs were first found in North America in 1855 by Ferdinand Hayden during a geological reconnaissance of the Upper Missouri, around the mouth of the Judith River in Montana. Among the rather broken and fragmentary remains collected were found several characteristically double-rooted teeth which were later to be referred to the genus *Monoclonius* ('single horn'). As was the case with *Hadrosaurus*, Joseph Leidy also described these first remains. Following these very early reports no other significant discoveries of ceratopids were made until 1872. This time, remains were discovered on the Union Pacific Railroad at Black Buttes Station about 50 miles from Green River in Wyoming. Again, and rather typically, the remains of this dinosaur, named *Agathaumas* ('marvellous') by Edward Drinker Cope, were very incomplete. They included backbones, leg bones and other scraps, but nothing which gave any clear clue as

Styracosaurus (right)
This interesting ceratopid had one of the most remarkable neck-frills. The frill was surrounded with the usual nodules of bone at the sides, but these became progressively longer round the back. The six most posterior pieces of bone were very long pointed spines that must have formed a very prominent visual display to threaten rivals or attract mates. The horn on its nose was, no doubt, a formidable weapon.

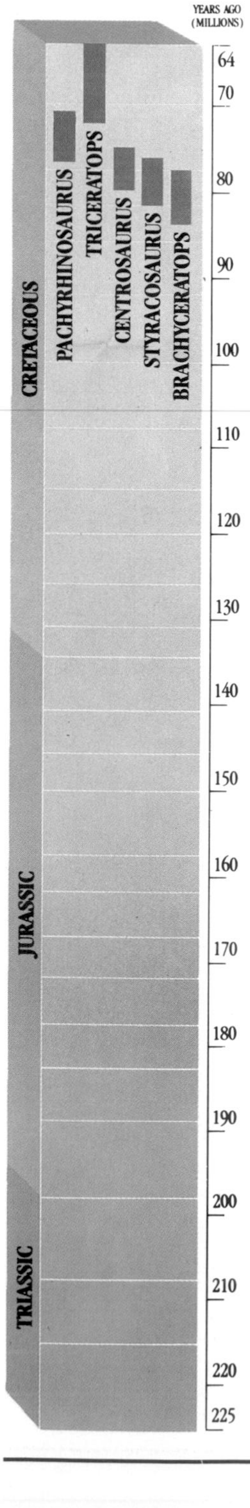

Time Chart (left)
The ceratopids were a very successful group in the late Cretaceous. The short-frilled forms were particularly abundant in the Red Deer River area of Alberta, which is of middle Upper Cretaceous age.

Triceratops (right)
The best known horned dinosaur, *Triceratops* was one of the largest members of the group. It might weigh up to 5·4 tonnes and reach a length of 30ft (9m). The neck frill was short, and rimmed by bony lumps. There were three sharp horns on the face, one on the snout, and one above each eye. The bony horn cores measure 3ft (90cm) long. so that they must have been considerably longer in life with the addition of the horn covering.

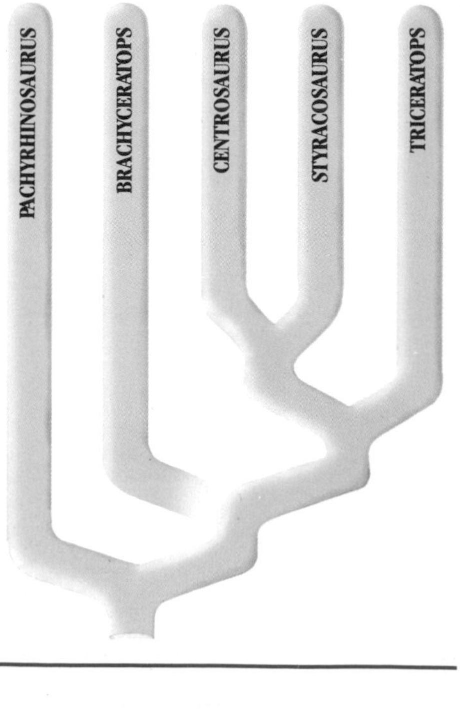

Family Tree (left)
The relations of the so-called short-frilled ceratopids are not clear. Each is so distinct that kinship is not at all obvious. *Centrosaurus* and *Styracosaurus* show some similarities: both have large nasal horns and elaborate frill margins. Where *Pachyrhinosaurus* fits is uncertain, and there is some doubt about the position of *Triceratops* as a short-frilled type at all.

Comparative Sizes (below)
1 *Styracosaurus:* l. 18ft (5·5m).
2 *Centrosaurus:* l. 20ft (6m).
3 *Triceratops:* l. 29·5ft (9m).

to the real identity of these dinosaurs. Indeed, although Cope and his assistants managed to collect quite a lot of remains (which we can now recognize as belonging to ceratopids) from Colorado, Alberta and Montana, none of these was well enough preserved to add anything new. The solution to this mystery came about through the activities of Cope's great rival, Othniel Charles Marsh — although Marsh himself was somewhat confused by the first remains that he was shown. These were a pair of very large bony horn cores which had been discovered in 1887 by George L. Cannon in Green Mountain Creek, near Denver, Colorado. Marsh initially thought that these remains, which were sent to him by a government geologist, belonged to an extinct buffalo. In fact he even named these bones *Bison alticornis* ('high-horned buffalo'), and suggested that it had only comparatively recently become extinct: Marsh was wrong! This specimen later became known as *Tri-*

ceratops alticornis ('high-horned three-horned face'). In 1888 John Bell Hatcher, another early dinosaur collector who subsequently became a world authority on these and other dinosaurs, was shown a massive horn core by a ranch owner in Niobrara County, Wyoming. This new specimen was shown to Marsh who immediately sent Hatcher back to Niobrara County to look for the remainder of the animal. Quite remarkably, this is exactly what Hatcher did with some style, returning in the following year with a skull weighing over 1 tonne. This was identified as the type *Triceratops horridus* ('terrifying three-horned-face'). Between 1889 and 1892, Hatcher collected dinosaurs continuously from this Niobrara County locality, discovering more than thirty complete or partial skulls and skeletons of ceratopian dinosaurs. All of these remains were sent to Marsh and are now either in the collections of or on display in the Peabody Museum, Yale University or at the United States National

Museum, Washington D.C. Following the frantic activity of the years of the Cope and Marsh rivalry, ceratopids continued to be discovered in North America. Between 1909 and 1916 some equally remarkable dinosaur collections were made along the Red Deer River in Canada. The collectors responsible for this were Barnum Brown and the Sternberg family, Charles Hazelius Sternberg and his sons, Charles, George and Levi. This all began in 1908, when a ranchman, John Wagner, showed Brown a rich deposit of dinosaur bones on the Red Deer River. Because the river was broad and slow-flowing, Brown decided that the best way to explore and collect was by boat. To do this, Brown and his assistants built a broad raft. Upon this they pitched a tent and stored their equipment for the expedition. They travelled slowly down river, stopping at likely places and setting off to explore and collect inland. At the end of the season when the weather became too cold to continue work, the raft was hauled

Map (above)
1 *Agathaumas*
2 *Brachyceratops*
3 *Centrosaurus*
4 *Diceratops*
5 *Monoclonius*
6 *Pachyrhinosaurus*
7 *Styracosaurus*
8 *Triceratops*

Centrosaurus (left)
This medium-sized ceratopid had a single horn on its snout, and small spines round the back of its neck frill. There were two horns on the posterior edge of the frill that pointed forwards. *Centrosaurus* had strong limbs and its feet were equipped with small hooves, rather like those of a rhinoceros. There is evidence that *Centrosaurus*, and other ceratopids, lived in herds of several dozen animals, and it is likely that they defended themselves communally, as do many living herbivores. The young animals and females might have remained in the middle, while the males formed a ring, facing outwards.

out and the materials stored until the next season. In this way large numbers of dinosaurs: ceratopids, hadrosaurs, and carnosaurs were discovered, many of which are to be found on display not only in North America, but in several museums around the world.

The next chapter in the story of the discovery of the ceratopian dinosaurs starts in the 1920s and continues, with interruptions, through to the present day. It centres on Asia, rather than North America. In the early 1920s there was considerable interest among scientists in North America in the fossils of Central Asia, because a prevailing theory of the time suggested that man's ancestors may be found there. With this in mind, a large expedition was mounted by the American Museum of Natural History in collaboration with the Mongolian government. Between 1922 and 1925 a series of expeditions was organized to map out the land and collect fossils from various parts of Mongolia. The results of this series of expeditions were

spectacular. The second and third years of the expedition saw the systematic collection of not the ancestors of man, but dinosaurs of many types, and small early mammals. Most of these were completely new to science. Of the dinosaurs, the most notable were the remains of *Protoceratops* which are described in the section preceding this. More than one hundred specimens were collected, many of complete animals. Not only that, but they also showed a complete age range, from tiny hatchlings up to fully grown adults. Perhaps one of the most famous discoveries of all was the collection of eggs and nest-sites of these animals. At the time this was the first ever discovery of a nest of dinosaur eggs (see also *Maiasaura* page 121). In addition to *Protoceratops*, other dinosaurs were discovered including *Pinacosaurus* (a large ankylosaur, page 165), as well as the small carnivorous dinosaurs *Oviraptor* (page 45), *Saurornithoides* (page 55), *Velociraptor* (page 56) and remains of a *Tarbosaurus* (page 72).

Further expeditions went to Mongolia shortly after the Second World War, this time from Russia, and collected many more dinosaurs. Much more recently there have been a series of jointly organized Polish-Mongolian expeditions to the Gobi Desert in the 1960s and 1970s which have also proved to be very successful. Interest has also been renewed in North America by the discovery of a spectacular new dinosaur locality in Alberta, which has so far revealed hundreds of remains of the ceratopian dinosaur *Centrosaurus* ('sharp point reptile'). These have been carefully collected during several field-seasons in recent years by a team of palaeontologists and voluntary helpers from the new Tyrrell Museum of Palaeontology at Drumheller in Alberta. Thus ceratopids are still attracting considerable interest and attention.

The larger and more spectacular ceratopid dinosaurs illustrated on these pages are both numerous and varied in appearance. However, they do share a considerable number of

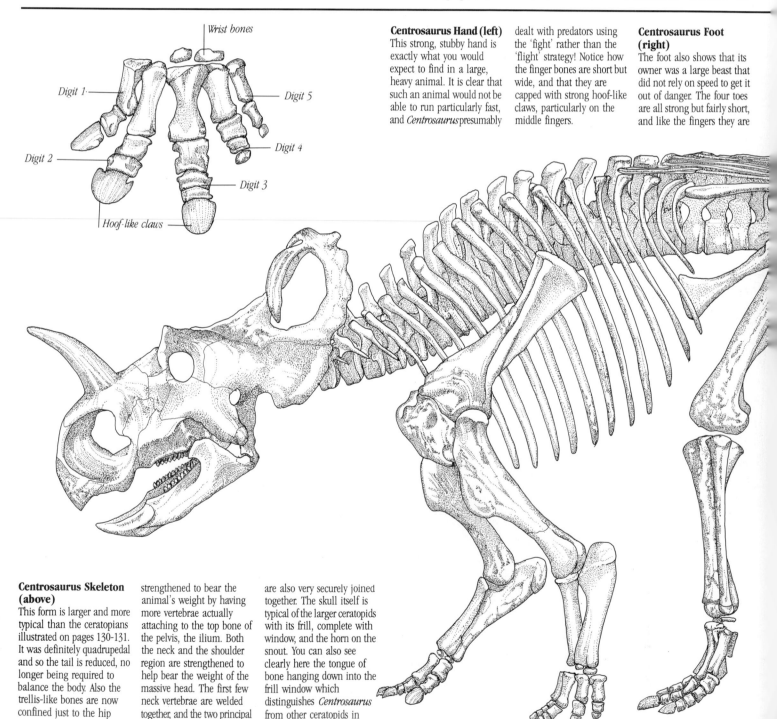

Wrist bones

Digit 1

Digit 2

Hoof-like claws

Digit 5

Digit 4

Digit 3

Centrosaurus Hand (left)
This strong, stubby hand is exactly what you would expect to find in a large, heavy animal. It is clear that such an animal would not be able to run particularly fast, and *Centrosaurus* presumably

dealt with predators using the 'fight' rather than the 'flight' strategy! Notice how the finger bones are short but wide, and that they are capped with strong hoof-like claws, particularly on the middle fingers.

Centrosaurus Foot (right)
The foot also shows that its owner was a large beast that did not rely on speed to get it out of danger. The four toes are all strong but fairly short, and like the fingers they are

Centrosaurus Skeleton (above)
This form is larger and more typical than the ceratopians illustrated on pages 130-131. It was definitely quadrupedal and so the tail is reduced, no longer being required to balance the body. Also the trellis-like bones are now confined just to the hip region. This has been

strengthened to bear the animal's weight by having more vertebrae actually attaching to the top bone of the pelvis, the ilium. Both the neck and the shoulder region are strengthened to help bear the weight of the massive head. The first few neck vertebrae are welded together, and the two principal bones of the shoulder girdle

are also very securely joined together. The skull itself is typical of the larger ceratopids with its frill, complete with window, and the horn on the snout. You can also see clearly here the tongue of bone hanging down into the frill window which distinguishes *Centrosaurus* from other ceratopids in this group.

features in common. They are all large, four-footed creatures with tails that were relatively short because they were no longer used as a counterbalance as in *Psittacosaurus*. The back legs are stout, pillar-like and considerably longer than the front legs. In fact the extreme difference in length between front and back legs seems to provide strong support for the idea that the large ceratopids *evolved* from originally bipedal ancestors not unlike *Psittacosaurus* or *Microceratops*. The forelimbs may be short, but they are very powerfully built with large crests of bone for the attachment of strong muscles. The muscles of the forelimb of these ceratopids can be reconstructed in quite some detail. This is because the shoulder and arm muscles were so powerful that they left distinctive patterns of large roughened areas and ridges on the shoulder and arm bones. By using modern animals for comparison it is possible to decide the arrangement of these muscles with a fair degree of confidence.

The need for such strong front legs is fairly obvious. These animals must have had extremely heavy heads, so that the front legs would have had to bear considerable weight, even when they were standing still. Add to this the fact that these animals swung their heads around to browse on plants, and also used them for fighting, and we can conclude that the power and strength of the front legs must have been quite remarkable.

Ceratopid Characteristics

The heads of all these ceratopids are considerably larger in proportion to body size than is the case in the protoceratopids. And here at last are developed the full set of ceratopid features, the sharp beak, large neck-frill and large horns. Some idea of the great weight of the head in the dinosaurs can be gained by looking at the structure of the neck vertebrae. The first three vertebrae immediately

behind the head are fused together into a solid piece of bone. All ceratopids (and some protoceratopids) show this type of modification which was undoubtedly a means of strengthening the top of the neck in order to be able to bear the great weight of the head.

The ceratopids chosen for illustration on pages 134-135 and 140-141 have been deliberately separated into two groups: short-frilled and long-frilled ceratopids respectively. *Centrosaurus* (sometimes referred to as *Monoclonius* instead), *Styracosaurus* ('spiked reptile') and *Triceratops* have been selected as representatives of the short-frilled type of ceratopid, although there are at least two other well known species: *Pachyrhinosaurus* ('thick-nosed reptile') and *Brachyceratops* ('short horned-face'). The skeleton of each of these animals is practically indistinguishable in general shape, and the *Centrosaurus* skeleton that we see illustrated is quite typical. A comparison with *Triceratops* for example would simply show that

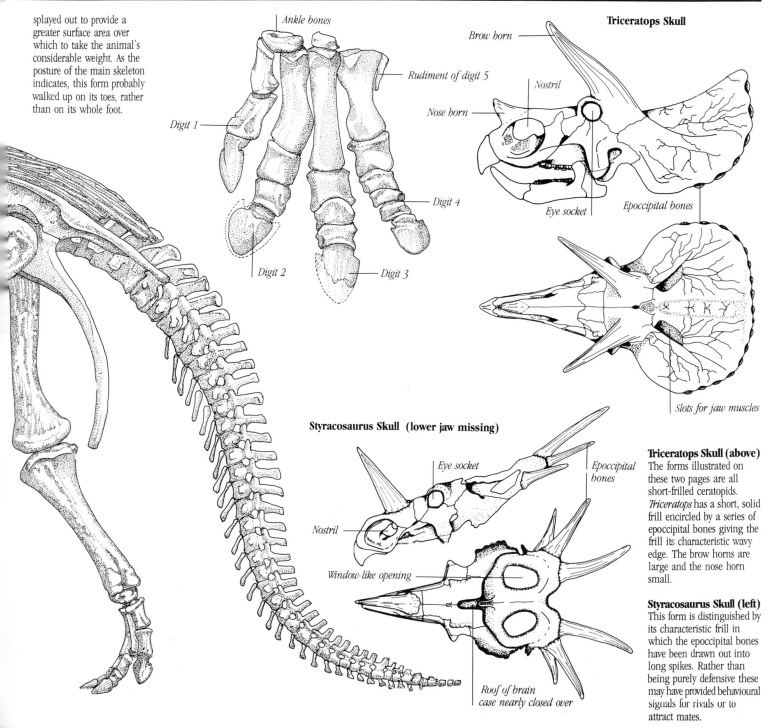

splayed out to provide a greater surface area over which to take the animal's considerable weight. As the posture of the main skeleton indicates, this form probably walked up on its toes, rather than on its whole foot.

Ankle bones

Rudiment of digit 5

Digit 1

Digit 4

Digit 2

Digit 3

Triceratops Skull

Brow horn

Nostril

Nose horn

Eye socket

Epoccipital bones

Slots for jaw muscles

Styracosaurus Skull (lower jaw missing)

Eye socket

Epoccipital bones

Nostril

Window-like opening

Roof of brain case nearly closed over

Triceratops Skull (above)
The forms illustrated on these two pages are all short-frilled ceratopids. *Triceratops* has a short, solid frill encircled by a series of epoccipital bones giving the frill its characteristic wavy edge. The brow horns are large and the nose horn small.

Styracosaurus Skull (left)
This form is distinguished by its characteristic frill in which the epoccipital bones have been drawn out into long spikes. Rather than being purely defensive these may have provided behavioural signals for rivals or to attract mates.

the *Triceratops* skeleton was more stoutly built than *Centrosaurus*, but this was simply a reflection of the fact that *Triceratops* was a larger and heavier animal. All the really obvious differences between these species are to be found in the skull.

Centrosaurus Described

Centrosaurus remains are found almost exclusively in the Red Deer River area of Alberta where it seems to have been remarkably abundant. It is known from several complete skeletons and detailed skin impressions. Despite this, there remains to this day much confusion about the name that should be applied to this dinosaur. Some describe it as *Monoclonius*, while others refer to it as *Centrosaurus*. The problem has arisen because of the very fragmentary nature of the early ceratopian material. The name *Monoclonius* was coined by Cope in 1876 for some broken fragments of a crest, and a few pieces of skeleton discovered in Montana (as described earlier). None of this material can be used for defining this type of dinosaur, or for comparing anything else with it, so the use of the name *Monoclonius* to describe any other dinosaur material could only be a matter of shrewd guesswork rather than strictly scientific comparison. *Centrosaurus* by contrast was described by Lawrence Lambe in 1904 and was based on another frill of a ceratopid this time from the Red Deer River. This admittedly fragmentary specimen does, however, have one crucial character present, and that is the rather curious tongue-shaped pieces of bone which point downward into the window-like openings of the frill. These do not appear in any other known ceratopid to date; so, imperfect though Lambe's specimen is, that piece of frill clearly characterises *Centrosaurus* and must take precedence. *Monoclonius*, interesting though it is from an historical point of view, has sadly to be looked upon as a dubiously named dinosaur.

Centrosaurus, in addition to possessing the unique tongue-shaped bones on its frill, has a very prominent nasal horn giving it quite a strong resemblance to a rhinoceros. There are also small eyebrow horns but these are very poorly developed compared to the nose horn. Most of the characters of the skull are similar to those seen in protoceratopids such as *Protoceratops* (pages 136-137). There is a pronounced parrot-like, toothless beak at the tip of the jaws, and the teeth, which are set in from the sides of the jaws to allow room for cheeks, form powerful cutting blades. The jaws of these larger ceratopids are better developed than the protoceratopids and have longer cutting blades with more teeth. The jaws are also operated by very powerful muscles which run down from the frill (as we saw in *Protoceratops*) but which this time attach to a large bar of bone that sticks up from the back end of the lower jaw. This process, termed the coronoid process (also seen in iguanodontids and hadrosaurids) provides extra leverage for the jaw-closing muscles.

Two other features in the skull not found in the protoceratopids are the so-called *epoccipital* bones and a secondary skull roof. Epoccipitals are small, rounded lumps of bone found around the edge of the frill, giving it an irregular wavy margin. In the case of *Centrosaurus* the epoccipitals are not very strongly developed. Precisely what their function was is not at all certain. Most likely, these lumps were decorative, and covered in life by horny layers of skin.

Such horny edging may have helped with individual recognition, thereby acting as signalling structures, rather than as a spiky defensive edge to deter predators.

The secondary skull roof can be seen most clearly in the top views of the skulls. In the area of the roof of the skull, just in front of the frill and between the raised ridges over the eyes, there is found a deep U-shaped notch. This notch represents the ingrown edges of the top of the skull roof which have grown up and over the original roof of the braincase. This rather complicated arrangement of bones probably reflects the changes that have taken place in ceratopian skulls when compared with more ordinary ornithischian dinosaur skulls, such as those of hypsilophodontids. Not only has the enormous frill been added to the back, but horns have been added to the nose and eyes, the skull has become much narrower and deeper, and huge muscles now operate the jaws. Some reinforcement of the skull would have been inevitable, and the adding of a second skull roof between and behind the eyes was probably essential in holding the skull together.

Looking at the remainder of the skeleton, the progressive trend toward a fully four-footed way of life, seen earlier in the protoceratopids, is now complete. The tail, which was still quite long and very deep in *Protoceratops* can now be seen to be quite short and slender, with only its tip resting on the ground, obviously of no use for counterbalancing the body. The peculiar bony rods, which ran along much of the length of the back and tail in most ornithischians and acted to stiffen the backbone so that it could be held fairly straight without sagging, are now simply concentrated across the spines immediately above the hip area. The connection between the backbone and hips is very greatly strengthened by increasing the number of vertebrae attaching to the pelvic bones from about 4-6, as seen in most dinosaurs, to about 10. The back legs are large and powerful with broad, hooved, four-toed feet. The rib cage is very large and deep and against this was slung the massive shoulders and forelimbs. As was noted with the protoceratopids, the bipedal ancestry of the ceratopids is very clearly shown in the obvious disparity between the lengths of the front and back legs.

The great size and weight of the head of *Centrosaurus* has produced several inevitable changes in the rest of the skeleton. As was noted with the protoceratopids, several of the neck vertebrae have become welded together, presumably to prevent dislocation of these bones when the head was being shaken or

used more violently, such as when defending itself against predatory dinosaurs. The shoulders and forelimbs also show evidence of great strengthening, in order to carry the heavy head. The two main shoulder bones are large and very tightly knitted together, thereby improving their strength for carrying weight and also their ability to anchor large and powerful shoulder muscles. That the shoulder muscles were powerful is indicated by large bony crests and ridges on the surface of both the shoulder and forelimb. As shown in the drawing on page 143, several of these muscles can be restored in their probable positions in life. The front feet are broad (five-toed), the inner ones with well developed hooves.

The powerful front legs and broad feet gave these animals great strength. This was not only simply to support the very heavy head, while walking, running or feeding; it would also have been necessary for fending off predators. The most likely predators of these dinosaurs were the giant tyrannosaurids of the late Cretaceous. When faced by the threat of a hunting tyrannosaurid, *Centrosaurus* probably had several options. It seems likely that *Centrosaurus* was a gregarious animal, in which case the largest and most powerful bull males may have defended the herd in groups. Armed with such formidable nose horns, these animals were very likely more than a match for any tyrannosaurid. However, herding animals do not remain packed tightly together all of the time; they have to spread out to find suitable food. Sneak attacks on isolated feeding animals may have been a good strategy for tyrannosaurids hunting such formidable creatures. The outcome of such attacks would depend upon numerous complicated factors: the respective ages of predator and prey, their agility, acceleration and top running speed, and many others beside. On occasion, tyrannosaurids must have cornered *Centrosaurus*. However, even when cornered by a full-sized *Tyrannosaurus*, *Centrosaurus* would have still been a considerable opponent. A tyrannosaurid would need to make its first bite a killing one, because its attacking lunge would leave it open to being severely gored by the nasal horn. When crouching low by spreading its front legs apart, *Centrosaurus* would be an elusive and dangerous target.

Other Species

Triceratops must be one of the best known of all dinosaurs; it has come to be known to the world at large through the labours of John Bell

Above: The most distinctive feature of this skull of *Pachyrhinosaurus*, a Tyrrell Museum of Palaeontology specimen, is the rough bony pad that extends along the upper surface of the snout region. Only two skulls of this dinosaur have been so far discovered.

Above: This skull on display in the National Museum of Natural History, Washington D.C., is identified as *Monoclonius flexus*. As can be seen, the skull is incomplete and many areas, including the nose horn, have had to be reconstructed in the laboratory.

Hatcher in Niobrara County, Wyoming. From this area Hatcher recovered thirty-two ceratopian skulls, almost all of them belonging to the genus *Triceratops*. There are 10 species of *Triceratops* currently recognized from these collections. These are distinguished by their size and general proportions, but it does seem very unlikely that there were in fact 10 distinct species living within a relatively short time period. More likely is the prospect that this number would be reduced if we were able to establish with some confidence young individuals, the normal range of variations within any single species population of *Triceratops*, and the differences between males and females. A study of the type done by Peter Dodson on *Protoceratops* may be one way of resolving this problem.

Nevertheless, all *Triceratops* share a number of common features. They have relatively short, but solid frills (there are no window-like openings as in *Centrosaurus*, and indeed most

other ceratopids). Around the fringe of the frill is an even row of conical epoccipital bones. In contrast to *Centrosaurus*, the eyebrow horns are very large and the nasal horn tends to be somewhat shorter. In fact the length of the nose horn may vary from individual to individual. The snout of *Triceratops* is also lower and longer than that of *Centrosaurus*. However, apart from these differences, the remainder of the skeleton is very similar in these two animals. Some *Triceratops* species were enormous. The head alone of *Triceratops horridus* ('horrible three-horned face') was 6·6ft (2m) long and the whole animal was probably 29·5ft (9m) long (even though its tail was very short). It may have weighed as much as 6 tonnes. More information about *Triceratops* is to be found in the following section: Ceratopids II.

Styracosaurus from the Belly River of Alberta has a rather extraordinary skull; it is long and low with a very prominent nose-horn like that of *Centrosaurus*. At first sight this seems to be a

long frilled ceratopid. However, if you look closely, the frill is actually short with large windows in it—just like *Centrosaurus*. However the epoccipitals, which are small nubbins in *Centrosaurus*, are developed into great long spikes which stick out backward. The visual effect of the spikes on the edge of the frill is quite striking and will be discussed later. Unfortunately all that is known of *Styracosaurus* is this extraordinary skull and a few other smaller skull fragments.

Pachyrhinosaurus from Alberta is another extraordinary ceratopid which has similar skull proportions to *Centrosaurus*. However, instead of a horn core on its nose, there is a broad, thick, rough plate of bone. Two skulls of this species have been discovered to date. The extraordinary roughness and irregularity of the nose-pad in these specimens tempts the suggestion that this might be a *pathological* feature developed after fracturing of an original horn core.

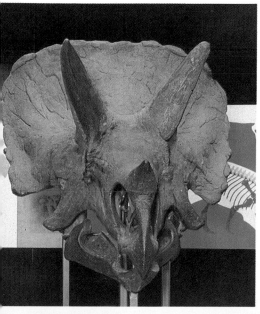

Left: This photograph graphically illustrates the massive size and robust construction of the skull of *Triceratops*. The eyebrow horns are noticeably larger than the nose horn, and the frill, which lacks window-like openings, is edged with an array of small epoccipital bones.

Below: The Smithsonian Institution's skeleton of *Triceratops prorsus*, the smallest species of *Triceratops*. The head is very large in proportion to the body, while the tail, no longer needed as a counterbalance as it was for bipedal ornithopods, has grown correspondingly shorter and just touches the ground.

On The Attack (above) An aggressive 5-tonne adult *Triceratops* charges a full-grown tyrannosaurid predator. The combination of its long facial horns and powerful build would have made it a formidable opponent for even the largest 'carnosaur'.

Below: This charging rhino invites comparison with *Centrosaurus*; were scenes like this enacted in late Cretaceous times?

The other major group of ceratopids comprises the long-frilled types considered here. The examples illustrated below and overleaf (*Chasmosaurus* 'ravine reptile', *Torosaurus* 'bull reptile', *Pentaceratops* 'five-horned face', *Anchiceratops* 'close-horned face') are all absolutely typical of this type of dinosaur. The body of these animals is practically identical to that of the short-frilled forms described earlier: they are, without exception, large lumbering quadrupedal dinosaurs.

The skulls of these creatures are even more bizarre than those of their short-frilled cousins. The general pattern seen in all these dinosaurs is for the frill to be greatly lengthened and somewhat lower than the short-frilled types, when seen in profile. As a result, the frill seems to have lain like a shield over the shoulder region of the animal, completely covering its neck. This would seem to suggest that their frills had some sort of defensive function, perhaps protecting the neck against the attacks of predators. In fact, as we shall see later, this is now considered to be an extremely unlikely function indeed. In addition to the variations in the proportions of the frill, the faces of these ceratopids are somewhat different from those of the short-frilled forms. Typically, they are not as deep, being long and low with a tapering muzzle. The arrangement of horns is also rather different. Whereas in the short-frilled forms (especially *Centrosaurus* and *Styracosaurus*) the nose horn is very long and pointed, the long-frilled types have very short, blunt nose horns, while the brow horns, which tend to be short in the short-frills, are long and pointed.

The best known long-frilled ceratopids are *Chasmosaurus*, *Pentaceratops*, *Torosaurus*, *Anchiceratops* and *Arrhinoceratops* ('no nose-horned face'), all of which come from the late Cretaceous of western North America. A few rather dubious types such as *Eoceratops* are also known, but these are discussed at the end of this section.

Chasmosaurus is known from several well-preserved skulls and skeletons which were discovered, along the Red Deer River in Alberta, by Lawrence Lambe and the Sternberg family. The skull of this ceratopid is very long and low. Its frill is large and has thick edges, which are fringed by low, rounded epoccipitals (lumps of bone edging the frill) which get progressively larger and more pointed toward each of the posterior corners of the frill. When viewed from above, the enormous size of the frill's window-like openings is very noticeable. Its back edge is formed by quite a thin bar of bone supported by a thin spar of bone projecting backward from the middle of the head. Presumably all the strength of the frill lay in the thick bones lying along either side of it. The enormous size of the openings immediately casts doubt on the idea that it was used as a defensive shield. The space between the thickened edges of the frill is scooped out on either side of the ridge which runs down its

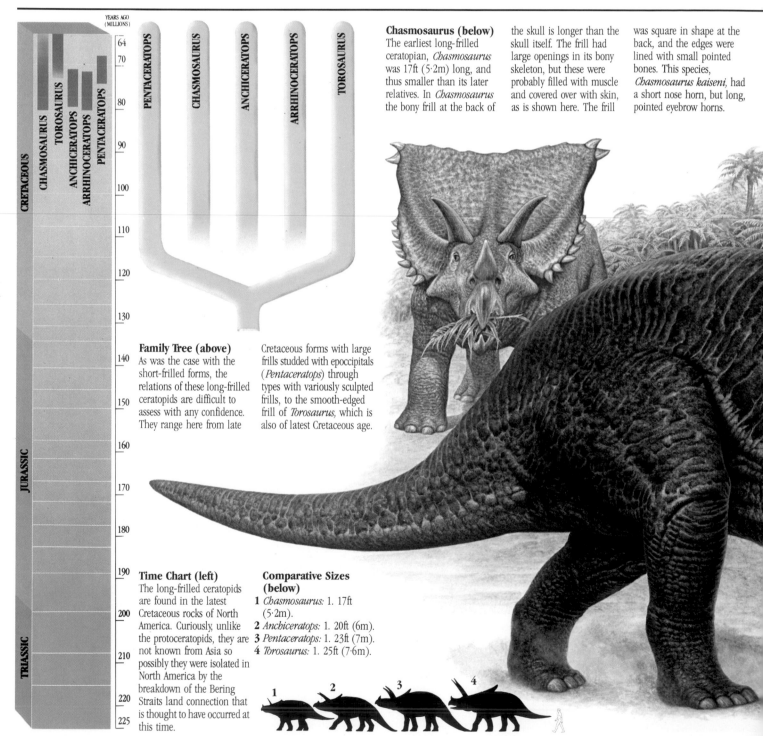

Chasmosaurus (below)
The earliest long-frilled ceratopian, *Chasmosaurus* was 17ft (5·2m) long, and thus smaller than its later relatives. In *Chasmosaurus* the bony frill at the back of the skull is longer than the skull itself. The frill had large openings in its bony skeleton, but these were probably filled with muscle and covered over with skin, as is shown here. The frill was square in shape at the back, and the edges were lined with small pointed bones. This species, *Chasmosaurus kaiseni*, had a short nose horn, but long, pointed eyebrow horns.

Family Tree (above)
As was the case with the short-frilled forms, the relations of these long-frilled ceratopids are difficult to assess with any confidence. They range here from late Cretaceous forms with large frills studded with epoccipitals (*Pentaceratops*) through types with variously sculpted frills, to the smooth-edged frill of *Torosaurus*, which is also of latest Cretaceous age.

Time Chart (left)
The long-frilled ceratopids are found in the latest Cretaceous rocks of North America. Curiously, unlike the protoceratopids, they are not known from Asia so possibly they were isolated in North America by the breakdown of the Bering Straits land connection that is thought to have occurred at this time.

Comparative Sizes (below)
1 *Chasmosaurus*: 1. 17ft (5·2m).
2 *Anchiceratops*: 1. 20ft (6m).
3 *Pentaceratops*: 1. 23ft (7m).
4 *Torosaurus*: 1. 25ft (7·6m).

YEARS AGO (MILLIONS)

CRETACEOUS
JURASSIC
TRIASSIC

PENTACERATOPS
CHASMOSAURUS
ANCHICERATOPS
ARRHINOCERATOPS
TOROSAURUS

middle. These two trough-shaped depressions almost certainly contained the enlarged jaw-closing muscles of these dinosaurs which plunge deep into spaces in the head just behind the eye, before attaching to the lower jaw. This arrangement is like that seen in *Protoceratops,* but on a much larger scale.

As well as the frill, the face deserves mention. It was stated earlier that most long-frilled ceratopids have long, pointed eyebrow horns and short blunt nose horns. *Chasmosaurus* already shows a variation on that theme: the eyebrow horns of the individual illustrated overleaf are really quite short and blunt, as is the nose horn. This combination of horn sizes characterizes a particular species of *Chasmosaurus—Chasmosaurus belli.* Another species, known as *Chasmosaurus kaiseni,* is also known from the Red Deer River. In most respects, the skulls of these two species are similar. The horns, however, differ strikingly: *Chasmosaurus kaiseni* has very long, pointed eyebrow horns

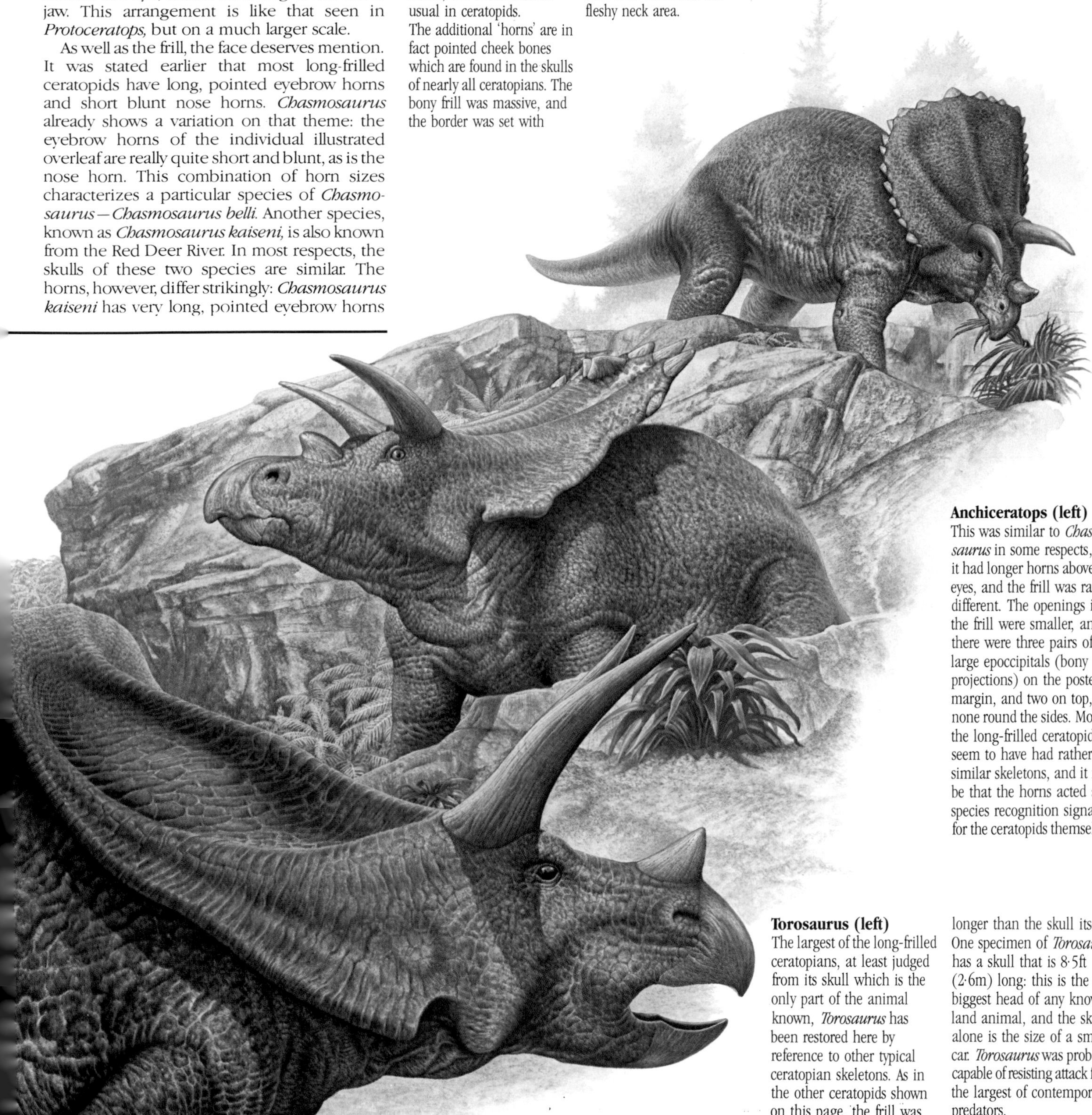

Pentaceratops (below)
As its name suggests ('five-horned face'), *Pentaceratops* was supposed to have five horns, two more than is usual in ceratopids.
The additional 'horns' are in fact pointed cheek bones which are found in the skulls of nearly all ceratopians. The bony frill was massive, and the border was set with

pointed bony nodules which were both decorative and an added defence against predators that might have tried to sink their teeth into the fleshy neck area.

Anchiceratops (left)
This was similar to *Chasmosaurus* in some respects, but it had longer horns above the eyes, and the frill was rather different. The openings in the frill were smaller, and there were three pairs of large epoccipitals (bony projections) on the posterior margin, and two on top, but none round the sides. Most of the long-frilled ceratopids seem to have had rather similar skeletons, and it may be that the horns acted as species recognition signals for the ceratopids themselves.

Torosaurus (left)
The largest of the long-frilled ceratopians, at least judged from its skull which is the only part of the animal known, *Torosaurus* has been restored here by reference to other typical ceratopian skeletons. As in the other ceratopids shown on this page, the frill was

longer than the skull itself. One specimen of *Torosaurus* has a skull that is 8·5ft (2·6m) long: this is the biggest head of any known land animal, and the skull alone is the size of a small car. *Torosaurus* was probably capable of resisting attack from the largest of contemporary predators.

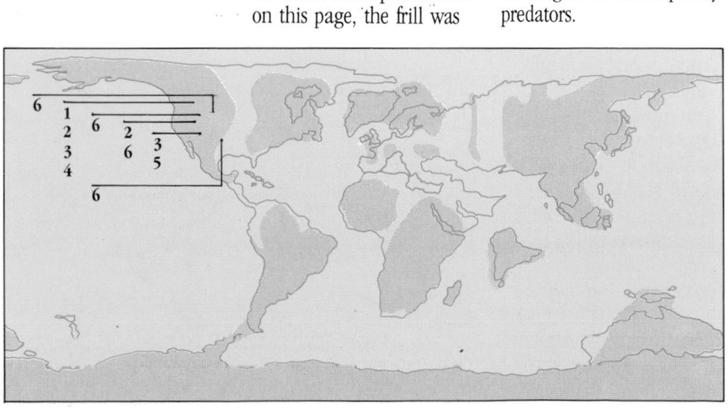

Map (right)
1 *Anchiceratops*
2 *Arrhinoceratops*
3 *Chasmosaurus*
4 *Eoceratops*
5 *Pentaceratops*
6 *Torosaurus*

(see colour illustration). The discovery of two such similar dinosaurs in the same geological deposit seems to point quite strongly to the possibility that the difference in brow horn size may in fact be an indicator of their sexes. We saw earlier in the case of *Protoceratops* how the shape of the nose and frill was associated with the sex of individuals. It seems equally possible that *Chasmosaurus kaiseni* (with the large brown horns) was a male individual, while the short-horned species, *C. belli*, may well have been the female. Unfortunately a detailed analysis to identify sexual characteristics in *Chasmosaurus* is not possible, because there are simply not enough skulls known to get sufficient scientific data for such an exercise.

Anchiceratops lived a little later in the Cretaceous Period than *Chasmosaurus* although it was also discovered on the Red Deer River. *Anchiceratops* is fairly similar to *Chasmosaurus kaiseni* as regards the shape of its skull; it has quite a long face, a short nose horn and long

pointed brow horns. The frill, however, is distinctive. The window-like openings are much smaller than in *Chasmosaurus* and three pairs of large, triangular epoccipitals are found along the back edge of the frill. There are also two epoccipitals which project forward from the middle of the back edge of the frill; these are smaller than, but vaguely reminiscent of, the curious tongue-shaped bones which project into the frill openings of *Centrosaurus*. Apart from this, these two genera are very similar.

Arrhinoceratops was a contemporary of *Anchiceratops;* both were found in the same area of the Red Deer River. The name of this ceratopid – 'no nose-horned face' – is particularly inappropriate because *Arrhinoceratops* does indeed have a nose horn. The peculiar name for this animal arose because William Parks, who first described this dinosaur in 1925, claimed that its skull did not have a *true* nose horn. There was clearly a 'lump' on the nose where a horn should be, but Parks believed that

it should be clearly visible as a *separate* bone, rather than just a thickening of the bones covering the nose area of the animal. This type of interpretation is now regarded as improbable since horns of this type would tend to weld themselves to the nose bones, and it is impossible to tell whether the bone was ever separate or not. However, despite the fact that Parks' name is inappropriate, the rules which govern the names given to animals make it impossible to change the name retrospectively.

Arrhinoceratops has large, pointed brow horns and the frill is quite large and broad, with two moderate-sized openings like those of *Anchiceratops*. The margins of its frill are wavy because of an even fringe of low, rounded epoccipitals. In many respects *Arrhinoceratops* resembles *Triceratops* very closely, the only obvious difference being the absence of openings in *Triceratops'* frill.

Pentaceratops was first described in 1923 by Henry Fairfield Osborn. The name was

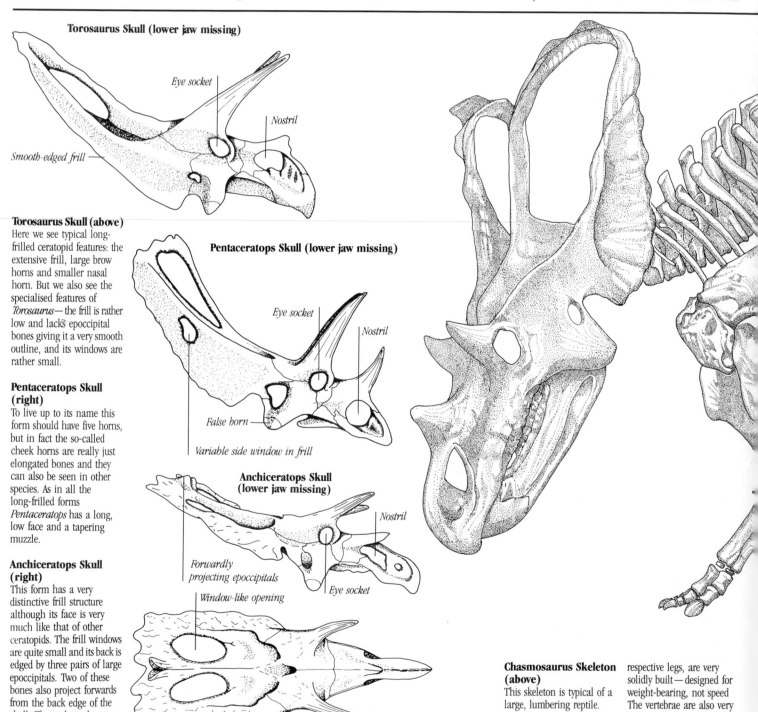

Torosaurus Skull (lower jaw missing)

Eye socket

Nostril

Smooth-edged frill

Torosaurus Skull (above)
Here we see typical long-frilled ceratopid features: the extensive frill, large brow horns and smaller nasal horn. But we also see the specialised features of *Torosaurus* — the frill is rather low and lacks epoccipital bones giving it a very smooth outline, and its windows are rather small.

Pentaceratops Skull (right)
To live up to its name this form should have five horns, but in fact the so-called cheek horns are really just elongated bones and they can also be seen in other species. As in all the long-frilled forms *Pentaceratops* has a long, low face and a tapering muzzle.

Anchiceratops Skull (right)
This form has a very distinctive frill structure although its face is very much like that of other ceratopids. The frill windows are quite small and its back is edged by three pairs of large epoccipitals. Two of these bones also project forwards from the back edge of the skull. The eyebrow horns are very long and pointed.

Pentaceratops Skull (lower jaw missing)

Eye socket

Nostril

False horn

Variable side window in frill

Anchiceratops Skull (lower jaw missing)

Nostril

Forwardly projecting epoccipitals

Eye socket

Window-like opening

Chasmosaurus Skeleton (above)
This skeleton is typical of a large, lumbering reptile. Both the hip and shoulder girdles, as well as their respective legs, are very solidly built — designed for weight-bearing, not speed. The vertebrae are also very large and strong, especially in the neck and back regions.

suggested to Osborn by William Diller Matthew to recognize the fact that in addition to the usual three horns of the head, this new specimen had two others formed by the long pointed cheek bones beneath and behind the eye (see illustration). In fact, as was the case in *Arrhinoceratops,* the name *Pentaceratops* turned out to be rather fanciful. These cheek bones are not particularly horn-like in some specimens and other ceratopids have equally large cheek bones. Nevertheless, we are again stuck with this rather misleading name.

All the remains of *Pentaceratops* come from the San Juan Basin of New Mexico, and are of a very large-frilled ceratopid. The brow horns are very long and pointed, the nose horn is of moderate size. The frill has many low triangular epoccipitals which run along its margins. The openings in the frill are large and rather like those of *Chasmosaurus.*

Torosaurus was, along with *Triceratops,* one of the last of the dinosaurs, appearing in the latest part of the Cretaceous Period. *Torosaurus* is known only from the character of its skull; none of the remainder of the skeleton has so far been identified. The skull, however, is quite remarkable. The genus is represented by two species, *Torosaurus gladius* and *Torosaurus latus,* both of which were first described by O. C. Marsh from material collected by Hatcher in Niobrara County, Wyoming.

Both of these species are represented by single skulls, each of which is incomplete. *Torosaurus latus* had a skull that was probably almost 8ft (2·4m) long when complete. Unfortunately the muzzle of the skull is not preserved, so it is not possible to give an exact measure of the length of the skull or the shape of the snout.

The arrangement of horns on the skull is similar to that seen in *Arrhinoceratops,* with a rather short nose horn and long pointed brow horns. The frill, however, is distinctive; it is very long and low, with very smooth edges exhibiting no sign of the epoccipitals seen in all other ceratopids. The frill also has moderately sized circular openings, unlike most other ceratopids. The smooth contours and smoothness of the frill contrast quite strongly with the features of the only other very late ceratopian genus *Triceratops,* which has a scalloped edge to its frill and no openings at all.

The inner surface of parts of the frill in this specimen of *Torosaurus* has proved to be of some interest because it reveals signs of a bone disease. This frill was examined in the 1930s by Dr Roy L. Moodie, a noted expert on bone disorders. The bone had a series of irregular holes and dimples in its surface. Dr Moodie's comments were rather surprising, because he showed that these lesions were identical to some found in the skeletons of prehistoric Indians. He diagnosed this disease as *Multiple Myeloma,* or perhaps the dinosaur equivalent of this disease, the pockmarking having been caused by the growth of small cancerous

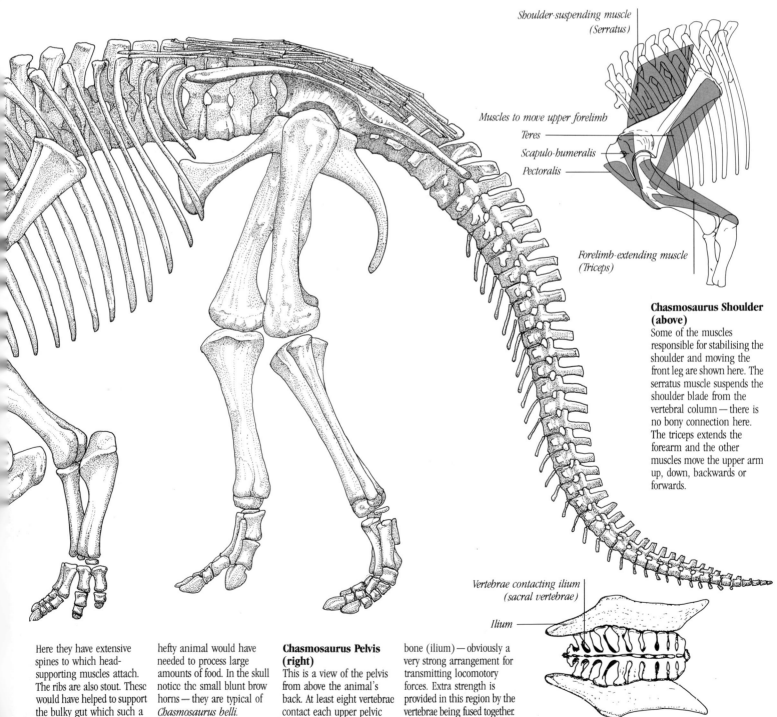

Chasmosaurus Shoulder (above)
Some of the muscles responsible for stabilising the shoulder and moving the front leg are shown here. The serratus muscle suspends the shoulder blade from the vertebral column — there is no bony connection here. The triceps extends the forearm and the other muscles move the upper arm up, down, backwards or forwards.

Chasmosaurus Pelvis (right)
This is a view of the pelvis from above the animal's back. At least eight vertebrae contact each upper pelvic bone (ilium) — obviously a very strong arrangement for transmitting locomotory forces. Extra strength is provided in this region by the vertebrae being fused together.

Here they have extensive spines to which head-supporting muscles attach. The ribs are also stout. These would have helped to support the bulky gut which such a hefty animal would have needed to process large amounts of food. In the skull notice the small blunt brow horns — they are typical of *Chasmosaurus belli.*

tumours within the bone. This is rather a chilling example of just how long cancers, in this case bone-cancer, have been around.

The other species of Torosaurus, T. gladius, is represented by another incomplete skull which may have reached a total length of 8·5ft (2·6m); this is the largest skull known of any land-living animal. The skull differs slightly in its general shape from that of T. latus in, for example, the position of the brow horns, the shape of the eye, and the angle of the frill. Again, whether these differences really justify the placing of these specimens in different species is an open question. It seems quite probable that both of these individuals belong to the same species and represent normal variations in shape due to age or sex differences. As we have seen before, however, such proposals are very difficult to prove scientifically.

Frill Classification

The division of the ceratopids into long-frilled and short-frilled types that we have used here is rather an arbitrary one, but it serves as a convenient way of dividing up a very varied group of animals into two more manageable groups. By doing this, we can learn about them more easily. However, there is built into this division the assumption that all the short-frilled ceratopids are more closely related to one another than to the long-frilled types, and vice versa. This assumption may or may not be true, and indeed there is still much debate about the significance of this division.

As an example of the problems that can be created by this kind of classification, let us look at the position of Triceratops— the best known of all ceratopids. Triceratops was described with the other short-frilled ceratopids on pages 134-139. However, although Triceratops does indeed have a relatively short frill, it does not share some of the other characteristics normally seen in the short-frilled forms. In particular, it has long pointed brow horns and a short nose horn: a combination typical of the long-frilled types that have just been described. The question then arises: is Triceratops really a long-frilled type of ceratopid with an unusually short frill, or is it a short-frilled type that is mimicking the horn arrangement usually found in long-frilled types? Or, even more importantly perhaps, does Triceratops prove that dividing the ceratopids into long- and short-frilled types is a complete waste of time?

One solution to the 'problem' of Triceratops was provided by Charles M. Sternberg. He decided that instead of looking at the overall length of the frill, it was more useful to study the individual bones from which it was made. Using this method he was able to divide the ceratopids into so-called 'long-squamosaled' and 'short-squamosaled' forms. (The squamosal is the bone that forms each side of the frill.) By doing this, Sternberg was able to include Triceratops with all the other 'long-frilled' forms described above, which may perhaps seem more satisfactory to our tidy minds. However, neat though this solution might seem to us, it is very difficult to be sure that what we have arrived at is a 'better' or more natural arrangement of these animals, rather than one that merely satisfies our sense of order.

Ceratopian Miscellany

In addition to the many well known ceratopids that we have looked at over the last few pages, there are several others whose names are also familiar to many, but are in fact very poorly known indeed. Monoclonius ('single shoot') is one obvious example; it was first described by Joseph Leidy in 1856 on the basis of a single tooth which had the characteristically double-fanged root found in all ceratopids. Several species of this genus were described in the 1870s on very poor, fragmentary material. As a result little is known about this genus, apart from the fact that it is a ceratopid from the Judith River in Montana. Despite this, Monoclonius is frequently illustrated in books about dinosaurs, creating the misleading impression that it is a very well-known form indeed.

Agathaumas sylvestris, a ceratopid from the Green River of Wyoming, was described by E. D. Cope. Again this was based on poor material: several bones from the back, hips and legs. None of these are of any use in characterizing a new type of ceratopid. Ceratops ('horned face') was an alternative name provided by O. C. Marsh for 'Bison alticornis' which finally became known as Triceratops alticornis, along with several other totally useless fragments.

Diceratops based on a partial skull from Niobrara County was originally supposed to differ from Triceratops from the same area because it lacked a nose horn (hence the name Diceratops, or 'two-horned face'). In fact the degree of development of the nose horn tends to vary quite a lot in Triceratops. It seems very probable that Diceratops is just a variant of the normal Triceratops and should be included in the latter genus.

Eoceratops ('dawn horned face') comes from the Red Deer River, Alberta and consists of a partial skull of another ceratopid. It was a young individual with long brow horns and a short nose horn, and a relatively short frill without any obvious epoccipitals. The two other well-known ceratopids found in this area are Centrosaurus and Chasmosaurus, but the skull of Eoceratops does not resemble that of Centrosaurus at all closely. Neither does it seem to resemble that of

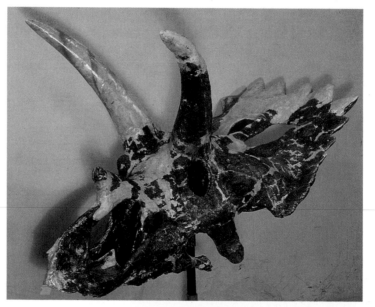

Left: Despite its name, Arrhinoceratops ('no nose horn') does have a small nose horn as this Tyrrell Museum skull confirms. Note the typically low tapering muzzle, the long pointed brow horns, the fairly small openings in the frill, and the even fringe of epoccipitals around the posterior edge of the frill.

Right: It would seem that a natural parallel can be drawn between the behaviour of rutting stags and the likely behaviour of long-frilled ceratopids. Frills may have been used for display, while males might lock horns in trials of strength to attract mates.

Right: The ceratopids are known almost exclusively from the Cretaceous rocks of north west America. Here the bones of a juvenile ceratopid are excavated from Dinosaur Provincial Park, Alberta, Canada.

Below: The body plan of Anchiceratops resembles that of the short-frilled ceratopids; distinguishing features are to be found in the skull, particularly in the form of the frill.

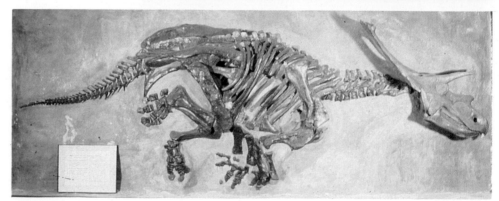

Chasmosaurus, since the frill is relatively short and there are no epoccipitals—hence the alternative name. However, the fact that it was a juvenile specimen may explain the differences. It is very probable that the frill of young *Chasmosaurus* was rather shorter than that of a fully-grown specimen (young *Protoceratops* show this characteristic), and the lack of epoccipitals may well be a result of their not being firmly attached to the frill in young individuals. I therefore suspect that *Eoceratops* is a young *Chasmosaurus* rather than a new type of ceratopid.

Ceratopian Behaviour

The great variety of ceratopian head shape has puzzled palaeontologists for a long time. Professor Edwin Colbert, a noted authority on dinosaurs, suggested that the development of a bewildering array of horns was essentially a random phenomenon. Each group of cera-

topids had independently developed its own pattern of horns and frill shapes as a common type of solution to a single problem, i.e. resisting predatory dinosaurs. He used for comparison the variety of horns displayed by African antelopes as evidence of a similar type of phenomenon.

Recent work, however, has suggested that the chief function of the horns of antelopes, and many of the larger, hoofed mammals of today, is to establish a form of social order among these animals, and for the maintenance of territories, especially between male animals (cf. the rutting of deer). The variety of horn and antler shapes, therefore, reflects special display functions allied to fighting behaviour, rather than simply serving to deter predators. Behaviour patterns tend to vary a great deal among living hoofed mammals, but they can nevertheless be divided into several fairly distinctive types. Small-horned types tend to swing their heads sideways at the flanks of opponents, and to show them off in side-on visual displays. Larger-horned types tend to use their horns either for head-to-head ramming (this is particularly well known in sheep and goats) or, alternatively like deer they can lock horns and have a complicated pushing-and-wrestling type of test of strength. Some animals, such as the recently extinct giant Irish Elk, had an enormous spread of antlers which was probably used in simple postural movements to display their antlers to the best advantage; these antlers were far too large and heavy to have been used for fighting.

The frills of ceratopids have also given rise to much speculation about their probable function, and the factors governing their variable shapes. Professor Ostrom suggested that the frill developed its shape in order to increase the effectiveness of the jaw-closing muscles which were attached to it. Unfortunately this does not seem to be the case in all examples when they are analysed mechanically. There are also ceratopids, such as *Styracosaurus,* with elaborate spikes around the frill edge which were clearly nothing whatever to do with jaw-closing muscles.

Jim Farlow and Peter Dodson reviewed the structure and function of ceratopian frills and horns in 1975. They concluded that the combination of variable horn arrangement and frill shape were most likely explained as having behavioural functions. Looking at the various types of ceratopian dinosaur they proposed the following:

(i) *Protoceratopids* probably behaved like small-horned antelopes. The low nasal horn may have been used to deliver sideways blows to the flanks of opponents. The moderately large frill may have also been used as a visual display signal; the larger the frill, the more dominant the animal in its social group. Most of the protoceratopids would have used similar sorts of behavioural strategies.

(ii) *Short-frilled ceratopids* tend to have large unpaired nose horns and their behaviour has been compared to that of rhinoceroses. The large nose horns would have been formidable weapons if used for fighting. To avoid the likelihood of severe injury resulting from combat, these animals probably relied heavily upon bluff displays and evasive manoeuvring. It is even possible that the short-frilled ceratopids were rather solitary animals, thereby reducing the need for combat in defence of their own territories.

Styracosaurus is unusual among the short-frilled ceratopids in its possession of long spikes on its frill margin. These probably formed a striking visual display when the head was waved about. Such development may have reduced the probability of combat between individuals and consequent severe injury. *Pachyrhinosaurus,* yet another unusual short-frilled ceratopid, may well have indulged in head-to-head pushing contests.

Triceratops, the problematic short-frilled form, has large eyebrow horns and more closely resembles the long-frilled ceratopids in this respect. It seems quite probable that *Triceratops* locked horns in pushing-and-twisting contests between individuals. The solid neck frill may well have acted as a shield to deflect the horns of opponents, and to protect the neck and shoulder muscles if either they slipped or failed to lock horns in such a contest of strength.

(iii) *Long-frilled ceratopids* would, by virtue of the great length of the frill, have been able to produce an impressive frontal threat display simply by nodding the head forward and swinging it from side to side. Such displays (as in *Styracosaurus*) may have reduced the need for direct combat between individuals. However, when combat did occur, then the brow horns may have locked together in pushing-and-wrestling contests.

The pose of the front legs in these ceratopids was probably quite variable. The front legs could be held directly beneath the body like pillars as in the colour illustrations, or alternatively held slightly apart with the feet more widely spaced. In the latter position these animals would be very stable and they may well have adopted this posture in combat.

All in all, the ceratopids are not only some of the most bizarre-looking of all known dinosaurs, but also the most interesting, allowing us many revealing insights into their possible way of life.

Above: *Torosaurus* is known only from skulls. However, these are huge, some measuring over 8ft (2·4m) in length, the largest recovered of any land-living animal. Note the relatively smooth edge to, and circular openings in the frill of this skull that is on display in the Peabody Museum.

Defensive Circle (right) Apart from their display function, ceratopian horns were also probably very powerful defensive weapons. Evidence of herding behaviour indicates that ceratopids may have formed defensive circles in order to protect their young as these *Chasmosaurus* are doing.

PACHYCEPHALOSAURS

Pachycephalosaurs ('thick headed reptiles') are a relatively rare and puzzling group of dinosaurs which lived toward the end of the Cretaceous Period. The history of their discovery is unusual. The first possible pachycephalosaur remains to be discovered consist of a single tooth from the Judith River Beds of Montana, which was found by Ferdinand Hayden. It was flattened and slightly curved and had serrations along its edges. This tooth was described by Joseph Leidy in 1856 and named *Troödon formosus* (*Troödon*: 'wounding tooth'). Leidy suggested that the tooth may have belonged to a large monitor lizard or some other extinct meat-eating reptile.

Little more material of this enigmatic reptile was discovered until just after the turn of the century. In 1902 Lawrence Lambe reported more similar *Troödon*-type teeth from the Belly River of Alberta, and in 1905 John Bell Hatcher described some more teeth from Wyoming. Hatcher was the first to propose that *Troödon*

teeth may have belonged to a dinosaur rather than to a large lizard. The fact that *Troödon* was only recognized as a series of teeth proved extremely unsatisfactory and confusing as we shall see.

At the same time that Lambe described the Belly River *Troödon* teeth (1902), he described two skull fragments, also from the Belly River Formation of Alberta, to which he gave the name *Stegoceras* ('horny roof'). The skull fragments were unusually thick and were at first thought, not unreasonably, to be from a ceratopian dinosaur. A little later Hatcher recognized that the fragments were from the back part of the skull, and were so different from any other known dinosaur that *Stegoceras* should be placed in an entirely new family. With the discovery of more fragments in later years Lambe was able to redescribe the skulls found in 1902 with more confidence, and he proposed that *Stegoceras* was a distant relative of the stegosaurids (pages 152-157).

Things became a little clearer in 1924 when Charles Gilmore was able to describe a skull and partial skeleton of a new dinosaur discovered on the Red Deer River in 1920 by George Sternberg. The material, although incomplete, gave a much clearer idea of the nature of the animals previously named *Troödon* and *Stegoceras*; the teeth near the front of the upper jaw were very similar to *Troödon*, while the head showed the great thickening of the skull roof which had caused such problems in the description of *Stegoceras*. Gilmore was able for the first time to describe the likely appearance of these creatures. And, incomplete though this specimen is, it is still today one of the few specimens which comprises more than just a skull. Gilmore named it *Troödon validus* because he claimed that the teeth were identical to *Troödon* described by Leidy. Most palaeontologists regard this as dubious practice, because using teeth alone for comparisons is extremely hazardous. In most reptiles teeth are

Time Chart (left)
Pachycephalosaurs have a solely Cretaceous time span. They may have originated in the latter half of the early Cretaceous (*Yaverlandia*), but by the late Cretaceous they were fairly widespread in North America and Asia. The discovery of *Majungatholus* also points to a southerly distribution.

Family Tree (below)
Pachycephalosaurs have been divided into high-domed (pachycephalosaurid) and low-domed (homalocephalid) forms. The differences probably reflect different behaviour patterns (head butting vs pushing). *Stygimoloch* may represent yet another group which had highly decorated skulls like modern deer. *Yaverlandia* may be an early pachycephalosaur but it is only known from a tiny fragment of skull.

Homalocephale (below)
This pachycephalosaur is remarkable since parts of its skeleton are known in addition to the skull. *Homalocephale*, as its name ('even head') suggests, had a flat head, and it lacked the massively thickened cranial roof that most of its relatives had. Nevertheless, *Homalocephale* did have a thickened skull roof lined with nodules of bone at the sides. The hip bones of *Homalocephale* are very wide, and it has been suggested that it gave birth to live young rather than laying eggs in typical dinosaurian fashion.

Time chart labels: STEGOCERAS, PACHYCEPHALOSAURUS, PRENOCEPHALE, HOMALOCEPHALE, MAJUNGATHOLUS, YAVERLANDIA

YEARS AGO (MILLIONS): 64, 70, 80, 90, 100, 110, 120, 130, 140, 150, 160, 170, 180, 190, 200, 210, 220, 225

Periods: CRETACEOUS, JURASSIC, TRIASSIC

'HOMALOCEPHALIDS': YAVERLANDIA, HOMALOCEPHALE, ORNATOTHOLUS, STYGIMOLOCH

'PACHYCEPHALOSAURIDS': STEGOCERAS, PRENOCEPHALE, PACHYCEPHALOSAURUS

Comparative Sizes (left)
1 *Stegoceras*: l. 6·5ft (2m)
2 *Homalocephale*: l. 10ft (3m).
3 *Pachycephalosaurus*: l. 26ft (8m).

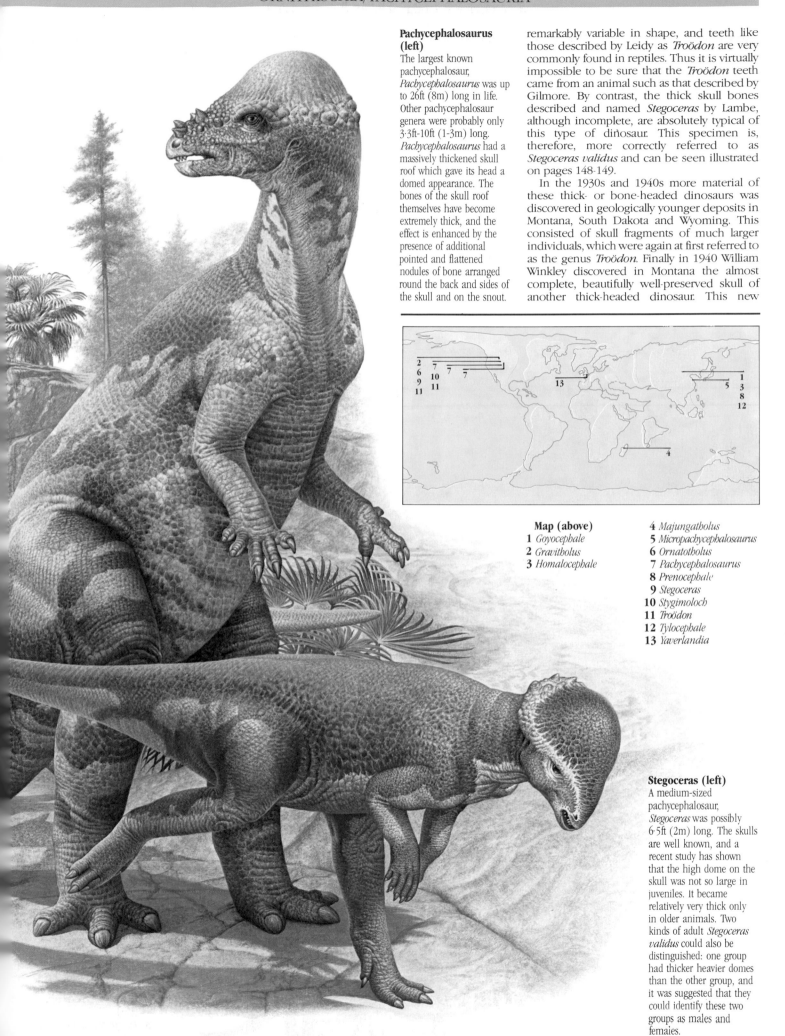

Pachycephalosaurus (left)

The largest known pachycephalosaur, *Pachycephalosaurus* was up to 26ft (8m) long in life. Other pachycephalosaur genera were probably only 3·3ft-10ft (1-3m) long. *Pachycephalosaurus* had a massively thickened skull roof which gave its head a domed appearance. The bones of the skull roof themselves have become extremely thick, and the effect is enhanced by the presence of additional pointed and flattened nodules of bone arranged round the back and sides of the skull and on the snout.

remarkably variable in shape, and teeth like those described by Leidy as *Troödon* are very commonly found in reptiles. Thus it is virtually impossible to be sure that the *Troödon* teeth came from an animal such as that described by Gilmore. By contrast, the thick skull bones described and named *Stegoceras* by Lambe, although incomplete, are absolutely typical of this type of dinosaur. This specimen is, therefore, more correctly referred to as *Stegoceras validus* and can be seen illustrated on pages 148-149.

In the 1930s and 1940s more material of these thick- or bone-headed dinosaurs was discovered in geologically younger deposits in Montana, South Dakota and Wyoming. This consisted of skull fragments of much larger individuals, which were again at first referred to as the genus *Troödon*. Finally in 1940 William Winkley discovered in Montana the almost complete, beautifully well-preserved skull of another thick-headed dinosaur. This new

Map (above)

1 *Goyocephale*
2 *Gravitholus*
3 *Homalocephale*
4 *Majungatholus*
5 *Micropachycephalosaurus*
6 *Ornatotholus*
7 *Pachycephalosaurus*
8 *Prenocephale*
9 *Stegoceras*
10 *Stygimoloch*
11 *Troödon*
12 *Tylocephale*
13 *Yaverlandia*

Stegoceras (left)

A medium-sized pachycephalosaur, *Stegoceras* was possibly 6·5ft (2m) long. The skulls are well known, and a recent study has shown that the high dome on the skull was not so large in juveniles. It became relatively very thick only in older animals. Two kinds of adult *Stegoceras validus* could also be distinguished: one group had thicker heavier domes than the other group, and it was suggested that they could identify these two groups as males and females.

specimen was so obviously different from *Stegoceras* (*'Troödon'*) that it was given a different generic name, *Pachycephalosaurus* ('thick-headed reptile'). The large size of the skull of this creature indicated that it probably had a body length of about 26ft (8m). Unfortunately although several skulls in varying states of completeness are known, there is very little skeletal information, so any body restorations are based largely upon guesswork and comparison with the little that is known about *Stegoceras*. Until *Pachycephalosaurus* was discovered, *Stegoceras* and its allies were known as Troödontids. However, since *Troödon* is a dubious name (based only on non-diagnostic teeth) a new family name was chosen by Sternberg in 1945: the Pachycephalosauridae. This name has stuck with us to the present day and, although the status of the family is now a matter of some scientific dispute as will be explained later, it remains a particularly descriptive term for these dinosaurs.

Further Discoveries

Since those early days a considerable number of remains of pachycephalosaurs have been discovered from many parts of the world. In addition to *Stegoceras* and *Pachycephalosaurus*, there are several rather imperfectly known North American pachycephalosaurs. *Stygimoloch* ('river of Hades [Hell Creek] devil') from the Hell Creek Formation of Montana is presently known from parts of the rear end of the skull. These are notable for the development of large, elaborate horn cores. In life these must have formed clusters of horns on either side of the domed skull roof. *Gravitholus* ('heavy-dome') is known from Alberta and consists of part of a very large, heavy dome which may in fact belong to *Pachycephalosaurus*. *Ornatotholus* ('ornate dome'), from the Red Deer River, Alberta, was first thought to be another species of *Stegoceras* which was characterized by having a rather low-domed

skull. Originally named *Stegoceras browni*, it has been proposed as a female of *Stegoceras validus*. However, Dr Peter Galton and Dr Hans-Dieter Sues have proposed that it is sufficiently different to merit the new name.

An apparently very primitive pachycephalosaur has been identified from the early Cretaceous of the Isle of Wight, southern England. It consists of a small fragment of the skull roof of an animal named *Yaverlandia* ('from Yaverland Point'). The outer surface has two low, rounded bulges. Peter Galton has identified this as a very primitive pachycephalosaur which had only developed a slight thickening of its skull roof. By comparing this small fragment of the skull with that of *Hypsilophodon*, Galton has been able to suggest that pachycephalosaurs may have evolved from small bipedal ornithopods similar to *Hypsilophodon*. No other clear pachycephalosaur remains have been recovered from Europe. However, central and eastern Asia

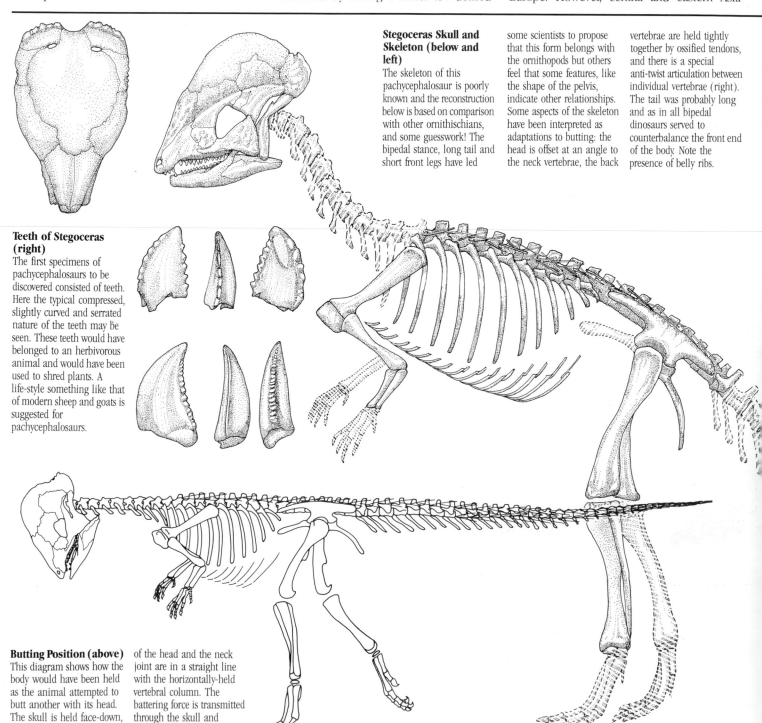

Stegoceras Skull and Skeleton (below and left)
The skeleton of this pachycephalosaur is poorly known and the reconstruction below is based on comparison with other ornithischians, and some guesswork! The bipedal stance, long tail and short front legs have led some scientists to propose that this form belongs with the ornithopods but others feel that some features, like the shape of the pelvis, indicate other relationships. Some aspects of the skeleton have been interpreted as adaptations to butting: the head is offset at an angle to the neck vertebrae, the back vertebrae are held tightly together by ossified tendons, and there is a special anti-twist articulation between individual vertebrae (right). The tail was probably long and as in all bipedal dinosaurs served to counterbalance the front end of the body. Note the presence of belly ribs.

Teeth of Stegoceras (right)
The first specimens of pachycephalosaurs to be discovered consisted of teeth. Here the typical compressed, slightly curved and serrated nature of the teeth may be seen. These teeth would have belonged to an herbivorous animal and would have been used to shred plants. A life-style something like that of modern sheep and goats is suggested for pachycephalosaurs.

Butting Position (above)
This diagram shows how the body would have been held as the animal attempted to butt another with its head. The skull is held face-down, so that the ramming surface of the head and the neck joint are in a straight line with the horizontally-held vertebral column. The battering force is transmitted through the skull and absorbed by the backbone.

(Mongolia and China) have produced several completely new types of pachycephalosaur in recent years. In Mongolia at least four have been identified: *Prenocephale, Tylocephale, Homalocephale* and *Goyocephale.*

Prenocephale ('sloping head') consists of an exceptionally well-preserved skull which bears a very strong resemblance to *Stegoceras.* The main difference is that *Prenocephale* has many rows of small bony knobs ornamenting the sides of the face and dome. *Tylocephale* ('swollen head') is rather similar in shape, although the skull is missing much of the snout and part of the dome. *Homalocephale* ('even head') does not have the high dome seen in the previous two Mongolian types, although like *Prenocephale* there are small rows of bony knobs about the sides of the face. *Goyocephale* ('decorated head') is another of these flat-headed pachycephalosaurs which is known from both partial skull and skeletal remains including much of the tail, the fore and hind

limbs. Unlike *Homalocephale,* which has a fairly flat, smooth skull roof, that of *Goyocephale* is rough and pitted rather like that of *Ornatotholus* of North America. *Goyocephale* also has a pair of large stabbing teeth in the upper and lower jaw.

China has two pachycephalosaurs to date: *Wannanosaurus* ('reptile from Wannan') and *Micropachycephalosaurus* ('tiny thick-headed reptile'). Both of these are flat-headed types of pachycephalosaur.

Finally and quite surprisingly a pachycephalosaur has also been reported from Madagascar: *Majungatholus* ('dome from Majunga'). So far this is only known from a fragment of a domed skull. Until *Majungatholus* was discovered the geographical distribution of pachycephalosaurs was quite typical of dinosaurs that seem to have arisen in middle to late Cretaceous times. As with the ceratopids, hadrosaurids, and dromaeosaurids, they were apparently restricted to the northern hemisphere and further restricted within that

hemisphere to western North America and Asia. Early in the Cretaceous Period, primitive pachycephalosaurs such as *Yaverlandia* (provided that Galton has correctly interpreted this tiny skull fragment) were probably widely distributed but relatively rare animals in northern continents. Later in the Cretaceous, with the division of the northern lands by seaways separating western North America and Asia from Europe, the later and more sophisticated pachycephalosaurs were confined to Asia and North America. Quite why they did not persist in Europe is not clear (unless *Yaverlandia,* the only European pachycephalosaur, has been misidentified). The presence of *Majungatholus* in Madagascar is, however, somewhat unexpected.

The Madagascar Fauna

Fossil remains from the late Cretaceous of Madagascar are unfortunately of rather poor

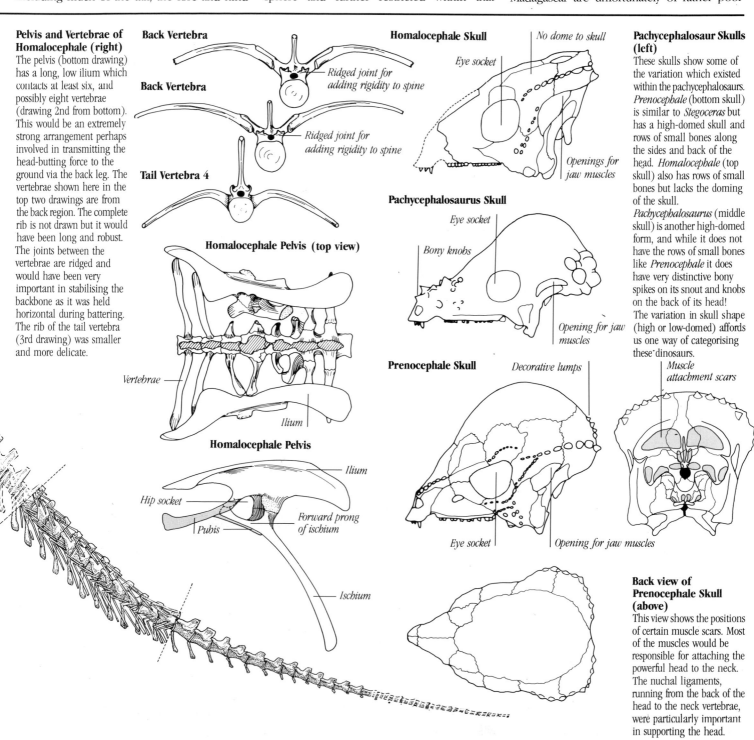

Pelvis and Vertebrae of Homalocephale (right)
The pelvis (bottom drawing) has a long, low ilium which contacts at least six, and possibly eight vertebrae (drawing 2nd from bottom). This would be an extremely strong arrangement perhaps involved in transmitting the head-butting force to the ground via the back leg. The vertebrae shown here in the top two drawings are from the back region. The complete rib is not drawn but it would have been long and robust. The joints between the vertebrae are ridged and would have been very important in stabilising the backbone as it was held horizontal during battering. The rib of the tail vertebra (3rd drawing) was smaller and more delicate.

Back Vertebra

Back Vertebra

Ridged joint for adding rigidity to spine

Ridged joint for adding rigidity to spine

Tail Vertebra 4

Homalocephale Pelvis (top view)

Vertebrae

Ilium

Homalocephale Pelvis

Ilium

Hip socket

Forward prong of ischium

Pubis

Ischium

Homalocephale Skull

No dome to skull

Eye socket

Openings for jaw muscles

Pachycephalosaurus Skull

Eye socket

Bony knobs

Opening for jaw muscles

Prenocephale Skull

Decorative lumps

Eye socket

Opening for jaw muscles

Muscle attachment scars

Back view of Prenocephale Skull (above)
This view shows the positions of certain muscle scars. Most of the muscles would be responsible for attaching the powerful head to the neck. The nuchal ligaments, running from the back of the head to the neck vertebrae, were particularly important in supporting the head.

Pachycephalosaur Skulls (left)
These skulls show some of the variation which existed within the pachycephalosaurs. *Prenocephale* (bottom skull) is similar to *Stegoceras* but has a high-domed skull and rows of small bones along the sides and back of the head. *Homalocephale* (top skull) also has rows of small bones but lacks the doming of the skull.
Pachycephalosaurus (middle skull) is another high-domed form, and while it does not have the rows of small bones like *Prenocephale* it does have very distinctive bony spikes on its snout and knobs on the back of its head! The variation in skull shape (high or low-domed) affords us one way of categorising these dinosaurs.

quality. Nevertheless those that have been found are of interest because they provide information on the likely land connections in the world at this time. Along with *Majungatholus* were also found the remains of a large sauropod dinosaur named *Titanosaurus madagascarensis*. This bears some similarities to *Saltasaurus*, the armoured South American sauropod. More bony armour of this type has also been reported from India. *Majungasaurus*, a medium-sized theropod is unfortunately too fragmentary for any fruitful comparisons to be drawn with theropods from elsewhere.

The fossil evidence then seems to point to land connections between South America, Africa-Madagascar and India in the late Cretaceous. In addition, we know that hadrosaurids, sauropods, and tyrannosaurids, as well as pachycephalosaur dinosaurs of similar types, are found in both the northern and southern continents in late Cretaceous times. Precisely how this distribution occurred is difficult to assess. There seem to be two alternative interpretations: either these families of dinosaur migrated across narrow seaways separating the northern and southern continents (perhaps between North and South America, which were very close) or alternatively, these dinosaurs were widely spread across both northern and southern continents *before* the continents divided. A really good record of fossils from the southern continents might help to decide which of the alternatives is correct, but this is not available at present.

Relationships

Because bone-head remains are so scarce, and even when found are usually just skulls or skull fragments, it has proved very difficult to decide how they relate to other dinosaurs generally. They are clearly ornithischians because they have the tell-tale horn-covered predentary beak in the lower jaw. However, their skulls are so highly modified by the great dome of bone that they show no overwhelming similarities to any of the other ornithischian groups.

The great thickening of the skull roof gives them a passing resemblance to the ankylosaurids. However, the similarity is more apparent than real because the thickening of the skull in ankylosaurids is created by the plastering of new bone on to the skull while in pachycephalosaurids it is the actual bones of the skull roof that become thicker.

In 1974 Doctors Teresa Maryanska and Halska Osmolska from Warsaw, Poland reviewed the pachycephalosaurs lately discovered in Mongolia and noted that pachycephalosaurs had an extraordinary pelvis, vaguely similar to that of ankylosaurids. On the basis of this and several other characteristics, they proposed that the pachycephalosaurs should be raised to the same level of importance as the ornithopods, stegosaurs, ceratopians and ankylosaurs, and categorized as a major group of ornithischians. This view is not accepted by all palaeontologists. For example, Dr Peter Galton prefers to consider them as rather unusual ornithopods. As noted earlier, he proposes that they evolved from hypsilophodontid-type ornithopods via forms such as the early Cretaceous *Yaverlandia*. The position of the pachycephalosaurs is very much an open question at present. Within the pachycephalosaur group, Maryanska and Osmolska have suggested that they may, perhaps, have been divided into low-domed and high-domed types: *Stegoceras*, *Pachycephalosaurus*, *Gravitholus*, *Tylocephale*, *Prenocephale*, *Stygimoloch* and *Majungatholus* being high-domed 'pachycephalosaurids'; while *Homalocephale*, *Goyocephale*, *Ornatotholus*, *Yaverlandia*, and *Micropachycephalosaurus* were low-domed 'homalocephalids'. Much more work needs to be done on these dinosaurs, and new and better material needs to be found, before any of these issues can be clarified.

Head-to-Head Butting

From quite an early date the enormously thickened dome of bone on the skulls of pachycephalosaurs has attracted attention and comment. It was not, however, until 1955 that Professor Edwin Colbert suggested a functional explanation of this feature; he proposed that it may have served as a protective zone for the head if it were used as a battering ram. This proposal was not elaborated upon by Professor Colbert at the time, but it has served as a spur to several palaeontologists in recent years, notably Dr Peter Galton (Bridgeport) and Dr Hans-Dieter Sues (Montreal).

Peter Galton agreed with Professor Colbert's proposal concerning the function of the thick skull roof in pachycephalosaurs and went on to discuss it further. He noted that like most ornithopods, the pachycephalosaur's backbone may well have been held horizontally — balanced at the hips. In addition, the head of these animals, instead of being held in-line with the bones of the neck, is offset from it at a sharp angle. So, the 'natural' position of the head would seem to be such that it pointed nose-downward while these animals walked or ran. Obviously there was no need for them to walk in this 'nose-down' position all of the time, because the neck was flexible and could be bent upward sharply so that the head could be held in a more normal raised position. However, the arrangement of the neck-head joint, which is unlike all other dinosaurs, does

Above: A cast of the skull of *Pachycephalosaurus* from the British Museum (Natural History) collection. Note the round bony knobs on the back of the skull, and the more pointed bony projections on the snout.

Below: This skull cast of *Stegoceras*—also from the BM (NH)—makes an interesting comparison with that of *Pachycephalosaurus* (above). The high bony dome (*Stegoceras:* 'horny roof') to the skull is present in both specimens, but *Stegoceras* lacks the profusion of knobbly projections, while its face is shorter and deeper. *Stegoceras* is known from the Belly River Formation of Alberta, Canada.

Above: Looking almost as if it had been sculpted from the rock, the skull of *Prenocephale* is excavated from the late Cretaceous sandstone at Nemegt in the Gobi Desert, Mongolia during the 1970 Polish-Mongolian Palaeontological Expedition. *Prenocephale* is a high-domed pachycephalosaurid; the frill of bony studs at the back of the skull is clearly visible.

allow the dome to be held forward in a 'battering' position. When you add to this the fact that the backbones fit together in an especially stiffened arrangement, and that in addition to the ossified tendons of the back, the joints between individual bones of the back have special grooved surfaces to stop them from twisting too much, then the design of these animals certainly does seem to fit in with the idea that they were able to use the head as a battering device.

The obvious question that has to be asked is why did they do this? Galton proposed that pachycephalosaurs did not just employ head-down charging to fend off predatory dinosaurs, but also used it as a part of their social life! He drew what seems to be a very appropriate comparison between pachycephalosaurs and living sheep and goats. These animals, especially the males, have large horns and are well known for their propensity to fight among themselves by head-to-head butting or

ramming—even females tend to butt one another though they do not have well-developed horns. In these animals, the butting behaviour is a part of a way of creating an ordered society. Especially among the males, the horns serve as visual signals of dominance: the larger the horns, the more dominant the male. However, when competing males have very similar-sized horns, then head butting is resorted to as a test of strength or endurance.

Mountain sheep have very large horns which help to absorb the initial shock of head-to-head butting; they also have special air-spaces at the front of their heads which serve to dull the shock that the brain would otherwise receive. Pachycephalosaurs differ from sheep and goats in the structure of their heads. Firstly, they do not have well-developed horns. There are small lumps and ridges around the dome on the skull roof of most pachycephalosaurs (especially *Stygimoloch* which has quite long spikes) but these are clearly ornamental rather than

functional. Secondly, there are no special air-spaces in the skull roof of pachycephalosaurs: the skull dome is solid bone right through to the brain cavity. These differences suggest that the impacts of head butting were carried straight through the skull roof across the brain cavity—giving it quite a severe shock—and then into the specially strengthened backbone. The brains of these dinosaurs were, fortunately for pachycephalosaurs, much smaller than those found in sheep and goats, and quite probably there were spaces around the brain itself which cushioned it from too severe a shock.

Dr Sues further elaborated on the mechanism of head butting in pachycephalosaurs by showing that the arrangement of bone in the skulls of these animals was ideally suited to transmitting shocks through the dome, around the sides of the head and then into the backbone. He was able to do this by using a photoelastic analysis of thin sections of the skull. He also noted that special ligaments running from the neck to the back of the head (nuchal ligaments) were very large and powerful, and helped to absorb a great deal of the shock of head clashes.

Life-Style

Pachycephalosaurs may well have lived rather like sheep and goats do today: in small groups in upland areas. Their social life was dependent upon the use of the head as a means of signalling the status of individuals. In most cases the visual signal would have been sufficient. However, when similarly-sized individuals met, the seniority of each would have to be decided by head-to-head pushing or butting contests. The low-domed 'homalocephalids' probably used head-to-head pushing contests rather than violent head-banging struggles because their skulls were not very strongly built. The high-domed forms undoubtedly indulged in violent head-butting contests. *Stygimoloch*, unusual among the high-domed pachycephalosaurids, may not have indulged in head butting at all, relying instead upon the visual effect of the tall bony spikes around its domed head to establish its place in the social hierarchy.

Head Butting (left)
Here we see two pachycephalosaurs indulging in the sort of violent head-butting contest for which their extraordinary skulls made them uniquely qualified. It is thought that such behaviour was a way of establishing a social hierarchy, allowing males in particular to achieve dominance over one another within the group.

Above: A dorsal view of the skull of *Homalocephale calathocercos,* another of the pachycephalosaurs discovered at Nemegt in the Gobi Desert, this time by the 1965 Polish-Mongolian Expedition. The skull of *Homalocephale,* a flat-headed type, is noticeably less heavily armoured; the two openings at the back are for the attachment of the jaw muscles.

The stegosaurids are a group of quite large, four-footed ornithischians that are characterized by their possession of a double row of tall spines which run down their backs. By far the best known of these dinosaurs is *Stegosaurus* (see below), several very fine specimens of which were discovered in North America toward the end of the last century.

The first stegosaurid remains to be described were those of an incomplete skeleton found in England and illustrated by Richard Owen in 1875. These remains were originally described as *Omosaurus armatus* (later renamed *Dacentrurus* 'pointed tail'). It was recognized as an armour-plated dinosaur, because among the remains were found large shield-like plates of bone. These early reports were, however, eclipsed by the discoveries made in North America in the late 1870s by teams of excavators in two quarries: one known as 'Quarry 13' in Albany County, Wyoming, the other as 'Quarry 1' in Fremont County, Colorado.

Quarry 13 was discovered in 1879 and was worked by a team of excavators led by William H. Reed, under the supervision of Othniel Marsh, between 1879 and 1882, and later with interruptions until 1887. This quarry produced the largest concentration of *Stegosaurus* ('roofed reptile') remains discovered to date. Quarry 1 was discovered in 1876 by M. P. Felch and his family. News of this discovery reached Marsh through newspaper reports. The following year Marsh sent Samuel Wendell Williston (later to become an eminent palaeontologist in his own right) to investigate the reported discovery. This quarry was worked for several years by Williston and although it did not produce as many stegosaurid remains as the Albany County Quarry, nevertheless it did produce a very fine, practically complete, skeleton of *Stegosaurus stenops*. Between 1877 and 1897 Marsh published numerous scientific articles describing parts of these new dinosaurs. Since the time of Owen and Marsh, several

other stegosaurids have been discovered which indicate that they were reasonably widely spread across the world.

Apart from *Stegosaurus* from North America, stegosaurids are also known from Europe: *Lexovisaurus* ('Lexovi reptile'), *Dacentrurus* and *Craterosaurus* ('bowl reptile'); Africa: *Kentrosaurus* ('prickly reptile') and *Paranthodon* ('beside Anthodon'); India: *Dravidosaurus* ('reptile from south India'); and China: *Huayangosaurus* ('Huayang reptile'), *Chialingosaurus* ('Chialing reptile'), *Wuerhosaurus* ('Wuerho reptile') and *Tuojiangosaurus* ('Tuojiang reptile'). The earliest stegosaurid remains identified so far are some odd plates and bones from the middle Jurassic of England, and the latest come from the late Cretaceous of India.

Stegosaur Distribution

The distribution of stegosaurids in time and space reveals an interesting pattern. The earliest

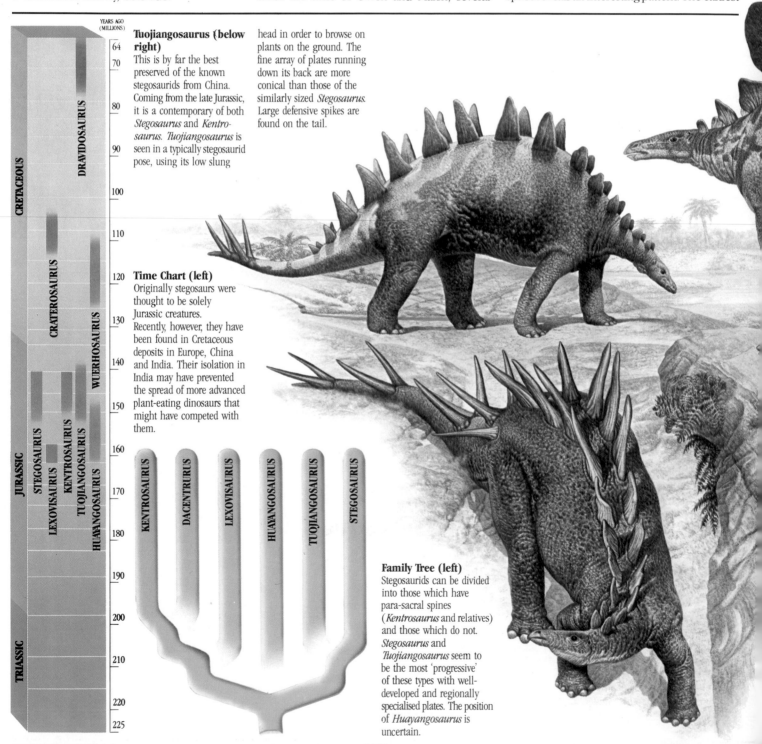

Tuojiangosaurus (below right)
This is by far the best preserved of the known stegosaurids from China. Coming from the late Jurassic, it is a contemporary of both *Stegosaurus* and *Kentrosaurus*. *Tuojiangosaurus* is seen in a typically stegosaurid pose, using its low slung head in order to browse on plants on the ground. The fine array of plates running down its back are more conical than those of the similarly sized *Stegosaurus*. Large defensive spikes are found on the tail.

Time Chart (left)
Originally stegosaurs were thought to be solely Jurassic creatures. Recently, however, they have been found in Cretaceous deposits in Europe, China and India. Their isolation in India may have prevented the spread of more advanced plant-eating dinosaurs that might have competed with them.

Family Tree (left)
Stegosaurids can be divided into those which have para-sacral spines (*Kentrosaurus* and relatives) and those which do not. *Stegosaurus* and *Tuojiangosaurus* seem to be the most 'progressive' of these types with well-developed and regionally specialised plates. The position of *Huayangosaurus* is uncertain.

stegosaurid remains are of the rather poorly known *Lexovisaurus* from the middle Jurassic of Oxfordshire (England). Shortly after this, in the late Jurassic, stegosaurids are found in North America, Africa and China as well as Europe. Looking at the map of the world at this time, the discovery of stegosaurids in North America, Africa and Europe seems quite reasonable, because these continents had all been in contact with one another up to this time, so we would expect their dinosaur faunas to be rather similar. However, the Chinese stegosaurids are not so readily explained. Eastern Asia seems to have been separated from the rest of the world by quite large seaways for much of the reign of the dinosaurs. In fact, it seems that it was not until quite late in the Cretaceous Period that a substantial link was established between western North America and eastern Asia. The most likely explanation for the Chinese stegosaurids is that they must have spread there quite early on in the Jurassic

Stegosaurus (left)

This North American form is by far the best known of the stegosaurids. Several fine skeletons have been recovered but this has not led to complete agreement about its appearance in life. The main areas of disagreement relate to the arrangement of the plates and the pose of the forelimbs: were they bent or straight? As can be seen, we have adopted a straight-legged pose and an array of upright plates staggered alternately along the back. They were probably used as heat transfer surfaces, while the sharp tail spikes were for defence.

Comparative Sizes (right)

1 *Stegosaurus*: 1. 20-24·6ft (6-7·5m).
2 *Tuojiangosaurus*: 1. 20ft (6m).
3 *Kentrosaurus*: 1. 8·2ft (2·5m).

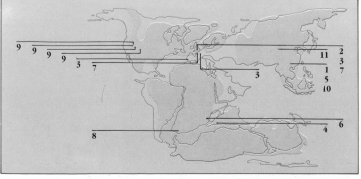

Kentrosaurus (left)

The pattern of spikes in *Kentrosaurus*, one of the smaller stegosaurids, so far known only from Tendaguru in Tanzania, is very distinctive. Those near the front of the body are flat and plate-like. However, by the middle of the back they have changed into narrow spines which continue to the end of the tail. In addition there is another pair of spines which point diagonally backwards from their attachment to the pelvis. Clearly these spines are primarily defensive in nature, and were intended to deter larger predators which risked impalement upon them. Whether *Kentrosaurus* could rush backwards at predators in the way that porcupines can do today is uncertain. The tail spines certainly look defensive in nature.

Map (left)

1 *Chialingosaurus*
2 *Craterosaurus*
3 *Dacentrurus*
4 *Dravidosaurus*
5 *Huayangosaurus*
6 *Kentrosaurus*
7 *Lexovisaurus*
8 *Paranthodon*
9 *Stegosaurus*
10 *Tuojiangosaurus*
11 *Wuerhosaurus*

by means of some sort of short-lived land connection between Europe and Asia. The sauropods of the Jurassic seem to show a similar pattern of movement. The late Jurassic was probably the most successful time for the stegosaurids, because in the Cretaceous they are far less abundant and widespread. Stegosaurids seem to go extinct in North America at the end of the Jurassic; no Cretaceous stegosaurid remains have ever been discovered in this area. Fragmentary remains of stegosaurids are, however, known from the early Cretaceous of Europe *(Craterosaurus)*, Africa *(Paranthodon)* and China *(Wuerhosaurus)*. By the late Cretaceous stegosaurids seem to be absent from all the continents except for India where *Dravidosaurus* seems to persist to the end of the Cretaceous Period.

The precise reason for this rather unusual distribution pattern is not easy to explain, and any explanation given here could be radically upset by any new discovery of stegosaurids.

However, the most reasonable interpretation that could be made is as follows: stegosaurids probably first evolved in the early to middle Jurassic Period and were able, because of the arrangement of the continents, to spread to most, if not all, the major continents. Thus, by the late Jurassic they were both diverse and widespread. The dawn of the Cretaceous Period marked a time of dramatic decline for most stegosaurids. The absence of stegosaurids in North America is very significant, because so much intensive collecting of Cretaceous dinosaurs has been done there that it seems inevitable that if stegosaurids had been around, some fossils would have been found by now. In all the other continents stegosaurids are found with much less frequency than during their heyday in the Jurassic, and by the mid-Cretaceous they seem to be extinct everywhere except India.

The survival of stegosaurids in India is interesting, because from the middle of the

Cretaceous onward, India was isolated from the rest of the world. Right up until the early part of the Cretaceous, India nestled against the southern end of Africa and presumably shared its fauna of dinosaurs with those of Africa. Once India began to drift away from Africa, then its fauna became isolated and it may perhaps have acted as a haven for, amongst others, the stegosaurids which elsewhere went extinct.

The cause of the widespread waning and extinction of stegosaurids in the Cretaceous has often been suggested to be the appearance of the ankylosaurs (pages 160-169). The ankylosaurs certainly show a pattern of emergence, diversification and extinction which seems to complement that of the stegosaurids. In the Jurassic ankylosaurs were scarce and not very widely distributed; they gradually increased in number and type in the early Cretaceous, reaching a peak in late Cretaceous times, before the final Cretaceous extinctions. It is certainly tempting to suggest that the rise of

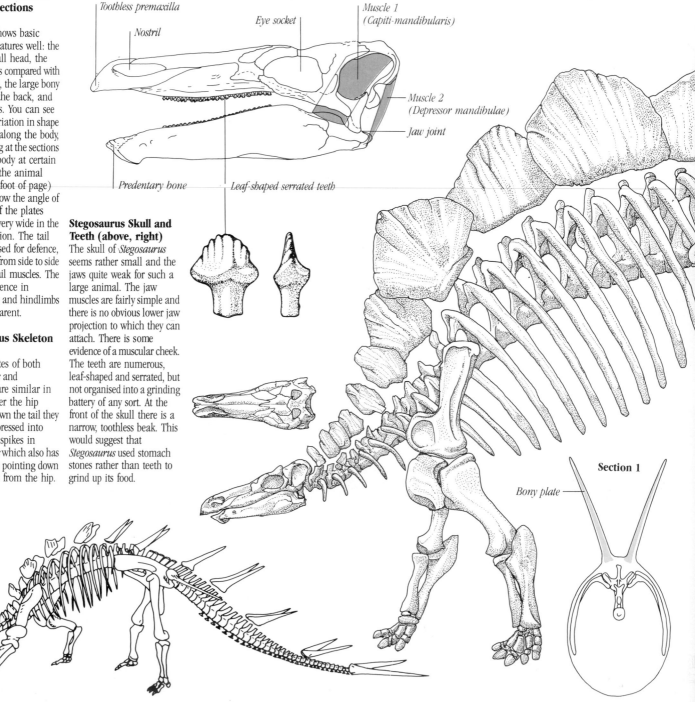

Stegosaurus Skeleton and Body Sections (centre)
This genus shows basic stegosaurid features well: the relatively small head, the short front legs compared with the back ones, the large bony plates along the back, and the tail spines. You can see clearly the variation in shape of the plates along the body, and by looking at the sections through the body at certain points along the animal (drawings at foot of page) you can see how the angle of attachment of the plates varies — it is very wide in the lower tail region. The tail spikes were used for defence, being swung from side to side by powerful tail muscles. The marked difference in length of fore and hindlimbs is readily apparent.

Kentrosaurus Skeleton (below)
The front plates of both *Kentrosaurus* and *Stegosaurus* are similar in shape, but over the hip region and down the tail they become compressed into long, narrow spikes in *Kentrosaurus* which also has an extra spike pointing down and outwards from the hip.

Stegosaurus Skull and Teeth (above, right)
The skull of *Stegosaurus* seems rather small and the jaws quite weak for such a large animal. The jaw muscles are fairly simple and there is no obvious lower jaw projection to which they can attach. There is some evidence of a muscular cheek. The teeth are numerous, leaf-shaped and serrated, but not organised into a grinding battery of any sort. At the front of the skull there is a narrow, toothless beak. This would suggest that *Stegosaurus* used stomach stones rather than teeth to grind up its food.

Toothless premaxilla
Nostril
Eye socket
Muscle 1 (Capiti-mandibularis)
Muscle 2 (Depressor mandibulae)
Jaw joint
Predentary bone
Leaf-shaped serrated teeth

Section 1
Bony plate

the ankylosaurs is associated in some way with the decline of the stegosaurids. The intriguing fact is that ankylosaurs are not found in India at all. Perhaps stegosaurids were able to survive in India because, through freakish geological conditions, India became isolated from the rest of the world in the early Cretaceous just at the time when the ankylosaurs were diversifying. One can only hope that new discoveries will confirm whether this explanation is anywhere near to the truth, or else disprove it.

Stegosaurid Anatomy

Stegosaurus gets its name – 'roofed reptile' – from the large bony plates found along its back; these were long thought to form some sort of protective shield ('roof') over the back of this animal. Apart from *Kentrosaurus* and *Tuojiangosaurus* which are both known from quite reasonable skeletons, *Stegosaurus* is the only

other really well known stegosaurid, most of the remainder are known from fragmentary pieces of skeleton alone. *Stegosaurus*, because it is well-preserved and well-described, will serve excellently as an example of this type of dinosaur.

The head of *Stegosaurus* is rather low and slender for such a large animal, with a narrow, toothless, horn-covered beak at the tip of its snout. Behind the beak the teeth are quite numerous, but are not arranged into a special cutting battery. Therefore it seems that the stegosaurids were not capable of grinding up plant food in their mouths in the way that some ornithopods and ceratopids could. The jaw muscles were also, so far as we can tell, quite simple, without the special mechanical devices for improving the efficiency of the jaw-closing muscles such as are seen in ceratopids. Despite this, the great size of these animals suggests that they had to consume large quantities of plant food to sustain themselves. It seems most likely

that these ornithischians used feeding techniques like those employed by the prosauropods and sauropods. They probably used their jaws to chop up crudely large quantities of plant food and then swallowed this quickly, passing it to a very large stomach where it was left slowly to ferment. Stomach stones may also have been used to help pulverize some of the tougher plant tissues.

The remainder of the body of *Stegosaurus* is striking in a number of ways, when compared with previous ornithischians. The plates found in two rows down the back of the animal are unique to stegosaurids, though they do tend to vary a bit in shape between different genera (compare skeleton drawings of *Stegosaurus* and *Kentrosaurus*).

In *Stegosaurus* the plates are quite small and flat, with irregular edges in the region immediately behind the head, becoming progressively taller and broader across the back. The largest plates of all are found just behind

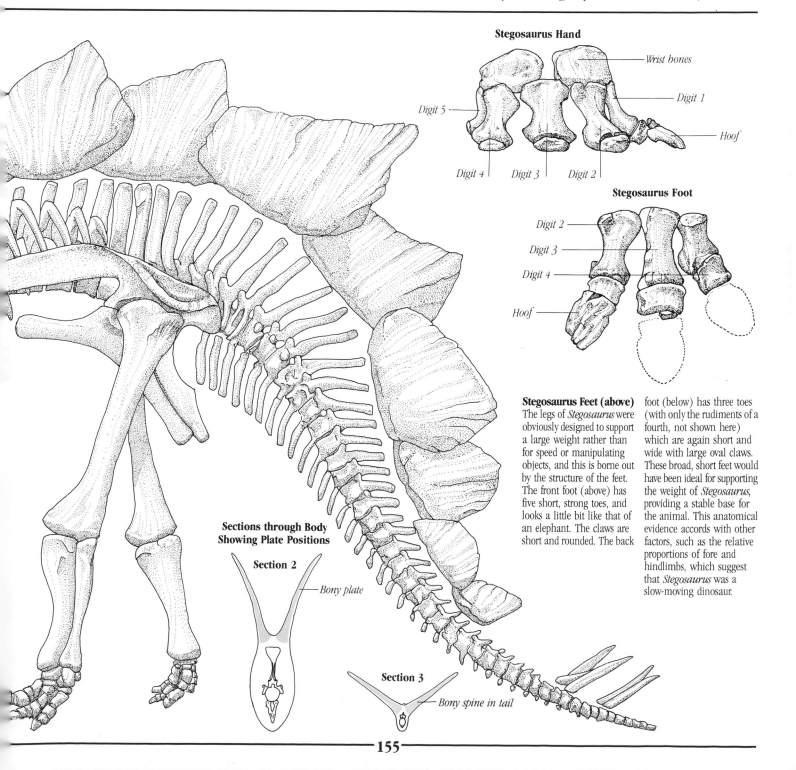

Stegosaurus Hand
Wrist bones
Digit 1
Digit 5
Hoof
Digit 4   Digit 3   Digit 2

Stegosaurus Foot
Digit 2
Digit 3
Digit 4
Hoof

Sections through Body Showing Plate Positions

Section 2
Bony plate

Section 3
Bony spine in tail

Stegosaurus Feet (above)
The legs of *Stegosaurus* were obviously designed to support a large weight rather than for speed or manipulating objects, and this is borne out by the structure of the feet. The front foot (above) has five short, strong toes, and looks a little bit like that of an elephant. The claws are short and rounded. The back foot (below) has three toes (with only the rudiments of a fourth, not shown here) which are again short and wide with large oval claws. These broad, short feet would have been ideal for supporting the weight of *Stegosaurus*, providing a stable base for the animal. This anatomical evidence accords with other factors, such as the relative proportions of fore and hindlimbs, which suggest that *Stegosaurus* was a slow-moving dinosaur.

the hip region. Beyond this there seem to be a few smaller plates (six pairs) before the end of the tail. The end of the tail also possesses bony plates but these are shaped as two pairs of long, thin pointed spikes. The precise arrangement of these bony plates along the back has been the subject of some debate over the years. Marsh, when he first described the skeleton in 1891, assumed that they formed a single line which ran right down the middle of the back of the animal with four pairs of spines on the tail. This was later disputed by other authorities, who suggested various alternative arrangements. In 1901 Lucas proposed that the plates were arranged in a double row of pairs of plates on either side of the backbone. A little later Lucas restored these in a staggered series of alternating pairs with only two pairs of tail spines—the pattern we illustrate. Restorations since the early part of this century have tended to vary between these alternative arrangements.

The source of this disagreement is the very well preserved skeleton of *Stegosaurus* in the Smithsonian Institution in Washington, D.C. A drawing of this skeleton as it was originally discovered is included below. As can be seen, the large bone plates are shown in a definite alternating pattern along the back of the skeleton. The question then arises: are these plates really in their natural arrangement? Lucas believed that they were, but Richard Lull and others claimed that the plates may have simply slipped past one another as the flesh of the carcass rotted during burial in lake sediments. These two viewpoints seem quite irreconcilable; however, as can be seen from the colour restoration and the skeletal drawings, the alternating arrangement of the plates is favoured here. Despite the fact that reptiles typically possess paired rows of armour, the

reason for preferring the alternating pattern stems from the work of Jim Farlow and his associates on the probable biological significance of stegosaurid plates. This is discussed in greater detail at the end of this section.

In addition to these large and obvious bony plates, *Stegosaurus* also has quite a well developed layer of bony knobs and bumps over other parts of its body. Again some of these can be seen in the drawing of the skeleton as it was found; these small bones were found in clusters around the throat area and were very probably widely spread in the skin all over this animal.

Another noteworthy feature of *Stegosaurus* is the remarkable difference in length between the fore and hindlimbs, a difference which is even more pronounced than that seen in the ceratopids. The forelimb is stout and powerful to support the weight of the animal, and the feet are broad, with five stubby toes, clearly designed for walking upon rather than grasping. The hindlimb is considerably longer than the

forelimb and is designed to be a pillar-like support for these slow-moving animals. This is particularly obvious if the proportions of the bones of the hind leg are compared with those of a fast runner such as *Hypsilophodon* (pages 106-107). The fast runner has a short thigh, a longer shin and slender, long toes; *Stegosaurus'* legs show the exact opposite of these proportions, with a long thigh, short shin and broad, short-toed feet.

Another feature of *Stegosaurus* is the almost legendary small size of the brain of this animal. One of the skulls of *Stegosaurus* was sufficiently well preserved for O. C. Marsh to be able to obtain a cast of the cavity in which the brain lay. This showed that the brain must have been very small, perhaps the smallest of any dinosaur. For an animal that grew to a length of 20ft (6m), and may have weighed 1·5 tonnes or more, to possess a brain that could have weighed no more than 2·5-2·8oz (70-80 grams) seems extraordinary. This observation more than any

Above: A *Stegosaurus* back plate is treated with a protective fluid at Dinosaur National Monument, Utah. As can be seen, the surface of the plate is finely grooved, a texture that suggests the presence of many blood vessels.

Below: This drawing shows the disposition of the skeleton of *Stegosaurus stenops* as it was found. The plates seem to lie in an alternating pattern but arguments persist as to whether this was how they were arranged in life.

Above: Excavated at Garden Park, Fremont County, Colorado in 1937, this is the Denver Museum's skeleton of *Stegosaurus stenops*. The comparative lengths of fore and hindlimbs are clearly illustrated in this photograph.

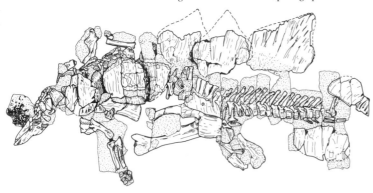

other must be responsible for the persistent and very widely held belief that all dinosaurs were dull and extremely stupid animals. Quite why *Stegosaurus* should possess such a small brain is not obvious. Many dinosaurs have quite respectably sized brains, particularly the carnivorous theropods. All we seem to be able to say at the moment is that the brain of *Stegosaurus*, although it was small, was evidently large enough for its needs! Associated with the very small brain of this animal is the fact that the spinal cord in the region of the hips was enormously enlarged. Again casts were made of this area which seemed to show that this part of the spine was over 20 times the size of the brain. This gave rise to the belief, again still widely held, that dinosaurs had a second brain in their tail.

This rather curious enlargement of the spinal cord almost certainly does *not* form a second brain. The enlargement of the spine at the hips probably marks the area where all the nerves of the back legs and tail met, forming a large relay station for messages or signals on their way to and from the brain. In addition to this, most land animals seem to store fat around this area of the spinal cord.

Apart from *Stegosaurus*, there are several other reasonably well-known stegosaurids. *Kentrosaurus* is a much smaller stegosaurid, reaching a length of about 8·2ft (2·5m), from the late Jurassic of Tanzania. Many remains of *Kentrosaurus* were found in East Africa between 1909 and 1912. Unfortunately the great majority of these fossils, which were preserved at the Humboldt Museum in Berlin, cannot now be found, and it seems likely that they were lost during World War II.

In comparison with *Stegosaurus*, *Kentrosaurus* has a clearly different plate and spine pattern. The anterior plates are like those of *Stegosaurus* being quite narrow and flattened, and these become slightly larger and more triangular towards the rear of the animal. However, instead of resembling the huge triangular plates above the hips of *Stegosaurus*, those of *Kentrosaurus* become taller and narrower and continue down the length of the tail as pairs of long, very sharp spines. In addition to this double row of spines there is another pair of 'para-sacral' spines attached to the hips on either side, which point obliquely downward and backward. The little that is known of the head of *Kentrosaurus* indicates a shape rather similar to that of *Stegosaurus*.

Tuojiangosaurus is the only other well-preserved stegosaurid. It comes from Zhucheng County, south-Central China and the remains indicate a *Stegosaurus*-sized animal with somewhat narrower spines over the hips and no para-sacral spines.

The other stegosaurids so far mentioned are based upon material which, though obviously stegosaurian (i.e. body plates or skulls and teeth), are not complete enough to provide details of their overall body shape and general characteristics. We can say, though, that *Lexovisaurus* and *Dacentrurus* appear to have possessed para-sacral spines like those of *Kentrosaurus*. *Huayangosaurus* is another very interesting stegosaurid which is only known so far from a complete skull. This skull is much more deep and square than that of *Stegosaurus*; it is also unusual because it still retains teeth at the front of the upper jaw which are not found in *Stegosaurus*. *Huayangosaurus* seems, therefore, to be a very primitive stegosaurid indeed, and if the remainder of its skeleton were to be discovered, it might well provide clues to the relationships of stegosaurids to the other ornithischian dinosaurs.

Stegosaurid Life-Style

Since they are so unusual when compared with most other dinosaurs, stegosaurid remains provide us with a considerable number of clues as to their way of life. The structure of their legs indicates that they were rather slow, lumbering creatures. The low position of the head was probably well suited to a habit of browsing on ferns, cycads and other low ground cover, rather than higher up in the trees where the ornithopods and sauropods presumably fed. The rather feeble jaws and teeth simply served as cutting devices and the plants (once swallowed) were probably stored for several days in a very large stomach which acted as a fermenting tank.

As slow-moving herbivores, these stegosaurids must have been preyed upon by the large carnosaurs of the time: *Allosaurus* and *Ceratosaurus*. In the past it was assumed by many palaeontologists that since stegosaurids were unable to run to escape such predators, they must have used some defensive tactics. The rows of huge plates and spines were regarded as a defensive armour, either like that of a porcupine with the upright plates acting as deterrents, or that they were armour plated like armadillos. Some scientists have proposed that the large plates of *Stegosaurus* lay flat against the sides of its body as a protective shield.

Looking at the skeleton of *Stegosaurus*, neither of these proposals seems particularly convincing. Most of the plates across the back are broad and not particularly sharp, hardly the equivalent of the sharp quills of a porcupine. On the other hand, if the plates were indeed laid flat, then they would scarcely form a complete bony covering to the flanks of the animal—great areas of belly and neck would still be very vulnerable.

In fact a recent (1977) suggestion by Jim Farlow and colleagues is that the large plates were nothing at all to do with protection against predators. The proposal was that the plates of *Stegosaurus* acted both as radiators and solar-panels for regulating the body temperature of the animal. The first clue that this might be the case was provided by some of the very earliest descriptions of these plates. It was noted that they were covered with lots of fine grooves which are usually associated with numerous small blood vessels running across the surface of the plates: hardly what you would expect of bony armour plating! When Farlow cut a thin section across one of these plates the result was quite unexpected. Instead of the expected solid bone, the plate was found to be a honeycomb of spaces. This implied that the plates of *Stegosaurus* were very richly supplied with blood, and raised the obvious question, what was all this blood doing in these plates? The answer seems now quite obvious: like most living reptiles *Stegosaurus* was using its blood rather like the water in the central-heating system of a house to regulate its body temperature.

Farlow tested this answer by looking at the shape of the *Stegosaurus* plates and their performance in a wind-tunnel. It appeared that the plates were the ideal shape for dissipating heat in a breeze, and so cooling these animals. However, they may also have been used like solar panels to absorb heat from the Sun to warm the animal should it become chilled. No doubt *Stegosaurus* was able to regulate precisely the amount of blood passing into its plates, and so exercise fine control over its body temperature. This explanation seems particularly convincing, and may have a bearing on the arrangement of the plates down the back of *Stegosaurus*. If the plates were used as radiators or solar-panels, then the staggered pattern is the one that would have provided the most efficient arrangement. *Stegosaurus*' actual defence against predators would undoubtedly have been the spike-bearing tail. The large, sharp double pair of bone spikes on the end of the tail could have inflicted severe injury on an attacking theropod.

The other stegosaurids such as *Kentrosaurus* do not have such broad, high plates across the back as *Stegosaurus*. Presumably these forms were much more porcupine-like, with their rump, hips and tail protected by long, sharp spikes. However, these forms do tend to possess broader, flatter plates near the shoulders and on the neck which may have served as a slightly less sophisticated temperature regulation arrangement.

Above: *Kentrosaurus* in the Humboldt Museum, East Berlin. The shapes of its dorsal plates are very different from those of *Stegosaurus*. Note also the backwardly-pointing para-sacral spines on the hips.

Left: One of the Chinese stegosaurids, this is *Tuojiangosaurus multispinus* on display in Beipei Museum. The discovery of stegosaurids in China is significant as it implies that although we think that Europe and Asia were separated by sea for most of the age of the dinosaurs, some brief land connection may have allowed them to spread into Asia during the late Jurassic period.

Body Armour (above) It has been suggested that the plates on *Stegosaurus*' back actually fulfilled the role of armour plating, protecting these slow-moving creatures from predators. In fact, as the drawing shows, even if the plates had lain flat on its back (which is improbable physiologically), the belly and flanks of *Stegosaurus* would still have been vulnerable to attack.

Until the discovery of *Heterodontosaurus* in 1962 (page 102), *Scelidosaurus* ('limb-reptile') was the earliest known ornithiscian dinosaur. It was first referred to by Richard Owen in 1859 who described remains recovered from early Jurassic rocks of Charmouth (Dorset) in southern England. Owen went on to describe and illustrate an assortment of bones under the name *Scelidosaurus* in 1861. A little later, in 1863, Owen described an almost complete skeleton of this animal. This latter skeleton forms the basis for the flesh reconstruction below. Fragmentary remains of another possible scelidosaurid—*Lusitanosaurus* ('Lusitania reptile')—have also been found in Portugal.

It has since been shown by Barney Newman that the odd bones that were described by Owen in 1861 were in fact a mixture of theropod *(Megalosaurus)* and ornithopod bones. Technically the name *Scelidosaurus* should apply to these bones alone, rather than the complete skeleton described in 1863, but this would clearly be absurd, and Barney Newman proposed that the rules governing the use of fossils' names should be suspended in this case so that the skeleton could 'adopt' the name *Scelidosaurus*. This is yet another example of the complicated tangles scientists can get into through naming fossil species on inadequate material.

Scelidosaurus Described

Scelidosaurus grew to at least 13ft (4m) in length and is now known not only from the original skeleton, but also from a very small partial skeleton found in a nodule of rock earlier this century, and some imperfect fragments discovered in 1980. And very recently (1985) a group of amateur collectors, Simon Barnsley, David Costain and Peter Langham, discovered and excavated a very exciting new skeleton from Charmouth. As a result of all these discoveries, *Scelidosaurus* is now a reasonably well understood dinosaur. As with the stegosaurs (seen earlier) and the ankylosaurs (to follow), *Scelidosaurus* had many bony plates embedded in its skin; these did not form the high, thin plates seen in stegosaurs, but more closely resemble the low, bony studs seen on the backs of most ankylosaurs.

The skull of *Scelidosaurus* is deeper and shorter than that of *Stegosaurus,* and not so heavily armoured as that of a typical ankylosaur. However, as with ankylosaurs, there is evidence of extra bony tissue being welded on to the surface of the skull and the sides of the lower jaw. The teeth are simple and leaf-shaped, extending right down towards the tip of the snout so that the horny beak, if it was present, must have been extremely small.

The skeleton of *Scelidosaurus* is quite heavily built, with pillar-like hind legs and broad four-toed feet. The form of the front legs is a bit of a mystery since none is presently known. An upper arm bone preserved with the newly discovered skeleton is quite large and heavily built; this suggests that *Scelidosaurus* was a quadruped, rather than a biped—as reconstructed here. The tail, however, is long judged by the standard of most ornithischians and may have at least partly counterbalanced the front part of the animal. As a result, most of the weight was probably carried by the hind legs.

The bony armour of *Scelidosaurus* appears to have formed a broad covering across the back and sides of the animal, judging by the way that the bony plates are found scattered along the back and across the ribs of the skeleton. Immediately behind the head, the bony plates on either side are arranged in clusters of three, a

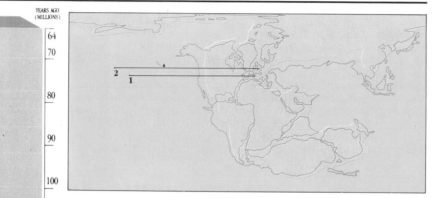

YEARS AGO (MILLIONS)

64
70
80
90
100
110
120
130
140
150
160
170
180
190
200
210
220
225

CRETACEOUS

JURASSIC

TRIASSIC

SCELIDOSAURUS

LUSITANOSAURUS

Map
1 *Lusitanosaurus*
2 *Scelidosaurus*

Time Chart (left)
Scelidosaurus is known from the early part of the Jurassic and is therefore one of the earliest ornithischian dinosaurs, and so very important in terms of the evolution of the Ornithischia as a whole. *Lusitanosaurus* may be another similar early armoured dinosaur.

Right: This specimen is part of the new find made by Barnsley, Costain and Langham and is extremely interesting because it shows, for the first time, the structure of the front end of *Scelidosaurus*' upper jaw. Six small, conical teeth can be seen. This part of the skull is missing from the very fine British Museum specimen—see above right. Behind is an array of leaf-shaped cheek teeth.

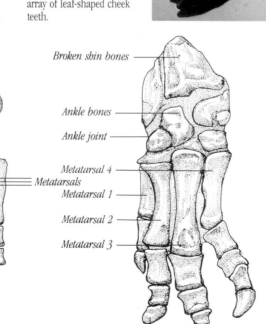

Shin and ankle bones

Claws

Broken shin bones

Ankle bones

Ankle joint

Metatarsal 4

Metatarsals

Metatarsal 1

Metatarsal 2

Metatarsal 3

Hoof-like claws

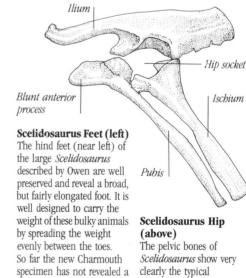

Ilium

Hip socket

Blunt anterior process

Ischium

Pubis

Scelidosaurus Feet (left)
The hind feet (near left) of the large *Scelidosaurus* described by Owen are well preserved and reveal a broad, but fairly elongated foot. It is well designed to carry the weight of these bulky animals by spreading the weight evenly between the toes. So far the new Charmouth specimen has not revealed a complete foot; the best pieces found to date are shown (far left).

Scelidosaurus Hip (above)
The pelvic bones of *Scelidosaurus* show very clearly the typical ornithischian pattern of bones, with pubis lying against the ischium.

curious pattern not seen anywhere else in the skeleton as can be appreciated by looking at the colour restoration below.

The rocks in which *Scelidosaurus* has been found are ones deposited at the bottom of a sea (rather than a lake or river). Indeed nearly all the other fossils found in these rocks are of sea-dwelling creatures such as ichthyosaurs and plesiosaurs. It is unusual to find the remains of land-living creatures on the sea-floor, and the only explanation would seem to be that carcasses of *Scelidosaurus* were occasionally washed down a nearby river into the sea before they sank and were buried by sediment, after which the process of fossilisation began.

The rocks in which it was buried, therefore, give us no clue to the way of life of *Scelidosaurus*. Most probably it was a fairly slow-moving plant eater which relied upon its armoured skin to protect it from the large theropods of the time. It is always possible that *Scelidosaurus* was capable of short bursts of speed to evade the larger theropods. The long tail, which might have counterbalanced the front of the body, may have permitted them to run for short distances on the hind legs alone.

Probable Relatives

The reason for dealing with *Scelidosaurus* on its own is because at the present time palaeontologists are undecided about its closest relatives. Some claim that they are the stegosaurs, while others suggest ankylosaur relationships, and yet others propose that it is an early ornithopod. This state of affairs has arisen for two main reasons. Firstly a detailed description of *Scelidosaurus* has never been published. This is now in the process of being rectified. For the past decade a team of people led by Ron Croucher in the laboratories of the British Museum (Natural History) have been carefully preparing in acid the large skeleton, described by Owen in 1863. The rock in which this skeleton was embedded has now been completely cleared away so that a full description can begin. The second problem is an evolutionary one. Being one of the early ornithischians, *Scelidosaurus* is primitive in many of its characters. Therefore, it does not have all the features associated with one particular ornithischian group. For example its feet, legs and tail are rather similar in shape to many ornithopods. Equally it has body armour like that of many ankylosaurs as well as a skull and hips reminiscent of stegosaurs. So, where does *Scelidosaurus* fit? My feeling is that of all the ornithischians currently known, the ankylosaurs seem to be its closest relatives. This *opinion* is based on three features: the development of extensive body armour, the arrangement of its teeth, and the fact that there is evidence of extra bone being welded onto the roof of the skull and the jaws; all of these features are found in ankylosaurs. Only time will tell whether this opinion is correct!

Scelidosaurus Skeleton (right)

For many years the large *Scelidosaurus* skeleton described by Richard Owen was on display in the BM (NH), looking like this. In recent years a team of laboratory preparators have carefully prepared this entire skeleton in acid baths in order to dissolve away the limestone. This difficult task is almost complete now and should result in *Scelidosaurus* being one of the best known of all early ornithischians.

Scelidosaurus (below)

This restoration is based upon illustrations prepared for Dr Alan Charig at the BM (NH). The back is studded with low conical bones and just behind the head these are modified into peculiar tricorn arrays perhaps for extra protection. The long tail may have counterbalanced the front of the body.

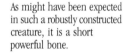

Below: The upper arm bone or humerus of *Scelidosaurus* has again been seen for the first time in the new specimen from Charmouth.

As might have been expected in such a robustly constructed creature, it is a short powerful bone.

Below: Yet another 'first', Barnsley, Costain and Langham also recovered from areas around the skeleton some fine skin impressions which show a mosaic of small, rounded scales embedded in the skin surface.

Size (below)
Scelidosaurus: l. 13ft (4m).

The other major group of armoured dinosaurs and the last of the major groups of dinosaurs that we shall be looking at are the ankylosaurs ('fused or joined-together reptiles'). Ankylosaurs are known from Jurassic and Cretaceous rocks worldwide. The unusual name refers to the fact that the bones in the skin of these animals tend to be fused together into great shield-like pieces of armour plating. In fact, this armour plating was so extensive that large slabs of bone were even welded onto the head, giving them quite a grotesque appearance. These were the tanks of the dinosaur era.

The ankylosaurs as a whole have a long and rather chequered history. Until quite recently they were very poorly understood. Fortunately, however, Dr Walter Preston Coombs Jr (Amherst) has completely restudied many of the known ankylosaurs and cleared away much confusion. And Dr Teresa Maryanska (Warsaw) has described several completely new ankylosaurs from Mongolia.

In general, ankylosaurs are medium sized (6·5-26·2ft, 2-8m long) heavily built, quadrupedal ornithischian dinosaurs; they all tend to have low, broad, heavily armoured heads. Their bodies are low and broad, the legs being short and powerful rather than long and graceful. Their backs and legs also tend to be covered in various patterns of bony plates and studs or spikes. The tail tends to be relatively short and in some cases bears a very large bony club.

Dr Coombs has been able to show that the ankylosaurs can be divided into two quite distinct families: the nodosaurids ('nodular reptiles') and the ankylosaurids. The differences between these two families are many, but one of the most obvious is the presence or absence of a tail club.

Nodosaurid Ankylosaurs

The first nodosaurid to be discovered was *Hylaeosaurus* ('woodland reptile') which was

found in 1833 in the Tilgate Forest area of Sussex in southern England. The fossil remains of *Hylaeosaurus* consisted of the front half of the skeleton embedded in a large piece of stone. This fossil was first described by Gideon Mantell and somewhat later by Richard Owen and, along with *Megalosaurus* and *Iguanodon*, was one of the founder members of Owen's *Dinosauria*. This fossil, which is now in the British Museum (Natural History) has, unfortunately, never been prepared out of the stone in which it is embedded. Nevertheless, the parts which are exposed seem to show an animal with rows of large, curved plates running down its back. Few other remains of *Hylaeosaurus* have been discovered to date, so that not a great deal is known about either its appearance or its relations with other ankylosaurs.

Another early British nodosaurid is *Polacanthus* ('many-spikes') which was discovered in 1865 by the Rev. William Fox. The skeleton, which consisted of the hind part of the animal

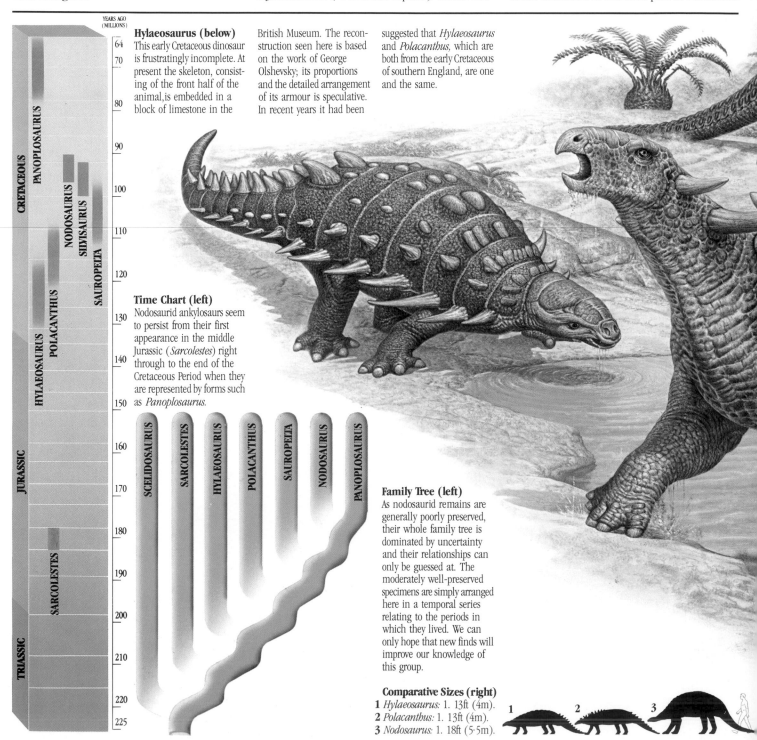

Hylaeosaurus (below)
This early Cretaceous dinosaur is frustratingly incomplete. At present the skeleton, consisting of the front half of the animal, is embedded in a block of limestone in the British Museum. The reconstruction seen here is based on the work of George Olshevsky; its proportions and the detailed arrangement of its armour is speculative. In recent years it had been suggested that *Hylaeosaurus* and *Polacanthus*, which are both from the early Cretaceous of southern England, are one and the same.

Time Chart (left)
Nodosaurid ankylosaurs seem to persist from their first appearance in the middle Jurassic (*Sarcolestes*) right through to the end of the Cretaceous Period when they are represented by forms such as *Panoplosaurus*.

Family Tree (left)
As nodosaurid remains are generally poorly preserved, their whole family tree is dominated by uncertainty and their relationships can only be guessed at. The moderately well-preserved specimens are simply arranged here in a temporal series relating to the periods in which they lived. We can only hope that new finds will improve our knowledge of this group.

Comparative Sizes (right)
1 *Hylaeosaurus*: 1. 13ft (4m).
2 *Polacanthus*: 1. 13ft (4m).
3 *Nodosaurus*: 1. 18ft (5·5m).

YEARS AGO (MILLIONS)

64 70 80 90 100 110 120 130 140 150 160 170 180 190 200 210 220 225

CRETACEOUS
JURASSIC
TRIASSIC

PANOPLOSAURUS
NODOSAURUS
SILVISAURUS
SAUROPELTA
POLACANTHUS
HYLAEOSAURUS
SARCOLESTES

SCELIDOSAURUS
SARCOLESTES
HYLAEOSAURUS
POLACANTHUS
SAUROPELTA
NODOSAURUS
PANOPLOSAURUS

Nodosaurus (below)
From what is known of the skeleton, the armour is the most distinctive feature of *Nodosaurus*. It seems to have consisted of broad bands of alternately large and small rounded nodules (hence its name). It is possible that the margins of the armour were fringed with tall spines as seems to have been the case with *Hylaeosaurus* and *Polacanthus*. The head of this colour reconstruction is conjectural, based upon that of *Panoplosaurus*, as no head was found with the skeleton in Albany County, Wyoming.

including many spines, various back and tail vertebrae, the hips and hind legs, had evidently weathered out of the cliffs on the coast of the Isle of Wight. It seems quite likely that much of the skeleton was present originally but that, once exposed by a cliff fall, much was lost by being washed out to sea. The frustrating thing about this specimen is that although it must have lived at about the same time as *Hylaeosaurus,* the parts of both skeletons do not overlap (one being the front half, the other the back half). It is therefore impossible to compare the two skeletons directly to *prove* that they belonged either to the same or to different animals. Quite recently (1979) Mr William T. Blows, an amateur collector of fossils who is continuing the tradition of collecting dinosaurs from the Isle of Wight established by the Rev. Fox, discovered some more *Polacanthus* material. Again this is far from complete, but it does include some very nice pieces of its armour-plated hide, and various bones from

the back of the animal. Some of these latter may help to solve the problem of the *Polacanthus-Hylaeosaurus* relationship. However, this awaits preparation of the original *Hylaeosaurus* skeleton.

The story of frustration revealed in the *Polacanthus-Hylaeosaurus* issue is by now a familiar one. The fossil remains are not well enough preserved to give precise information about these interesting animals, and indeed this problem applies very strongly to nearly all ankylosaurs. In some geological formations ankylosaur-type bony plates can be very abundant, but these always seem to be isolated bones, presumably scattered from rotting carcasses. Very few nodosaurids are known at all well, and many of the reconstructions of these animals seen in books are based on little more than guesswork. Bearing this fact in mind, we shall simply look at a few details of the anatomy of some of the better known members of nodosaurid group.

Polacanthus (below left)
As has been the case with the other nodosaurids, much of this reconstruction is conjectural. The skeleton of *Polacanthus* lacks the head and much of the front half of the body before the pelvis—apart from the spines, which were found scattered near the remainder of the fossil. So even their position is a matter of guess work. The long dorsal spines may have formed a protective frill around the sides of the body to guard the flanks and legs of *Polacanthus* when under attack.

Map (right)
1 *Dracopelta*
2 *Hylaeosaurus*
3 *Minmi*
4 *Nodosaurus*
5 *Panoplosaurus*
6 *Polacanthus*
7 *Sarcolestes*
8 *Sauropelta*
9 *Silvisaurus*
10 *Struthiosaurus*

Nodosaurus ('nodular [lumpy] reptile') was first mentioned by Marsh in 1889, but was only described in some detail in 1921 by Richard Lull on the basis of partial remains of the skeleton. *Nodosaurus* remains come from the late Cretaceous of Wyoming and Kansas. *Nodosaurus* gives us a fair idea of how most nodosaurids must have looked. The skeleton is about 18ft (5·5m) long and the whole of its upper surface is studded with bony plates forming a very thick and heavy protective coat. The pattern of armour plating seen in *Nodosaurus* consists of regular bands of larger and smaller bony plates. This would have undoubtedly conferred upon this animal both considerable strength and a certain amount of flexibility. The hind legs are pillar-like in order to support the heavy body, and the feet are naturally short and broad. The pelvis is rather a different shape to that of other ornithischians because the ilium at the top of the hip is greatly enlarged and overhangs the legs, while the lower hip bones (pubis and ischium) are very much reduced. Large leg muscles attached to the underside of the ilium, while its upper surface was covered by extensive armour-plating. The front legs of *Nodosaurus* are not very well preserved but were undoubtedly, as shown here, short and powerfully built to support the great weight of the body. The shoulders were similarly very strong and in many cases clearly scarred by powerful muscles.

The skull of *Nodosaurus* is unfortunately not known to date; however, that of another late Cretaceous North American nodosaurid, *Panoplosaurus* ('fully plated reptile'), is very well preserved (see right). The skull of all known nodosaurids seems to resemble that of *Panoplosaurus*. Unlike the ankylosaurids (pages 164-169) the nodosaurid skull is rather narrow with a more pointed snout, and lacks the horn-like projections from the rear corners of the skull. There is also an opening on the side of the skull behind the eye, which is not seen in ankylosaurids. The teeth are quite simple, leaf-shaped and rather similar to those of stegosaurs. Indeed although the jaws are massive, they are not specially modified for grinding in the way that the jaws and teeth of ceratopids and hadrosaurids were. The front of both upper and lower jaws ends in a toothless, horn-covered beak.

Silvisaurus ('forest reptile') is another nodosaurid which was described by Theodore Eaton Jr. in 1960. It consisted of a skull and partial skeleton collected from Ottawa county,

Kansas and is dated at early Cretaceous. Measuring about 8ft (2·5m) in length, this small armoured dinosaur is slightly unusual in that it has 8 or 9 small pointed teeth near the front of its upper jaw — the area covered by a horny beak in most other ankylosaurs. This does not mean that *Silvisaurus* had no horny beak at all, merely that the upper beak was quite small and situated right at the tip of the upper jaw.

Sauropelta ('shielded reptile') is another early Cretaceous nodosaurid described by Professor John Ostrom in 1970. Again the material of this animal is far from complete, even though abundant remains have been recovered in recent years. One specimen of *Sauropelta* includes a very well-preserved tail which clearly tapers toward the tip and lacks the club characteristic of ankylosaurids. The body armour is also quite well preserved in several specimens and seems to show transverse rows of alternating large low bony studs and smaller pebbly armour. Towards the sides of the animal

the larger studs seem to be taller and spike-like, and probably formed a fringe of defensive spikes protecting the sides of the animal from attack by predators.

In addition to these admittedly poorly known animals there are several other even less well known nodosaurids. *Struthiosaurus* ('ostrich reptile') is known from the latest Cretaceous of southern Europe (France, Hungary, Austria) and especially from localities in an area originally known as Transylvania in Rumania. These remains are particularly interesting because all the dinosaurs from this area (including a sauropod, a hadrosaurid and an iguanodontid) are *dwarf* species. *Struthiosaurus* is the smallest of all known nodosaurids, measuring no more than 6·5ft (2m) in length. Why all these dinosaurs should be so small is a mystery. One explanation is that they lived on small islands, whereon there has been shown to be a surprisingly common tendency toward miniaturization. Several Mediterranean islands

Left: The massive construction of the nodosaurid skull is plainly seen in this picture of *Panoplosaurus*. Large slabs of bone are plastered all over the skull.

Panoplosaurus Skull (right)
From above (near right) the details of the armour plating are clear; the grooves show where the slabs of bone join. From below one can see the toothless beak on the snout, the teeth, the internal nostrils and the braincase behind.

Nodosaurus Skeleton (right)
It is a sad fact that nodosaurids are very poorly known at present. This reconstruction of *Nodosaurus textilis* is based on Richard Swann Lull's work, and has been given additional material from other nodosaurids. The specimen is badly preserved and so the skull is 'borrowed' from *Panoplosaurus*, while the shoulders are those of *Sauropelta*. The armour plating is distinctive, con-

sisting of bands of rounded nodules. It is not known whether this animal had a fringe of longer spikes, as other nodosaurids did.

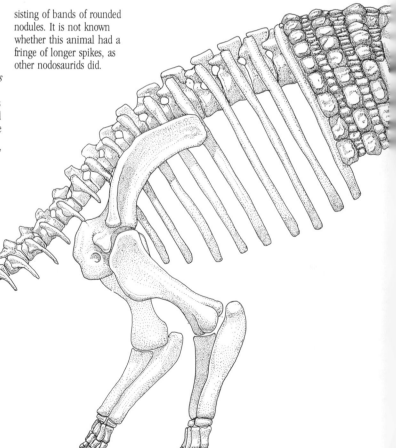

'Pseudo-acromion process'

Shoulder blade

Shoulder joint

Nodosaur Shoulder Blade (above)
This shoulder blade belongs to *Sauropelta* and is typical of the type seen in nodosaurids. Its most outstanding feature, and one in which it differs from that of ankylosaurids, is the large pseudo-acromion process which overhangs the shoulder joint and which

may have improved the mechanical advantage of some of the shoulder muscles. It is possible that this allowed nodosaurids to crouch against the ground for protection against predators, relying on their armour to withstand any attack (see also drawing of nodosaurid defensive strategy on page 168).

are known to have had miniature elephants and even today Madagascar still has a fauna which includes a dwarf hippopotamus. So perhaps these dinosaurs were island dwellers as well.

Other important but very poorly known nodosaurids include *Minmi* (named after Minmi Crossing where it was found), the first Australian ankylosaur which was discovered in early Cretaceous rocks near Roma, Queensland. *Minmi* is only known from a small portion of the back and parts of a foot. *Dracopelta* ('armoured dragon') is a small late Jurassic nodosaurid from Portugal. This new species described by Galton in 1980 is known from part of a rib cage with several types of armour plate preserved in position. *Sarcolestes* ('flesh robber'), mistakenly identified as a meat-eating dinosaur, comes from the middle Jurassic of Cambridgeshire. It consists only of an incomplete piece of jaw which seems to be typically ankylosaurian in that it has a large piece of armour-plating welded to its outer

surface. This is the earliest record of a nodosaurid from anywhere in the world. *Priodontognathus* ('saw-toothed jaw') of uncertain age may be a fragment of ankylosaur jaw from England, and *Cryptodraco* ('hidden dragon') is an ankylosaurian thigh bone from the late Jurassic of Cambridgeshire.

Apart from these interesting but very fragmentary records of nodosaurid ankylosaurs, there are many other commonly named nodosaurids which are unfortunately very dubious indeed. These include *Acanthopholis* ('thorn bearer'), *Brachypodosaurus* ('short-footed reptile'), *Hoplitosaurus* ('hoplite reptile'), *Polacanthoides* ('like many spikes'), *Onychosaurus* ('crawling reptile'), *Palaeoscincus* ('ancient skink') and *Priconodon* ('saw cone-shaped tooth'). All of these are based on fossil specimens that are inadequate for scientific comparison with other species and should therefore be considered as 'nomina dubia' or dubious names.

Many other names have been proposed for nodosaurids but these have proved to be incorrect. For example *Struthiosaurus* has, over the years, been given the following names, all of which are incorrect: *Cretaeomus, Danubiosaurus, Danubriosaurus, Hoplosaurus, Leipsanosaurus, Lepanosaurus, Pleuropeltis, Pleuropeltus, Rhodanosaurus*. This is not the only example of a variety of names applying to a single fossil genus. In this case it very forcefully makes the point that the original material of *Struthiosaurus* was extremely poorly understood. As a result, each time more ankylosaur material was discovered in southern Europe it was given a new name because it could not be compared adequately with the original. Obviously this sort of phenomenon can bedevil scientific research on groups such as this because it can take such an inordinate length of time to track down all these different names and undertake the necessary work to prove that they are incorrect.

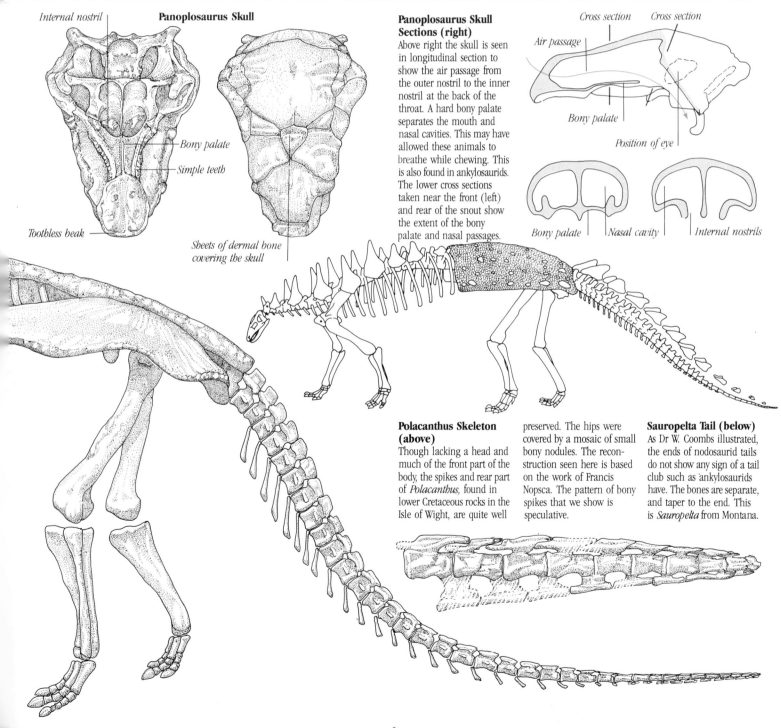

Panoplosaurus Skull

Internal nostril

Bony palate

Simple teeth

Toothless beak

Sheets of dermal bone covering the skull

Panoplosaurus Skull Sections (right)
Above right the skull is seen in longitudinal section to show the air passage from the outer nostril to the inner nostril at the back of the throat. A hard bony palate separates the mouth and nasal cavities. This may have allowed these animals to breathe while chewing. This is also found in ankylosaurids. The lower cross sections taken near the front (left) and rear of the snout show the extent of the bony palate and nasal passages.

Cross section   *Cross section*

Air passage

Bony palate

Position of eye

Bony palate   Nasal cavity   Internal nostrils

Polacanthus Skeleton (above)
Though lacking a head and much of the front part of the body, the spikes and rear part of *Polacanthus*, found in lower Cretaceous rocks in the Isle of Wight, are quite well

preserved. The hips were covered by a mosaic of small bony nodules. The reconstruction seen here is based on the work of Francis Nopsca. The pattern of bony spikes that we show is speculative.

Sauropelta Tail (below)
As Dr W. Coombs illustrated, the ends of nodosaurid tails do not show any sign of a tail club such as ankylosaurids have. The bones are separate, and taper to the end. This is *Sauropelta* from Montana.

The second group of ankylosaurs known as ankylosaurids are described in this section. Ankylosaurids may be distinguished from the nodosaurid ankylosaurs in a number of ways. Ankylosaurids have broad, armoured heads which are about as wide as they are long. Large triangular horns are found at the rear corners of the skull, and the sides of the head are completely closed in by bone. The bony armour-plating covering the body tends to have very few tall spines and the tail is highly modified to form a heavy bony club.

While nodosaurids are found in rocks which vary in age between the middle Jurassic and the late Cretaceous, the ankylosaurids appear to be restricted in time to the Cretaceous. Ankylosaurids also appear to have been much less widespread geographically, having been recovered with certainty only from western North America and eastern Asia (Mongolia and China). As was the case with nodosaurids, remains of ankylosaurid-type dinosaurs are quite abundant. Unfortunately, these remains tend to be isolated pieces of armour-plating or other skeletal fragments, which cannot be identified with any great confidence. This abundance of poor material has therefore tended to generate many invalid or extremely dubious names. Again we have to be grateful to Dr Walter Coombs Jr and Dr Teresa Maryanska for their detailed work which has, over the last decade, helped to clarify what, until recently, has been a very confusing group of dinosaurs.

In order to discuss some of the main features of ankylosaurids, we shall look at what is known of the dinosaur illustrated in the foreground below: *Euoplocephalus* ('true plated head').

Euoplocephalus Described

The first remains of the animal later to be known as *Euoplocephalus* were recovered from the Red Deer River of Alberta in 1902; they consisted of a partial head and incomplete skeleton. Lawrence Lambe created the name *Stereocephalus* ('twin-head') for this skeleton. Unfortunately this particular name had already been used for an insect! So Lambe changed it to *Euoplocephalus* in 1910. Other remains of armoured dinosaurs were found in the same general area in subsequent years. Some of these remains were named *Dyoplosaurus* ('doubly armoured reptile'), others were named *Scolosaurus* ('thorn-reptile') and *Anodontosaurus* ('toothless reptile'). Coombs eventually realized, after studying these separate species carefully, that they were all parts of the same type of animal and renamed them all *Euoplocephalus*.

All of this material, which includes skulls, several partial skeletons and fairly complete armour, provides enough information for a reasonably accurate picture of *Euoplocephalus* to be drawn. The reconstructions seen here are based on the work of Dr Kenneth Carpenter (Boulder, Colorado). In common with all the

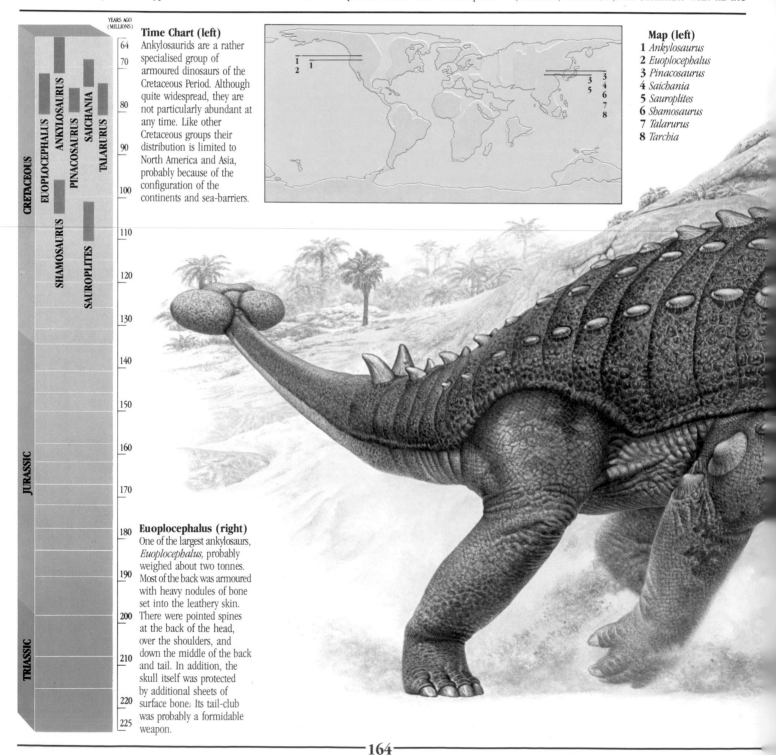

Time Chart (left)
Ankylosaurids are a rather specialised group of armoured dinosaurs of the Cretaceous Period. Although quite widespread, they are not particularly abundant at any time. Like other Cretaceous groups their distribution is limited to North America and Asia, probably because of the configuration of the continents and sea-barriers.

YEARS AGO (MILLIONS)

64
70
80
90
100
110
120
130
140
150
160
170
180
190
200
210
220
225

CRETACEOUS
JURASSIC
TRIASSIC

EUOPLOCEPHALUS
ANKYLOSAURUS
PINACOSAURUS
SAICHANIA
TALARURUS
SHAMOSAURUS
SAUROPLITES

Map (left)
1 *Ankylosaurus*
2 *Euoplocephalus*
3 *Pinacosaurus*
4 *Saichania*
5 *Sauroplites*
6 *Shamosaurus*
7 *Talarurus*
8 *Tarchia*

Euoplocephalus (right)
One of the largest ankylosaurs, *Euoplocephalus*, probably weighed about two tonnes. Most of the back was armoured with heavy nodules of bone set into the leathery skin. There were pointed spines at the back of the head, over the shoulders, and down the middle of the back and tail. In addition, the skull itself was protected by additional sheets of surface bone. Its tail-club was probably a formidable weapon.

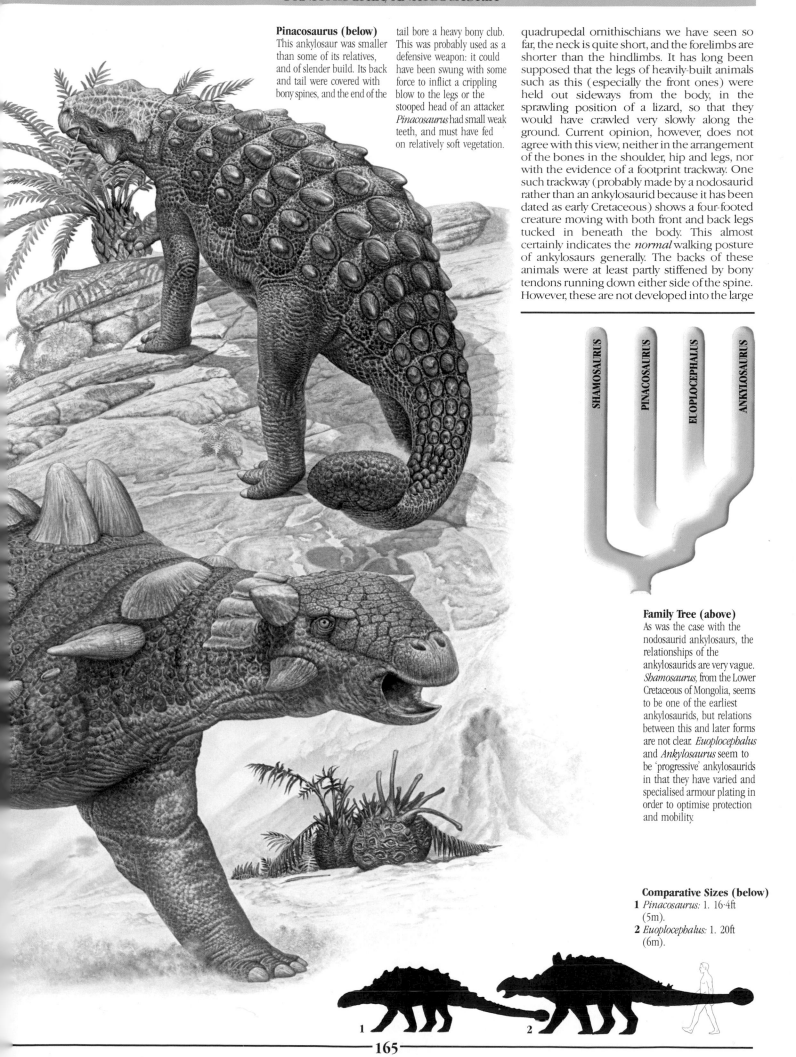

Pinacosaurus (below)
This ankylosaur was smaller than some of its relatives, and of slender build. Its back and tail were covered with bony spines, and the end of the tail bore a heavy bony club. This was probably used as a defensive weapon: it could have been swung with some force to inflict a crippling blow to the legs or the stooped head of an attacker. *Pinacosaurus* had small weak teeth, and must have fed on relatively soft vegetation.

quadrupedal ornithischians we have seen so far, the neck is quite short, and the forelimbs are shorter than the hindlimbs. It has long been supposed that the legs of heavily-built animals such as this (especially the front ones) were held out sideways from the body, in the sprawling position of a lizard, so that they would have crawled very slowly along the ground. Current opinion, however, does not agree with this view, neither in the arrangement of the bones in the shoulder, hip and legs, nor with the evidence of a footprint trackway. One such trackway (probably made by a nodosaurid rather than an ankylosaurid because it has been dated as early Cretaceous) shows a four-footed creature moving with both front and back legs tucked in beneath the body. This almost certainly indicates the *normal* walking posture of ankylosaurs generally. The backs of these animals were at least partly stiffened by bony tendons running down either side of the spine. However, these are not developed into the large

SHAMOSAURUS
PINACOSAURUS
EUOPLOCEPHALUS
ANKYLOSAURUS

Family Tree (above)
As was the case with the nodosaurid ankylosaurs, the relationships of the ankylosaurids are very vague. *Shamosaurus,* from the Lower Cretaceous of Mongolia, seems to be one of the earliest ankylosaurids, but relations between this and later forms are not clear. *Euoplocephalus* and *Ankylosaurus* seem to be 'progressive' ankylosaurids in that they have varied and specialised armour plating in order to optimise protection and mobility.

Comparative Sizes (below)
1 *Pinacosaurus:* 1. 16·4ft (5m).
2 *Euoplocephalus:* 1. 20ft (6m).

1
2

lattice-like arrangements seen across the hips of hadrosaurids (pages 118-119 and 124-125), but appear much more sporadically in this area. The region where they are best developed is toward the end of the tail—near the tail-club. These tendons probably served two purposes in life. Firstly, they provided firm anchorage for the tail-swinging muscles; secondly, they stiffened the end of the tail in order to prevent 'whip-lash' effects from damaging the bones near the tail-club. The main part of the tail had no ossified tendons and could therefore be swung freely from side to side.

The dominant characteristic of this animal is, however, the bony armour-plating. The ground plan for the arrangement of the armour lies in the skin, practically all of which is embedded with small, bony studs. On the back and tail the studded skin is divided up into bands of much larger bony plates of various shapes running across the body. Over the neck there are two bands, the first appears to consist of two large,

slightly ridged plates, followed by a second ring with a whorl of very large, oblique blunt spikes. These are arranged so as to give not only protection, but also a great deal of flexibility to the neck. Behind this area, the back is covered by four bands of armour studded with rows of large but quite low, keeled plates. Across the hips there are three further bands which are covered by a mosaic of disc-shaped studs. The front part of the tail is also banded, with four rows of keeled spikes which get progressively smaller, except for the middle two spikes on the last band. Beyond this region the tail lacks the bands of bone, but is studded with small bony nodules. The shoulders, arms and thighs were probably also covered with variously sized bony plates, but their arrangement is not at all well understood.

What we have then is a large animal (20ft, 6m or more in length) weighing something like two tonnes. Rather than being an enormous, very slow-moving creature somewhat like a

gigantic tortoise, it is here pictured as a surprisingly agile animal, perhaps more like a modern rhinoceros which, although it is large and heavy, is by no means slow-moving.

The degree to which ankylosaurids were armoured is quite remarkable, as can be appreciated by looking at the skulls of *Euoplocephalus*, *Pinacosaurus* and *Saichania*. Large slabs of bone are plastered all over the exposed surfaces of the skull and jaws forming an almost impregnable covering; these must have given them almost complete immunity to attacks by the large theropods of the time. Two rather exceptional skulls of *Euoplocephalus* in the American Museum of Natural History show that these dinosaurs even went so far as to develop bony eyelids! Both of these skulls are preserved with curved bony plates inside the eye socket which undoubtedly closed rather like steel shutters to protect the delicate eye from the talons of theropods. Although such bony eyelids have only been found in *Euoplocephalus*

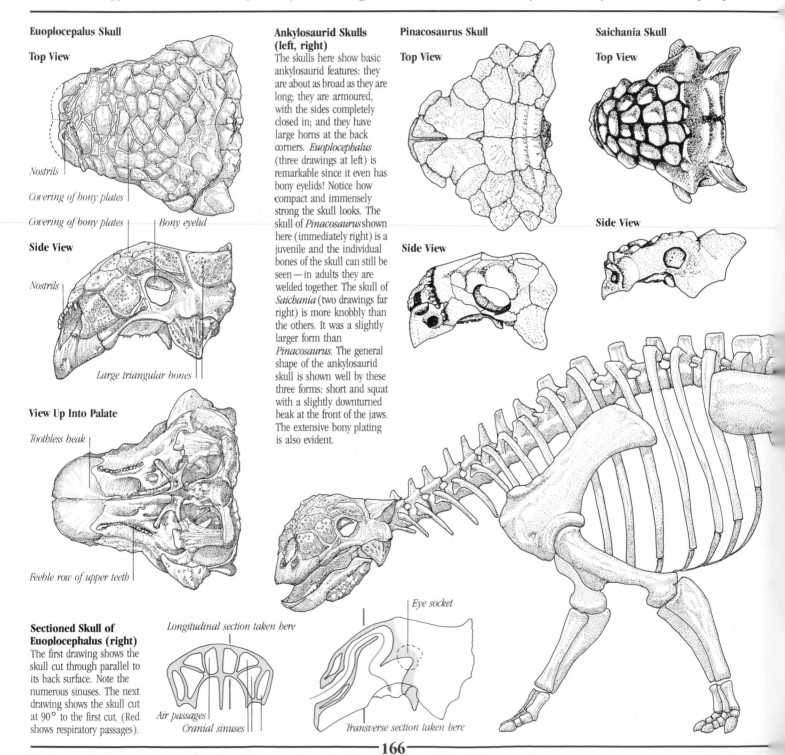

Euoplocepalus Skull

Top View

Nostrils

Covering of bony plates

Covering of bony plates   *Bony eyelid*

Side View

Nostrils

Large triangular bones

View Up Into Palate

Toothless beak

Feeble row of upper teeth

Sectioned Skull of Euoplocephalus (right)
The first drawing shows the skull cut through parallel to its back surface. Note the numerous sinuses. The next drawing shows the skull cut at 90° to the first cut. (Red shows respiratory passages).

Longitudinal section taken here

Air passages
Cranial sinuses

Ankylosaurid Skulls (left, right)
The skulls here show basic ankylosaurid features: they are about as broad as they are long; they are armoured, with the sides completely closed in; and they have large horns at the back corners. *Euoplocephalus* (three drawings at left) is remarkable since it even has bony eyelids! Notice how compact and immensely strong the skull looks. The skull of *Pinacosaurus* shown here (immediately right) is a juvenile and the individual bones of the skull can still be seen—in adults they are welded together. The skull of *Saichania* (two drawings far right) is more knobbly than the others. It was a slightly larger form than *Pinacosaurus*. The general shape of the ankylosaurid skull is shown well by these three forms: short and squat with a slightly downturned beak at the front of the jaws. The extensive bony plating is also evident.

Eye socket

Transverse section taken here

Pinacosaurus Skull

Top View

Side View

Saichania Skull

Top View

Side View

to date, it seems quite likely that other ankylosaurids possessed them.

Nasal Passages

Nodosaurid nasal passages are relatively simple paired tubes which run from the nostrils directly to the back of the throat. By contrast ankylosaurid nasal tubes follow an S-shaped course through the head and on either side of these there are additional passages (sinuses). These elaborate sinuses may have had several purposes in life. Similar sorts of complicated passages in the heads of hadrosaurids have been interpreted as allowing for an improved sense of smell, or for making characteristic noises. Teresa Maryanska believes that they served to filter, warm and moisten the air which these animals breathed. In *Pinacosaurus* ('plank reptile') and *Saichania* ('beautiful') skulls recovered from Mongolia, Maryanska has discovered thin curved bones within the nasa

passages which look strikingly similar to the turbinal or scroll bones found in the noses of mammals. These bones are covered by membranes which filter, warm and moisten the air we breathe, so that a similar function in ankylosaurids does seem reasonable.

With regard to the structure of the ankylosaurid brain, we are fortunate that an endocranial cast of *Euoplocephalus* has been illustrated and described by Dr Coombs. This seems to show a fairly typical reptile brain cavity. The only unusual characteristic is the large, divergent pair of olfactory stalks which run towards the complex nasal passages. The relatively small size of the parts of the brain concerned with co-ordination and general activity compared with some other dinosaurs, such as ornithopods, tends to confirm the notion that these animals were slower-moving than their agile, bipedal contemporaries.

Because ankylosaurs were large and heavy animals, their leg muscles were of necessity

extremely powerful. One fortunate result of this for the palaeontologist is that the muscles have left remarkably clear scars on the areas where they were originally attached to the bones. Walter Coombs was able to analyse these muscle scars and used them to build up a detailed picture of the arrangement of muscles in the hips and shoulders of ankylosaurs. Some of the muscles are indicated in the diagrams below. There is, of course, no way in which we can be *absolutely* certain about the muscular arrangement proposed here. However, by comparing the *known* arrangement of muscles in the shoulders and hips of crocodiles with the pattern of muscle scars in ankylosaurs, we believe that we can get fairly close to the original pattern. The general impression gained from the arrangement and likely size of the muscles of both fore and hindlimbs is that they were designed to generate great power and moved the limbs quite slowly. Some of the muscles show interesting arrangements.

Shoulder and Hip Muscles (right)
Although the muscles are labelled here with just one function, this is merely their primary function. Usually muscles exert quite a complex force. For example, the coracobrachialis pulls forwards, but also inwards and upwards. Ankylosaurids needed powerful leg muscles to support and move their rather large, heavy bodies. Notice the bulky muscles arising from the back of the hip region. In most reptiles these pull the leg back, but here they are also responsible for swinging the tail, a very important part of the ankylosaurid defensive armoury.

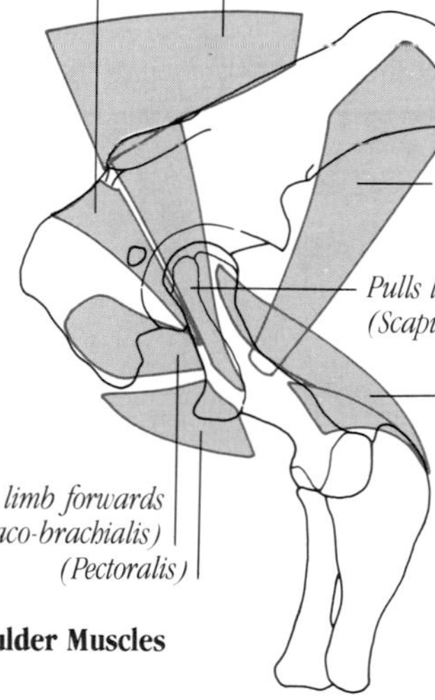

Pulls limb upwards
(*Supracoracoideus*)

Shoulder suspender
(*Serratus*)

Pulls limb back
(*Teres*)

Pulls limb upwards
(*Scapulo-humeralis anterior*)

Lower arm extensor
(*Triceps*)

Pulls limb forwards
(*Coraco-brachialis*)
(*Pectoralis*)

Shoulder Muscles

Hip Muscles

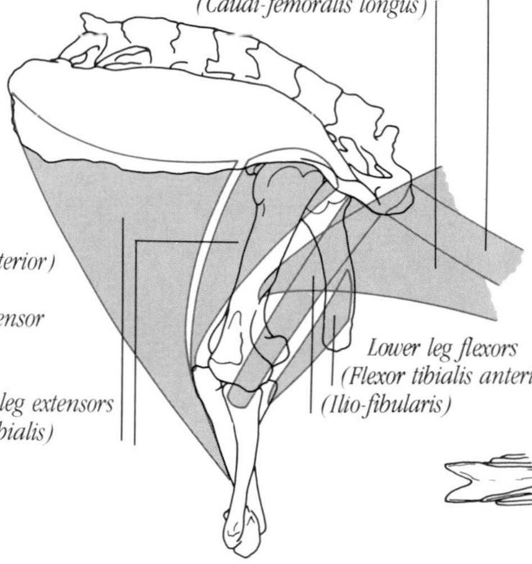

Club-swinging muscles
(*Ilio-caudalis*)
(*Caudi-femoralis longus*)

Lower leg flexors
(*Flexor tibialis anterior*)
(*Ilio-fibularis*)

Lower leg extensors
(*Ilio-tibialis*)

Tail of Ankylosaurus magniventris (below)
The tail club is unique to ankylosaurids. It is formed from bones embedded in the skin which have become greatly enlarged and fused to each other and to the tail vertebrae. It forms two lobes, one each side of the vertebral column, and could be swung from side to side by the powerful tail muscles, and so used as a weapon.

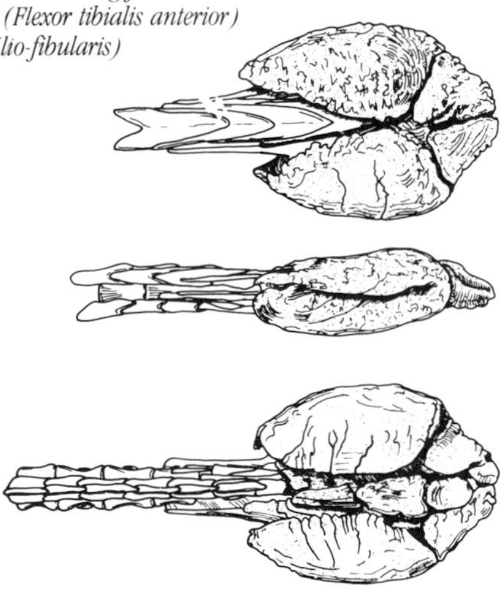

Euoplocephalus Skeleton (below)
In this ankylosaurid skeleton you can see the characteristic armoured head with its toothless beak, the shortish neck, the strongly-built legs and the tail club. The legs are tucked in, underneath the body, more like the situation in mammals than in most reptiles. The vertebral spines in the hip region are welded together, giving extra attachment area for hip muscles, and also extra strength to transmit the powerful locomotory thrust of the leg. The relative size of the tail club can be fully appreciated in the plan view (bottom).

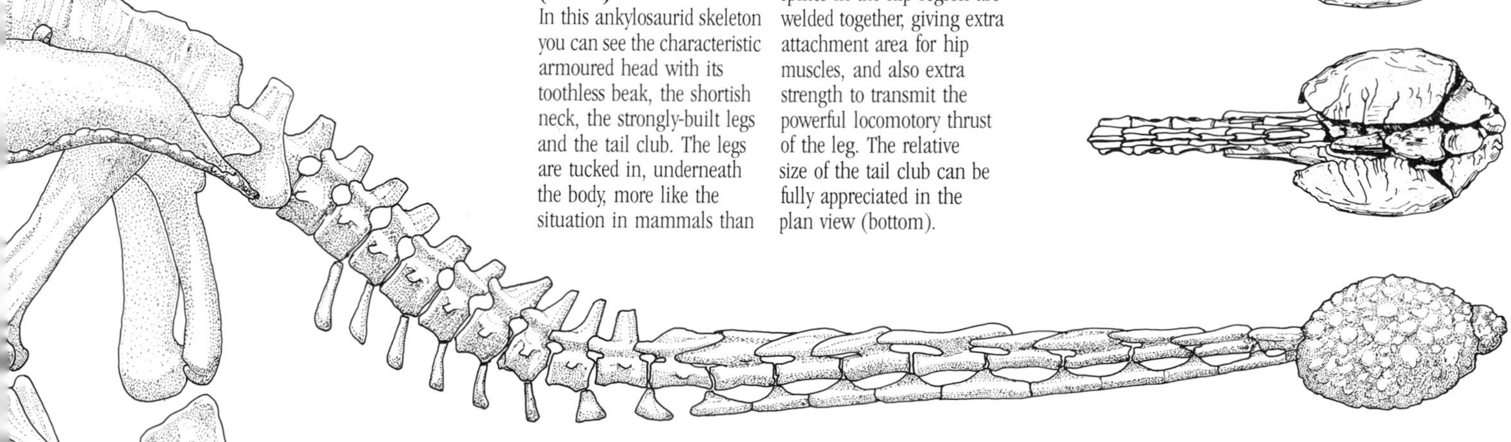

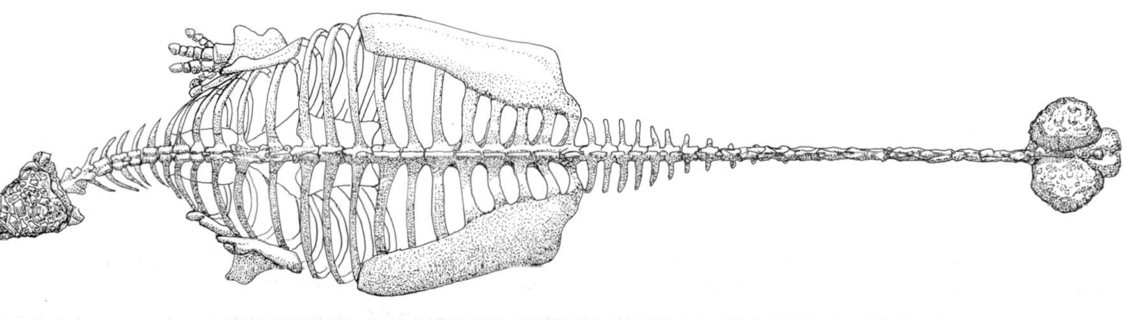

In the case of ankylosaurid hindlimb there are a cluster of muscles which run from the tail up towards the pelvis and hindlimb. In most ornithischian dinosaurs (see *Hypsilophodon* page 106-107) these were solely concerned with moving the hind leg powerfully backwards. While this would no doubt have been one function of these muscles in ankylosaurids, there was undoubtedly another function which was to provide the power to swing the heavy tail-club. Some of these muscles ran the length of the tail (M. caudi-femoralis longus) and attached to the ossified tendons clustered around the tail-club.

Defensive Strategies

Both ankylosaurids and nodosaurids lived at times when theropods were many and varied in type. The differences between these two types of armoured dinosaur suggest that they used different tactics to avoid or resist predators.

(i) Armour-plating. First (and most obviously) the well-developed bony armour plating would have acted as a deterrent to all but the largest and most powerful of the theropods. There are, however, a few differences in the pattern of the bony armour in the two groups. The ankylosaurids, as we have just seen with *Euoplocephalus*, have armour plating which is divided into bands which are studded with variably-sized bony plates. Only the front end of the tail seems to be plated. This arrangement confers not only protection, but gives these animals a surprising degree of flexibility of movement, and of course a free-swinging tail-club. Nodosaurids, at least on the evidence of *Sauropelta* for which there is a reasonably well-preserved skin, have a much more extensive armour; this is not so clearly divided into flexible bands and seems to extend to the end of the tail. The large, protective bony studs are very numerous and tend to develop into long, pointed spikes forming a fringe along the sides of the animal. *Panoplosaurus* (=*Palaeoscincus*) seem to show the same sort of arrangement. Other nodosaurids, such as the earlier form *Polacanthus*, do not have well-preserved skins to show the clear arrangement of its armour. Nevertheless, these did bear numerous large, sharply pointed spikes embedded in the skin either along the back and tail, or around the sides of the animal.

The heads of both nodosaurids and ankylosaurids are extensively plated by bone, but whether nodosaurids possessed bony eyelids like those of *Euoplocephalus* is not known.

(ii) Defensive weapons. Nodosaurids possess no obvious defensive weapons unless, like porcupines today, they were able to run backwards at their predators and attempt to wound or impale them on their spikes. This strategy does not seem very likely because the spikes of nodosaurids are not really comparable with the very long, sharp, detachable quills of porcupines.

Ankylosaurids by contrast possessed the unique tail-club. Several of the bones embedded in the skin at the end of the tail are greatly enlarged and have become fused to one another, and to the last few tail bones, to form a very heavy club. The rear half of the tail is not apparently heavily-armoured so that the long muscles of the tail, which are anchored to the hips and legs, were capable of swinging the club from side to side. The size and weight of an ankylosaurid club can be appreciated from the drawings on page 167.

The tail-club is an unusual weapon among dinosaurs (or any other animal groups for that matter!). The spike-adorned tail of *Stegosaurus* is perhaps the nearest equivalent. The club, however, would have been an extremely useful weapon. The likely predators of ankylosaurids would have been the tyrannosaurid theropods, all of which were extremely large, bipedal predators with very small forelimbs. The way in which a tyrannosaurid would have attempted to deal with an ankylosaurid would have been to try to overturn one. Once on its back, the ankylosaur would probably be unable to right itself, and the predator would be able to gorge itself on the relatively poorly-protected belly of the unfortunate creature. However, to do any of this, the tyrannosaurid would have to get close to the ankylosaurid in order to be able to use its hind legs, and perhaps its jaws, to catch one side of the animal and flip it over. Ankylosaurids were probably quite mobile creatures, and no doubt would have avoided the lunges of a tyrannosaurid quite skilfully. In addition, the ankylosaurid would attempt to position itself so that it could swing its club at the legs of its assailant. One telling blow from an ankylosaurid club could have been fatal to a tyrannosaurid. Standing as they did on two legs, these heavy creatures would have been relatively unstable, and if caught on the ankles by a scything blow could well have been sent crashing to the ground with the risk of breaking their legs or pelvis. Any such injury would have been fatal to a 4-5 tonne tyrannosaurid, because it would have been unable to rise from the ground, and would undoubtedly have been devoured by other tyrannosaurids in turn.

To sum up, it would seem that both groups of ankylosaurs were well able to withstand attacks from large theropods. The ankylosaurids were no doubt both fairly agile, with heavy but flexible body armour, and they possessed a very effective defensive weapon—the heavy tail-club. The nodosaurids by contrast seem to have been rather more heavily-armoured and did not possess the tail-club as a defensive weapon. Presumably their strategy for survival was simply to 'weather the storm', relying on their heavier and more complete armour to protect them against predators, much as tortoises do today. This passive means of defence may in fact provide an alternative explanation for the peculiar structure of their shoulder muscles which might have allowed them to *retract* the front legs very powerfully (more so than ankylosaurids). Perhaps when attacked by predators, nodosaurids dug their claws into the ground and retracted their legs, thereby anchoring themselves to the ground. By doing this they would have been able to resist attempts by large theropods to turn them onto their backs. Also, by pulling themselves closer to the ground, the long spikes which form a fringe along the sides of the body would have created a spiky apron to protect the legs and sides of the creature under attack.

All in all, the ankylosaurs seem to be a most remarkable group of dinosaurs. Only one other group of animals comes close to them in general appearance, and these are the extinct South American glyptodonts—extinct relatives of the armadillos. These animals had bony shields covering their heads and backs, and a tail covered in rings of bone. Some glyptodonts such as *Doedicurus* had a mace-like spiky club which resembles the ankylosaurid club, and probably served the same sort of defensive function. Glyptodonts lived long after the reign of the dinosaurs, during the late Pleistocene Epoch (a mere 500,000 years ago), but they had to contend with equally fierce predators, such as the marsupial sabre-toothed cats (*Thylacosmilus*). The spiky club was presumably a very effective defensive weapon at close-quarters.

Ankylosaurid Genera

Apart from *Euoplocephalus,* which has been looked at in some detail, there are several other reasonably well-established ankylosaurids, but only two are known from North Amerca. *Ankylosaurus* ('fused reptile'), the only other North American form, was one of the largest ankylosaurids known, growing up to 33ft (10m) long. The remains of this species have been recovered from Alberta and Montana.

Several genera are known from eastern Asia. *Pinacosaurus* ('plank reptile'), also incorrectly referred to as *Syrmosaurus, Ninghsiasaurus* and *Virminicaudus,* was first described by Charles Gilmore from material collected in the Gobi Desert during the American Museum-Mongolian expedition. A newly discovered skull of a young *Pinacosaurus* is a rare example in which the bones which normally form a solid covering to the skull have not yet firmly attached themselves, so that the pattern of true

Defensive Strategies (above and left)
These drawings illustrate the different ways in which ankylosaurs may have defended themselves against predators. *Hylaeosaurus,* a nodosaurid, adopts a passive defence, clutching the ground with its strong limbs and relying on its body armour and fringe of spikes to deter the attacker. The ankylosaurid *Euoplocephalus,* however, is more active in its self defence, swinging its big tail-club in order to topple and so disable the tyrannosaurid.

skull bones is revealed for the first time. This may prove to be of great help when trying to discover the relationships of ankylosaurs to other ornithischians. Reaching a maximum body length of 16·4ft (5m), *Pinacosaurus* was a relatively slender-built ankylosaurid.

Saichania ('beautiful') consists of the skull and much of the front part of the skeleton of a 23ft (7m) long ankylosaurid from Mongolia. First described in 1977 by Dr Maryanska, it has a broad, knobbly skull (see illustration). As preserved, the armour reveals many different types of plates, including spiked half-rings around the neck, and low backwardly-pointing spikes across the back similar to those of *Pinacosaurus*.

Talarurus ('basket-tail') is a 16-23ft (5-7m) long ankylosaurid from Bayn Shireh in southern Mongolia. At present this is not fully described but comprises skull and skeleton remains in the Palaeontological Institute of the Academy of Sciences, Moscow (see below).

Tarchia ('brain'), from the Barun Goyot formation of Mongolia, is known from an incomplete skull. The skull, which is about the same size as that of *Saichania* has a much larger braincase: hence the name!

Shamosaurus ('Gobi reptile') was described in 1983 from material collected from the early Cretaceous of Mongolia. This and the poorly-known *Sauroplites* ('hoplite reptile') are the earliest ankylosaurids known. The skull, the only part so far described, is typically ankylosaurid, being low, broad and having bony horns at the posterior corners.

Many genera of ankylosaurid are rather dubiously established. For example *Amtosaurus* ('Amtgay reptile') from Bayn Shireh in Mongolia may well be the same as *Talarurus* from the same area. While *Heishanosaurus* '('Heishan reptile'), *Peishanosaurus* ('Peishan reptile'), *Lametasaurus* ('Lameta reptile') and *Stegosaurides (Stegosauroides)* ('Stegosaur form') are all very dubiously established types.

When we consider the geographical distribution of ankylosaurids, it is clear that good species are known only from western North America and eastern Asia. Only two late Cretaceous species are definitely known in North America, *Euoplocephalus* and *Ankylosaurus,* while at least six species are established in Asia ranging from the early Cretaceous right through to the end. This distribution pattern suggests that ankylosaurids originated in Asia during the early Cretaceous and were able to migrate into western North America, perhaps via the Bering Straits, in the late Cretaceous. This certainly accords with the distribution of tyrannosaurids and 'saurolophine' hadrosaurids in the late Cretaceous. The nature of this late Cretaceous link is peculiar, because the ceratopids, a very diverse group in the late Cretaceous of North America, never managed to spread back across the Bering Straits into Asia, as one might expect in the light of the distribution of other dinosaurs.

Right: Parts of the skull and body armour of the Mongolian ankylosaur *Shamosaurus scutatus.* The general shape of the skull and the bony projections jutting out from it are typically ankylosaurian.

Left: The BM (NH) specimen of *Scolosaurus* (= *Euoplocephalus) cutleri* which is from the Belly River Formation at Red Deer River, Alberta. We are looking down on the back of the fossil, which lacks its skull, and the nature of the bony armour bands studded with plates, embedded in its skin are clear to see.

Left: The skull and partial skeleton of *Saichania* are gradually exposed during excavations at Khulsan in the Gobi Desert undertaken by the 1971 Polish-Mongolian Palaeontological Expedition. The skull (right) is covered with knobbly studs, while a multitude of triangular spikes can be made out around the neck and back. *Saichania's* forelimbs were also found to be fairly well preserved.

Above: Another Mongolian ankylosaurid: *Talarurus plicatospinus.* This is a very well preserved skeleton, and this view nicely shows the rather squat posture and broad hippo-like chest typical of ankylosaurs. The body was evidently covered in bony nodules, but there is no evidence of any tall, *Euoplocephalus*-like spikes projecting from the back or tail of this animal. Note the heavily armoured head.

PTEROSAURS

The following section of the book is devoted to a few of the other groups of animals that were contemporaries of the dinosaurs during the Mesozoic Era. It is not intended to be a completely comprehensive review, but it serves to highlight some of the more interesting non-dinosaurian types.

The pterosaurs or 'wing reptiles' were contemporaries of the dinosaurs throughout the Triassic, Jurassic and Cretaceous Periods; they also appear to be quite close relatives of the dinosaurs. Both dinosaurs and pterosaurs evolved from small, agile archosaurs in the late Triassic. However, while the dinosaurs rose to dominance on land, the pterosaurs became the first specialist flying vertebrates.

Because of the constraints imposed upon flying animals, their bodies were of necessity extremely light and delicate; this factor, allied to the fact that they lived in the air, militates very strongly against their remains being preserved as fossils. Nevertheless numerous, sometimes spectacularly well-preserved fossils of pterosaurs have been discovered over the last two centuries which provide ample evidence of pterosaurian biology. The vast majority of fossil remains of pterosaurs come from marine deposits; this has led to the widespread belief that they lived lives similar to those of modern sea-birds such as terns and albatrosses. However, it is also probable that there were a considerable number of inland forms, but (for the reasons mentioned above) the likelihood of fossilised remains of these types being preserved is extremely slight.

Early Discoveries

One of the earliest discoveries of any pterosaur dates back to 1784, when an Italian naturalist Cosmo Alessandro Collini discovered a well preserved skeleton in a limestone quarry in Eichstätt (southern Germany). The small size and extraordinary light construction of the fossil proved most perplexing to those who first studied it. Collini assumed that it was some sort of aquatic creature, while others suggested bat or bird-like affinities. It was not until the early years of the 19th century that the reptilian nature of this fossil was established by the eminent French comparative anatomist, Georges Cuvier. Cuvier recognised that the fourth finger of the creature was enormously elongated and speculated that it supported a wing. On the strength of these observations he named the fossil *Pterodactylus* ('wing finger') — a reptile totally unlike any found living today. Despite Cuvier's pronouncements, several scientists (notably one named Johannes Wagler) persisted with the idea that *Pterodactylus* was a swimmer and provided a restoration of this creature as a penguin-like animal. The debate over the habits of *Pterodactylus* rumbled on into the 1830s as more remains were discovered both in Britain and Europe. In 1837 Hermann von Meyer pointed out that several bones of the *Pterodactylus* had openings for air passages (pneumatic ducts) running through them. The only sensible interpretation for this was that these skeletons were lightened specifically for flight, in the same way as those of living birds.

Being such extraordinarily specialised creatures, at least by conventional reptilian standards, pterodactyls attracted a great deal of interest in the latter half of the century. E. T. Newton was able to show in 1888 that pterosaurs (*Scaphognathus*, 'tusk jaw', from the early Jurassic of Yorkshire, England) had a remarkably bird-like brain. One fine partial skull of *Scaphognathus* was preserved in such a way

that a natural endocranial cast was obtained. This suggested that pterosaurs had bird-like intelligence, as indeed befitted such obviously sophisticated flying creatures. Newton's original work was amply confirmed by the palaeoneurologist Tilly Edinger in the early 1940s. Upon preparation, a small well-preserved specimen of *Pterodactylus* revealed a very fine endocranial cast (more perfect than that of Newton's) confirming the remarkable similarity in brain structure between these two groups, right down to the pattern of folds in the surface of the brain itself.

The early work on pterosaurs was reviewed by Professor Harry Govier Seeley in his book *Dragons of the Air* in 1901. Seeley concluded that the pterosaurs (ornithosaurs as he called them) were remarkable among reptiles. They were highly specialised flying creatures with large brains and therefore high levels of sensitivity and control; they had complex lungs and a bird-like air-sac system — again associated with high levels of activity. He also reasoned that they must have had very efficient fully divided bird- or mammal-like hearts. All this

pointed to the strong probability that pterosaurs were endothermic ('warm blooded'), highly active creatures more similar to bats and birds than to the lizards of today. If Seeley was correct, then small creatures such as this should have possessed an insulation layer of fur or feather-like material to prevent excessive rates of heat loss especially when flying. Claim and counterclaim had been made concerning the absence of a furry covering to pterosaurs ever since it was first suggested from fossil remains examined by Goldfuss in the 1830s. Finally in 1970 A. G. Sharov (Moscow) collected several pterosaur fossils from the Jurassic of Kazakhstan. Some of these rocks preserved fossils in remarkable detail. One such fossil was named *Sordes pilosus* ('hairy devil') because fine impressions were left around the body of not only the wings, but also a 'furry' covering — finally confirming Seeley's conclusion of 1901.

North America also had its share of pterosaurs. Again the Cope-Marsh feud figures in the story of the early recognition of pterosaurs from North America. In 1870 O. C. Marsh and Colonel William F. Cody ('Buffalo Bill') led an expedition

Above: *Pterodactylus kochi.*
This specimen is very well preserved, as are many fossils from the Bavarian limestone. This is a small, probably juvenile individual; note the short 'pterodactyloid' tail.

Right: *Rhamphorhynchus.*
This is a cast from the British Museum (Natural History) and shows one of the very fine 'rhamphorhynchoid' pterosaurs (note the long tail). It even bears the impression of wing membranes and the tail-kite.

from Yale College (as the University was then known) into the Rockies. In late Cretaceous rocks of western Kansas, Marsh discovered not only large marine reptiles (plesiosaurs and mosasaurs), but also the first remains of pterosaurs (broken finger bones). At first these were puzzling, because although they seemed similar to the pterosaur remains of Europe, they indicated animals with wing-spans of 23ft (7m) or so — far larger than any previously reported. By 1872 both Marsh and Cope had enough pterosaur material from Kansas to merit naming them. Marsh named his *Pterodactylus* after the European types, while Cope chose the name *Ornithochirus* ('bird arm'). More material collected by S. W. Williston for Marsh revealed several unusual features, which prompted Marsh to propose a new name, *Pteranodon* ('winged and toothless'), for his Kansas *Pterodactylus*; this was an extraordinary creature with a long pointed, toothless beak, a long bony crest at the back of the skull and an enormous wing-span.

Until quite recently *Pteranodon* was thought to have been the largest of all flying vertebrates.

In 1972, however, opinions were forced to change. Douglas Lawson (California) found the remains of some ultra-large pterosaurs at Big Bend National Park in Texas. Although far from complete, these remains, called *Quetzalcoatlus* ('feathered serpent' — named after an Aztec god) indicate the existence of pterosaurs with 50ft (15m) wing-spans (equivalent in size to a small light-aircraft).

The prevailing view of pterosaur habits is that they were large, broad winged, bat-like gliders. Their relatively small hindlimbs were supposed to have left them incapable of walking effectively on land, forcing them to shuffle along on all-fours with the fourth finger swept up in the air. In view of this it seems likely that they roosted on oceanic islands where they would have been safe from predators (especially dinosaurs). These traditional views have been challenged in recent years by Dr Kevin Padian (California), as we shall see later.

Pterosaurs Described

Eudimorphodon ('true two-form tooth') comes from the late Triassic of Italy and is therefore a very early pterosaur; it was described quite recently by Dr Rupert Wild (Stuttgart). The skull of *Eudimorphodon* is long and tapering (reminiscent of that of some 'coelurosaurs' with a large eye and enlarged braincase. The snout is slender but possesses a row of well-developed spiky teeth; those near the front of the jaw are simple spikes, while

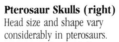

'Pterodactyloid'

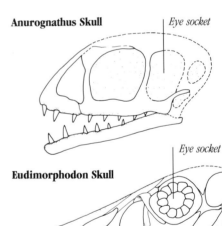

Pterosaur Sizes (right)
Here we see a typical medium to large-sized 'rhampho-rhynchoid' with 6·6ft (2m) wing-span (near right) and a large 'pterodactyloid' with 39ft (12m) wing-span. Much smaller 'sparrow-sized' pterosaurs are also known.

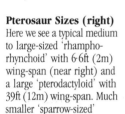

'Rhamphorhynchoid'

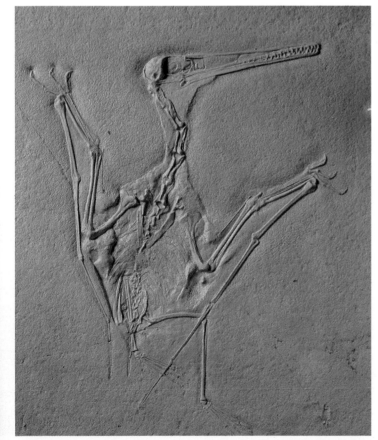

Pterosaur Skulls (right)
Head size and shape vary considerably in pterosaurs. *Anurognathus* (top) has a 'primitive' shape with a deep skull, while *Eudimorphodon* and *Dorygnathus* show the more typical long-snouted head. *Pterodaustro* has a comb-like array of teeth, possibly for sieving plankton.

Left: This an adult *Pterodactylus kochi* also from Bavaria (compare with the juvenile shown on the opposite page). Note in particular how much longer the neck and head are in the adult individual.

Anurognathus Skull   *Eye socket*

Eudimorphodon Skull   *Eye socket*

Dorygnathus Skull   *Eye socket*

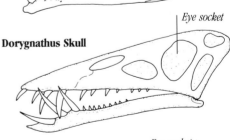

Pterodaustro Skull   *Eye socket*

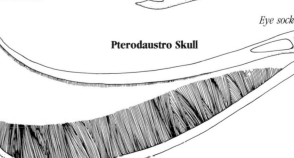

those further back in the jaws are complicated by the development of sharp jagged spikes. The long snout and arrangement of the teeth indicate a diet of fish for this creature; these may well have been plucked from the surface of the water using the long sharp teeth at the tip of the snout.

The remainder of the skeleton is typical of early pterosaurs. The neck is flexible, but relatively short; the trunk is quite short and compact so that it can support the immensely long wings; several bones are fused together to support the pelvis; and the tail is long and stiffened by a series of thin bony rods reminiscent of those in the tail of dromaeosaurid dinosaurs.

The forelimbs are fairly typical of most pterosaurs with short, stout upper arm and forearm bones attached to a powerful shoulder girdle; thse fingers are grossly modified to support the wing membrane. The first three fingers of the hand are 'normal' in that they are relatively short and end in sharp, curved claws; the fourth finger is, however, enormously elongated with four long jointed sections supporting a narrow leathery wing membrane.

The hindlimbs are also remarkable. The hips are well developed and the legs are arranged and proportioned remarkably like those of small theropod dinosaurs or birds. Incidentally, unlike many life-like illustrations of pterosaurs, their feet and legs are not twisted backward as in modern bats but are arranged quite normally. There are four well-developed walking toes and a rather unusual, narrow, spined fifth toe.

Rhamphorhynchus ('narrow beak') comes from the late Jurassic limestones of southern Germany (Bavaria) and is known in remarkable

detail. Many of the specimens of complete animals include partial evidence of wing membranes, some of these even give an impression of the nature of the fibrous tissue in the wing and its arrangement.

The skull of *Rhamphorhynchus* is very similar in proportions to that of *Eudimorphodon*. The main difference lies in the arrangement of the teeth. Unlike *Eudimorphodon* all the teeth are long, forwardly-pointing spikes, while the tips of both upper and lower jaws are long, slender and toothless. The tip of the jaws may have been covered in a horny sheath which was used to spear fish.

The remainder of the skeleton seems practically identical to that of *Eudimorphodon*. The impressions of the wing membranes in *Rhamphorhynchus* have been noted not only along the wings, but also on the hindlimbs and feet. A small kite-shaped membrane has also been preserved on the end of the tail giving it a rudder-like appearance.

Dimorphodon ('two-form tooth') from the early Jurassic of Britain (Lyme Regis) is another pterosaur which has the fairly standard *Eudimorphodon*-type body shape. It is, however, worthy of note because of the unusually deep snout of the creature. The skull is obviously large in proportion to its body, and yet still retains a very light construction with thin spars of bone connecting the important areas of the skull (braincase, eye sockets, jaws). This pterosaur derives its name from its teeth; those near the front of the jaw are tall and spiky, while those at the rear are very small and numerous.

The reason for the unusual shape of the skull in *Dimorphodon* is not immediately apparent, but was presumably related to its diet. Unlike

the two previous examples, *Dimorphodon* may have preyed upon insects or small vertebrates which it caught either on the wing or on the ground; this sort of diet would best suit the type of teeth in this skull.

Pterodactylus ('wing finger') comes from the late Jurassic of southern Germany (Bavaria) from the same deposits in which *Rhamphorhynchus* is found. *Pterodactylus*, however, shows a radical departure in shape from that seen in the three previous examples. Its head is even longer and more slender and the teeth somewhat reduced in size and number; the neck is considerably longer; the tail is notably much reduced in length, and the fifth toe (which is long and spine-like in previous examples) is almost gone. This pattern of features is common to most of the later pterosaurs of the Jurassic and Cretaceous Periods; these have as a consequence been called 'pterodactyloids', as opposed to the earlier forms which are frequently termed 'rhamphorhynchoids'. The 'pterodactyloid' design was evidently quite successful, because by the beginning of the Cretaceous the 'rhamphorhynchoids' were all extinct. *Pterodactylus* (of which there are several species) was a small, presumably highly manoeuvrable flyer, and may well have preyed upon small insects caught upon the wing.

Pteranodon ('winged and toothless') represents one of the high points in pterosaur evolution. These huge pterosaurs of the late Cretaceous are structurally quite similar to *Pterodactylus*. However, the skull is even more elongate with a long, narrow, completely toothless beak, behind which the skull had a long counterbalancing crest.

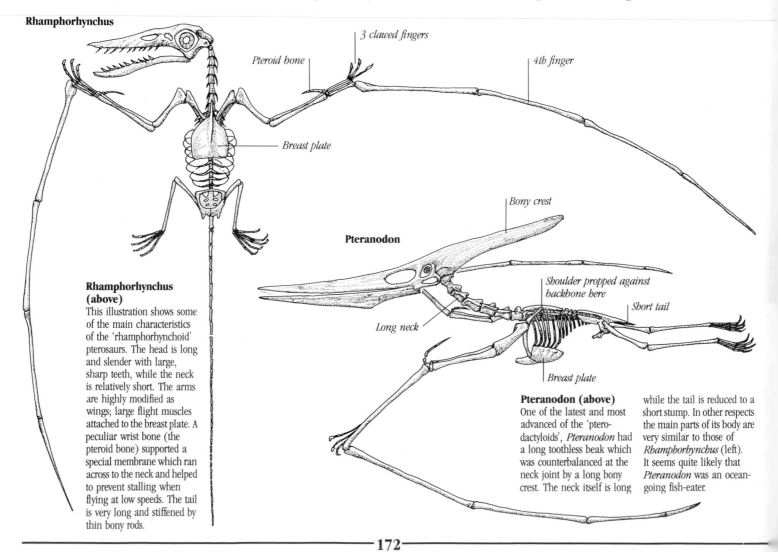

Rhamphorhynchus

3 clawed fingers

Pteroid bone

4th finger

Breast plate

Bony crest

Pteranodon

Shoulder propped against backbone here

Short tail

Long neck

Breast plate

Rhamphorhynchus (above)
This illustration shows some of the main characteristics of the 'rhamphorhynchoid' pterosaurs. The head is long and slender with large, sharp teeth, while the neck is relatively short. The arms are highly modified as wings; large flight muscles attached to the breast plate. A peculiar wrist bone (the pteroid bone) supported a special membrane which ran across to the neck and helped to prevent stalling when flying at low speeds. The tail is very long and stiffened by thin bony rods.

Pteranodon (above)
One of the latest and most advanced of the 'ptero-dactyloids', *Pteranodon* had a long toothless beak which was counterbalanced at the neck joint by a long bony crest. The neck itself is long while the tail is reduced to a short stump. In other respects the main parts of its body are very similar to those of *Rhamphorhynchus* (left). It seems quite likely that *Pteranodon* was an ocean-going fish-eater.

It seems very likely that *Pteranodon* was an ocean-going pterosaur, broadly equivalent to the albatrosses of today. Its beak was undoubtedly horn-covered and there was a pouch of skin between the lower jaws which served to store fish, just as pelicans do today. The crest, which was evidently variably developed, probably served to counterbalance the long snout, especially when plucking fish from the ocean surface.

Pterodaustro ('southern wing') and *Dsungaripterus* ('wing from Jungarr') represent remarkably divergent types of pterodactyloid; both are from the early Cretaceous. *Pterodaustro* from Argentina displays a remarkably fine comb-like arrangement of teeth. Very probably *Pterodaustro* was a plankton feeder skimming over the surface with its lower jaw in the water and combing out minute animals and plants on its teeth. *Dsungaripterus* from Xinjiang (Sinkiang) in China is remarkable for

the unusual crest on its skull and its peculiar jaws and teeth. The skull alone is 16in (41cm) long. What its diet may have been is a complete mystery.

Pterosaur Habits

In the late 1970s and early 1980s Dr Kevin Padian reviewed pterosaur biology in some detail to see if he agreed with general opinions held concerning pterosaur habits. A detailed review of pterosaur anatomy, in particular that of various 'rhamphorhynchoids', enabled him to suggest that (i) most pterosaurs were active *fliers*, rather than gliders as often supposed; (ii) that pterosaurs were able to flap their wings using a system very similar to that of living birds; (iii) that the wing in pterosaurs was very narrow and *not* attached to the hindlimb as often proposed; (iv) that the hindlimb was very like that of birds and theropod dinosaurs and,

since pterosaurs could not have walked on all-fours because of limitations in the wing, they must have walked or run *bipedally* on land!

Most of these proposals (i-iii) are quite acceptable and are regarded as much-needed improvements to our view of pterosaur life-styles. The suggestion that pterosaurs could walk and run bipedally, however, is still quite controversial. Padian provided a remarkable reconstruction of *Dimorphodon* scampering along with its wing neatly folded back, and the long tail counterbalancing the body at the hips. There does, however, seem to be rather a large part of the body in front of the feet for a dynamic balance to be feasible, and exactly how the larger tailless 'pterodactyloids' would have managed is not clear. Nevertheless, despite these slight misgivings, Dr Padian has done a great service in highlighting many aspects of pterosaurian biology that have been overlooked for many years.

Left: The partial remains of *Rhamphorhynchus longimanus* which were found in Bavarian slate. This specimen was evidently partially rotted and disturbed before burial. Despite this, the head and one of the wings are well preserved.

Above: *Dsungaripterus* is a remarkable form from China. The front of the jaws are shaped like long forceps and were probably covered in horn. The teeth behind are broad and flattened. These animals may have winkled out shellfish and snails.

Below: One of the earlier pterosaurs, *Dimorphodon*, like *Anurognathus* (page 171), had a more typical reptile-like skull with large, heavy jaws and teeth. The large spaces and thin bony struts in the head were weight-saving features.

Dimorphodon (left)
This new reconstruction of *Dimorphodon* in a running position is based on the work of Dr Kevin Padian. The legs appear to have been well-suited for running, and the head is counterbalanced by the tail, and in part by the long fourth finger which supported the wing membrane.

This view is in marked contrast to most drawings of pterosaurs on the ground in which they are seen on all-fours with arms and legs spread out. While this posture seems plausible for 'primitive' tailed pterosaurs, the later tailless forms, such as *Pteranodon*, present enormous problems of balance.

The crocodiles are a remarkable group of reptiles which, like the pterosaurs, are quite close relatives of the dinosaurs; they appear to have evolved from archosaurian ancestors during the late Triassic. However, their history is very different from that of the pterosaurs and dinosaurs because crocodiles have survived right through to the present day. For some reason they avoided the extinctions that affected so many groups of animals at the end of the Cretaceous. One of the most notable characters of this group is its enormous conservatism. Once crocodiles appeared in the Triassic Period as moderate to large-sized semi-aquatic predators their fate was sealed, and they have changed relatively little in body-form since then.

Modern crocodilians are found in tropical and subtropical environments and are of two major types. One group, the crocodylids, consists of the crocodiles and alligators of almost world-wide distribution; the gavialids comprise the slender-snouted fish-eating gavials (gharials) of India.

The ferocious alligators and crocodiles have relatively broad diets taking fish, large vertebrates (including humans!) and carrion whenever possible. Large vertebrates are generally caught in or near water by stealth. The attributes that allow crocodilians to feed in this way summarise many of their typical features. Crocodilians are long-bodied reptiles with a long and extremely powerful tail which is used for swimming, and as a defensive lash on land. The limbs are relatively short in proportion to their body length and are used for manoeuvring and steering in water. On land crocodiles and alligators mostly walk with a slow, measured stride with the belly held quite high off the ground. Although their legs do not seem particularly powerful, crocodiles are capable of short bursts of fast running on land either to catch prey or return quickly to the water. While these comments apply to adult crocodiles, this is not true of young crocodilians; these by contrast have disproportionately long legs and are remarkably active on land as well as in the water. Unlike the adults, young crocodiles feed on small vertebrates (frogs, fish) and a variety of insects and can, on occasions, even be found climbing in low shrubs in pursuit of their prey! Adults use the powerful tail to swim close to potential prey, they remain almost completely submerged, with just eyes and nostrils breaking the water. The eyes are specially positioned on top of the skull, and the nostrils are similarly located right at the tip of the snout and have special valves to close them off when the animals are completely submerged. Crocodiles also have a special bony roof to the mouth so that the air passage from the nostrils to the lungs is separated from the mouth — a neat way of avoiding drowning when trying to breathe while semi-submerged. The jaws of crocodiles are long and lined with large conical teeth which are very deeply rooted in the jaws. These jaws and teeth are well suited to overcoming large active prey such as wild pigs or antelope; the skull is also very heavily constructed in order to withstand the severe stresses and strains of violently struggling animals. Once killed, either directly or by drowning, the prey generally has to be dismembered prior to swallowing. This is done in a variety of ways: moderate-sized prey tends to be lifted out of the water and vigorously shaken from side to side until it is torn into pieces that can be swallowed with ease; larger prey are more difficult and their carcasses are often wedged under rocks or fallen trees beneath water. This

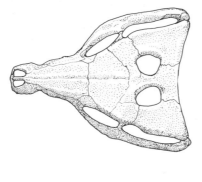

Above: Contemporary crocodiles are ferocious predators in tropical lakes and streams. Their prey ranges from large fish that are swallowed whole to much larger animals, such as antelopes, which are usually caught at water-holes when they come down to drink. Crocodiles are not able to chew off large pieces of meat as a lion can, so they have to tear such carcasses apart underwater. The crocodiles are one of the existing links to the Mesozoic Era. They survived the mass-extinction at the end of the Cretaceous.

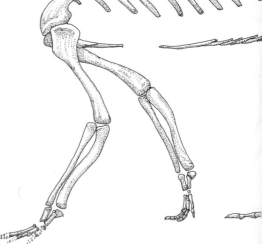

Protosuchus Skeleton and Skull (above and right)
These two reconstructions of the late Triassic crocodile *Protosuchus* are based on the work of Charles Mook and Edwin Colbert. Compared with modern crocodilians, *Protosuchus* is rather unusual. Its head is low and broad, and the snout, which is so typically long in modern forms, is really quite short and narrow. The remainder of the skeleton is also noteworthy. This was a small animal (c. 3·3ft, 1m long) and it had a slender build with a short trunk and long legs that lifted the belly quite high off the ground. Its back was armour-plated quite extensively (not shown here). *Protosuchus* may have spent much of its time on land.

Above: The little-known and studied gharial (*Gavialis gangeticus*) is an exclusively fish-eating crocodilian. Note the long snout lined with sharp teeth for gripping slippery fish. The lump on the tip of the snout develops in mature individuals.

Left: Crocodilians are very agile when young, chasing and catching insects in particular. This habit even takes them into trees in pursuit of prey. This young alligator has obviously graduated to larger prey but is being rather ambitious in his attempt to catch this fledgling egret.

Right: This well-preserved crocodile skull dates from the early part of the Tertiary Period. The proportions of the snout provide a clue to its probable diet; the long slender snout is similar to that seen in fish-eating types today (see photograph at top right).

allows the crocodile to take a firm hold of a desired portion (such as a leg) and then twist violently round and round underwater, using legs and tail, until the piece is torn off. All these peculiar manoeuvres are necessary because crocodiles have stabbing teeth rather than slicing teeth, and are therefore unable to chew off pieces of any prey too big to be swallowed whole.

Another notable feature of crocodiles and alligators is the heavy bony armour-plating of their backs. The body armour is undoubtedly valuable protection against predators, particularly for younger crocodiles which may be preyed upon by birds and large monitor lizards. The need for well-developed armour in adults is less obvious because there are no natural predators of these animals, and presumably simply reflects its importance for the young animals. However, another rather unexpected 'use' for body armour seems to be emerging from recent work by Frey and Reiss in Tübingen. They have demonstrated that the body armour is firmly attached to the muscles and bones of the back and lends a great deal of support to this area of the back above the hips during locomotion on land. In fact, it could be that the development of body armour down the back was a crucial step in the evolutionary line that in the Triassic led to the dinosaurs appearing on land.

Gharials (or gavials) are a peculiar group of fish-eating crocodiles which are today restricted to Indian rivers. They are quite large animals characterised by a very long and narrow snout fringed with even, sharply-pointed teeth. These adaptations are ideally suited to fish-eating and are not seen developed to quite the same degree in other living crocodiles.

Mesozoic Crocodilians

In the Mesozoic, crocodilians of various sorts are known, some from very well preserved fossil material. Some such examples are described below. *Protosuchus* ('first crocodile') is a small (3·3ft, 1m long) primitive crocodilian from the late Triassic or possibly early Jurassic of Arizona. It was first described by Barnum Brown in the 1930s from material originally collected by Navajo Indians and later from more fossils including 6 partial skeletons. In 1951 Professor Edwin Colbert and Charles Mook described the best material of *Protosuchus*. *Protosuchus* has rather different proportions from modern crocodiles. The head is quite short and broad, with a rather narrow snout. The neck and back are also short and the tail is of only moderate length—generally a much more 'compact' creature than those of today. The limbs accentuate the differences as well; as in all archosaurs the hindlimbs are longer than the forelimbs, but again the limbs are remarkably long for a crocodilian.

Protosuchus was evidently primarily a terrestrial crocodilian, an active land-living predator. This conclusion accords not only with the proportions of the body and limbs, but also with the head which has eyes and nostrils positioned on the side of the head rather than on top as in modern crocodilians.

Orthosuchus ('straight crocodile') is another early crocodilian, this time from the late Triassic of Lesotho (southern Africa). Orthosuchus was discovered by a team of collectors from the South African Museum (Cape Town) in 1963. Described in detail in 1975 by Dr Diane Nash (Bath, UK) Orthosuchus bears a strong resemblance to Protosuchus in its general proportions. Again it is rather a short-bodied creature. However, its limbs appear somewhat shorter than those of Protosuchus and there is less disparity between fore and hindlimbs. The skull has a rather unusual pattern of teeth compared with that of Protosuchus, but otherwise its proportions are remarkably similar. Nash proposed that the narrow-snouted form of the skull and relatively feeble teeth may indicate that Orthosuchus preyed upon fish rather than larger terrestrial vertebrates and suggested, albeit tentatively, that Orthosuchus may have inhabited swampy areas to avoid competition with early carnivorous dinosaurs and large predatory thecodontians.

More typical crocodilians are found in the Jurassic Period. Teleosaurus ('end reptile') and Steneosaurus ('narrow reptile') are two reasonably well-known early Jurassic forms. These types of crocodile appear to have been marine or possibly estuarine inhabitants. They have

typical long-bodied crocodile-like bodies, and have notably elongate snouts lined with thin sharp teeth indicating that they were primarily fish eaters. Despite their obvious preference for the aquatic habitat, these forms retained the typical heavily-armoured body and well-developed limbs and feet—unlike the next type.

Metriorhynchus ('long snout') and Geosaurus ('rock reptile') are members of a very distinctive group of Jurassic crocodilians sometimes referred to as thallatosuchians ('sea crocodiles'). These long-snouted, presumably fish-eating crocodiles were completely un-armoured and their limbs were modified into turtle-like flippers or paddles. The paddle-like limbs, however, were not the main propulsive organs; this was the tail which was similarly modified into fish-like form by the development of a tail fin. The end of the tail was bent sharply downward in order to strengthen the fin in the same way as in the tail fins of the dolphin-like ichthyosaurs (see pages 178-180). For some reason these 'sea crocodiles' were not particularly successful because they seem to have gone extinct in late Jurassic times.

Modern types of crocodile begin to appear toward the end of the Jurassic Period in the form of crocodiles such as Goniopholis a 6·5-10ft (2-3m) long, reasonably typical crocodile which is found fairly widespread across Europe at about this time. Two rather fine Goniopholis skeletons were found at Bernissart among the many Iguanodon carcasses. Whether Goniopholis was actually scavenging the carcasses or was merely preserved there by accident is impossible to decide.

In addition to Goniopholis, another interesting crocodilian specimen was found among the Iguanodon carcasses at Bernissart. This tiny crocodilian, less than 3ft (1m) long, was named Bernissartia by Louis Dollo in 1885. Bernissartia was small but well-armoured, and had rather peculiar teeth in its jaws. The front teeth were normal simple spikes; the posterior teeth, however, were unusually broad and flattened—

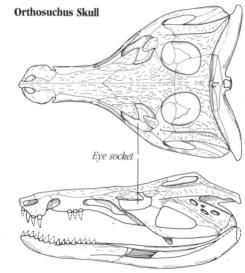

Orthosuchus Skull

Eye socket

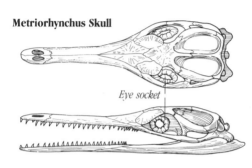

Metriorhynchus Skull

Eye socket

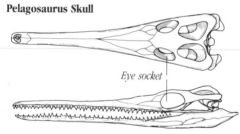

Pelagosaurus Skull

Eye socket

Crocodile Skulls (right)
The variety of skull shapes in crocodilians can be appreciated here. Orthosuchus from the late Triassic of southern Africa is broad and short-snouted as is Protosuchus (page 174). Metriorhynchus and Pelagosaurus show an extreme elongation of the snout that suggests a fish diet, while Crocodylus is a broad and powerful general predator.

Left: This fossilised bony armour plate (or scute) of Diplocynodon is typically crocodilian having a rough and pitted texture.

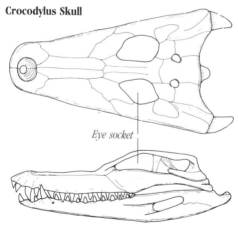

Crocodylus Skull

Eye socket

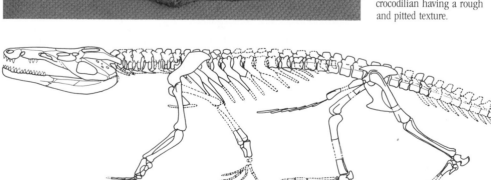

Orthosuchus Skeleton (below)
Based on Diane Nash's study of new material collected from Southern Africa in the 1960s, this reconstruction of Orthosuchus is broadly similar to Protosuchus (page 174). The jaws and rather feeble teeth suggest that Orthosuchus was a swamp-dweller feeding on fish, rather than a land-living predator.

shaped more like crushing plates than piercing teeth. Perhaps these unusual little crocodiles had a varied diet including shellfish. The blunt posterior teeth may have served as crushing plates to crack open the hard shells of clams, while the sharp front teeth could be used for grasping more conventional soft-bodied prey such as fish.

During the Cretaceous Period, the crocodilians were very abundant and widespread, far more so than today. This probably reflects the fact that the conditions were much milder than they are at the present time. Records of warmth-loving plants from the Mesozoic Era indicate that tropical or subtropical conditions extended into the temperate and subarctic regions of today.

One of the most remarkable of the Cretaceous crocodiles comes from the Rio Grande in Texas. Named *Deinosuchus* ('terrible crocodile') or *Phobosuchus* ('fearsome crocodile') this is the largest crocodile so far found. Although incomplete, *Deinosuchus* had a skull measuring 6ft (1·8m) in length. If this creature had the proportions of a typical crocodile then it may have attained a length of 40-50ft (12-15m). It seems quite possible that *Deinosuchus* preyed upon dinosaurs in the late Cretaceous. *Deinosuchus* was either a typical amphibious crocodile preying upon occasional wading sauropods or hadrosaurs, or as some have proposed it may have been a short-bodied, longer-legged terrestrial predator of dinosaurs. It would obviously be interesting to find more remains of this remarkable crocodilian.

Recent Crocodilians

In addition to the comments already made about living crocodiles, a few other points need to be considered because they have a bearing on later sections of this book concerned with the origin of dinosaurs (page 186) and the debate on the physiology of dinosaurs (page 188).

Crocodile ankles As was mentioned earlier, crocodiles are able to adopt an unusually high gait when they walk (i.e. the belly is held very high off the ground). As a result the legs are drawn in very nearly underneath the body. This so-called 'semi-erect' position is a more efficient method of walking than the sprawling posture used by most other reptiles in which the belly is very close to the ground and the legs splay outward. However, in order to walk like this crocodiles have developed rather special ankle joints which have a special swivel section in the middle; this permits powerful twisting movements to occur at the ankle during the 'high walk'. As was seen (page 36), the unusual ankle and 'high walk' of the crocodile figure large in the origin of dinosaur walking methods.

Crocodilian behaviour It has often been alleged in the past that reptiles are rather 'simple' creatures and therefore incapable of the complex types of behaviour seen in living mammals and birds. On this basis it has been argued that as several types of dinosaur seem to show evidence of complex behaviour, dinosaurs must be more like mammals and birds than reptiles.

Hugh Cott, an authority on crocodilians, has been able to show quite conclusively that crocodiles are capable of very complex behaviour indeed. One of the best examples of such behaviour is the exhibition of parental care in the Nile crocodile. In this species the hatchling crocodiles call to their parents from the nest mound. This stimulates the parent crocodiles to break open the nest and release the young; these are then carried in the jaws of the parents to special 'nurseries' where their growth and development is watched over to prevent predators from taking the young. They are finally released when they are large enough to defend themselves against potential predators. All this information is comparatively recent work based on the field observations of Hugh Cott who has done more than anyone else to further our understanding of these remarkable animals. Its implications with regard to our view of dinosaurs and their possible behavioural patterns as well as those of living reptiles have been of great value.

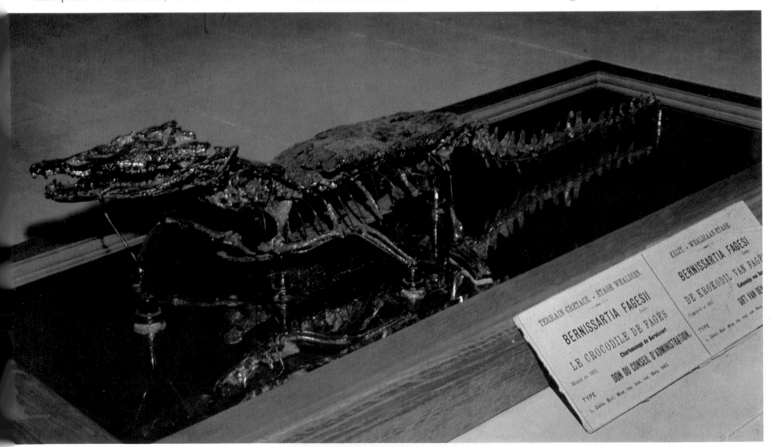

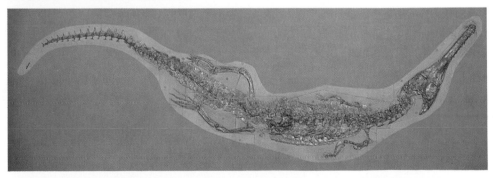

Above: *Bernissartia fagesii*; this remarkable little crocodile was found among the *Iguanodon* skeletons at Bernissart. It may have been scavenging the flesh of the dinosaur carcasses when it was buried. However, the blunt rear teeth may point to a diet of shellfish. It was named after Gustav Fagès, the manager of the mine at Bernissart.

Right: *Steneosaurus*, a Jurassic crocodile, is typical of a variety that became well adapted to a purely aquatic way of life in the Mesozoic. Note the long body well suited to swimming, and the relatively small forelimbs. A diet of fish is indicated by the long snout. This was most probably an estuarine rather than an ocean-going form.

In addition to the various archosaurian types of reptile (pterosaurs and crocodiles), a number of other groups of reptiles co-existed with the dinosaurs during the Mesozoic Era. Many of these were aquatic forms of considerable variety. Representatives of these types of reptile are described below.

Ichthyosaurs

Of all the varied reptilian types the ichthyosaurs ('fish reptiles') are by far the most highly adapted to an aquatic life-style. They seem to have occupied the niche now taken by porpoises of the present day. The earliest ichthyosaurs date back to the late Triassic. Even these, however, are clearly ichthyosaurs and give few clues to the earlier origin of these reptiles. Ichthyosaurs were particularly abundant in the Jurassic Period, although their remains extend into the late Cretaceous as well.

Mixosaurus ('mixed reptile') from the late Triassic is an early ichthyosaur that already possesses a full range of ichthyosaur characteristics. The head is drawn out into a long thin snout fringed with small spiky teeth; the eyes are unusually large and supported by a circular array of bones which probably improved the focusing abilities. The body is smooth and streamlined for efficient movement through the water and the neck is notably absent in profile view; this was achieved by great compression of the neck vertebrae (a similar phenomenon is seen in porpoises today). The limbs are modified into paddles which may have been used for steering rather than for propulsion. The tail is long and tapering, but near its base the spines are notably elongate suggesting the presence of an auxiliary fin to assist the propulsive action of the tail.

Temnodontosaurus ('cutting toothed reptile') is an example of an early Jurassic ichthyosaur; it was one of the largest of all ichthyosaurs, some individuals reaching lengths of as much as 30ft (9m). Originally described as *Ichthyosaurus* on the basis of a single tooth by William Conybeare in 1822, the original has unfortunately been lost. In his review of lower Jurassic ichthyosaurs of Britain Dr Chris McGowan (Ontario) designated another complete skeleton from a similar locality as a new representative of this genus. The form of this ichthyosaur is little different from that of *Mixosaurus* except that its snout has a greater number of teeth, the eye is a little larger and, most notably the tail has a more fish-like shape. Instead of the enlarged fin near the base of the tail of *Mixosaurus, Temnodontosaurus* has its tail bones curved down near their tip to support a broad paddle-like fin. Skin impressions of several ichthyosaurs have been found at several localities in southern Germany which reveal that the tail 'fluke' also extended upward, and was presumably supported by a stiffened bar of tissue. A fish-like dorsal fin was also present along the back to improve stability.

Ophthalmosaurus ('eye reptile'), also from the Jurassic, was named for the particularly large size of its eyes. Although typically ichthyosaurian, *Ophthalmosaurus* is notable for its apparent total lack of teeth.

Our knowledge of the feeding and reproductive habits of ichthyosaurs has been improved by the discovery of several beautifully-preserved ichthyosaur skeletons which include the fossilized soft tissues within the rib cage. Examination of these reveals that ichthyosaurs fed upon cephalopods, fish and occasionally pterosaurs. Several skeletons have also revealed the presence of embryos within the body cavity of a mother ichthyosaur; one such appears to have been preserved at the moment of birth of the young baby! As in porpoises, the baby was born tail first. The necessity of bearing live young, rather than laying eggs as many reptiles do, reflects the fact that ichthyosaurs were so highly adapted to life in the water that they were unable even to crawl onto land to lay their eggs in the manner of living turtles.

Plesiosaurs

Plesiosaurs ('ribbon reptiles') are another very important group of marine reptiles of the Mesozoic. Less obviously fish-like than the ichthyosaurs, they were nevertheless well

Ichthyosaur Skull

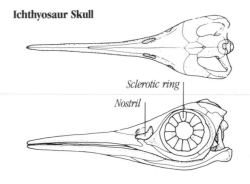

Sclerotic ring

Nostril

Above: This finely preserved fossil of *Ichthyosaurus acutirostris* shows not only the details of the skeleton (including the 'kink' in the tail), but also the outline of the skin.

Ichthyosaur Skeleton (below)
Many ichthyosaur skeletons have been found. The streamlined body shape is very similar to that of fast-swimming porpoises.

Ophthalmosaurus Skull (above right)
The skull of this Jurassic ichthyosaur has a very long, slender, toothless snout, and a large eye socket with a ring of bony plates.

Plesiosaur Skull (below right)
This is a typical plesiosaur skull. The snout is broad and flat, and armed with large teeth. These creatures may have fed on fish.

Plesiosaur Skull

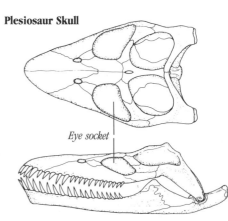

Eye socket

Ichthyosaur

Cryptoclidus (below)
This long-necked plesiosaur is shown in a fast swimming position with front flippers fully raised ready to be swept downwards powerfully. (Reconstruction based on the work of Dr David Brown).

Plesiosaur

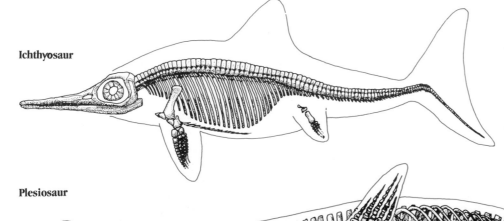

adapted for a marine existence. Unlike the ichthyosaurs, many plesiosaurs have relatively short tails and long necks. The body is broad and quite compact with closely-set strong ribs and well-developed gastralia lining the belly area. The limbs are also very large and bear well-developed paddles which were undoubtedly their main means of propulsion. A careful study of plesiosaur paddles and limb girdles by Dr Jane Robinson revealed that instead of being pulled backward and forward like the oars of a rowing boat, the paddles were flapped up and down much like the 'wings' of a penguin or the paddles of a turtle.

The long-necked or 'plesiosauroid' plesiosaurs, such as *Elasmosaurus* ('plated reptile') and *Plesiosaurus* ('ribbon reptile') had relatively small heads armed with sharply-pointed teeth. Most probably these were fish-eaters using the neck rather like a sling to 'throw' the head at the prey in a very rapid darting movement.

Short-necked or 'pliosauroid' plesiosaurs seem to have been more like the killer whales of today. Powerfully built with enormous heads — one particularly large pliosauroid, *Kronosaurus* ('time reptile') from Queensland, Australia, has a head nearly 8ft (2·4m) long — these animals must have been formidable predators of most aquatic creatures including other plesiosaurs, ichthyosaurs (if it could catch them!), giant turtles and large ammonites. They lived at the same time as the mosasaurs.

On a historical note, *Elasmosaurus*, a very long-necked Cretaceous 'plesiosauroid' from Kansas, may well have been the unwitting cause of the bitter but highly productive feud between O. C. Marsh and E. D. Cope. According to Adrian Desmond who has researched the history of the Marsh-Cope feud, the event which sparked off the aggressively competitive spirit between these two men occurred after Cope had described the newly-discovered skeleton of *Elasmosaurus* in 1868. In so doing he had mistakenly placed the head of the animal on the tip of its tail! At a meeting between Marsh and Cope, Marsh was able to demonstrate to Cope that he had made this rather important mistake. Cope, a man of fiery disposition, found his own mistake hard to bear and this event irrevocably soured what had up to that time been a fairly cordial relationship between these two men.

Placodonts and Mosasaurs

Placodonts ('flat teeth') are a rather odd group of Triassic reptiles that seem to have taken to a mollusc diet very early on. The neck and trunk of these creatures is relatively short and generally covered in well-developed bony armour. The tail is fairly short and was evidently not always used for swimming. The limbs are short and powerful. Evidently these animals walked across the sea floor and used their claws

Above: This well-preserved plesiosaur skull, which is fossilised in a slab of limestone, is in the British Museum (Natural History) collection. Note the large, sharply-pointed teeth.

Placochelys (below) This placodont reptile skeleton shows clearly the generally turtle-like nature of these creatures. The back was very heavily armoured. The legs were flipper-like.

Above: The skeleton of the 10ft (3m) long plesiosaur *Cryptoclidus oxoniensis* as it used to be mounted in the Marine Reptile gallery of the British Museum (Natural History).

Placodont Skulls (below and right) The head of *Placochelys* (below left) is very short-jawed and powerfully constructed. The teeth are short and block-like. Their

absence from the front of the jaws suggests this area was covered by a horny beak. The skull of *Placodus* is seen in side view and looking into the roof of the mouth with the lower jaw removed

(bottom). *Placodus* retains peg-like teeth at the front of the jaws, which were used to pluck shellfish from river beds. These would have been cracked open by the massive crushing teeth.

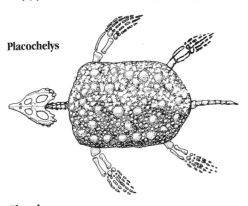

Placochelys

Placochelys Skull — *Eye socket*

Placodus Skull — *Eye socket*

Crushing teeth — *Peg-like teeth*

Placodus Skeleton (below) With its armour plating removed, *Placodus* looks

much like other reptiles. Its body is quite short and is supported by powerful legs that splay outwards.

Roof of mouth

Placodus

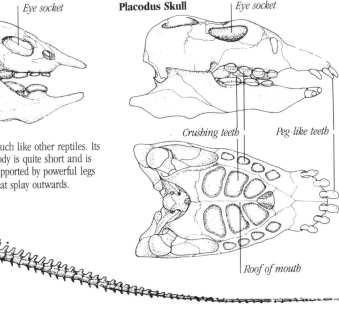

to prize clams and suchlike from rocky ledges or crevices.

The head betrays their preference for shellfish quite clearly. The teeth are highly modified. At the front of the jaws they are blunt and forwardly-pointing in order to grasp potential food; behind these teeth the sides of the jaws and roof of the mouth are covered by large, flat crushing plates. The skull also has large areas at the back for the attachment of powerful muscles to operate the jaws. These features all clearly point to a diet of hard-shelled molluscs, such as clams or mussels. The extraordinary degree of armour plating found in these animals presumably reflects the fact that they were slow-moving and therefore open to attack from various aquatic predators.

Mosasaurs ('reptiles from the Meuse') were very large (15-30ft, 4·5-9m long) marine lizards that evolved in the late Cretaceous. They are especially abundant in the Cretaceous rocks of northern Europe (Maastricht, Holland) and Kansas (USA).

The head is long and the jaws armed with long, sharp fangs—a standard pattern for most aquatic predators. The neck is quite short and the body behind particularly long and slender. As in ichthyosaurs the tail was the main swimming organ, while the limbs, which are paddle-like, were used for steering. The feet and hands have long, delicate toes which were probably webbed.

In the shape and arrangement of its bones, the skull is very similar to that of living monitor lizards. Such similarities even extend to the structure of the lower jaw, which has an extra joint half way along its length. Because of these similarities, it is suspected that living monitor lizards are close relatives of the mosasaurs.

Mosasaurs may well have been fish eaters but many were sufficiently large to have taken a whole range of large vertebrate prey. One or two mosasaurs show slightly unusual types of teeth: for example *Globidens* ('globe tooth') has rather flattened teeth which may well reveal a placodont-like predilection for shellfish.

Turtles

The earliest turtles are Triassic. A good example of a Triassic turtle is *Proganochelys* ('first turtle'). In the same way as modern turtles and tortoises, *Proganochelys* had a well-developed bony carapace; however, it seems unlikely that the head, tail or legs could be withdrawn inside the shell. Again like modern turtles, this Triassic type had a horny beak covering its jaws; however *unlike* modern forms it did retain some teeth on the roof of its mouth; the teeth may have helped to hold slippery fish in the mouth before they were swallowed.

One of the most impressive of dinosaur contemporaries among the turtles was *Archelon* ('ancient turtle'). This Cretaceous turtle grew to over 12ft (3·6m) in length. Its carapace was well developed and its flipper-like limbs were very large. A well-developed shell would have been absolutely essential to a Cretaceous turtle given the profusion of large marine predators at this time.

Proganochelys Skull

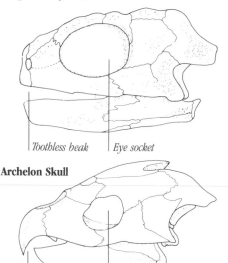

Toothless beak | Eye socket

Archelon Skull

Hooked beak | Eye socket

Above: Here we see the 'business end' of a late Cretaceous mosasaur. Apparently quite close relatives of the living monitor lizards, these must have been savage predators in the Cretaceous seas. The large head is armed with pointed teeth, while the limbs are modified into swimming flippers.

Below: *Protostega gigas* is a large marine turtle on display in the Smithsonian Institution, Washington D.C. Note the large flippers and poorly developed shell.

Below: A very well preserved shell of the turtle *Pleurosternon bullocki.* Turtle fossils are often either skulls or shells, rarely both together.

Turtle Skulls (above)
Proganochelys (top) is an early turtle of the Triassic Period. The skull is already typically turtle-like with toothless horn-covered jaws, large eyes and a short head. *Archelon* (lower) was a gigantic late Cretaceous form. The hooked beak suggests it may have fed on slow-moving shellfish.

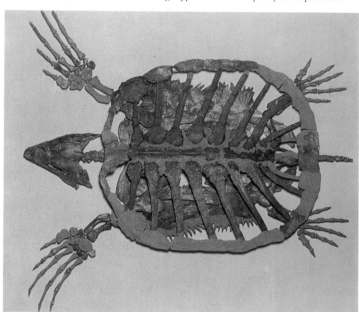

The lizards and snakes are by far the most successful of modern reptiles, with about 6,000 species alive today. The first lizards appear in late Triassic rocks and these relatively small, agile, insectivorous creatures have remained virtually unchanged to the present day—apart from some relatively short-lived variants (notably the large predatory mosasaurs mentioned earlier).

The 'secret' of the success of lizards is hard to define with certainty. One factor may be that the typical shape of lizards (slender, long-bodied, sprawling legs, small head) ideally suits them to particular ecological niches; they are just better at being 'lizards' than anything else! However, side-stepping the circularity of that last proposition, one of the most popular explanations for their success over the past 200 million years is based on an analysis of the way in which the skull and jaw bones are linked together in a movable chain of bones.

One of the key innovations in lizard design—in fact it is the only significant change

Sphenodon Skull

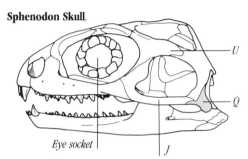

Eye socket

Kuehneosaurus Skull

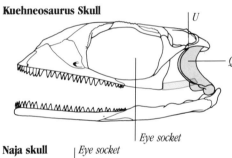

Eye socket

Naja skull *Eye socket*

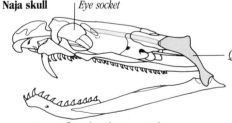

Bones of jaw loosely connected

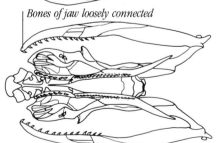

that has taken place if you compare the very earliest reptiles to lizards—can be found on the side of the head. The arch of bone possessed by non-lizard reptiles, marked (J) below, has disappeared (compare the drawings of *Sphenodon* and *Kuehneosaurus*). The result of this change is quite profound since the removal of bone J now permits the bone Q (a pillar-like bone that forms the joint with the lower jaw) to swing backward and forward. This means first of all that the lower jaw can be slid fore and aft. Secondly, movement of Q also operates a series of joints within the skull of the lizard. The net result of this series of interlinked joints is that the snout can be raised and lowered. It would appear that the development of this mobility both in the lower and the upper jaws of lizards was very important. Perhaps it allowed lizards to feed more effectively on insects (the staple diet of many lizards) by allowing them greater precision of jaw closure. This unusual hingeing system may also have acted as a type of a 'shock-absorber' in the skull; this may have been of some value since it would tend to cushion the lizard's brain against the jarring effect caused by snapping the jaws shut on its prey. The violent snapping action of the jaws is a necessary adaptation both to catch very fast-moving insects, and also to crack open their hard external skeletons. Whatever the true explanation is, it seems inevitable that mobility of the jaws was of considerable value because it is developed in almost all living lizards.

The fossil record of lizards is poor, largely because lizards tend to live in dry uplands away from the areas that are most likely to produce fossils, and because they are so small and their skeletons are consequently very easily destroyed. Nevertheless, several fossil lizards are known. One of these is *Kuehneosaurus* ('Kühne's reptile') from the late Triassic of Britain. Despite its early appearance, this was already a highly specialised gliding lizard; its ribs are enormously elongate and formed gliding membranes which allowed the animal to glide from tree-to-tree. A small living lizard from Malaya (*Draco volans*, 'flying dragon') has similar long ribs which are also used for gliding.

Lizard Skull Flexing

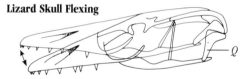

Lizard Skull Movements (above)
The ability of bone Q to move to and fro is used by lizards to tilt the snout up and down. The mechanism allows them to feed very efficiently.

Below: This photograph shows the front portion of the skeleton of *Pleurosaurus goldfussi*, a small lizard-like reptile from the late Jurassic Period. Compare the shape of the skull with the drawings on this page.

Snakes

Snakes have an even worse fossil record than lizards. The first remains of snakes are known from the late Cretaceous of North America (*Coniophis*, 'Coniacian snake') and Patagonia (*Dinilysia*, 'terrible destroyer').

The main differences between lizards and snakes are fairly technical anatomical ones. Simple features such as the absence of legs are not sufficiently precise because there are several legless lizards ('slow-worms', 'glass-snakes' etc). One particular feature can be mentioned because it continues a trend seen in the lizards. This relates to the flexibility of the skull bones. If we compare a lizard and snake skull, we can see that not only has bone J been lost but also the arch of bone above it (U) has gone. As a result, the bone (Q) which supports the lower jaw has only the flimsiest attachment to the skull—giving a great deal of mobility to the lower jaw. In addition both sides of the lower jaw are separate, and the skull bones are even more loosely joined together than those of the lizard. The result of these changes has been to make the whole snake head incredibly flexible, so allowing it to swallow very large animal prey.

The other notable feature of snakes is the variety of methods that they use for killing their prey. The large boas, pythons and anacondas use constriction to suffocate their prey. Other types of snake (notably the viper family) are able to inject deadly venoms into their victims. Some venomous snakes have permanently erect fangs, either at the rear of the jaws (back-fanged snakes), or at the front (elapids). The most specialised fangs are those of the vipers. The teeth at the front of their mouths are specially modified in the form of hypodermic needles through which they can squirt venom from glands in the roof of the mouth. When not in use, the fangs may be folded back against the roof of the mouth. However, when they are about to make a 'strike' the fangs are swung forward through the action of the jointed bones of the skull roof. Whether vipers had evolved in late Cretaceous times when snakes first appeared is uncertain.

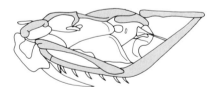

Viperid Fang Erection

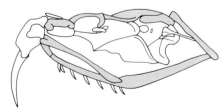

Snake Fangs (above)
The flexibility of skull developed by lizards was further adapted in two ways by snakes: allowing them to swallow large prey, and to deploy erectile fangs to inject venom into a victim. Seen here is the mechanism of fang erection (red). With jaws closed the fangs are folded back, but when the jaws open they swing forward ready to strike.

Lizard and Snake Skulls (above)
Sphenodon (top) shows the typical skull shape of an early lizard. Note the positions of the bony arches J (jugal) and U (upper temporal) and the bone Q (quadrate) which forms part of the jaw joint. *Kuehneosaurus* is an early true lizard. Note that J has been lost leaving bone Q free to swing backwards and forwards. The snake skull (bottom drawings) shows that arches J and U have both been lost. Both sides of the lower jaw are separate, while the skull bones are loosely connected, features which allow the snake to swallow large prey.

MAMMAL-LIKE REPTILES & MAMMALS

The last group of dinosaur contemporaries that we shall be looking at are the mammal-like reptiles and mammals. These represent a very important group of animals in the fossil record. The mammal-like reptiles were particularly abundant in the Permian and early part of the Triassic but rapidly declined in abundance towards the close of the Triassic Period. The disappearance of the mammal-like reptiles at the end of the Triassic heralds the arrival of two new groups: the dinosaurs which rapidly rise to dominate the land for the remaining 140 million years or so of the Mesozoic Era; and, the first true mammals. Rather than being large, dominant creatures as they are today, these early mammals were small, shrew-like, probably nocturnal, insectivorous creatures and so they remained throughout the remainder of the Mesozoic Era — literally and figuratively in the shadow of the dinosaurs. So far as we can tell, things might have continued like this right up to the present day had it not been for the mysterious event which occurred at the end of the Cretaceous Period. At this time, 64 million years ago, the dinosaurs quite suddenly went extinct, as did a variety of other creatures. However, from the point of view of the mammals which somehow survived the Cretaceous extinction event, the most important feature was the disappearance of the dinosaurs, because within the space of a few million years the mammals underwent a quite spectacular evolutionary radiation. Not only did they evolve into large land-living animals of all shapes and sizes, they also evolved into sea creatures — the whales and dolphins, seals and sea cows — and invaded the air in the form of bats. The enormity of this radiation makes it seem as though it represents the pent-up 'energy' of 140 million years of mammals waiting in the wings for the dinosaurs finally to leave the stage. A part of the wide radiation of mammals in the early Tertiary included some fairly small, almost rat-like creatures which are of particular interest to us because they were the first primates, a group from which our own human species was eventually to arise a mere 2-3 million years ago.

So, even though the mammals were relatively insignificant elements of the terrestrial fauna during the Jurassic and Cretaceous Periods, they are nevertheless an extremely important group in the fossil record and both they and their ancestors, the mammal-like reptiles, deserve some consideration.

Pelycosaurs

The earliest known mammal-like reptiles are called pelycosaurs ('sail reptiles') and are first found in rocks of late Carboniferous age. *Archaeothyris* ('ancient opening') is a very early representative which is known from very fragmentary remains from Nova Scotia. In its general features it is small and lizard-like — much like most of the other small insectivorous early reptiles. It does, however, bear one particular distinguishing feature which is the small single opening on the side of the skull just behind the eye. This one character sets this little reptile apart from all others of the time, because it is found only in the synapsids or mammal-like reptiles and, in a highly modified form, in mammals too.

From these small beginnings, the pelycosaurs evolved into some of the dominant terrestrial animals of the early Permian. Pelycosaurs are particularly common fossils in the early Permian 'Red Bed' rocks of Texas and neighbouring areas of the USA. There appear to be three main types of pelycosaur, the large long-bodied and long-snouted ophiacodonts (named after *Ophiacodon* or 'snake tooth') of which *Varannosaurus* ('monitor lizard reptile') is a good example. The relatively long snout and rather small spiky teeth have been interpreted by many as indicating an aquatic, fish-eating way of life. The other two groups are far better known and quite spectacular animals: the sphenacodonts (*Dimetrodon*) and the edaphosaurs (*Edaphosaurus*).

Dimetrodon ('two long teeth') was a large predatory creature of the early Permian. Compared with *Varannosaurus*, it has a much shorter, deeper skull, the jaws of which are armed with large sharp-edged teeth. The remainder of the skeleton is very similar to that of *Varannosaurus* except that the dorsal spines are enormously long giving the appearance of a large fan perched on the back.

One early suggestion was that this sail-like structure was literally used as a sail so that these animals could swim more easily. This idea was not taken at all seriously. The most favoured explanation is that the sail of *Dimetrodon* was

Archaeothyris Skull

Eye socket

Synapsid opening

Ophiacodon Skull

Eye socket

Left: This view of *Varanops brevirostris* clearly shows the classic sprawling posture of a typical pelycosaur. Even though the legs are quite long, their splayed position means that the belly is low-slung.

Right: This magnificent skeleton from the Field Museum of Natural History, Chicago, shows a victim's-eye view of the ferocious *Dimetrodon grandis*. Note the large skull and jaws befitting a fierce predator such as this.

Pelycosaur Skulls (above)
Archaeothyris (top) is the earliest well-described pelycosaur, a small lizard-like creature of the late Carboniferous. *Ophiacodon* (bottom) from the Permian is a larger form that was clearly a predator. It may have been aquatic.

Edaphosaurus Skull

Eye socket

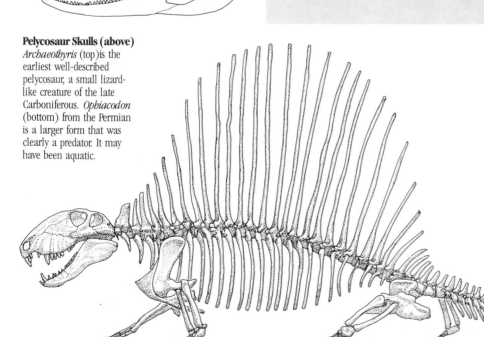

Dimetrodon Skeleton (left)
This reconstruction shows all the main anatomical attributes of this sail-backed sphenacodont: the large head, sprawling limbs, and tall 'sail' of spines.

Edaphosaurus Skull (above)
Similar in overall size to *Dimetrodon*, *Edaphosaurus* was however an herbivore. The teeth are blunt and modified to form large grinding plates for crushing plants.

involved in body temperature regulation (see also *Spinosaurus, Ouranosaurus* and stegosaurids). The spines were undoubtedly covered by thin skin, and by controlling the amount of blood flowing through the sail it could have acted as either a solar panel: the heat from the Sun falling on the sail warming the blood and the body; or as a radiator: in the case of the animal being too warm, the blood in the sail could be cooled either in a breeze or in the shade so that the body temperature could be lowered very quickly. Calculations have been made in order to estimate how long it would take reptiles of the size of *Dimetrodon*—with or without a sail—to warm up in the morning by basking in the Sun. The answer seems to be that possesing a sail allows a reptile to warm itself much more quickly. This may well have been a distinct advantage to early Permian predators.

Edaphosaurus ('Earth reptile') also from the early Permian, was another large-sailed pelycosaur. *Edaphosaurus*, however, was an herbivore; the skull is again short, but its teeth are shorter and blunter than those of *Dimetrodon*, and the inner sides of the jaws are modified in the form of large food-grinding knobbly tooth plates. These features indicate that *Edaphosaurus* fed on tough vegetation. Another peculiarity lies in the structure of the sail.Unlike the spines of *Dimetrodon* which are quite smooth, those of *Edaphosaurus* are very knobbly; this feature may have increased surface area and therefore the efficiency of its temperature-regulating sail.

At the very beginning of the late Permian, a fairly dramatic change seems to take place among these early mammal-like reptiles. The pelycosaurs which were so abundant in early times dwindled and rapidly became extinct and their place seems to have been taken by another type of mammal-like reptile group known as the therapsids.

Therapsids

The therapsids ('beast arch') were a varied group of mammal-like reptiles which differ from the earlier pelycosaurs in a number of ways. One of the most obvious changes is in the body proportions and posture. Therapsids tend to have relatively short tails, unlike the long lizard-like tails of pelycosaurs. Their limbs are rather longer and could be held not only in the sprawled position, but also in a much more efficient position tucked beneath the body. This 'dual or variable gait' as it is known is very similar to that of crocodiles. The combination of a short-tailed, rather compact body with the

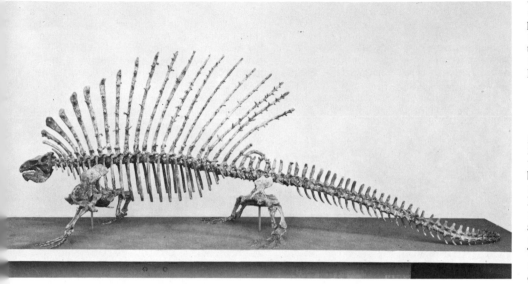

Above: Another very fine exhibit from the Field Museum, Chicago, this is the herbivorous sail-backed pelycosaur, *Edaphosaurus poconias.* The spines of the sail are quite distinct from those of *Dimetrodon;* they are very knobbly, a feature that may have increased the surface area, and thus the efficiency, of the sail.

Therapsid Skulls (right)
Delphinognathus (top) shows the fairly typical skull shape of an early Permian therapsid. The head is heavily-built and sloping; the teeth are large and chisel-like. *Dicynodon* (middle) is typical of the dicynodont therapsids which were very abundant in the late Permian and Triassic. Apart from the large 'eye-teeth', their jaws were toothless and no doubt covered in a horny sheath. These creatures were about the size of modern sheep.

Delphinognathus Skull

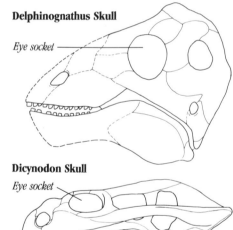

Eye socket

Dicynodon Skull

Eye socket

Horn-covered beak

Cynognathus Skull

Eye socket

Incisors Canine Cheek teeth

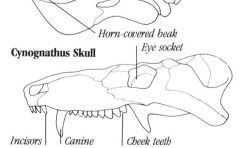

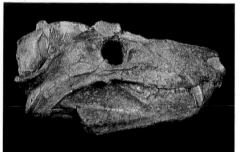

Cynognathus Skull (above and left)
The two illustrations of *Cynognathus* show that this was an advanced carnivore. The teeth are differentiated into small incisors at the front, large canines behind, and broader, sharp-edged slicing teeth at the back. The similarity to a modern dog is quite striking.

variable gait potential of the legs seems to represent a major advance over the arrangements seen in pelycosaurs, and suggests that these may have been much more active types of animal.

Increased activity is also probably reflected in the structure of the jaws and teeth of the therapsids. Some of the early carnivores such as *Lycaenops* ('wolf-face') of the late Permian had large heads and teeth which are specialised for dealing with large prey. *Lycaenops* has small nipping teeth at the tip of the jaws, but immediately behind these are a pair of huge stabbing teeth, followed by a few smaller chewing teeth. As the name of this predator suggests, these are indeed rather wolf-like creatures, and their long legs would have made them quite fast runners.

Various sabre-toothed therapsids resembling *Lycaenops* appeared during the late Permian but they do not appear to survive beyond the close of the Permian Period.

Alongside these fearsome predators are found a peculiar assortment of herbivores. Some early forms developed stout, powerful bodies, large knobbly heads and blunt chipping teeth and were known as dinocephalians ('terrible heads') because of their rather grotesque appearance. These were, however, relatively short lived and were replaced by another equally odd group of herbivores known as dicynodonts ('two dog teeth').

Dicynodonts were extremely numerous in late Permian times and in fact persist in fewer numbers right into the late Triassic. Their body form is surprisingly constant featuring relatively short, stout legs, and a barrel-like body. Their heads, however, are the most interesting part.

The name dicynodont refers to the fact that most of them only had two large tusks in the upper jaw. All their other teeth were lost (except in one or two rather primitive forms) and were replaced by a turtle-like horny beak. This was evidently a very successful ploy judging by their great abundance in late Permian rocks. It would appear that the jaws of these creatures were very versatile and able to cope with most types of vegetation. This may have been assisted by the extraordinary mobility (both fore and aft, and side to side) of the lower jaw.

At the end of the Permian the majority of carnivorous therapsids and many of the herbivorous therapsids (excluding the dicynodonts) had gone extinct. These were in turn replaced by yet another group of mammal-like reptiles, this time known as cynodonts ('dog teeth').

Cynodonts

A few cynodonts appear in the latest Permian but they first begin to be abundant in early Triassic times. This time the changes which distinguish therapsids from cynodonts are much more subtle. From our point of view the most important changes are to be found in the jaws and teeth. The teeth are even more specialised than those of therapsids, being divided into small sharp incisors at the tip of the jaws, a large stabbing canine tooth, and behind this a row of complex cheek teeth. Unlike typical reptiles, each cheek tooth has a broad crown which develops a series of blunt points. This arrangement allowed the cynodonts to chew their food very efficiently, unlike most other reptiles. The teeth in the lower jaw are also lodged in a large single bone to which all the jaw muscles are attached; this is a much stronger arrangement than that of earlier mammal-like reptiles. Finally the complicated

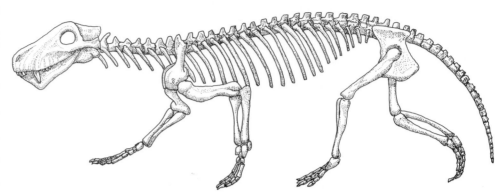

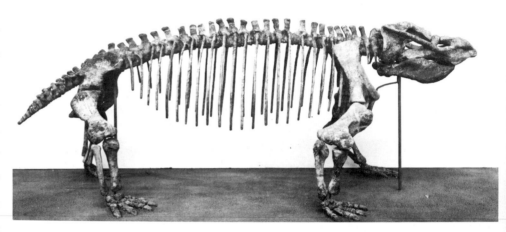

Lycaenops (above)
This was a therapsid mammal-like reptile of the late Permian. As can be seen here the skeleton is much less lizard-like than that of a pelycosaur. The legs are tucked in beneath the body and the tail is quite short. The large stabbing teeth reveal that *Lycaenops* was a carnivorous predator.

Below: *Aulacocephalodon peavoti* was a dicynodont mammal-like reptile. Therapsids like this were particularly abundant in the late Permian and Triassic. This was a rather unprepossessing creature to look at, with stout legs and a tubby body. It was an herbivore, the prey of animals like *Lycaenops*.

Probelesodon (below and bottom)
One of the more advanced types of cynodont, *Probelesodon* from South America was a small, nimble predator. The photograph of the finely preserved skull (bottom) shows the large spaces behind the eyes for the jaw muscles.

Morganucodon Skull (right)
A close relative of *Megazostrodon, Morganucodon* remains come from South Wales. This is an early mammal, and the drawing shows clearly the four types of teeth. It is based on the work of Dr Mussett and Professor Kermack.

Morganucodon Skull

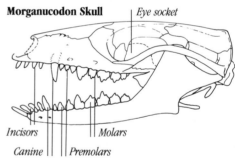

Eye socket

Incisors

Canine

Premolars

Molars

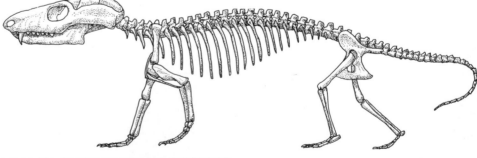

cheek teeth made it necessary for the jaw muscles to be not only powerful, but also quite sophisticated in order that opposing teeth could be brought together powerfully and in exactly the right position for the most effective cutting or crushing action.

These changes give a vivid impression of cynodonts as highly active and very efficient animals of the Triassic. They evolved not only into small, agile carnivores such as *Probelesodon* ('before lovely tooth') from South America, but also various herbivorous, lightly-built types. Towards the end of the Triassic, however, even the active and versatile cynodonts declined and

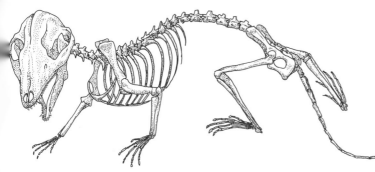

Above: This living rufous spectacled elephant shrew (*Elephantulus rufescens*) is an animal which we believe exists in a very similar way to Mesozoic mammals such as *Megazostrodon* (below left) and *Morganucodon* (opposite page). Nocturnal, it spends its time scurrying in search of insects. Great sensitivity and agility are absolutely essential for this style of life.

Left: This model of *Megazostrodon* comes from a display in the British Museum (Natural History). It shows the strong resemblance between this early mammal and modern shrews.

Megazostrodon Skeleton (left)
The real breakthrough in our understanding of early mammals came with the chance discovery by Dr Ione Rudner of a partial skeleton and skull of this tiny creature in 1966. The skeleton (based on the work of Jenkins and Parrington) looks like that of an agile insectivore.

creature named *Megazostrodon* ('big girdled tooth') which was found in Lesotho in 1966. *Megazostrodon* was a tiny shrew-like creature. So far as we can tell it was an early mammal. Some of the reasons for believing this can be found in its jaws and teeth. The teeth are divided into four types (incisors, canines, premolars and molars). Unlike the cynodonts which have simple cheek teeth, those of *Megazostrodon* fall into premolar and molar types. This implies that *Megazostrodon* had a 'milk set' and a 'permanent set' of teeth only, rather than the continuously replaced teeth of reptiles; this also implies that *Megazostrodon* may have suckled its young on milk—a key mammalian character. The molar teeth also show very precise wear surfaces caused by opposing teeth rubbing past one another; this precision bite is another mammal character.

These features, and a few other more technical ones, make it highly probable that *Megazostrodon* was a very early mammal. The combination of large eyes, a long nose, sharp spiky teeth, and nimble limbs suggests that *Megazostrodon* and many other early mammals of the Triassic, Jurassic and Cretaceous were nocturnal insectivores, little different in most respects from living shrews.

Mammal features in advanced cynodonts Several of the later cynodonts show many very mammal-like features, notably complex teeth, great agility etc, and they may indeed have been very mammal-like in appearance. Many palaeontologists have speculated on the possibility that cynodonts might have generated their own body heat and had hair-covered skin rather than scaly bodies.

The curiously cyclical nature of origin, radiation and extinction in the evolution of the mammal-like reptiles from pelycosaurs to therapsids, then cynodonts, finally culminating in late Triassic mammals was reviewed recently (1982) by Dr Tom Kemp (Oxford). This curious pattern may reflect how the process of evolution of animals as complex as living mammals may have had to occur in stepwise fashion from less biologically complex lizard-like pelycosaurs. In retrospect, each step appears to mark a distinct advance towards the ultimate mammalian condition.

went extinct. This final phase in the evolution of the mammal-like reptiles marked the time of the rise of two groups: the true mammals and the dinosaurs.

Mammals

Living mammals are quite distinct from the reptiles of today. Briefly summarised the main differences are as follows. Reptiles have scaly skin, lay eggs, rely on the Sun to warm their bodies and have relatively simple teeth. Mammals in contrast have soft hair-covered skin, bear live young (except for the duck-billed platypus and spiny echidna of S. E. Asia and Australia), suckle their young on mothers' milk, generate their own body heat rather than relying on the Sun, and have complicated teeth.

Turning to the fossil record, these clear-cut differences become blurred, or at least extremely difficult to establish, since they are dependent mostly upon soft anatomical features (skin structure, hair, mammary glands, and body temperature control), none of which preserve in fossils. As a result, the first true mammals are recognised as fossils almost by weight of opinion, rather than anything more scientific.

One of the best preserved early mammals is a

This chapter will deal with several controversial issues which involve the dinosaurs, namely their origins, their physiological status (were they 'warm-blooded' or not?), the ancestry of birds, and finally that perennial problem, why did the dinosaurs go extinct at the end of the Cretaceous Period?

Dinosaur Origins

The question of the origin of dinosaurs is one that has puzzled palaeontologists for many years. The issue we shall be addressing here is not so much one of *which* particular group of archosaurs evolved into dinosaurs, although that is important in itself, but rather *why* did dinosaurs appear in late Triassic times and then prove so successful for the next 140 million years. This is particularly relevant because, as we have seen earlier, true mammals had also evolved in the late Triassic.

Looking at the animals inhabiting the world today, it must seem obvious that the mammals are a very important group indeed. They are found in all habitats from polar ice caps to tropical rainforests, hot deserts to arctic tundra, in the sea, up trees, in the air and burrowing underground. Compared with the reptiles which are only found in any great numbers in the tropics, they are obviously very successful animals. The question that poses itself then is this: if mammals are so much more successful than reptiles in the present day, why were they not so successful in the Mesozoic Era? Several attempts have been made to answer this question, some of these are examined below.

Dinosaur Posture

One of the most prominent theories attempting to explain dinosaur success in the Triassic has been put forward by Dr Alan Charig (London). Its principal claim is that the success of dinosaurs is related to their ability to walk with erect limbs.

As was explained earlier, dinosaurs can be distinguished from other archosaur reptiles by changes that have taken place at the hip, knee and ankle; these enable their legs to be tucked directly beneath the body to act not only as pillar-like supports but also to provide a longer stride and more effective walking and running abilities. According to Dr Charig the circumstances that led to this change in posture can be traced back to large semi-aquatic archosaurs (proterosuchians) of the late Permian or early Triassic. These large, swamp-dwelling creatures are supposed to have developed large, paddling hind legs which were, in later archosaurs of the Triassic Period, used as powerful hindlimbs on land. Whatever the actual reason, the archosaurs of the early and middle Triassic were characterised by their carnivorous way of life and an ability to assume a more erect posture, as seen in living crocodiles. The best comparison may perhaps be with the late Permian carnivorous therapsids such as *Lycaenops* with their 'dual' or 'variable gait' limbs.

Some middle Triassic archosaurs of this type (such as *Ticinosuchus*) were quite large creatures (10-13ft, 3-4m long) and were probably the top carnivores of the time. The large skulls with dagger-like teeth and the relatively efficient running abilities of these archosaurs are supposed to have endowed them with superior predatory abilities compared with the contemporary carnivorous cynodonts. As a result of competition between the carnivorous archosaurs and cynodonts, the cynodonts rapidly declined in middle to late

Triassic times leaving the archosaurs as dominant carnivores. By late Triassic times the improvements in limb posture which had begun in the earlier Triassic in these variably-gaited archosaurs finally resulted in the evolution of true dinosaurs.

It is argued that becaue of their superior running and walking abilities, the early carnivorous dinosaurs of the late Triassic proved to be excessively efficient at preying upon the surviving herbivorous cynodonts and dicynodonts. As a consequence, in the early part of the late Triassic the first dinosaurs had caused the extinction of all the herbivorous mammal-like reptiles and a few other aberrant groups of reptiles (e.g. rhynchosaurs and aëtosaurs). Under the circumstances, there would have been intense competition between the various carnivorous dinosaurs of the late Triassic because of the general absence of herbivores to prey upon. There must, therefore, have been very strong evolutionary 'pressure' in favour of some early dinosaurs becoming herbivorous in order to capitalise on the vegetation that was not being consumed by other vertebrates, and simultaneously to provide a more balanced fauna of herbivores and carnivores.

Changing Fortunes (below)

This time chart logs the relative abundances of (red) the synapsid, or mammal-like, reptiles and their descendants, the mammals, and (grey) archosaurs and their descendants, the birds. The synapsids flourished in the Permian and Triassic, but in the late Triassic were replaced by the dinosaurs which dominated the Earth in the Jurassic and Cretaceous. Following the Cretaceous extinction of the dinosaurs, the relative abundance of mammals and birds rose very dramatically.

Indeed that is what is seen in the latest Triassic with the appearance of a variety of herbivorous dinosaurs: the relatively large-bodied prosauropod saurischians and the smaller, fleet-footed fabrosaurid and heterodontosaurid ornithischians.

Thus the faunal succession of mammal-like reptiles to dinosaurs in the late Triassic is interpreted as an inevitable consequence of progressive improvements in the limb posture. The 'variable-gaited' carnivorous archosaurs causing first the extinction of the carnivorous cynodonts, then the herbivorous cynodonts with the consequent rise of carnivorous erect-gaited archosaurs (dinosaurs!) and the subsequent evolution of herbivorous dinosaurs to fill the niches vacated by the herbivorous cynodonts and dicynodonts.

Elegant though this argument undoubtedly is, there are one or two disquieting aspects to it. First, if mammal-like reptiles had already evolved a variable-gait walking technique in the late Permian, why was its apparent re-invention by archosaurs in the Triassic Period so devastatingly effective. The cynodonts were in possession of just as effective, if not more effective, walking and running techniques as

Dinosaur Posture (left)

This restoration of *Diplodocus* is based on the work of Hay and Tornier who believed it had a sprawling posture. As we see, this is totally unrealistic. In fact dinosaurs were able to walk with fully-erect limbs.

Right: One major issue that has been raised in relation to the success of the dinosaurs in the late Triassic concerns the nature of the climate. The presence of 'Red Bed' rocks, similar to these in Australia, has been used to support the idea that it was very arid then.

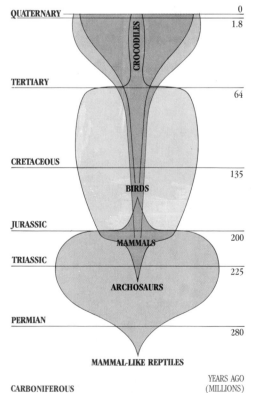

		YEARS AGO (MILLIONS)
QUATERNARY		0
	CROCODILES	1.8
TERTIARY		64
CRETACEOUS		135
	BIRDS	
JURASSIC		200
	MAMMALS	
TRIASSIC	ARCHOSAURS	225
PERMIAN		280
	MAMMAL-LIKE REPTILES	
CARBONIFEROUS		

the contemporary archosaurs. Secondly the account of the origin of herbivorous dinosaurs seems rather improbable. The likelihood of carnivores causing the extinction of their prey animals runs counter to current ecological theory. Predator numbers follow prey abundance very closely under normal conditions, so that the extinction of its prey would be followed by extinction of the predator.

Climatic Change

Another model which has been used to explain the rise of the dinosaurs is based on an interpretation of the climatic conditions which prevailed in the late Triassic.

This theory has had several advocates, notably Dr Pamela Robinson (London), and it stems from the fact that many of the late Triassic rocks are characteristically red in colour. This has been widely interpreted as indicating that seasonal, hot and arid conditions prevailed. The red coloration of the rocks is due to their being literally 'rusty'. If it is true that the late Triassic was a time of hot dry conditions, then considerations can be given to the type of animals that could best survive then.

Comparing reptiles and mammals it can be seen that reptiles are on the whole very economical types of animals, well suited to dry, desert environments. Reptile skin is scaly and impervious to water so they do not tend to dry out in the Sun; they also lose very little water in their urine; they do not generate their own body heat, so they do not need to eat a great deal of food simply to generate heat. Reptiles seem well designed to live in areas where there is little water, little food and plenty of heat (desert conditions). Mammals on the other hand find it unexpectedly hard to tolerate these conditions. All mammals sweat to keep cool and in hot deserts are constantly losing water through their skin; they also lose rather a lot of water in their urine (certainly by comparison with reptiles); and they require a constant source of food to fuel the internal heat production system. In general mammals find hot deserts particularly stressful because of the high temperatures, lack of water and general unavailability of food.

Perhaps then, if we are looking for a cause for the rise of the dinosaurs instead of the mammals at the end of the Triassic we need look no further than this. Widespread desert

conditions would have favoured a reptilian type of creature because of its generally economical life-style. Once the dinosaur-type reptiles were firmly established on land, the mammals had no opportunity to replace them.

Again this solution is both simple and elegant. The only real dispute tends to revolve around the evidence for a world-wide desert-type climate in the Triassic and the true significance of 'Red Bed' rocks. It is claimed by some that 'Red Bed' type rocks are being deposited today in areas that have high seasonal temperature *and* high rainfall. Obviously these issues will need to be settled before this explanation can become widely accepted.

Opportunistic Dinosaurs

In the last few years a rather different type of theory has been proposed by Dr Mike Benton (Belfast). This theory claims that rather than invoking some element of competition between mammals and dinosaurs, perhaps dinosaurs were simply given the opportunity to evolve in the late Triassic because some unknown factor had caused the extinction of the previously abundant groups.

Right: This is a skin impression from the hadrosaurid *Edmontosaurus*. All reptiles have scaly skin, a feature that is of great advantage to them in hot, dry desert conditions because very little water is lost through it.

Below: If the climatic change theory is correct, then perhaps this photograph provides us with a vivid impression of the harsh arid conditions that prevailed in the late Triassic, which may have allowed dinosaurs to succeed mammal-like reptiles (synapsids).

Above: A display of the sauropod *Diplodocus* and the ornithopod *Iguanodon.* The pressure required to pump blood to *Diplodocus*' brain when its head was raised would have been enormous. Is this evidence that dinosaurs had fully divided hearts like endothermic mammals?

Detailed analysis of fossil finds from rocks in the Triassic seems to reveal a pattern of extinctions towards the end of the Triassic among many reptile groups (mammal-like reptiles, rhynchosaurs, various archosaurs). It would seem from this record of events that the dinosaurs simply evolved into the spaces left by all the forms that had gone extinct and that therefore a chance event (whatever caused these extinctions) may have given the dinosaurs the chance that they had been waiting for.

This seems to be yet another highly plausible explanation of the rise of the dinosaurs. Obviously this interpretation is heavily dependent upon the accuracy of the recorded fossils from the late Triassic and will probably stand or fall on this evidence over the next few years.

Dinosaurs and 'Warm Blood'

The fourth and final theory to explain dinosaur success in the Triassic has had one notable advocate in recent years, Dr Bob Bakker. This theory has its roots in the general observation that was made at the beginning of the chapter about the timing of the origin of mammals and dinosaurs *and* the self-evident superiority of mammals in the present-day.

The argument is quite simple and can be stated as follows: mammals are superior to reptiles today; the reason for this superiority is that they are 'warm-blooded'—to be more accurate the term is *endothermic* ('internal heat')—as a consequence of which they are more active and intelligent animals than living reptiles. Since mammals and dinosaurs evolved at practically the same time, the endothermic mammals should have prevailed. For the dinosaurs to have radiated at the expense of the mammals, dinosaurs must have been as 'competitive' as mammals and therefore *must* have been endothermic or 'warm-blooded'. The argument is basically sound and the logic impeccable, but as the debate over the past decade has shown, the case for endothermy in dinosaurs is far from proven.

Above: This skeleton of *Daspletosaurus* in Ottawa shows clearly several attributes of theropod dinosaurs that have been linked to endothermy: an erect gait, bipedality, and the generally active 'air' of the creature.

Right: The sprawling posture of today's reptiles, such as this varanid lizard, is radically different from that of the dinosaurs. Some have interpreted this variance as evidence in favour of endothermy (warm-bloodedness) in dinosaurs.

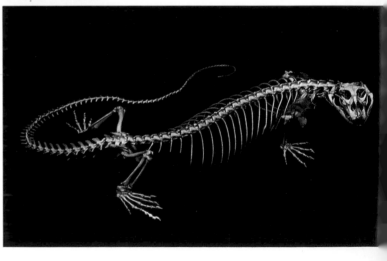

The body temperature of dinosaurs (something that can never be actually established) has become a major palaeontological issue in the last decade. Dr Bob Bakker has single-mindedly and virtually single-handedly pursued his belief that dinosaurs were endothermic for more than a decade and really whether he is right or wrong (much current opinion seems to be against his views), his contributions to our appreciation of the biology of both dinosaurs and living reptiles and mammals have been of enormous value.

As explained in the previous section, the crux of Bakker's argument comes from the simple observation that mammals and dinosaurs appear to have evolved at about the same time in the late Triassic. Bearing in mind that living (endothermic) mammals are almost completely dominant over the (ectothermic) reptiles, the interpretation that can be put on the events of the late Triassic is that dinosaurs must have been as efficient as the mammals, and they must have been endothermic. Taking this argument as a reasonable working hypothesis Bakker then set about garnering evidence from the fossil remains of dinosaurs in an attempt to 'prove' that they were endothermic.

Dinosaur posture Dinosaurs are, as we have seen, characterised by a fully erect gait; the legs are drawn underneath the body and appear to have operated very effectively on land. Dinosaurian reptiles differ from living reptiles because living reptiles display a primitive sprawling posture, with the legs held out to the sides of the body. Looking at our present-day animals, the only ones with limb postures resembling those of dinosaurs are the mammals and birds—both of which are endothermic. The proposition that Bakker made was that only animals with an endothermic physiology are capable of walking with an erect gait; therefore dinosaurs must have been endotherms.

The basic argument has been built upon in two ways. Professor Ostrom modified the reasoning and proposed that rather than simply an erect gait, it was the ability to walk bipedally (as many dinosaurs did, some mammals and all birds do) that was a crucial feature linked to endothermy. Another posturally-related proposition was based on the height of the head above the heart. An upright posture also coincides with an elevated head and neck in all dinosaurs. Taking an extreme example, the

Below: This is a cast of the brain cavity of *Triceratops*. Although it may be hard to appreciate, the brain is not only quite large by reptile standards, but it is also quite complicated in structure, which indicates that these animals were not un-intelligent.

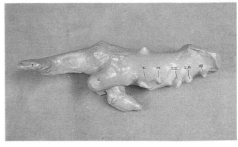

Heart Systems (below) In the toad, deoxygenated blood from the body (blue) returns to the heart where it is mixed (mauve) with oxygenated blood (red) from the lungs. This rather 'leaky' system works for the ectothermic toad. In the case of the reptile, blood in the heart is not mixed to the same extent, although a pressure-sensitive valve allows blood to mix in some conditions. In endothermic mammals, birds, (and perhaps dinosaurs?), the heart is fully divided: no mixing can occur. This is the most efficient circulatory system.

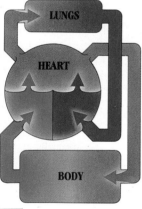

Toad (undivided heart)

Reptile (semi-divided heart)

Endotherm (fully divided heart)

LUNGS

HEART

BODY

■ **Oxygenated blood**   ■ **Deoxygenated blood**   ■ **Mixed blood**

high activity levels can only be sustained by endotherms. As we shall see later this may not be true.

Brain-size and behaviour Mammals and birds both possess large brains and exhibit a great deal of what we might call 'intelligent' activity. Ectothermic reptiles have relatively smaller brains and are not renowned for their intellectual prowess. There would appear to be an important link between endothermy and brain size amongst vertebrates. Large brains are highly complex structures which need constant supplies of food, oxygen *and* an even temperature in order to function properly. The endothermic regime of mammals and birds supplies these requirements and can therefore maintain a large brain. Reptiles with their ectothermic regime can supply food and oxygen moderately efficiently (though the levels do tend to vary slightly), but their body temperature does tend to vary in a normal 24 hour cycle; they therefore seem unable to support a large brain.

At first sight this seems to counter the argument for endothermy in dinosaurs very effectively; dinosaurs are notorious for their lack of brain power. However, all is not lost! Dr Jim Hopson (Chicago) has estimated brain size in a whole range of dinosaurs and by comparing ratios of brain size to body size has revealed that most dinosaurs have at least typical reptilian-sized brains. More interesting still, however, is his observation that among the theropods, *Stenonychosaurus* (page 54) had a brain equivalent in size to that of some living birds and mammals. Indeed among the dinosaurs, the theropods and ornithopods seem to have been of above average reptile brain-size. Thus at least a few dinosaurs did have large and presumably complex brains more like those of living animals and birds.

This argument about 'intelligence' in dinosaurs has been extended into the field of behaviour as well. As we have already seen, dinosaurs have left various clues about their behaviour: nesting activities, care of their young, herding, visual and auditory recognition systems etc. It has been proposed on the basis of this 'evidence' that dinosaurs had very complex behaviour patterns more comparable to those of mammals and birds than to reptiles. This type of argument, however, seems based more on ignorance of reptile behaviour than sound logic. As we saw a little earlier, crocodiles are capable of extremely complex behaviour. Dinosaur behaviour therefore may well fall within the normal range of reptile behaviour.

Latitudinal spread of dinosaurs The report of dinosaur remains from the Yukon area of North America and footprints from Spitzbergen has also been used as evidence of endothermy in dinosaurs. The argument

dinosaur *Brachiosaurus*: if we consider the action of the heart which has to pump blood all the way up its neck to its brain, we realise that it would have to generate very high blood pressure to raise the blood that distance. However, if, like all modern reptiles, the heart was not fully divided into a lung circulation and a body-and-head circuit, then the high pressure in the body-and-head circuit would cause massive bleeding in the thin blood vessels of the lungs. *Brachiosaurus* must therefore have had a fully divided heart, so that the blood pressure in the lung circuit could be lower than that in the body-and-head circuit. Again only the endothermic mammals and birds today have a fully divided heart; since dinosaurs also had a divided heart, they may have been endothermic.

This group of arguments seems positive and compelling evidence of endothermy in dinosaurs. They have been countered, however, by the following comments: just because dinosaurs have an erect posture it does not necessarily follow that they were endothermic; an erect posture may have been a design feature which simply allowed dinosaurs to grow large (large animals with sprawling legs are a

physical impossibility!); also what about the humble chamaeleon, this is a living ectotherm with an erect gait!

Activity levels Linked to the previous point about the posture, we can go on to consider the way in which dinosaurs may have moved. The arguments have concentrated on the small agile types of dinosaur (particularly theropods and ornithopods). Taking *Deinonychus* as an example, we have seen that it was a remarkably specialised predator. Not only could it run fast (judging by its limb proportions) but it had a special balancing tail and had a large offensive claw on its hind foot; the latter would have obliged *Deinonychus* to leap at its prey or slash at it while standing on one foot.

What we have then is an extremely sophisticated type of dinosaur able to do a whole range of things that we would not normally associate with the usual scope of activity of a living ectothermic lizard or crocodile. The high activity levels implied in the life-style of *Deinonychus* are more compatible with the high activity levels seen in living endotherms.

Again this is a very compelling argument. Ultimately it depends upon the assumption that supposes that in order to survive in such high latitudes (near the Arctic Circle) dinosaurs must have been able to generate body heat internally. Ectothermic reptiles are incapable of surviving at such high latitudes because they cannot use the Sun to warm their bodies sufficiently.

This argument was countered by Professor Ostrom who pointed out that in the Mesozoic the latitudinal bands of climate were very different from those that exist today. The plants that were contemporaries of the dinosaurs in these high latitudes were of sub-tropical type. Thus, even at high latitudes the climate was warm and mild in Mesozoic times. Such distributional patterns cannot therefore be used to support arguments concerning the physiology of dinosaurs in either direction.

Predator/prey relationships One of the most novel of Bakker's arguments in favour of endothermy in dinosaurs depended on being able to take censuses of communities of animals from the fossil record. Again his idea was simple and quite elegant. Endothermic and ectothermic animals require different amounts of food in order to survive — what we might term their 'running costs'. Endothermic mammals and birds have high running costs because much of the food that they eat (80 per cent or more) is simply burned up (in a chemical sense) to produce body heat. Ectothermic reptiles need to take in far less food than endotherms because very little of it is used to generate heat. A working approximation is that an ectotherm needs about 10 per cent (or less) of the food requirements of an endotherm.

Bakker used this basic observation to make the following prediction. Since a balance is usually found in nature between the number of predator and prey animals, surely if we take a census of the fossil record, then the actual ratio of fossil predator to prey animals may indicate the physiology of these creatures. The results of his survey seem to support his claim. Looking first at ancient fossil 'communities' of ecto-thermic amphibians and reptiles, he noted that predator and prey were about equally represented. Dinosaur 'communities' seemed to show small numbers of predators and large numbers of prey. Finally looking at (endothermic) Tertiary mammal 'communities' he found again small numbers of predators balanced by large numbers of prey.

The similarity in pattern of predators to prey in dinosaur and early mammal 'communities' was striking, and prompts the suggestion that community structure among dinosaurs resembled that of mammals and therefore that predatory dinosaurs (at least) were endothermic.

Predator/Prey Ratios (left)
One lion (an endotherm) consumes on average about the same as 10 crocodiles (ectotherms) i.e. ten times more than a similar-sized crocodile. Thus to be in natural balance, endotherms need to have prey that are ten times more numerous than those needed by ectothermic predators. High predator to prey ratios among dinosaurs seemed to confirm Robert Bakker's ideas that they were indeed endotherms. However, further work has led to doubts being voiced about his conclusions.

This very novel approach has been challenged by several workers, notably Dr Alan Charig (London) who has pointed out that there are enormous difficulties and many suppositions that have to be made when estimating numbers of fossils in Bakker's alleged 'communities'. Other workers have also begun to assess predator/prey ratios in modern ectothermic communities and curiously seem to find that ectothermic predators make up only 10 per cent or so of the potential prey population — the sort of figure that would have been expected of an endothermic predator. The picture, therefore, is yet again far from clear. The repercussions of Bakker's novel idea have nevertheless posed many problems even for scientists working on living groups.

Bone structure (histology) For a long time evidence from the internal structure of the bones of dinosaurs and other animals has strongly favoured the notion that dinosaurs were endothermic. Looked at simply the case seems very clear-cut. If we compare thin, polished sections of bone from a lizard, a dinosaur and a mammal then we are immediately struck by the great similarity between

Right: This crocodile can consume enough food at one time to last it for several days before it is driven by hunger to pursue its next victim. A similar-sized meal might last an endothermic lion a matter of hours rather than days.

Below: A superb display of dinosaur predator and dinosaur prey in Fort Worth Museum, Texas. Having successfully brought down this *Camptosaurus,* how long would the ensuing meal have satisfied a large 'carnosaur' like *Allosaurus?*

dinosaur and mammal bone. The highly vascularised bone of endothermic mammals seems virtually identical to that of dinosaurs. This similarity is linked with the high activity levels and endothermic status of mammals and by implication of dinosaurs as well.

However various scientists, particularly Dr Armand de Ricqlès (Paris) and Dr Robin Reid (Belfast), have begun to look in detail at the structure of bone and the factors that govern its appearance under the microscope. It now appears that highly vascular bone is found in many reptiles while poorly vascular bone is found in small birds and mammals; highly vascular bone is of two types, one type is formed very quickly and is associated with fast-growing animals, the other type of vascular bone is specially designed to help bones to carry heavy loads.

So yet again the categories are less clear-cut than was first thought. The type of bone found in dinosaurs is that which would have allowed them to grow very quickly (as would be expected of an animal that had to grow to the size of an adult dinosaur) and also would have made the bones well able to carry heavy loads

(a natural prerequisite of most dinosaur bones!). The evidence for dinosaurs being endothermic on the basis of bone structure is therefore not very strong.

Birds and dinosaurs Finally there is the claim that birds (which are endothermic) evolved from dinosaurs. If this claim is correct, then dinosaurs, at least those close to the ancestry of birds, may have been endothermic as well.

Conclusions Convincing though the arguments for 'warm-blooded' dinosaurs appeared at first we have seen that there is doubt about most of them.

The present view of most palaeontologists involved in this subject is roughly as follows:

i) Dinosaurs lived at a time of very mild climatic conditions, with no strong seasons and high average temperatures.

ii) Dinosaurs were mostly very big animals. Being big has its advantages because large animals lose and gain heat only very slowly compared with small ones.

iii) Dinosaurs may well have had a fully divided heart which would have made them capable of high activity levels.

Taking these three main factors into account, dinosaurs may well have been ectothermic reptiles (which meant they did not have to eat enormous quantities of food) which were able to keep the temperature of their bodies constant and warm by being very large and living in a warm mild climate. Given these conditions and a fully divided heart, they could have been warm-bodied, highly active creatures (like mammals and birds today) without any of the costs associated with being an endotherm. Perhaps this combination of features was a key to their success in the Mesozoic Era.

Dinosaurs and Birds

The proposition that birds and reptiles are fairly closely related has not really been seriously disputed in the past. The presence of scales on the legs of birds and the fact that both birds and reptiles lay shelled eggs seems ample proof of some distant evolutionary ancestor. The more precise question of which of the various reptile groups currently recognised is closest to the ancestry of birds has, however, exercised many biologists' minds.

The issue of bird origins came to the forefront of biological and evolutionary thinking in 1861 with the discovery of the fossilised skeleton of a bird-like creature in a limestone quarry near Solnhofen (southern Germany). The limestones were of late Jurassic age and were of a peculiarly fine-grained high quality stone that was used in printing processes. As a consequence not only were the bones of the skeleton very finely preserved but also impressions of the original feathers of this early bird had been left around the skeleton.

The skeleton was named *Archaeopteryx lithographica* ('ancient wing from lithographic limestone') by Hermann von Meyer and the specimen was eventually acquired from Dr Karl Häberlein, its discoverer, by the British Museum (Natural History). In 1877 another skeleton in an even better state of preservation (it included a well preserved skull most of which was missing from the first skeleton) was obtained in the same general area by Ernst Häberlein (Karl Häberlein's son). This was subsequently sold to the Berlin Museum of Natural History. No more material of *Archaeopteryx* was recorded until 1956 when another headless specimen was discovered. Since that time another two specimens have turned up in collections, having lain unrecognised for some time. One of these, some fragments of leg and wing bone, was thought to belong to a pterosaur until in 1970 Professor Ostrom noticed the feather impressions around them. Finally, a fifth specimen was identified: another very well-preserved skeleton which had been discovered in 1951 but which had been thought to be another skeleton of *Compsognathus* until it was recognised as *Archaeopteryx* in 1973.

Archaeopteryx Described

The impression of feathers provides an immediate clue to the relationships of *Archaeopteryx* because, notwithstanding Kurzanov's dubious claims regarding *Avimimus*, birds are the only vertebrates known to possess feathers.

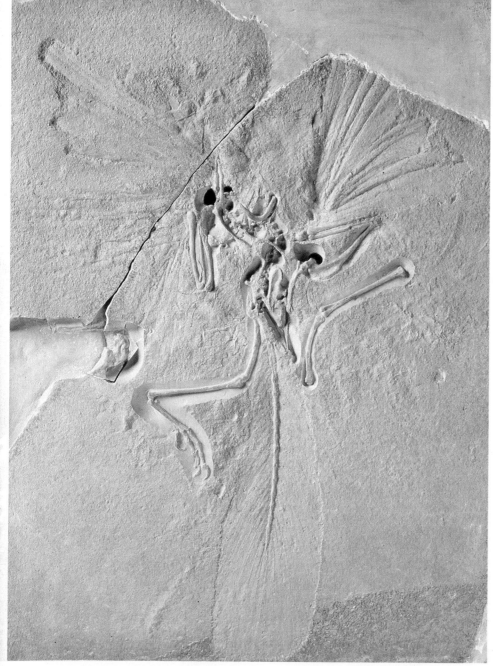

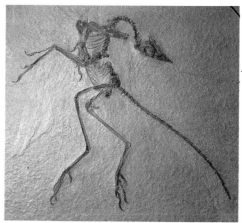

Left: This is the London specimen of *Archaeopteryx lithographica* which is kept in the British Museum (Natural History). Since it was first discovered in 1861, it has been surrounded by controversy. In 1985 some scientists, including Sir Fred Hoyle, wrongly expressed doubts about the authenticity of the feather impressions, claiming they were printed on the specimen as an elaborate hoax.

Above: Discovered in 1951, the Eichstätt *Archaeopteryx* shows no obvious feather impressions. It was labelled as *Compsognathus,* a small 'coelurosaur', until 1973, when it was recognised and described by Dr Peter Wellnhofer. It is a fine specimen, and it emphasises the point that *Archaeopteryx* and small coelurosaurian dinosaurs are very alike, and so by implication may be closely related.

Euparkeria Skull

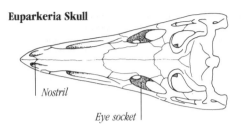

Nostril

Eye socket

Archaeopteryx Skull

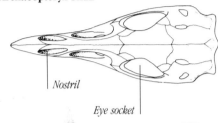

Nostril

Eye socket

Pigeon Skull

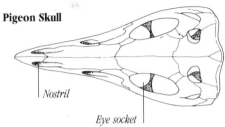

Nostril

Eye socket

So *Archaeopteryx* is an early bird, but one with some rather unusual features.

The head has a fairly long narrow snout. However, while superficially bird-like, the jaws are in fact lined with small, sharply pointed teeth. All modern birds by contrast lack teeth and have horny beaks or bills instead. The eye of *Archaeopteryx* is large, as is the brain; both of these are bird-like features—although it should perhaps be mentioned that small theropod dinosaurs share these features as well! The neck is slender and swan-like, while the back is somewhat long and more flexible than that of typical birds. Also the attachment between the hips and backbone is not nearly as extensive as it is in birds. The tail is long and bony, like that of a typical reptile and quite unlike that of birds in which the tail is reduced to a small fleshy stump: the 'Parson's Nose'.

The 'wings' of *Archaeopteryx* are not quite the same as those of birds because they still have three separate, *clawed* fingers. The shoulders do however have a distinctly bird-like 'wishbone' or furcula which is supposed to represent the fused collar bones (clavicles) of primitive reptiles. The hips seem bird-like in that the configuration of bones seems to show that the pubis lay parallel to the ischium as it did in the primitive ornithischian dinosaurs, although there is some dispute about this. The legs and feet are also slim and generally

bird-like with a reversed (though rather short) first toe on the foot. One other feature notably lacking in *Archaeopteryx* and found in the other flying forms (birds *and* pterosaurs) is the presence of air ducts running into the long bones to give them added lightness.

Given all these features, what do they tell us about *Archaeopteryx*'s nearest relatives? The pointed teeth in the jaws, the claws on its hand, and the long bony tail, all signify reptilian forebears, but the question is, which *particular* reptile group is closest.

In the late 1860s and early 1870s the British palaeontologist Thoms Henry Huxley was an ardent advocate of a dinosaur relationship with birds. At the time, dinosaurs as a group were still rather poorly understood but Huxley had noted many similarities between the hips and legs of dinosaurs and birds. However, as the new dinosaur discoveries from the American mid-West came rolling in during the 1870s and 1880s these relationships became less clear as the bewildering variety of dinosaurs started to emerge.

The whole issue of bird origins was comprehensively summarised by Gerhard Heilmann in a book on the subject which was published in 1926. In this book Heilmann dealt at length with all the anatomical factors that seemed to have any relevance to bird origins, including the anatomy and embryology of

Comparative Skulls (above)

From above, the skulls of *Euparkeria*, *Archaeopteryx*, and *Columba* (the pigeon) look fairly similar. This tends to lend support to Heilmann's contention that birds have evolved from thecodontian archosaurs (*Euparkeria*) rather than 'coelurosaur'-type dinosaurs. This is, however, rather misleading because the skull of *Euparkeria* is very different in side view.

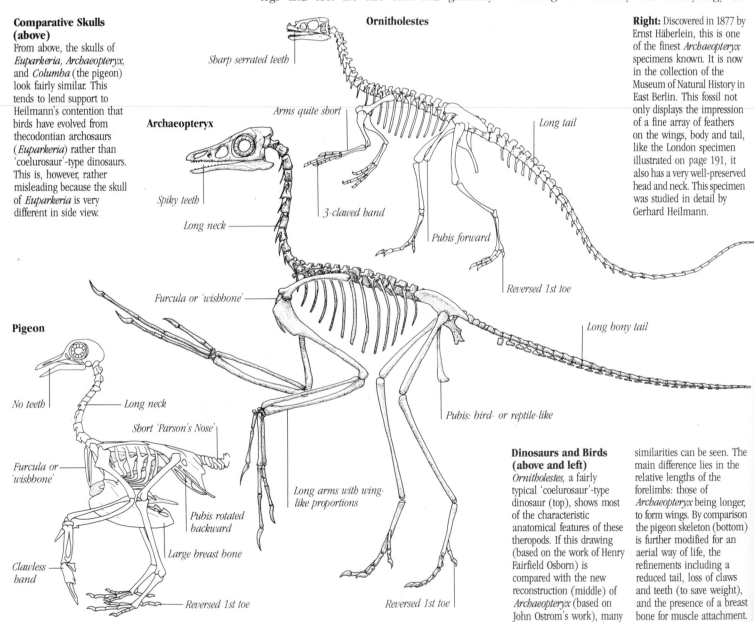

Ornitholestes

Sharp serrated teeth

Arms quite short

Long tail

Archaeopteryx

Spiky teeth

Long neck

Furcula or 'wishbone'

3-clawed hand

Pubis forward

Reversed 1st toe

Long bony tail

Pigeon

No teeth

Long neck

Short 'Parson's Nose'

Furcula or 'wishbone'

Pubis rotated backward

Large breast bone

Clawless hand

Reversed 1st toe

Long arms with wing-like proportions

Reversed 1st toe

Pubis: bird- or reptile-like

Right: Discovered in 1877 by Ernst Häberlein, this is one of the finest *Archaeopteryx* specimens known. It is now in the collection of the Museum of Natural History in East Berlin. This fossil not only displays the impression of a fine array of feathers on the wings, body and tail, like the London specimen illustrated on page 191, it also has a very well-preserved head and neck. This specimen was studied in detail by Gerhard Heilmann.

Dinosaurs and Birds (above and left)

Ornitholestes, a fairly typical 'coelurosaur'-type dinosaur (top), shows most of the characteristic anatomical features of these theropods. If this drawing (based on the work of Henry Fairfield Osborn) is compared with the new reconstruction (middle) of *Archaeopteryx* (based on John Ostrom's work), many

similarities can be seen. The main difference lies in the relative lengths of the forelimbs: those of *Archaeopteryx* being longer, to form wings. By comparison the pigeon skeleton (bottom) is further modified for an aerial way of life, the refinements including a reduced tail, loss of claws and teeth (to save weight), and the presence of a breast bone for muscle attachment.

modern birds and reptiles, the anatomy of *Archaeopteryx*, and the anatomy of a whole range of fossil reptiles. The outcome of this masterly review of the problem was as follows. Of all the reptile groups that can be considered as the ancestors of birds, the most likely candidates were archosaurs; within this category the 'coelurosaurs' among the saurischian dinosaurs were by far the best candidates. Unfortunately, as Heilmann pointed out, dinosaurs did not possess collar bones (clavicles) in their shoulders, so a 'coelurosaur' ancestry for birds was out of the question. After all, how could a bird with a well-developed wishbone (formed from the fused clavicles) ever have evolved from an animal that did not have such a bone? Caught by this one irreconcilable problem Heilmann therefore proposed that the resemblance between 'coelurosaurs' and birds was a result of evolutionary convergence, and thus proposed that birds must have evolved from more primitive archosaurs such as those found in early and middle Triassic rocks. He postulated that a group of these reptiles may have taken to the habit of living in trees where they became small agile creatures in which feathers may have first evolved as parachuting devices either to break their fall or allow them to glide from tree to tree, thereby providing the first stage which resulted in the origin of feathers, flight and birds.

Heilmann's review was so thorough and authoritative that it was not seriously questioned until the early 1970s when three alternative proposals appeared in fairly quick succession.

1970: ornithischians and birds In 1970 Peter Galton proposed that the 'bird-hipped' (ornithischian) dinosaurs were the closest relatives of birds. Galton was in fact reviving a rather old idea that had been dismissed by Heilmann in 1926. His argument, if looked at carefully, was rather evasive because he had to admit that all known ornithischian dinosaurs were far too specialised to have given rise to birds. So he was forced to propose that birds arose from an unknown archosaur of middle Triassic age which possessed a bird-like pelvis. So far no such creature has been found, and Peter Galton now admits he was wrong.

1972: crocodiles and birds In 1972 Dr Alick Walker (Newcastle) proposed that modern birds share several features in common with a Triassic crocodile-like archosaur named *Sphenosuchus*. The detailed similarities were rather complex ones relating to the arrangement of the skull bones, as well as more general ones concerning the structure of the shoulders, fore-limbs and ankle of embryo birds and crocodiles.

Walker's proposals were essentially that birds evolved from a primitive, lightly-built, crocodile-like group of archosaurs some of which took to tree-climbing, essentially as Heilmann had

proposed, while others became amphibious and developed into true crocodiles.

One curious aspect of Walker's work is that little account was taken of the structure of *Archaeopteryx* which must surely receive some attention when bird origins are discussed. Interesting and provocative though Alick Walker's ideas are, it seems that he too has begun to recant in favour of the third and last proposal.

1973: theropods and birds In 1973 Professor John Ostrom revived the idea of a 'coelurosaur' ancestry for birds. A careful anatomical review of *Archaeopteryx* revealed that it shared over 20 features in common with 'coelurosaur'-type dinosaurs. The major problem of the lack of a 'collar-bone' or clavicle in theropods was shown not to be a problem at all, because several theropods did in fact possess clavicles (see page 47). In any case some embryological evidence suggests that the 'wish-bone' is not equivalent to 'collar bones' at all.

Some of Ostrom's most telling points in favour of a theropod ancestry for *Archaeopteryx* and therefore of birds can be summarised as follows. First, he claimed that the hips of *Archaeopteryx* were not bird-like at all but rather were crushed into the bird-like arrangement during fossilisation; in life, therefore, they may have closely resembled the arrangement seen in theropod dinosaurs. Secondly, the forelimbs of theropods and *Archaeopteryx* are remarkably similar down to the minutest detail and thirdly, the hindlimbs and feet of *Archaeopteryx* are also very similar to those of theropods. In the light of Ostrom's long list of similarities, the question arises: could all these detailed similarities have arisen through convergent evolution? The answer would seem to be a resounding no!

This is not to say that the debate is now closed. Dr Sam Tarsitano and Dr Max Hecht are recent ardent advocates of Heilmann's original proposals of a more distant Triassic archosaur ancestor of birds. They claim to have found major faults with Ostrom's original work. Also several embryologists claim that the three fingers of the modified hand of living birds could not possibly have evolved from the three fingers of the theropod hand because the hand of birds is composed of the 2nd, 3rd and 4th fingers while in theropods the fingers are the 1st, 2nd and 3rd ones! Quite where this leaves *Archaeopteryx*, which also appears to have a theropod-like hand of fingers 1, 2 and 3, is a matter of some embarrassment – does it mean that *Archaeopteryx* was merely a feathered dinosaur and not related to birds at all?

Obviously the debate over the origins of birds is far from over even though a strong consensus of opinion now favours a theropod/ 'coelurosaur' ancestry.

The Origin of Flight

Almost as contentious an issue as the origin of birds, the origin of flight has also aroused much attention. There are in essence two main schools of thought: flight either evolved in fast-running ground animals or from gliding tree-dwellers.

Flying from the ground Leading advocates of this theory have been S.W. Williston (1879), F.B. Nopsca (1907) and J.H. Ostrom (1974). The general notion is that bird ancestors were, like 'coelurosaurs', fast-running creatures. The development of wings is therefore seen as a means of adding propulsion (in Nopsca's and Williston's interpretation). This idea is not regarded with great enthusiasm by most palaeontologists because the 'proto-

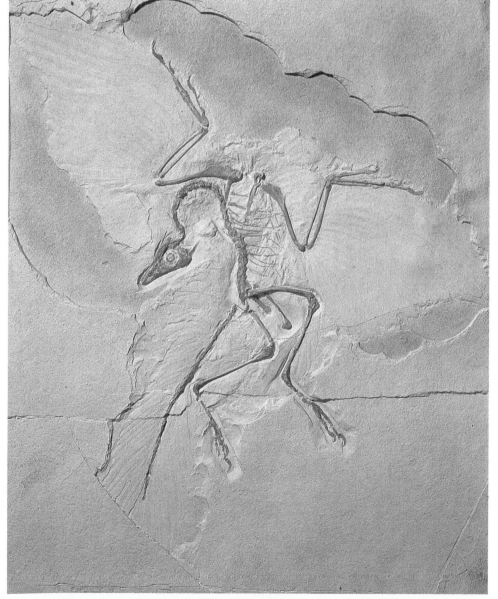

Below: The origin of flight in birds, and vertebrates in general, is a matter of some dispute. From an energetic point of view, it is far easier for an animal to begin flying by parachuting or gliding, as Stephen Winkworth's model of *Pteranodon* here illustrates.

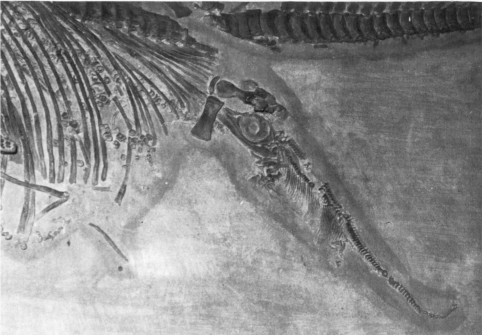

wings' would create either a lot of drag or lift, neither of which will help the animal run any more quickly.

John Ostrom's idea provides a novel twist to these earlier ideas in that he imagines *Archaeopteryx* as, at best, a very poor flier. Feeding on flying insects, he imagines that its feathered arms ('wings') were used as traps to help catch insects; these arms, he argues, allowed *Archaeopteryx* to make short fluttering jumps upwards to help it catch insects, thereby providing the first step toward active flapping flight.

Gliding from trees By far the most popular theory of the origin of flight is that proposed by Heilmann. Flight is seen as developing in stages from the efforts of tree-dwelling 'proto-birds' which used feathered limbs to break their fall and/or glide from tree to tree. Such gliding adaptations (using skin, ribs etc.) are seen in a host of tree-dwelling vertebrates living today — from frogs, to snakes and lizards, squirrels and monkeys. The advantages of gliding are great in that they save the time and energy that would have to be expended going down one tree and then up the next. The move from gliding to powered flight is then a relatively minor matter of modifying muscles and joints in order to flap the wings.

Although this issue is difficult to resolve with any degree of certainty, I favour Heilmann's interpretation. There are certain bio-mechanical problems associated with fast ground-running with wings outspread: as lift is generated so traction with the ground would be lessened. It seems more feasible that gliding from trees allowed intermittent flying patterns to be developed, and a gradual modification of gliding surfaces into wings to be achieved.

Extinction of the Dinosaurs

The last and perhaps most controversial issue to concern dinosaurs relates to their eventual downfall. For an enormously long period of time, slightly in excess of 140 million years — from the end of the Triassic until the close of the Cretaceous Period — dinosaurs of one sort or another dominated the terrestrial environments of the world. At the same time other groups of reptiles dominated the two other physical environments, air and water. In the sea the dominant predators appear to have

been the sleek ichthyosaurs and remarkable plesiosaurs, and to a lesser extent crocodiles and mosasaurs. In the air the pterosaurs seem to have been dominant for the early part of the Mesozoic, but in the Cretaceous their radiation may have been limited by the appearance of newly-evolved birds. Then, apparently quite suddenly, the dinosaurs went extinct 64 million years ago at the end of the Cretaceous Period. The extinction of the dinosaurs at this time has, quite unfairly, been the primary focus of attention for a large number of scientists, as well as the public at large. This is perhaps understandable, the dinosaurs were large and extremely interesting forms of life and have provoked a great deal of public interest in fossil animals as a whole. However, their prominent position has provoked a great number of theories which have attempted to explain the extinction of dinosaurs *alone*. An example of this type of thinking is one theory that was put forward quite seriously by a palaeontologist many years ago, which proposed that the small Mesozoic mammals took to the habit of eating dinosaurs' eggs. The end result of this change of diet was the over-predation of eggs leading to the extinction of the dinosaurs.

A few moments reflection are probably all that are needed to come to a decision about this particular theory. In the first place, it is exceedingly improbable that the change to an egg-eating diet by mammals should have caused the extinction of *all* dinosaur species; after all we cannot even be sure they all laid eggs! Secondly, many egg-eating species are known today but these show no sign whatever of causing the extinction of their prey; indeed it is biological 'common-sense' not to cause the extinction of the organisms that you feed upon otherwise you will surely hasten your own end!

Notwithstanding these immediate and obvious objections to such a theory, one much more important observation can be made which renders it a complete non-starter. At the end of the Cretaceous Period, it was not simply the ornithischian and saurischian dinosaurs that went extinct, but also pterosaurs, mosasaurs, plesiosaurs, and ichthyosaurs among the vertebrate animals, as well as ammonites and calcareous (chalky) plankton. The end of the Cretaceous marked the time of what is called a mass-extinction, that is to say the extinction of

Above: Frozen in time, this remarkable fossil shows the moment of birth of a baby ichthyosaur, tail first, from its mother. It is a graphic illustration that not all reptiles lay eggs, which in turn rebuts the argument that egg-eating mammals were the cause of the mass-extinction at the end of the Cretaceous Period.

Below: This ammonite is just one example of a vast array of marine animals that went extinct at the close of the Cretaceous Period. While it is all very well to try to explain the extinction of the land-living dinosaurs in isolation, such explanations more often than not founder when they have to account for ammonite extinctions.

not just one or two species, but a whole range of near and distantly related forms. As we have seen from the fossil record of dinosaurs alone which we have traced in some detail in this book, extinction is the eventual fate of all species. Indeed, no matter how optimistic we might feel at the present, even our human species is almost certainly destined for extinction in the end. Thus we would expect to find species originating, diversifying and finally becoming extinct throughout the fossil record. For the most part that is indeed the pattern that seems to emerge. However, at apparently irregular intervals, notably the Permian-Triassic and the Cretaceous-Tertiary boundaries, mass-extinctions appear to have occurred. Such events would not have been predicted from what we know of the process of evolution. The simultaneous extinction of a whole range of species, both closely and distantly related, implies that some common cause or event must have been responsible. The possibility

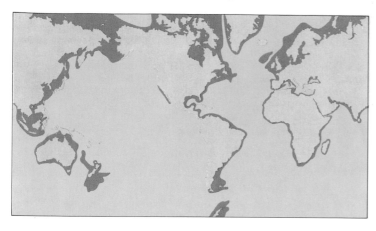

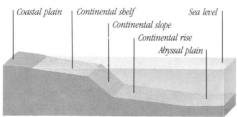

Continental Shelves (left and below left)
The continental shelves (dark brown) reveal the real extent of the continents below sea level. The links that exist today between North America and Asia, and the countries of Northern Europe, can be clearly seen. The section through a continental margin (below left) shows the relation between a continental shelf and other major submarine features. These areas are densely populated by marine organisms. A large drop in sea level as a result of the formation of the super-continent of Pangaea, such as that proposed in the Permo-Triassic, would have had catastrophic effects on the animals living on the continental shelf, and may explain the mass-extinction.

Below: The excavation of a plesiosaur skeleton of Jurassic age at Fletton near Peterborough in England. Plesiosaurs lasted until the end of the Cretaceous. The cause of their extinction, like that of the dinosaurs, remains unexplained.

towards one another. In the late Permian the continents appear to have fused together to form one gigantic supercontinent named Pangaea. The potential effects of the formation of Pangaea upon the ecosystems of the Earth may hold the key to the mass-extinction phenomenon at this time. It has been suggested that the formation of Pangaea would have dramatically changed the conditions for marine organisms in a number of ways.

First, at least 50 per cent of the area of the continental shelf surrounding each of the continents would have been 'lost' where the continents actually joined together. This would restrict the area available for marine species to exist and presumably also the total number capable of living in this sea.

Secondly, the joining together of continental shelves would have reduced species diversity because there would be competition between previously isolated species and only the most vigorous would survive. Thus in the end fewer species would be more widely spread.

Thirdly, the joining together of the continents may have caused a temporary halt in sea-floor spreading activity at the mid-oceanic ridges and marginal continental trenches (subduction zones). As a result the huge ocean ridges may have collapsed back into the Earth's crust. If this happened then there would have been an enormous increase in the capacity of the oceans causing a large drop in the sea-level. Some estimates have proposed that the sea-level may have dropped by over 200 feet—perilously close to the top of the continental shelf. Since most of the marine organisms tend to live in or on the continental shelves the effect of a drop in sea-level of this magnitude may have been catastrophic.

What we have therefore is a single unified explanation for the mass-extinctions at the end of the Permian. All can be seen as a natural consequence of the chance formation of Pangaea as a result of continental movements. The evidence from the marine fauna is also backed up by evidence from the terrestrial fauna. Here, although extinctions are not nearly so marked, the diversity of species drops noticeably as animals originally confined to one continent find that they are able to spread almost world-wide at the expense of others (e.g. the dicynodont *Lystrosaurus* has been found in India, Antarctica, South Africa and Central Asia in early Triassic times). The geophysical and fossil evidence therefore seems to be in remarkable accord with this theory to explain the mass-extinction.

that all the species went extinct purely coincidentally seems too remote for most scientists to give it serious consideration. Therefore, returning briefly to our first dinosaur extinction theory, the likelihood that egg-eating mammals caused the extinction of ammonites, chalky plankton, ichythyosaurs (which bore live young!) etc. cannot be entertained seriously.

I have dwelt on the egg-eating mammal theory not because it is particularly contemptible, but rather because it serves as an excellent example of a whole range of theories which have been advanced simply to explain the extinction of the dinosaurs at the end of the Cretaceous. No consideration is given to the other animals that went extinct simultaneously.

Mass-Extinctions

Two mass-extinctions were mentioned above. Both of these 'events' are particularly prominent in the fossil record: one at the end of the

Permian Period and the other at the end of the Cretaceous Period. Although the former 'event' precedes the era of the dinosaurs, it has aroused a great deal of interest and deserves some consideration here, because it can be compared with the events of the late Cretaceous.

Permo-Triassic extinctions The fossil record of marine animals shows a remarkable mass-extinction at the end of the Permian as a result of which up to 70 per cent of all known groups went extinct. This is a more dramatic but less heavily publicised mass-extinction that the one that involved the dinosaurs. Evidence of the dramatic marine mass-extinction has prompted many explanations. One of the most popular theories at present is based upon our knowledge of plate tectonics ('continental drift', see also pages 15-17).

Coincident with the mass-extinction event, the various continents of the late Palaeozoic world, which had up till then been separate and drifting across the oceans, seem to have drifted

Cretaceous-Tertiary Extinctions

If we exclude from consideration those theories which explain the extinctions at the end of the Cretaceous Period in terms of the dinosaurs alone, we are left with just two main theories which attempt to explain the mass-extinction: a 'cosmic' theory and a climatic change theory.

Cosmic explanation A long-standing theory to explain the Cretaceous extinctions has been one which favours some sort of global cosmic influence. One of the favourites in this category has been the possibility of a star exploding in a nearby constellation and forming a supernova. The effects of this supernova would be to bathe the Earth's surface in deadly cosmic rays which could have caused the widespread extinctions. This has always run into the problem of explaining how the deadly cosmic rays killed some groups but left others, such as the birds, mammals, crocodiles and turtles, to survive apparently unscathed. Secondly there do not appear from astrophysical observations to be many good candidates within nearby constellations of the remnants of stars that may have caused such a supernova at this time.

Such cosmic theorising, however, has had an unexpected boost in recent years as a result of the work of Luis Alvarez, his son Walter Alvarez and colleagues in California. While carrying out routine sampling of sediments from the late Cretaceous of Gubbio (Italy) they discovered unexpectedly high levels of a rare element named iridium. Iridium is a heavy metal which is not normally found in large amounts in the Earth's crust. What iridium there is on Earth is concentrated in the molten core. It would have sunk there at the time of the formation of the Earth 4,500 million years ago when the Earth was still molten rock. One potential source of iridium, however, is extra-terrestrial: from meteorites, asteroids and comets.

The iridium 'spike' or anomaly was explained by Alvarez and his team as evidence of a truly massive meteorite impact at the end of the Cretaceous Period. Examination of clays of late Cretaceous age from elsewhere in the world turned up similar iridium 'spikes' confirming the widespread nature of the iridium-rich layer.

Scientists attempting to account for this phenomenon theorised that the iridium may have been introduced into these sediments as dust. This dust could have been created by the impact of a massive (6-9 mile, 10-15km wide) meteorite with the Earth. Such a collision would have caused a massive explosion as the meteorite scorched its way through the atmosphere and then impacted the Earth's crust. The meteorite would have vaporised on impact and an enormous cloud of dust and steam would have risen into the atmosphere. The resulting cloud of steam and dust is held to be the main cause of the extinctions. It is proposed that if the cloud shrouded the Earth for an appreciable length of time, several weeks or even months so the predictions go, then the biological effects would have been dramatic. Shrouding the Earth in dust and water vapour would cut out the light from the Sun which is essential for plant growth on land and at sea (phyto-plankton). These are the organisms at the bottom of th food pyramid upon which life on Earth is almost totally dependent. If the Earth was shrouded for an appreciable length of time then the damage to ecosystems on land and in the sea would have been profound. Most of the animals near the top of the pyramid, the great carnivores and herbivores of the time, would go extinct. In fact the creatures best able to survive in the short term may well have been the smaller opportunistic scavenging types of animals: mammals, lizards and snakes, croco-diles, rather than the larger, more specialised types.

Thus, as in the case of the Permo-Triassic extinctions, the meteorite impact theory also has the benefit of linking a chance event with natural and understandable biological reper-cussions. A large body of scientists now endorse this particular theory very strongly although there is still much discussion about its finer aspects.

Much debate has centred on the nature of the extra-terrestrial bombardment that the Earth is thought to have experienced, and the celestial mechanism that may have set it off. Rather than being the result of a meteor impact, some scientists argue that the iridium anomaly might have been caused by a rain of comets that, judging by the stratigraphic evidence, is

believed to strike the Earth every 26 million years or so. Such comets might be 'shaken out' of the Oort Cloud—a vast field of comets that orbits the Sun at a distance of about 9 million million miles—by the action of some cosmic agency. There are three major theories of how this might come about.

The first envisages that the Sun is part of a binary star system i.e. it has a (so far undis-covered) companion star circling it in a highly elliptical orbit, which periodically exerts gravitational influence on the Oort Cloud, causing comets to be hurled towards the inner Solar System. The second theory ascribes this gravitational influence to the presence of a tenth planet (Planet X, also undiscovered to date) which may be orbiting the Sun in a sharply inclined orbit which is constantly changing as a result of the gravitational influences of the other planets, and which may thus intersect the cometary disc only at very

long intervals. Such a planet might also account for observed anomalies in the orbit of Neptune.

The third explanation takes as its starting point the nature of the Solar System's orbit around the centre of our galaxy. The Milky Way galaxy is shaped rather like a disc with a bulbous centre; the Sun and the planets slowly orbit this centre and in doing so bob up and down through the plane of the galaxy rather like riders on a merry-go-round. It has been postulated that the passage through the denser dust clouds in the galactic plane might be the cause of comets being hurled out of their normal orbits.

All these theories have their ardent propo-nents, and also their vociferous critics who can find fault with the astrophysical assumptions underlying them. However, in contrast to the 'cosmic school' there are several palaeon-tologists who favour a less dramatic explanation of the end of the Mesozoic Era.

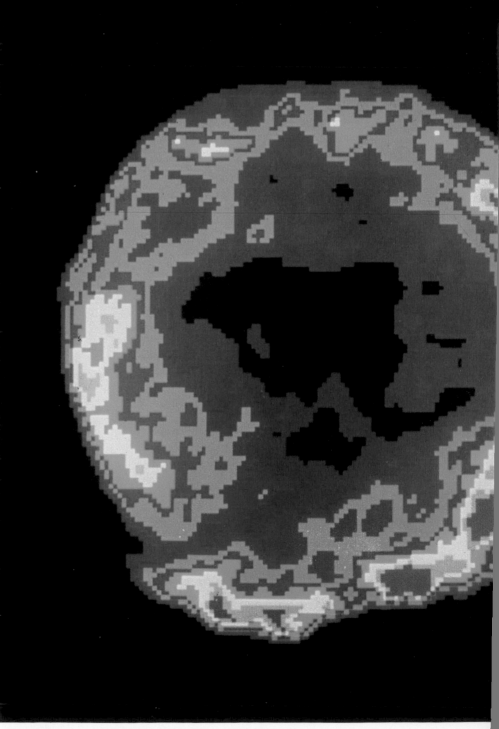

Climatic change theory This theory has had several advocates, notably Leigh Van Valen and Robert Sloan, in the last decade. Their contention is that the events of the late Cretaceous were not quick and dramatic, as proponents of the cosmic theories believe, but were the culmination of changes in climate that had begun in the early part of the late Cretaceous.

Careful analysis of geological sections from North America has revealed, according to Van Valen and Sloan, a marked but gradual change in plant and animal types. About 5 to 10 million years from the end of the Cretaceous Period the vegetation was very lush with abundant tropical and sub-tropical species of plants; these conditions supported a rich and varied dinosaur fauna. However, towards the close of the Cretaceous the flora changed markedly to one dominated by cool, temperate woodland plants; the dinosaurs became fewer in variety and various small mammals were more conspicuous elements in the fauna.

The implication is that the climate deteriorated towards the end of the Cretaceous Period. The consequent change in plant types supported less varied dinosaur types while the cooler conditions favoured the insulated endothermic mammals rather than the uninsulated ecto-thermic dinosaurs. The story that seems to be emerging from these studies is thus one of slower, climatically induced change.

What may the cause of this climatic change have been? One possible cause may be, yet again, continental drift. In the late Cretaceous, continental movement had separated all the major continents. Indeed, all the sea-floor spreading activity may have resulted in appreciably raised sea-levels (exactly the reverse of the late Permian!) resulting in shallow seas dividing, for example, west from east North America, Asia from Europe and subdividing Africa. The effect of all these separate continental areas may have been to alter ocean currents, wind patterns and consequently climatic patterns from the prevailing mild conditions of the Jurassic and Cretaceous to the cooler, more seasonal, conditions which seem to mark the late Cretaceous.

Drawing Conclusions

Could climatic changes induced by continental drift explain the late Cretaceous extinctions? While they might explain terrestrial extinctions, the marine extinctions are not so readily understood. The idea is that lower global temperatures affected the plankton. Many types of plankton are notoriously temperature sensitive; perhaps this was the reason for the extinction among chalky plankton. If such was the case, then climatic changes may have indeed induced extinctions in the sea because plankton forms the base of the food pyramid upon which plesiosaurs, mosasaurs and ammonites may have depended.

In the final analysis, neither of these theories is entirely satisfactory. Were the late Cretaceous extinctions almost instantaneous or more gradual? Could the iridium 'spike' have been caused by volcanic activity associated with great tectonic activity in the late Cretaceous? Could the marine extinctions really have been caused by climatic changes as proposed above?

At the moment a great deal of work is being undertaken by scientists to try to find answers to these and many other questions. For example efforts are being made to try to correlate geological sections from various areas, particularly in North America, to see whether or not they show *exactly* similar timings of the Cretaceous extinctions. This is extremely difficult (perhaps it will prove impossible) work, but if a clear answer emerges it will surely bring us very close to the answer to this perplexing 64 million year old question.

Above: This photograph shows the team of explorers who discovered the Hoba West meteorite in 1920. The largest meteorite discovered to date, this would be dwarfed by the one that is supposed by some authorities to have caused the end of the dinosaurs and other Mesozoic organisms.

Left: Tycho's Supernova. This striking picture is a radio-telescope image of the remnants of a supernova which occurred in 1572 AD. The ring-like structure represents the radio emission from the supernova blast wave. Remnants of a stellar explosion of this type which occurred 64 million years ago would be needed to link such an event to the extinctions at the end of the Cretaceous.

Right: Comet Ikeya-Seki, vivid in the night sky. One theory favours comet showers resulting from disturbances in the Oort Cloud as the agent of periodic extinctions on the Earth.

To give some impression of how wide-spread dinosaur discoveries are, a map of the world has been provided with many of the dinosaur localities marked. Many of these sites have already been described earlier in the book, under the various sections devoted to the individual groups of dinosaurs.

The overwhelming impression that is gained from studying the map is that dinosaur fossils are remarkably widespread. Almost all of the continents (excluding Antarctica) have produced dinosaur remains. Even Antarctica no doubt contains fossil dinosaurs, the obvious problem, however, is that the rocks of the appropriate age are mostly covered by ice-sheets. The fact that the early Triassic *Lystrosaurus* (a mammal-like reptile) has been discovered here shows that Antarctica has not always been an inhospitable ice-bound continent as it is today.

A map of discoveries of dinosaurs made in the middle of the last century would have looked very different from the one we see here. At that time, dinosaur remains were only known from Europe (England and Germany) and North America, as a result of the pioneering work of Gideon Mantell in Britain, Hermann von Meyer in Gemany and Ferdinand Vandiveer Hayden in Montana, North America. From these rather modest beginnings the rate of dinosaur discoveries increased dramatically in the second half of the nineteenth century. Most of the finds were centred on North America.

North America

The first important discovery around the 1850s was that Hayden found several dinosaur localities both in western and eastern North America. Then, in the late 1870s, further dramatic discoveries in Wyoming and Colorado attracted the attention of the two rival palaeontologists, Othniel Charles Marsh and Edward Drinker Cope. The feverish activities of these two scientists, and perhaps more importantly their hired teams of explorers and excavators, resulted in the discovery of dinosaurs right across the continent from New England in the east to Utah and Colorado in the west. North America has been an extremely fine hunting ground for dinosaurs. Not only have some localities proved to be particularly rich in dinosaur remains — notably those in Wyoming, Colorado, Montana and Alberta — but they have also revealed dinosaurs from all three periods of the Mesozoic. Triassic and early Jurassic dinosaurs have been recovered from Arizona and Connecticut in particular. In fact very recently (1985) Robert Long reported the discovery of a new, extremely early dinosaur from the Painted Desert of Arizona. This may be one of the earliest dinosaurs found to date, but as yet it has not been fully prepared or described. Jurassic, and particularly late Jurassic, rocks are those of Utah, Colorado and Wyoming where some of the most spectacular discoveries have been made. Cretaceous finds are largely from the late Cretaceous of States such as Montana, Alberta and New Mexico. Early Cretaceous discoveries are less abundant on the whole, although significant finds have been made in southern Montana and South Dakota.

South America

In the latter half of the nineteenth century dinosaurs were also discovered in South America. Interest in fossils had been stimulated by the work of Georges Cuvier and Richard Owen who were both able to describe fossil material of giant extinct mammals brought back by early explorers of that continent — notably one Charles Darwin during the voyage of the *Beagle*. Most dinosaur discoveries have been made in southern Brazil and Argentina where Mesozoic rocks are quite widespread. While much of the early work revolved around chance discoveries, careful and systematic collection in the last few years by teams led by José Bonaparte have begun to discover very important, well-preserved remains.

Europe

Western Europe has a long tradition of dinosaur discovery and excavation, but, despite this, its collections have been largely outshone by the more dramatic discoveries elsewhere in the world. Some of the best Triassic deposits are in Germany, where the famous *Plateosaurus* quarries of Halberstadt and Trössingen were excavated earlier this century. Jurassic rocks, although quite widespread, have never produced really good fossil skeletons. The best are from the quarries of central-western Britain; the ones that have produced the partial remains of creatures such as *Megalosaurus, Eustreptospondylus* and *Cetiosauriscus,* but never the wonderful, fully articulated, huge dinosaur skeletons found in North America or China. The late Jurassic lagoon deposits of southern Germany have, however, yielded the beautifully preserved small skeletons of *Archaeopteryx* and *Compsognathus.*

Early Cretaceous rocks have been a little more generous, yielding many skeletons of *Iguanodon* in southern England, Belgium, Germany and Spain in particular. Little else is well preserved. Later Cretaceous rocks are also frustratingly poor. Some well-preserved remains are known from Rumania (Transylvania) and the dinosaur egg locality of southern France (Aix-en-Provence), but most remains are fragmentary and poor.

Central Asia

Until the early 1920s and the American Museum Central Asiatic Expeditions, virtually nothing was known of the fossil remains of this area. The Central Asiatic Expedition revealed rich dinosaur-bearing rocks in Mongolia which were subsequently explored by Russian and Polish Expeditions in the 1940s and more recent decades. Finds from this area, particularly in the late Cretaceous of the Gobi Desert, have proved as interesting and exciting as those from North America at the turn of the century. Notable among them are the discoveries of *Tarbosaurus, Saurolophus,* various ankylosaurs, pachycephalosaurs and a host of small theropods and large sauropods.

China

China has extensive Triassic, Jurassic and Cretaceous exposures that have begun to yield enormous numbers of dinosaurs in recent years. Early chance discoveries in north-eastern China (*Mandschurosaurus*) at the turn of the century were followed by systematic excavations by Chinese palaeontologists in the 1930s and 1940s and the discovery of *Lufengosaurus* from the Triassic. This was followed by work in

Localities of Dinosaur Discoveries Worldwide

Cretaceous and Jurassic exposures, which has produced some quite spectacular finds, notably those from Sichuan Province.

Australia and India

Again, discoveries of dinosaurs date back to the early part of this century. Most remains have so far been frustratingly poor, but it seems to be only a matter of time before rich dinosaur-bearing localities are discovered. Recent Australian finds include *Austrosaurus, Mutta-burrasaurus* and *Fulgurotherium.*

First reports of dinosaurs in India date back to the latter half of the nineteenth century (notably the sauropod *Titanosaurus*). More recently the Kota area of central India has revealed abundant remains of the early Jurassic dinosaur *Barapasaurus.* The interesting late Cretaceous stegosaur *Dravidosaurus* was found in southern India.

Africa

Finds of dinosaurs in Africa are quite widespread: ranging from the Triassic and early Jurassic exposures in southern Africa that have produced prosauropods such as *Massospondylus* and *Anchisaurus* and the ornithopods *Lesotho-saurus* and *Heterodontosaurus;* through the late Jurassic deposits of Tanzania that have revealed forms such as *Brachiosaurus, Dicraeo-saurus* and *Kentrosaurus;* to the Cretaceous deposits of the central Sahara, Niger and Morocco that have yielded large sauropods, *Ouranosaurus* and the peculiar *Spinosaurus.*

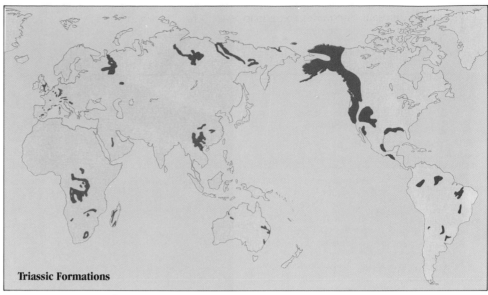

Triassic Formations

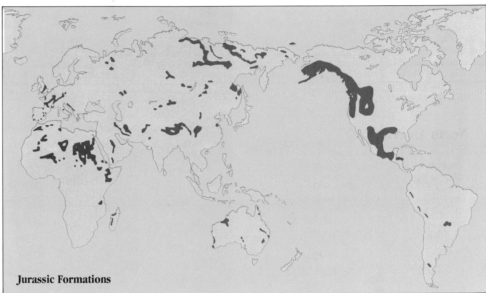

Jurassic Formations

Left: This map shows many of the important localities worldwide where dinosaur discoveries have been made. It is at once obvious how widespread was the dispersal of the dinosaurs on land. New expeditions will no doubt extend the picture even further.

Top: This map shows those exposures of Triassic rocks that are currently charted. Important finds from this Period include *Coelophysis* (USA), *Plateosaurus* (West Germany), *Anchisaurus* (South Africa) and Robert Long's new dinosaur from the Arizona desert.

Above: Notable among the finds from Jurassic rocks are many of the large sauropods, the small theropod *Compsognathus* from South Germany, and two very early ornithischians, *Scelidosaurus* (England) and *Heterodontosaurus* (South Africa).

Below: Fossils finds in Cretaceous rocks are many; they include numerous ceratopians from Canada and North America, an abundance of hadrosaurids and iguanodontids, and most of the recent spectacular discoveries from Mongolia and China.

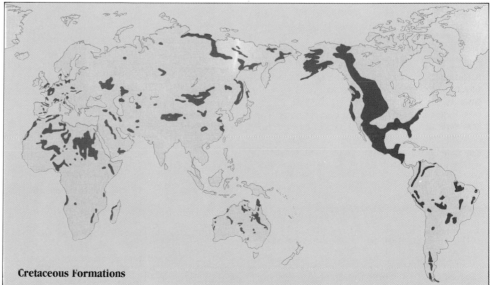

Cretaceous Formations

The purpose of this listing is to show the major institutions where dinosaur skeletons, casts, or fossil remains are on display around the world, and to indicate the most important specimens that particular collections hold. Wherever possible, full postal addresses have been included. This list is obviously not exhaustive, and the editor would welcome correspondence from the curators of any museums that have been inadvertently left out, or, where appropriate, information to update the listing of specimens on display. The list is split into four broad continental groups: Africa, the Americas, Asia and Australia, and Europe.

AFRICA

Morocco

The Museum of Earth Sciences
Rabat
Cetiosaurus
Rebbachisaurus

Niger

Musée National du Niger
B.P. No 248,
Niamey
Ouranosaurus

South Africa

Bernard Price Institute
of Palaeontology
University of Witwatersrand,
Jan Smuts Avenue,
Johannesburg 2001
Melanorosaurus

South African Museum
PO Box 61,
Cape Town,
South Africa 8000
Anchisaurus
Heterodontosaurus
Massospondylus
Melanorosaurus

Zimbabwe

National Museum of Zimbabwe
Harare
Syntarsus
Vulcanodon

THE AMERICAS

Argentina

Museo Argentino de Ciencias
Naturales
Av. Angel Gallardo 470,
1405 Buenos Aires
Antarctosaurus
Mussaurus
Noasaurus
Riojasaurus
Saltasaurus
Titanosaurus

Museum of La Plata University
La Plata
Centrosaurus
Diplodocus

Brazil

Museu Nacional
20942 Quinto da Boa Vista,
São Cristovao,
Rio de Janeiro 20940
Various sauropods

Canada

Dinosaur Provincial Park
Patricia,
Alberta
Excavation in progress

National Museum of Natural
Sciences
Ottawa,
Ontario KA1 OM8
Anchiceratops
Daspletosaurus
Dromiceiomimus
Leptoceratops
Panoplosaurus
Styracosaurus
Triceratops
Various hadrosaurids

Provincial Museum of Alberta
12845 102 Avenue,
Edmonton,
Alberta T5N OM6
Ankylosaurus model
Corythosaurus model
Lambeosaurus
Struthiomimus model

Redpath Museum
McGill University,
859 Sherbrook Street West,
Quebec H3A 2K6
Majungatholus
Saurornithoides
Zephyrosaurus

Royal Ontario Museum
Toronto,
Ontario M5S 2C6
Albertosaurus
Allosaurus
Camptosaurus
Chasmosaurus
Corythosaurus
Edmontosaurus
Hadrosaurus
Lambeosaurus
Ornithomimus
Parasaurolophus
Prosaurolophus

Tyrrell Museum of
Palaeontology
PO Box 7500,
Drumheller,
Alberta
Albertosaurus
Centrosaurus
Coelophysis
Corythosaurus
Dromaeosaurus
Hadrosaurus
Hypacrosaurus
Lambeosaurus
Ornitholestes
Saurornitholestes
Tyrannosaurus

Zoological Gardens
Calgary,
Alberta
Outdoor display of models

Mexico

Natural History Museum
Mexico City
Diplodocus cast

United States of America

Academy of Natural Sciences
19th & The Parkway,
Logan Square,
Philadelphia,
Pennsylvania 19103
A new display is under
construction; exhibits will
include:
Brachyceratops
Corythosaurus

Deinonychus
Hadrosaurus
'*Supersaurus*' leg
Tenontosaurus

American Museum of Natural
History
Central Park West/79th St,
New York,
New York 10024
Albertosaurus
Allosaurus
Anatosaurus
Apatosaurus
Camptosaurus
Coelophysis
Corythosaurus
Lambeosaurus
Montanoceratops
Monoclonius
Ornitholestes
Panoplosaurus
Plateosaurus
Protoceratops
Psittacosaurus
Saurolophus
Stegosaurus
Styracosaurus
Triceratops
Tyrannosaurus

Amherst College
Pratt Museum,
Amherst,

Massachusetts 01002
Anchisaurus

Buffalo Museum of Science
Buffalo,
New York
Allosaurus
Psittacosaurus
Triceratops

Carnegie Museum of Natural
History
4400 Forbes Avenue,
Pittsburgh,
Pennsylvania 15213
Allosaurus
Apatosaurus
Camarasaurus
Camptosaurus
Corythosaurus
Diplodocus
Dryosaurus
Protoceratops
Stegosaurus
Tyrannosaurus

Denver Museum of Natural
History
City Park,
Denver,
Colorado 80205
Anatosaurus
Diplodocus
Stegosaurus
Tyrannosaurus

Cleveland Museum of Natural
History
Wade Oval,
University Circle,
Cleveland,
Ohio 44106
Allosaurus
Haplocanthosaurus

Dinosaur National
Monument
PO Box 128,
Jensen,
Utah 84035
A vast quarry site where
excavation is still in progress.
Dinosaurs found here include:
Allosaurus
Apatosaurus
Camarasaurus
Camptosaurus
Ceratosaurus
Dryosaurus
Stegosaurus

Earth Sciences Museum
Brigham Young University,
Provo,
Utah 84602
'*Supersaurus*'
'*Ultrasaurus*'

Field Museum of Natural
History
Roosevelt Road at Lake Shore
Drive,

Above: The spacious main hall of the British Museum (Natural History) provides a magnificent setting for the Museum's permanent exhibition: *Dinosaurs and their living relatives.* In the foreground we see a cast of the skeleton of the 85ft (26m) long sauropod *Diplodocus*; behind that is a cast of the skeleton of *Triceratops.* Normally this hall is thronging with adults and children— living (and noisy!) proof of the enduring fascination of dinosaurs.

Chicago,
Illinois 60605
Albertosaurus
Apatosaurus
Diplodocus
Lambeosaurus
Protoceratops

Forth Worth Museum of
Science
1501 Montgomery Street,
Forth Worth,
Texas 76107
Allosaurus
Camptosaurus

Houston Museum of Natural
Science
Houston,
Texas
Diplodocus

Los Angeles County Museum
900 Exposition Boulevard,
Los Angeles,
California 90007
Allosaurus
Camptosaurus
Corythosaurus
Dilophosaurus
Edmontosaurus
Parasaurolophus
Tyrannosaurus

Museum of Comparative
Zoology
Harvard University,
Cambridge,
Massachusetts 02138
Heterodontosaurus
Plateosaurus
Scutellosaurus
Staurikosaurus

Museum of Northern Arizona
Box 720,
Flagstaff,
Arizona 86001
Coelophysis
Scutellosaurus

Museum of Palaeontology
University of California,
Berkeley,
California 94720
Dilophosaurus

Museum of the Rockies
Montana State University,
Bozeman,
Montana 59715
Maiasaura

National Museum of Natural
History
Smithsonian Institution,
Washington D.C. 20560
Albertosaurus
Allosaurus
Brachyceratops
Camarasaurus
Camptosaurus
Diplodocus
Edmontosaurus
Stegosaurus
Thescelosaurus
Triceratops

Peabody Museum of Natural
History
Yale University,
170 Whitney Avenue,
PO Box 6666,
New Haven,
Connecticut 06511
Apatosaurus

Camarasaurus
Camptosaurus
Claosaurus
Deinonychus
Monoclonius
Stegosaurus
Torosaurus

University of Michigan Exhibit
Museum
Alexander G. Ruthven Museums,
1109 Geddes Avenue,
Ann Arbor,
Michigan 48109
Allosaurus
Anatosaurus
Stegosaurus

University of Wyoming
Geological Museum,
Box 3254,
Laramie,
Wyoming 82071
Anatosaurus
Anchiceratops
Apatosaurus
Tyrannosaurus

Utah Museum of Natural
History
University of Utah,
Salt Lake City,
Utah 84112
Allosaurus
Barosaurus
Camptosaurus
Stegosaurus

ASIA AND AUSTRALIA

Australia

Australian Museum
PO Box A285,
Sidney,
New South Wales 2000
Dilophosaurus

Queensland Museum
Gregory Terrace,
Fortitude Valley,
Queensland 4006
Muttaburrasaurus
Rhoetosaurus

China

Beipei Museum
Beipei,
Sichuan Province
Omeisaurus
Tuojiangosaurus
Yangchuanosaurus

Institute of Vertebrate
Palaeontology and
Palaeoanthropology
PO Box 643,
Beijing
Lufengosaurus
Mamenchisaurus
Psittacosaurus
Shantungosaurus
Tsintaosaurus
Yangchuanosaurus

India

Geology Studies Unit
Indian Statistical Institute,
Calcutta
Barapasaurus
Lametasaurus

Japan

National Science Museum
Tokyo
Permanent display includes
Nipponosaurus

Mongolia

Mongolian Academy of
Sciences
Geological Institute,
Ulan Bator
Bactrosaurus
Nemegtosaurus
Opisthocoelicaudia
Oviraptor
Protoceratops
Psittacosaurus
Saurornithoides
Tarbosaurus

EUROPE

Austria

Natural History Museum
Vienna
Ouranosaurus
Struthiosaurus

Belgium

Bernissart Museum
Bernissart,
Hainaut
Iguanodon

Institut Royal des Sciences
Naturelles de Belgique
Rue Vautier 29,
B-1040 Brussels
Craspedodon
Iguanodon from Bernissart
'Megalosaurus'
Orthomerus

Federal Republic of
Germany

Bavarian State Collection for
Palaeontology and Historical
Geology
Richard-Wagner-Strasse 10/2,
8000 Munich 2
Compsognathus

Geological and
Palaeontological Institute
University of Münster,
Pferdegasse 3,
D4400 Münster
Iguanodon

Institute and Museum of
Geology and Palaeontology
University of Tübingen,
Sigwartstrasse 10
7400 Tübingen 1
Coelophysis
Hypsilophodon
Kentrosaurus
Plateosaurus

Senckenberg Nature Museum
Forschungsinstitut Senckenberg,
Senckenberganlage 25,
6000 Frankfurt 1
Anatosaurus
Diplodocus
Iguanodon
Plateosaurus
Protoceratops
Triceratops
Tyrannosaurus

State Museum for Natural
History
Arsenalplatz 3,
D7140 Ludwigsburg 1
Plateosaurus

France

National Museum of Natural
History
Institute of Palaeontology,

8 rue Buffon,
F-75005 Paris
Compsognathus
Diplodocus
Iguanodon
Ouranosaurus
Protoceratops
Tarbosaurus
Triceratops

German Democratic
Republic

Natural History Museum
Humboldt University,
Unter den Linden 6,
108 Berlin
Archaeopteryx
Brachiosaurus
Dicraeosaurus
Dryosaurus
Elaphrosaurus
Kentrosaurus

Italy

Museo Civico di Storia
Naturale di Venezia
S. Croce 1730,
30125 Venice
Ouranosaurus

Poland

Dinosaur Park
Chorzow,
Silesia
Models of Mongolian
dinosaurs including:
Saichania
Saurolophus
Tarbosaurus

Institute of Palaeobiology
Al Zwirki I Wigury 93,
02-089 Warsaw
Many specimens from the
Polish-Mongolian expeditions
are studied here including:
Deinocheirus
Gallimimus
Homalocephale
Nemegtosaurus
Pinacosaurus
Protoceratops
Opisthocoelicaudia
Saichania
Tarbosaurus
Velociraptor

Sweden

Palaeontological Museum
Uppsala University,
PO Box 256,
751 05 Uppsala
Euhelopus

United Kingdom

Birmingham Museum
Dept of Natural History
Chamberlain Square,
Birmingham B3 3DH
Allosaurus
Triceratops

British Museum
(Natural History)
Cromwell Road,
London SW7 5BD
Diplodocus
Euoplocephalus
Gallimimus
Hypsilophodon
Iguanodon
Protoceratops eggs
Triceratops
Specimens held in store include:
Brachiosaurus

Cetiosauriscus
Dacentrurus
Hylaeosaurus
'Megalosaurus'
Mochlodon
Polacanthus
Proceratosaurus
Scelidosaurus
Struthiosaurus
Titanosaurus

Crystal Palace Park
Sydenham,
London SE20
Display of Waterhouse Hawkins'
19th Century dinosaur models

The Dinosaur Museum
Icen Way,
Dorchester,
Dorset DT1 1EW
Hypsilophodon
Iguanodon
Stegosaurus model
Tyrannosaurus model

Hunterian Museum
The University,
Glasgow G12 8QQ
Iguanodon footprints
Triceratops

The Leicestershire Museums
96 New Walk,
Leicester LE1 6TD
New sauropod: ?*Cetiosaurus*

Museum of Isle of Wight
Geology
Sandown Library,
High Street,
Sandown,
Isle of Wight PO36 8AF
Hypsilophodon
Iguanodon
Yaverlandia

Royal Scottish Museum
Chambers Street,
Edinburgh EH1 1JF
Allosaurus
Triceratops
Footprint trackway

Sedgwick Museum
Cambridge University,
Downing Street,
Cambridge CB2 3EQ
Iguanodon

University Museum
Parks Road,
Oxford OX1 3PW
Camptosaurus
Cetiosaurus
Dacentrurus
Eustreptospondylus
Iguanodon
Megalosaurus
Metriacanthosaurus

USSR

Central Geological and
Prospecting Museum
Leningrad
Diplodocus
Mandschurosaurus

Palaeontological Institute
Academy of Sciences,
Profsoyuznaya 113,
Moscow 117321
Avimimus
Bactrosaurus
Bagaceratops
Iguanodon orientalis
Prohadrosaurus
Procheneosaurus
Protoceratops
Psittacosaurus
Saurolophus
Talarurus
Tarbosaurus

A

Aberrant
Unusual, out of the ordinary.

Abraded
Worn down.

Absolute dating
A means of estimating the age of rocks with some degree of accuracy using measurements of radioactive isotopes.

Adductor
Closer (i.e. jaw adductor muscle is a jaw-closing muscle).

Aestivate
To hide away and become inactive during periods of drought.

Aëtosaurs
Heavily-armoured, plant-eating archosaurs of the Triassic Period.

Algae
Aquatic plants, both small and large.

Ammonites
Extinct coiled shellfish that were abundant in Mesozoic seas, relatives of squid, octopus and *Nautilus* today.

Amniotes
Tetrapods whose embryos develop within an amniotic membrane e.g. reptiles, mammals and birds.

Amphibious
Able to live both in water and on land.

Anapsid
A reptile group including the living turtles and tortoises characterised by having no skull openings behind the eye socket.

Angiosperms
Flowering plants.

Archaeothyris
The earliest pelycosaur.

Archosaurs
A major group of reptiles including the dinosaurs, pterosaurs, thecodontians — all of which are extinct — and the living crocodiles.

Arthropods
Animals with jointed legs, e.g. insects, spiders, crabs and shrimps.

Articulated
Jointed together or jointed.

Asiamerica
The land areas of Asia and America joined by a land bridge formed by the Bering Straits in the Mesozoic Era.

B

Bacteria
Microscopically small organisms.

Biped
An habitually two-footed creature.

BM (NH)
British Museum (Natural History).

Brachiopods
Shelled sea creatures that look a little like clams and oysters but are not closely related.

Browsers
Those animals that feed on high foliage (shrubs and trees).

Burlap
Strips of hessian sacking soaked in plaster-of-Paris and used to bandage fossils in the field.

C

Cadaver
A carcass of a dead animal.

Calcite
A mineral found abundantly in the Earth's crust as a variant of chalk ($CaCO_3$).

Cambrian Period
The most ancient of the Palaeozoic time zones, rocks from this period show the first traces of fairly complicated animal life.

Cantilever
A beam or lever that projects outward from its support (e.g. the tail of a dinosaur projects from the pelvis as a cantilever and so balances the front part of the body).

Carapace
A hard outer covering to the body, such as the shell of a tortoise.

Caudal
Of or from the tail.

Cellulose
Chemical that forms the bulk of plant cell walls — tough and indigestible to most animals.

Cenozoic/Kainozoic
'Recent life': the Era since the time of the dinosaurs i.e. from 64 million years ago to the recent, historical past.

Champsosaurs
Early aquatic lizard-like reptiles.

Chevrons
Bones hanging below the tail.

Cladogram
A diagram representing the family tree of groups of organisms.

Class
Below the level of *Phylum*, this is an important grouping among animals, as for example into the Classes *Amphibia, Reptilia, Mammalia* and *Aves* (birds).

Classification
The process of ordering or cataloguing organisms into groups which are related by descent.

Clavicle
Collar bone.

Collagen
A protein that forms fine, tough strands which make up ligaments and tendons and strengthens bones.

Colonial
Living together in colonies of like individuals.

Community
The local environment of an organism.

Comparative anatomy
A branch of biology which relies on the ability to compare and contrast the attributes of one animal with another in order to understand them more fully.

Comparative dating
A technique for estimating the age of rocks based on their characteristic fossils; these can be compared with those from rocks elsewhere, as similarly aged rocks are expected to have similar fossil species.

Conifers
Cone-bearing trees such as firs, pines and yews.

Conservation
The procedure used to ensure that a fossil once excavated does not deteriorate.

Continental Drift
The phenomenon of continental movement (Drift) on tectonic plates in the Earth's crust.

Coprolites
Fossilised dung.

Coronoid process
A tall prong of bone on the lower jaw for the attachment of jaw-closing muscles.

Cranial
Relating to the cranium or braincase.

Cretaceous Period
The third Period in the Mesozoic Era. It lasted from 135 million years ago until the extinction of the dinosaurs about 64 million years ago.

Crocodylids
Alligators and crocodiles.

Cursorial
Fast-running.

Cycads
Squat, rather palm-tree-like plants that were particularly abundant in the Mesozoic Era.

Cynodonts
Advanced types of mammal-like reptiles of the Triassic Period.

D

Decay
To rot, to disintegrate (see also **radioactive decay**).

Dentition
Teeth.

Deposit (geological)
Accumulation of rock.

Depyritisation
The chemical process (which can severely damage fossil specimens) whereby iron pyrites spontaneously converts into iron sulphate and acids.

Dermal bone
Bone formed within the skin.

Diapsid
A reptile group, including the dinosaurs, as well as crocodiles, lizards, snakes and descendants of the birds, characterised by having a pair of openings immediately behind the eye socket.

Dicynodonts
Curious pig-like therapsids of the Permian and Triassic Periods, often with just two tusks in the upper jaw.

Dimorphism
The characteristic of having two forms — usually sexual. For example, if males and females of the same species look different, then the species is said to exhibit sexual dimorphism.

Dinosaur
A special type of land-living reptile with an erect gait — a member of the archosaur group — that flourished between 225 and 64 million years ago. Dinosaurs can be classified in two orders: Saurischia and Ornithischia. The term is from the Greek, meaning 'terrible, or fearfully great reptile'.

'Dinosauroid'
Dale Russell's name for his imaginative reconstruction of how the theropod dinosaur *Stenonychosaurus* might have looked if it had not gone extinct 64 million years ago.

Disarticulated
Pulled apart, broken up.

Dispersal
The process of spreading out, in a geographic sense.

Distal
Furthest from the point of attachment to the body (opposite of proximal).

Diurnal
Active during daylight hours (as opposed to nocturnal).

Divergence
Moving away from, changing in form in an evolutionary sense.

Dorsal
From above (opposite of ventral).

E

Echinoderms
Sea urchins and their relatives.

Ecology
The study of the relationship between organisms and the environment.

Ectothermic
'Cold-blooded' — relying mainly on external sources of heat (i.e. the Sun's rays) to maintain an even working body temperature.

Embryo
An animal in its earliest stages of development.

Endocranial cast
A sediment in-fill of the brain cavity.

Endocranial cavity
The cavity in the skull for the brain and associated soft parts.

Endothermic
'Warm-blooded' — being able to generate heat internally by means of chemical reactions in order to regulate the body temperature.

Epoccipital
Small bone edging the frill on the skulls of ceratopian dinosaurs.

Erosion
The result of weathering on exposed rocks.

Euramerica
The land areas of Europe and America which were joined for much of the Mesozoic Era.

Eurasia
The land areas of Europe and Asia joined as they are today.

Euryapsid
A reptile group, exclusively aquatic and now extinct (e.g. plesiosaurs and ichthyosaurs) characterised by a single opening high up on the side of the skull behind the eye socket.

Evolution
A gradual change in the characteristics of a population of organisms over a series of generations brought about through natural selection.

Evolve
To change in form or appearance over successive generations.

Exposure
An area where bare rock is exposed to the erosive action of the weather.

Extensor muscle
A muscle which straightens a joint, as opposed to a flexor muscle.

Extinction
The death of a species.

F

Family
A grouping of similar genera.

Fauna
Animals.

Femur
Upper leg or thigh-bone.

Fenestra
Window-like opening in skull.

Fibula
Shin bone (see also **tibia**).

Flexor muscle
A muscle which bends a joint, as opposed to an extensor which straightens a joint.

Flora
Plants.

Foliage
Leaves, branches and twigs.

Forelimbs
Front legs or arms/wings.

Fossil
A fossil is the preserved remains of something that once lived. It can be formed in a number of way, usually involving burial and chemical change.

Fossilisation
The process that leads to the formation of fossils.

The Fossil Record
The history of life on Earth as revealed by fossil remains.

Furcula
The 'wish-bone' of birds.

Fused
Joined, welded together very firmly.

G

Gait
Characteristics of movement.

Gastralia
Belly ribs.

'Gastric mill'
A muscular portion of the stomach used to grind up food — often with the assistance of gastroliths or 'stomach stones'.

Gastroliths
'Stomach stones' used either for pounding up food or as ballast.

Gavialids
Slender-snouted, fish-eating crocodiles of India.

Genealogy
The study of family-trees.

Genus
A grouping to which several species belong.

Geographical distribution
The localities where an animal or plant may be found.

Geological timescale
A timescale of the history of the Earth arrived at by a combination of comparative and absolute dating of rocks and their fossils worldwide.

Geologist
A person who studies rocks.

Geology
The science of the study of rocks.

Ginkgo
The maidenhair tree of East Asia; the sole survivor of a once abundant group of gymnosperm trees.

Gizzard
As '**gastric mill**'.

Gondwana
The 'southern continents' in the Triassic Period, comprising South America, Africa, India, Antarctica and Australia.

Graptolites
Curious fossils, especially in Palaeozoic rocks, that look like scratch marks made by a saw.

Graviportal
Slow-moving, lumbering.

Grazers
Those animals that feed on grasses (and other low-lying vegetation).

Gymnosperms
Non-flowering plants (in general).

H

Hadrosaurine
Non-crested hadrosaurid.

Hindlimbs
Back or rear legs.

Histology
The study of the fine structure of body tissues.

Humerus
Upper arm bone.

Hyperextended
Over-straightened, bent backwards on itself.

I

Ichnology
The study of footprints as preserved in rocks.

Ichthyosaurs
Marine reptiles of the Mesozoic Era; these were the most highly specialised of swimming reptiles with streamlined, fish-shaped bodies.

Ilium
One of the bones of the pelvis; it is connected to the vertebral column (backbone).

Infraorder
A category smaller than Suborder but bigger than Family; used in the classification of animals.

Insectivores
Insect-eaters.

Iridium
A heavy metal element found in meteorites and the Earth's core.

Iron pyrites
'Fool's gold'; an iron-based mineral that occurs widely in all types of rocks.

Ischium
One of the pelvic bones; it points downward and backward from the hip socket.

Isotope
One of a set of chemically identical types of atom which differ in their weight and stability. Unstable isotopes are radioactive and 'decay' to form more stable isotopes. Isotope analysis is used in dating some types of rock.

IVPP
Institute of Vertebrate Palaeontology and Palaeoanthropology, Beijing, China.

J

Jurassic Period
The second period in the Mesozoic Era; it lasted from 200-135 million years ago.

K

Kinematics
The study of movement by a system of links and joints.

Kuehneosaurus
An early gliding lizard of the Triassic Period.

L

Lambeosaurine
Relating to hadrosaurids with large tubular crests on skull.

Lateral
From the outside; external (opposite of medial).

Laurasia
The 'northern continents' in the Triassic Period, comprising North

America, Europe and Asia. Separated from Gondwana by Tethys.

Lepidosaurs
Lizards and snakes.

Ligaments
Tough sheets or threads of protein (collagen) which support joints between bones.

M

Macroevolution
Large-scale evolutionary change.

Mantle
The region of the Earth's interior between the outer crust and the core.

Mass-extinction
The simultaneous extinction of a whole range of species.

Medial
From the inside or inner (opposite of lateral).

Mesozoic
'Middle life': the period of time (Era) between 225-64 million years ago when the dinosaurs reigned supreme — incorporates the Triassic, Jurassic and Cretaceous Periods.

Metacarpals
Long bones in the upper part of the hand that form the palm.

Metatarsals
Long bones in the upper part of the foot.

Mosasaurs
A group of aquatic reptiles that appeared at the end of the Cretaceous Period and did not survive beyond that time. Large predators of the seas, these forms appear to be relatives of modern monitor lizards.

Musculature
The arrangement of muscles of an animal.

Muzzle
The front part of the head around the jaws and nostrils.

N

Natural selection
The notion that those organisms that are best adapted to prevailing conditions will survive to perpetuate their kind i.e. the environment 'selects' the fittest organisms. A quintessential part of Charles Darwin's Theory of Evolution.

Neural spine
A spine rising above a vertebra and protecting the spinal cord.

Nocturnal
Being active at night, rather than during daylight hours.

Nuchal ligaments
Neck ligaments (from *ligamentum nuchae*).

O

Omnivore
An animal with a diet of both plant and animal food.

Order
A category of animals that includes a variety of similar families.

Ornithischian
One of the two major Orders of dinosaurs (see also **saurischian**) which is based on hip structure. In ornithischians the pubis lies parallel to the ischium (as in birds). The group

is entirely herbivorous and includes ornithopods, stegosaurs, ceratopians, ankylosaurs and pachycephalosaurs.

Overburden
The rock lying directly above a fossil that is in the process of being excavated.

P

Pachyderm
Literally 'thick-skinned' mammals, such as the rhinoceros, hippopotamus and elephant living today.

Palaeomagnetism
The magnetic bearing left in rocks from the time when they first solidified.

Palaeontologist
A person who studies fossils.

Palaeontology
The study of fossils.

Palaeozoic
'Ancient life': the period of time (Era) between 600-225 million years ago comprising the Cambrian, Ordovician, Silurian, Devonian, Carboniferous and Permian Periods. This was the Era *before* the dinosaurs who lived in the Mesozoic.

Palpebral
Small bone found in the rim of the eye socket, especially in ornithischian dinosaurs.

Pangaea
The enormous supercontinent formed in late Permian times when all the continents of the Earth collided.

Para-sacral spines
Bony spikes projecting from the hip region in stegosaurs.

Pareiasaurids
Large, early plant-eating reptiles of the Permian Period.

Pathological
Relating to the study of disease.

Pelvis
The hip region of the skeleton.

Pelycosaurs
Mammal-like reptiles of the Carboniferous and Permian Periods; some have distinctive 'sails' on their backs.

Percolate
To penetrate gradually with water (and dissolved minerals).

Permineralisation
Deposition of minerals inside a bony fossil.

Petrification
'Turning to stone': the replacement, by minerals, of the original hard tissues of a fossilised organism, so that it becomes stone-like in nature.

Phanerozoic
'Visible life': the time on Earth between 600 million years ago and today during which recognisable animal and plant remains are known.

Photoelastic studies
The use of light to measure the flexibility of materials.

Phylum
One of the major groupings of the Animal Kingdom.

Physiology
The study of the processes of life in animals and plants.

Phytosaurs
Early crocodile-like archosaurs of the Triassic.

Piscivores
Fish eaters.

Placodonts
Curious shellfish-eating, heavily-armoured, turtle-like reptiles of the Triassic Period.

Plate tectonics
The study of the large plates which make up the Earth's crust, and their relative movements.

Plenum
A concept used in religious teaching which is founded on the idea that the Creator formed all Earthly life in its infinite variety on just one occasion, thereby excluding the possibility of extinctions.

Plesiosaurs
Marine reptiles of the Mesozoic Era which swam using large flippers.

Pleurocoel
A cavity in the sides of vertebrae.

'Polywachs'
Polyethylene glycol granules; used in the conservation of fossil bones.

Posture
Normal standing or walking position of an animal.

Precambrian
Referring to the vast Period of time (before the Cambrian Period) that elapsed while the Earth cooled and became a solid planet which eventually developed its own climate and ecosystems with simple forms of life (4,500-600 million years ago).

Predatory
Preying upon other animals; referring to a hunting-and-killing style of life.

Predentary bone
A small crescent-shaped bone found at the tip of the lower jaw in ornithischian dinosaurs alone.

Premaxilla
A paired bone at the front of the upper jaw of nearly all vertebrates.

Preservation
The general condition or 'state' (of a fossil specimen).

Process
A bony projection (in an anatomical sense).

Procolophonids
Small, primitive, plant-eating reptiles of the Permian Period.

Proterosuchians
Hook-nosed, crocodile-like thecodontians of the late Permian Period.

Proximal
Nearest to the point of attachment to the body (opposite of distal).

Pterosaurs
The flying reptiles of the Mesozoic Era; these are distant cousins of the dinosaurs.

Pubis
One of the pelvic bones, this usually points downward and forward from the hip socket. In some reptiles; ornithischian dinosaurs, segnosaurids and birds, the pubis lies parallel to the ischium.

'Pyrite disease'
Spontaneous destruction of fossil specimens which contain high concentrations of iron pyrites.

Q

Quadruped
An habitually four-footed creature.

Quaternary Period
The recent prehistoric past which has been dominated by the arrival of Man; 1·8 million years ago to the present day.

R

Radioactive decay
The disintegration of an unstable isotope into a more stable isotope with the production of radiation (energy).

Radiometrics
Measurement of radioactive decay.

Radius
One of the two forearm bones (see also **ulna**).

Recurved
Curved backwards (of teeth).

Resonator
A device for increasing sound levels by vibrating in sympathy with the source of the sound.

Rhynchosaurs
Squat, pig-like creatures with a curious hooked beak from the late Triassic Period.

'Ridges'
High mountain ranges on the sea-floor, marking the point where new sea-floor is emerging from the interior of the Earth.

Rigor mortis
Stiffening of the body following death.

Rostral bone
A bone found at the tip of the upper jaw in ceratopian dinosaurs only.

Rutting
Mating behaviour of deer.

S

Sacral ribs
Special strong ribs that connect the vertebral column to the pelvis.

Sacrum
The region of the backbone which is attached to the pelvis by means of sacral ribs.

Saurischian
One major grouping of the dinosaurs (based on hip structure) in which the pubis is long and points forward and downward from the hip socket; includes the carnivorous theropods and the herbivorous sauropodomorphs.

Saurolophine
Referring to hadrosaurids with slender spikes on head.

Sauropodomorphs
Large herbivorous saurischian dinosaurs including the prosauropods and sauropods.

Sclerotic ossicles
Bones found in the sclera or 'white' of the eye.

Scutes
Bony or horny plates embedded in the skin, particularly of reptiles.

Sedimentary rocks
Rocks that have formed from sediments such as sands and clays.

Serrated
With a notched edge like the cutting edge of a saw.

Shales
A rock type composed mainly of clay that splits into thin wafers.

Silica
One of several abundant minerals in the Earth's crust based on the element silicon.

Silt
Grains, or finely broken pieces of rock that slowly settle out of water.

Sinuses
Spaces within the body.

Solar-panels
Flat surfaces that are able to absorb the warmth of the Sun.

Specialised
Modified in a particular way.

Species
A group of animals which look the same and can breed together — something which it is impossible to prove in fossil animals.

Squamosal
A bone near the top rear corner of a reptile skull. In ceratopians it is greatly enlarged to form part of the frill.

Stereoscopic
Relating to an ability to perceive a three-dimensional image.

Stratigraphy
The study of the pattern of rock layers (strata).

Stratum
A rock layer.

Stromatolites
Banded rocks that were made by blue-green algae; abundant in the Precambrian in particular.

Suborder
A category smaller than Order but bigger than Infraorder; used in the classification of animals.

Supercontinents
Extra large continents formed by the joining together of several continental areas i.e. Laurasia, Gondwana, Pangaea.

Supernova
The last phase in the life of certain types of star, when it annihilates itself in an enormous explosion.

Superorder
A category bigger than Order but smaller than Class; used in the classification of animals.

Suture
A line where bones meet.

Synapsid
A reptile group, to which the mammals are distantly related, characterised by a single opening low down on the skull behind the eye socket.

T

Talons
Sharp claws.

Taphonomy
The study of the processes of decay and fossilisation in order to understand the circumstances that may have led to organisms being preserved in particular ways.

Termitarium
A termite mound.

Terrestrial
On or of the Earth's surface — land-dwelling.

Tertiary Period
This follows the Cretaceous Period and charts the rise of mammals from 64 million years ago up to the recent past (1·8 million years ago, the start of the Quaternary Period).

Tethys
A sea which in former times separated Laurasia from Gondwana. A remnant of this seaway is the Mediterranean.

Tetrapods
Vertebrates with four limbs e.g. amphibians, reptiles, mammals *and* birds.

Thecodontians
Early archosaurs of the Permian and Triassic Periods which form the group from which all of the more advanced archosaurs (pterosaurs, dinosaurs, crocodiles) evolved in the Triassic Period.

Therapsids
Mammal-like reptiles of the late Permian and early Triassic Periods.

Theropods
A wide range of predatory saurischian dinosaurs, most of which were bipedal; commonly divided into two artificial groupings as 'coelurosaurs' (small theropods), and 'carnosaurs' (big theropods).

Tibia
The main shin bone (one of two, see also **fibula**).

Tooth battery
A large number of interlocking teeth arranged in a jaw to form a cutting or grinding surface.

'Trenches'
Deep gulleys found at the edges of tectonic plates where ocean crust is sinking back into the mantle.

Triassic Period
The first period of the Mesozoic Era; it lasted from 225-200 million years ago, and the dinosaurs first appeared towards its close.

Tripodal
Of, or with, three feet.

Trochanter
A bony lump on the femur to which muscles are attached.

U

Ulna
One of the two forearm bones (see also **radius**).

V

'Variable gait'
The ability to walk in a variety of ways depending upon how the legs are positioned.

Variation
The range of appearance of organisms of the same general type of species.

Vascular
Of or relating to the blood.

Ventral
From beneath (opposite of dorsal).

Vertebra
An individual bone of the back (vertebral column = backbone).

Vertebrates
Animals with backbones e.g. fish, amphibians, reptiles, birds and mammals.

W

Wealden
An area of south east England comprised of rocks of early Cretaceous age.

Z

Zygapophyses
Usually peg-like bones that help to hold vertebrae together, and prevent them from slipping apart.

PICTURE CREDITS

The publishers wish to thank the many private individuals, museum photographic archives and picture agencies who have generously supplied photographs for inclusion in this book, and by courtesy of whom they are reproduced. All photographs are here credited by page number.

The Academy of Natural Sciences, Philadelphia: 12 top left; 120 upper
ARDEA: 170 upper (Pat Morris); 181 (Pat Morris); 191 right (Pat Morris)
Bayerische Staatssammlung für Paläontologie und historische Geologie, Munich: 42
W.T. Blows: 18 top left; 49 lower; 120 middle (D. Tanke); 144 middle
Brigham Young University: 91 left and lower right (Mark Philbrick)
British Museum (Natural History), courtesy of the Trustees: 35; 48 lower; 61 middle; 67 upper; 72 upper; 109 lower right; 120 lower; 127 upper left; 133 lower; 162; 169 upper left; 173 upper right and lower right; 177 lower; 179 left; 180 lower right; 191 left; 197 upper; 200/1.
Carnegie Museum of Natural History: 18/9; 90; 108/9
Bruce Coleman Ltd: 33 (WWF/Hirsch and Müller); 43 lower (Hans Reinhard); 48 upper (Jen and Des Bartlett); 52 left (Joseph van Wormer); 97 (Gerald Cubitt); 102 left (Udo Hirsch); 102 right (Masood Qureshi); 109 upper (Gunter Ziesler); 139 lower right (Bob Campbell); 145 upper (Hans Reinhard); 174 (Norman Myers); 175 upper left (Donn Renn); 175 upper (Peter Jackson); 185 upper (Mark Boulton); 190 upper (Jen and Des Bartlett)
Daily Mirror Syndication International: 9 (part of montage)
Denver Museum of Natural History Photo Archives: 22 top; 85

upper; 156 upper right
Express Newspapers: 9 (part of montage)
Field Museum of Natural History, Chicago: 132; 182; 183 upper and lower left; 184 upper
Fort Worth Museum of Science and History: 190 lower
GeoScience Features: 186/7
Hasselblad: 16 upper
K.H. Hilpert: 25 lower
Stephen Hutt, Museum of Isle of Wight Geology: 18 top right, 108 upper
Imitor: 8 top; 10 all excluding middle left; 12 top middle and top right; 170 lower; 171; 175 bottom; 176; 178; 179 right; 184 lower; 185 lower; 187 upper right; 189; 193; 194 upper right; 195
Institute of Palaeobiology, Warsaw: 13 lower; 49 upper; 61 lower; 73 upper; 84; 96/7; 150/1; 151; 169 lower left
Institut Royal des Sciences Naturelles de Belgique: 12 lower; 22 lower; 25 both upper; 26 upper (E. Casier); 28; 28/9; 31 upper; 32 (L. Dollo); 32/3; 177 upper.
Institute of Vertebrate Palaeontology and Palaeoanthropology, Beijing/ Dong Zhiming: 126; 133 upper left
Jet Propulsion Laboratory/NASA: 16 lower
S.M. Kurzanov, Moscow Academy of Sciences: 37 top right; 52 left; 72 lower; 114 lower; 115 upper; 127 upper right; 132/3; 133 upper right; 169 upper and lower right (all photographs by A.N. Tarassenco)
Los Angeles County Natural History Museum: 66/7
Dr James H. Madsen: 19 lower
The Mansell Collection: 11 lower; 20
Dr. A.C. Milner: 13 top; 24/5; 67 lower; 79 upper left and right; 85

lower; 156 lower right; 157
Pat Morris Photographic: 34/5 lower; 91 lower middle; 180 upper; 194 lower right
Museo Civico di Storia Naturale, Venice: 115 lower (E. Ruffert)
NHPA: 34/5 upper (G.I. Bernard); 188 lower (G.I. Bernard)
Dr D.B. Norman: 8 middle; 11 top right; 19 top; 26 lower; 27 top left; 29; 31 lower; 36; 103 lower; 108 lower left; 158; 159 both; 187 upper left
NRAO (National Radio Astronomy Observatory): 196/7
Oxford University Museum: 10 middle left; 11 top left
Péabody Museum of Natural History, Yale University: 61 top right; 145 lower
Science Photo Library: 173 left (Sinclair Stammers); 183 lower right (Sinclair Stammers); 194 upper left (Martin Dohrn)
Senckenberg Museum, Frankfurt: 114 upper; 139 upper; 188/9 (all photographs by E. Haupt).
Smithsonian Institution: 8/9; 37 top left; 138 lower right; 139 lower left; 180 lower left
South African Museum, Cape Town: 78 upper; 79 lower right; 103 upper
The Sun: 9 (part of montage)
D. Tanke: 120 middle (via W.T. Blows)
Tübingen University, Museum for Geology and Palaeontology: 78/9
Tyrrell Museum of Palaeontology, Alberta: 42/3; 60/1; 73 lower; 120/1; 126/7; 138 lower left; 144 upper
US Department of the Interior, National Park Service: 84/5; 91 upper right; 156 upper left
US Naval Observatory: 197 lower

ARTWORK CREDITS

Many of the drawings of skeletons and fossil bones in this book are based on the original reconstructions made by the scientists who described or have studied the specimens. The publishers would like here to acknowledge, with thanks, these sources. Some drawings have been modified from the originals in the light of new evidence, or sometimes to show specific anatomical features, such as musculature. These are identified here by an asterisk.

9: A.P. Santa-Luca (*Heterodontosaurus* hip); J.H. Ostrom (*Compsognathus* hip). 27: D.B. Norman (*Iguanodon*). 28/9: D.B. Norman (*Iguanodon*). 30: Mark Hallett (*Iguanodon* reconstructions). 30/1: D.B. Norman (*Iguanodon*). 32/3: D.B. Norman (*Iguanodon*). 34: R. Reisz (*Petrolacosaurus*); R.F. Ewer (*Euparkeria*). 35: A.J. Charig (postures). 36: J. Bonaparte (*Saurosuchus*); R.A. Thulborn (ankle structures*); A.J. Charig (hip joints). 40/1: J.H. Ostrom (*Compsognathus*); E.H. Colbert (*Coelophysis*); H.F. Osborn (*Ornitholestes*). 46/7: D. Russell (*Struthiomimus* skeleton* and skull, *Dromiceiomimus* skull); A.S. Romar (*Struthiomimus* foot); A.G. Russell and E. Nicholls (*Struthiomimus* hand and gastralia); R. Barsbold (*Oviraptor* shoulder and middle skull); H.F. Osborn (*Oviraptor* top skull); H. Osmolska (*Oviraptor* bottom skull); D.B. Norman (shoulders and hips). 52/3: S.M. Kurzanov (*Avimimus*); H. Osmolska (*Elmisaurus*); R. Barsbold and A. Perle (*Segnosaurus*, *Adasaurus* and *Erlikosaurus*); C. Camp (*Segisaurus*); J. Bonaparte and J. Powell (*Noasaurus*); A.K. Rozhdestvensky (*Therizinosaurus*); Dong Zhiming (*Shanshanosaurus*). 55: D. Russell and R. Seguin ('dinosauroid'*). 58/9: J.H. Ostrom (*Deinonychus*); D.B. Norman (head, skull and shoulder musculature); H.F. Osborn (*Velociraptor* skull). 64/65: C.W. Gilmore (*Ceratosaurus* skeleton and hip, *Allosaurus* skull and vertebrae); O.C. Marsh (*Ceratosaurus* skull); J. Madsen (*Allosaurus* hand and foot); S.P. Welles (*Dilophosaurus*); Dong Zhiming (*Yangchuanosaurus*). 70/1: D. Russell (*Allosaurus* hatchling, *Albertosaurus* and *Daspletosaurus* skulls); A. Maleev (*Tyrannosaurus* hand and

foot, *Tarbosaurus* skull); H.F. Osborn (*Tyrannosaurus* pelvis); B.H. Newman (*Tyrannosaurus* skeleton*). 73: B.H. Newman (*Tyrannosaurus* rising from ground*). 76/7: F. von Huehne (*Plateosaurus* skeleton and skull); P.M. Galton (anchisaurid posture, *Plateosaurus* hand* and foot*); A.J. Charig (*Plateosaurus* tooth); O.C. Marsh (*Anchisaurus* skeleton and skull); J. Bonaparte (*Coloradia* skull). 82/3: W.J. Holland (*Diplodocus* skeleton*, hand and foot); J. Nowinski (*Nemegtosaurus*, *Dicraeosaurus* and *Antarctosaurus* skulls); C.W. Gilmore (*Apatosaurus* skeleton*); O.C. Marsh (*Apatosaurus* skeleton*). 88/9: W Janensch (*Brachiosaurus* skeleton, skull, rib and vertebrae); C.W. Gilmore (*Camarasaurus*); F. von Huehne (*Brachiosaurus* hand). 94/5: J. Bonaparte and J. Powell (*Saltasaurus* and *Laplatasaurus*); S. Jain (*Barapasaurus*); H.G. Seeley (*Ornithopsis*); M. Borsuk-Bialynicka (*Opisthocoelicaudia*); Dong Zhiming (*Omeisaurus*); M. Cooper (*Vulcanodon*); A.S. Woodward (*Cetiosauriscus* skeleton); J. Bonaparte (*Cetiosauriscus* chevron). 100/1: A.P. Santa-Luca (*Heterodontosaurus* skeleton, hip, hand and foot); P.M. Galton (*Lesothosaurus* skeleton); A.J. Charig and A.W. Crompton (*Heterodontosaurus* skull); R.A. Thulborn (*Lesothosaurus* skull*). 106/7: P.M. Galton (*Hypsilophodon*, *Dryosaurus* skull); J.H. Ostrom (*Tenontosaurus* skull); P. Dodson (*Tenontosaurus* hand and foot). 109: O. Abel (*Hypsilophodon* foot). 112/3: P. Taquet (*Ouranosaurus* skeleton and skull*); D.B. Norman (*Iguanodon*); C.W. Gilmore (*Camptosaurus*); A. Bartholomai and R. Molnar (*Muttaburrasaurus*). 115: G. Heilmann (*Iguanodon* feeding). 118/9: J. Horner (*Edmontosaurus* skeleton*); C.W. Parks (*Edmontosaurus* hand and foot); R.S. Lull and N. Wright (hadrosaur pelves, *Kritosaurus* skull*, *Anatosaurus* skull*); C.W. Gilmore (*Bactrosaurus* skull*); L. Lambe (*Edmontosaurus* skull); D.B. Norman (hadrosaurid skull). 124/5: C.W. Parks (*Parasaurolophus* skeleton*); J.H. Ostrom (*Parasaurolophus* skulls, sections through crests*); P. Dodson (*Corythosaurus* and *Lambeosaurus* skulls); R.S. Lull and N. Wright (*Prosaurolophus* and *Saurolophus* skulls). 130/1: C.M.Sternberg (*Protoceratops* skeleton*); H.F. Osborn (*Psittacosaurus* skeleton); B. Brown and E.M. Schlaijker (*Protoceratops* skull);

J.H. Ostrom (ceratopian teeth); H. Osmolska (*Bagaceratops* skull). 133 P. Dodson, after B. Brown and E.M. Schlaijker (*Protoceratops* skulls). 136/7: C.W. Gilmore (*Centrosaurus* skeleton, hand and foot); O.C. Marsh (*Triceratops* skull); C.M. Sternberg (*Styracosaurus* skull). 142/3: R.S. Lull (*Chasmosaurus* pelvis, *Torosaurus*, *Pentaceratops* and *Anchiceratops* skulls); R.S. Lull and C.W. Gilmore (*Chasmosaurus* skeleton*); D.B. Norman (shoulder musculature). 148/9: L. Lambe (*Stegoceras* skeleton* and skull*); R. Barsbold (*Stegoceras* teeth); T. Maryanska and H. Osmolska (*Homalocephale* pelvis, vertebrae and skull, *Prenocephale* skulls); P.M. Galton and P. Watts (*Pachycephalosaurus* skull). 154/5: C.W. Gilmore (*Stegosaurus*); W. Hennig (*Kentrosaurus*). 156: C.W. Gilmore (*Stegosaurus* skeleton). 158/9: B.H. Newman (*Scelidosaurus* skeleton from a photograph). 162/3: W.P. Coombs (nodosaur shoulder blade, *Panoplosaurus* skulls and skull sections, *Sauropelta* tail); R.S. Lull (*Nodosaurus* skeleton*); F.B. Nopsca (*Polacanthus* skeleton). 166/7: W.P. Coombs (*Euoplocephalus* skulls and skull sections, *Ankylosaurus* tail club, shoulder and hip muscles); K. Carpenter (*Euoplocephalus* skeleton); T. Maryanska (*Pinacosaurus* and *Saichania* skulls). 170/1: Wann Langston (all pterosaurs). 172/3: A.S. Romer; (*Rhamphorhynchus** and *Pteranodon**); K. Padian (*Dimorphodon*). 174/5: E.H. Colbert and C.C. Mook (*Protosuchus*). 176: D. Nash (*Orthosuchus*); A.S. Romer (*Metriorhynchus*); B. Kurten (*Pelagosaurus*). 178/9: A.S. Romer (*Ophthalmosaurus*, ichthyosaur skull, plesiosaur skull, *Placodus*, *Placochelys*); D.S. Brown (*Cryptoclidus*). 180/1: A.S. Romer (*Proganochelys*, *Archelon*, *Sphenodon*, *Kuehneosaurus*, snake fangs); T. Frazzetta (lizard skull flexing); W.N. McFarland, F.H. Pough, J.B.Heiser and T.J. Cade (*Naja* skull). 182/3: R. Reisz (*Archaeothyris*); A.S. Romer and L. Price (*Ophiacodon*, *Dimetrodon* and *Edaphosaurus* skull); T.S. Kemp (*Delphinognathus*, *Drynodon* and *Cynognathus* skulls). 184/5: A.S. Romer (*Lycaenops*); T.S. Kemp (*Probelesodon*); D.M. Kermack and K.A. Kermack (*Morganucodon*); F. Jenkins and R. Parrington (*Megazostrodon*). 192/3: G. Heilmann (*Euparkeria*, '*Archaeopteryx* and pigeon skulls, pigeon skeleton*); H.F. Osborn (*Ornitholestes*); J.H. Ostrom (*Archaeopteryx*).